Second Workshop on Figurative Language Processing 2020

Online
9 July 2020

ISBN: 978-1-7138-1378-1

ACL 2020

Figurative Language Processing

Proceedings of the Second Workshop

July 9, 2020

Introduction

Figurative language processing is a rapidly growing area in Natural Language Processing (NLP), including processing of metaphors, idioms, puns, irony, sarcasm, as well as other figures. Characteristic to all areas of human activity (from poetic to ordinary to scientific) and, thus, to all types of discourse, figurative language becomes an important problem for NLP systems. Its ubiquity in language has been established in a number of corpus studies, and the role it plays in human reasoning has been confirmed in psychological experiments. This makes figurative language an important research area for computational and cognitive linguistics, and its automatic identification and interpretation indispensable for any semantics-oriented NLP application.

This workshop is the second in a series of biannual workshops on Figurative Language Processing. This new workshop series builds upon the successful start of the Metaphor in NLP workshop series (at NAACL– HLT 2013, ACL 2014, NAACL–HLT 2015, NAACL–HLT 2016), expanding its scope to incorporate the rapidly growing body of research on various types of figurative language such as sarcasm, irony and puns, with the aim of maintaining and nourishing a community of NLP researchers interested in this topic. The workshop features both regular research papers and two shared tasks on metaphor and sarcasm detection. In the regular research track, we received 20 research paper submissions and accepted 9 (3 oral presentations and 6 posters). The featured papers cover a range of aspects of figurative language processing such as metaphor identification (Dankers et al.; Zayed, McCrae and Buitelaar), metaphor in the visual modality (Bizzoni and Dobnik), annotation of oxymorons (La Pietra and Massini), satirical and humorous headline generation (Weller et al.; Horvitz et al.) and recognising euphemisms and dysphemisms (Felt and Riloff). The workshop program also features a keynote talk by Marilyn Walker, Department of Computer Science, University of California Santa Cruz, on the topic of "Generating Expressive Language by Mining User Reviews".

The two shared tasks on metaphor and sarcasm detection serve to benchmark various computational approaches to metaphor and sarcasm, clarifying the state of this steadily growing field and facilitating further research.

For the metaphor shared task, we used the VU Amsterdam Metaphor Corpus (VUA) corpus as one of the corpora for the shared tasks. New to this year's benchmarking tasks, we added a corpus of TOEFL essays written by non-native speakers of English annotated for metaphor (a subset from the publicly available ETS Corpus of Non-Native Written English), allowing us to broaden the genres covered in the task and in accordance with findings in the literature demonstrating the potential of information on metaphor usage for assessing English proficiency of students.

The shared task was organized into four tracks: a Verbs track and an All Content Part-of-Speech track for both VUA and TOEFL. Overall, there were 1,224 submissions from 71 teams. There were 805 submissions from the 14 teams who submitted system papers; one paper was withdrawn before publication. In terms of performance, the current published state-of-art on VUA corpus has been matched by the best participating system, while a new state-of-art was established for the TOEFL corpus. We observed the following general trends: (1) Transformer architectures were highly popular and resulted in competitive performance; (2) New sources of information were explored by participants, such as fine-grained POS, spell-corrected variants of words (for TOEFL data), sub-word level information (e.g., character embeddings), idioms, sensorimotor and embodiment-related information; (3) The relative performance rankings of teams were largely consistent between VUA and TOEFL datasets; (4) Performance of participating systems was generally better on Verbs than on the All POS tracks, across both corpora.

The shared task on sarcasm detection was designed to benchmark the usefulness of modeling conversation context (i.e., all the prior dialogue turns) for sarcasm detection. Two types of social media content are used as training data for the two tracks – microblogging platforms such as Twitter and online discussion forums such as Reddit. Overall, we received an overwhelming number of submissions: 655 for the Reddit track and 1070 for the Twitter track. The CodaLab leaderboard showcases results from 39 systems for the Reddit track and 38 systems for the Twitter track, respectively. Out of all submissions, 14 shared task system papers were submitted. Almost all the submitted systems have used the transformer-architecture that seems to perform better than RNN-architectures, even without any task-specific fine-tuning. The best system has shown the usefulness of augmenting "other" dataset(s) during training. In terms of context, novel approaches include: CNN-LSTM based summarization of the prior dialogue turns, time-series fusion with proxy labels, an ensemble of a variety of transformers with different depth of context, aspect-based sentiment classification for the immediate context, etc. When explicitly modeling the number of turns, systems have shown better accuracy with a depth of a maximum of three prior turns. In the future, we plan to continuously grow the training corpus, collecting data from a variety of subreddits, in case of Reddit, and different topics from Twitter.

We wish to thank everyone who showed interest and submitted a paper, all of the authors for their contributions, the members of the Program Committee for their thoughtful reviews, the invited speaker for sharing her perspective on the topic, and all the attendees of the workshop. All of these factors contribute to a truly enriching event!

Workshop co–chairs:
Beata Beigman Klebanov, Educational Testing Service (USA)
Ekaterina Shutova, University of Amsterdam (The Netherlands)
Patricia Lichtenstein, University of California, Merced (USA)
Smaranda Muresan, Columbia University (USA)
Chee Wee (Ben) Leong, Educational Testing Service (USA)
Anna Feldman, Montclair State University (USA)
Debanjan Ghosh, Educational Testing Service (USA)

Organizers:

Beata Beigman Klebanov, Educational Testing Service (USA)
Ekaterina Shutova, University of Amsterdam (The Netherlands)
Patricia Lichtenstein, University of California, Merced (USA)
Smaranda Muresan, Columbia University (USA)
Chee Wee (Ben) Leong, Educational Testing Service (USA)
Anna Feldman, Montclair State University (USA)
Debanjan Ghosh, Educational Testing Service (USA)

Program Committee:

Khalid Alnajjar, University of Helsinki (Finland)
Yulia Badryzlova, National Research University Higher School of Economics (Russia)
Suma Bhat, University of Illinois at Urbana-Champaign (USA)
Paul Cook, University of New Brunswick (Canada)
Ellen Dodge, Google (USA)
Jonathan Dunn, University of Canterbury (New Zealand)
Anjalie Field, Carnegie Mellon University (USA)
Michael Flor, Educational Testing Service (USA)
Mark Granroth-Wilding, University of Helsinki (Finland)
Mika Hämäläinen, University of Helsinki (Finland)
Veronique Hoste, Ghent University (Belgium)
Eduard Hovy, Carnegie Mellon University (USA)
Rebecca Hwa, University of Pittsburgh (USA)
Hyeju Jang, University of British Columbia (Canada)
Valia Kordoni, Humboldt-Universitaet zu Berlin (Germany)
Mark Last, Ben-Gurion University of the Negev (Israel)
Mark Lee, University of Birmingham (UK)
Els Lefever, LT3, Ghent University (Belgium)
Jean Maillard, Facebook AI (USA)
Katja Markert, Heidelberg University (Germany)
James Martin, University of Colorado Boulder (USA)
Michael Mohler, Language Computer Corporation (USA)
Elena Musi, University of Liverpool (UK)
Preslav Nakov, Qatar Computing Research Institute, HBKU (Qatar)
Srini Narayanan, Google Research (USA)
Thierry Poibeau, CNRS (France)
Vinodkumar Prabhakaran, Google Research (USA)
Marek Rei, University of Cambridge (UK)
Ellen Riloff, University of Utah (USA)
Sarah Rosenthal, IBM Research (USA)
Paolo Rosso, University of Politècnica de València (Spain)
Giovanni Da San Martino, Qatar Computing Research Institute (Qatar)
Eyal Sagi, University of St. Francis (USA)
Agata Savary, University of Tours (France)
Sabine Schulte im Walde, University of Stuttgart (Germany)
Samira Shaikh, University of North Carolina, Charlotte (USA)
Thamar Solorio Martinez, University of Houston (USA)

Kevin Stowe, TU Darmstadt, UKP Lab (Germany)
Tomek Strzalkowski, Rensselaer Polytechnic Institute (USA)
Stan Szpakowicz, University of Ottawa (Canada)
Marc Tomlinson, Language Computer Corporation (USA)
Yulia Tsvetkov, Carnegie Mellon University (USA)
Aline Villavicencio, University of Sheffield (UK)

Invited Speaker:

Marilyn Walker, University of California Santa Cruz (USA)

Table of Contents

Conference Program

Thursday July 9, 2020

12:50   *Sarcasm Detection Using an Ensemble Approach*
Jens Lemmens, Ben Burtenshaw, Ehsan Lotfi, Ilia Markov and Walter Daelemans

12:55   *A Transformer Approach to Contextual Sarcasm Detection in Twitter*
Hunter Gregory, Steven Li, Pouya Mohammadi, Natalie Tarn, Rachel Draelos and Cynthia Rudin

13:00   *Transformer-based Context-aware Sarcasm Detection in Conversation Threads from Social Media*
Xiangjue Dong, Changmao Li and Jinho D. Choi

A Report on the 2020 Sarcasm Detection Shared Task

Debanjan Ghosh[1], Avijit Vajpayee[1], and Smaranda Muresan[2]
[1] Educational Testing Service
[2]Data Science Institute, Columbia University
{dghosh, avajpayee}@ets.org
smara@columbia.edu

Abstract

Detecting sarcasm and verbal irony is critical for understanding people's actual sentiments and beliefs. Thus, the field of sarcasm analysis has become a popular research problem in natural language processing. As the community working on computational approaches for sarcasm detection is growing, it is imperative to conduct benchmarking studies to analyze the current state-of-the-art, facilitating progress in this area. We report on the shared task on sarcasm detection we conducted as a part of the 2nd Workshop on Figurative Language Processing (FigLang 2020) at ACL 2020.

Turns	Message
$Context_1$	The [govt] just confiscated a \$180 million boat shipment of cocaine from drug traffickers.
$Context_2$	People think 5 tonnes is not a lot of cocaine.
$Response$	Man, I've seen more than that on a Friday night!

Table 1: Sarcastic replies to conversation context in Reddit. *Response* turn is a reply to $Context_2$ turn that is a reply to $Context_1$ turn

1 Introduction

Sarcasm and verbal irony are a type of figurative language where the speakers usually mean the opposite of what they say. Recognizing whether a speaker is ironic or sarcastic is essential to downstream applications for correctly understanding speakers' intended sentiments and beliefs. Consequently, in the last decade, the problem of irony and sarcasm detection has attracted a considerable interest from computational linguistics researchers. The task has been usually framed as a binary classification task (sarcastic vs. non-sarcastic) using either the utterance in isolation or adding contextual information such as conversation context, author context, visual context, or cognitive features (Davidov et al., 2010; Tsur et al., 2010; González-Ibáñez et al., 2011; Riloff et al., 2013; Maynard and Greenwood, 2014; Wallace et al., 2014; Ghosh et al., 2015; Joshi et al., 2015; Muresan et al., 2016; Amir et al., 2016; Mishra et al., 2016; Ghosh and Veale, 2017; Felbo et al., 2017; Ghosh et al., 2017; Hazarika et al., 2018; Tay et al., 2018; Oprea and Magdy, 2019; Majumder et al., 2019; Castro et al., 2019; Ghosh et al., 2019).

In this paper, we report on the shared task on sarcasm detection that we conducted as part of the 2nd Workshop on Figurative Language Processing (FigLang 2020) at ACL 2020. The task aims to study the role of conversation context for sarcasm detection. Two types of social media content are used as training data for the two tracks - microblogging platform such as Twitter and online discussion forum such as Reddit.

Table 1 and Table 2 show examples of three turn dialogues, where *Response* is the sarcastic reply. Without using the conversation context $Context_i$, it is difficult to identify the sarcastic intent expressed in *Response*. The shared task is designed to benchmark the usefulness of modeling the entire conversation context (i.e., all the prior dialogue turns) for sarcasm detection.

Section 2 discusses the current state of research on sarcasm detection with a focus on the role of context. Section 3 provides a description of the shared task, datasets, and metrics. Section 4 contains brief summaries of each of the participating systems whereas Section 5 reports a comparative evaluation of the systems and our observations about trends in designs and performance of the systems that participated in the shared task.

1

Proceedings of the Second Workshop on Figurative Language Processing, pages 1–11
July 9, 2020. ©2020 Association for Computational Linguistics
https://doi.org/10.18653/v1/P17

Turns	Message
$Context_1$	This is the greatest video in the history of college football.
$Context_2$	Hes gonna have a short career if he keeps smoking . Not good for your health
$Response$	Awesome !!! Everybody does it. That's the greatest reason to do something.

Table 2: Sarcastic replies to conversation context in Twitter. *Response* turn is a reply to $Context_2$ turn that is a reply to $Context_1$ turn

2   Related Work

A considerable amount of work on sarcasm detection has considered the utterance in isolation when predicting the sarcastic or non-sarcastic label. Initial approaches used feature-based machine learning models that rely on different types of features from lexical (e.g., sarcasm markers, word embeddings) to pragmatic such as emoticons or learned patterns of contrast between positive sentiment and negative situations (Davidov et al., 2010; Veale and Hao, 2010; González-Ibáñez et al., 2011; Liebrecht et al., 2013; Riloff et al., 2013; Maynard and Greenwood, 2014; Joshi et al., 2015; Ghosh et al., 2015; Ghosh and Muresan, 2018). Recently, deep learning methods have been applied for this task (Ghosh and Veale, 2016; Tay et al., 2018). For excellent surveys on sarcasm and irony detection see (Wallace, 2015; Joshi et al., 2017).

However, when recognizing sarcastic intent even humans have difficulties sometimes when considering an utterance in isolation (Wallace et al., 2014). Recently an increasing number of researchers have started to explore the role of contextual information for irony and sarcasm analysis. The term context loosely refers to any *information* that is available beyond the utterance itself (Joshi et al., 2017). A few researchers have examined author context (Bamman and Smith, 2015; Khattri et al., 2015; Rajadesingan et al., 2015; Amir et al., 2016; Ghosh and Veale, 2017), multi-modal context (Schifanella et al., 2016; Cai et al., 2019; Castro et al., 2019), eye-tracking information (Mishra et al., 2016), or conversation context (Bamman and Smith, 2015; Wang et al., 2015; Joshi et al., 2016; Zhang et al., 2016; Ghosh et al., 2017; Ghosh and Veale, 2017).

Related to shared tasks on figurative language analysis, recently, Van Hee et al. (2018) have conducted a SemEval task on irony detection in Twitter focusing on utterances in isolation. Besides the binary classification task of identifying the ironic tweet the authors also conducted a multi-class irony classification to identify the specific *type* of irony: whether it contains verbal irony, situational irony, or other types of irony. In our case, the current shared task aims to study the role of conversation context for sarcasm detection. In particular, we focus on benchmark the effectiveness of modeling the conversation context (e.g., all the prior dialogue turns or a subset of the prior dialogue turns) for sarcasm detection.

3   Task Description

The design of our shared task is guided by two specific issues. First, we plan to leverage a particular type of context — the entire prior conversation context — for sarcasm detection. Second, we plan to investigate the systems' performance on conversations from two types of social media platforms: Twitter and Reddit. Both of these platforms allow the writers to mark whether their messages are sarcastic (e.g., #sarcasm hashtag in Twitter and "/s" marker in Reddit).

The competition is organized in two phases: training and evaluation. By making available common datasets and frameworks for evaluation, we hope to contribute to the consolidation and strengthening of the growing community of researchers working on computational approaches to sarcasm analysis.

3.1   Datasets

3.1.1   Reddit Training Dataset

Khodak et al. (2017) introduced the self-annotated Reddit Corpus which is a very large collection of sarcastic and non-sarcastic posts (over one million) curated from different subreddits such as politics, religion, sports, technology, etc. This corpus contains self-labeled sarcastic posts where users label their posts as sarcastic by marking "/s" to the end of sarcastic posts. For any such sarcastic post, the corpus also provides the full conversation context, i.e., all the prior turns that took place in the dialogue.

We select the training data for the Reddit track from Khodak et al. (2017). We considered a couple of criteria. First, we choose sarcastic responses with at least two prior turns. Note, for many responses in our training corpus the number of turns is much more. Second, we curated sarcastic responses from a variety of subreddits such that no single subreddit (e.g., politics) dominates the training corpus. In addition, we avoid responses from subreddits that we believe are too specific and narrow (e.g., subreddit dedicated to a specific video game) that might not generalize well. The non-sarcastic partition of the training dataset is collected from the same set of subreddits that are used to collect sarcastic responses. We finally end up in selecting 4,400 posts (as well as their conversation context) for the training dataset equally balanced between sarcastic and non-sarcastic posts.

3.1.2 Twitter Training Dataset

For the Twitter dataset, we have relied upon the annotations that users assign to their tweets using hashtags. The sarcastic tweets were collected using hashtags: *#sarcasm* and *#sarcastic*. As non-sarcastic utterances, we consider sentiment tweets, i.e., we adopt the methodology proposed in related work (Muresan et al., 2016). Such sentiment tweets do not contain the sarcasm hashtags but include hashtags that contain positive or negative sentiment words. The positive tweets express direct positive sentiment and they are collected based on tweets with positive hashtags such as *#happy, #love, #lucky*. Likewise, the negative tweets express direct negative sentiment and are collected based on tweets with negative hashtags such as *#sad, #hate, #angry*. Classifying sarcastic utterances against sentiment utterances is a considerably harder task than classifying against random objective tweets since many sarcastic utterances also contain sentiment terms. Here, we are relying on *self-labeled* tweets, thus, it is always possible that sarcastic tweets were mislabeled with sentiment hashtags or users did not use the #sarcasm hashtag at all. We manually evaluated around 200 sentiment tweets and found very few such cases in the training corpus. Similar to the Reddit dataset we apply a couple of criteria while selecting the training dataset. First, we select sarcastic or non-sarcastic tweets only when they appear in a dialogue (i.e., begins with "@"-user symbol) and at least have two or more prior turns as conversation context. Second, for the non-sarcastic posts, we maintain a strict upper limit (i.e., not-greater than 10%) for any sentiment hashtag. Third, we apply heuristics such as avoiding short tweets, discarding tweets with only multiple URLs, etc. We end up selecting 5,000 tweets for training balanced between sarcastic and non-sarcastic tweets.

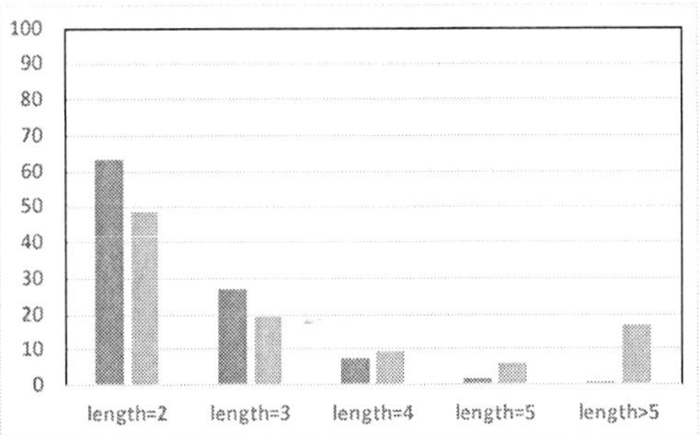

Figure 1: Plot of Reddit (blue) and Twitter (orange) training datasets on the basis of context length. X-axis represents context length (i.e., number of prior turns) and Y-axis represents the % of training utterances.

Figure 1 presents a plot of number of training utterances on the basis of context length, for Reddit and Twitter tracks respectively. We notice, although the numbers are comparable for utterances with context length equal to two or three, for Twitter corpus, utterances with a higher number of context (i.e., prior turns) is much higher.

3.1.3 Evaluation Data

The Twitter data for evaluation is curated similarly to the training data. For Reddit, we do not use Khodak et al. (2017) rather collected new sarcastic and non-sarcastic responses from Reddit. First, for sarcastic responses we utilize the same set of subreddits utilized in the training dataset, thus, keeping the same genre between the evaluation and training. For the non-sarcastic partition, we utilized the same set of subreddits and submission threads as the sarcastic partition. For both tracks the evaluation dataset contains 1800 instances partitioned equally between the sarcastic and the non-sarcastic categories.

3.2 Training Phase

In the first phase, data is released for training and/or development of sarcasm detection models (both Reddit and Twitter). Participants can choose to partition the training data further to a validation set for preliminary evaluations and/or tuning of hyper-parameters. Likewise, they can also elect to perform cross-validation on the training data.

3.3 Evaluation Phase

In the second phase, instances for evaluation are released. Each participating system generated predictions for the evaluation instances, for up to N

models. [1] Predictions are submitted to the CodaLab site and evaluated automatically against the gold labels. CodaLab is an established platform to organize shared-tasks (Leong et al., 2018) because it is easy to use, provides easy communication with the participants (e.g., allows mass-emailing) as well as tracks all the submissions updating the leaderboard in real-time. The metrics used for evaluation is the average F1 score between the two categories - sarcastic and non-sarcastic. The leaderboards displayed the Precision, Recall, and F1 scores in the descending order of the F1 scores, separately for the two tracks - Twitter and Reddit.

4 Systems

The shared task started on January 19, 2020, when the training data was made available to all the registered participants. We released the evaluation data on February 25, 2020. Submissions were accepted until March 16, 2020. Overall, we received an overwhelming number of submissions: 655 for the Reddit track and 1070 for the Twitter track. The CodaLab leaderboard showcases results from 39 systems for the Reddit track and 38 systems for the Twitter track, respectively. Out of all submissions, 14 shared task system papers were submitted. In the following section we summarize each system paper. We also put forward a comparative analysis based on their performance and the choice of features/models in Section 5. Interested readers can refer to the individual teams' papers for more details. But first, we discuss the baseline classification model that we used.

4.1 Baseline Classifier

We use prior published work as the baseline that used conversation context to detect sarcasm from social media platforms such as Twitter and Reddit (Ghosh et al., 2018). Ghosh et al. (2018) proposed a *dual LSTM architecture* with hierarchical attention where one LSTM models the conversation context and the other models sarcastic response. The hierarchical attention (Yang et al., 2016) implements two levels of attention – one at the word level and another at the sentence level. We used their system based on only the immediate conversation context (i.e., the immediate prior turn). [2] This is denoted as $LSTM_{attn}$ in Table 3 and Table 4.

<hr>

[1] N is set to 999.

[2] `https://github.com/Alex-Fabbri/deep_learning_nlp_sarcasm`

4.2 System Descriptions

We describe the participating systems in the following section (in alphabetical order).

abaruah (Baruah et al., 2020): Fine-tuned a BERT model (Devlin et al., 2018) and reported results on varying maximum sequence length (corresponding to varying level of context inclusion from just response to entire context). They also reported results of BiLSTM with FastText embeddings (of response and entire context) and SVM based on char n-gram features (again on both response and entire context). One interesting result was SVM with discrete features performed better than BiLSTM. They achieved best results with BERT on response and most immediate context.

ad6398 (Kumar and Anand, 2020): Report results comparing multiple transformer architectures (BERT, SpanBERT (Joshi et al., 2020), RoBERTa (Liu et al., 2019)) both in single sentence classification (with concatenated context and response string) and sentence pair classification (with context and response being separate inputs to a Siamese type architecture). Their best result was with using RoBERTa + LSTM model.

aditya604 (Avvaru et al., 2020): Used BERT on simple concatenation of last-k context texts and response text. The authors included details of data cleaning (de-emojification, hashtag text extraction, apostrophe expansion) as well experiments on other architectures (LSTM, CNN, XLNet (Yang et al., 2019)) and varying size of context (5, 7, complete) in their report. The best results were obtained by BERT with 7 length context for Twitter dataset and BERT with 5 context for Reddit dataset.

amitjena40 (Jena et al., 2020): Used a time-series analysis inspired approach for integrating context. Each text in conversational thread (context and response) was individually scored using BERT and Simple Exponential Smoothing (SES) was utilized to get probability of final response being sarcastic. They used the final response label as a pseudo-label for scoring the context entries, which is not theoretically grounded. If final response is sarcastic, the previous context dialogue cannot be assumed to be sarcastic (with respect to its preceding dialogue). However, the effect of this error is attenuated due to exponentially decreasing contribution of context to final label under SES scheme.

Rank	Lb. Rank	Team	P	R	F1	Approach
1	1	miroblog	0.834	0.838	0.834	BERT + BiLSTM + NeXtVLAD + Context Ensemble + Data Augmentation
2	2	andy3223	0.751	0.755	0.750	RoBERTa-Large (all the prior turns)
3	6	taha	0.738	0.739	0.737	BERT+ Local Context Focus
4	8	tanvidadu	0.716	0.718	0.716	RoBERTa-Large (last two prior turns)
5	9	nclabj	0.708	0.708	0.708	RoBERTa + Multi-Initialization Ensemble
6	12	ad6398	0.693	0.699	0.691	RoBERTa + LSTM
7	16	kalaivani.A	0.679	0.679	0.679	BERT (isolated response)
8	17	amitjena40	0.679	0.683	0.678	TorchMoji + ELMO + Simple Exp. Smoothing
9	21	burtenshaw	0.67	0.677	0.667	Ensemble of SVM, LSTM, CNN-LSTM, MLP
10	26	salokr	0.641	0.643	0.639	BERT + CNN + LSTM
11	31	adithya604	0.605	0.607	0.603	BERT (concatenation of prior turns and response)
12	-	baseline	0.600	0.599	0.600	$LSTM_{attn}$
13	32	abaruah	0.595	0.605	0.585	BERT-Large (concatenation of response and its immediate prior turn)

Table 3: Performance of the best system per team and baseline for the Reddit track. We include two ranks - ranks from the submitted systems as well as the Leaderboard ranks from the CodaLab site

AnandKumaR (Khatri and P, 2020): Experimented with using traditional ML classifiers like SVM and Logisitic Regression over embeddings through BERT and GloVe (Pennington et al., 2014). Using BERT as a feature extraction method as opposed to fine-tuning it was not beneficial and Logisitic Regression over GloVe embeddings outperformed them in their experiment. Context was used in their best model but no details were available about the depth of context usage (full vs. immediate). Additionally, they only experimented with Twitter data and no submission was made to the Reddit track. They provided details of data cleaning measures for their experiments which involved stopword removal, lowercasing, stemming, punctuation removal and spelling normalization.

andy3223 (Dong et al., 2020): Used the transformer-based architecture for sarcasm detection, reporting the performance of three architecture, BERT, RoBERTa, and ALBERT (Lan et al., 2019). They considered two models, the *target-oriented* where only the target (i.e., sarcastic response) is modeled and *context-aware*, where the context is also modeled with the target. The authors conducted extensive hyper-parameter search, and set the learning rate to 3e-5, the number of epochs to 30, and use different seed values, 21, 42, 63, for three runs. Additionally, they set the maximum sequence length 128 for the *target-oriented* models while it is set to 256 for the *context-aware* models.

burtenshaw (Lemmens et al., 2020): Employed an ensemble of four models - LSTM (on word, emoji and hashtag representations), CNN-LSTM (on GloVe embeddings with discrete punctuation and sentiment features), MLP (on sentence embeddings through Infersent (Conneau et al., 2017)) and SVM (on character and stylometric features). The first three models (except SVM) used the last two immediate contexts along with the response.

duke_DS (Gregory et al., 2020): Here the authors have conducted extensive set of experiments using discrete features, DNNs, as well as transformer models, however, reporting only the results on the Twitter track. Regarding discrete features, one of novelties in their approach is including a *predictor* to identify whether the tweet is political or not, since many sarcastic tweets are on political topics. Regarding the models, the best performing model is an ensemble of five transformers: BERT-base-uncased, RoBERTa-base, XLNet-base-cased, RoBERTa-large, and ALBERT-base-v2.

kalaivani.A (kalaivani A and D, 2020): Compared traditional machine learning classifiers (e.g., Logistic Regression/Random Forest/XGBoost/Linear SVC/ Gaussian Naive Bayes) on discrete bag-of-word features/Doc2Vec features with LSTM models on Word2Vec embeddings (Mikolov et al., 2013) and BERT models. For context usage they report results on using isolated response, isolated context and context-response combined (unclear as to how deep the context usage is). The best performance for their experiments was by BERT on isolated response.

miroblog (Lee et al., 2020): Implemented a classifier composed of BERT followed by BiLSTM and NeXtVLAD (Lin et al., 2018) (a differentiable pooling mechanism which empirically performed better than Mean/Max pooling). [3] They employed an ensembling approach for including varying length context and reported that gains in F1 after context of length three are negligible. Just with these two contributions alone, their model outperformed all others. Additionally, they devised a novel approach of data augmentation (i.e., Contextual Response Augmentation) from unlabelled conversational contexts based on next sentence prediction confidence score of BERT. Leveraging large-scale unlabelled conversation data from web, their model outperformed the second best system by 14% and 8.4% for Twitter and Reddit respectively (absolute F1 score).

nclabj (Jaiswal, 2020): Used a majority-voting ensemble of RoBERTa models with different weight-initialization and different levels of context length. Their report shows that previous 3 turns of dialogues had the best performance in isolation. Additionally, the present results comparing other sentence embedding architectures like Universal Sentence Encoder (Cer et al., 2018), ELMo (Peters et al., 2018) and BERT.

salokr/vaibhav (Srivastava et al., 2020) : Employed a CNN-LSTM based architecture on BERT embeddings to utilize the full context thread and the response. The entire context after encoding through BERT is passed through CNN and LSTM layers to get a representation of the context. Convolution and dense layers over this summarized context representation and BERT encoding of response make up the final classifier.

taha (ataei et al., 2020): Reported experiments comparing SVM on character n-gram features, LSTM-CNN models, Transformer models as well as a novel usage of aspect based sentiment classification approaches like Interactive Attention

Networks(IAN) (Ma et al., 2017), Local Context Focus(LCF)-BERT (Zeng et al., 2019) and BERT-Attentional Encoder network (AEN) (Song et al., 2019). For aspect based approaches, they viewed the last dialogue of conversational context as aspect of the target response. LCF-BERT was their best model for the Twitter task but due to computational resource limitations they were not able to try it for Reddit task (where BERT on just the response text performed best).

tanvidadu (Dadu and Pant, 2020): Fine-tuned RoBERTa-large model (355 Million parameters with over a 50K vocabulary size) on response and its two immediate contexts. They reported results on three different types of inputs: response-only model, concatenation of immediate two context with response, and using an explicit separator token between the response and the final context. The best result is reported in the setting where they used the separation token.

5 Results and Discussions

Table 3 and Table 4 present the results for the Reddit track and the Twitter track, respectively. We show the rank of the submitted systems (best result from their submitted reports) both in terms of the system submissions (out of 14) as well as their rank on the Codalab leaderboard. Note, for a couple of entries we observe a discrepancy between their best reported system(s) and the leaderboard entries. For the sake of fairness, for such cases, we selected the leaderboard entries to present in Table 3 and Table 4. [4]

Also, out of the 14 system descriptions *duke_DS* and *AnadKumR* report the performance on the Twitter dataset, only. For overall results on both tracks, we observe majority of the models outperformed the $LSTM_{attn}$ baseline (Ghosh et al., 2018). Almost all the submitted systems have used the transformer-architecture that seems to perform better than RNN-architecture, even without any task-specific fine-tuning. Although most of the models are similar and perform comparably, we observe a particular system - miroblog - has outperformed the other models in both the tracks by posting an improvement over the 2nd ranked system by more than 7% F1-score in the Reddit track and by 14% F1-score in the Twitter track.

---

[3] VLAD is an acronym of "Vector of Locally Aggregated Descriptors" (Lin et al., 2018).

[4] Also, for such cases (e.g., abaruah, under the *Approach* column we reported the approach described in the system paper that is not necessarily reflect the scores of Table 3.

Rank	Lb. Rank	Team	P	R	F1	Approach
1	1	miroblog	0.932	0.936	0.931	BERT + BiLSTM + NeXtVLAD + Context Ensemble + Data Augmentation
2	2	nclabj	0.792	0.793	0.791	RoBERTa + Multi-Initialization Ensemble
3	3	andy3223	0.791	0.794	0.790	RoBERTa-Large (all the prior turns)
4	5	ad6398	0.773	0.774	0.772	RoBERTa + LSTM
5	6	tanvidadu	0.772	0.772	0.772	RoBERTa-Large (last two prior turns)
6	8	duke_DS	0.758	0.767	0.756	Ensemble of Transformers
7	11	amitjena40	0.751	0.751	0.750	TorchMoji + ELMO + Simple Exp. Smoothing
8	13	salokr	0.742	0.746	0.741	BERT + CNN + LSTM
9	16	burtenshaw	0.741	0.746	0.740	Ensemble of SVM, LSTM, CNN-LSTM, MLP
10	21	abaruah	0.734	0.735	0.734	BERT-Large (concatenation of response and its immediate prior turn)
11	24	taha	0.731	0.732	0.731	BERT
12	27	kalaivani.A	0.722	0.722	0.722	BERT (isolated response)
13	28	adithya604	0.719	0.721	0.719	BERT (concatenation of prior turns and response)
14	35	AnadKumR	0.690	0.690	0.690	GloVe + Logistic Regression
15	-	baseline	0.700	0.669	0.680	$LSTM_{attn}$

Table 4: Performance of the best system per team and baseline for the Twitter track. We include two ranks - ranks from the submitted systems as well as the Leaderboard ranks from the CodaLab site

In the following paragraphs, we inspect the performance of the different systems more closely. We discuss a couple of particular aspects.

Context Usage: One of the prime motivating factors for conducting this shared task was to investigate the role of contextual information. We notice the most common approach for integrating context was simply concatenating it with the response text. Novel approaches include :

1. Taking immediate context as aspect for response in Aspect-based Sentiment Classification architectures (**taha**)

2. CNN-LSTM based summarization of entire context thread (**salokr**)

3. Time-series fusion with proxy labels for context (**amitjena40**)

4. Ensemble of multiple models with different depth of context (**miroblog**)

5. Using explicit separator between context and response when concatenating (**tanvidadu**)

Depth of Context: Results suggest that beyond three context turns, gains from context information are negligible and may also reduce the performance due to sparsity of long context threads. The depth of context required is dependent on the architecture and CNN-LSTM based summarization of context thread (**salokr**) was the only approach that effectively used the whole dialogue.

Discrete vs. Embedding Features The leaderboard was dominated by Transformer based architectures and we saw submissions using BERT or RoBERTa and other variants. Other sentence embedding architectures like Infersent, CNN/LSTM over word embeddings were also used but had middling performances. Discrete features were involved in only two submissions (**burtenshaw** and **duke_DS**) and were the focus of **burtenshaw** system.

Leveraging other datasets The large difference between the best model (**miroblog**) and other systems can be attributed to their dataset augmentation strategies. Using just the context thread as a negative example when the context+response is a positive example, is a straight-forward approach for augmentation from labeled dialogues. Their novel contribution lies in leveraging large-scaled unlabelled dialogue threads, showing another use of BERT by using NSP confidence score for assigning pseudo-labels.

Analysis of predictions: Finally, we conducted an error analysis based on the predictions of the systems. We particularly focused on addressing two questions. First, we investigate whether any particular pattern exists in the evaluation instances that are wrongly classified by the majority of the systems. Second, we compare the predictions of the top-performing systems to identify instances correctly classified by the candidate system but missed by the remaining systems. Here, we attempt to recognize specific characteristics that are unique to a model, if any.

Instead of looking at the predictions of all the systems we decided to analyze only the *top-three* submissions in both tracks because of their high performances. We identify 80 instances (30 sarcastic) from the Reddit evaluation dataset and 20 instances (10 sarcastic) from the Twitter evaluation set, respectively, that are missed by all the top-performing systems. Our interpretation of this finding is that all these test instances more or less belong to a variety of topics including sarcastic remarks on baseball teams, internet bills, vaccination, etc., that probably do not generalize well during the training. For both Twitter and Reddit, we also found many sarcastic examples that contain common non-sarcastic markers such as laughs (e.g., "haha"), jokes, positive-sentiment emoticons (e.g., :)) in terms of Twitter track. We did not find any correlation to context length. Most of the instances contain varied context length, from two to six.

While analyzing the predictions of individual systems we noted that **miroblog** correctly identifies the most number of predictions for both the tracks. In fact, miroblog has successfully predicted over two hundred examples (with almost equal distribution of sarcastic and non-sarcastic instances) in comparison to the second-ranked and third-ranked systems for both tracks. As stated earlier, this can be attributed to their data augmentation strategies that have assisted miroblog's models to generalize best. However, we still notice that instances with subtle humor or positive sentiment are missed by the best-performing models even if they are pre-trained on a very large-scale corpora. We foresee models that are able to detect subtle humor or witty wordplay will perform even better in a sarcasm detection task.

6 Conclusion

This paper summarizes the results of the shared task on sarcasm detection using conversation from two social media platforms (Reddit and Twitter),

organized as part of the 2nd Workshop on the Figurative Language Processing at ACL 2020. This shared task aimed to investigate the role of conversation context for sarcasm detection. The goal was to understand how much conversation context is needed or helpful for sarcasm detection. For Reddit, the training data was sampled from the standard corpus from Khodak et al. (2017) whereas we curated a new evaluation dataset. For Twitter, both the training and the test datasets are new and collected using standard hashtags. We received 655 submissions (from 39 unique participants) and 1070 submissions (from 38 unique participants) for Reddit and Twitter tracks, respectively. We provided brief descriptions of each of the participating systems who submitted a shared task paper (14 systems).

We notice that almost every submitted system have used transformer-based architectures, such as BERT and RoBERTa and other variants, emphasizing the increasing popularity of using pre-trained language models for various classification tasks. The best systems, however, have employed a clever mix of ensemble techniques and/or data augmentation setups, which seem to be a promising direction for future work. We hope that some of the teams will make their implementations publicly available, which would facilitate further research on improving performance on the sarcasm detection task.

References

kalaivani A and Thenmozhi D. 2020. Sarcasm identification and detection in conversion context using BERT. In *Proceedings of the Second Workshop on Figurative Language Processing, Seattle, WA, USA.*

Silvio Amir, Byron C Wallace, Hao Lyu, and Paula Carvalho Mário J Silva. 2016. Modelling context with user embeddings for sarcasm detection in social media. *arXiv preprint arXiv:1607.00976.*

Taha Shangipour ataei, Soroush Javdan, and Behrouz Minaei-Bidgoli. 2020. Applying Transformers and aspect-based sentiment analysis approaches on sarcasm detection. In *Proceedings of the Second Workshop on Figurative Language Processing, Seattle, WA, USA.*

Adithya Avvaru, Sanath Vobilisetty, and Radhika Mamidi. 2020. Detecting sarcasm in conversation context using Transformer based model. In *Proceedings of the Second Workshop on Figurative Language Processing, Seattle, WA, USA.*

David Bamman and Noah A Smith. 2015. Contextualized sarcasm detection on twitter. In *Ninth International AAAI Conference on Web and Social Media*.

Arup Baruah, Kaushik Das, Ferdous Barbhuiya, and Kuntal Dey. 2020. Context-aware sarcasm detection using BERT. In *Proceedings of the Second Workshop on Figurative Language Processing, Seattle, WA, USA*.

Yitao Cai, Huiyu Cai, and Xiaojun Wan. 2019. Multimodal sarcasm detection in twitter with hierarchical fusion model. In *Proceedings of the 57th Annual Meeting of the Association for Computational Linguistics*, pages 2506–2515.

Santiago Castro, Devamanyu Hazarika, Verónica Pérez-Rosas, Roger Zimmermann, Rada Mihalcea, and Soujanya Poria. 2019. Towards multimodal sarcasm detection (an _obviously_ perfect paper). In *Proceedings of the 57th Annual Meeting of the Association for Computational Linguistics*, pages 4619–4629.

Daniel Cer, Yinfei Yang, Sheng-yi Kong, Nan Hua, Nicole Limtiaco, Rhomni St John, Noah Constant, Mario Guajardo-Cespedes, Steve Yuan, Chris Tar, et al. 2018. Universal sentence encoder. *arXiv preprint arXiv:1803.11175*.

Alexis Conneau, Douwe Kiela, Holger Schwenk, Loic Barrault, and Antoine Bordes. 2017. Supervised learning of universal sentence representations from natural language inference data. *arXiv preprint arXiv:1705.02364*.

Tanvi Dadu and Kartikey Pant. 2020. Sarcasm detection using context separators in online discourse. In *Proceedings of the Second Workshop on Figurative Language Processing, Seattle, WA, USA*.

Dmitry Davidov, Oren Tsur, and Ari Rappoport. 2010. Semi-supervised recognition of sarcastic sentences in twitter and amazon. In *Proceedings of the Fourteenth Conference on Computational Natural Language Learning*, CoNLL '10.

Jacob Devlin, Ming-Wei Chang, Kenton Lee, and Kristina Toutanova. 2018. Bert: Pre-training of deep bidirectional transformers for language understanding. *arXiv preprint arXiv:1810.04805*.

Xiangjue Dong, Changmao Li, and Jinho D. Choi. 2020. Transformer-based context-aware sarcasm detection in conversation threads from social media. In *Proceedings of the Second Workshop on Figurative Language Processing, Seattle, WA, USA*.

Bjarke Felbo, Alan Mislove, Anders Søgaard, Iyad Rahwan, and Sune Lehmann. 2017. Using millions of emoji occurrences to learn any-domain representations for detecting sentiment, emotion and sarcasm. In *Proceedings of the 2017 Conference on Empirical Methods in Natural Language Processing*, pages 1615–1625. Association for Computational Linguistics.

Aniruddha Ghosh and Tony Veale. 2016. Fracking sarcasm using neural network. In *Proceedings of NAACL-HLT*, pages 161–169.

Aniruddha Ghosh and Tony Veale. 2017. Magnets for sarcasm: Making sarcasm detection timely, contextual and very personal. In *Proceedings of the 2017 Conference on Empirical Methods in Natural Language Processing*, pages 482–491. Association for Computational Linguistics.

Debanjan Ghosh, Alexander R Fabbri, and Smaranda Muresan. 2018. Sarcasm analysis using conversation context. *arXiv preprint arXiv:1808.07531*.

Debanjan Ghosh, Alexander Richard Fabbri, and Smaranda Muresan. 2017. The role of conversation context for sarcasm detection in online interactions. *arXiv preprint arXiv:1707.06226*.

Debanjan Ghosh, Weiwei Guo, and Smaranda Muresan. 2015. Sarcastic or not: Word embeddings to predict the literal or sarcastic meaning of words. In *Proceedings of the 2015 Conference on Empirical Methods in Natural Language Processing*, pages 1003–1012, Lisbon, Portugal. Association for Computational Linguistics.

Debanjan Ghosh and Smaranda Muresan. 2018. " with 1 follower i must be awesome: P". exploring the role of irony markers in irony recognition. *arXiv preprint arXiv:1804.05253*.

Debanjan Ghosh, Elena Musi, Kartikeya Upasani, and Smaranda Muresan. 2019. Interpreting verbal irony: Linguistic strategies and the connection to the type of semantic incongruity. *arXiv preprint arXiv:1911.00891*.

Roberto González-Ibáñez, Smaranda Muresan, and Nina Wacholder. 2011. Identifying sarcasm in twitter: A closer look. In *ACL (Short Papers)*, pages 581–586. Association for Computational Linguistics.

Hunter Gregory, Steven Li, Pouya Mohammadi, Natalie Tarn, Rachel Ballantyne, and Cynthia Rudin. 2020. A Transformer approach to contextual sarcasm detection in twitter. In *Proceedings of the Second Workshop on Figurative Language Processing, Seattle, WA, USA*.

Devamanyu Hazarika, Soujanya Poria, Sruthi Gorantla, Erik Cambria, Roger Zimmermann, and Rada Mihalcea. 2018. Cascade: Contextual sarcasm detection in online discussion forums. In *Proceedings of the 27th International Conference on Computational Linguistics*, pages 1837–1848. Association for Computational Linguistics.

Nikhil Jaiswal. 2020. Neural sarcasm detection using conversation context. In *Proceedings of the Second Workshop on Figurative Language Processing, Seattle, WA, USA*.

Amit Kumar Jena, Aman Sinha, and Rohit Agarwal. 2020. C-net: Contextual network for sarcasm detection. In *Proceedings of the Second Workshop on Figurative Language Processing, Seattle, WA, USA*.

Aditya Joshi, Pushpak Bhattacharyya, and Mark J Carman. 2017. Automatic sarcasm detection: A survey. *ACM Computing Surveys (CSUR)*, page 73.

Aditya Joshi, Vinita Sharma, and Pushpak Bhattacharyya. 2015. Harnessing context incongruity for sarcasm detection. In *Proceedings of the 53rd Annual Meeting of the Association for Computational Linguistics and the 7th International Joint Conference on Natural Language Processing (Volume 2: Short Papers)*, volume 2, pages 757–762.

Aditya Joshi, Vaibhav Tripathi, Pushpak Bhattacharyya, and Mark Carman. 2016. Harnessing sequence labeling for sarcasm detection in dialogue from tv series 'friends'. *CoNLL 2016*, page 146.

Mandar Joshi, Danqi Chen, Yinhan Liu, Daniel S Weld, Luke Zettlemoyer, and Omer Levy. 2020. Spanbert: Improving pre-training by representing and predicting spans. *Transactions of the Association for Computational Linguistics*, 8:64–77.

Akshay Khatri and Pranav P. 2020. Sarcasm detection in tweets with BERT and GloVe embeddings. In *Proceedings of the Second Workshop on Figurative Language Processing, Seattle, WA, USA*.

Anupam Khattri, Aditya Joshi, Pushpak Bhattacharyya, and Mark Carman. 2015. Your sentiment precedes you: Using an author's historical tweets to predict sarcasm. In *Proceedings of the 6th Workshop on Computational Approaches to Subjectivity, Sentiment and Social Media Analysis*, pages 25–30, Lisboa, Portugal. Association for Computational Linguistics.

Mikhail Khodak, Nikunj Saunshi, and Kiran Vodrahalli. 2017. A large self-annotated corpus for sarcasm. *arXiv preprint arXiv:1704.05579*.

Amardeep Kumar and Vivek Anand. 2020. Transformers on sarcasm detection with context. In *Proceedings of the Second Workshop on Figurative Language Processing, Seattle, WA, USA*.

Zhenzhong Lan, Mingda Chen, Sebastian Goodman, Kevin Gimpel, Piyush Sharma, and Radu Soricut. 2019. Albert: A lite bert for self-supervised learning of language representations. *arXiv preprint arXiv:1909.11942*.

Hankyol Lee, Youngjae Yu, and Gunhee Kim. 2020. Augmenting data for sarcasm detection with unlabeled conversation context. In *Proceedings of the Second Workshop on Figurative Language Processing, Seattle, WA, USA*.

Jens Lemmens, Ben Burtenshaw, Ehsan Lotfi, Ilia Markov, and Walter Daelemans. 2020. Sarcasm detection using an ensemble approach. In *Proceedings of the Second Workshop on Figurative Language Processing, Seattle, WA, USA*.

Chee Wee Leong, Beata Beigman Klebanov, and Ekaterina Shutova. 2018. A report on the 2018 vua metaphor detection shared task. In *Proceedings of the Workshop on Figurative Language Processing*, pages 56–66.

CC Liebrecht, FA Kunneman, and APJ van den Bosch. 2013. The perfect solution for detecting sarcasm in tweets# not. In *Proceedings of the 4th Workshop on Computational Approaches to Subjectivity, Sentiment and Social Media Analysis*.

Rongcheng Lin, Jing Xiao, and Jianping Fan. 2018. Nextvlad: An efficient neural network to aggregate frame-level features for large-scale video classification. In *Proceedings of the European Conference on Computer Vision (ECCV)*, pages 0–0.

Yinhan Liu, Myle Ott, Naman Goyal, Jingfei Du, Mandar Joshi, Danqi Chen, Omer Levy, Mike Lewis, Luke Zettlemoyer, and Veselin Stoyanov. 2019. Roberta: A robustly optimized bert pretraining approach. *arXiv preprint arXiv:1907.11692*.

Dehong Ma, Sujian Li, Xiaodong Zhang, and Houfeng Wang. 2017. Interactive attention networks for aspect-level sentiment classification. *arXiv preprint arXiv:1709.00893*.

Navonil Majumder, Soujanya Poria, Haiyun Peng, Niyati Chhaya, Erik Cambria, and Alexander Gelbukh. 2019. Sentiment and sarcasm classification with multitask learning. *IEEE Intelligent Systems*, 34(3):38–43.

Diana Maynard and Mark A Greenwood. 2014. Who cares about sarcastic tweets? investigating the impact of sarcasm on sentiment analysis. In *Proceedings of LREC*.

Tomas Mikolov, Ilya Sutskever, Kai Chen, Greg S Corrado, and Jeff Dean. 2013. Distributed representations of words and phrases and their compositionality. In *Advances in Neural Information Processing Systems*, pages 3111–3119.

Abhijit Mishra, Diptesh Kanojia, Seema Nagar, Kuntal Dey, and Pushpak Bhattacharyya. 2016. Harnessing cognitive features for sarcasm detection. In *Proceedings of the 54th Annual Meeting of the Association for Computational Linguistics*, pages 1095–1104, Berlin, Germany.

Smaranda Muresan, Roberto Gonzalez-Ibanez, Debanjan Ghosh, and Nina Wacholder. 2016. Identification of nonliteral language in social media: A case study on sarcasm. *Journal of the Association for Information Science and Technology*, 67(11):2725–2737.

Silviu Oprea and Walid Magdy. 2019. Exploring author context for detecting intended vs perceived sarcasm. In *Proceedings of the 57th Annual Meeting of the Association for Computational Linguistics*, pages 2854–2859.

Jeffrey Pennington, Richard Socher, and Christopher D Manning. 2014. Glove: Global vectors for word representation. *Proceedings of the Empiricial Methods in Natural Language Processing (EMNLP 2014)*, 12.

Matthew E Peters, Mark Neumann, Mohit Iyyer, Matt Gardner, Christopher Clark, Kenton Lee, and Luke Zettlemoyer. 2018. Deep contextualized word representations. *arXiv preprint arXiv:1802.05365*.

Ashwin Rajadesingan, Reza Zafarani, and Huan Liu. 2015. Sarcasm detection on twitter: A behavioral modeling approach. In *Proceedings of the Eighth ACM International Conference on Web Search and Data Mining*, pages 97–106. ACM.

Ellen Riloff, Ashequl Qadir, Prafulla Surve, Lalindra De Silva, Nathan Gilbert, and Ruihong Huang. 2013. Sarcasm as contrast between a positive sentiment and negative situation. In *Proceedings of the 2013 Conference on Empirical Methods in Natural Language Processing*, pages 704–714.

Rossano Schifanella, Paloma de Juan, Joel Tetreault, and Liangliang Cao. 2016. Detecting sarcasm in multimodal social platforms. In *Proceedings of the 2016 ACM on Multimedia Conference*, pages 1136–1145. ACM.

Youwei Song, Jiahai Wang, Tao Jiang, Zhiyue Liu, and Yanghui Rao. 2019. Attentional encoder network for targeted sentiment classification. *arXiv preprint arXiv:1902.09314*.

Himani Srivastava, Vaibhav Varshney, Surabhi Kumari, and Saurabh Srivastava. 2020. A novel hierarchical BERT architecture for sarcasm detection. In *Proceedings of the Second Workshop on Figurative Language Processing, Seattle, WA, USA*.

Yi Tay, Anh Tuan Luu, Siu Cheung Hui, and Jian Su. 2018. Reasoning with sarcasm by reading in-between. In *Proceedings of the 56th Annual Meeting of the Association for Computational Linguistics (Volume 1: Long Papers)*, pages 1010–1020. Association for Computational Linguistics.

Oren Tsur, Dmitry Davidov, and Ari Rappoport. 2010. Icwsm-a great catchy name: Semi-supervised recognition of sarcastic sentences in online product reviews. In *ICWSM*.

Cynthia Van Hee, Els Lefever, and Véronique Hoste. 2018. Semeval-2018 task 3: Irony detection in english tweets. In *Proceedings of The 12th International Workshop on Semantic Evaluation*, pages 39–50.

Tony Veale and Yanfen Hao. 2010. Detecting ironic intent in creative comparisons. In *European Conference on Artificial Intelligence*, volume 215, pages 765–770, Lisbon, Portugal.

Byron C Wallace. 2015. Computational irony: A survey and new perspectives. *Artificial Intelligence Review*, 43(4):467–483.

Byron C Wallace, Do Kook Choe, Laura Kertz, and Eugene Charniak. 2014. Humans require context to infer ironic intent (so computers probably do, too). In *ACL (2)*, pages 512–516.

Zelin Wang, Zhijian Wu, Ruimin Wang, and Yafeng Ren. 2015. Twitter sarcasm detection exploiting a context-based model. In *International Conference on Web Information Systems Engineering*, pages 77–91, Miami, Florida. Springer.

Zhilin Yang, Zihang Dai, Yiming Yang, Jaime Carbonell, Russ R Salakhutdinov, and Quoc V Le. 2019. Xlnet: Generalized autoregressive pretraining for language understanding. In *Advances in neural information processing systems*, pages 5754–5764.

Zichao Yang, Diyi Yang, Chris Dyer, Xiaodong He, Alex Smola, and Eduard Hovy. 2016. Hierarchical attention networks for document classification. In *Proceedings of NAACL-HLT*, pages 1480–1489.

Biqing Zeng, Heng Yang, Ruyang Xu, Wu Zhou, and Xuli Han. 2019. Lcf: A local context focus mechanism for aspect-based sentiment classification. *Applied Sciences*, 9(16):3389.

Meishan Zhang, Yue Zhang, and Guohong Fu. 2016. Tweet sarcasm detection using deep neural network. In *Proceedings of COLING 2016, The 26th International Conference on Computational Linguistics: Technical Papers*, pages 2449–2460.

Augmenting Data for Sarcasm Detection
with Unlabeled Conversation Context

Hankyol Lee
RippleAI
Seoul, Korea
hklee@rippleai.co

Youngjae Yu
RippleAI & SNU
Seoul, Korea
yj.yu@rippleai.co

Gunhee Kim
RippleAI & SNU
Seoul, Korea
gunhee@snu.ac.kr

Abstract

We present a novel data augmentation technique, CRA (Contextual Response Augmentation), which utilizes conversational context to generate meaningful samples for training. We also mitigate the issues regarding unbalanced context lengths by changing the input-output format of the model such that it can deal with varying context lengths effectively. Specifically, our proposed model, trained with the proposed data augmentation technique, participated in the sarcasm detection task of FigLang2020, have won and achieves the best performance in both Reddit and Twitter datasets.

1 Introduction

The performance of many NLP systems largely depends on their ability to understand figurative languages such as irony, sarcasm, and metaphor (Pozzi et al., 2016). The results from the Sentiment Analysis task held in SemEval-2014 (Martínez-Cámara et al., 2014), for example, show that apparent performance drops occur when the figurative language is involved in the task. This work aims, in particular, to design a model that identifies sarcasm in the conversational context. More specifically, the goal is to determine whether a response is sarcastic or not, given the immediate context (*i.e.* only the previous dialogue turn) and/or the full dialogue thread (if available). For evaluation of our model, we participated in the FigLang2020 sarcasm challenge[1], and have won the competition as our model is ranked 1 out of 35 teams for the Twitter dataset and 1 out of 34 teams for the Reddit dataset.

We summarize our technical contributions to win the challenge as follows:

1. We propose a new data augmentation technique that can successfully leverage the structural patterns of the conversational dataset. Our technique, called CRA(Contextual Response Augmentation), utilizes the conversational context of the unlabeled dataset to generate new training samples.

2. The context lengths (*i.e.* previous dialogue turns) are highly variable across the dataset. To cope with such imbalance, we propose a context ensemble method that exploits multiple context lengths to train the model. The proposed format is easily applicable to any Transformer (Vaswani et al., 2017) encoders without changing any model architecture.

3. We propose an architecture where the Transformer Encoder is stacked with BiLSTM (Schuster and Paliwal, 1997) and NeXtVLAD (Lin et al., 2018). We observe that NeXtVLAD, a differentiable pooling layer, proves more effective than simple non-parametric mean/max pooling methods.

2 Approach

The task of our interest is, given response (r_1) and its previous conversational context ($c_1, c_2, \cdots, c_n$), to predict whether the response r_1 is sarcastic or not (See an example in Figure 2). We below discuss our model (section 2.1), training details (section 2.2) and the proposed data augmentation techniques (section 2.3).

	$train_{data}$	$valid_{data}$	$test_{data}$
Twitter	4000	1000	1800
Reddit	3520	880	1800

Table 1: Dataset Splitting.

---

[1] https://competitions.codalab.org/competitions/22247.

Proceedings of the Second Workshop on Figurative Language Processing, pages 12–17
July 9, 2020. ©2020 Association for Computational Linguistics
https://doi.org/10.18653/v1/P17

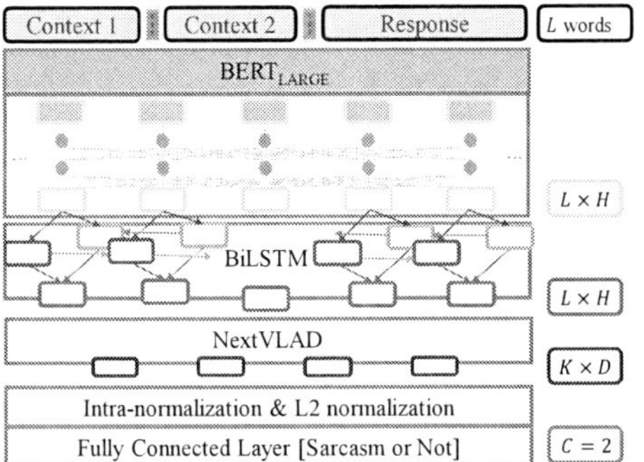

Figure 1: The architecture of our best performing model for sarcasm detection.

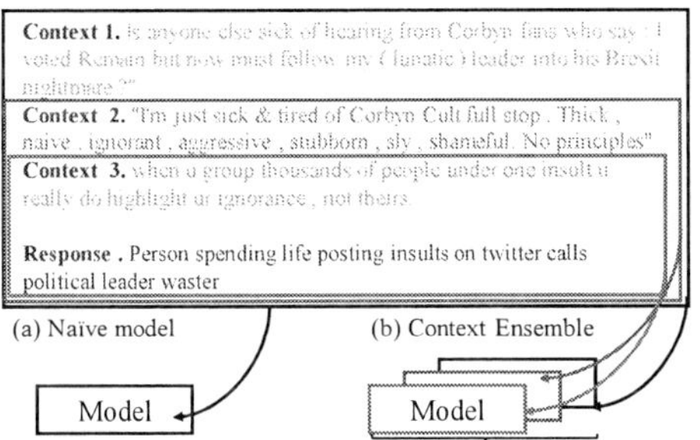

Figure 2: Illustration of the context ensemble method for Sarcasm detection. We train multiple models with different context window sizes, and ensemble them for inference.

2.1 The Model

Figure 1 describes the architecture of our best performing model. The model broadly consists of two parts: the transformer (BERT) (Devlin et al., 2018) and pooling layers, which are decomposed into BiLSTM (Schuster and Paliwal, 1997) and NeXtVLAD (Lin et al., 2018) as an improved version of NetVLAD (Arandjelovic et al., 2016). Reportedly, NetVLAD is a CNN-model that is highly effective and more resistant to over-fitting than usual temporal models such as LSTM or GRU (Lin et al., 2018). The Implementation of these models are as follows:

- BERT(large-cased): 24-layer, 1024-hidden and 16-heads.

- BiLSTM: 2-layer, 1024-hidden and 0.25-dropout.

- NeXtVLAD: 8-groups, 4-expansion, 128-number of clusters and 512-cluster size.

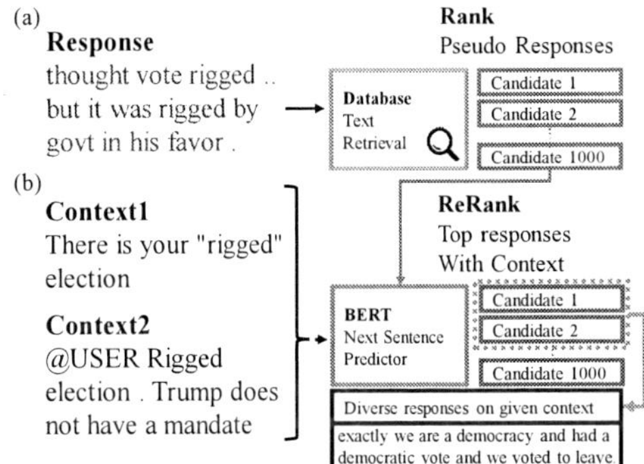

Figure 3: Overview of the proposed Contextual Response Augmentation (CRA). Using (a) Text query retrieval on sarcasm database and (b) Reranking best responses conditioned on a given context, we obtain various pseudo responses that are useful for training.

2.2 Training Details

We use the entropy loss on the last softmax layer in the model. The training batch size is 4 for all the experiments. We adopt the cyclic learning rate (Smith, 2017), where the initial learning rate is 1e-6, and the moment parameters are (0.825, 0.725).

Dataset Splitting. We further split the provided training set ($training_{data}$) into the training ($train_{data}$) and validation ($valid_{data}$) set as in Table 1. We use $valid_{data}$ for early stopping and the model performance validation during the training phase.

Context Ensemble. Figure 2 depicts the idea of the context ensemble method to cope with highly variable context lengths in the dataset. Instead of using the training data as their original forms only (Figure 2(a)), we consider multiple context window sizes as separate data, which can naturally balance out the proportion of short and long context (Figure 2(b)).

2.3 Data Augmentation

Van Hee et al. (2018) and Ilić et al. (2018) have observed that in the case of Twitter, fueling additional data from the same domain did not help much the performance for detecting sarcasm and irony. However, this does not mean that the data augmentation would fail to improve sarcasm detection. We use two techniques to augment the training data according to whether the data are labeled or not. Especially, our data augmentation method named Contextual Response Augmentation (CRA) can take advantage of unlabeled dialogue threads, which are abundant and cheaply collectible. Fig-

	An unsarcastic sample		
c1	Dont mind me, its just a gun		
c2	The dude in the front row is like 'Are we gonna do something?'		
	It's the perfect example of how the bystander effect works, even amongst police (or whatever they are)		
c3	100% if they were alone and saw this they'd doay something to the guy.		
	But together you get a pack mentality.		
r1	Unfortunately, the police are sometimes the victimizers		
	A sarcastic sample		
c1	Trump won Wisconsin by 27,000 votes. 300,000 voters were turned away by the states strict Voter ID law. There is your ïggedëlection ."		
c2	@USER Rigged election . Trump does not have a mandate . Period.		
r1	@USER @USER @USER exactly we are a democracy and had a democratic vote and we voted to leave		

Table 2: Samples generated from unlabeled dataset

Metric	Precision		Recall		F1	
dataset	$twitter_{valid}$	$reddit_{valid}$	$twitter_{valid}$	$reddit_{valid}$	$twitter_{valid}$	$reddit_{valid}$
T+BiLSTM+NeXtVLAD	0.8295	0.6414	0.8816	0.7867	0.8548	0.7067
T+BiLSTM+MaxPool	0.8558	0.6620	0.8182	0.7092	0.8366	0.6848
T+BiLSTM+MeanPool	0.7339	0.6881	0.8683	0.5837	0.7954	0.6316
T+NeXtVLAD	0.8163	0.5891	0.8785	0.7976	0.8462	0.6777
T+BiLSTM+NeXtVLAD	0.8747	0.6938	0.9219	0.8187	0.8977	0.7513
T+BiLSTM+MaxPool	0.8318	0.6624	0.8751	0.7910	0.8529	0.7210
T+BiLSTM+MeanPool	0.7856	0.6089	0.8792	0.8070	0.8298	0.6941
T+NeXtVLAD	0.8525	0.6888	0.9101	0.7792	0.8804	0.7313

Table 3: Sarcasm detection performance on the validation set. The upper and lower part of the table respectively denote the performance before and after data augmentation is applied. We set the context length to 3 for all models.

ure 3 illustrates the overview of our CRA method whose details are presented in section 2.3.2.

2.3.1 Augmentation with Labeled Data

Each training sample consists of contextual utterances, a response and its label ("SARCASM" or "NOT_SARCASM"): $[c_1, c_2, \cdots, c_n, r_1, l_1]$. Our idea is to take the context sequence $[c_1, c_2, \cdots, c_n]$ as a new datapoint and label it as "NOT_SARCASM". As shown in Figure 2, without the response $[r_1]$, the sequence could not be labeled as "SARCASM". We hypothesize that these newly generated negative samples help the model better focus on the relationship between the response $[r_1]$ and its contexts $[c_1, c_2, \cdots, c_n]$. Also, we balance out the number of negative samples by creating positive samples via back-translation methods (Bérard et al. (2019); Zheng et al. (2019)), which simply translate the sentences into another language and then back to the original language to obtain possibly rephrased data points. For the back-translation, we have used 3 languages [French, Spanish, Dutch].

2.3.2 Augmentation with Unlabeled Data

We also generate additional training samples using the unlabeled data: $[c_1, c_2, \cdots, c_n, r_1]$. This approach is tremendously useful since a huge amount of unlabeled dialogue threads can be collected at little cost. As shown in Figure 3, the procedures for unlabeled augmentation are as follows:

1. We encode each response in the labeled training set using the BERT trained on natural inference tasks (Reimers and Gurevych, 2019).

2. Given unlabeled data $[c_1, c_2, \cdots, c_n, r_1]$, we encode $[r_1]$ and find the most similar top $k(= 1000)$ data from the labeled database. We denote them as $\{r_{t,1}, \cdots, r_{t,k}\}$.

3. We rank the top k candidates according to the next sentence prediction (NSP) confidence of BERT[2]. That is, we input $[c_1, c_2, \cdots, c_n, sep, r_{t,i}]$ to BERT, and compute the NSP confidence of $r_{t,i}$ for all $i \in \{1, \cdots, k\}$. We then select the most confident response r_t^* with its label l_t^* and make a new data point $[c_1, c_2, \cdots, c_n, r_t^*, l_t^*]$.

Table 2 shows some samples generated from this technique. The quality of generated data depends undoubtedly on the degree of contextual conformity and similarity between the initial responses. We find, however, that adding more data makes the quality of the augmented data better as the label transfer noise becomes attenuated. In summary, besides the standard datasets shown in Table 7, we

---

[2] We fine-tune BERT only for the next sentence prediction task using the corpora in Table 7 and the $training_{data}$

Teams	Precision	Recall	F1
miroblog	**0.932**	**0.936**	**0.931**
nclabj	0.792	0.793	0.791
Andy3223	0.7910	0.7940	0.790
DeepBlueAI	0.78	0.785	0.779
ad6398	0.773	0.775	0.772
miroblog	**0.834**	**0.838**	**0.834**
Andy3223	0.751	0.755	0.75
DeepBlueAI	0.749	0.750	0.749
kevintest	0.746	0.746	0.746
Taha	0.738	0.739	0.737

Table 4: The FigLang2020 Sarcasm Scoreboard for Twitter (upper) and Reddit (below) dataset. Our method miroblog achieves the best performance in both datasets with significant margins.

$twitter_{valid}$	Precision	Recall	F1
no augmentation	0.8294	0.8816	0.8547
labeled augmentation	0.8676	0.8550	0.8613
unlabeled augmentation	0.8747	0.9219	0.8977

Table 5: Sarcasm detection performance according to data augmentation on the $twitter_{valid}$ dataset.

further crawled 100,000 texts from both Twitter and Reddit for the augmentation with unlabeled data.

3 Experiments

We first report the quantitative results by referring to the statistics in the official evaluation server [3] of the FigLang2020 sarcasm challenge as of the challenge deadline (*i.e.* April 16, 2020, 11:59 p.m. UTC). Table 4 summarizes the results of the competition, where our method named miroblog shows significantly better performance than other participants in both Twitter and Reddit dataset. We report Precision (P), Recall (R), and F1 scores as the official metrics.

3.1 Further Analysis

We perform further empirical analysis to demonstrate the effectiveness of the proposed ideas. We compare different configurations of pooling layers, context ensemble, and data augmentation.

Pooling Layers. Table 3 shows the comparison of sarcasm detection performance between NeXtVLAD and other pooling methods in performance. When coupled with BiLSTM, NeXtVLAD achieves better performance than max, and mean pooling methods.

Context Ensemble. Table 6 shows the comparison with different context ensemble methods.

[3]https://competitions.codalab.org/competitions/22247.

$twitter_{valid}$	Precision	Recall	F1
Ensemble (max context)	0.8558	0.8182	0.8366
Ensemble (3 context)	0.8320	0.8288	0.8304
Single (3 context)	0.8147	0.8052	0.8099

Table 6: Sarcasm detection performance according to the ensemble methods on the $twitter_{valid}$ dataset.

Reference	Name	Size
Ptáček et al. (2014)	Platek	57041
Riloff et al. (2013)	Riloff	1570
Khodak et al. (2017)	SARC-v2	321748
Khodak et al. (2017)	SARC-v2-pol	14340
Van Hee et al. (2018)	SemEval-2018-irony	3851
-	Web Crawled	100000

Table 7: The standard datasets and the crawled dataset (for unlabeled augmentation) used in the experiments.

We use the baseline (Transformer+BiLSTM+ Max-pooling) and train it without augmenting the training set. F1 scores of the model are better in the order of (a) ensemble with maximum context, (b) ensemble with three contexts and (c) no context. The performance gap with or without context ensemble implies that balancing out the samples in terms of context length is important. On the other hand, the performance gap between (a) and (b) is only 0.006, indicating that the use of older than three recent conversational contexts is scarcely helpful.

Data Augmentation. Table 5 compares the sarcasm detection results when the data augmentation is applied or not. The augmentation with labeled data increases the F1 score from 0.854 to 0.861. The augmentation with unlabeled data further enhances performance from 0.861 to 0.897. The results demonstrate that both augmentation techniques help with the performance.

3.2 Error Analysis

In order to better understand when our data augmentation methods are effective, we further analyze some examples of the following three cases according to whether the proposed labeled and unlabeled data augmentation (DA) is applied or not: (i) the prediction is wrong without DA but correct with DA, (ii) the prediction is correct without DA but wrong with DA, and (iii) the prediction is wrong with and without DA. In other words, (i) is the case where DA helps, (ii) is the one where DA hurts, and (iii) is the one where DA fails to improve.

Table 8 shows some examples of these three cases. (i) The initial steps of the CRA involve finding similar training samples from the labeled database. Thus, after applying CRA, samples containing specific hashtags, *e.g.* #NotReally #Relax,

	(i) The prediction is wrong without DA but correct with DA.	
c1	Any practice could be anyone's last practice. Yes.
c2	@USER report: tom brady struck by lighting after leaving practice.
r1	[SARCASM] @USER Report: Tom Brady abducted by space aliens during practice. #NotReally #Relax

	(ii) The prediction is correct without DA but wrong with DA	
c1	@USER @USER @USER The racist trump is a Russian puppet. He's a loser who's trying to destroy our constitution and hand this Country over to Putin. He steals with the help of his white nationalist supporters. He should be removed from Office and put in prison.
c2	@USER @USER @USER And who's drinking the koolaide ? Mueller said no collusion or obstruction after spending $ 30 million investigating - with full access to the White House. White Nationists unsubstantiated conspiracy theory. Trump will win 2020 because people see him succeed through the nonsense.
r1	[NOT_SARCASM] @USER @USER @USER You didn't bother to read the Mueller report, did you? It was Barr who falsely exonerated your beloved cult leader. Read the Mueller report. Until you do, don't propagate this lie. Educate yourself and read the report or shut up. You ' ll believe anything except the truth.
r2	[SARCASM] you not worry i are so blind, deaf. I KNOW you have lost your sight (with regard) listened to your cult leaders and Faux News and some Republicans.

	(iii) The prediction is wrong with and without DA.	
c1	I love this land called America #VPDExperiment #VPDDay @USER and @USER at @USER.
c2	The 30 Best Things to do in Washington DC: URL @USER @USER @USER Makes me just want to bow out of this whole thing right now... LOL
c3	@USER @USER @USER Noooooo! It's just the way I edit. I'm trying all sorts of styles this 30 days. No competition being done.
r1	[SARCASM] @USER @USER @USER Sorry, I forgot to use the font! I'm loving your videos. Its giving me ideas and inspiration for some stuff I'd like to try.

Table 8: Examples of three cases where data augmentation helps, hurts, or fails to improve the sarcasm predction.

are included in the training set. We observe that theses tags tend to occur with the samples that are labeled "SARCASM", and thus CRA helps the model learn the correlation between the hashtags and the labels. (ii) The augmented response ($r2$) contains the phrase "cult leader" as in the original response ($r1$). The corresponding label, however, is "SARCASM". When the newly added samples do not match the context, or the labels are incorrect, CRA degrades the prediction. (iii) The third case arises mostly when the situation is subtle and requires external knowledge beyond the given context. In order for the model to correctly classify the response as "SARCASM", the model requires to understand the tag #VPD(Video Per Day). It is not clear what #VPD is from the context, and without such knowledge, the model may still make incorrect predictions.

4   Conclusion

We proposed a new data augmentation technique, CRA (Contextual Response Augmentation), that utilizes the conversational context of the unlabeled data to generate meaningful training samples. We demonstrated that the method boosts the perfor-mance of sarcasm detection significantly. The employment of both augmentations with labeled and unlabeled data enables the system to achieve the best F1 scores to win the FigLang2020 sarcasm challenge on both datasets of Twitter and Reddit.

References

Relja Arandjelovic, Petr Gronat, Akihiko Torii, Tomas Pajdla, and Josef Sivic. 2016. Netvlad: Cnn architecture for weakly supervised place recognition. In *Proceedings of the IEEE conference on computer vision and pattern recognition*, pages 5297–5307.

Alexandre Bérard, Ioan Calapodescu, and Claude Roux. 2019. Naver labs europe's systems for the wmt19 machine translation robustness task. In *arXiv preprint arXiv:1907.06488*.

Jacob Devlin, Ming-Wei Chang, Kenton Lee, and Kristina Toutanova. 2018. Bert: Pre-training of deep bidirectional transformers for language understanding. *arXiv preprint arXiv:1810.04805*.

Suzana Ilić, Edison Marrese-Taylor, Jorge A Balazs, and Yutaka Matsuo. 2018. Deep contextualized word representations for detecting sarcasm and irony. *arXiv preprint arXiv:1809.09795*.

Mikhail Khodak, Nikunj Saunshi, and Kiran Vodrahalli.

2017. A large self-annotated corpus for sarcasm. *arXiv preprint arXiv:1704.05579*.

Rongcheng Lin, Jing Xiao, and Jianping Fan. 2018. Nextvlad: An efficient neural network to aggregate frame-level features for large-scale video classification. In *Proceedings of the European Conference on Computer Vision (ECCV)*, pages 0–0.

Eugenio Martínez-Cámara, M Teresa Martín-Valdivia, L Alfonso Urena-López, and A Rturo Montejo-Ráez. 2014. Sentiment analysis in twitter. *Natural Language Engineering*, 20(1):1–28.

Federico Alberto Pozzi, Elisabetta Fersini, Enza Messina, and Bing Liu. 2016. *Sentiment analysis in social networks*. Morgan Kaufmann.

Tomáš Ptáček, Ivan Habernal, and Jun Hong. 2014. Sarcasm detection on czech and english twitter. In *Proceedings of COLING 2014, the 25th International Conference on Computational Linguistics: Technical Papers*, pages 213–223.

Nils Reimers and Iryna Gurevych. 2019. Sentence-bert: Sentence embeddings using siamese bert-networks. In *Proceedings of the 2019 Conference on Empirical Methods in Natural Language Processing*. Association for Computational Linguistics.

Ellen Riloff, Ashequl Qadir, Prafulla Surve, Lalindra De Silva, Nathan Gilbert, and Ruihong Huang. 2013. Sarcasm as contrast between a positive sentiment and negative situation. In *Proceedings of the 2013 Conference on Empirical Methods in Natural Language Processing*, pages 704–714.

Mike Schuster and Kuldip K Paliwal. 1997. Bidirectional recurrent neural networks. *IEEE transactions on Signal Processing*, 45(11):2673–2681.

Leslie N Smith. 2017. Cyclical learning rates for training neural networks. In *2017 IEEE Winter Conference on Applications of Computer Vision (WACV)*, pages 464–472. IEEE.

Cynthia Van Hee, Els Lefever, and Véronique Hoste. 2018. Semeval-2018 task 3: Irony detection in english tweets. In *Proceedings of The 12th International Workshop on Semantic Evaluation*, pages 39–50.

Ashish Vaswani, Noam Shazeer, Niki Parmar, Jakob Uszkoreit, Llion Jones, Aidan N Gomez, Łukasz Kaiser, and Illia Polosukhin. 2017. Attention is all you need. In *Advances in neural information processing systems*, pages 5998–6008.

Renjie Zheng, Hairong Liu, Mingbo Ma, Baigong Zheng, and Liang Huang. 2019. Robust machine translation with domain sensitive pseudo-sources: Baidu-osu wmt19 mt robustness shared task system report. *arXiv preprint arXiv:1906.08393*.

A Report on the 2020 VUA and TOEFL Metaphor Detection Shared Task

Chee Wee Leong[1], Beata Beigman Klebanov[1],
Chris Hamill[1], Egon Stemle[2,3*], Rutuja Ubale[1†] and Xianyang Chen[1]
[1]Educational Testing Service
[2]Eurac Research, Institute for Applied Linguistics
[3]Masaryk University, Faculty of Informatics
{cleong,bbeigmanklebanov,chamill,xchen002}@ets.org
[†]rubale@etscanada.ca
[*]egon.stemle@eurac.edu

Abstract

In this paper, we report on the shared task on metaphor identification on VU Amsterdam Metaphor Corpus and on a subset of the TOEFL Native Language Identification Corpus. The shared task was conducted as apart of the ACL 2020 Workshop on Processing Figurative Language.

1 Introduction

Metaphor use in everyday language is a way to relate our physical and familiar social experiences to a multitude of other subjects and contexts (Lakoff and Johnson, 2008); it is a fundamental way to structure our understanding of the world even without our conscious realization of its presence as we speak and write. It highlights the unknown using the known, explains the complex using the simple, and helps us to emphasize the relevant aspects of meaning resulting in effective communication.

Metaphor has been studied in the context of political communication, marketing, mental health, teaching, assessment of English proficiency, among others (Beigman Klebanov et al., 2018; Gutierrez et al., 2017; Littlemore et al., 2013; Thibodeau and Boroditsky, 2011; Kaviani and Hamedi, 2011; Kathpalia and Carmel, 2011; Landau et al., 2009; Beigman Klebanov et al., 2008; Zaltman and Zaltman, 2008; Littlemore and Low, 2006; Cameron, 2003; Lakoff, 2010; Billow et al., 1997; Bosman, 1987); see chapter 7 in Veale et al. (2016) for a recent review.

We report on the second shared task on automatic metaphor detection, following up on the first shared task held in 2018 (Leong et al., 2018). We present the shared task and provide a brief description of each of the participating systems, a comparative evaluation of the systems, and our observations about trends in designs and performance of the systems that participated in the shared task.

2 Related Work

Over the last decade, automated detection of metaphor has become an popular topic, which manifests itself in both a variety of approaches and in an increasing variety of data to which the methods are applied. In terms of methods, approaches based on feature-engineering in a supervised machine learning paradigm explored features based on concreteness and imageability, semantic classification using WordNet, FrameNet, VerbNet, SUMO ontology, property norms, and distributional semantic models, syntactic dependency patterns, sensorial and vision-based features (Bulat et al., 2017; Köper and im Walde, 2017; Gutierrez et al., 2016; Shutova et al., 2016; Beigman Klebanov et al., 2016; Tekiroglu et al., 2015; Tsvetkov et al., 2014; Beigman Klebanov et al., 2014; Dunn, 2013; Neuman et al., 2013; Mohler et al., 2013; Hovy et al., 2013; Tsvetkov et al., 2013; Turney et al., 2011; Shutova et al., 2010; Gedigian et al., 2006); see Shutova et al. (2017) and Veale et al. (2016) for reviews of supervised as well as semi-supervised and unsupervised approaches. Recently, deep learning methods have been explored for token-level metaphor detection (Mao et al., 2019; Dankers et al., 2019; Gao et al., 2018; Wu et al., 2018; Rei et al., 2017; Gutierrez et al., 2017; Do Dinh and Gurevych, 2016).

In terms of data, researchers used specially constructed or selected sets, such as adjective noun pairs (Gutierrez et al., 2016; Tsvetkov et al., 2014), WordNet synsets and glosses (Mohammad et al., 2016), annotated lexical items (from a range of word classes) in sentences sampled from corpora (Özbal et al., 2016; Jang et al., 2015; Hovy et al., 2013; Birke and Sarkar, 2006), all the way to annotation of all words in running text for metaphoricity (Beigman Klebanov et al., 2018; Steen et al., 2010); Veale et al. (2016) review various annotated datasets.

Proceedings of the Second Workshop on Figurative Language Processing, pages 18–29
July 9, 2020. ©2020 Association for Computational Linguistics
https://doi.org/10.18653/v1/P17

3 Task Description

The goal of this shared task is to detect, at the word level, all content word metaphors in a given text. We are using two datasets – VUA and TOEFL, to be described shortly. There are two tracks for each dataset, for a total of four tracks: **VUA All POS, VUA Verbs, TOEFL All POS**, and **TOEFL Verbs**. The **AllPOS** track is concerned with the detection of all content words, i.e., nouns, verbs, adverbs and adjectives that are labeled as metaphorical while the **Verbs** track is concerned only with verbs that are metaphorical. We excluded all forms of *be*, *do*, and *have* for both tracks. For each dataset, each participating individual or team can elect to compete in the All POS track, Verbs track, or both. The competition is organized into two phases: training and testing.

3.1 Datasets

3.1.1 VUA corpus

We use the VU Amsterdam Metaphor Corpus (VUA) (Steen et al., 2010). The dataset consists of 117 fragments sampled across four genres from the British National Corpus: Academic, News, Conversation, and Fiction. The data is annotated using the MIPVU procedure with a strong inter-annotator reliability of $\kappa > 0.8$ (Steen et al., 2010). The VUA dataset and annotations is the same as the one used in the first shared task on metaphor detection (Leong et al., 2018), where the reader is referred for further details.

3.1.2 TOEFL corpus

This data labeled for metaphor was sampled from the publicly available ETS Corpus of Non-Native Written English[1] and was first introduced by (Beigman Klebanov et al., 2018). The annotated data comprises essay responses to eight persuasive/argumentative prompts, for three native languages of the writer (Japanese, Italian, Arabic), and for two proficiency levels – medium and high. The data was annotated using the protocol in Beigman Klebanov and Flor (2013), that emphasized argumentation-relevant metaphors:

> "Argumentation-relevant metaphors are, briefly, those that help the author advance her argument. For example, if you are arguing against some action because it would drain resources, *drain* is a metaphor that helps you advance your argument, because it presents the expenditure in a very negative way, suggesting that resources would disappear very quickly and without control." Beigman Klebanov and Flor (2013)

Average inter-annotator agreement was $\kappa = 0.56$-0.62, for multiple passes of the annotation (see (Beigman Klebanov et al., 2018) for more details). We use the data partition from Beigman Klebanov et al. (2018), with 180 essays as training data and 60 essays as testing data.

Tables 1 and 2 show some descriptive characteristics of the data: the number of texts, sentences, tokens, and class distribution information for Verbs and AllPOS tracks for the two datasets.

Datasets	VUA		TOEFL	
	Train	**Test**	**Train**	**Test**
#texts	90	27	180	60
#sents	12,123	4,081	2,741	968

Table 1: Number of texts and sentences for both VUA and TOEFL datasets.

To facilitate the use of the datasets and evaluation scripts beyond this shared task in future research, the complete set of task instructions and scripts are published on Github[2]. We also provide a set of features used to construct one of the baseline classification models for prediction of metaphor/non-metaphor classes at the word level, and instructions on how to replicate that baseline.

3.2 Training phase

In this first phase, data is released for training and/or development of metaphor detection models. Participants can elect to perform cross-validation on the training data, or partition the training data further to have a held-out set for preliminary evaluations, and/or set apart a subset of the data for development/tuning of hyper-parameters. However the training data is used, the goal is to have N final systems (or versions of a system) ready for evaluation when the test data is released.

---

[1] https://catalog.ldc.upenn.edu/LDC2014T06

[2] https://github.com/EducationalTestingService/metaphor /tree/master/NAACL-FLP-shared-task, https://github.com/EducationalTestingService/metaphor/ /tree/master/TOEFL-release

Datasets	VUA				TOEFL			
	Verbs		All POS		Verbs		All POS	
	Train	Test	Train	Test	Train	Test	Train	Test
#tokens	17,240	5,873	72,611	22,196	7,016	2,301	26,737	9,014
%M	29%	−	18%	−	13%	−	7%	−

Table 2: Number of tokens and percentage of metaphors breakdown for VUA and TOEFL datasets.

3.3 Testing phase

In this phase, instances for evaluation are released.[3] Each participating system generated predictions for the test instances, for up to N models.[4] Predictions are submitted to CodaLab[5] and evaluated automatically against the gold-standard labels. Submissions were anonymized. The only statistics displayed were the highest score of all systems per day. The total allowable number of system submissions per day was limited to 5 per team per track. The metric used for evaluation is the F1 score (least frequent class/label, which is "metaphor") with Precision and Recall also available via the detailed results link in CodaLab.

The shared task started on January 12, 2020 when the training data was made available to registered participants. On February 14, 2020, the testing data was released. Submissions were accepted until April 17, 2020. Table 3 shows the submission statistics for systems with a system paper. Generally, there were more participants in the VUA tracks than in TOEFL tracks, and in All POS tracks than in Verbs tracks. In total, 13 system papers were submitted describing methods for generating metaphor/non-metaphor predictions.

	#teams	#submissions
VUA-AllPOS	13	210
VUA-Verbs	11	167
TOEFL-AllPOS	9	247
TOEFL-Verbs	9	181

Table 3: Participation statistics for all tracks.

4 Systems

We first describe the baseline systems. Next, we briefly describe the general approach taken by every team. Interested readers can refer to the teams' papers for more details.

4.1 Baseline Classifiers

We make available to shared task participants a number of features from prior published work on metaphor detection, including unigram features, features based on WordNet, VerbNet, and those derived from a distributional semantic model, POS-based, concreteness and difference in concreteness, as well as topic models.

We adopted three informed baselines from prior work. As **Baseline 1: UL + WordNet + CCDB**, we use the best system from Beigman Klebanov et al. (2016). The features are: lemmatized unigrams, generalized WordNet semantic classes, and difference in concreteness ratings between verbs/adjectives and nouns (UL + WN + CCDB).[6] **Baseline 2: bot.zen** is one of the top-ranked systems in the first metaphor shared task in 2018 by Stemle and Onysko (2018) that uses a bi-directional recursive neural network architecture with long-term short-term memory (LSTM BiRNN) and implements a flat sequence-to-sequence neural network with one hidden layer using TensorFlow and Keras in Python. The system uses fastText word embeddings from different corpora, including learner corpus and BNC data. Finally, **Baseline 3: BERT** is constructed by fine-tuning the BERT model (Devlin et al., 2018) in a standard token classification task: After obtaining the contextualized embeddings of a sentence, we apply a linear layer followed by softmax on each token to predict whether it is metaphorical or not. Chen et al. (2020) gives more details about the architecture of this baseline. For Verbs tracks, we tune the system on All POS data and test on Verbs,

---

[3]In principle, participants could have access to the test data by independently obtaining the VUA corpus. The shared task was based on a presumption of fair play by participants.
[4]We set N=12.
[5]https://competitions.codalab.org/competitions/22188

[6]Baseline 1 is "all-16" in Beigman Klebanov et al. (2018)

as this produced better results during preliminary experimentation than training on Verbs only.

4.2 System Descriptions

illiniMet: RoBERTa embedding + Linguistic features + Ensemble Gong et al. (2020) used RoBERTa to obtain a contextualized embedding of a word and concatenate it with features extracted from linguistic resources (e.g. WordNet, VerbNet) as well as other features (e.g. POS, topicality, concreteness) previously used in the first shared task (Leong et al., 2018) before feeding them into a fully-connected Feedforward network to generate predictions. During inference, an ensemble of three independently trained models using different train/development splits is proposed to yield a final prediction based on majority vote. Using just RoBERTa without linguistic features in an ensemble also generates competitive performance.

DeepMet: Global and local text information + Transformer stacks Su et al. (2020) proposed a reading comprehension paradigm for metaphor detection, where the system seeks to understand the metaphoricity role of each word token in a shorter sequence within a given sentence. Features belonging to five different categories are provided as inputs to the network i.e. global text context, local text context, query word, general POS, fine-grained POS. The features are then mapped onto embeddings before going into Transformer stacks and ensemble for inference. An ablation experiment was also performed with the observation that fine-grained POS and global text features are the most helpful for detecting metaphors.

umd_bilstm: Bi-LSTM + Embeddings + Unigram Lemmas + Spell Correction Kuo and Carpuat (2020) explored the effectiveness of additional features by augmenting the basic contextual metaphor detection system developed by Gao et al. (2018) with one-hot unigram lemma features in addition to GloVe and ELMo embeddings. The authors also experimented with a spell-corrected version of TOEFL data and found it further improves the performance of the Bi-LSTM system.

atr2112: Residual Bi-LSTM + Embeddings + CRF + POS + WN Rivera et al. (2020) proposed a deep architecture that takes as inputs ELMo embeddings that represent words and lemmas, along with POS labels and WordNet synsets. The inputs are processed by a residual Bi-LSTM, then by a number of additional layers, with a final CRF sequence labeling step to generate predictions.

Zenith: Character embeddings + Similarity Networks + Bi-LSTM + Transformer Kumar and Sharma (2020) added lexical and orthographic information via character embeddings in addition to GloVe and ELMo embeddings for an enriched input representation. The authors also constructed a similarity metric between the literal and contextual representations of a word as another input component. A Bi-LSTM network and Transformer network are trained independently and combined in an ensemble. Eventually, adding both character-based information and similarity network are the most helpful, as evidenced by results obtained using cross-validation on the training datasets.

rowanhm: Static and contextual embeddings + concreteness + Multi-layer Perceptron Maudslay et al. (2020) created a system that combines the concreteness of a word, its static embedding and its contextual embedding before providing them as inputs into a deep Multi-layer Perceptron network which predicts word metaphoricity. Specifically, the concreteness value of a word is formulated as a linear interpolation between two reference vectors (concrete and abstract) which were randomly initialized and learned from data.

iiegn: LSTM BiRNN + metadata; combine TOEFL and VUA data Stemle and Onysko (2020) used an LSTM BiRNN classifier to study the relationship between the metadata in the TOEFL corpus (proficiency, L1 of the author, and the prompt to which the essay is responding) and classifier performance. The system is an extension of the authors' system for the 2018 shared task (Stemle and Onysko, 2018) that served as one of the baseline in the current shared task (see section 4.1). Analyzing the training data, the authors observed that essays written by more proficient users had significantly more metaphors, and that essays responding to some of the prompts had significantly more metaphors than other prompts; however, using proficiency and prompt metadata explicitly in the classifier did not improve performance. The authors also experimented with combining VUA and TOEFL data.

Duke Data Science: BERT, XNET language models + POS tags as features for a Bi-LSTM classifier Liu et al. (2020) use pre-trained BERT and XLNet language models to create contextualized embeddings, which are combined with

POS tags to generate features for a Bi-LSTM for token-level metaphor classification. For the testing phase, the authros used an ensemble strategy, training four copies of the Bi-LSTM with different initializations and averaging their predictions. To increase the likelihood of prediction of a metaphor label, a token is declared a metaphor if: (1) its predicted probability is higher than the threshold, or (2) if its probability is three orders of magnitude higher than the median predicted probability for that word in the evaluation set.

chasingkangaroos: RNN + BiLSTM + Attention + Ensemble Brooks and Youssef (2020) use an ensemble of RNN models with Bi-LSTMs and bidirectional attention mechanisms. Each word was represented by an 11-gram and appeared at the center of the 11-gram; each word in the 11-gram was represented by a 1,324 dimensional word embedding (concatenation of ELMo and GloVe embeddings). The authors experimented with ensembles of models that implement somewhat different architecture (in terms of attention) and models trained on all POS and on a specific POS.

Go Figure!: BERT + multi-task + spell correction + idioms + domain adaptation Chen et al. (2020) baseline system (also one of the shared task baselines, see section 4.1) uses BERT – after obtaining the contextualized embeddings of a sentence, a linear layer is applied followed by softmax on each token to predict whether it is metaphorical or not. The authors spell-correct the TOEFL data, which improves performance. Chen et al. (2020) present two multi-task settings: In the first, metaphor detection on out-of-domain data is treated as an auxiliary task; in the second, idiom detection on in-domain data is the auxiliary task. Performance on TOEFL is helped by the first multi-task setting; performance on VUA is helped by the second.

UoB team: Bi-LSTM + GloVe embeddings + concreteness Alnafesah et al. (2020) explore ways of using concreteness information in a neural metaphor detection context. GloVe embeddings are used as features to an SVM classifier to learn concreteness values, training it using human labels of concreteness. Then, for metaphor detection, every input word is represented as a 304-dimensional vector – 300 dimensions are GloVe pre-trained embeddings, plus probabilities for the four concreteness classes. These representations of words are given as input to a Bi-LSTM which outputs a sequence of labels. Results suggest that explicit concreteness information helps improve metaphor detection, relative to a baseline that uses GloVe embeddings only.

zhengchang: ALBERT + BiLSTM Li et al. (2020) use a sequence labeling model based on ALBERT-LSTM-Softmax. Embeddings produced by BERT serve as input to BiLSTM, as well as to the final softmax layer. The authors report on experiments with inputs to BERT (single-sentence vs pairs; variants using BERT tokenization), spell-correction of the TOEFL data, and CRF vs softmax at the classification layer.

PolyU-LLT: Sensorimotor and embodiment features + embeddings + n-grams + logistic regression classifier Wan et al. (2020) use sensorimotor and embodiment features. They use the Lancaster Sensorimotor norms (Lynott et al., 2019) that include measures of sensorimotor strength for about 40K English words across six perceptual modalities (e.g., touch, hearing, smell), and five action effectors (mouth/throat, hand/arm, etc), and embodiment norms from Sidhu et al. (2014). The authors also use word, lemma, and POS n-grams; word2vec and GloVe word embeddings, as well as cosine distance measurements using the embeddings. The different features are combined using logistic regression and other classifiers.

5 Results and Discussion

Table 4 present the results for All POS and Verbs tracks for VUA data. Table 5 present the results for All POS and Verbs tracks for TOEFL data.

5.1 Trends in system design

The clearest trend in the 2020 submissions is the use of deep learning architectures based on BERT (Devlin et al., 2018) – more than half of the participating systems used BERT or its variant. The usefulness of BERT for metaphor detection has been shown by Mao et al. (2019), where a BERT-based system posted F1 = 0.717 on VUA AllPOS, hence our use of a BERT-based system as Baseline 3.

Beyond explorations of neural architectures, we also observe usage of new lexical, grammatical, and morphological information, such as fine-grained POS, spell-corrected variants of words (for TOEFL data), sub-word level information (e.g., character embeddings), idioms, sensorimotor and embodiment-related information.

Rank	Team	P	R	F1
	All POS			
1	DeepMet	.756	.783	.769
2	Go Figure!	.721	.748	.734
3	illiniMet	.746	.715	.730
4	rowanhm	.727	.709	.718
5	Baseline 3: BERT	.712	.725	.718
6	zhengchang	.696	.729	.712
7	chasingkangaroos	.702	.704	.703
8	Duke Data Science	.662	.699	.680
9	Zenith	.630	.716	.670
10	umd_bilstm	.733	.601	.660
11	atr2112	.599	.672	.633
12	PolyU-LLT	.556	.660	.603
13	iiegn	.601	.591	.596
14	UoB team	.653	.548	.596
15	Baseline 2: bot.zen	.612	.575	.593
16	Baseline 1: UL + + WN + CCDB	.510	.696	.589
	Verbs			
1	DeepMet	.789	.819	.804
2	Go Figure!	.732	.823	.775
3	illiniMet	.761	.781	.771
4	Baseline 3: BERT	.725	.789	.756
5	zhengchang	.706	.811	.755
6	rowanhm	.734	.779	.755
7	Duke Data Science	.712	.749	.730
8	Zenith	.667	.775	.717
9	umd_bilstm	.597	.806	.686
10	atr2112	.652	.718	.683
11	PolyU-LLT	.608	.703	.652
12	iiegn	.587	.691	.635
13	Baseline 2: bot.zen	.605	.666	.634
14	Baseline 1: UL + + WN + CCDB	.527	.698	.600

Table 4: **VUA Dataset**: Performance and ranking of the best system per team and baselines, for All POS track (top panel) and for Verbs track (bottom panel).

5.2 Performance wrt 2018 shared task

Since the same VUA dataset was used in 2020 shared task as in the 2018 shared task, we can directly compare the performance of the best systems to observe the extent of the improvement. The best system in 2018 performed at F1 = 0.651; the best performance in 2020 is more than 10 points better – F1 = 0.769. Indeed, the 2018 best performing system would have earned the rank of 11 in the 2020 All POS track, suggesting that the field has generally moved to more effective models than those proposed for the 2018 competitions.

The best result posted for the 2020 shared task is on par with state-of-art for VUA All POS task: Dankers et al. (2019) reported F1 = 0.769 for a multi-task learning setting utilizing emotion-related information. The best results obtained by participants of the 2020 shared task for TOEFL are state-of-the-art, improving upon Baseline 1, which is the best published result for this dataset

Rank	Team	P	R	F1
	All POS			
1	DeepMet	.695	.735	.715
2	zhengchang	.755	.666	.707
3	illiniMet	.709	.697	.703
4	Go Figure!	.669	.717	.692
5	Duke Data Science	.688	.651	.669
6	Baseline 3: BERT	.701	.563	.624
7	Zenith	.607	.634	.620
8	umd_bilstm	.629	.593	.611
9	iiegn	.596	.579	.587
10	PolyU-LLT	.523	.602	.560
11	Baseline 2: bot.zen	.590	.517	.551
12	Baseline 1: UL + + WN + CCDB	.488	.576	.528
	Verbs			
1	DeepMet	.733	.766	.749
2	zhengchang	.735	.720	.728
3	illiniMet	.731	.707	.719
4	Go Figure!	.747	.661	.702
5	Duke Data Science	.687	.707	.697
6	Baseline 3: BERT	.624	.694	.657
7	Zenith	.669	.638	.653
8	umd_bilstm	.668	.562	.611
9	PolyU-LLT	.584	.609	.596
10	Baseline 2: bot.zen	.566	.595	.580
11	Baseline 1: UL + + WN + CCDB	.504	.641	.564
12	iiegn	.622	.487	.546

Table 5: **TOEFL Dataset**: Performance and ranking of the best system per team and baselines, for All POS track (top panel) and for Verbs track (bottom panel).

(Beigman Klebanov et al., 2018).

5.3 Performance across genres: VUA

Table 6 shows performance by genre for the VUA data All POS track. The patterns are highly consistent across systems, and replicate those observed for the 2018 shared task – Academic and News genres are substantially easier to handle than Fiction and Conversation. The gap between the best and worst performance across genres for the same system remains wide – between 11.4 F1 points and 24.3 F1 points. Somewhat encouragingly, the gap is narrower for the better performing systems – the top 6 systems show the smallest gaps between best and worst genres (11.4-14.0).

5.4 Performance on VUA vs TOEFL data

Table 7 shows performance and ranks of the best systems for teams that participated in both VUA and TOEFL AllPOS tracks, along with baselines. Overall, the relative performance rankings are consistent – F1 scores are correlated at $r = .92$ and team ranks are correlated at $r = 0.95$ across the two datasets. All teams posted better performance on the VUA data than on the TOEFL

Team	All VUA	Acad.	Conv.	Fiction	News	Best to Worst
atr2112	.633	.716 (1)	.510 (4)	.558 (3)	.641 (2)	.206
chasingkangaroos	.703	.761 (1)	.599 (4)	.651 (3)	.714 (2)	.162
PolyU-LLT	.603	.719 (1)	.482 (3)	.476 (4)	.634 (2)	.243
DeepMet	**.769**	**.810** (1)	**.681** (4)	**.718** (3)	**.790** (2)	.129
UoB team	.596	.686 (1)	.485 (4)	.511 (3)	.582 (2)	.201
iiegn	.596	.669 (1)	.521 (4)	.500 (4)	.626 (2)	.169
umd_bilstm	.660	.724 (1)	.537 (4)	.606 (3)	.670 (2)	.187
illiniMet	**.730**	**.768** (1)	**.654** (4)	**.688** (3)	**.743** (2)	.114
rowanhm	.718	.760 (1)	.631 (4)	.678 (3)	.730 (2)	.129
Zenith	.670	.730 (1)	.566 (4)	.583 (3)	.697 (2)	.164
Duke Data Science	.680	.742 (1)	.572 (4)	.617 (3)	.697 (2)	.170
Go Figure!	**.734**	**.784** (1)	**.644** (4)	**.692** (3)	**.741** (2)	.140
zhengchang	.712	.752 (1)	.634 (4)	.669 (3)	.723 (2)	.118
Baseline 3: BERT	.718	.767 (1)	.640 (4)	.684 (3)	.719 (2)	.127
Baseline 2: bot.zen	.593	.673 (1)	.487 (4)	.521 (3)	.602 (2)	.186
Baseline 1: UL+ +WN+CCDB	.589	.721 (1)	.472 (3)	.458 (4)	.606 (2)	.263
Av. rank among genres	–	1.00	3.81	3.19	2.00	.169

Table 6: **VUA Dataset**: Performance (F1-score) of the best systems submitted to All-POS track by genre subsets of the test data. In parentheses, we show the rank of the given genre within all genres for the system. The last column shows the overall drop in performance from best genre (ranked 1) to worst (ranked 4). The top three performances for a given genre are boldfaced.

Team	VUA (rank)	TOEFL (rank)	Diff.
Baseline 1: UL+ +WN+CCDB	.59 (12)	.53 (12)	.06
Baseline 2: bot.zen	.59 (11)	.55 (11)	.04
Baseline 3: BERT	.72 (4)	.62 (6)	.09
PolyU-LLT	.60 (9)	.56 (10)	.04
DeepMet	.77 (1)	.72 (1)	.05
iiegn	.60 (10)	.59 (9)	.01
umd_bilstm	.66 (8)	.61 (8)	.05
illiniMet	.73 (3)	.70 (3)	.03
Zenith	.67 (7)	.62 (7)	.05
Duke Data Science	.68 (6)	.67 (5)	.01
Go Figure!	.73 (2)	.69 (4)	.04
zhengchang	.71 (5)	.71 (2)	.01

Table 7: **VUA vs TOEFL**: Performance (F1 scores) and rankings of participants in both VUA and TOEFL All POS competitions. Column 4 shows the difference in F1 performance between VUA and TOEFL data.

data; the difference (see column 4 in Table 7) averaged 4 F1 points, ranging from just half a F1 point (zhengchang) to 5 F1 points (DeepMet, umd_bilstm, Zenith). The BERT baseline posted a relatively large difference of 9 F1 points; this could be because BNC data is more similar to the data on which BERT has been pre-trained than TOEFL data. We note, however, that participating systems that used BERT showed a smaller performance gap between VUA and TOEFL data; in zhengchang the gap is all but eliminated. This suggests that a BERT-based system with parameters optimized for performance on TOEFL data

can close this gap.

Considering TOEFL data as an additional genre, along with the four genres represented in VUA, we observe that it is generally harder than Academic and News, and is commensurate with Fiction in terms of performance, for the three systems with best VUA All POS performance (DeepMet: 0.72 both, Go Figure!: 0.69 both, illiniMet: 0.69 for VUA Fiction, .70 for TOEFL); a caveat to this observation is that the difference between VUA and TOEFL is not only in genre but in the metaphor annotation guidelines as well.

5.5 Performance by proficiency: TOEFL

Table 8 shows performance for All POS track on the TOEFL data by the writer's proficiency level – high or medium. We note that the quality of the human annotations does not appear to differ substantially by proficiency: The average inter-annotator agreement for the high proficiency essays was $\kappa = 0.619$, while it was $\kappa = 0.613$ for the medium proficiency essays. We observe that generally systems tend to perform better on the higher proficiency essays, although two of the 12 systems posted better performance on the medium proficiency data. However, even though the medium proficiency essays might have deficiencies in grammar, spelling, coherence and other properties of the essay that could interfere with metaphor detection, we generally observe relatively small differences in performance by proficiency – up to 3.5 F1 points, with a few exceptions (zhengchang, Go Figure!). Interestingly, automatic correction of spelling errors does not seem to guarantee a smaller gap in performance (see Chen et al. (2020), Go Figure!).

Team	All	High	Med.	Diff.
PolyU-LLT	.560	.567 (1)	.552 (2)	.015
DeepMet	**.715**	**.724** (1)	**.706** (2)	.018
iiegn	.587	.592 (1)	.583 (2)	.009
umd_bilstm	.611	.620 (1)	.601 (2)	.019
illiniMet	**.703**	**.717** (1)	**.690** (2)	.027
Zenith	.620	.637 (1)	.604 (2)	.033
Duke Data Science	.669	.660 (2)	**.677** (1)	.017
Go Figure!	.692	.713 (1)	.671 (2)	.042
zhengchang	**.707**	**.741** (1)	.674 (2)	.067
Baseline 3: BERT	.624	.636 (1)	.612 (2)	.024
Baseline 2: bot.zen	.551	.535 (2)	.567 (1)	.032
Baseline 1: UL+ WordNet+CCDB	.528	.533 (1)	.524 (2)	.009
Av. rank	–	1.16	1.83	.03

Table 8: **TOEFL Dataset**: Performance (F1-score) of the best systems submitted to All-POS track by proficiency level (high, medium) subsets of the test data. In parentheses, we show the rank of the given proficiency level within all levels for the system. The last column shows the overall drop in performance from best proficiency level (ranked 1) to worst (ranked 4). The top three performances for a given genre are boldfaced.

5.6 Part of Speech

Table 9 shows the performance of the systems submitted to the All POS tracks for VUA and TOEFL data broken down by part of speech (Verbs, Nouns, Adjectives, Adverbs). As can be observed both from the All POS vs Verbs tracks (Tables 4 and 5) and from Table 9, performance on Verbs is generally better than on All POS.[7]

For VUA data, all but one systems perform best on Verbs, followed by Adjectives and Nouns, with the worst performance generally observed for Adverbs. These results replicate the findings from the 2018 shared task and follow the proportions of metaphors in the respective parts of speech, led by Verbs (30%), Adjectives (18%), Nouns (13%), Adverbs (8%). The average gap between best and worst POS performance has also stayed similar – 11 F1 points (it was 9% in 2018).

For the TOEFL data, the situation is quite different. Adjectives lead the scoreboard for all but 3 systems, with Adverbs and Verbs coming next, while Nouns proved to be the most challenging category for all participating systems. Furthermore, the gap between best and worst POS performance is large – 17 F1 points on average, ranging between 11 and 22 points. The best performance on Nouns is only F1 = 0.641; it would have ranked 10th out of 12 on Adjectives. The proportions of metaphorically used Verbs (13%), Adjectives (8%), Nouns (4%), and Adverbs (3%) (based on training data) perhaps offer some explanation of the difficulty with nouns, since nominal metaphors seem to be quite rare. Stemle and Onysko (2020) observed that metaphors occur more frequently in responses to some essay prompts that to others among the 8 prompts covered in the TOEFL dataset; moreover, for some prompts, a metaphor is suggested in the prompt itself and occurs frequently in responses (e.g. whether *broad* knowledge is better than specialized knowledge). It is possible that prompt-based patterns interact with POS patterns in ways that affect relative ease or difficulty of POS for metaphor identification.

6 Acknowledgements

As organizers of the shared task, we would like to thank all the teams for their interest and participation. We would also like to thank Ton Veale, Eyal Sagi, Debanjan Ghosh, Xinhao Wang, and Keelan Evanini for their helpful comments on the paper.

---

[7]Performance on Verbs track and performance on Verbs as part of All POS track might differ, since for Verbs track, participants could train their system on verbs-only data, whereas we took submissions to All POS track and analyzed by POS for Table 9.

Team	All-POS	Verbs	Adjectives	Nouns	Adverbs	Best to Worst
VUA Dataset						
atr2112	.633	.683 (1)	.602 (2)	.595 (3)	.560 (4)	.12
chasingkangaroos	.703	.737 (1)	.678 (2)	.678 (2)	.648 (4)	.09
PolyU-LLT	.603	.625 (1)	.595 (2)	.581 (3)	.552 (4)	.07
DeepMet	.769	.800 (1)	.733 (3)	.749 (2)	.732 (4)	.07
UoB team	.596	.626 (1)	.587 (2)	.569 (3)	.506 (4)	.12
iiegn	.596	.635 (1)	.581 (2)	.558 (3)	.513 (4)	.12
umd_bilstm	.660	.700 (1)	.642 (2)	.630 (3)	.514 (4)	.19
illiniMet	.730	.770 (1)	.693 (3)	.705 (2)	.633 (4)	.14
rowanhm	.718	.753 (1)	.660 (3)	.706 (2)	.644 (4)	.11
Zenith	.670	.715 (1)	.621 (3)	.637 (2)	.612 (4)	.10
Duke Data Science	.680	.724 (1)	.614 (4)	.654 (2)	.625 (3)	.11
Go Figure!	.734	.775 (1)	.683 (3)	.708 (2)	.681 (4)	.09
zhengchang	.712	.755 (1)	.655 (4)	.684 (2)	.659 (3)	.10
Baseline 3: BERT	.718	.756 (1)	.672 (3)	.695 (2)	.672 (3)	.08
Baseline 2: bot.zen	.593	.637 (1)	.564 (2)	.553 (3)	.513 (4)	.12
Baseline 1: UL + WN + CCDB	.589	.616 (1)	.557 (3)	.564 (2)	.542 (4)	.07
Av. rank among POS	–	1.00	2.69	2.38	3.81	.11
TOEFL Dataset						
PolyU-LLT	.560	.587 (2)	.630 (1)	.462 (4)	.517 (3)	.17
DeepMet	.715	.749 (3)	.757 (2)	.610 (4)	.800 (1)	.19
iiegn	.587	.617 (3)	.667 (1)	.465 (4)	.632 (2)	.20
umd_bilstm	.611	.652 (2)	.693 (1)	.478 (4)	.627 (3)	.22
illiniMet	.703	.718 (3)	.770 (2)	.609 (4)	.786 (1)	.18
Zenith	.620	.650 (2)	.703 (1)	.505 (4)	.600 (3)	.20
Duke Data Science	.669	.697 (3)	.725 (2)	.555 (4)	.741 (1)	.19
Go Figure!	.692	.697 (2)	.749 (1)	.641 (4)	.691 (3)	.11
zhengchang	.707	.728 (3)	.759 (1)	.620 (4)	.731 (2)	.14
Baseline 3: BERT	.624	.644 (2)	.689 (1)	.541 (4)	.583 (3)	.15
Baseline 2: bot.zen	.551	.565 (2)	.611 (1)	.485 (4)	.490 (3)	.13
Baseline 1: UL + WN + CCDB	.528	.543 (2)	.618 (1)	.415 (4)	.531 (3)	.20
Av. rank among POS	–	2.42	1.25	4.00	2.33	.17

Table 9: **VUA and TOEFL Datasets by POS**: Performance (F1-score) of the best systems submitted to All-POS track by POS subsets of the test data. In parentheses, we show the rank of the given POS within all POS for the system. The last column shows the overall drop in performance from best POS (ranked 1) to worst (ranked 4).

References

Ghadi Alnafesah, Harish Tayyar Madabushi, and Mark Lee. 2020. Augmenting neural metaphor detection with concreteness. In *Proceedings of the Second Workshop on Figurative Language Processing*, Seattle, WA.

Beata Beigman Klebanov, Daniel Diermeier, and Eyal Beigman. 2008. Lexical cohesion analysis of political speech. *Political Analysis*, 16(4):447–463.

Beata Beigman Klebanov and Michael Flor. 2013. Argumentation-relevant metaphors in test-taker essays. In *Proceedings of the First Workshop on Metaphor in NLP*, pages 11–20.

Beata Beigman Klebanov, Chee Wee Leong, and Michael Flor. 2018. A corpus of non-native written English annotated for metaphor. In *Proceedings of the 2018 Conference of the North American Chapter of the Association for Computational Linguistics: Human Language Technologies, Volume 2 (Short Papers)*, pages 86–91, New Orleans, Louisiana. Association for Computational Linguistics.

Beata Beigman Klebanov, Chee Wee Leong, E Dario Gutierrez, Ekaterina Shutova, and Michael Flor. 2016. Semantic classifications for detection of verb metaphors. In *Proceedings of the 54th Annual Meeting of the Association for Computational Linguistics (Volume 2: Short Papers)*, volume 2, pages 101–106.

Beata Beigman Klebanov, Chee Wee Leong, Michael Heilman, and Michael Flor. 2014. Different texts, same metaphors: Unigrams and beyond. In *Proceedings of the Second Workshop on Metaphor in NLP*, pages 11–17.

Richard M Billow, Jeffrey Rossman, Nona Lewis, Deberah Goldman, and Charles Raps. 1997. Observing expressive and deviant language in schizophrenia. *Metaphor and Symbol*, 12(3):205–216.

Julia Birke and Anoop Sarkar. 2006. A clustering approach for nearly unsupervised recognition of nonliteral language. In *11th Conference of the European Chapter of the Association for Computational Linguistics*.

Jan Bosman. 1987. Persuasive effects of political metaphors. *Metaphor and Symbol*, 2(2):97–113.

Jennifer Brooks and Abdou Youssef. 2020. Metaphor detection using ensembles of bidirectional recurrent neural networks. In *Proceedings of the Second Workshop on Figurative Language Processing*, Seattle, WA.

Luana Bulat, Stephen Clark, and Ekaterina Shutova. 2017. Modelling metaphor with attribute-based semantics. In *Proceedings of the 15th Conference of the European Chapter of the Association for Computational Linguistics: Volume 2, Short Papers*, volume 2, pages 523–528.

Lynne Cameron. 2003. *Metaphor in educational discourse*. A&C Black.

Xianyang Chen, Chee Wee Leong, Michael Flor, and Beata Beigman Klebanov. 2020. Go figure! multitask transformer-based architecture for metaphor detection using idioms: Ets team in 2020 metaphor shared task. In *Proceedings of the Second Workshop on Figurative Language Processing*, Seattle, WA.

Verna Dankers, Marek Rei, Martha Lewis, and Ekaterina Shutova. 2019. Modelling the interplay of metaphor and emotion through multitask learning. In *Proceedings of the 2019 Conference on Empirical Methods in Natural Language Processing and the 9th International Joint Conference on Natural Language Processing (EMNLP-IJCNLP)*, pages 2218–2229, Hong Kong, China. Association for Computational Linguistics.

Jacob Devlin, Ming-Wei Chang, Kenton Lee, and Kristina Toutanova. 2018. Bert: Pre-training of deep bidirectional transformers for language understanding. *arXiv preprint arXiv:1810.04805*.

Erik-Lân Do Dinh and Iryna Gurevych. 2016. Token-level metaphor detection using neural networks. In *Proceedings of the Fourth Workshop on Metaphor in NLP*, pages 28–33.

Jonathan Dunn. 2013. What metaphor identification systems can tell us about metaphor-in-language. In *Proceedings of the First Workshop on Metaphor in NLP*, pages 1–10.

Ge Gao, Eunsol Choi, Yejin Choi, and Luke Zettlemoyer. 2018. Neural metaphor detection in context. In *Conference on Empirical Methods in Natural Language Processing*.

Matt Gedigian, John Bryant, Srini Narayanan, and Branimir Ciric. 2006. Catching metaphors. In *Proceedings of the Third Workshop on Scalable Natural Language Understanding*, pages 41–48. Association for Computational Linguistics.

Hongyu Gong, Kshitij Gupta, Akriti Jain, and Suma Bhat. 2020. Illinimet: Illinois system for metaphor detection with contextual and linguistic information. In *Proceedings of the Second Workshop on Figurative Language Processing*, Seattle, WA.

E Dario Gutierrez, Guillermo Cecchi, Cheryl Corcoran, and Philip Corlett. 2017. Using automated metaphor identification to aid in detection and prediction of first-episode schizophrenia. In *Proceedings of the 2017 Conference on Empirical Methods in Natural Language Processing*, pages 2923–2930.

E Dario Gutierrez, Ekaterina Shutova, Tyler Marghetis, and Benjamin Bergen. 2016. Literal and metaphorical senses in compositional distributional semantic models. In *Proceedings of the 54th Annual Meeting of the Association for Computational Linguistics (Volume 1: Long Papers)*, volume 1, pages 183–193.

Dirk Hovy, Shashank Shrivastava, Sujay Kumar Jauhar, Mrinmaya Sachan, Kartik Goyal, Huying Li, Whitney Sanders, and Eduard Hovy. 2013. Identifying metaphorical word use with tree kernels. In *Proceedings of the First Workshop on Metaphor in NLP*, pages 52–57.

Hyeju Jang, Seungwhan Moon, Yohan Jo, and Carolyn Rose. 2015. Metaphor detection in discourse. In *Proceedings of the 16th Annual Meeting of the Special Interest Group on Discourse and Dialogue*, pages 384–392.

Sujata S Kathpalia and Heah Lee Hah Carmel. 2011. Metaphorical competence in esl student writing. *RELC Journal*, 42(3):273–290.

Hossein Kaviani and Robabeh Hamedi. 2011. A quantitative/qualitative study on metaphors used by persian depressed patients. *Archives of Psychiatry and Psychotherapy*, 4(5-13):110.

Maximilian Köper and Sabine Schulte im Walde. 2017. Improving verb metaphor detection by propagating abstractness to words, phrases and individual senses. In *Proceedings of the 1st Workshop on Sense, Concept and Entity Representations and their Applications*, pages 24–30.

Tarun Kumar and Yashvardhan Sharma. 2020. Character aware models with similarity learning for metaphor detection. In *Proceedings of the Second Workshop on Figurative Language Processing*, Seattle, WA.

Kevin Kuo and Marine Carpuat. 2020. Evaluating a bilstm model for metaphor detection in toefl essays. In *Proceedings of the Second Workshop on Figurative Language Processing*, Seattle, WA.

George Lakoff. 2010. *Moral politics: How liberals and conservatives think*. University of Chicago Press.

George Lakoff and Mark Johnson. 2008. *Metaphors we live by*. University of Chicago press.

Mark J Landau, Daniel Sullivan, and Jeff Greenberg. 2009. Evidence that self-relevant motives and metaphoric framing interact to influence political and social attitudes. *Psychological Science*, 20(11):1421–1427.

Chee Wee Leong, Beata Beigman Klebanov, and Ekaterina Shutova. 2018. A report on the 2018 vua metaphor detection shared task. In *Proceedings of the Workshop on Figurative Language Processing*, pages 56–66.

Shuqun Li, Jingjie Zeng, Jinhui Zhang, Tao Peng, Liang Yang, and Hongfei Lin. 2020. Albert-BiLSTM for sequential metaphor detection. In *Proceedings of the Second Workshop on Figurative Language Processing*, Seattle, WA.

Jeannette Littlemore, Tina Krennmayr, James Turner, and Sarah Turner. 2013. An investigation into metaphor use at different levels of second language writing. *Applied linguistics*, 35(2):117–144.

Jeannette Littlemore and Graham Low. 2006. Metaphoric competence, second language learning, and communicative language ability. *Applied linguistics*, 27(2):268–294.

Jerry Liu, Nathan OʹHara, Alex Rubin, Rachel Draelos, and Cynthia Rudin. 2020. Metaphor detection using contextual word embeddings from transformers. In *Proceedings of the Second Workshop on Figurative Language Processing*, Seattle, WA.

Dermot Lynott, Louise Connell, Marc Brysbaert, James Brand, and James Carney. 2019. The Lancaster sensorimotor norms: multidimensional measures of perceptual and action strength for 40,000 English words. *Behavior Research Methods*, pages 1–21.

Rui Mao, Chenghua Lin, and Frank Guerin. 2019. End-to-end sequential metaphor identification inspired by linguistic theories. In *Proceedings of the 57th Annual Meeting of the Association for Computational Linguistics*, pages 3888–3898, Florence, Italy. Association for Computational Linguistics.

Rowan Hall Maudslay, Tiago Pimentel, Ryan Cotterell, and Simone Teufel. 2020. Metaphor detection using context and concreteness. In *Proceedings of the Second Workshop on Figurative Language Processing*, Seattle, WA.

Saif Mohammad, Ekaterina Shutova, and Peter Turney. 2016. Metaphor as a medium for emotion: An empirical study. In *Proceedings of the Fifth Joint Conference on Lexical and Computational Semantics*, pages 23–33.

Michael Mohler, David Bracewell, Marc Tomlinson, and David Hinote. 2013. Semantic signatures for example-based linguistic metaphor detection. In *Proceedings of the First Workshop on Metaphor in NLP*, pages 27–35.

Yair Neuman, Dan Assaf, Yohai Cohen, Mark Last, Shlomo Argamon, Newton Howard, and Ophir Frieder. 2013. Metaphor identification in large texts corpora. *PloS one*, 8(4):e62343.

Gözde Özbal, Carlo Strapparava, and Serra Sinem Tekiroglu. 2016. Prometheus: A corpus of proverbs annotated with metaphors. In *LREC*.

Marek Rei, Luana Bulat, Douwe Kiela, and Ekaterina Shutova. 2017. Grasping the finer point: A supervised similarity network for metaphor detection. In *Proceedings of the 2017 Conference on Empirical Methods in Natural Language Processing*, pages 1537–1546.

Andrés Torres Rivera, Antoni Oliver, Salvador Climent, and Marta Coll-Florit. 2020. Neural metaphor detection with a residual bilstm-crf model. In *Proceedings of the Second Workshop on Figurative Language Processing*, Seattle, WA.

Ekaterina Shutova, Douwe Kiela, and Jean Maillard. 2016. Black holes and white rabbits: Metaphor identification with visual features. In *Proceedings of the 2016 Conference of the North American Chapter of the Association for Computational Linguistics: Human Language Technologies*, pages 160–170.

Ekaterina Shutova, Lin Sun, Elkin Darío Gutiérrez, Patricia Lichtenstein, and Srini Narayanan. 2017. Multilingual metaphor processing: Experiments with semi-supervised and unsupervised learning. *Computational Linguistics*, 43(1):71–123.

Ekaterina Shutova, Lin Sun, and Anna Korhonen. 2010. Metaphor identification using verb and noun clustering. In *Proceedings of the 23rd International Conference on Computational Linguistics*, pages 1002–1010. Association for Computational Linguistics.

David Sidhu, Rachel Kwan, Penny Pexman, and Paul Siakaluk. 2014. Effects of relative embodiment in lexical and semantic processing of verbs. *Acta psychologica*, 149:32–39.

Gerard J Steen, Aletta G Dorst, J Berenike Herrmann, Anna Kaal, Tina Krennmayr, and Trijntje Pasma. 2010. *A method for linguistic metaphor identification: From MIP to MIPVU*, volume 14. John Benjamins Publishing.

Egon Stemle and Alexander Onysko. 2018. Using language learner data for metaphor detection. In *Proceedings of the Workshop on Figurative Language Processing*, New Orleans,LA.

Egon Stemle and Alexander Onysko. 2020. Testing the role of metadata in metaphor identification. In *Proceedings of the Second Workshop on Figurative Language Processing*, Seattle, WA.

Chuandong Su, Fumiyo Fukumoto, Xiaoxi Huang, Jiyi Li, Rongbo Wang, and Zhiqun Chen. 2020. Deepmet: A reading comprehension paradigm for token-level metaphor detection. In *Proceedings of the Second Workshop on Figurative Language Processing*, Seattle, WA.

Serra Sinem Tekiroglu, Gözde Özbal, and Carlo Strapparava. 2015. Exploring sensorial features for metaphor identification. In *Proceedings of the Third Workshop on Metaphor in NLP*, pages 31–39.

Paul H Thibodeau and Lera Boroditsky. 2011. Metaphors we think with: The role of metaphor in reasoning. *PloS one*, 6(2):e16782.

Yulia Tsvetkov, Leonid Boytsov, Anatole Gershman, Eric Nyberg, and Chris Dyer. 2014. Metaphor detection with cross-lingual model transfer. In *Proceedings of the 52nd Annual Meeting of the Association for Computational Linguistics (Volume 1: Long Papers)*, volume 1, pages 248–258.

Yulia Tsvetkov, Elena Mukomel, and Anatole Gershman. 2013. Cross-lingual metaphor detection using common semantic features. In *Proceedings of the First Workshop on Metaphor in NLP*, pages 45–51.

Peter D Turney, Yair Neuman, Dan Assaf, and Yohai Cohen. 2011. Literal and metaphorical sense identification through concrete and abstract context. In *Proceedings of the Conference on Empirical Methods in Natural Language Processing*, pages 680–690. Association for Computational Linguistics.

Tony Veale, Ekaterina Shutova, and Beata Beigman Klebanov. 2016. Metaphor: A computational perspective. *Synthesis Lectures on Human Language Technologies*, 9(1):1–160.

Mingyu Wan, Kathleen Ahrens, Emmanuele Chersoni, Menghan Jiang, Qi Su, Rong Xiang, and Chu-Ren Huang. 2020. Using conceptual norms for metaphor detection. In *Proceedings of the Second Workshop on Figurative Language Processing*, Seattle, WA.

Chuhan Wu, Fangzhao Wu, Yubo Chen, Sixing Wu, Zhigang Yuan, and Yongfeng Huang. 2018. Thu ngn at naacl-2018 metaphor shared task: Neural metaphor detecting with cnn-lstm model. In *Proceedings of the Workshop on Figurative Language Processing*, New Orleans,LA.

Gerald Zaltman and Lindsay H Zaltman. 2008. *Marketing metaphoria: What deep metaphors reveal about the minds of consumers*. Harvard Business Press.

DeepMet: A Reading Comprehension Paradigm for Token-level Metaphor Detection

Chuandong Su[1,2], **Fumiyo Fukumoto**[2]**, Xiaoxi Huang**[1]**, Jiyi Li**[2],
Rongbo Wang[1] **and Zhiqun Chen**[1]

[1]College of Computer Science and Technology, Hangzhou Dianzi University,
Hangzhou 310018, China
[2]Department of Computer Science and Engineering, University of Yamanashi,
Yamanashi 400-8510, Japan
{suchuandong,huangxx,wangrongbo,chenzq}@hdu.edu.cn
fukumoto@yamanashi.ac.jp
garfieldpigljy@gmail.com

Abstract

Machine metaphor understanding is one of the major topics in NLP. Most of the recent attempts consider it as classification or sequence tagging task. However, few types of research introduce the rich linguistic information into the field of computational metaphor by leveraging powerful pre-training language models. We focus a novel reading comprehension paradigm for solving the token-level metaphor detection task which provides an innovative type of solution for this task. We propose an end-to-end deep metaphor detection model named DeepMet based on this paradigm. The proposed approach encodes the global text context (whole sentence), local text context (sentence fragments), and question (query word) information as well as incorporating two types of part-of-speech (POS) features by making use of the advanced pre-training language model. The experimental results by using several metaphor datasets show that our model achieves competitive results in the second shared task on metaphor detection.

1 Introduction

Metaphor is one of the figurative languages and often used to express our thoughts in daily conversations. It is deeply related to human cognitive processes (Lakoff and Johnson, 2003). Metaphor is used to implicitly refer one concept to another concept, usually triggered by a verb (Steen et al., 2010). For example, the verb "drink" in *"car drinks gasoline"* is a metaphorical usage. Other parts of speech can also be used metaphorically (Tsvetkov et al., 2014). For example, the noun "angel" in *"she is an angel"* and the adjective "bright" in *"your idea is very bright"* are also metaphorical uses. Metaphor computation technologies are helpful for most NLP tasks such as machine translation, dialogue systems, content analysis, and machine reading comprehension. Of these, token-level metaphor detec-

tion is the basic technology for metaphor understanding. Its task is to give a text sequence and determine whether a token in the given text sequence is a metaphor or literal. The second shared task on metaphor detection[1] aims to promote the development of metaphor detection technology. This task provides two data sets, VU Amsterdam Metaphor Corpus (VUA) (Steen, 2010) and TOEFI (a subset of ETS corpus of non-native written English) (Klebanov et al., 2018), each with two tasks. Each dataset has two tasks, i.e., verb metaphor detection and all POS metaphor detection. Previous research (Wu et al., 2018; Gao et al., 2018; Mao et al., 2019) has been limited to treat them as the text classification task or sequence tagging task without deeply investigating and leveraging the linguistic information that may be proper for the specific metaphor understanding task.

Motivated by the previous work mentioned in the above, we propose an end-to-end neural based method named DeepMet for detecting metaphor by transforming the token-level metaphor detection task into the reading comprehension task. Our approach encodes the global text, local text and question information as well as incorporating the POS features on two granularity. To improve the performance further, we also leverage the powerful pre-training language models. The F1 score of our best model reaches 80.4% and 76.9% in the verbal track and the all POS track of the VUA data set, and 74.9% and 71.5% in the verbal track and the all POS track of the TOEFL data set, respectively. Our source codes are available online[2].

The main contributions of our work can be summarized: (1) We propose a novel reading comprehension paradigm for token-level metaphor detection task. (2) We design a metaphor detec-

---

[1]https://competitions.codalab.org/competitions/22188
[2]https://github.com/YU-NLPLab/DeepMet

30

Proceedings of the Second Workshop on Figurative Language Processing, pages 30–39
July 9, 2020. ©2020 Association for Computational Linguistics
https://doi.org/10.18653/v1/P17

tion model based on the reading comprehension paradigm which makes use of the advanced pre-training language model to encode global, local, and question information of the text as well as two types of POS auxiliary features. We also introduced a metaphor preference parameter in the cross-validation phase to improve the model performance. (3) The experimental results on several metaphor datasets show that our model is comparable to the state-of-the-art metaphor detection, especially we verified that fine-grained POS (FGPOS) features contribute to performance improvement in our model.

2 Related Work

2.1 Metaphor Detection

As a common language phenomenon, the metaphor was first studied by linguists and psycho-linguists (Wilks, 1975; Glucksberg, 2003; Group, 2007). Metaphor is related to the human cognitive process, and the essential mechanism of metaphor is the conceptual mapping from the source domain to the target domain (Lakoff and Johnson, 2003). Metaphor understanding involves high-level semantic analysis and thus requires special domain knowledge (Tsvetkov et al., 2014).

There are three types of metaphor detection methods. One is a lexicon and rule-based methods (Dodge et al., 2015; Mohler et al., 2013), while these methods need manual creation of rules which is extremely costly. The second is a corpus-based statistical algorithm. It has been studied to construct manual features such as unigrams (Klebanov et al., 2014), bag-of-words features (Köper and im Walde, 2016), concreteness, abstractness (Turney et al., 2011; Tsvetkov et al., 2014), and sensory features (Shutova et al., 2016). The disadvantage of this method is that it cannot detect rare usages of metaphors as we can hardly deal with all these unexpected linguistic phenomena. The third is a metaphor detection algorithm based on deep learning. With a recent surge of interest in neural networks, metaphor detection based on deep learning techniques has been intensively studied. Wu et al. (2018) proposed a metaphor detection model based on Convolutional Neural Network (CNN) and Bidirectional Long Short-Term Memory (BiLSTM) (Graves and Schmidhuber, 2005). They utilized Word2Vec (Mikolov et al., 2013) as text representation, and POS and word clusters information for additional features. Their method performed

the best in the NAACL-2018 metaphor shared task (Leong et al., 2018) with an ensemble learning strategy. Gao et al. (2018) proposed a metaphor detection model using global vectors for word representation (GloVe) (Pennington et al., 2014) and deep contextualized word representations (ELMo) (Peters et al., 2018) as text representations. They applied BiLSTM as an encoder. The accuracy of their method surpasses Wu et al.'s method. Mao et al. (2019) presented two metaphor detection models inspired by the theory of metaphor linguistics (Metaphor Identification Procedure (MLP) (Steen et al., 2010) and Selectional Preference Violation (SPV) (Wilks, 1975)), with BiLSTM as the encoder and Glove and ELMo as the word embeddings. The method is currently SOTA on metaphor detection tasks. Despite some successes, approaches explored so far use classification or sequence labeling and the encoder is based on shallow neural networks such as CNN or BiLSTM, ignoring to make use of different aspects of contexts simultaneously.

Several efforts have been made to cope with shallow neural network architectures. One attempt is Transformer based methods (Vaswani et al., 2017) such as GPT (Radford et al., 2018), BERT (Devlin et al., 2018), RoBERTa (Liu et al., 2019),and XL-Net (Yang et al., 2019). Our backbone network be based on RoBERTa, which uses robustly optimized BERT pretraining approach to improve the performance on many NLP tasks.

2.2 Reading Comprehension

The reading comprehension in NLP assesses a machine's understanding of NL by measuring its ability to answer questions based on a given text/document. The answer to this question may be either explicit or implicit in the text and needs to be inferred based on knowledge and logic (Seo et al., 2016; Wang and Jiang, 2016; Shen et al., 2017). It is a crucial task in NLP and a lot of approaches are presented. McCann et al. showed that many NLP tasks can be translated into reading comprehension tasks, e.g., the sentiment analysis task can be regarded as the reading comprehension task that answers the polarity of a sentence based on a given text (McCann et al., 2018). Levy et al. (2017) translated the information extraction task into the reading comprehension task with good results. Li et al. (2019) attempted to use reading comprehension to solve the NER task and also achieved good performance on multiple NER datasets.

Inspired by the previous work mentioned in the above, we utilize a paradigm based on reading comprehension and propose a Transformer-based encoder for metaphor detection.

3 Methodology

3.1 A Reading Comprehension Paradigm for Token-level Metaphor Detection

Let S ($|S| = n$) be a sentence and $w_i \in V$ be the i-th word within the sentence, where V is the data set vocabulary and the total number of words of sentence is n. Similarly, let Q ($|Q| = m$) be a query word sequence within the sentence S and $q_j \in V'$ be the j-th query word with in Q, where V' is the query word vocabulary and the total number of query words is m. As shown in Figure 1, the task of the token-level metaphor detection is to predict a label sequence Y ($|Y| = m$), where each $y_j \in Y$ refers to the predicted label of q_j and $y_j \in \{1,0\}$ (1 denotes *metaphor* and 0 indicates *literal*). The goal of the task is to estimate the conditional probability $P(Y \mid S, Q)$.

We note that the length of the sequence Q is smaller than that of S. This is because metaphors are generally triggered by some POS such as verbs, nouns, adjectives, and adverbs (Steen et al., 2010; Wilks, 1975). Other POS such as punctuation, prepositions, and conjunctions are unlikely to trigger metaphors. Therefore, we set the POS of a query sequence word to a verb, nouns, adjectives, and adverbs. We consider the token-level metaphor detection task to be a reading comprehension task based on a given context and query words, while previous research has regarded it as a classification or sequence tagging task.

The form of converted reading comprehension paradigm can be defined as triple (S, q_j, y_j) ($S, q_j \in Q, y_j \in Y$). The goal of the task is to estimate the conditional probability $P(y_j|S, q_j)$. For example, when the context is "car drinks gasoline" and the question is the query word "car", the correct label is 0 (literal). If the query word is changed to "*drink*", the correct label is 1 (metaphor).

Metaphor detection is a metaphor comprehension problem, and the reading comprehension task is more in line with the definition of natural language comprehension problems. In addition, reading comprehension paradigms can avoid unnecessary training. When constructing a training set triples, we can filter query words that can not be a

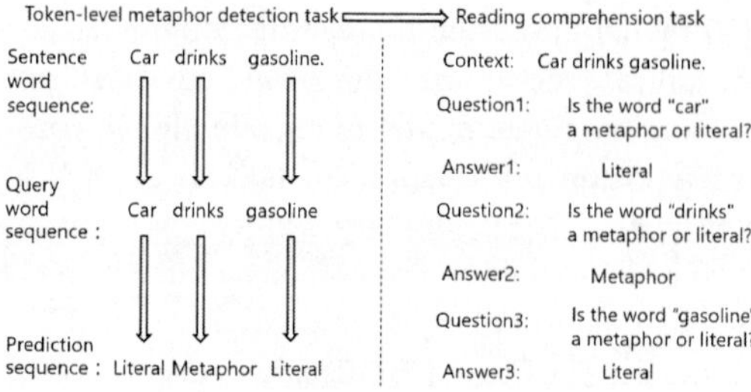

Figure 1: Schematic diagram of metaphor detection task translated into reading comprehension task.

metaphor.

3.2 DeepMet: An End-to-End Neural Metaphor Detector

We build an end-to-end neural metaphor detection model based on the reading comprehension paradigm, and the architecture is shown in Figure 2. We use the improved BERT embedding layer (Devlin et al., 2018) to represent the input information, use the byte pair encoding (BPE) algorithm (Shibata et al., 1999) to obtain the token, and use the position code represented by the yellow dots and the segment code represented by the blue dots to represent the position information of the token and distinguish the different token segments. A special classification token $[CLS]$ will be added before the first token, and special segment separation tokens $[SEP]$ will be added between different sentences. The final input is the addition of token, position encoding, and segment encoding. The improvement of our embedding layer is to use five features as input. The red dots represent the global text context, that is, the original text data. Green dots represent the local text context obtained by cutting the original text data with a comma. Orange dots indicate the features of the question, which is the query word. The purple dots indicate the general POS features, that is, the POS of the query word is represented by the POS of the verb, adjective, noun, etc. Light blue dots represent FGPOS features, using Penn Treebank POS Tags (Santorini, 1990) to represent POS, and FGPOS has a wider variety of POS features than general POS features. Different features are separated by a special segment separation token $[SEP]$.

The backbone network of our model (DeepMet) uses the Transformer encoder layer (Vaswani et al., 2017) of the siamese architecture, which uses two Transformer encoder layers to process different fea-

32

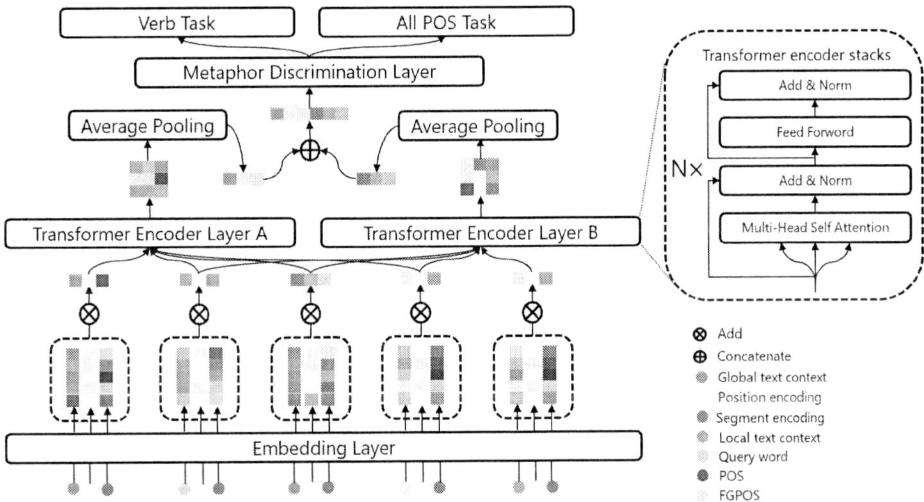

Figure 2: The overall architecture of our model (DeepMet).

ture combinations. The Transformer encoder layer A processes global text features, and the Transformer encoder layer B processes local text features. The query word and two POS features are shared by the two Transformer encoder layers. Specifically, the feature input order of Transformer coding layer A is global text context, query word, POS, FGPOS, and the feature input order of Transformer coding layer B is local text context, query word, POS, FGPOS, and the features are separated by special segment separation token $[SEP]$. The two Transformer encoder layers share weight parameters, which not only learns global and local information from different perspectives but also avoids double storage of weight parameters. The Transformer encoder layer is composed of stacked multi-headed self-attention encoders and its formula is shown in Formula (1)–(5).

$$Q^i, K^i, V^i = W_q h^{i-1}, W_k h^{i-1}, W_v h^{i-1} \quad (1)$$

$$S^i = softmax(\frac{Q^i K^i}{\sqrt{d_k}}) \quad (2)$$

$$Attention(Q, K, V) = h^i = S^i V^i \quad (3)$$

$$head_j = Attention(QW_q^j, KW_k^j, VW_v^j) \quad (4)$$

$$MultiHead(Q, K, V) = Concat_{j=1}^n(head_j)W_o \quad (5)$$

Among them, i is the i-th self-attention block, Q, K, and V are query matrix, key matrix, and value matrix, h is the hidden state, W_q, W_k, W_v, W_o are all self-attention mechanism weight matrices, d_k is a scaling factor to counteract the effect of excessive dot product growth, j is the j-th self-attention head and function $Concat$ is the tensor concatenation. The Transformer encoder also includes residual connections, feedforward networks (FFN), and batch normalization (BN) (Vaswani et al., 2017).

The output of these two Transformer encoder layers is a metaphor information matrix with dimensions of maximum sequence length and hidden state size, respectively. Then these two matrices are reduced by average pooling to obtain high-level metaphor feature vector with length of hidden state size, including global semantic features and local semantic features, respectively, and then stitching these two vectors into the metaphor discrimination layer. The metaphor discriminating layer first performs a dropout operation to alleviate overfitting then uses an FFN containing two neurons to obtain a metaphor discriminant vector with length equal to 2, and finally performs a $softmax$ function to obtain the metaphor and literal probability. As shown in formula (6).

$$y_\tau = softmax(V^T x + b) \quad (6)$$

y_τ is a real value vector representing metaphor and literal probability, V and b are the FFN parameter matrix. In the process of training the model, we use the parameter weight of pre-training language models published by Facebook (RoBERTa) (Liu et al., 2019) to fine-tune the Transformer encoder layers. The metaphor discrimination layer will use the training method to train the model through the Adam optimizer with the adaptive learning rate. The final training goal is the cross-entropy loss function $\mathcal{L}$, which contains the loss functions $\mathcal{L}_0$ and $\mathcal{L}_1$ of the two subtasks (verb task and all POS task of metaphor detection), as shown in Formulas (7)–(9).

$$\mathcal{L}_0 = \mathcal{L}_1 = -\sum_{i=1}^{M}(\hat{y}\log y_{\tau 0} + (1 - \hat{y})\log y_{\tau 1}) \quad (7)$$

$$\mathcal{L} = \mathcal{L}_0 T(t) + \mathcal{L}_1(1 - T(t)) \quad (8)$$

$$T(t) = \begin{cases} 1 & \text{if } t \text{ is } VERB \\ 0 & \text{if } t \text{ is } ALLPOS \end{cases} \quad (9)$$

where $T(t)$ ($t \in \{VERB, ALLPOS\}$) is the task selection function, M is the number of training data samples, $\hat{y}$ is the real label of the data, $y_{\tau 0}$ and $y_{\tau 1}$ represent the prediction probability of whether the data belongs to metaphor and literal respectively, and $y_{\tau 0}, y_{\tau 1} \in [0, 1]$, $y_{\tau 0} + y_{\tau 1} = 1$. During the training process, we use the multi-task mode to train the metaphor detector to improve the training efficiency. Therefore, the final parameters in the task-specific metaphor feature extractor for the two subtasks is the same.

We use cross-validation to train the model to improve the training set utilization efficiency. We introduce a metaphor preference parameter α in this process to improve the metaphor recognition effect, as shown in formula (10).

$$P_i = \begin{cases} M & \frac{1}{N}\sum_{i=j}^{N} DeepMet_j(d_i) \geq \alpha \\ L & \frac{1}{N}\sum_{i=j}^{N} DeepMet_j(d_i) < \alpha \end{cases} \quad (10)$$

where N is the number of cross-validation folds, the function $DeepMet_j$ ($0 \leq j \leq N$) is the metaphor recognizer we designed, d_i (i is the index of the validation data) is the validation data and P_i is the final prediction result and the results are M (metaphor) and L (literal meaning) respectively. Since the metaphor data sets are imbalanced, the model recall rate can be effectively improved by adjusting the metaphor preference parameter α. For details, refer to the section 4.

4 Experiments and Analysis

4.1 Data Sets and Exploratory Data Analysis

We used four benchmark datasets: (1) VUA[3] (Steen, 2010) is currently the largest publicly available metaphor detection data set. Both of the NAACL-2018 metaphor shared task and second shared task on metaphor detection use VUA as the evaluation data set. There are two tracks, i.e., verbs and all POS metaphor detection. (2) TOEFI[4] (Klebanov et al., 2018) is a subset of ETS corpus of non-native written English. It is also used as the evaluation data set in the second shared task on metaphor detection with two tracks, verbs and all POS metaphor detection. (3) MOH-X[5] (Mohammad et al., 2016) is a verb metaphor detection database with the data from WordNet (Miller, 1998) example sentences. The average sentence length of MOH-X is the shortest among the four data sets. (4) The TroFi[6] (Birke and Sarkar, 2006) is a verb metaphor detection dataset consisting of sentences from the 1987-89 Wall Street Journal Corpus Release 1 (Charniak et al., 2000). The average sentence length of TroFi is the longest among the four data sets.

We first sampled the four data sets into four new (S, q_i, y_j) triple data sets following the requirements of the reading comprehension paradigm. In this paper, we focus on the VUA and TOEFI as the evaluation data set. MOH-X and TOEFI are used as auxiliary data sets to verify the performance of our designed metaphor detector. We made exploratory data analysis on the data sets of VUA and TOEFI. The label distribution of data sets is shown in Figure 3.

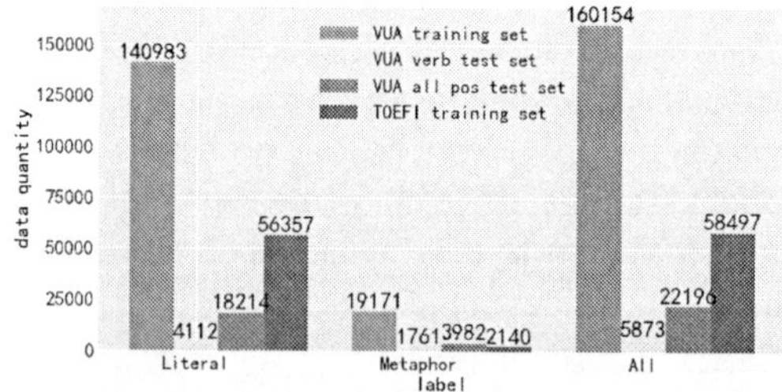

Figure 3: Distribution of label categories.

There are more literal data in VUA and TOEFI than metaphor data, indicating that both data sets are unbalanced. Unbalanced data sets may affect the performance of metaphor detectors. The distribution of the sentence length in the data set is shown in Figure 4.

As we can see from Figure 4 that the distribution of the sentence length distribution by both training

---

[3]http://ota.ahds.ac.uk/headers/2541.xml

[4]https://catalog.ldc.upenn.edu/LDC2014T06
[5]http://saifmohammad.com/WebPages/metaphor.html
[6]http://natlang.cs.sfu.ca/software/trofi.html

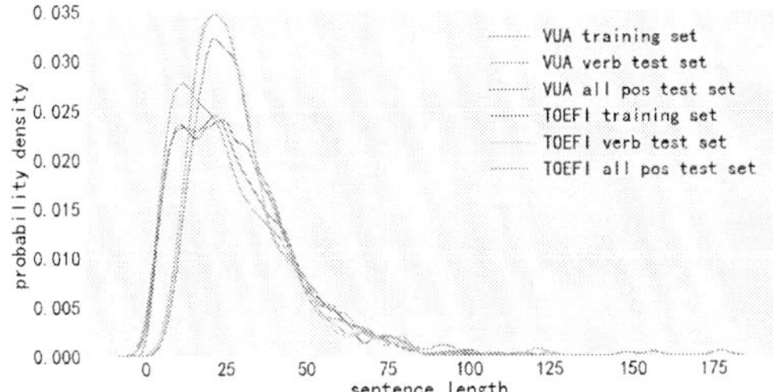

Figure 4: Sentence length distribution of different data sets.

and test set are similar. Similarly, the distribution of query word's POS and its label in the data sets are shown in Figure 5 and Figure 6. The most likely POS of query words triggering metaphor in the two data sets are verbs, nouns, and adjectives. We can delete the triplet data of query words whose POS are other than those POS as these query words are few possibilities as a trigger metaphor.

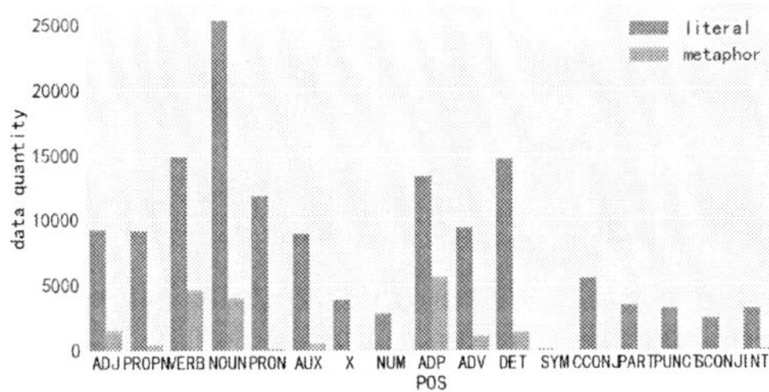

Figure 5: The relationship between POS and label of query words in VUA dataset.

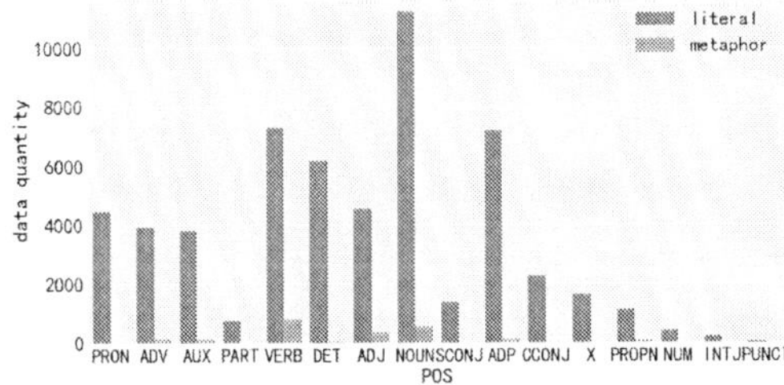

Figure 6: The relationship between POS and label of query words in TOEFI dataset.

4.2 Baselines

We use four baselines to compare the performance of different metaphor detectors: (1) Word2Vec+CNN+BiLSTM+Ensemble (Wu et al., 2018) is the best model in the NAACL-2018 Metaphor Shared Task. The model is based on a sequence tagging paradigm by using CNN and BiLSTM as encoders, Word2Vec, POS tags and word clusters as features, and it is further improved performance through ensemble learning. (2) ELMo+BiLSTM (Gao et al., 2018) is a metaphor detection model based on classification and sequence labeling paradigm by using ELMo as feature representations, and BiLSTM as an encoder. (3) Glove+ELMo+BiLSTM+Attention (Mao et al., 2019) is a metaphor detection model based on sequence tagging paradigm by using GloVe and ELMo as feature representations, BiLSTM and attention mechanism as encoders. To the best of our knowledge, this model is the best among others in the benchmark data sets. (4) BERT+BiLSTM (Mao et al., 2019) is a metaphor detection model based on the sequence labeling paradigm with BERT output vector as the feature and BiLSTM as the encoder.

4.3 Data Preprocessing and Hyperparameters Setting

Our evaluation metrics for metaphor detection tasks are accuracy (A), precision (P), recall (R) and F1 measure (F1), which are the most commonly used evaluation metrics for metaphor detection tasks. We used the default hyperparameters of RoBERTa (Liu et al., 2019) and estimated them by using a grid search within a reasonable range. Each value of the hyperparameters is shown in Table 1.

First, we preprocess the data into the triple format (S, q_i, y_j) required by the reading comprehension paradigm. We remove triples whose query words are punctuation marks, and it was included about 10% among the data. We use the Spacy[7] framework to obtain the query word POS and FG-POS features needed by the experiments. The pre-training language model directly encodes the data into dynamic word embeddings. The best model parameter weight in the validation set is the final model parameter weight. We divided the data into two folds, training and verification sets consisting of 90% and 10% of the data, respectively. We used ten folds cross-validation throughout the experi-

Table 1: The value of the hyperparameters.

Hyperparameters	Vaule
Sequencey length	128
Batches	16
Initial learning rate	1e-5
Dropout rate	0.2
Epochs	3
Cross-validation folds	10

---

[7]https://spacy.io

ments.

4.4 Experimental results and Analysis

The results are shown in Table 2. Overall, we can see that our metaphor detector (DeepMet) attained at the best performance in each of the four metaphor detection data sets. To verify the factors that affect the performance of DeepMet, we conducted ablation experiments on the model. The results are shown in Table 3.

The experimental results show that FGPOS features have a greater impact on the model than POS features, which shows that the fine-grained POS information provided by FGPOS features is better than ordinary POS information. At the level of the model structure, we also designed corresponding ablation experiments. The experimental results show that the influence of Transformer encoder layer A on the model is greater than that of Transformer encoder layer B, which indicates that the global text information extracted by Transformer encoder layer A is better than local text information extracted by Transformer encoder layer B. Moreover, the ensemble learning of DeepMet with different hyperparameters can also improve about a 3% in the F1 score.

From the experimental results of metaphor detection on four datasets, we can see that the metaphor detection model based on the reading comprehension paradigm can achieve competitive results. Global and local information and two POS features are also helpful to improve the performance of the model. Global and local information contains two kinds of granularity context, which is helpful for the model to extract different granularity text features. FGPOS and POS contain two kinds of granularity POS information, which give the model more abundant query word features. POS features are related to the POS of query words, which can capture implicit knowledge of the model. One reason why DeepMet is better than the previous baseline is that the reading comprehension paradigm can model the nature of the metaphor comprehension problem better, and the Transformer encoder works well than that of general deep learning models such as CNN and BiLSTM.

Moreover, metaphors are used less frequently than ordinary words, and all of the experimental data are unbalanced data sets, i.e., the number of literal sentences are larger than those of metaphor sentences. We thus introduced the metaphor pref-

erence parameter α to help the recall value of the model. The results are shown in Figure 7.

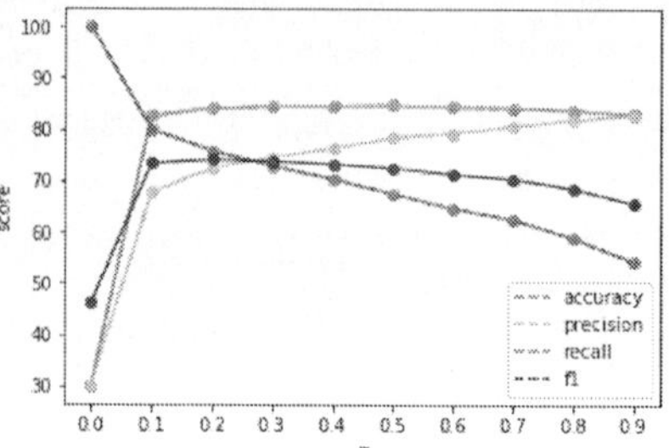

Figure 7: Influence of metaphor preference parameter α on model performance in VUA verb task test set.

As can be seen clearly from Figure 7, the recall score can be improved by using lower α, while the accuracy will be reduced if α is too small. Our experiments show that the best F1 score can be obtained by controlling the metaphor preference parameter α to 0.2 or 0.3.

Through the experiments, we can conclude: (1) Metaphor detection based on the reading comprehension paradigm is feasible, and we obtained competitive results. (2) Ablation experiments indicate that global information, local information, and POS are helpful for metaphor detection. (3) In the cross-validation stage, the introduction of metaphor preference parameter and model ensemble learning can further improve the performance of the metaphor detector.

4.5 Error Analysis

We analyzed the data which could not predict correctly. The ambiguous annotation will make our model incorrectly predict. For example, *"The Health Secretary accused the unions of 'posturing and pretending' to run a 999 service yesterday"* (VUA ID: a7w-fragment01_29), in which the underlined words are labeled as metaphors. Although our model detects "accused" as the literal meaning, it is difficult for even human to judge whether *"accused"* is a metaphor or literal meaning. It is also challenging to detect metaphors triggered by multiple words. For example, *"I stared at Jackson Chatterton , and at last sensed the drama that lay behind his big calm presence."* (VUA ID: ccw-fragment04_2095). In our model, the detection result of *"big"* is a false negative, and *"drama that lay behind his big calm presence"* triggers metaphor together. However, our model only questions one word at a time, so it causes misjudgment that *"big"*

Table 2: Performance of different models on different datasets. * indicates $p<0.01$ in two-tailed t-test, bold indicates best result.

Model	Dataset	A	P	R	F1
Word2Vec+CNN+BiLSTM+Ensemble	VUA-verb	-	60.0	76.3	67.2
ELMo+BiLSTM	VUA-verb	81.4	68.2	71.3	69.7
Glove+ELMo+BiLSTM+Attention	VUA-verb	82.1	69.3	72.3	70.8
BERT+BiLSTM	VUA-verb	80.7	66.7	71.5	69.0
DeepMet	VUA-verb	**88.0**	**78.9**	**81.9**	**80.4***
Word2Vec+CNN+BiLSTM+Ensemble	VUA-allpos	-	60.8	70.0	65.1
ELMo+BiLSTM	VUA-allpos	93.1	71.6	73.6	72.6
Glove+ELMo+BiLSTM+Attention	VUA-allpos	**93.8**	73.0	75.7	74.3
BERT+BiLSTM	VUA-allpos	92.9	71.5	71.9	71.7
DeepMet	VUA-allpos	91.6	**75.6**	**78.3**	**76.9***
DeepMet	TOEFI-verb	-	73.3	76.6	74.9
DeepMet	TOEFI-allpos	-	69.5	73.5	71.5
ELMo+BiLSTM	MOH-X	77.2	79.1	73.5	75.6
Glove+ELMo+BiLSTM+Attention	MOH-X	79.8	77.5	83.1	80.0
BERT+BiLSTM	MOH-X	78.1	75.1	81.8	78.2
DeepMet	MOH-X	**92.3**	**93.3**	**90.3**	**91.8***
ELMo+BiLSTM	TroFi	74.6	70.7	71.6	71.1
Glove+ELMo+BiLSTM+Attention	TroFi	75.2	68.6	76.8	72.4
BERT+BiLSTM	TroFi	73.4	70.3	67.1	68.7
DeepMet	TroFi	**77.0**	**72.1**	**80.6**	**76.1***

Table 3: Experimental results of ablation experiments. w/o indicates ablation of features or network structures.

Model	Dataset	A	P	R	F1
DeepMet	VUA-verb	88.0	78.9	81.9	80.4
w/o POS	VUA-verb	86.0	76.7	76.8	76.7
w/o FGPOS	VUA-verb	85.1	72.7	80.5	76.4
w/o Transformer Encoder Layer A	VUA-verb	85.7	75.4	77.3	76.4
w/o Transformer Encoder Layer B	VUA-verb	85.6	73.9	80.2	76.9
w/o ensemble learning	VUA-verb	86.2	76.2	78.3	77.2
DeepMet	VUA-allpos	91.6	75.6	78.3	76.9
w/o POS	VUA-allpos	90.5	74.7	71.2	72.9
w/o FGPOS	VUA-allpos	89.8	70.5	74.2	72.3
w/o Transformer Encoder Layer A	VUA-allpos	90.2	73.2	71.2	72.2
w/o Transformer Encoder Layer B	VUA-allpos	90.6	74.0	73.2	73.6
w/o ensemble learning	VUA-allpos	90.5	73.8	73.2	73.5

is not a metaphor.

5 Conclusion and Future Work

This paper proposed a reading comprehension paradigm for metaphor detection. According to this reading comprehension paradigm, we designed an end-to-end neural metaphor detector, which processes global and local information of the text through the transformer encoder, and introduces two POS with different granularity as additional features. Throughout the experiments on four metaphor detection data sets, we found that the model works well, and a competitive result is achieved good performance in the second metaphor detection sharing task. We also designed ablation experiments to verify the influence factors of the model and found that fine-grained POS and global text information is more helpful to the metaphor

detection ability of the model.

There are a number of interesting directions for future work: (1) Metaphor is a special figurative language and we will extend our research methods to other figurative languages such as metonymy, simile, satire, and pun. (2) We will introduce linguistic theory into our framework to make a deep learning model more explanatory. (3) Through error analysis, we find that the multiple words trigger metaphor will affect the performance of the metaphor detection model. We will consider the multi-word question metaphor detection based on the reading comprehension paradigm.

Acknowledgments

We are grateful to the anonymous reviewers for their insightful comments and suggestions. This work was supported in part by the Grant-in-aid for JSPS, the Support Center for Advanced Telecommunications Technology Research Foundation under Grant 17K00299, the Humanities and Social Sciences Research Program Funds from the Ministry of Education of China under Grant 18YJA740016, and the Major Projects of the National Social Science Foundation of China under Grant 18ZDA290.

References

Julia Birke and Anoop Sarkar. 2006. A clustering approach for nearly unsupervised recognition of nonliteral language. In *11th Conference of the European Chapter of the Association for Computational Linguistics*.

E Charniak, D Blaheta, N Ge, K Hall, J Hale, and M Johnson. 2000. Bllip 1987-89 wsj corpus release 1. linguistic data consortium ldc2000t43.

Jacob Devlin, Ming-Wei Chang, Kenton Lee, and Kristina Toutanova. 2018. Bert: Pre-training of deep bidirectional transformers for language understanding. *arXiv preprint arXiv:1810.04805*.

Ellen Dodge, Jisup Hong, and Elise Stickles. 2015. MetaNet: Deep semantic automatic metaphor analysis. In *Proceedings of the Third Workshop on Metaphor in NLP*. Association for Computational Linguistics.

Ge Gao, Eunsol Choi, Yejin Choi, and Luke Zettlemoyer. 2018. Neural metaphor detection in context. In *Proceedings of the 2018 Conference on Empirical Methods in Natural Language Processing*. Association for Computational Linguistics.

Sam Glucksberg. 2003. The psycholinguistics of metaphor. *Trends in Cognitive Sciences*, 7(2):92–96.

Alex Graves and Jürgen Schmidhuber. 2005. Framewise phoneme classification with bidirectional lstm and other neural network architectures. *Neural Networks*, 18(5-6):602–610.

Pragglejaz Group. 2007. MIP: A method for identifying metaphorically used words in discourse. *Metaphor and Symbol*, 22(1):1–39.

Beata Beigman Klebanov, Ben Leong, Michael Heilman, and Michael Flor. 2014. Different texts, same metaphors: Unigrams and beyond. In *Proceedings of the Second Workshop on Metaphor in NLP*. Association for Computational Linguistics.

Beata Beigman Klebanov, Chee Wee (Ben) Leong, and Michael Flor. 2018. A corpus of non-native written english annotated for metaphor. In *Proceedings of the 2018 Conference of the North American Chapter of the Association for Computational Linguistics: Human Language Technologies, Volume 2 (Short Papers)*. Association for Computational Linguistics.

Maximilian Köper and Sabine Schulte im Walde. 2016. Distinguishing literal and non-literal usage of german particle verbs. In *Proceedings of the 2016 Conference of the North American Chapter of the Association for Computational Linguistics: Human Language Technologies*. Association for Computational Linguistics.

George Lakoff and Mark Johnson. 2003. *Metaphors We Live By*. University of Chicago Press.

Chee Wee (Ben) Leong, Beata Beigman Klebanov, and Ekaterina Shutova. 2018. A report on the 2018 VUA metaphor detection shared task. In *Proceedings of the Workshop on Figurative Language Processing*. Association for Computational Linguistics.

Omer Levy, Minjoon Seo, Eunsol Choi, and Luke Zettlemoyer. 2017. Zero-shot relation extraction via reading comprehension. *arXiv preprint arXiv:1706.04115*.

Xiaoya Li, Jingrong Feng, Yuxian Meng, Qinghong Han, Fei Wu, and Jiwei Li. 2019. A unified mrc framework for named entity recognition. *arXiv preprint arXiv:1910.11476*.

Yinhan Liu, Myle Ott, Naman Goyal, Jingfei Du, Mandar Joshi, Danqi Chen, Omer Levy, Mike Lewis, Luke Zettlemoyer, and Veselin Stoyanov. 2019. Roberta: A robustly optimized bert pretraining approach. *arXiv preprint arXiv:1907.11692*.

Rui Mao, Chenghua Lin, and Frank Guerin. 2019. End-to-end sequential metaphor identification inspired by linguistic theories. In *Proceedings of the 57th Annual Meeting of the Association for Computational Linguistics*. Association for Computational Linguistics.

Bryan McCann, Nitish Shirish Keskar, Caiming Xiong, and Richard Socher. 2018. The natural language decathlon: Multitask learning as question answering. *arXiv preprint arXiv:1806.08730*.

Tomas Mikolov, Ilya Sutskever, Kai Chen, Greg S Corrado, and Jeff Dean. 2013. Distributed representations of words and phrases and their compositionality. In *Advances in neural information processing systems*, pages 3111–3119.

George A Miller. 1998. *WordNet: An electronic lexical database*. MIT press.

Saif Mohammad, Ekaterina Shutova, and Peter Turney. 2016. Metaphor as a medium for emotion: An empirical study. In *Proceedings of the Fifth Joint Conference on Lexical and Computational Semantics*. Association for Computational Linguistics.

Michael Mohler, David Bracewell, Marc Tomlinson, and David Hinote. 2013. Semantic signatures for example-based linguistic metaphor detection. In *Proceedings of the First Workshop on Metaphor in NLP*, pages 27–35.

Jeffrey Pennington, Richard Socher, and Christopher Manning. 2014. Glove: Global vectors for word representation. In *Proceedings of the 2014 Conference on Empirical Methods in Natural Language Processing (EMNLP)*. Association for Computational Linguistics.

Matthew E Peters, Mark Neumann, Mohit Iyyer, Matt Gardner, Christopher Clark, Kenton Lee, and Luke Zettlemoyer. 2018. Deep contextualized word representations. *arXiv preprint arXiv:1802.05365*.

Alec Radford, Karthik Narasimhan, Tim Salimans, and Ilya Sutskever. 2018. Improving language understanding by generative pre-training. *URL https://s3-us-west-2. amazonaws. com/openai-assets/researchcovers/languageunsupervised/language understanding paper. pdf*.

Beatrice Santorini. 1990. Part-of-speech tagging guidelines for the penn treebank project.

Minjoon Seo, Aniruddha Kembhavi, Ali Farhadi, and Hannaneh Hajishirzi. 2016. Bidirectional attention flow for machine comprehension. *arXiv preprint arXiv:1611.01603*.

Yelong Shen, Po-Sen Huang, Jianfeng Gao, and Weizhu Chen. 2017. Reasonet: Learning to stop reading in machine comprehension. In *Proceedings of the 23rd ACM SIGKDD International Conference on Knowledge Discovery and Data Mining*, pages 1047–1055.

Yusuxke Shibata, Takuya Kida, Shuichi Fukamachi, Masayuki Takeda, Ayumi Shinohara, Takeshi Shinohara, and Setsuo Arikawa. 1999. Byte pair encoding: A text compression scheme that accelerates pattern matching. Technical report, Technical Report DOI-TR-161, Department of Informatics, Kyushu University.

Ekaterina Shutova, Douwe Kiela, and Jean Maillard. 2016. Black holes and white rabbits: Metaphor identification with visual features. In *Proceedings of the 2016 Conference of the North American Chapter of the Association for Computational Linguistics: Human Language Technologies*. Association for Computational Linguistics.

Gerard Steen. 2010. *A method for linguistic metaphor identification: From MIP to MIPVU*, volume 14. John Benjamins Publishing.

Gerard J. Steen, Aletta G. Dorst, J. Berenike Herrmann, Anna A. Kaal, and Tina Krennmayr. 2010. Metaphor in usage. *Cognitive Linguistics*, 21(4).

Yulia Tsvetkov, Leonid Boytsov, Anatole Gershman, Eric Nyberg, and Chris Dyer. 2014. Metaphor detection with cross-lingual model transfer. In *Proceedings of the 52nd Annual Meeting of the Association for Computational Linguistics (Volume 1: Long Papers)*. Association for Computational Linguistics.

Peter D Turney, Yair Neuman, Dan Assaf, and Yohai Cohen. 2011. Literal and metaphorical sense identification through concrete and abstract context. In *Proceedings of the Conference on Empirical Methods in Natural Language Processing*, pages 680–690. Association for Computational Linguistics.

Ashish Vaswani, Noam Shazeer, Niki Parmar, Jakob Uszkoreit, Llion Jones, Aidan N Gomez, Łukasz Kaiser, and Illia Polosukhin. 2017. Attention is all you need. In *Advances in neural information processing systems*, pages 5998–6008.

Shuohang Wang and Jing Jiang. 2016. Machine comprehension using match-lstm and answer pointer. *arXiv preprint arXiv:1608.07905*.

Yorick Wilks. 1975. A preferential, pattern-seeking, semantics for natural language inference. *Artificial intelligence*, 6(1):53–74.

Chuhan Wu, Fangzhao Wu, Yubo Chen, Sixing Wu, Zhigang Yuan, and Yongfeng Huang. 2018. Neural metaphor detecting with CNN-LSTM model. In *Proceedings of the Workshop on Figurative Language Processing*. Association for Computational Linguistics.

Zhilin Yang, Zihang Dai, Yiming Yang, Jaime Carbonell, Russ R Salakhutdinov, and Quoc V Le. 2019. Xlnet: Generalized autoregressive pretraining for language understanding. In *Advances in neural information processing systems*, pages 5754–5764.

Context-Driven Satirical Headline Generation

Zachary Horvitz   Nam Do   Michael L. Littman
Department of Computer Science
Brown University
Providence, RI 02912
{zachary_horvitz,nam_do,michael_littman}@brown.edu

Abstract

While mysterious, humor likely hinges on an interplay of entities, their relationships, and cultural connotations. Motivated by the importance of context in humor, we consider methods for constructing and leveraging contextual representations in generating humorous text. Specifically, we study the capacity of transformer-based architectures to generate funny satirical headlines, and show that both language models and summarization models can be fine-tuned to regularly generate headlines that people find funny. Furthermore, we find that summarization models uniquely support satire-generation by enabling the generation of topical humorous text. Outside of our formal study, we note that headlines generated by our model were accepted via a competitive process into a satirical newspaper, and one headline was ranked as high or better than 73% of human submissions. As part of our work, we contribute a dataset of over 15K satirical headlines paired with ranked contextual information from news articles and Wikipedia.

1   Introduction

Despite long-term interest in the foundations of humor, work to date in the NLP community on humorous text has largely relied on surface-level features (e.g., puns). We study employing richer contextual representations to generate satirical news headlines, which necessitate a balance between funniness and topicality. While our particular focus is humor, our methods are broadly applicable to tasks that require reasoning over textual knowledge.

Consider the following satirical headline from The Onion (TheOnion.com):

TC Energy Says Keystone Pipeline Failed Due To Protestors Making It Lose Confidence In Itself

In addition to knowing the connection between failure and self-confidence, processing the humor of this headline presupposes knowing (or inferring):

1. TC Energy Oversaw the Keystone XL Pipeline.

2. The Keystone XL pipeline failed amid protests.

Thus, satirical news requires an appreciation of a real-world, non-funny context.

Existing literature on the psychology of humor emphasizes the role of complex representations and relationships (Morreall, 2016; Martin, 2010; Attardo, 2001; Raskin, 1985; Attardo, 2014). Psychologists have offered multiple theories of humor. According to "Superiority Theory," jokes hinge on the power-relations between entities, while "Relief Theory" ventures that humor releases conflict between desires and inhibitions. "Incongruity Theory" sees humor as emerging from low-probability juxtapositions between objects and events.

Regardless of the theoretical framework, moving from surface-level features to a deeper analysis of humor requires an implicit calculus of entities, their relationships, and even cultural connotations. Recent NLP and NLG research has sought to apply psychological hypotheses to understand and generate humorous text. J.T. Kao (2016) applied the incongruity framework to analyze and predict the funniness of puns, and found that puns rated funnier tended to be more ambiguous. Building on the aforementioned work, Yu et al. (2018) applied neural models to pun generation, and He et al. (2019) found that puns could be procedurally created by inserting low-probability (as determined by a language model) homophones into non-funny sentences.

Other related work has established style-transfer and translation approaches for sarcasm generation. For example, Mishra et al. (2019) introduced a pipeline for converting an input sentence to a sarcastic form by neutralizing its sentiment, translating it into strong positive sentiment, and then combining it with a negative event. This pairing creates

Proceedings of the Second Workshop on Figurative Language Processing, pages 40–50
July 9, 2020. ©2020 Association for Computational Linguistics
https://doi.org/10.18653/v1/P17

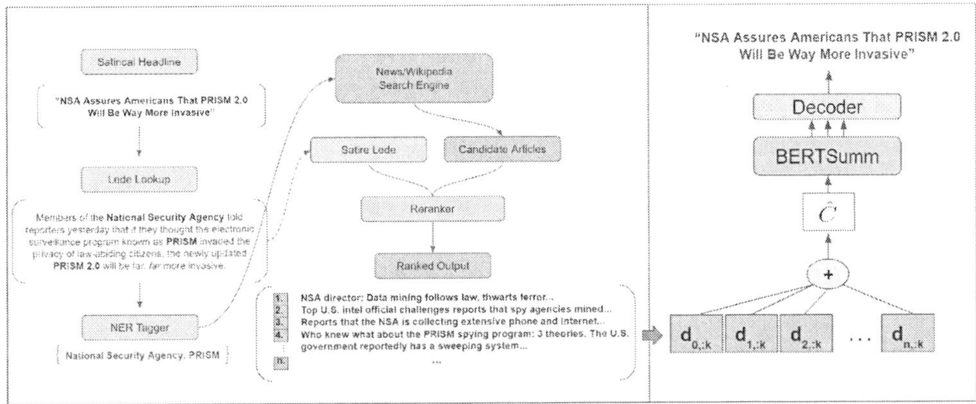

Figure 1: Pipeline for retrieving real-world textual context for a satirical headline. The extracted context is combined into a synthetic document, which is used as the input to a pretrained abstractive summarization model. The pipeline extracts named entities from the lede of the satirical article. These named entities are queried on Wikipedia and CNN. The results are then ranked by comparing their similarity to the original article across several metrics. We task the model with decoding the original satirical headline.

an incongruity between the underling event and sentiment expressed in the sentence. In contrast to pun wordplay or sarcasm, satirical headlines require a significantly richer context. Therefore, we explore satirical headlines as a testbed for humor generation that leverages richer contextual features.

Recent work in satire has explored the curation of corpora mapping from non-satirical to satirical forms. West and Horvitz (2019) built a corpus of unfunny headlines via a game that asks crowdworkers to make minimal edits that render satirical headlines unfunny and then analyzed structural differences between matched pairs of serious and satirical headlines. Taking an alternative approach, Hossain et al. (2019) introduced a corpus of news headlines with one-word edits While both of the aforementioned research efforts make inroads into understanding the rules underlying satire, both of the collected datasets are relatively small and curated. More importantly, both datasets do not consider the broader context that forms the basis of the joke.

Beyond puns and sarcasm, there has been little research on the generation of humorous text. Notable exceptions include Alnajjar and Hämäläinen (2018), who apply evolutionary algorithms and a master-apprentice approach to transform English movie titles into "creative" titles related to Saudi Arabia, and Winters et al. (2019) who automatically extract schemas from ranked lists of one-liner jokes. Rather than generation, the emphasis thus far has

been on humor classification and ranking. Work by Shahaf et al. (2015) built classifiers to rank the funniness of submissions to the New Yorker Magazine caption contest, and Hossain et al. (2019) have introduced a headline-editing evaluation task.

Raskin (2012) notes that both humor detection and generation research have been hindered by "the difficulty of accessing a context sensitive, computationally based world model," but that "such difficulties are eliminated when the humor analysis is done with a system capable of capturing the semantics of text." Our work follows the second vein: we build on recent advances in contextual embeddings and summarizing architectures to extract meaningful features from text, and leverage them for conditional headline generation. We treat the satire generation task as one of taking a real-world text input, and generating a satirical headline output.

We propose a novel approach (as detailed in Figure 1) wherein we first construct a dataset of real-world context–satirical headline pairs in which the context is constructed by procedurally retrieving and ranking real-world stories, events and information related to the entities that appear in the original satirical headline. Then, we fine-tune BertSum, a state-of-the-art abstractive summarization architecture pretrained on news corpora, to encode the real-word context and generate the original satirical headline.

Our contributions are as follows: (1) we introduce a novel approach for modeling satirical news headlines as conditioned on a real-world context, and an information retrieval pipeline for constructing the real-world context for a given real satirical headline; (2) we generate a dataset of more than 15K real-world context–satirical headline pairs for conditional humor generation; (3) we formulate satirical headline generation as an abstractive summarization task, mapping from a real-world text document to a humorous headline, and (4) we show that both the language and summarization models can be fine-tuned to generate headlines that people find funny. We find that summarization models best support satire generation by enabling humorous text that is both coherent and topical.

The context-based model appears to capture aspects of a "humor transformation" that include "edgy"/taboo topics and the satirical news register. Additionally, our model appears to learn how to mimic known principles of humor, including false-analogy, and to use incongruous relationships between entities and ideas. We compare the context-based approach to a context-free language modeling baseline. While the context-free approach can produce funny results, we find that people rate the context-based approach as generating funnier headlines. The context-based approach is also able to generalize, and generate headlines for unseen news contexts. Together, the results demonstrate that summarization models, which provide rich textual feature extraction, may offer important tools for future work in computational humor.

In machine generation of humor, it is important to control for the possibility that the humor is emerging from amusing generation failures. Our comparisons with non-satirical baselines evince that, fortunately, annotators are laughing *with* our model, not *at* it.

2 Our Approach

We now provide background on our methods.

2.1 Headline Representation

We model a satirical headline S_i as a function of an underlying latent joke J_i, which is, in turn, dependent on real-word context C_i,

$$S_i = \text{HEADLINE}(J_i), J_i = \text{HUMOR}(C_i).$$

The goal of satirical news generation is then to map from context C_i to a satirical headline S_i.

2.2 Retrieving Real World Context

Hossain et al. (2019) attribute the lack of progress in computational humor research to "the scarcity of public datasets." In previous work, humans have been an essential in the labeling of these corpora. However, in the present work, we introduce an automatic, scalable pipeline for recovering background information for a satirical joke. We reconfigure the problem of matching headlines to a context as an unsupervised information retrieval task. The flow of our pipeline is displayed in Figure 1. We leverage the paradigm introduced by West and Horvitz (2019) of translating from funny text (a known satirical headline) to an unfunny related document. However, we expand this mapping to include a larger textual context.

In satirical headlines, the full "joke" may never be explicitly stated. However, the first line in a satirical article, referred to as the *lede*, contextualizes the headline by providing a grammatical, extended description and introducing named entities.

1. For a given satirical headline, we look up its lede, the first sentence in the body of the original satirical article.

2. We run the SpaCy Named Entity Recognition Tagger to extract named entities from the lede (Honnibal and Montani, 2017).

3. We then query these named entities on the news site CNN.com to retrieve contemporaneous news content published the week that the satirical article was written, along with all paragraphs from those entities' Wikipedia entries.

The output of our pipeline (Figure 1) is a dictionary that maps satirical headlines to a ranked list of Wikipedia paragraphs and CNN news articles. We then combine these results into an aggregate text document to serve as fodder for training and evaluating.

2.3 Building a Synthetic Document

To build our aggregate context document, we take the first k sentences from the top n most relevant ranked documents $\{d_0, ..., d_{n-1}\}$. This synthetic document of retrieved entity text serves as the approximation of the real world context:

$$\hat{C}_i = [d_0; ...; d_{n-1}] \approx C_i.$$

Once we have mapped every satirical headline to a corresponding context, we then train our model to approximate:

$$\hat{C}_i \mapsto S_i.$$

In other words, we train our summarization model to encode the contextual representation, augment it with pretrained embeddings, and then decode the original satirical headline.

2.4 Datasets

We retrieve documents for 15199 satirical Onion headlines.

To build our training and testing datasets, we include the first four sentences from the top two CNN articles and from the top three remaining documents by rank. (This design biases our contextual document towards news content, when it is available). We then trim these aggregate contexts, which we refer to as synthetic documents, down to approximately 512 tokens. We experimented with several document-creation schemes, including building a larger corpus by stochastically sampling from the different text sources.

The resulting dataset comprises over document–headline pairs. We employed human annotators to confirm that our retrieved documents are regularly relevant to the original satirical article. These results are included in the Appendix (See A.1).

For our news-based context-free baseline model, we used the roughly 10K real news headlines from the Unfun.me corpus. As an additional baseline, we trained the model on the 2758 unfunned-satirical pairs provided in the corpus. Each satirical headline had multiple "unfunned" candidates, so we ensured that no such duplicates appeared in both the train and test corpora.

We used an 85-15 train-test split for all satire models.

2.5 Models

We leverage recent breakthroughs in document summarization by employing the abstractive summarization model introduced by Liu and Lapata (2019)(Nallapati et al., 2016). The architecture is state-of-the-art on the CNN-DailyMail Test.[1] Their architecture, BERTSum, augments BERT (Devlin et al., 2018) (Bidirectional Encoder Representations from Transformers) with sentence embeddings to build document-level encodings. These

encoder embeddings are then fed to a Transformer decoder (Vaswani et al., 2017). The BERTSum encoder is then secondarily pretrained on an extractive summarization task before finally being fine-tuned on an abstractive summarization task. For our work, we fine-tuned a BERTSum model pretrained for abstractive and extractive summarization on 286K CNN and Daily Mail articles.

We settled on three main fine-tuning schemes, which yielded three distinct context-based models. For the **Encoder-Weighted-Context** (E-Context) model, we trained the encoder and decoder with learning rates of 0.002 and 0.02, respectively. For the **Abstractive-Context** (A-Context) model, we trained the network on contexts that had been preprocessed by the pretrained abstractive summarizer. For **Decoder-Weighted-Context** (D-Context), we trained the decoder with a learning rate of 0.02, and an encoder with learning rate 0.00002. For all models, we used batches of size 200, a warmup of 500, and decayed the learning rate using the function implemented by Liu and Lapata (2019).

We applied these varied schemes as a means of exploring the relationship between learning a new encoder representation and fine-tuning a new 'satirical' decoder atop the pretrained summarization encoder module. Additionally, we include the abstractive approach to test the value of a more concise document formulation.

For the context-free baselines, we fine-tuned Hugging Face's large GPT-2 model on the satirical headlines in our corpus (Radford et al., 2019; Wolf et al., 2019). We also fine-tuned the GPT-2 model on a corpus of 10K real news headlines from the Unfun.me corpus.

3 Experimental Design

We tested our models by sampling headline generations and evaluating their quality via crowdsourcing.

3.1 Satire Generation

We began by greedily generating headlines from our baseline models: the GPT-2 context-free satire model and the GPT-2 context-free news model. Since language models only condition on the previous tokens in a sequence, generating diverse outputs requires random sampling. However, we found that common approaches (such as Top-k and Top-p sampling) rapidly degraded headline quality. Thus, from our validation set of 1955 satirical head-

---

[1] https://paperswithcode.com/sota/document-summarization-on-cnn-daily-mail

lines collected from The Onion, we extracted the first two words from each headline, and used these two words as prompts for greedy generation. For the context-based modes, we generated headlines by feeding in the synthetic documents from our test set. In contrast to our language-model baselines, our context-based model never sees any segment of the original satirical headline.

3.2 Satire Generation Evaluation

We employed human annotators to evaluate the performance of different models on the satire-generation task. Workers on Amazon Mechanical Turk answered three questions for every generation: (1) Is the headline coherent? (2) Does the headline sound like The Onion? and (3) Is the headline funny? To control for funniness induced by incoherence, we instructed annotators to mark all 'incoherent' headlines as not funny.

For each generated headline, we received three unique annotations. To qualify, annotators must have come from the United States, have had more than 50 annotations approved in previous studies, and have had an annotation approval rating higher than 95%.

We had 750 headlines annotated for each model. Labels were determined by majority agreement $(2/3+)$.

4   Results

This section describe the results of our evaluation.[2]

Table 1: Model Comparison

Model	Coherence	Onion	Funny	F | C
Onion (Gold)	**99.5%**	**86.6%**	**38.2%**	**38.4%**
Satire GPT-2	86.5%	57.7%	6.9%	7.9%
News GPT-2	**89.2%**	36.9%	2.4%	2.7%
D-Context	88.4%	**58.8%**	**9.4%**	10.4%
E-Context	80.2%	57.8%	8.7%	**10.8%**
A-Context	85.3%	54.9%	8.8 %	10.3%

[2]We excluded the model trained on the Unfun.me corpus, as only 2.5% of its generations were rated as funny, and 64% of generations were simply duplicates of the original input context. The redundant generations likely resulted from the small corpus size, and the significant word-overlap between the 'unfunned' input and labels.

4.1   Quantitative Results

Table 2 contrasts the performance of the different headline-generation techniques as rated by the annotators. Coherence, Onion and Funny columns describe the majority vote among the three annotators for the category. Column $F|C$ contains the probability of a headline being rated funny, given that it is rated coherent. Because all funny annotations were also by default rated coherent, we computed $F|C$ by dividing the number of Funny headlines by Coherent headlines.

We also collected annotations for original Onion headlines, which we compared to the results for each of our models. As expected, expert-generated satirical headlines from The Onion perform best on the Coherence, Onion and Funny metrics, as well as $F|C$. In contrast, the news-based model was judged as Coherent, but not rated well on the humor-related metrics.

Importantly, the D-Context model achieved the highest Funny rating among all models, followed by the E-Context model. (The former had a Funny score $\sim 4\times$ that of the News GPT-2 baseline). Additionally, the context-based models received higher Funny scores than the Satire GPT-2 language model (a 2% increase, approximately). This delta is especially impressive given that the context-free satirical language model was prompted with the first two words of a true satirical headline.

These results support the claim that context-based models more regularly produce funny generations than the context-free approaches. Additionally, all satire-trained models substantially outperformed the News GPT-2 baseline, providing critical evidence that the humor judgments are not simply due to awkward machine-generated language, but are a consequence of the fact that the models are learning to generate coherent, humorous text.

While the D-Context was rated over 8% more coherent than the E-Context model, a smaller fraction of the coherent generations are rated Funny. Our examinations of these generations reveal that primarily fine-tuning the decoder on satire may lead to coherent, but more standardized generations that are less conditioned on context. However, we measured the quantitative similarity of generations for all context-based models to their input document (See A.2), and found that all models produced generations that were as similar to their input document as the original satirical headline.

We will now examine the patterns that characterize these generations.

4.2 Qualitative Analysis

In our initial analyses of the characteristic behaviors of the models, we have observed a transformation from events referenced in the context into a "newsy" register, the introduction of expressions of uncertainty, sweeping generalizations, and incongruous juxtapositions (see Figure 2).

The adoption of a newsy tone is readily apparent; the model invents "studies" and "reports" even when none are mentioned in the original context. Additionally, common forms include "X announces/unveils Y," where X and Y are extracted from the context, or are particularly polarizing topics from The Onion corpus, like "abortion" or "sex."

The model also refers to general entities often referenced by Onion writers. These include common satirical terms for everyday people, like 'area man.' When the model employs these characters, it tends to decode out more observational headlines, like *area man just wants to know what he 's doing*, that are less related to the given context. Our Decoder-Weighted-Model exhibited this behavior more often.

The context-based generations also introduce apparent "incongruities" in a variety of ways. For example, the models catch the satirical news trick of juxtaposing a 'study' with an unscientific remark. For example: *study finds americans should be more obese by now*. Another, most obvious example of incongruity is the mention of absurd, yet contextually relevant events (e.g. *study finds majority of americans still in oil spill*).

However, the most fascinating cases are when the reality articulated in the input context is inverted. For example, *god admits he's not the creator* when the context very much states that He is. Similarly, in Figure 2, we see *scientists discover that oil spills caused by natural causes*, when the context argues quite the opposite. This juxtaposition works as a humorous construction and suggests that the model has latched onto something like a general principle.

We submitted these two generated headlines, along with others, to the Brown Noser[1], Brown University's campus satirical newspaper:

- *God Unveils New Line of Sex*

<hr>

[1] http://thenoser.com/

- *U.S. Asks Pugs If they Can Do Anything*

Staff writers rated the latter as high as or better than 73% of writer submissions. Both were accepted for publication and express several aspects of observed humor transformation captured by our context-based models. The first juxtaposes newsy language (for example, Unveils, New line of, U.S.) with incongruous entities like 'God' and 'Sex.' The second relates pugs to U.S. governmental affairs. The latter article was published with an accompanying article written by a human satirical writer (See A.3).

4.3 Sensitivity Analysis

The latent space of Transformer-based architectures is fundamentally difficult to analyze. However, our summarization approach gives us the ability to probe the relationship between context and output: We can perturb the input context and examine the resulting change to the decoding headline. Thus far, we have observed that our model is less sensitive to changes to the context in the form of adjectives or negations than it is to changes in the entities. Additionally, key terms in the context can activate certain headlines. For example, mentions of the Royal family tend to prompt the same original headline: *Royal baby born in captivity*. However, in other instances, the entire tone of the resulting headline can be changed by single verb substitution. For example:

> "harriet hall of science based medicine reviewed the film in an article entitled ' does the movie fed up make sense ? ' . the film [**makes/disputes**] the claim that drinking one soda a day will increase a child's chance of becoming obese by 60 %"
>
> 1. **makes**: study finds americans should be more obese by now
> 2. **disputes**: study finds average american has no idea how to get overweight

In both cases, the model introduced a fictional study. However, the latter appears to capture the uncertainty around the disputed claim that one can become obese by drinking a soda. Future work is necessary to explore the relationship between context and output.

Input: a creator deity or creator god [often called the creator] is a deity or god responsible for the creation of the earth , world , and universe in human religion and mythology . in monotheism , the single god is often also the creator . a number of monolatristic traditions separate a secondary creator from a primary transcendent being , identified as a primary creator...
E-Context: god 's name a big hit / god admits he 's not the creator
D-Context: god 's god calls for greater understanding of all the things
A-Context: god admits he 's not a good person
Onion: Biologists Confirm God Evolved From Chimpanzee Deity
GPT-2 Satire: biologists confirm
GPT-2 News: biologists confirm human ancestor

Input: the jet propulsion laboratory is a federally funded research and development center and nasa field center...on 26 november 2011 , nasa's mars science laboratory mission was successfully launched for mars ... the rover is currently helping to determine whether mars could ever have supported life , and search for evidence of past or present life on mars ...
E-Context: nasa announces plan to put down mars / nasa announces plan to hunt mars
D-Context: nasa launches new mission to find out what life is doing
A-Context: mars scientists successfully successfully successfully successfully
Onion: Coke-Sponsored Rover Finds Evidence Of Dasani On Mars
GPT-2 Satire: coke - a little too much
GPT-2 News: coke - the new 'dancing with the stars'

Input: the boston globe called for a nationwide refutation of trump's 'dirty war' against the news media, with the hashtag enemy of none. more than 300 news outlets joined the campaign. the new york times called trump's attacks 'dangerous to the lifeblood of democracy...
E-Context: trump vows to destroy all his words / trump: ' i 'm not the best guy in the world '
D-Context: trump vows to destroy all the things he 's doing
A-Context: trump : ' we 're not going to let people know what it is '
Onion: Trump's Attacks On The Press
GPT-2 Satire: trump'sick and tired of hearing' trump say
GPT-2 News: trump'sick of being in the middle of a fight'

Input: a 2014 study of the effects of the oil spill on bluefin tuna funded by national oceanic and atmospheric administration...found that tuna and amberjack that were exposed to oil from the spill developed deformities of the heart and other organs that would be expected to be fatal or at least life-shortening . the scientists said that their findings would most likely apply to other large predator fish and even to humans.. bp was guilty of gross negligence and willful misconduct . he described bp's actions as 'reckless ...
E-Context: study finds majority of americans still in oil spill
/ study finds majority of tuna spills now in danger of human suffering
D-Context: scientists discover that oil spills caused by natural causes
A-Context: report : bluefin fish may have been killed by fish
Onion: Shrimp Boat Captain Worn Out From Long Day Of Putting Human Face On Crisis
GPT-2 Satire: shrimp boat to be built in new york
GPT-2 News: shrimp boat sinks in gulf

Figure 2: A sample of documents (abbreviated) and resulting generations. These generations incorporate entities from the context while maintaining Onion-like language. This includes irreverent, observational tone, and the addition of frequently Onion corpus terms like "study" and "announces." We also observed that generations could invert facts expressed within the context (e.g. *God admitting he is **not** the creator*, or *oil spills result from natural causes*). We observe the decoder-weighted model resorting to more casual, repetitive language (e.g. *"all the things..."*).

4.4 Topical Generation for News Stories

We can apply our model to novel news stories. While all of our training headlines were collected before COVID-19 was declared a pandemic in March 2020, our model shows an ability to generalize to pandemic-related news stories and generate topical headlines (Figure 3). We preprocessed the beginning of CNN articles from April 2020 with the pretrained BERTsum model to generate concise abstracts, and then input these summaries into our networks. Our models appear to condition on these new contexts and generate related satirical headlines.

> **Input:** president donald trump doubled down on an unproven therapy for the novel coronavirus . without citing evidence , he said it's a "great " and "powerful" anti-malaria drug " . trump said it ' s
>
> - trump doubles down on prescription drug that can cause coronavirus
>
> **Input:** questions over whether downing street was fully transparent about the prime minister's health . but important issues risk overshadowing the true picture of the uk's struggle against coronavirus . the uk is on a similar, grim trajectory as the uk is
>
> - nation 's love of coronavirus now a little more complex
>
> **Input:** president donald trump announced tuesday he is halting funding to the world health organization while a review is conducted . trump said the review would cover the " role in severely mismanaging and covering up the spread of coronavirus " . trump has sought to assign blame elsewhere , including at the who and in the news media
>
> - world health organization unveils new " ' plan to cover up coronavirus

Figure 3: We preprocessed CNN articles from April using the pretrained abstractive summarization model provided by Liu and Lapata (2019). Our approach appears to generalize to these novel news contexts.

The resulting generations incorporate named entities from the context, and embed them in a humorous generation.

5 Future Work

We intend to further investigate the latent and embedding spaces of our model, and hope to better elucidate the neural-logic that transposes everyday events into humorous language.

Additionally, our context-driven approach allows us to examine the relationship between real-world, input events, and the resulting satirical output. We plan to continue probing this relationship, and to refine our understanding of the processes underlying our generations, and how their relationship to real-world events can be interpreted within proposed theories of humor, including the Script-Based Semantic Theory of Humor (See A.4).

While we treat document retrieval as a prepossessing step, we can also explore including retrieval in end-to-end training, as employed by Guu et al. (2020).

Lastly, we are fascinated by the potential for leveraging other text-based contextual representations, ranging from alternative types of document and longer-form text, to graph-encoded representations of events and entities. These approaches can provide alternative blends of depth, concision, and structure.

6 Conclusion

We introduced a methodology and formalization for modeling satirical news headlines as conditioned on a real-world context, and presented an information retrieval pipeline for constructing that context. We found that pretrained abstractive summarization models provide powerful feature extractors atop these rich contextual representations. Conditioning on such contextual documents enabled the generation of topical satire that people determined to be funnier than headlines generated via context-free methods. Additionally, we discovered that the approach generalizes to new topics and circumstances.

Moving beyond the focus on generating satirical headlines, we believe that variations of our approach are broadly applicable to tasks ranging from information retrieval and dialogue to reading comprehension. Our work provides further evidence that neural architectures, augmented with task-relevant contextual information, have the potential to reason about sub-textual concepts, including the subtleties of humor.

Acknowledgments

Special thanks to Ellie Pavlick for providing valuable feedback through the course of this research. Additionally, we are grateful to Jacob Lockwood, an editor of the Brown Noser Satirical Newspaper, for offering the necessary human talent to parlay our model's output into a full satirical article (Figure 4).

This work is supported in part by the ONR PERISCOPE MURI award N00014-17-1-2699.

References

Khalid Alnajjar and Mika Hämäläinen. 2018. A master-apprentice approach to automatic creation of culturally satirical movie titles. In *Proceedings of the 11th International Conference on Natural Language Generation*, pages 274–283, Tilburg University, The Netherlands. Association for Computational Linguistics.

Salvatore Attardo. 2001. *Humorous Texts: A Semantic and Pragmatic Analysis*. Mouton de Gruyter.

Salvatore Attardo. 2014. Humor in language. In *Oxford Research Encyclopedia of Linguistics*. Oxford University Press.

Salvatore Attardo and Victor Raskin. 1991. Script theory revis(it)ed: Joke similarity and joke representation model. *HUMOR: International Journal of Humor Research*, 4(3/4):293–348.

Jacob Devlin, Ming-Wei Chang, Kenton Lee, and Kristina Toutanova. 2018. BERT: pre-training of deep bidirectional transformers for language understanding. *CoRR*, abs/1810.04805.

Kelvin Guu, Kenton Lee, Zora Tung, Panupong Pasupat, and Ming-Wei Chang. 2020. Realm: Retrieval-augmented language model pre-training. *ArXiv*, abs/2002.08909.

He He, Nanyun Peng, and Percy Liang. 2019. Pun generation with surprise. In *Proceedings of the 2019 Conference of the North American Chapter of the Association for Computational Linguistics: Human Language Technologies, Volume 1 (Long and Short Papers)*, pages 1734–1744, Minneapolis, Minnesota. Association for Computational Linguistics.

Matthew Honnibal and Ines Montani. 2017. spaCy 2: Natural language understanding with Bloom embeddings, convolutional neural networks and incremental parsing. To appear.

Nabil Hossain, John Krumm, and Michael Gamon. 2019. "president vows to cut <taxes> hair": Dataset and analysis of creative text editing for humorous headlines. In *Proceedings of the 2019 Conference of the North American Chapter of the Association for Computational Linguistics: Human Language Technologies, Volume 1 (Long and Short Papers)*, pages 133–142, Minneapolis, Minnesota. Association for Computational Linguistics.

N. D. Goodman J.T. Kao, R. Levy. 2016. A computational model of linguistic humor in puns. *Cognitive Science*.

Yang Liu and Mirella Lapata. 2019. Text summarization with pretrained encoders. In *EMNLP/IJCNLP*.

Rod A Martin. 2010. *The Psychology of Humor: An Integrative Approach*. Elsevier.

Abhijit Mishra, Tarun Tater, and Karthik Sankaranarayanan. 2019. A modular architecture for unsupervised sarcasm generation. In *Proceedings of the 2019 Conference on Empirical Methods in Natural Language Processing and the 9th International Joint Conference on Natural Language Processing (EMNLP-IJCNLP)*, pages 6144–6154, Hong Kong, China. Association for Computational Linguistics.

John Morreall. 2016. Philosophy of humor. In Edward N. Zalta, editor, *The Stanford Encyclopedia of Philosophy*, winter 2016 edition. Metaphysics Research Lab, Stanford University.

Ramesh Nallapati, Bowen Zhou, Cicero dos Santos, Çağlar Gu̇l̇çehre, and Bing Xiang. 2016. Abstractive text summarization using sequence-to-sequence RNNs and beyond. In *Proceedings of The 20th SIGNLL Conference on Computational Natural Language Learning*, pages 280–290, Berlin, Germany. Association for Computational Linguistics.

Alec Radford, Jeffrey Wu, Rewon Child, David Luan, Dario Amodei, and Ilya Sutskever. 2019. Language models are unsupervised multitask learners. OpenAI Blog.

Victor Raskin. 1985. *Semantic Mechanisms of Humor*. Reidel.

Victor Raskin. 2012. A little metatheory: Thought on what a theory of computational humor should look like. In *AAAI Fall Symposium: Artificial Intelligence of Humor*.

Dafna Shahaf, Eric Horvitz, and Robert Mankoff. 2015. Inside jokes: Identifying humorous cartoon captions. In *Proc. ACM SIGKDD International Conference on Knowledge Discovery and Data Mining (KDD)*.

Ashish Vaswani, Noam Shazeer, Niki Parmar, Jakob Uszkoreit, Llion Jones, Aidan N. Gomez, Lukasz Kaiser, and Illia Polosukhin. 2017. Attention is all you need. *ArXiv*, abs/1706.03762.

Robert West and Eric Horvitz. 2019. Reverse-engineering satire, or "paper on computational humor accepted despite making serious advances". *CoRR*, abs/1901.03253.

Thomas Winters, Vincent Nys, and Danny De Schreye. 2019. Towards a general framework for humor generation from rated examples. *Proceedings of the 10th International Conference on Computational Creativit*, pages 274–281. Association for Computational Creativity; University of North Carolina at Charlotte, USA.

Thomas Wolf, Lysandre Debut, Victor Sanh, Julien Chaumond, Clement Delangue, Anthony Moi, Pierric Cistac, Tim Rault, R'emi Louf, Morgan Funtowicz, and Jamie Brew. 2019. Huggingface's transformers: State-of-the-art natural language processing. *ArXiv*, abs/1910.03771.

Zhiwei Yu, Jiwei Tan, and Xiaojun Wan. 2018. A neural approach to pun generation. In *Proceedings of the 56th Annual Meeting of the Association for Computational Linguistics (Volume 1: Long Papers)*, pages 1650–1660, Melbourne, Australia. Association for Computational Linguistics.

A Appendices

A.1 Dataset Evaluation

We employed 62 annotators via Amazon Mechanical Turk to evaluate the relevance of a sample of our retrieved documents to the original satirical articles. Annotators must (1) have come from the United States, (2) have had more than 50 annotations approved in previous studies, and (3) have an annotation approval rating higher than 95%. We evaluated the retrieved documents for 1500 of the satirical headlines. For each article, we present three different annotators with the satirical headline, lede and the top five retrieved documents from our ranker, each trimmed to contain only the title and the first three sentences of content. We asked annotators to evaluate how "relevant" each context document is relative to the satirical article, with relevant being defined as either (1) the context document covering the event discussed by the satirical article, or (2) the context document provides useful context to understand the satirical article. Table 2

Table 2: Top 5 Retrieved Document Relevance

Consensus	Top 1	Top 2	Top 3	Top 4	Top 5
≥ 1	86.7%	96.3%	97.7%	98.5%	99.0%
Majority	48.3%	61.5%	69.1%	74.5%	80.7%

describes the result of the evaluation. The first row indicates the percentage of all headlines where at least one annotator considered one of the top n retrieved documents to be relevant. The second gives the fraction of headlines where 2/3+ annotators agreed that at least one of the top n retrieved documents was relevant to the original satirical article.

For approximately 80% of the headlines, a majority of annotators deemed at least one of the top five retrieved documents to be relevant. For 99% of headlines, at least one annotator believed that one of the top five retrieved documents were relevant. These results indicate our automatic pipeline systematically retrieves relevant articles. We believe that we could further improve retrieval accuracy via (1) filtering out satirical headlines less likely to have contextual information (e.g. "Nervous New Driver Going To Stick To Sidewalks Until He's More Confident"), (2) human labeling of the corpus, and/or (3) training a reranker with human labels on a subset of the corpus.

A.2 Generation Relevance to Context

To evaluate the extent to which our generations incorporate the input context, we performed quantitative evaluations of similarity. For each contextual model, we computed the Jaccard index between each headline in the test set and its corresponding input context. We then normalized these scores by the *average* Jaccard index between that headline and every context. This metric captures similarity to the specific context, relative to an arbitrary context.

Table 3: Generation-to-Context Similarity

Model	Normalized Jaccard (Avg.)
Onion	5.0
Summarizer	9.9
D-Context	6.2
E-Context	6.7
A-Context	6.0

Table 3 contains the generation-to-context similarity score for each model. These values were computed by tokenizing the headline and input, stemming tokens, and filtering out stopwords.

Critically, we see that all models receive scores significantly greater than 1. This result indicates that the headlines are substantially more similar to their input context than to an arbitrary one. As expected, the pretrained summarization model (with no satirical fine-tuning) receives the highest generation-to-content similarity score. Additionally, D-Context, which has an attenuated encoder learning rate, is less contextually relevant than E-Context.

However, most notably, all models produce generations that are more relevant to the input context than to the original satirical headline. These quantitative evaluations reveal that our architecture's generations are not only funny, but apt.

A.3 Satirical Newspaper Publication

After our headlines were accepted into the Brown Noser's April 2020 issue, Jacob Lockwood, an undergraduate satirical writer, volunteered to write an accompanying article (See Figure 4). We are enthusiastic about the potential for future AI–Human satirical collaborations.

U.S. Asks Pugs If They Can Do Anything

Figure 4: A satirical headline generated by our model was published in the Brown Noser Satirical Newspaper, and accompanied by an article written by a human satirical writer. The article can be found here.

A.4 The Script-Based Semantic Theory of Humor

The Script-Based Semantic Theory of Humor (SSTH) (Raskin, 1985) provides a framework for interpreting our model's output. According to SSTH, for a text to be "funny" it must satisfy the following conditions:

1. The text is compatible, fully or in part, with two different scripts.

2. The two scripts with which the text is compatible are opposite in a special sense (Raskin, 1985).

Many of our generations exhibit these properties. For example, consider the generated headline from Figure 2:

God Admits He's Not The Creator

Within this generation, there is at least one possible script opposition:

1. God as the divine creator (as described in the context).

which opposes the script:

2. A person making an admission to the media.

These opposing scripts are related via the logical mechanism of false-analogy: God is a famous entity, and thus likely to appear in the news, but God is also a deity, *not* a person, and is infallible (West and Horvitz, 2019; Attardo and Raskin, 1991). Consider another example generation:

Royal Baby Born in Captivity

With opposing scripts:

1. The royal baby is a human.

2. The baby is, like an animal, born into captivity.

These two scripts are again related through the mechanism of false-analogy: The royal baby is a baby, like an animal born in captivity. However, the baby is human, making it unlikely to be born in captivity.

It remains unclear whether our architecture is explicitly modeling "opposing scripts" in its latent space, or rather translating entities from the context into headlines with Onion-style language. However, in either case, our approach is incorporating contextual entities, using contextual information, and generating text that imitates the properties of humor.

Sarcasm Detection using Context Separators in Online Discourse

Tanvi Dadu * and **Kartikey Pant** *
Netaji Subhas Institute of Technology, New Delhi, India
International Institute of Information Technology, Hyderabad, India
`tanvid.co.16@nsit.net.in`
`kartikey.pant@research.iiit.ac.in`

Abstract

Sarcasm is an intricate form of speech, where meaning is conveyed implicitly. Being a convoluted form of expression, detecting sarcasm is an assiduous problem. The difficulty in recognition of sarcasm has many pitfalls, including misunderstandings in everyday communications, which leads us to an increasing focus on automated sarcasm detection. In the second edition of the Figurative Language Processing (FigLang 2020) workshop, the shared task of sarcasm detection released two datasets, containing responses along with their context sampled from Twitter and Reddit.

In this work, we use $RoBERTa_{large}$ to detect sarcasm in both the datasets. We further assert the importance of context in improving the performance of contextual word embedding based models by using three different types of inputs - *Response-only*, *Context-Response*, and *Context-Response (Separated)*. We show that our proposed architecture performs competitively for both the datasets. We also show that the addition of a separation token between context and target response results in an improvement of 5.13% in the *F1-score* in the Reddit dataset.

1 Introduction

Sarcasm is a sophisticated form of speech, in which the surface meaning differs from the implied sense. This form of expression implicitly conveys the message making it hard to detect sarcasm in a statement. Since speech in sarcasm is dependent in context, it is tough to resolve the speaker's intentions unless given insights into the circumstances of the sarcastic response. These insights or contextual information may include the speaker of the response, the listener of the response, and how its content relates to the preceding discourse.

Recognizing sarcasm is critical for understanding the actual sentiment and meaning of the discourse. The difficulty in the recognition of sarcasm causes misunderstandings in everyday communication. This difficulty also poses problems to many natural language processing systems, including summarization systems and dialogue systems. Therefore, it is essential to develop automated sarcasm detectors to help understand the implicit meaning of a sarcastic response.

The sarcasm detection shared task held at the second edition of the Figurative Language Processing (FigLang 2020) workshop proposes two datasets from different social media discourse platforms for evaluation. The first dataset contains user conversations from Twitter, while the second dataset contains Reddit conversation threads. Both datasets contain contextual information in the form of posts of the previous dialogue turns. Their primary aim is to understand the importance of conversational contextual information in improving the detection of sarcasm in a given response.

In this work, we explore the use of contextualized word embeddings for detecting sarcasm in the responses sampled from Reddit as well as Twitter. We outline the effect of adding contextual information, from previous dialogue turns, to the response, for both the datasets. We further explore the importance of separation tokens, differentiating discourse context from the target response while detecting sarcasm.

2 Related Works

Davidov et al. (2010) approached the task of sarcasm detection in a semi-supervised setting, investigating their algorithm in two different forms of text, tweets from Twitter, and product reviews from Amazon. Subsequently, González-Ibáñez et al. (2011) explored this task in a supervised set-

---

Both authors contributed equally to the work.

Proceedings of the Second Workshop on Figurative Language Processing, pages 51–55
July 9, 2020. ©2020 Association for Computational Linguistics
https://doi.org/10.18653/v1/P17

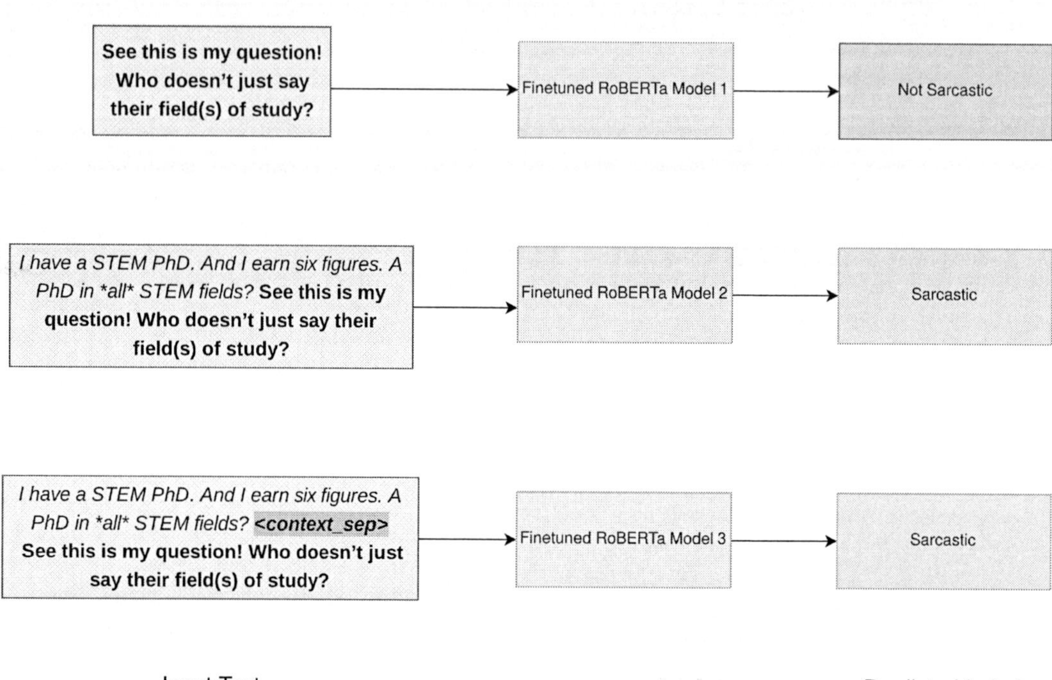

Figure 1: Architecture of our proposed approach.

ting, using SVM and logistic regression. They also release a dataset of 900 tweets to the public domain, entailing tweets containing sarcastic, positive, or negative content. Moreover, there has been significant work done to detect sarcasm in a multi-modal setting, primarily including visual cues. While Schifanella et al. (2016) proposed a multi-modal methodology to exploit features from both text and image, Cai et al. (2019) investigated instilling attribute information from social media posts to propose a model leveraging hierarchical fusion.

Ghosh et al. (2018) investigated the use of Long Short-Term Memory (LSTM) networks with sentence-level attention for modeling both the responses under consideration and the conversation context preceding it. They execute their models on responses sampled from two social media plat-forms, Twitter and Reddit. They concluded that contextual information is vital for detecting sarcasm by showing that the LSTM network modeling the context and the response outperforms the LSTM network that models only the target response. This observation is in sync with other similar tasks like irony detection, as highlighted by Wallace et al. (2014), which claimed that human annotators consistently rely on contextual information to make judgments.

The use of other turns of dialogue as contextual information has been explored well in previous works. Bamman and Smith (2015) investigated the use of "author and addressee" features apart from the conversation context, but observed only a minimal impact of modeling conversation context. Oraby et al. (2017) investigated using "pre" and "post" messages from debate forums and Twitter conversations to identify whether rhetorical questions are used sarcastically or not. They observe that using the "post" message as context improved the *F1-score* for the sarcastic class. Joshi et al. (2016) showed that sequence labeling algorithms outperform traditional classical statistical methods, obtaining a gain of 4% in *F1-score* on their proposed dataset.

The use of pre-trained contextual word representations has been explored in multiple tasks in NLP, including text classification. Recently released models such as BERT (Devlin et al., 2018) and RoBERTa (Liu et al., 2020), exploit the use of pre-training and bidirectional transformers to enable efficient solutions obtaining state-of-the-art performance. Pre-trained embeddings significantly outperform the previous state-of-the-art in similar problems such as humor detection (Weller and Seppi, 2019), and subjectivity detection (Pant et al., 2020).

3 Approach

This section outlines the approach used to detect sarcasm in the Reddit and Twitter datasets. Our approach utilizes contextualized word embeddings with three different inputs, as explained in the following paragraphs.

The use of pretrained contextualized word embeddings has been applied to achieve state-of-the-art results for various downstream tasks (Devlin et al., 2018; Liu et al., 2020). Devlin et al. (2018) proposed BERT that leverages context from both left and right representations in each layer of the bidirectional transformer. The model is pretrained and released in the public domain, and can be trained in a simpler, yet efficient manner without having to make significant architectural changes for a specific task.

RoBERTa (Liu et al., 2020) is a replication study of BERT, trained on a dataset twelve times larger with bigger batches as compared to BERT. RoBERTa makes use of larger byte-pair encoding(BPE) vocabulary that helps to achieve better results than BERT on various downstream tasks. We use $RoBERTa_{large}$ and finetune it for the task using varying hyperparameters for different inputs.

We use the following three different types of input to study the effect of context on the performance of $Roberta_{large}$ to detect sarcasm:

1. **Response-only** : Input containing only the target response.

2. **Context-Response** : Input containing target response appended to the related context (containing previous responses).

3. **Context-Response (Separated)**: Input containing a separation token separating target response from context (containing previous responses).

Split/Dataset	Reddit	Twitter
Training	2.491	3.867
Testing	4.254	3.164

Table 1: The average number of contexts per post.

4 Experiments

4.1 Dataset

Two datasets containing an equal number of sarcastic and non-sarcastic responses were sampled from Twitter and Reddit by the authors of the shared task. The Twitter dataset comprises $5,000$ English tweets, and the Reddit dataset contains $4,400$ Reddit posts along with their context, which is an ordered list of dialogues. The sarcastic response, present in both datasets, is the reply to the last dialogue turn in the context list.

From Table 1, we infer that the dataset suffers from a significant mismatch in the average number of context responses between the training and testing split. This mismatch is particularly evident in the Reddit dataset, where the training split contains 1.71 times the number of contexts provided on average as compared to the testing split. We observe a similar mismatch, in the opposite direction, with the testing split containing 1.22 times the average number of contexts as compared to the training split. We argue that this mismatch in training and test splits in terms of context lengths, adds a layer of complexity to the problem. Consequently, we use the last two dialogues as the context in the *Context-Response* input and *the Context-Response (Separated)* input.

4.2 Experimental Setting

In this subsection, we outline the experimental setup for the sarcasm detection task and present the results obtained on the blind test set. For experiments, we used $RoBERTa_{large}$ having $355M$ parameters with a $50,265$ vocabulary size. For validation, we trained and evaluated our model for three

Input	F1-score	Precision	Recall
Response-only	0.752	0.752	0.753
Context-Response	0.772	0.772	0.772
Context-Response (Separated)	0.771	0.771	0.771

Table 2: Experimental Results for the Twitter test dataset.

Input	F1-score	Precision	Recall
Response-only	0.679	0.679	0.679
Context-Response	0.681	0.684	0.692
Context-Response (Separated)	0.716	0.716	0.718

Table 3: Experimental Results for the Reddit test dataset.

different inputs using a $90 - 10$ train-validation split.

We finetune $RoBERTa_{large}$ with a learning rate of $1 * 10^{-5}$ for 3 epochs. We used a sequence length of 50 for the *Response-only* input and 256 for the other two types of inputs, *Context-Response* input and *Context-Response (Separated)* input. We evaluate all our models on the following metrics: *F1 score*, *Precision-1* and *Recall-1*.

4.3 Results

In Table 2 and Table 3, we illustrate the effect of adding contextual information to the target response. We see an increase of 2.6% and 0.3% in *F1-score* upon including previous contexts with the response in the Twitter dataset and Reddit dataset respectively.

We also investigate the effect of adding a separation token between contextual information and the target response in the predictive performance of the model. We observe a 5.13% increase in *F1-score* in the Reddit dataset but a 0.1% decrease in *F1-score* in the Twitter dataset. We observe a similar pattern as the *F1-score* in both of its constituent metrics of *Precision* and *Recall*.

5 Conclusion

This work presents the importance of context while detecting sarcasm from responses sampled from Twitter and Reddit. Our proposed architecture using three different inputs performs competitively for both datasets showing that the addition of contextual information to target response improves the performance of the fine-tuned contextual word embeddings for detecting sarcasm. We further show that the addition of a separation token between context and target response also performs com-

petitively, markedly showing an improvement of 5.13% in the *F1-score* of Reddit dataset. Future works include exploring different contextual cues, including user-specific attribute information and extending this hypothesis to other figurative speeches like irony detection and humor detection.

References

David Bamman and Noah A. Smith. 2015. Contextualized sarcasm detection on twitter. In *ICWSM*.

Yitao Cai, Huiyu Cai, and Xiaojun Wan. 2019. Multimodal sarcasm detection in twitter with hierarchical fusion model. pages 2506–2515.

Dmitry Davidov, Oren Tsur, and Ari Rappoport. 2010. Semi-supervised recognition of sarcasm in twitter and Amazon. In *Proceedings of the Fourteenth Conference on Computational Natural Language Learning*, pages 107–116, Uppsala, Sweden. Association for Computational Linguistics.

Jacob Devlin, Ming-Wei Chang, Kenton Lee, and Kristina Toutanova. 2018. Bert: Pre-training of deep bidirectional transformers for language understanding.

Debanjan Ghosh, Alexander Fabbri, and Smaranda Muresan. 2018. Sarcasm analysis using conversation context. *Computational Linguistics*, 44:1–56.

Roberto González-Ibáñez, Smaranda Muresan, and Nina Wacholder. 2011. Identifying sarcasm in twitter: A closer look. In *Proceedings of the 49th Annual Meeting of the Association for Computational Linguistics: Human Language Technologies*, pages 581–586, Portland, Oregon, USA. Association for Computational Linguistics.

Aditya Joshi, Vaibhav Tripathi, Pushpak Bhattacharyya, and Mark J. Carman. 2016. Harnessing sequence labeling for sarcasm detection in dialogue from TV series 'Friends'. In *Proceedings of The*

20th SIGNLL Conference on Computational Natural Language Learning, pages 146–155, Berlin, Germany. Association for Computational Linguistics.

Yinhan Liu, Myle Ott, Naman Goyal, Jingfei Du, Mandar Joshi, Danqi Chen, Omer Levy, Mike Lewis, Luke Zettlemoyer, and Veselin Stoyanov. 2020. Roberta: A robustly optimized bert pretraining approach. In *International Conference on Learning Representations*. Accepted.

Shereen Oraby, Vrindavan Harrison, Amita Misra, Ellen Riloff, and Marilyn Walker. 2017. Are you serious?: Rhetorical questions and sarcasm in social media dialog.

Kartikey Pant, Tanvi Dadu, and Radhika Mamidi. 2020. Towards detection of subjective bias using contextualized word embeddings. In *Companion Proceedings of the Web Conference 2020*, WWW '20, page 75–76, New York, NY, USA. Association for Computing Machinery.

Rossano Schifanella, Paloma Juan, Joel Tetreault, and Liangliang Cao. 2016. Detecting sarcasm in multimodal social platforms.

Byron C. Wallace, Do Kook Choe, Laura Kertz, and Eugene Charniak. 2014. Humans require context to infer ironic intent (so computers probably do, too). In *ACL*.

Orion Weller and Kevin D. Seppi. 2019. Humor detection: A transformer gets the last laugh. In *EMNLP/IJCNLP*.

Sarcasm Detection in Tweets with BERT and GloVe Embeddings

Akshay Khatri
Department of Information Technology
National Institute of Technology
Karnataka, Surathkal
akshaykhatri0011@gmail.com

Pranav P
Department of Information Technology
National Institute of Technology
Karnataka, Surathkal
hsr.pranav@gmail.com

Abstract

Sarcasm is a form of communication in which the person states opposite of what he actually means. It is ambiguous in nature. In this paper, we propose using machine learning techniques with BERT and GloVe embeddings to detect sarcasm in tweets. The dataset is preprocessed before extracting the embeddings. The proposed model also uses the context in which the user is reacting to along with his actual response.

1 Introduction

Sarcasm is defined as a sharp, bitter or cutting expression or remark and is sometimes ironic (Gibbs et al., 1994). To identify if a sentence is sarcastic, it requires analyzing the speaker's intentions. Different kinds of sarcasm exist like propositional, embedded, like-prefixed and illocutionary (Camp, 2012). Among these, propositional requires the use of context.

The most common formulation of sarcasm detection is a classification task (Joshi et al., 2017). Our task is to determine whether a given sentence is sarcastic or not. Sarcasm detection approaches are broadly classified into three types (Joshi et al., 2017) . They are: Rule based, deep learning based and statistical based. Rule based detectors are simple, they just look for negative response in a positive context and vice versa. It can be done using sentiment analysis. Deep learning based approaches use deep learning to extract features and the extracted features are fed into a classifier to get the result. Statistical approach use features related to the text like unigrams, bigrams etc and are fed to SVM classifier.

In this paper, we use BERT embeddings (Devlin et al., 2018) and GloVe embeddings (Pennington et al., 2014) as features. They are used for getting vector representation of words. These embeddings are trained with a machine learning algorithm. Before extracting the embeddings, the dataset also needs to be processed to enhance the quality of the data supplied to the model.

2 Literature Review

There have been many methods for sarcasm detection. We discuss some of them in this section. Under rule based approaches, Maynard and Greenwood (2014) use hashtag sentiment to identify sarcasm. The disagreement of the sentiment expressed by the hashtag with the rest of the tweet is a clear indication of sarcasm. Vaele and Hao (2010) identify sarcasm in similes using Google searches to determine how likely a simile is. Riloff et al. (2013) look for a positive verb and a negative situation phrase in a sentence to detect sarcasm.

In statistical sarcasm detection, we use features related to the text to be classified. Most approaches use bag-of-words as features (Joshi et al., 2017). Some other features used in other papers include sarcastic patterns and punctuations (Tsur et al., 2010), user mentions, emoticons, unigrams, sentiment-lexicon-based features (González-Ibáñez et al., 2011), ambiguity-based, semantic relatedness (Reyes et al., 2012), N-grams, emotion marks, intensifiers (Liebrecht et al., 2013), unigrams (Joshi et al., 2015), bigrams (Liebrecht et al., 2013), word shape, pointedness (Ptáček et al., 2014), etc. Most work in statistical sarcasm detection relies on different forms of Support Vector Machines(SVMs) (Kreuz and Caucci, 2007). (Reyes et al., 2012) uses Naive Bayes and Decision Trees for multiple pairs of labels among irony, humor, politics and education. For conversational data,sequence labeling algorithms perform better than classification algorithms (Joshi et al., 2016). They use SVM-HMM and SEARN as the sequence labeling algorithms (Joshi et al., 2016).

Proceedings of the Second Workshop on Figurative Language Processing, pages 56–60
July 9, 2020. ©2020 Association for Computational Linguistics
https://doi.org/10.18653/v1/P17

For a long time, NLP was mainly based on statistical analysis, but machine learning algorithms have now taken over this domain of research providing unbeaten results. Dr. Pushpak Bhattacharyya, a well-known researcher in this field, refers to this as "NLP-ML marriage". Some approaches use similarity between word embeddings as features for sarcasm detection. They augment these word embedding-based features with features from their prior works. The inclusion of past features is key because they observe that using the new features alone does not suffice for an excellent performance. Some of the approaches show a considerable boost in results while using deep learning algorithms over the standard classifiers. Ghosh and Veale (2016) use a combination of CNN, RNN, and a deep neural network. Another approach uses a combination of deep learning and classifiers. It uses deep learning(CNN) to extract features and the extracted features are fed into the SVM classifier to detect sarcasm.

3   Dataset

We used the twitter dataset provided by the hosts of shared task on Sarcasm Detection. Initial analysis reveals that this is a perfectly balanced dataset having 5000 entries. There are an equal number of sarcastic and non-sarcastic entries in it. It includes the fields label, response and context. The label specifies whether the entry is sarcastic or non-sarcastic, response is the statement over which sarcasm needs to be detected and context is a list of statements which specify the context of the particular response. The test dataset has 1800 entries with fields ID(an identifier), context and response.

Most of the time, raw data is not complete and it cannot be sent for processing(applying models). Here, preprocessing the dataset makes it suitable to apply analysis on. This is an extremely important phase as the final results are completely dependent on the quality of the data supplied to the model. However great the implementation or design of the model is, the dataset is going to be the distinguishing factor between obtaining excellent results or not. Steps followed during the preprocessing phase are: (Mayo)

- Check out for null values - Presence of null values in the dataset leads to inaccurate predictions. There are two approaches to handle this:
  - Delete that particular row - We will be using this method to handle null values.
  - Replace the null value with the mean, mode or median value of that column - This approach cannot be used as our dataset contains only text.

- Tokenization and remove punctuation - Process of splitting the sentences into words and also remove the punctuation in the sentences as they are of no importance for the given specific task.

- Case conversion - Converting the case of the dataset to lowercase unless the case of the whole word is in uppercase.

- Stopword removal - These words are a set of commonly used words in a language. Some common English stop words are "a", "the", "is", "are" and etc. The main idea behind this procedure is to remove low value information so as to focus on the important information.

- Normalization - This is the process of transforming the text into its standard form. For example, the word "gooood" and "gud" can be transformed to "good", "b4" can be transformed to "before", ":)" can be transformed to "smile" its canonical form.

- Noise removal - Removal of all pieces of text that might interfere with our text analysis phase. This is a highly domain dependent task. For the twitter dataset noise can be all special characters except hashtag.

- Stemming - This is the process of converting the words to their root form for easy processing.

Both training and test data are preprocessed with the above methods. Once the above preprocessing steps have been applied we are ready to move to the model development.

4   Methodology

In this section, we describe the methods we used to build the model for the sarcasm detection.

4.1   Feature Extraction

Feature extraction is an extremely important factor along with pre-processing in the model building process. The field of natural language processing(NLP), sentence and word embeddings are majorly used to represent the features of the language. Word embedding is the collective name for a set of feature learning techniques in natural language processing where words or phrases from the vocabulary are mapped to vectors of real numbers. In our research, we used two types of embeddings for the feature extraction phase. One being **BERT(Bidirectional Encoder Representations from Transformers)** word embeddings (Devlin et al., 2018) and the other being **GloVe(Global Vectors) embeddings** (Pennington et al., 2014).

4.1.1 BERT embeddings

'Bert-as-service' (Xiao, 2018) is a useful tool for the generation of the word embeddings. Each word is represented as a vector of size 768. The embeddings given by BERT are contextual. Every sentence is represented as a list of word embeddings. The given training and test data has response and context as two fields. Embeddings for both context and response were generated. Then, the embeddings were combined in such a way that context comes before response. The intuition to this being that it is the context that elicits a response from a user. Once the embeddings are extracted, the sequence of the embeddings were padded to get them to the same size.

4.1.2 GloVe embeddings

The results given by BERT not being up to the mark led us to search for a twitter specific embedding and thus we chose GloVe embeddings specifically trained for twitter. It uses unsupervised learning for obtaining vector representation of words. The embeddings given by GloVe are non-contextual. Here we decided to choose GloVe twitter sentence embeddings for training the models as it would capture the overall meaning of the sentence in a relatively lesser amount of memory. This generated a list of size 200 for each input provided. Once the sentence embeddings were extracted, the context and the response were combined such that context comes before response. Context embeddings were generated independent of the response so that the sentiment of response would not effect the sentiment of the context.

4.2 Training and Predictions

After extraction of the word embeddings, the next step is to train these to build a model which can be used to predict the class of test samples. Classifiers like Linear Support Vector Classifier(LSVC), Logistic Regression(LR), Gaussian Naive Bayes and Random Forest were used. Scikit-learn (Pedregosa et al., 2011) was used for training these models. Word embeddings were obtained for the test dataset in the same way mentioned before. Now, they are ready for predictions.

5 Reproducibility

5.1 Experimental Setup

Google colab with 25GB RAM was used for the experiment, which includes extraction of embedding, training the models and prediction.

5.2 Extracting BERT embeddings

We use the bert as a service for generating the BERT embeddings. We spin up BERT as a service server and create a client to get the embeddings. We use the uncased_L-12_H-768_A-12 pretrained BERT model to generate the embeddings.

All of the context(i.e 100%) provided in the dataset was used for this study. Word embeddings for the response and context are generated separately. Embeddings for each word in the response is extracted separately and appended to form a list. Every sentence in the context is appended one after the other. The same is done for response embeddings. The embeddings of the context and that of response fields are concatenated to get the final embedding.

5.3 Extracting the GLOVE embeddings

We used genism to download glove-twitter-200 pretrained model. Embeddings for the response and context are extracted separately. Sentences in the given context are appended to form a single sentence. Later we generate the sentence embeddings for response and context separately. The context embeddings and response embeddings are concatenated to generate the final embedding.

5.4 Training the model

We use the Scikit-learn machine learning library to train the classifiers(SVM, Logistic Regression, Gaussian Naive Bayes and Random Forest). Trained models are saved for later prediction. Using the saved models, we predict the test samples as SARCASM or NOT_SARCASM.

6 Results

The result was measured using the metric F-measure. F-measure is a measure of a test's ac-

Classifier	F-measure
Linear Support Vector Classifier	0.598
Logistic Regression	0.6224
Gaussian Naive Bayes	0.373
Random Forest	0.577

Table 1: Results with BERT embeddings excluding context

Classifier	F-measure
Linear Support Vector Classifier	0.616
Logistic Regression	0.630

Table 2: Results with BERT embeddings including both context and response

curacy and is calculated as the weighted harmonic mean of the precision and recall of the test (Zhang and Zhang, 2009). Now, we discuss the results obtained with BERT and GloVe separately.

6.1 With BERT

Among the classifiers mentioned in the previous section, a good result was received from SVM and logistic regression, with the latter giving the best results. Table 1 shows the results of training the classifiers only on the response and excluding the context. Table 2 shows the results obtained with BERT including the context. It is clear that taking the context into consideration boosts the result.

6.2 With GloVe

The results for this approach gave much better results when compared to the BERT embedding approach. Also, GloVe was much faster than BERT. Among the two classifiers logistic regression gave the better results of the two. Table 3 shows the results obtained with GloVe.

7 Conclusion

Sarcasm detection can be done effectively using word embeddings. They are extremely useful as they capture the meaning of a word in a vector representation. Even though BERT gives contextual

Classifier	F-measure
Linear Support Vector Classifier	0.679
Logistic Regression	0.690

Table 3: Results with GloVe embeddings including both context and response

word representations i.e the same word occuring multiple times in a sentence may have different vectors, it didn't perform to the mark when compared to GloVe which gives the same vector for a word occuring multiple times. However, this cannot be generalized. It may depend on the dataset. Among the classifiers, logistic regression always outperformed the other classifiers used in this study.

Acknowledgments

We would like to thank Dr. Anand Kumar M for his immense support, patient guidance and enthusiastic encouragement throughout the research work. We would also like to thank the reviewers for their useful suggestions to improvise the paper.

References

Elisabeth Camp. 2012. Sarcasm, pretense, and the semantics/pragmatics distinction. *Noûs*, 46(4):587–634.

Jacob Devlin, Ming-Wei Chang, Kenton Lee, and Kristina Toutanova. 2018. Bert: Pre-training of deep bidirectional transformers for language understanding. *arXiv preprint arXiv:1810.04805*.

Aniruddha Ghosh and Tony Veale. 2016. Fracking sarcasm using neural network. In *Proceedings of the 7th workshop on computational approaches to subjectivity, sentiment and social media analysis*, pages 161–169.

R.W. Gibbs, R.W. Gibbs, Cambridge University Press, and J. Gibbs. 1994. *The Poetics of Mind: Figurative Thought, Language, and Understanding*. The Poetics of Mind: Figurative Thought, Language, and Understanding. Cambridge University Press.

Roberto González-Ibáñez, Smaranda Muresan, and Nina Wacholder. 2011. Identifying sarcasm in twitter: A closer look. In *Proceedings of the 49th Annual Meeting of the Association for Computational Linguistics: Human Language Technologies: Short Papers - Volume 2*, HLT '11, page 581–586, USA. Association for Computational Linguistics.

Aditya Joshi, Pushpak Bhattacharyya, and Mark J Carman. 2017. Automatic sarcasm detection: A survey. *ACM Computing Surveys (CSUR)*, 50(5):1–22.

Aditya Joshi, Vinita Sharma, and Pushpak Bhattacharyya. 2015. Harnessing context incongruity for sarcasm detection. In *Proceedings of the 53rd Annual Meeting of the Association for Computational Linguistics and the 7th International Joint Conference on Natural Language Processing (Volume 2: Short Papers)*, pages 757–762, Beijing, China. Association for Computational Linguistics.

Aditya Joshi, Vaibhav Tripathi, Pushpak Bhattacharyya, and Mark James Carman. 2016. Harnessing sequence labeling for sarcasm detection in dialogue from tv series 'friends'. In *CoNLL*.

Roger Kreuz and Gina Caucci. 2007. Lexical influences on the perception of sarcasm. In *Proceedings of the Workshop on Computational Approaches to Figurative Language*, pages 1–4, Rochester, New York. Association for Computational Linguistics.

Christine Liebrecht, Florian Kunneman, and Antal van den Bosch. 2013. The perfect solution for detecting sarcasm in tweets #not. In *Proceedings of the 4th Workshop on Computational Approaches to Subjectivity, Sentiment and Social Media Analysis*, pages 29–37, Atlanta, Georgia. Association for Computational Linguistics.

Diana Maynard and Mark Greenwood. 2014. Who cares about sarcastic tweets? investigating the impact of sarcasm on sentiment analysis. In *Proceedings of the Ninth International Conference on Language Resources and Evaluation (LREC-2014)*, pages 4238–4243, Reykjavik, Iceland. European Languages Resources Association (ELRA).

Matthew Mayo. A general approach to preprocessing text data. `https://www.kdnuggets.com/2017/12/general-approach-preprocessing-text-data.html`.

F. Pedregosa, G. Varoquaux, A. Gramfort, V. Michel, B. Thirion, O. Grisel, M. Blondel, P. Prettenhofer, R. Weiss, V. Dubourg, J. Vanderplas, A. Passos, D. Cournapeau, M. Brucher, M. Perrot, and E. Duchesnay. 2011. Scikit-learn: Machine learning in Python. *Journal of Machine Learning Research*, 12:2825–2830.

Jeffrey Pennington, Richard Socher, and Christopher D. Manning. 2014. Glove: Global vectors for word representation. In *Empirical Methods in Natural Language Processing (EMNLP)*, pages 1532–1543.

Tomáš Ptáček, Ivan Habernal, and Jun Hong. 2014. Sarcasm detection on Czech and English twitter. In *Proceedings of COLING 2014, the 25th International Conference on Computational Linguistics: Technical Papers*, pages 213–223, Dublin, Ireland. Dublin City University and Association for Computational Linguistics.

Antonio Reyes, Paolo Rosso, and Davide Buscaldi. 2012. From humor recognition to irony detection: The figurative language of social media. *Data Knowledge Engineering*, 74:1–12.

Ellen Riloff, Ashequl Qadir, Prafulla Surve, De Lalindra Silva, Nathan Gilbert, and Ruihong Huang. 2013. Sarcasm as contrast between a positive sentiment and negative situation. *EMNLP*, pages 704–714.

Oren Tsur, Dmitry Davidov, and Ari Rappoport. 2010. Icwsm - a great catchy name: Semi-supervised recognition of sarcastic sentences in online product reviews.

Tony Vaele and Yanfen Hao. 2010. Detecting ironic intent in creative comparisons. In *European Conference on Artificial Intelligence*, volume 215, pages 765–770.

Han Xiao. 2018. bert-as-service. `https://github.com/hanxiao/bert-as-service`.

Ethan Zhang and Yi Zhang. 2009. *F-Measure*, pages 1147–1147. Springer US, Boston, MA.

C-Net: Contextual Network for Sarcasm Detection

Amit Kumar Jena, Aman Sinha* and Rohit Agarwal*

Indian Institute of Technology (Indian School of Mines) Dhanbad, India
{amitjena40, amansinha091, agarwal.102497}@gmail.com

Abstract

Automatic Sarcasm Detection in conversations is a difficult and tricky task. Classifying an utterance as sarcastic or not in isolation can be futile since most of the time the sarcastic nature of a sentence heavily relies on its context. This paper presents our proposed model, C-Net, which takes contextual information of a sentence in a sequential manner to classify it as sarcastic or non-sarcastic. Our model showcases competitive performance in the Sarcasm Detection shared task organised on CodaLab and achieved 75.0% F1-score on the Twitter dataset and 66.3% F1-score on Reddit dataset.

1 Introduction

Sarcasm detection plays a crucial role in improving the effectiveness of chatbot systems. Sentiment classification systems can fail in the absence of a robust sarcasm detection system. A sarcastic sentence can express a negative sentiment even with the presence of positive or neutral sentiment words in that sentence. Hence, accurate detection of sarcasm can take an artificially intelligent agent closer to imitate human behaviour and enable it to better understand true intentions and emotions of humans (Joshi et al., 2018).

This paper represents work on the Sarcasm Detection shared task which is a part of the Second Workshop on Figurative Language Processing, co-located with ACL 2020. The shared task aims to investigate and understand how much conversation context is needed or helpful for Sarcasm Detection. Two datasets, one of Reddit and the other of Twitter, were provided for developing and testing multiple sarcasm detection systems.

In this paper, we present our study on the effectiveness of contextual information to decide if an

utterance is sarcastic or not. For this, the baseline models were first created using traditional machine learning algorithms like logistic regression, SVM etc. which were trained to classify utterances without considering their contextual information. Sequence models like vanilla RNN and LSTM were trained similarly. Then different types of word embeddings (ELMo and Glove) and sentence embedding (DeepMoji) to capture emotional states in the sentences were also experimented to detect incongruities within the text. The latest state-of-the-art transformer based models like BERT, XLNet and RoBERTa were also used for classifying sentences in isolation. Our investigations for creating systems which can use the context information effectively in a sequential manner led to the creation of our proposed model, which showed decent performances in both the test datasets.

2 Related Works

The evolution of various trends in Sarcasm detection research can be seen in (Joshi et al., 2017). Sarcasm detection was initially performed using rule-based approaches. (Riloff et al., 2013) presented rule-based classifiers that look for a positive verb and a negative situation phrase in a sentence. (Maynard and Greenwood, 2014) proposed using hashtag sentiment as an indicator for sarcasm and (Liu et al., 2014) introduced POS sequences and semantic imbalance as features. Statistical feature-based approaches were also used for this task e.g. (Reyes and Rosso, 2012) introduced features related to ambiguity, unexpectedness, emotional scenario, etc. to better capture situational dependencies for the presence of sarcasm.

Machine learning algorithms were also used for sarcasm detection. Majority of work in sarcasm detection earlier relied on SVM ((Joshi et al., 2015); (Tepperman et al., 2006); (Kreuz and Caucci,

---

* Equal contribution.

Proceedings of the Second Workshop on Figurative Language Processing, pages 61–66
July 9, 2020. ©2020 Association for Computational Linguistics
https://doi.org/10.18653/v1/P17

Dataset	Train	Test
Reddit	4400	1800
Twitter	5000	1800

Table 1: Dataset statistics.

2007); (Tsur et al., 2010); (Davidov et al., 2010)). (Riloff et al., 2013) compared rule-based techniques with an SVM-based classifier. (Reyes et al., 2013) used Naive Bayes and decision trees for multiple pairs of labels among irony, humor, politics and education. (Bamman and Smith, 2015) used binary logistic regression for their work.

The importance of context information was first presented in (Wallace et al., 2014) which described their annotation study where annotators repeatedly asked for context information to judge a text to be sarcastic or not. Many times they changed their previously given labels to a text after being shown the context behind it. (Rajadesingan et al., 2015) and (Bamman and Smith, 2015) tried to include the author context by analysing the author's past tweets and sentiments. To consider the conversational context, (Wang et al., 2015) and (Joshi et al., 2016) used a sequence labeling approach. (Wang et al., 2015) also tried to use the topical context of a text, since some topics are more likely to generate sarcasm as compared to other topics.

Recent works in this domain include deep learning methods such as (Ghosh et al., 2018) included several types of Long Short-Term Memory (LSTM) networks that can model both, the conversation context and the response. (Hazarika et al., 2018) used CNNs to incorporate various contextual information. (Potamias et al., 2019) used pre-trained RoBERTa weights combined with an RCNN to capture contextual information to detect sarcasm.

3 Data

The dataset used for this study was provided in the shared task on Sarcasm Detection, organized at Codalab. It included two separate datasets, Twitter and Reddit, each of them having equal no. of sarcastic and non-sarcastic responses. For each response provided in the dataset, the conversation context consists of an ordered list of previous dialogues. Table 1 shows the size of the train and test sets of both the datasets. From Figure 1, we can see that we have variable number of sentences in the context set of responses, ranging from 2 to 20.

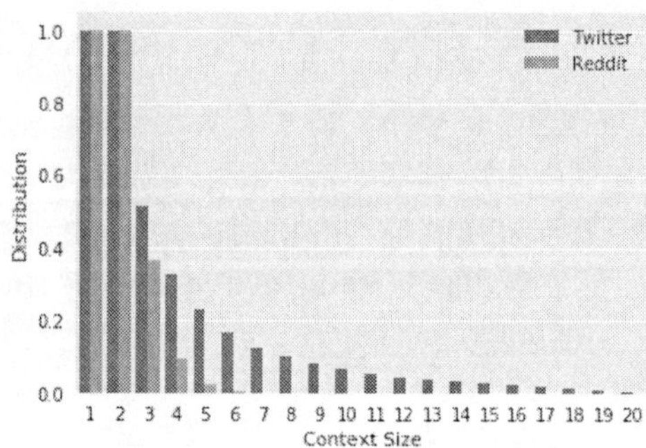

Figure 1: Context set size distribution. The x-axis shows the size of context sets in both the training datasets. The y-axis shows the percentage of data containing that much context size.

4 Methods

We used three kinds of approaches to experiment in this task. First, methods that classified utterances in isolation were investigated. Then, approaches that considered partial conversation context for classifying texts were experimented. Finally, methods that can potentially utilise the complete conversation context information were looked into.

4.1 Baseline models

We experimented with traditional machine learning based approaches like logistic regression, Naive Bayes classifier, SVM etc. first for sarcasm detection by treating the response sentences in isolation. Sequential models like RNNs can easily model a sequential data hence, they are widely used in Natural Language Processing. Basic RNN and LSTM variants were also used in experiments for this task.

4.2 Pretrained Networks

We used Deepmoji (Felbo et al., 2017) in order to investigate the correlation between emotion and presence of sarcasm in sentences. ELMo (Peters et al., 2018) provides contextualized word representation where embeddings of each word is actually a function of the entire sentence containing that word. This may help in capturing local semantic incongruities within a sentence, which is an indicator of sarcasm. Recently introduced transformer models like BERT (Devlin et al., 2019), XLNet (Yang et al., 2019) and RoBERTa (Liu et al., 2019) have given state-of-the-art results on various NLP tasks. Experiments were performed with these models to classify utterances as sarcastic or not-sarcastic.

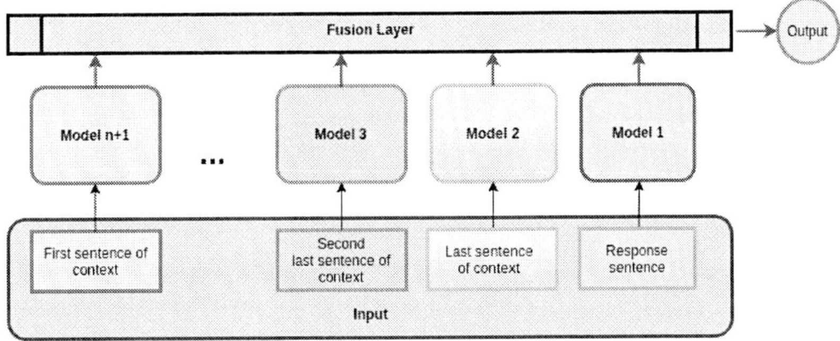

Figure 2: **C-Net Architecture**: Here, 'n' is the maximum size of the context set. Model-1, 2, 3... n+1 are BERT (base-uncased) models which are trained separately on the response sentences, last sentence of context sets, second last sentence of context sets and so on till the first sentence of context sets respectively. Probability values generated by these n+1 models are used by the Fusion Layer to generate another probability value as output, which tells about the possibility of sarcasm presence in the response.

4.3 C-Net

Sarcasm detection can be attributed to information like emotional state, the topic of the conversation, etc. which can be extracted from the conversation context of an utterance. Manually annotating a huge corpus of text data can be a tedious task. We propose our model Contextual-Network (C-Net) for Sarcasm Detection, which uses pseudo-labeling to provide labels for the context sentences by giving them the same label as the response sentence. This is followed by a fusion layer as shown in Figure 2. Training in this way helps in including the contextual information in the model and therefore aid in detecting situations that may lead to the occurrence of a sarcastic sentence in the near future.

By using pseudo labels for training BERT on context sentences, we assigned a score to each context sentence. These scores told about the probability of the conversation leading to a sarcastic response, if that particular context sentence was present in the conversation. This helped in analysing how sarcasm generating situations build up during conversations.

For this model, we used Simple Exponential Smoothing (SES) in the fusion layer, which is a time series forecasting method for univariate data without a trend or seasonality. Forecasts produced using exponential smoothing methods are weighted averages of past observations, with the weights decaying exponentially as the observations get older.

The mathematical expression for Simple Exponential Smoothing (SES) is given by

$$y_{t+1} = \alpha(y_t + (1 - \alpha)y_{t-1} + (1 - \alpha)^2 y_{t-2} + ...)$$

where $\alpha \in (0, 1)$ controls the rate at which the influence of the observations at previous time steps decays exponentially. Here y_{t-1}, y_{t-2}, and so on, are scores predicted by Model 2, Model 3 and so on till Model n+1 respectively. These scores are the probability of the response being sarcastic if these context sentences were present in the conversation anytime before the response. y_t is the probability of response being sarcastic, predicted by Model 1. C-Net takes all these scores into consideration and gives the final output value y_{t+1}, as shown in Figure 2. In this way the method is capable of handling the complete context set.

Hence, generating probability values by giving pseudo-labels to context sentences and combining those values using simple exponential smoothing helps in making a more accurate prediction of sarcasm in conversation.

5 Implementation

5.1 Methods using response only

The training datasets were split into a 90% training set and 10% validation set. We used Fastai tokenizer for pre-processing the datasets and then applied various basic machine learning algorithms for sentence classification. We also used the torchtext library and spacy tokenizer to pre-process the dataset before using Vanilla RNN and bidirectional LSTM models. Both the models were trained for 10 epochs.

We used transformer architectures available within the Huggingface's transformers library and trained them using Gradual Unfreezing and Slanted Triangular Learning Rates (Howard and Ruder, 2018). The learning rate for the last layer was

Method	Twitter	Reddit
Response Only Set		
Logistic Regression	0.685	0.622
Naive Bayes	0.673	0.626
SGD Classifier	0.668	0.626
XGBoost	0.672	0.617
SVM	0.632	0.334
Vanilla RNN	0.478	0.463
Bi-LSTM	0.497	0.481
DeepMoji	0.679	0.633
ELMo	0.684	0.544
ELMo+DeepMoji	0.681	0.518
XLNet (base-cased)	0.712	0.598
BERT (base-uncased)	**0.733**	0.671
RoBERTa (base)	0.680	**0.678**
Fixed Context Set		
C-Net+LR	0.747	0.650
C-Net+SES	**0.750**	**0.663**
Complete Context Set		
Time-stamping	0.710	0.500

Table 2: Results on test datasets (F1-scores)

1e-4 and for other layers, it was 1e-5. The batch size used was 16 and the model was trained with half-precision settings on 16 GB GPU.

Pre-trained torchMoji was used to generate 2304 dimensional sentence encoding for each response sentence. Using ELMo we obtained 1024 dimensional word vectors. The sentence vectors for each response was obtained by averaging the word-vectors. We also concatenated the ELMo representation of each response sentence with the DeepMoji representation of the same sentence to make the sentence representations richer. Then we applied logistic regression to classify the sentence representations obtained by the above-said approaches.

5.2 Methods using fixed context set

We observe that two fixed context utterances are always available for each response in both the datasets. Thus, we create a C-Net with 3 models. Model 1 uses response, Model 2 uses the latest context and Model 3 uses the second latest context. For the training of each model, the output target is the label of response. Thus, we train each model in the lieu of detecting sarcasm in response.

As we see in Figure 2, the fusion layer works on the probability values generated by the BERT (base-uncased) models to give an output. The fusion layer can be either a Logistic Regression or a Simple

Exponential Smoothing model. Since the sequence of dialogues in a conversation matters in deciding the polarity or emotion of future dialogues, simple exponential smoothing was used to take advantage of the sequential nature of the dataset.

5.3 Method using complete context set

In order to include the complete context set for training, we used Timestamping to preserve the sequence of sentences. In this method, two bert-base-uncased models were trained separately on the response only set and all the context sentences. Also, for all the context sentences, a special marker was concatenated at the end which would make the model aware of the position of that sentence in a conversation. Output probabilities by these two models were used to get label for the response.

6 Reproducibility

To reproduce the best results mentioned in this paper, C-Net with SES should be used, utilising the two latest context sentences associated with each response. The pre-trained BERT (base-uncased) model, provided in the transformers library by Huggingface (Wolf et al., 2019), was trained similarly as mentioned in the implementation section using the fastai library (Howard and Gugger, 2020). While fine-tuning BERT on response sentences, the learning rates used were ranging between 1e-5 to 1e-4. But while training on Context sentences, the learning rates used were ranging between 1e-6 to 1e-5. The optimum parameter α for SES was found out from the training set with a grid search. In our experiments, it was found out that the value 0.395 for α best fits the Twitter training data and 0.2 best fits the Reddit training data.

7 Results

From Table 2, it can be seen that the BERT classifier performed the best on Twitter dataset and RoBERTa model performed the best on the Reddit dataset when compared to all methods over *response only* set. Overall, the C-Net model gave the best results as compared to all the approaches on the twitter test dataset.

The results in the case of C-Net for both the fusion methods (LR and SES) are better as compared to the results of the BERT classifier trained only on response in the twitter data. However, this is not true for the Reddit dataset. The BERT and RoBERTa model trained only on response sentences in the Reddit dataset performed better as compared to the C-Net approach. This is counterintuitive as per the theory that context information helps in sarcasm detection. However, it's possible that the Reddit response-only dataset contains many flags for sarcasm, which are also present in the large dataset the models were pre-trained with. Further pre-training of the models on the target Reddit and Twitter dataset may further improve the results.

8 Conclusion

In this paper, we compared the performances of various approaches for the Sarcasm Detection task. We experimented with traditional machine learning based approaches, and the latest state-of-the-art transformer architectures. The results obtained show that our proposed model, C-Net, has the potential to effectively use the conversation context of an utterance to capture the sarcastic nature of a conversation.

The variable number of context sentences for each response sentence makes it difficult to capture the long range dependency. Hence, as future work, approaches that can effectively deal with variable context set size can be investigated.

References

David Bamman and Noah A. Smith. 2015. Contextualized sarcasm detection on twitter. In *ICWSM*.

Dmitry Davidov, Oren Tsur, and Ari Rappoport. 2010. Semi-supervised recognition of sarcastic sentences in twitter and amazon. In *Proceedings of the Fourteenth Conference on Computational Natural Language Learning*, CoNLL '10, page 107–116, USA. Association for Computational Linguistics.

Jacob Devlin, Ming-Wei Chang, Kenton Lee, and Kristina Toutanova. 2019. Bert: Pre-training of deep bidirectional transformers for language understanding. *ArXiv*, abs/1810.04805.

Bjarke Felbo, Alan Mislove, Anders Søgaard, Iyad Rahwan, and Sune Lehmann. 2017. Using millions of emoji occurrences to learn any-domain representations for detecting sentiment, emotion and sarcasm. In *Proceedings of the 2017 Conference on Empirical Methods in Natural Language Processing*, pages 1615–1625, Copenhagen, Denmark. Association for Computational Linguistics.

Debanjan Ghosh, Alexander R. Fabbri, and Smaranda Muresan. 2018. Sarcasm analysis using conversation context. *Computational Linguistics*, 44(4):755–792.

Devamanyu Hazarika, Soujanya Poria, Sruthi Gorantla, Erik Cambria, Roger Zimmermann, and Rada Mihalcea. 2018. Cascade: Contextual sarcasm detection in online discussion forums. *ArXiv*, abs/1805.06413.

Jeremy Howard and Sylvain Gugger. 2020. fastai: A layered api for deep learning. *Information*, 11:108.

Jeremy Howard and Sebastian Ruder. 2018. Fine-tuned language models for text classification. *ArXiv*, abs/1801.06146.

Aditya Joshi, Pushpak Bhattacharyya, and Mark J. Carman. 2017. Automatic sarcasm detection: A survey. *ACM Comput. Surv.*, 50(5).

Aditya Joshi, Pushpak Bhattacharyya, and Mark J. Carman. 2018. *Investigations in Computational Sarcasm*, 1st edition. Springer Publishing Company, Incorporated.

Aditya Joshi, Vinita Sharma, and Pushpak Bhattacharyya. 2015. Harnessing context incongruity for sarcasm detection. In *Proceedings of the 53rd Annual Meeting of the Association for Computational Linguistics and the 7th International Joint Conference on Natural Language Processing (Volume 2: Short Papers)*, pages 757–762, Beijing, China. Association for Computational Linguistics.

Aditya Joshi, Vaibhav Tripathi, Pushpak Bhattacharyya, and Mark J. Carman. 2016. Harnessing sequence labeling for sarcasm detection in dialogue from TV series 'Friends'. In *Proceedings of The 20th SIGNLL Conference on Computational Natural Language Learning*, pages 146–155, Berlin, Germany. Association for Computational Linguistics.

Roger J. Kreuz and Gina M. Caucci. 2007. Lexical influences on the perception of sarcasm. In *Proceedings of the Workshop on Computational Approaches to Figurative Language*, FigLanguages '07, page 1–4, USA. Association for Computational Linguistics.

Peng Liu, Wei Chen, Gaoyan Ou, Tengjiao Wang, Dongqing Yang, and Kai Lei. 2014. Sarcasm detection in social media based on imbalanced classification. In *Web-Age Information Management*, pages 459–471, Cham. Springer International Publishing.

Yinhan Liu, Myle Ott, Naman Goyal, Jingfei Du, Mandar Joshi, Danqi Chen, Omer Levy, Mike Lewis, Luke Zettlemoyer, and Veselin Stoyanov. 2019. Roberta: A robustly optimized bert pretraining approach. *ArXiv*, abs/1907.11692.

Diana Maynard and Mark Greenwood. 2014. Who cares about sarcastic tweets? investigating the impact of sarcasm on sentiment analysis. In *Proceedings of the Ninth International Conference on Language Resources and Evaluation (LREC'14)*, pages 4238–4243, Reykjavik, Iceland. European Language Resources Association (ELRA).

Matthew Peters, Mark Neumann, Mohit Iyyer, Matt Gardner, Christopher Clark, Kenton Lee, and Luke Zettlemoyer. 2018. Deep contextualized word representations. In *Proceedings of the 2018 Conference of the North American Chapter of the Association for Computational Linguistics: Human Language Technologies, Volume 1 (Long Papers)*, pages 2227–2237, New Orleans, Louisiana. Association for Computational Linguistics.

Rolandos Alexandros Potamias, Georgios Siolas, and A. Stafylopatis. 2019. A transformer-based approach to irony and sarcasm detection. *ArXiv*, abs/1911.10401.

Ashwin Rajadesingan, Reza Zafarani, and Huan Liu. 2015. Sarcasm detection on twitter: A behavioral modeling approach. In *Proceedings of the Eighth ACM International Conference on Web Search and Data Mining*, WSDM '15, page 97–106, New York, NY, USA. Association for Computing Machinery.

Antonio Reyes and Paolo Rosso. 2012. Making objective decisions from subjective data: Detecting irony in customer reviews. *Decision Support Systems*, 53:754–760.

Antonio Reyes, Paolo Rosso, and Tony Veale. 2013. A multidimensional approach for detecting irony in twitter. *Lang. Resour. Eval.*, 47(1):239–268.

Ellen Riloff, Ashequl Qadir, Prafulla Surve, Lalindra De Silva, Nathan Gilbert, and Ruihong Huang. 2013. Sarcasm as contrast between a positive sentiment and negative situation. In *Proceedings of the 2013 Conference on Empirical Methods in Natural Language Processing*, pages 704–714, Seattle, Washington, USA. Association for Computational Linguistics.

Joseph Tepperman, David Traum, and Shrikanth Narayanan. 2006. Yeah right: Sarcasm recognition for spoken dialogue systems.

Oren Tsur, Dmitry Davidov, and Ari Rappoport. 2010. Icwsm - a great catchy name: Semi-supervised recognition of sarcastic sentences in online product reviews. In *ICWSM*.

Byron C. Wallace, Do Kook Choe, Laura Kertz, and Eugene Charniak. 2014. Humans require context to infer ironic intent (so computers probably do, too). In *Proceedings of the 52nd Annual Meeting of the Association for Computational Linguistics (Volume 2: Short Papers)*, pages 512–516, Baltimore, Maryland. Association for Computational Linguistics.

Zelin Wang, Zhijian Wu, Ruimin Wang, and Yafeng Ren. 2015. Twitter sarcasm detection exploiting a context-based model. In *Proceedings, Part I, of the 16th International Conference on Web Information Systems Engineering — WISE 2015 - Volume 9418*, page 77–91, Berlin, Heidelberg. Springer-Verlag.

Thomas Wolf, Lysandre Debut, Victor Sanh, Julien Chaumond, Clement Delangue, Anthony Moi, Pierric Cistac, Tim Rault, R'emi Louf, Morgan Funtowicz, and Jamie Brew. 2019. Huggingface's transformers: State-of-the-art natural language processing. *ArXiv*, abs/1910.03771.

Zhilin Yang, Zihang Dai, Yiming Yang, Jaime G. Carbonell, Ruslan Salakhutdinov, and Quoc V. Le. 2019. Xlnet: Generalized autoregressive pretraining for language understanding. In *NeurIPS*.

Applying Transformers and Aspect-based Sentiment Analysis approaches on Sarcasm Detection

Taha Shangipour ataei, Soroush Javdan and Behrouz Minaei-Bidgoli
Computer Engineering Department
Iran University of Science and Technology
Tehran, Iran
`taha_shangipour,soroush_javdan@comp.iust.ac.ir`
`b_minaei@iust.ac.ir`

Abstract

Sarcasm is a type of figurative language broadly adopted in social media and daily conversations. The sarcasm can ultimately alter the meaning of the sentence, which makes the opinion analysis process error-prone. In this paper, we propose to employ bidirectional encoder representations transformers (BERT), and aspect-based sentiment analysis approaches in order to extract the relation between context dialogue sequence and response and determine whether or not the response is sarcastic. The best performing method of ours obtains an F1 score of 0.73 on the Twitter dataset and 0.734 over the Reddit dataset at the second workshop on figurative language processing Shared Task 2020.

1 Introduction

We are living in the age of social media. Many consider it as a revolution. Social media creates a variety of new possibilities; for instance, today, people can express their thought with just a tap of a finger. In the twitter platform, people are twitting around 500 million tweets per day, and it is estimated that over 2.8 million comments are posted on the Reddit every single day. This vast amount of data present an enormous opportunity for businesses, and researchers alogn with a significant number of challenges. Many companies and researchers have been interested in these data to investigate the opinion, emotions, and other aspects of them.

The usage of informal language and noisy content within social media presents many difficulties toward the opinion and emotion analysis problems. One of the main challenges in this criteria is the appearance of figurative language such as sarcasm. The sarcasm can alter the meaning of the sentence ultimately, and consequently, make the opinion analysis process error-prone. For instance, criticism may use positive words to convey a negative message. In recent years there was a growing trend to address the Sarcasm Detection problem among Natural Language Processing (NLP) researchers. Many approaches tackle the Sarcasm Detection problem by considering contextual information, instead of using utterance solely. For instance, Bamman and Smith (2015) utilized author context along with the environment and audience context, and Mishra et al. (2016) used cognitive features, Ghosh et al. (2018) made use of conversational context.

The Sarcasm Detection shared task[1] is aimed to detect sarcasm based on the conversation context. Given the current utterance and conversation history, the models are expected to decide if the utterance is sarcastic or not. We test our models on the dataset from both Twitter and Reddit. Both utterance and the conversation history have been used as input. We applied the transformer-based model and adopted aspect-based sentiment analysis approaches to address the problem.

The remnant of this paper is organized as follows: Section 2 reviews related work. Section 3 describes the datasets. Section 4 explains our methodology. Section 5 shows the results of each dataset in detail. Lastly, section 6 provides conclusions and our plans for future research.

2 Related works

There have been several attempts to solve the Sarcasm Detection problem with rule-based approaches. Bharti et al. (2015) presented two rule-based classifiers for two different types of tweet structure, the first one used to detect sarcasm in tweets that have a contradiction between negative sentiment and positive situation. The second classifier applied to tweets that start with interjection

---

[1] https://competitions.codalab.org/competitions/22247

Proceedings of the Second Workshop on Figurative Language Processing, pages 67–71
July 9, 2020. ©2020 Association for Computational Linguistics
https://doi.org/10.18653/v1/P17

words. The former classifier applied parsed-based lexicon generation to identify phrases that display sentiment, and indicate the sarcastic label whenever a negative phrase occurs in a positive sentence. The latest classifier used interjections and intensifiers that occur together in order to predict sarcasm. Maynard and Greenwood (2014) suggests that hashtag sentiment is an essential symbol of sarcasm, and authors often used hashtags to emphasize sarcasm. They propose the tweet is sarcastic whenever the hashtags' sentiments do not agree with the rest of the tweet.

Besides the requirement for in-depth knowledge of the domain and much manual work, rule-based methods are usually not the best performers in terms of prediction quality. Because of the high cost of the rule-based methods, many researchers put there focus on machine learning approaches. Different types of models and features have been adopted to tackle this problem. Mukherjee and Bala (2017) addressed the problem in both supervised and unsupervised settings. They utilized Naïve Bayes as a classifier and C-means clustering, which is one of the most widely used fuzzy clustering algorithms. Joshi et al. (2016) adopted a sequence labeling techniques (SVM-HMM and SEARN) and indicated that sequence labeling algorithms outperform the classification algorithms in conversational data.

With the development of computational hardware and deep learning in recent years, many deep learning methods have been proposed to address the sarcasm detection problem. Amir et al. (2016) proposed a Convolutional Neural Network-based architecture that jointly learns and exploits embeddings for the users' content and utterances. Ghosh and Veale (2016) used the complication of the Convolutional Neural Network and Recurrent Neural Network. They used two layers of Convolutional Neural Network, followed by two layers of Long Short-Term Memory(LSTM). The output of LSTM layers fed to a Fully Connected Neural Network in order to produce a higher-order feature set. Diao et al. (2020) proposed a novel multi-dimension question answering network in order to detect sarcasm. They utilized conversation context information. A deep memory network based on BiLSTM and attention mechanisms have been adopted to extract the factors of sarcasm.

3   Dataset

Two corpora were used in Sarcasm Detection shared task, which both of them are balanced. The Twitter corpus consists of 5000 data samples for the train and 1800 for the test set. On the other hand, Reddit corpus contains 4400 data samples for the train and 1800 for the test set. Training datasets have four columns:

- ID: a unique identifier for each data sample

- Context: an ordered list of dialogues

- Response: reply to the last post or tweet of Context dialogues

- Label: indicate wheter the responce is sarcastic or not

Figure 1 shows the distribution of dialogue turns in each dataset.

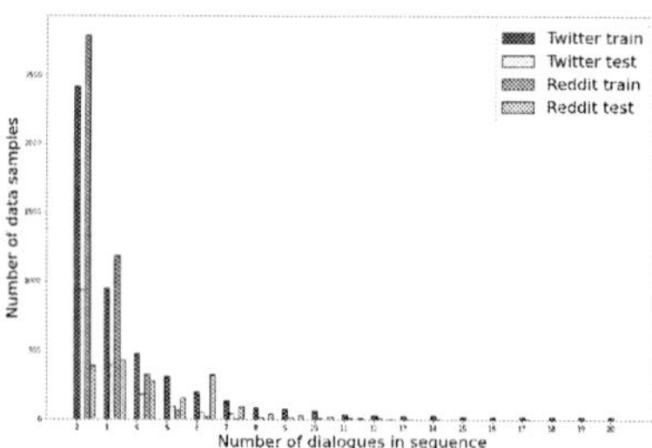

Figure 1: distribution of dialogues turns.

Moreover, we used a balanced dataset proposed at (Khodak et al., 2017) with 1 million data samples over Reddit comments as an additional dataset.

4   Methodology

In this section we describe models and technquies that we used to address sarcasm detection problem.

4.1   Preprocessing

Hashtag segmentation: the hashtag is a type of metadata used on social media starting with a number sign, #, which helps users find messages with the same topic. We apply word segmentation on hashtags, for example '#BlackHistoryMonth' is segmented as 'Black History Month.'

Misc.:   We removed all of the @USER mentions and <URL> tags.

4.2 Word Embedding:

GloVe (Pennington et al., 2014) is an unsupervised method for extracting word vector representation for our raw data. We also employed Fasttext(Mikolov et al., 2018) embedding because they are derived from character n-gram and thus are useful for misspelled words and social media contents.

4.3 Models:

NBSVM: We used the NBSVM model introduced by Wang and Manning (2012), which is a combination of Naïve Bayes and support vector machine, and is known as an excellent baseline for many NLP tasks. As input, we utilized the TF-IDF matrix with character n-gram features with n-gram range from 2 to 6. We applied this method over both datasets. Also, we tried different input data for the NBSVM model. The different combinations of 'response' column, 'context' column have been used as input.

BERT: Bidirectional Encoder Representation from Transformer (BERT) (Devlin et al., 2018) was released by the Google research team and achieved state of the art in many NLP tasks. BERT is pre-trained on a huge corpus of data sources. As input, we experiment with the 'response' column solely, 'context' column solely, and the concatenation of 'context' and 'response' column. We trained the model with three epochs, a batch size of 8, and a learning rate of 2e-5. For maximum sequence length, the 128 yield best result.

BERT-SVM: We used logits from the final layer of BERT as input for a support vector machine model with a linear kernel. We trained the model with three epochs, a batch size of 8, and a learning rate of 2e-5. For maximum sequence length, the 128 yield best result.

BERT-LR: We used logits from the final layer of BERT as input for a logistic regression model. We trained the model with three epochs, a batch size of 8, and a learning rate of 2e-5. For maximum sequence length, the 128 yield best result.

XLNET: XLNet (Yang et al., 2019) is a generalized autoregressive pretraining method. Since it outperforms BERT on 20 different NLP tasks, we train this method over the Reddit dataset. We trained the model with three epochs, a batch size of 8, and a learning rate of 2e-5. For maximum sequence length, the 128 yield best result.

Bi-GRU-CNN+BiLSTM-CNN: CNN is suitable for detecting patterns, and by changing kernel sizes, it also can detect different patterns regardless of their positions. RNN is a sequence of network blocks linked to each other, and each of them passes a message to the next one, this feature enables the network to demonstrate dynamic temporal behavior for a time sequence. We employ a neural network architecture built on top of a concatenation of glove embedding and the fastText embedding, both of them with 300 dimensions. Then, the network splits into two parallel parts. The first part combines a bidirectional gated recurrent unit (GRU) with 128 hidden units and a convolutional layer with a kernel size of 2 and 64 hidden units. The second part combines a BiLSTM with 128 hidden units and a convolutional layer with a kernel size of 2 and 64 hidden units. Finally, we concatenate global max pooling and global average pooling of parallel parts and feed them to a dense layer and then through a softmax layer for the classification purpose.

After reviewing some aspect-based sentiment analysis methods, we found some similarities between these models and sarcasm detection problems, so we attempted to change aspect-based sentiment analysis and adapt it sufficiently to address the Sarcasm Detection problem. For all the following models, the number of training epochs has been set to 10.

IAN: IAN (Ma et al., 2017) has two attention layers that learn context and target interactively and make representation for both separately. We replace the context of the ABSA with the last dialogue in the 'context' column of the sarcasm datasets and target with the 'response' column. We utilized 300 hidden units for both LSTM and attention parts. We run this method on both datasets.

LCF-BERT: LCF-BERT (Zeng et al., 2019) is a method based on multi-head self-attention, it employs context features dynamic mask (CDM) and context features dynamic weighted (CDW) layers along with a BERT-shared layer to extract long-term internal dependencies of local context and global context in aspect-based sentiment classification problem. We alter the model input so it can perform on the sarcastic dataset. As input, we used 'response' and the last dialogue in the 'context' column. The BERT-base-uncased with a maximum sequence length of 80 has been used as a BERT-shared layer.

BERT-AEN: AEN-BERT (Song et al., 2019) is another method proposed for the aspect-based sentiment classification that we borrowed for this task. This method introduces an attentional encoder network as a solution for the RNN problem with long-term pattern recognition. It also applies a BERT-base-uncased pre-trained model with a maximum sequence length of 80. We also used hidden units of 300 for the attention part. We modify the model input so it can work on the sarcastic dataset. As input, we used 'response' and the last dialogue in the 'context' column.

5 Results

On twitter corpus, the performance of NBSVM as a simple model is quite impressive. As long as the data is from social media and might contain informal and misspelling content using character n-gram TFIDT matrix can yield excellent performance. As features, we used different combinations of 'response' column, 'context' column. However, taking the 'response' column as a feature solely produced the best result. We also test models with and without preprocessing steps. However, adding the preprocessing step did not show a significate change in the results. As expected, BERT achieved the second-best position on the scoreboard. We used a different set of features, but again using the 'response' column solely scored the best among others. Furthermore, LCF-BERT, which is an aspect-based sentiment classification method, scored the best on the Twitter dataset because aspect-based sentiment classification methods consider input data as two different sections and try to learn them interactively. The complete results with more details are shown in Table. 1.

Method	Score
Base-line	
NBSVM	0.691
Transformers	
BERT-base-cased	0.726
Bi-GRU-CNN+BiLSTM-CNN	0.660
Aspect-based	
LCF-BERT	**0.730**
IAN	0.648
BERT-AEN	0.651

Table 1: Models performance over Twitter dataset

Unlike our experience on the Twitter dataset, NBSVM did not perform well on the Reddit dataset. It appears that the Reddit dataset is more complicated and challenging than twitter. However, using an additional dataset, around 1 million data points, boosted the NBSVM result around 7 percent. For NBSVM, we used the same feature as it was used for the twitter dataset. BERT performance was the best on this dataset, regardless of additional data. For BERT-SVM and BERT-LR, we only utilized the 'response' column as input. Moreover, for XL-Net, we used the 'response' column with 100,000 random data points from the additional dataset. Furthermore, for the aspect-based sentiment analysis models, we used the last dialogue 'context' column and 'response' column as our input. The complete results with more details are shown in Table. 2.

Method	Score
Base-line	
NBSVM	0.675
Transformers	
BERT-base-cased	**0.734**
BERT-SVM	0.647
BERT-LR	0.649
Bi-GRU-CNN+BiLSTM-CNN	0.660
XLNet	0.698
Aspect-based	
IAN	0.502
BERT-AEN	0.612

Table 2: Models performance over Reddit dataset

6 Conclusion

Our proposed methods ranked 5 out of 37 groups for the Reddit dataset and ranked 25 out of 36 for the Twitter dataset. This result shows the strength of the BERT pre-trained model on sarcasm detection and its combination with aspect-based sentiment analysis models, which take data as two separate parts and learn them interactively. Also, additional data can improve performance slightly better. It is noteworthy to mention that NBSVM performance as a simple baseline with the TFIDF matrix with character n-gram was quite impressive. For future work, a combination of contextual and character-based embedding could lead to better performance. Moreover, since social media content usually contains misspelling and informal data, more complicated preprocessing techniques like social media content normalization might be more helpful than proposed techniques.

References

Silvio Amir, Byron C Wallace, Hao Lyu, and Paula Carvalho Mário J Silva. 2016. Modelling context with user embeddings for sarcasm detection in social media. *arXiv preprint arXiv:1607.00976*.

David Bamman and Noah A Smith. 2015. Contextualized sarcasm detection on twitter. In *Ninth International AAAI Conference on Web and Social Media*.

Santosh Kumar Bharti, Korra Sathya Babu, and Sanjay Kumar Jena. 2015. Parsing-based sarcasm sentiment recognition in twitter data. In *2015 IEEE/ACM International Conference on Advances in Social Networks Analysis and Mining (ASONAM)*, pages 1373–1380. IEEE.

Jacob Devlin, Ming-Wei Chang, Kenton Lee, and Kristina Toutanova. 2018. Bert: Pre-training of deep bidirectional transformers for language understanding. *arXiv preprint arXiv:1810.04805*.

Yufeng Diao, Hongfei Lin, Liang Yang, Xiaochao Fan, Yonghe Chu, Kan Xu, and Di Wu. 2020. A multi-dimension question answering network for sarcasm detection. *IEEE Access*.

Aniruddha Ghosh and Tony Veale. 2016. Fracking sarcasm using neural network. In *Proceedings of the 7th workshop on computational approaches to subjectivity, sentiment and social media analysis*, pages 161–169.

Debanjan Ghosh, Alexander R Fabbri, and Smaranda Muresan. 2018. Sarcasm analysis using conversation context. *Computational Linguistics*, 44(4):755–792.

Aditya Joshi, Vaibhav Tripathi, Pushpak Bhattacharyya, and Mark Carman. 2016. Harnessing sequence labeling for sarcasm detection in dialogue from tv series 'friends'. In *Proceedings of The 20th SIGNLL Conference on Computational Natural Language Learning*, pages 146–155.

Mikhail Khodak, Nikunj Saunshi, and Kiran Vodrahalli. 2017. A large self-annotated corpus for sarcasm. *arXiv preprint arXiv:1704.05579*.

Dehong Ma, Sujian Li, Xiaodong Zhang, and Houfeng Wang. 2017. Interactive attention networks for aspect-level sentiment classification. *arXiv preprint arXiv:1709.00893*.

Diana G Maynard and Mark A Greenwood. 2014. Who cares about sarcastic tweets? investigating the impact of sarcasm on sentiment analysis. In *LREC 2014 Proceedings*. ELRA.

Tomas Mikolov, Edouard Grave, Piotr Bojanowski, Christian Puhrsch, and Armand Joulin. 2018. Advances in pre-training distributed word representations. In *Proceedings of the International Conference on Language Resources and Evaluation (LREC 2018)*.

Abhijit Mishra, Diptesh Kanojia, Seema Nagar, Kuntal Dey, and Pushpak Bhattacharyya. 2016. Harnessing cognitive features for sarcasm detection. In *Proceedings of the 54th Annual Meeting of the Association for Computational Linguistics (Volume 1: Long Papers)*, pages 1095–1104, Berlin, Germany. Association for Computational Linguistics.

Shubhadeep Mukherjee and Pradip Kumar Bala. 2017. Sarcasm detection in microblogs using naïve bayes and fuzzy clustering. *Technology in Society*, 48:19–27.

Jeffrey Pennington, Richard Socher, and Christopher D Manning. 2014. Glove: Global vectors for word representation. In *Proceedings of the 2014 conference on empirical methods in natural language processing (EMNLP)*, pages 1532–1543.

Youwei Song, Jiahai Wang, Tao Jiang, Zhiyue Liu, and Yanghui Rao. 2019. Attentional encoder network for targeted sentiment classification. *arXiv preprint arXiv:1902.09314*.

Sida Wang and Christopher Manning. 2012. Baselines and bigrams: Simple, good sentiment and topic classification. In *Proceedings of the 50th Annual Meeting of the Association for Computational Linguistics (Volume 2: Short Papers)*, pages 90–94, Jeju Island, Korea. Association for Computational Linguistics.

Zhilin Yang, Zihang Dai, Yiming Yang, Jaime Carbonell, Russ R Salakhutdinov, and Quoc V Le. 2019. Xlnet: Generalized autoregressive pretraining for language understanding. In *Advances in neural information processing systems*, pages 5754–5764.

Biqing Zeng, Heng Yang, Ruyang Xu, Wu Zhou, and Xuli Han. 2019. Lcf: A local context focus mechanism for aspect-based sentiment classification. *Applied Sciences*, 9(16):3389.

Sarcasm Identification and Detection in Conversion Context using BERT

Kalaivani A, Thenmozhi D
Department of Computer Science and Engineering,
SSN College of Engineering (Autonomous),
Affiliated to Anna University, Tamilnadu, India.
kalaiwind@gmail.com, theni_d@ssn.edu.in

Abstract

Sarcasm analysis in user conversion text is automatic detection of any irony, insult, hurting, painful, caustic, humour, vulgarity that degrades an individual. It is helpful in the field of sentimental analysis and cyberbullying. As an immense growth of social media, sarcasm analysis helps to avoid insult, hurts and humour to affect someone. In this paper, we present traditional Machine learning approaches, Deep learning approach (RNN-LSTM) and BERT (Bidirectional Encoder Representations from Transformers) for identifying sarcasm. We have used the approaches to build the model, to identify and categorize how much conversion context or response is needed for sarcasm detection and evaluated on the two social media forums that is Twitter conversation dataset and Reddit conversion dataset. We compare the performance based on the approaches and obtained the best F1 scores as 0.722, 0.679 for the Twitter forums and Reddit forums respectively.

1 Introduction

Social media have shown a rapid growth of user counts and have been object of scientific and sentiment analysis as in (Kalaivani A and Thenmozhi D, 2018). Sarcasm occurs frequently in user-generated content such as blogs, forums and micro posts, especially in English, and is inherently difficult to analyze, not only for a machine but even for a human. Sarcasm Analysis is useful for several applications such as sentimental analysis, opinion mining, hate speech identification, offensive and abusive language detection, advertising and cyber bullying.

(Debanjan Ghosh et al., 2018) performed to identify how much context is needed to find the conversion context is sarcastic or not and

analysed the verbal irony tweets using LSTM with more different attention mechanism and still facing the problem with the usage of slangs, rhetorical questions, usage of numbers and usage of non-vocabulary tweets. In recent years, several research works are performed in sarcasm detection in the Natural Language Processing community (Aditya Joshi at el., 2017).

In Figurative Language 2020 Task 2: shared task on sarcasm detection in social media forums. It focuses to identify the given conversion text is sarcastic or not and find how much context is helpful for sarcasm identification have modelled either the given instance may be isolated or combined. It focuses on two social media forums that are Twitter conversion dataset and Reddit conversion dataset (Khodak et al., 2017). For both the datasets, the organizer provides the context and response that is the response is reply to the context and the context is a full dialogue conversation thread. The computational task is to detect and identify the sarcasm and to understand how much conversation context is needed or helpful for sarcasm detection.

The challenges of this shared task include: a) small dataset is hard to train the complex models; b) the characteristics of the language on social media forums difficulties such as non-vocabulary words and ungrammatical context c) how much conversion text to detect sarcasm and the usage of slangs, rhetorical questions, Capitalized words, numbers, Abbreviations, pro-longed words, hashtags, URL, Repetitions of Punctuations, Contractions, Continuous words without spaces.

We address the problem in hash tags, continuation of words without spaces, URL and to classify which context is helpful to find sarcasm. To address the problem, we pre-processed the text by using Machine learning libraries like NTLK, Gensim and classified by using different traditional machine learning techniques, deep learning technique and finally we obtained the

Proceedings of the Second Workshop on Figurative Language Processing, pages 72–76
July 9, 2020. ©2020 Association for Computational Linguistics
https://doi.org/10.18653/v1/P17

best result by using BERT models. The tasks are independently evaluated by macro-F1 metrics.

2   Related Work

(Aniruddha Ghosh and Tony Veale, 2016) used neural network semantic model to capture the temporal text patterns for shorter texts. As an example, in this model classified "I Just Love Mondays!" correctly as sarcasm, but it failed to classify "Thank God It's Monday!" as sarcasm, even though both are similar at the conceptual level. (Keith Cortis et al., 2017) performed in the SemEval-2017 shared task to detect the sentiment, humour and to predict the sentiment score of companies' stocks in the smaller texts.

(Raj Kumar Gupta and Yinping Yang, 2017) performed in the shared task of SemEval-2017 Task 4 to detect sarcasm by used the SVM Based classifier and developed the CrystalNest to analyse the features combining sarcasm score derived, sentiment scores, NRC lexicon, n-grams, word embedding vectors, and part-of-speech features.

(David Bamman and Noah A. Smith, 2015) used the predictive features and analysed the utterance on Twitter based on the properties of author, audience and environment features. (Mondher Bouazizi and Tomoaki Otsuki, 2016) used the pattern-based approach to detect sarcasm and analysed the four features such as sentiment-related features, punctuation-related features, syntactic and semantic features, pattern-related features and classification done by the classifiers such as Random Forest, Support Vector Machine, k Near-est Neighbours and Maximum Entropy.

(Meishan Zhang et al., 2016) used the bi-directional gated recurrent neural network and discrete model to detect sarcasm and analyse the local and conceptual information and perform the process in Glove word embedding. (Malave N et al., 2020) used the context-based evaluation based on the data and to determine the user behaviour and context information to detect sarcasm. (Yitao Cai et al., 2019) used the multi-modal hierarchical fusion model to detect the multi-modal sarcasm for tweets consisting of texts and images in Twitter.

3   Data and Methodology

In our approach, we have used Twitter and Reddit dataset given by Figurative Language processing 2020 shared task on sarcasm detection. The dataset is given with columns namely, label, context and response where the response is the reply of context and the context is the full conversion dialogue and it is separated as C1, C2, C3 etc. C2 is the reply of the C1 context and C3 is the reply of C2 context respectively. Both the datasets consists of the labels namely SARCASM and NOT_SARCASM. In the Twitter dataset, the train data has 5000 conversion tweets in that 2500 sarcasm tweets and 2500 not sarcasm tweets and the test data has 1800 tweets.

In the Reddit dataset, the train data has 4400 conversion tweets in that 2200 sarcasm tweets and 2200 non sarcasm tweets and the test data have 1800 tweets. we have the pre-processed the text to removal of @USER, URL and the pro longed words like "ohhhhhh" and replace the words like F * * king as Fucking, replace the question tags like Didn't as Did not, removal of hashtags and separate the words into the continuous space less sentence. Tweet tokenizer is used to tokenize the word and to get the vocabulary words.

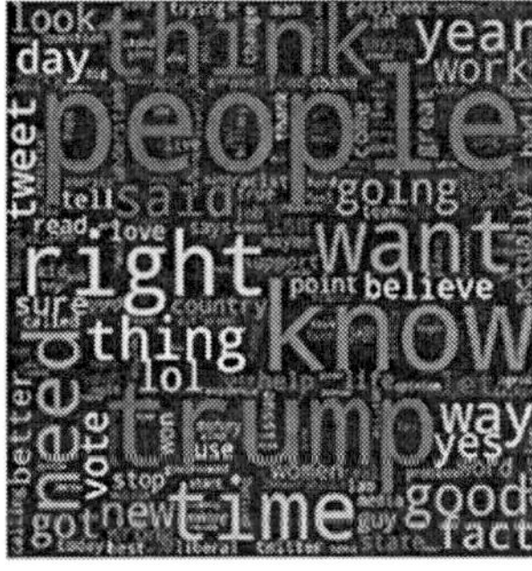

Figure 1: Sarcastic words

Figure 2: Not Sarcastic Words

We have employed the traditional machine learning techniques, Recurrent Neural Network with LSTM (RNN-LSTM) and BERT. In the machine learning approach, first, we have used the utterance of combined context and response (CR) for detecting the sarcasm and then pre-processed data using Gensim libraries to remove the hashtags, punctuation, white spaces, numeric content, stop words and then convert into lower text. We have used the word cloud to identify and categorize the most sarcastic words and non-sarcastic words which are appeared in sarcasm message and not sarcasm message as shown below in Figure 1 and Figure 2.

Models	Combined Context and Response (CR)		Response (R)	
	Doc2Vec	Tfidf	Doc2Vec	Tfidf
LR	0.513	**0.7296**	0.509	**0.7132**
RF	0.513	0.6764	0.527	0.7038
XGB	0.534	0.6876	0.533	0.6928
SVC	0.507	**0.7212**	0.506	0.7016
NB	0.505	**0.7394**	0.512	**0.7106**

Table 1: Accuracies of the models based on the feature extraction of the utterance of combined and isolated text – Twitter data

Models	Combined Context and Response (CR)		Response(R)	
	Doc2Vec	Tfidf	Doc2Vec	Tfidf
LR	0.5061	**0.552**	0.497	**0.597**
RF	0.4947	0.539	0.505	0.564
XGB	0.4965	**0.565**	0.500	0.582
SVC	0.5029	0.538	0.493	0.587
NB	0.4977	0.549	0.493	**0.595**

Table 2: Accuracies of the models based on the feature extraction of the utterance of combined and isolated text – Reddit data

We have performed Doc2Vec transformer and Tfidf Vectorizer for feature extraction and classified by using the Logistic Regression (LR), Random Forest Classifier (RF), XGBoost Classifier (XGB), Linear Support vector machine (SVC), Gaussian Naïve Binomial (NB). By using Tfidf Vectorizer, we got the 28761 features for 5000 tweets. Table 1 presents the cross validation accuracies of the different machine learning classifiers in the Twitter data as mentioned above. Table 2 presents the cross validation accuracies of the models based on the feature extraction in the Reddit data.

In Twitter data, we have chosen the scores which are above 0.70 from the cross validation accuracies of the machine learning techniques. Based on the cross validation scores, we have obtain the best accuracies score in SVM, logistic regression and NB classifiers of the combined

context text (CR) in Tfidf vectorizer and the best accuracies score in Logistic regression and Gaussian NB models of the isolated response (R) text in Tfidf vectorizer. In Reddit data, we have chosen the scores which are above 0.55 from the cross validation accuracies of the machine learning techniques. Based on the cross validation scores, we have obtain the best accuracies score in logistic regression and XGBoost Classifier of the combined text (CR) in Tfidf vectorizer and the best accuracies score in Logistic regression and Gaussian NB models of the isolated response text (R) in Tfidf vectorizer. In both the dataset, the result shows Doc2Vec transformer is not performed well because of non-grammatical sentences and Tfidf Vectorizer performs well when compared with the Doc2Vec transformer in dialogue conversion thread.

In the RNN-LSTM Method, we have used the combined context text with response to perform the pre-process using NLTK libraries, tokenize the word by using the word tokenizer and lemmatize the word after that to remove the stop words. Finally, we have obtained the train data has 325382 words total, with a vocabulary size of 32756, max sentence length is 568 and the test data has 30782 words total, with a vocabulary size of 8824, Max sentence length is 467. We used the Word2Vec embedding model for the embedding the words and obtain the 32668 unique tokens. We have evaluated using the RNN-LSTM and trained the deep learning models with a batch size 128 and dropout 0.2 for 5 epochs to build the model. We got the accuracy is 0.4890 which is low when compared with the machine learning approach.

In the BERT model, Google research team releases BERT (Devlin et al., 2018) and achieve good performance on many NLP tasks. We have used the combined context text, isolated context, and isolated response to perform the model. We have used the Bert uncased model for training the model, batch size is 32, learning rate is 2e-5, and number of train epochs is 3.0. Warmup is a period of time where the learning rate is small and gradually increases usually helps training. Warmup proportion is 0.1 and the model configuration is checkpoints is 300, summary steps is 100. We got the accuracy is 0.77 score. We have compared over all cross validation accuracies scores, BERT performs good than the machine learning approaches and deep learning technique.

Type	Precision	Recall	F1 score
BERT(CR)	0.672	0.673	0.671
BERT(C)	0.695	0.701	0.693
BERT(PCRW)	0.704	0.705	0.703
BERT(PCW)	0.703	0.703	0.703
BERT(PC1RW)	0.677	0.678	0.677
BERT(PC1W)	0.689	0.690	0.689
RNN-LSTM(CR)	0.361	0.361	0.361
BERT(R)	**0.722**	**0.722**	**0.722**
BERT(PC2R)	0.658	0.685	0.645
BERT(PR)	0.706	0.706	0.706
SVM(CR)	0.646	0.647	0.646
NB(CR)	0.672	0.672	0.672
NB(R)	0.632	0.632	0.632
LR(R)	0.642	0.643	0.642

Table 3: Results for Twitter Dataset

Type	Precision	Recall	F1 score
BERT(C)	0.587	0.589	0.585
BERT(CR)	0.493	0.492	0.477
BERT(R)	**0.679**	**0.679**	**0.679**
BERT(PR)	0.638	0.638	0.637
LR(CR)	0.526	0.526	0.526
LR(R)	0.563	0.564	0.563
NB(R)	0.557	0.557	0.557
SVC(R)	0.551	0.551	0.550
XGB(R)	0.539	0.543	0.528
SVC(CR)	0.516	0.516	0.516
XGB(CR)	0.544	0.544	0.544

Table 4: Results for Reddit Dataset

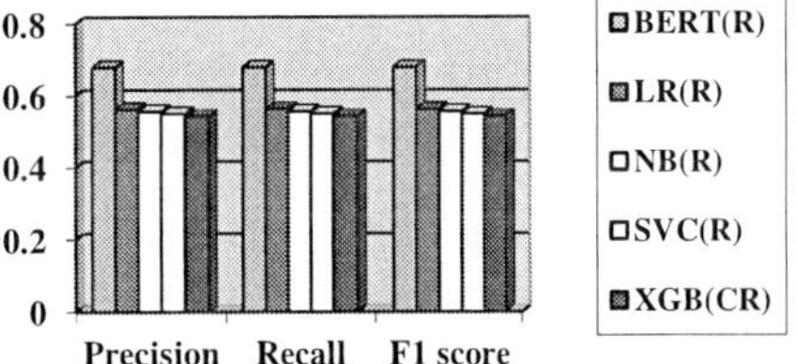

Figure 4: Results analysis for Reddit Dataset

4   Results

We have evaluated the test data of Twitter and Reddit dataset which is shared by Figurative Language processing 2020 shared task organizers. The performance is evaluated by using the metrics as precision, recall and F1 score. We have chosen the classifiers to predict the test data based on the performance of the cross validation of training data. We have performed to predict the test data by using various combinations of Conversion context and response that are CR represents the combined context of sentences with response, C represents the combined full context of sentences without response, PCRW represents the processed combined context of meaningful words and response, PCW represents the combined full context of meaningful words without response,

PC1RW represents the processed isolated first context of meaningful words and response, PC1W represents the isolated first context of meaningful words without response, R represents the response, PC1R represents the processed second context with response, PR represents the processed response. The results of the approaches are presented in the Table 3 shows the response text from conversion dialogue by using BERT have higher performance than others for the shared task of the Twitter dataset and the Table 4 shows   BERT response text from conversion dialogue thread performs well for the shared task of the Reddit dataset. The best results have obtained by using BERT model with the isolated response(R) text for both the Twitter and Reddit dataset respectively. We have noticed that the BERT performs well in continuous conversion dialogues or continuous sentences with previous dialogues compared with the meaningful words from conversion context. In both the dataset, the RNN-LSTM performs poor than the SVM, NB and LR because of the smaller dataset. The machine learning approach performs better with the smaller dataset. But the BERT model performs

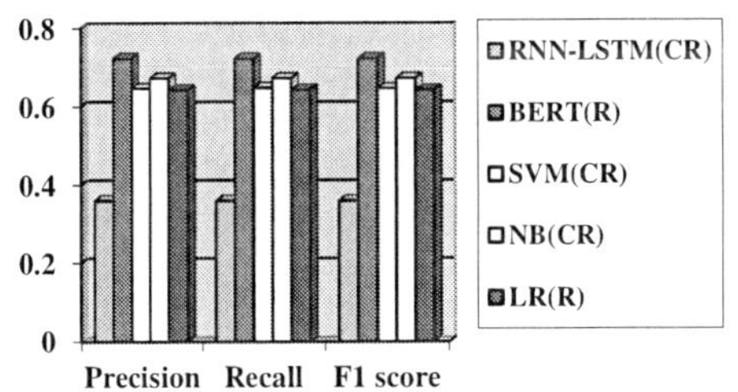

Figure 3: Results analysis for Twitter Dataset

well for the response text of both the Twitter and Reddit dataset with the non-grammatical sentences even the data size is small. Figure 3 shows the chart representations of the performance analysis of the different methods in the Twitter data. Figure 4 shows the chart representations of the performance analysis of the different methods in the Reddit data.

5   Conclusion

We have implemented traditional machine learning, deep learning approach and BERT model for identifying the sarcasm from Conversion dialogue thread and to detecting sarcasm from social media. The approaches are evaluated on Figurative Language 2020 dataset. The given utterance of combined text and isolated text are preprocessed and vectorized using word embeddings in deep learning models. We have employed RNN-LSTM to build the model for both the datasets. The instances are vectorized using Doc2Vec and TFIDF score for traditional machine learning models. The classifiers namely Logistic Regression (LR), Random Forest Classifier (RF), XGBoost Classifier (XGB), Linear Support vector machine (SVC), Gaussian Naïve Binomial (NB) were employed to build the models for both the Twitter and Reddit datasets. BERT uncased model with isolated response context gives better results for both the datasets respectively. The performance may be improved further by using larger datasets.

References

Joshi, A., Bhattacharyya, P., and Carman, M. J. 2017. Automatic sarcasm detection: A survey. *ACM Computing Surveys (CSUR)*, 50(5), 73.

Ghosh, D., Fabbri, A. R., and Muresan, S. 2018. Sarcasm analysis using conversation context. *Computational Linguistics*, 44(4), 755-792.

Khodak, M., Saunshi, N., and Vodrahalli, K. 2017. A large self-annotated corpus for sarcasm. arXiv preprint arXiv:1704.05579.

Aniruddha Ghosh, and Tony Veale. 2016. Fracking Sarcasm using Neural Network", *research gate publication*, Conference Paper. DOI: 10.13140/RG.2.2.16560.15363.

Keith Cortis, Andre Freitas, Tobias Daudert, Manuela Hurlimann, Manel Zarrouk, Siegfried Handschuh, and Brian Davis. 2017. SemEval-2017 Task 5: Fine-Grained Sentiment Analysis on Financial Microblogs and News", *Proceedings of the 11th International Workshop on Semantic Evaluations* , pages 519–535, Association for Computational Linguistics.

Raj Kumar Gupta, and Yinping Yang. 2017. CrystalNest at SemEval-2017 Task 4: Using Sarcasm Detection for Enhancing Sentiment Classification and Quantification, ACM.

David Bamman and Noah A. Smith. 2016. Contextualized Sarcasm Detection on Twitter, *Association for the Advancement of Artificial Intelligence (www.aaai.org)*.

Mondher Bouazizi And Tomoaki Otsuki (Ohtsuki),. 2016. A Pattern-Based Approach for Sarcasm Detection on Twitter, *IEEE. Translations and content mining*, Digital Object Identifier 10.1109/ACCESS.2016.2594194

Kalaivani A and Thenmozhi D. 2019. Sentimental Analysis using Deep Learning Techniques, *International journal of recent technology and engineering*, ISSN: 2277-3878.

Meishan Zhang, Yue Zhang, and Guohong Fu,. 2016. Tweet Sarcasm Detection Using Deep Neural Network, *Proceedings of COLING 2016, the 26th International Conference on Computational Linguistics: Technical Papers*, pages 2449–2460.

Malave N., and Dhage S.N. 2020. Sarcasm Detection on Twitter: User Behavior Approach. In: Thampi S. et al. (eds) Intelligent Systems, Technologies and Applications. *Advances in Intelligent Systems and Computing, vol 910. Springer, Singapore.* DOI https://doi.org/10.1007/978-981-13-6095-4_5.

Yitao Cai, Huiyu Cai and Xiaojun Wan. 2019. Multi-Modal Sarcasm Detection in Twitter with Hierarchical Fusion Model, *Proceedings of the 57th Annual Meeting of the Association for Computational Linguistics*, pages 2506–2515 Association for Computational Linguistics.

Jacob Devlin, Ming-Wei Chang, Kenton Lee, and Kristina Toutanova. 2018. Bert: Pre-training of deep bidirectional transformers for language understanding. arXiv preprint arXiv:1810.04805.

Neural Sarcasm Detection using Conversation Context

Nikhil Jaiswal
TCS Research, New Delhi, India
`nikhil.jais@tcs.com`

Abstract

Social media platforms and discussion forums such as Reddit, Twitter, etc. are filled with figurative languages. Sarcasm is one such category of figurative language whose presence in a conversation makes language understanding a challenging task. In this paper, we present a deep neural architecture for sarcasm detection. We investigate various pre-trained language representation models (PLRMs) like BERT, RoBERTa, etc. and fine-tune it on the Twitter dataset[1]. We experiment with a variety of PLRMs either on the twitter utterance in isolation or utilizing the contextual information along with the utterance. Our findings indicate that by taking into consideration the previous three most recent utterances, the model is more accurately able to classify a conversation as being sarcastic or not. Our best performing ensemble model achieves an overall F1 score of 0.790, which ranks us second[2] on the leaderboard of the Sarcasm Shared Task 2020.

1 Introduction

Sarcasm can be defined as a communicative act of intentionally using words or phrases which tend to transform the polarity of a positive utterance into its negative counterpart and vice versa. The significant increase in the usage of social media channels has generated content that is sarcastic and ironic in nature. The apparent reason for this is that social media users tend to use various figurative language forms to convey their message. The detection of sarcasm is thus vital for several NLP applications such as opinion minings, sentiment analysis, etc (Maynard and Greenwood, 2014). This leads to a considerable amount of research in the sarcasm detection domain among the NLP community in recent years.

The Shared Task on Sarcasm Detection 2020 aims to explore various approaches for sarcasm detection in a given textual utterance. Specifically, the task is to understand how much conversation context is needed or helpful for sarcasm detection. Our approach for this task focuses on utilizing various state-of-the-art PLRMs and fine-tuning it to detect whether a given conversation is sarcastic. We apply an ensembling strategy consisting of models trained on different length conversational contexts to make more accurate predictions. Our best performing model **(Team name - nclabj)** achieves an F1 score of 0.790 on the test data in the CoadaLab evaluation platform.

2 Problem Description

The dataset assigned for this task is collected from the popular social media platform, Twitter. Each training data contains the following fields: "label" (i.e., "SARCASM" or "NOTSARCASM"), "response" (the Tweet utterance), "context" (i.e., the conversation context of the "response"). Our objective here is to take as input a response along with its optional conversational context and predict whether the response is sarcastic or not. This problem can be modeled as a binary classification task. The predicted response on the test set is evaluated against the true label. Three performance metrics, namely, Precision, Recall, and F1 Score are used for final evaluation.

3 Related Work

Various attempts have been made for sarcasm detection in recent years (Joshi et al., 2017). Researchers have approached this task through different methodologies, such as framing it as a sense disambigua-

---

[1] The dataset is provided by the organizers of Sarcasm Shared Task FigLang-2020

[2] We are ranked 8th with an F1 score of 0.702 on the Reddit dataset leaderboard using the same approach. But we do not describe those results here as we could not test all our experiments within the timing constraints of the Shared Task.

Proceedings of the Second Workshop on Figurative Language Processing, pages 77–82
July 9, 2020. ©2020 Association for Computational Linguistics
https://doi.org/10.18653/v1/P17

tion problem (Ghosh et al., 2015) or considering sarcasm as a contrast between a positive sentiment and negative situation (Riloff et al., 2013; Maynard and Greenwood, 2014; Joshi et al., 2015, 2016b; Ghosh and Veale, 2016). Recently, few works have taken into account the additional context information along with the utterance. (Wallace et al., 2014) demonstrate how additional contextual information beyond the utterance is often necessary for humans as well as computers to identify sarcasm. (Schifanella et al., 2016) propose a multi-modal approach to combine textual and visual features for sarcasm detection. (Joshi et al., 2016a) model sarcasm detection as a sequence labeling task instead of a classification task. (Ghosh et al., 2017) investigated that the conditional LSTM network (Rocktäschel et al., 2015) and LSTM networks with sentence-level attention on context and response achieved significant improvement over the LSTM model that reads only the response. Therefore, the new trend in the field of sarcasm detection is to take into account the additional context information along with the utterance. The objective of this Shared Task is to investigate how much of the context information is necessary to classify an utterance as being sarcastic or not.

4   System Description

We describe our proposed system for sarcasm detection in this section. We frame this problem as a binary classification task and apply a transfer learning approach to classify the tweet as either sarcastic or not. We experiment with several state of the art PLRMs like BERT (Devlin et al., 2019), RoBERTa (Liu et al., 2019), as well as pre-trained embeddings representations models such as ELMo (Peters et al., 2018), USE (Cer et al., 2018), etc. and fine-tune it on the assigned Twitter dataset. We briefly review these models in subsections 4. For fine-tuning, we add additional dense layers and train the entire model in an end to end manner. Figure 1 illustrates one such approach for fine-tuning a RoBERTa model. We sequentially unfreeze the layers with each ongoing epoch. We apply a model ensembling strategy called "majority voting", as shown in Figure 2 to come out with our final predictions on the test data. In this ensemble technique, we take the prediction of several models and choose the label predicted by the maximum number of models.

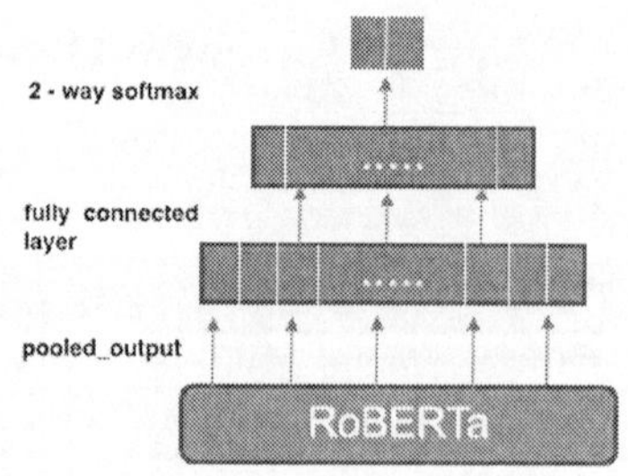

Figure 1: The proposed methodology to fine-tune a RoBERTa model

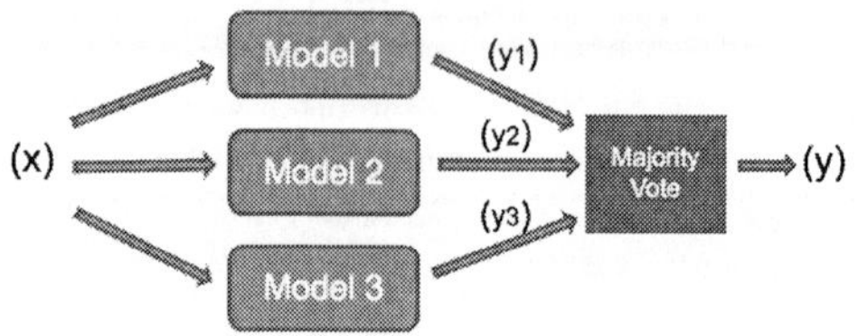

Figure 2: The majority voting ensemble methodology consisting of three sample models

4.1   Embeddings from Language Models (ELMo)

ELMo introduces a method to obtain deep contextualized word representation. Here, the researchers build a bidirectional Language model (biLM) with a two-layered bidirectional LSTM architecture and obtain the word vectors through a learned function of the internal states of biLM. This model is trained on 30 million sentence corpus, and thus the word embeddings obtained using this model can be used to increase the classification performance in several NLP tasks. For our task, we utilize the ELMo embeddings to come out with a feature representation of the words in the input utterance and pass it through three dense layers to perform the binary classification task.

4.2   Universal Sentence Encoder (USE)

USE presents an approach to create embedding vector representation of a complete sentence to specifically target transfer learning to other NLP tasks. There are two variants of USE based on trade-offs in compute resources and accuracy. The first variant uses an encoding sub-graph of the transformer architecture to construct sentence embeddings (Vaswani et al., 2017) and achieve higher performance figures. The second variant is a light model that uses a deep averaging network (DAN) (Iyyer et al., 2015) in which first the input embedding for words and bi-grams are averaged and then passed through a feedforward neural network to obtain sentence embeddings. We utilize the USE embeddings from the Transformer architecture on our data and perform the classification task by passing them through three dense layers.

4.3 Bidirectional Encoder Representations from Transformers (BERT)

BERT, a Transformer language model, achieved state-of-the-art results on eleven NLP tasks. There are two pre-training tasks on which BERT is trained on. In the first task, also known as masked language modeling (MLMs), 15% of words are randomly masked in each sequence, and the model is used to predict the masked words. The second task, also known as the next sentence prediction (NSP), in which given two sentences, the model tries to predict whether one sentence is the next sentence of the other. Once the above pre-training phase is completed, this can be extended for classification related task with minimal changes. This is also known as BERT fine-tuning, which we apply for our sarcasm detection task. In the paper, two models ($BERT_{BASE}$ & $BERT_{LARGE}$) are released depending on the number of transformer blocks (12 vs. 24), attention heads (12 vs. 16), and hidden units size (768 vs. 1024). We experiment with $BERT_{LARGE}$ model for our task, since it generally performs better as compared to the $BERT_{BASE}$ model.

4.4 Robustly Optimized BERT Approach (RoBERTa)

RoBERTa presents improved modifications for training BERT models. The modifications are as follows: 1. training the model for more epochs (500K vs. 100K) 2. using bigger batch sizes (around 8 times) 3. training on more data (160GB vs. 16 GB). Apart from the above parameters changes, byte-level BPE vocabulary is used instead of character-level vocabulary. The dynamic masking technique is used here instead of the static masking used in BERT. Also, the NSP task is removed following some recent works that have questioned the necessity of the NSP loss (Sun et al., 2019; Lample and Conneau, 2019). Summarizing, RoBERTa is trained with dynamic masking, sentences without NSP loss, large batches, and a larger byte-level BPE.

Notation	Description	Seq. Length
RESP	only response	70
CON1	previous 1 turn followed by response	130
CON2	previous 2 turns followed by response	180
CON3	previous 3 turns followed by response	230
CON	entire context followed by response	450

Table 1: Different Variants of Data

5 Experiments and Results

5.1 Dataset Preparation

The dataset assigned for this task is collected from Twitter. There are 5,000 English Tweets for training, and 1,800 English Tweets for testing purpose. We use 10% of the training data for the validation set to tune the hyper-parameters of our model. We apply several preprocessing steps to clean the given raw data. Apart from the standard preprocessing steps such as lowercasing the letters, removal of punctuations and emojis, expansion of contractions, etc., we remove the usernames from the tweets. Also, since hashtags generally consist of phrases in CamelCase letters, we split them into individual words since they carry the essential information about the tweet.

To incorporate contextual information along with a given tweet, we prepare the data in the manner, as shown in Table 1. For data in which only the previous two turns are available, for them, only those two turns are considered in CON3 & CON case illustrated in Table 1. We fix the maximum sequence length based on the coverage of the data (greater than 90th percentile) in the training and test set. This sequence length is determined by considering each word as a single token.

5.2 Implementation Details

Here, we describe a detailed set up of our experiments and the different hyper-parameters of our models for better reproducibility. We experiment with various advanced state-of-the-art methodologies such as ELMo, USE, BERT, and RoBERTa. We use the validation set to tune the hyper-parameters. We use Adam (Kingma and Ba, 2014) optimizer in all our experiments. We use dropout regularization (Srivastava et al., 2014) and early stopping (Yao et al., 2007) to prevent overfitting. We use a batch size of $\{2, 4, 8, 16\}$ depending on the model size and the sequence length.

Firstly, the data is prepared as mentioned in subsection 5.1. For fine-tuning ELMo, USE, and $BERT_{LARGE}$ models, we use the module from Ten-

Model	ELMo			USE			BERT$_{\text{LARGE}}$		
Data	Pr	Re	F1	Pr	Re	F1	Pr	Re	F1
RESP	0.688	0.690	0.688	0.728	0.728	0.728	0.720	0.735	0.716
CON1	0.677	0.679	0.676	0.718	0.718	0.718	0.714	0.719	0.712
CON2	0.652	0.670	0.643	0.715	0.715	0.715	0.729	0.731	0.729
CON3	0.697	0.697	0.697	0.719	0.725	0.717	0.741	0.758	0.737
CON	0.699	0.699	0.699	0.704	0.705	0.704	0.734	0.734	0.734

Table 2: We compare the fine-tuning of different individual models **ELMo** and **USE** and **BERT**$_{\text{LARGE}}$ on different variants of Twitter test data. The metric Precision (Pr), Recall (Re) and F1 Score (F1) denotes the test set results.

Model	RoBERTa$_{\text{LARGE}}$ A				RoBERTa$_{\text{LARGE}}$ B			
Data	ID	Pr	Re	F1	ID	Pr	Re	F1
RESP	1	0.742	0.745	0.742	6	0.744	0.744	0.744
CON1	2	0.751	0.756	0.750	7	0.752	0.753	0.751
CON2	3	0.751	0.751	0.750	8	0.763	0.764	0.763
CON3	4	**0.773**	**0.778**	**0.772**	9	0.766	0.766	0.766
CON	5	0.759	0.760	0.759	10	0.757	0.757	0.757

Table 3: We compare the fine-tuning of **RoBERTa**$_{\text{LARGE}}$ model on different variants of Twitter test data. We fine-tune this model twice on the same train and validation data with different weight initialization. We represent each of these results with a unique ID to utilize them in the ensemble network.

Description	Models IDs	Pr	Re	F1
Top 3 RoBERTa A	**3, 4, 5**	0.773	0.775	0.772
Top 3 RoBERTa B	**8, 9, 10**	0.778	0.779	0.778
Top 3 RoBERTa A & B	**4, 8, 9**	**0.790**	**0.792**	**0.790**
Top 5 RoBERTa A & B	**4, 5, 8, 9, 10**	0.788	0.789	0.787

Table 4: We compare the ensembling results based on several combinations of RoBERTa$_{\text{LARGE}}$ models. Bold font denotes the best results.

sorflow Hub [345] and wrap it in a Keras Lambda layer whose weights are also trained during the fine-tuning process. We add three dense layers {512, 256, 1} with a dropout of 0.5 between these layers. The relu activation function is being applied between the first two layers whereas sigmoid is used at the final layer. ELMo and USE models are trained for 20 epochs while BERT$_{\text{LARGE}}$ is trained for 5 epochs. During the training, only the best model based on the minimum validation loss was saved by using the Keras ModelCheckpoint callback. Instead of using a threshold value of 0.5 for binary classification, a whole range of threshold values from 0.1 to 0.9 with an interval of 0.01 is experimented on the validation set. The threshold value for which the highest validation accuracy is obtained is selected as the final threshold and is being applied on the test set to get the test class predictions.

For fine-tuning RoBERTa$_{\text{LARGE}}$ model, we use the fastai (Howard and Gugger, 2020) framework and utilize PLRMs from HuggingFace's Transformers library (Wolf et al., 2019). HuggingFace library contains a collection of state-of-the-art PLRMs which is being widely used by the researcher and practitioner communities. Incorporating HuggingFace library with fastai allows us to utilize powerful fastai capabilities such as Discriminate Learning Rate, Slanted Triangular Learning Rate and Gradual Unfreezing Learning Rate on the powerful pretrained Transformer models. For our experiment, first of all, we extract the pooled output (i.e. the last layer hidden-state of the first token of the sequence (CLS token) further processed by a linear layer and a Tanh activation function). It is then passed through a linear layer with two neurons followed by a softmax activation function. We use a learning rate of 1e-5 and utilize the "1cycle" learning rate policy for super-convergence, as suggested by (Smith, 2015). We gradually unfreeze the layers and train on a 1cycle manner. After unfreezing the last three layers, we unfreeze the entire layers

[3]https://tfhub.dev/google/elmo/2
[4]https://tfhub.dev/google/universal-sentence-encoder-large/3
[5]https://tfhub.dev/tensorflow/bert_en_uncased_L-24_H-1024_A-16/1

and train in the similar 1cycle manner. We stop the training when the validation accuracy does not improve consecutively for three epochs.

We use a simple ensembling technique called majority voting to ensemble the predictions of different models to further improvise the test accuracy.

5.3 Results and Error Analysis

Here, we compare and discuss the results of our experiments. First, we summarize the results of the individual model on the test set using different variants of data in Tables 2 & 3. From Table 2, we can observe that adding context information of specific lengths helps in improving the classification performance in almost all the models. USE results are better as compared to the ELMo model since Transformers utilized in the USE are able to handle sequential data comparatively better than that as LSTMs being used in ELMo. On the other hand, $BERT_{LARGE}$ outperforms USE with the increase in the length of context history. The highest test accuracy by $BERT_{LARGE}$ is obtained on the CON3 variant of data which depicts the fact that adding most recent three turns of context history helps the model to classify more accurately. This hypothesis is further supported from the experiments when a similar trend occurs with the $RoBERTa_{LARGE}$ model. Since the results obtained by RoBERTa are comparatively better than other models, we train this model once again on the same train and validation data with different weight initialization. By doing this, we can have a variety of models to build our final ensemble architecture. The evaluation metrics used are Precision (Pr), Recall (Re), F1-score (F1).

As observed in Table 3, RoBERTa fine-tuned on the CON3 variant of data outperforms all other approaches. In the case of fine-tuning PLRMs like $BERT_{LARGE}$ & $RoBERTa_{LARGE}$ on this data, we can observe the importance of most recent three turns of context history. From the experiments, we conclude that on increasing the context history along with the utterance, the model can learn a better representation of the utterance and can classify the correct class more accurately. Finally, RoBERTa model outperforms every other model because this model is already an optimized and improved version of the BERT model.

Table 4 summarizes the results of our various ensemble models. For ensembling, we choose different variants of best performing models on the test data and apply majority voting on it to get the final test predictions. We experiment with several combinations of the models and report here the results of some of the best performing ensembles. We can observe that the ensemble model consisting of top three individual models gave us the best results.

6 Conclusion & Future Work

In this work, we have presented an effective methodology to tackle the sarcasm detection task on the twitter dataset by framing it as a binary classification problem. We showed that by fine-tuning PLRMs on a given utterance along with its specific length context history, we could successfully classify the utterance as being sarcastic or not. We experimented with different length context history and concluded that by taking into account the most recent three conversation turns, the model was able to obtain the best results. The fine-tuned $RoBERTa_{LARGE}$ model outperformed every other experimented models in terms of precision, recall, and F1 score. We also demonstrated that we could obtain a significant gain in the performance by using a simple ensembling technique called majority voting.

In the future, we would like to explore with these PLRMs on other publicly available datasets. We also aim to dive deep into the context history information and derive insights about the contextual part, which helps the model in improvising the classification result. We also wish to investigate more complex ensemble techniques to observe the performance gain.

References

Daniel Cer, Yinfei Yang, Sheng-yi Kong, Nan Hua, Nicole Limtiaco, Rhomni St. John, Noah Constant, Mario Guajardo-Cespedes, Steve Yuan, Chris Tar, Yun-Hsuan Sung, Brian Strope, and Ray Kurzweil. 2018. Universal sentence encoder. *CoRR*, abs/1803.11175.

Jacob Devlin et al. 2019. BERT: pre-training of deep bidirectional transformers for language understanding. In *Proceedings of the 2019 Conference of the North American Chapter of the Association for Computational Linguistics: Human Language Technologies*.

Aniruddha Ghosh and Tony Veale. 2016. Fracking sarcasm using neural network.

Debanjan Ghosh, Alexander Richard Fabbri, and Smaranda Muresan. 2017. The role of conversation context for sarcasm detection in online interactions. *CoRR*, abs/1707.06226.

Debanjan Ghosh, Weiwei Guo, and Smaranda Muresan. 2015. Sarcastic or not: Word embeddings to predict the literal or sarcastic meaning of words. In *Proceedings of the 2015 Conference on Empirical Methods in Natural Language Processing*, pages 1003–1012, Lisbon, Portugal. Association for Computational Linguistics.

Jeremy Howard and Sylvain Gugger. 2020. Fastai: A layered api for deep learning. *Information*, 11(2):108.

Mohit Iyyer, Varun Manjunatha, Jordan Boyd-Graber, and Hal Daumé III. 2015. Deep unordered composition rivals syntactic methods for text classification. In *Proceedings of the 53rd Annual Meeting of the Association for Computational Linguistics and the 7th International Joint Conference on Natural Language Processing (Volume 1: Long Papers)*, pages 1681–1691, Beijing, China. Association for Computational Linguistics.

Aditya Joshi, Pushpak Bhattacharyya, Mark Carman, and Vaibhav Tripathi. 2016a. Harnessing sequence labeling for sarcasm detection in dialogue from tv series 'friends'.

Aditya Joshi, Pushpak Bhattacharyya, and Mark J. Carman. 2017. Automatic sarcasm detection: A survey. *ACM Comput. Surv.*, 50(5).

Aditya Joshi, Vinita Sharma, and Pushpak Bhattacharyya. 2015. Harnessing context incongruity for sarcasm detection. In *Proceedings of the 53rd Annual Meeting of the Association for Computational Linguistics and the 7th International Joint Conference on Natural Language Processing (Volume 2: Short Papers)*, pages 757–762, Beijing, China. Association for Computational Linguistics.

Aditya Joshi, Vaibhav Tripathi, Kevin Patel, Pushpak Bhattacharyya, and Mark James Carman. 2016b. Are word embedding-based features useful for sarcasm detection? *CoRR*, abs/1610.00883.

Diederik Kingma and Jimmy Ba. 2014. Adam: A method for stochastic optimization. *International Conference on Learning Representations*.

Guillaume Lample and Alexis Conneau. 2019. Cross-lingual language model pretraining. *CoRR*, abs/1901.07291.

Yinhan Liu, Myle Ott, Naman Goyal, Jingfei Du, Mandar Joshi, Danqi Chen, Omer Levy, Mike Lewis, Luke Zettlemoyer, and Veselin Stoyanov. 2019. Roberta: A robustly optimized BERT pretraining approach. *CoRR*, abs/1907.11692.

Diana Maynard and Mark Greenwood. 2014. Who cares about sarcastic tweets? investigating the impact of sarcasm on sentiment analysis. In *Proceedings of the Ninth International Conference on Language Resources and Evaluation (LREC'14)*, pages 4238–4243, Reykjavik, Iceland. European Language Resources Association (ELRA).

Matthew Peters, Mark Neumann, et al. 2018. Deep contextualized word representations. In *Proceedings of the 2018 Conference of the North American Chapter of the Association for Computational Linguistics: Human Language Technologies, Volume 1 (Long Papers)*.

Ellen Riloff, Ashequl Qadir, Prafulla Surve, Lalindra De Silva, Nathan Gilbert, and Ruihong Huang. 2013. Sarcasm as contrast between a positive sentiment and negative situation. In *Proceedings of the 2013 Conference on Empirical Methods in Natural Language Processing*, pages 704–714, Seattle, Washington, USA. Association for Computational Linguistics.

Tim Rocktäschel, Edward Grefenstette, Karl Hermann, Tomáš Kočiský, and Phil Blunsom. 2015. Reasoning about entailment with neural attention.

Rossano Schifanella, Paloma Juan, Joel Tetreault, and Liangliang Cao. 2016. Detecting sarcasm in multimodal social platforms.

Leslie N. Smith. 2015. No more pesky learning rate guessing games. *CoRR*, abs/1506.01186.

Nitish Srivastava, Geoffrey E Hinton, et al. 2014. Dropout: a simple way to prevent neural networks from overfitting. *Journal of Machine Learning Research*.

Yu Sun, Shuohuan Wang, Yu-Kun Li, Shikun Feng, Xuyi Chen, Han Zhang, Xin Tian, Danxiang Zhu, Hao Tian, and Hua Wu. 2019. ERNIE: enhanced representation through knowledge integration. *CoRR*, abs/1904.09223.

Ashish Vaswani, Noam Shazeer, Niki Parmar, Jakob Uszkoreit, Llion Jones, Aidan N. Gomez, undefine-dukasz Kaiser, and Illia Polosukhin. 2017. Attention is all you need. In *Proceedings of the 31st International Conference on Neural Information Processing Systems*, NIPS'17, page 6000–6010, Red Hook, NY, USA. Curran Associates Inc.

Byron C. Wallace, Do Kook Choe, Laura Kertz, and Eugene Charniak. 2014. Humans require context to infer ironic intent (so computers probably do, too). In *Proceedings of the 52nd Annual Meeting of the Association for Computational Linguistics (Volume 2: Short Papers)*, pages 512–516, Baltimore, Maryland. Association for Computational Linguistics.

Thomas Wolf, Lysandre Debut, Victor Sanh, Julien Chaumond, Clement Delangue, Anthony Moi, Pierric Cistac, Tim Rault, Rémi Louf, Morgan Funtowicz, and Jamie Brew. 2019. Huggingface's transformers: State-of-the-art natural language processing.

Yuan Yao, Lorenzo Rosasco, and Andrea Caponnetto. 2007. On early stopping in gradient descent learning. *Constructive Approximation*, 26:289–315.

Context-Aware Sarcasm Detection Using BERT

Arup Baruah[1], Kaushik Amar Das[1], Ferdous Ahmed Barbhuiya[1], and Kuntal Dey[2]
[1]IIIT Guwahati, India
[2]IBM Research, New Delhi, India
arup.baruah@gmail.com, kaushikamardas@gmail.com,
ferdous@iiitg.ac.in, kuntadey@in.ibm.com

Abstract

In this paper, we present the results obtained by BERT, BiLSTM and SVM classifiers on the shared task on *Sarcasm Detection* held as part of *The Second Workshop on Figurative Language Processing*. The shared task required the use of conversational context to detect sarcasm. We experimented by varying the amount of context used along with the response (*response* is the text to be classified). The amount of context used includes (i) zero context, (ii) last one, two or three utterances, and (iii) all utterances. It was found that including the last utterance in the dialogue along with the response improved the performance of the classifier for the Twitter data set. On the other hand, the best performance for the Reddit data set was obtained when using only the response without any contextual information. The BERT classifier obtained F-score of 0.743 and 0.658 for the Twitter and Reddit data set respectively.

1 Introduction

Figurative language refers to texts where the intended meaning does not coincide with the literal meanings of the words and sentences that are used (Glucksberg, 2001). An example of such a sentence is *"The economic impact of Covid-19 that we have seen so far is just the tip of the iceberg"*. The *principle of compositionality* which states the meaning of a sentence can be obtained by combining the meaning of the constituent words do not apply in such sentences. Some of the types of figurative language are metaphor, idioms, similie, personification, hyperbole, understatement, analogy, irony, and sarcasm.

The Second Workshop on Figurative Language Processing, co-located with ACL 2020, had two shared tasks: *Methaphor Detection* and *Sarcasm Detection*. The shared task on sarcasm detection is

a binary classification task where it is required to determine if the final response given in a conversation dialogue is sarcastic or not. So, the task was sarcasm detection given the context in which the response was made. To capture the context the full dialogue thread was provided. The task was held for two different data sets: the Twitter dataset and the Reddit dataset.

In this paper, we describe the work we performed for context aware sarcasm detection for both the data sets. We used the Bidirectional Encoder Representations from Transformers (BERT), Bidirectional Long Short-Term Memory (BiLSTM) and Support Vector Machine (SVM) classifiers in our study. The rest of this paper is structured as follows: section 2 discusses the related work that has been performed on automatic sarcasm detection, section 3 describes the data set used in this shared task, section 4 discusses the approach we used in our study, and section 6 discusses the results we obtained.

2 Related Work

Joshi et al. (2017) provides a comprehensive survey of the work performed in the field of automatic sarcasm detection. As mentioned in this survey, the use of context information beyond the target text is one of the three milestones in the research related to automatic sarcasm detection. Three types of context has been mentioned in this study: author-specific context, conversational context, and topical context. Our work in this shared task makes use of the conversational context to assist classification.

Ghosh et al. (2017) found that modeling both conversational context and response improves the F1 score for sarcasm detection by 6 to 11% compared to modeling only the response. Conditional LSTM classifiers and LSTM classifiers with attention were used in this study. Hazarika et al. (2018)

Proceedings of the Second Workshop on Figurative Language Processing, pages 83–87
July 9, 2020. ©2020 Association for Computational Linguistics
https://doi.org/10.18653/v1/P17

Type	Total	POS	NEG	Max Utterances	Min Utterances	Max Length	Min Length
Train	5000	2500	2500	20	2	1213	27
Test	1800	-	-	18	2	786	24

Table 1: Twitter Dataset Statistics

Type	Total	POS	NEG	Max Utterances	Min Utterances	Max Length	Min Length
Train	4400	2200	2200	8	2	422	12
Test	1800	-	-	13	2	646	19

Table 2: Reddit Dataset Statistics

combined both content and contextual information to detect sarcasm. The contextual information captured user traits and topical information of the discussion forum. The contextual information used in Bamman and Smith (2015) consisted of author information, audience information, and the tweet against which the response is made. The contextual information was combined with content information to make the final classification. It was found that combining all the four types of features yielded the best accuracy while using only the content features resulted in the worst accuracy.

Ilic et al. (2018) used an ELMo based BiLSTM classifier to detect sarcasm and obtained superior performance on 6 out of the 7 datasets used in the study.

3 Data Set

The shared task on sarcasm detection required detecting sarcasm for two different data sets: the Twitter Dataset and the Reddit Dataset. Tables 1 and 2 show the statistics of the two data sets. As can be seen from the tables, both the train data sets are balanced with 50% of the instances labelled as *sarcasm* and 50% labelled as *not sarcasm*. The tables also list the minimum and maximum number of utterances included from the conversational dialogue apart from the response. As can be seen, the Twitter train set included from 2 to 20 utterances, the Twitter test set included from 2 to 18 utterances, the Reddit train set included from 2 to 8 utterances, and the Reddit test set included from 2 to 13 utterances. It was observed that for 48%, 52%, and 63% of the total instances in the Twitter train, Twitter test, and Reddit train data set only two utterances were present in the dialogue. In the case of the Reddit test data set, 24% of the instances had only

two utterances. The rest of the instances had more than two utterances in the dialogue.

The two tables also show the minimum and the maximum length (in terms of number of tokens) of the string obtained by concatenating the response and all the utterances in the conversational dialogue. This length varied from 27 to 1213 for Twitter train data set, from 24 to 786 for Twitter test data set, from 12 to 422 for Reddit data set, and from 19 to 646 for Reddit data set. Although the maximum length is high, it was seen that 73% and 75% of the instances in the Twitter train and test had length less than 150, and 99% and 75% of the instances in Reddit train and test data set had length less than 100 respectively.

4 Methodology

This section discusses the details required for reproducing the results. It mentions the preprocessing steps, the architecture of the classifiers used, and hyperparameter values.

4.1 Preprocessing

The preprocessing performed includes the removal of the *USER* and *URL* tokens from the response and utterances in the dialogue. The text was also converted to lower-case.

4.2 Classifiers

In our study, we used BiLSTM, BERT, and SVM classifiers.

4.2.1 BiLSTM

The BiLSTM classifier (Hochreiter and Schmidhuber, 1997) we used had a single BiLSTM layer of 100 units. The output from the BiLSTM layer is fed to a fully connected layer of 100 units through a max pooling layer. After applying dropout on

the output from the fully connected layer, it was
fed to an output layer having a single unit. The
hyperparameter values used for the classifier are
listed in table 3.

Parameter	Value
Number of LSTM units	100
LSTM dropout	0.25
Recurrent dropout	0.10
Units in 1st Dense layer	100
Activation Function for 1st Dense layer	ReLU
Rate for dropout layer	0.25
Units in 2nd Dense layer	1
Activation Function for 2nd Dense layer	sigmoid
Optimizer	Adam
Learning Rate	2e-5
Loss Function	Binary cross-entropy

Table 3: Hyperparameters for the BiLSTM model

For the BiLSTM classifier, the text was represented using the pre-trained fastText embeddings. The 300-dimensional fastText embeddings
[1] trained on Wikipedia 2017, UMBC webbase corpus and statmt.org news dataset were used in our
study.

4.2.2 BERT

BERT (Devlin et al., 2019) is a transformer based
architecture (Vaswani et al., 2017). It is a bidirectional model. As opposed to static embeddings that are produced by fastText, BERT produces contextualized word embeddings where the
vector for the word is computed based on the context in which it appears.

In our study, we used the uncased large version
of BERT [2]. This version has 24 layers and 16 attention heads. This model generates 1024 dimensional
vector for each word. We used 1024 dimensional
vector of the Extract layer as the representation
of the text. Our classification layer consisted of
a single Dense layer. This layer used the *sigmoid*
activation layer. The classifier was trained using
the *Adam* optimizer with a learning rate of 2e-5.
The *binary crossentropy* loss function was used.

4.2.3 SVM

The Support Vector Machine (SVM) classifier we
used in our study was trained using the TF-IDF
features of character n-grams (1 to 6). The *linear*
kernel was used for the classifier and hyperparameter C was set to 1.0.

5 Experiments

In our experiments, we concatenated the response
with a varied number of utterances from the dialogue. It this way we varied the amount of context
that was used to detect sarcasm. While concatenating, the utterances were concatenated in the reverse
order so that the last utterances appeared at the start
of the string. The individual utterances were separated from each other using a special token. We
performed the following types of experiments:

1. Used only the response without any context

2. Used the response along with the last utterance from the dialogue

3. Used the response along with the last two utterance from the dialogue

4. Used the response along with the last three
   utterance from the dialogue

5. Used the response along with all the utterances from the dialogue

6 Results and Discussion

Tables 4 and 5 shows the results that our classifiers
obtained on the test data sets. The scores mentioned
in the tables were obtained from the submission
page of the shared task in CodaLab [3].

We cross validated our models by retaining 20%
of the train set as our development set. This technique has a disadvantage that the model we submit
does not see 20% of the instances from the train set.
So, the other form of cross validation we performed
is the 5-Fold cross validation. The development set
results were used to filter out some of the models
and hyperparameter values (as we did not use grid
search). The implementation details of our models
and the hyperparameter values used are discussed
in section 4.

As can be seen from table 4, the best F-score of
0.743 was obtained by the BERT classifier for the

---

[1] https://fasttext.cc/docs/en/english-vectors.html
[2] https://github.com/google-research/bert

[3] https://competitions.codalab.org/competitions/22247

Classifier	Validation Technique	Amount of conversational context used	Max Seq Length	Precision	Recall	F1
BERT	5-fold CV	Only Response	70	0.741	0.741	0.741
BERT	5-fold CV	Response+Last Utterance	140	**0.744**	**0.748**	**0.743**
BERT	5-fold CV	Response+Last 2 Utterances	180	0.500	0.500	0.500
BERT	5-fold CV	Response+Last 3 Utterances	260	0.500	0.250	0.334
BERT	5-fold CV	Response+All Utterances	300	0.734	0.735	0.734
BERT	20% holdout	Response+All Utterances	300	0.724	0.725	0.724
BiLSTM	20% holdout	Response+All Utterances	300	0.673	0.674	0.672
BiLSTM	20% holdout	Response+All Utterances	1213	0.671	0.674	0.669
SVM	20% holdout	Response+All Utterances	1213	0.676	0.676	0.676
Baseline	-	-	-	-	-	0.670

Table 4: Results on Twitter test Dataset

Classifier	Validation Technique	Amount of conversational context used	Max Seq Length	Precision	Recall	F1
BERT	5-fold CV	Only Response	70	**0.658**	**0.658**	**0.658**
BERT	5-fold CV	Response+Last Utterance	120	0.635	0.636	0.635
BERT	5-fold CV	Response+Last 2 Utterances	180	0.491	0.490	0.478
BERT	5-fold CV	Response+Last 3 Utterances	260	0.500	0.250	0.334
BERT	5-fold CV	Response+All Utterances	150	0.595	0.605	0.585
BERT	20% holdout	Response+All Utterances	150	0.587	0.591	0.583
Baseline	-	-	-	-	-	0.600

Table 5: Results on Reddit test Dataset

Twitter data set when only the response and the last utterance in the conversational dialogue was used. The maximum sequence length of 140 was used for this run. This result, however, is close to the F-score of 0.741 obtained using only the response (without any conversational context). On including the last two and the last three utterances from the dialogue, the performance of the BERT classifier degraded considerably with F-score of 0.500 and 0.334 respectively. The reason for this could be that the sequence length was increased for these runs to accommodate the extra contextual information. However, the majority of the instances were of shorter length. Thus, the zero-padding performed on the shorter instances might have degraded the performance. However, it was also found that the performance of the classifier improved considerably (compared to including last two and last three utterances as mentioned above) to an F-score of 0.734 when all the utterances in the context were used and the maximum sequence length was set to 300.

The BiLSTM and SVM classifier obtained F-scores of 0.672 and 0.676 respectively on the Twitter data set. All the utterances were used for these runs.

As can be seen from table 5, the best F-score of 0.658 was obtained for the Reddit data set when only the response was used without any utterance from the dialogue. The maximum sequence length was set to 70 for this run. On using the last utterance along with the response, an F-score of 0.635 was obtained. Just like it happened for the Twitter data set, the performance of the classifier degraded to F-score of 0.478 and 0.334 when the last two and the last three utterances were used respectively. On using all the utterances with a maximum sequence length of 150, the performance again improved to 0.585.

Overall, our best performing runs performed better than the base line scores that were obtained using a BiLSTM with attention based classifier (Ghosh et al., 2018). The classifiers obtained the ranks 14/36 and 21/37 in the leaderboard. However, as our best performing runs were submitted beyond the last date of the competition they have been removed from the leaderboard.

7 Conclusion

In our work, we found that including context in the form of the last utterance in a dialogue chain slightly improved the performance of the BERT classifier for the Twitter data set compared to just using the response alone. For the Reddit data set, including the context did not improve the performance. The best performance for the Reddit data set was obtained when using only the response. Approaches other that only concatenating the utterances to make use of the context needs to be investigated as future work.

References

David Bamman and Noah A. Smith. 2015. Contextualized sarcasm detection on twitter. In *Proceedings of the Ninth International Conference on Web and Social Media, ICWSM 2015, University of Oxford, Oxford, UK, May 26-29, 2015*, pages 574–577. AAAI Press.

Jacob Devlin, Ming-Wei Chang, Kenton Lee, and Kristina Toutanova. 2019. BERT: Pre-training of deep bidirectional transformers for language understanding. In *Proceedings of the 2019 Conference of the North American Chapter of the Association for Computational Linguistics*, pages 4171–4186, Minneapolis, Minnesota. Association for Computational Linguistics.

Debanjan Ghosh, Alexander R Fabbri, and Smaranda Muresan. 2018. Sarcasm analysis using conversation context. *Computational Linguistics*, 44(4):755–792.

Debanjan Ghosh, Alexander Richard Fabbri, and Smaranda Muresan. 2017. The role of conversation context for sarcasm detection in online interactions. In *Proceedings of the 18th Annual SIGdial Meeting on Discourse and Dialogue, Saarbrücken, Germany, August 15-17, 2017*, pages 186–196. Association for Computational Linguistics.

Sam Glucksberg. 2001. *Understanding Figurative Language: From Metaphor to Idioms*. Oxford University Press, New York.

Devamanyu Hazarika, Soujanya Poria, Sruthi Gorantla, Erik Cambria, Roger Zimmermann, and Rada Mihalcea. 2018. CASCADE: contextual sarcasm detection in online discussion forums. In *Proceedings of the 27th International Conference on Computational Linguistics, COLING 2018, Santa Fe, New Mexico, USA, August 20-26, 2018*, pages 1837–1848. Association for Computational Linguistics.

Sepp Hochreiter and Jürgen Schmidhuber. 1997. Long short-term memory. *Neural computation*, 9(8):1735–1780.

Suzana Ilic, Edison Marrese-Taylor, Jorge A. Balazs, and Yutaka Matsuo. 2018. Deep contextualized word representations for detecting sarcasm and irony. In *Proceedings of the 9th Workshop on Computational Approaches to Subjectivity, Sentiment and Social Media Analysis, WASSA@EMNLP 2018, Brussels, Belgium, October 31, 2018*, pages 2–7. Association for Computational Linguistics.

Aditya Joshi, Pushpak Bhattacharyya, and Mark James Carman. 2017. Automatic sarcasm detection: A survey. *ACM Comput. Surv.*, 50(5):73:1–73:22.

Ashish Vaswani, Noam Shazeer, Niki Parmar, Jakob Uszkoreit, Llion Jones, Aidan. N. Gomez, Lukasz Kaiser, and Illia Polosukhin. 2017. Attention is All you Need. In *Advances in Neural Information Processing Systems 30*, pages 5998–6008. Curran Associates, Inc.

Transformers on Sarcasm Detection with Context

Amardeep Kumar
Indian Institute of Technology
(ISM), Dhanbad
adkr6398@gmail.com

Vivek Anand
IIIT Hyderabad, India
vivek.a@research.iiit.ac.in

Abstract

Sarcasm Detection with Context, a shared task of Second Workshop on Figurative Language Processing (co-located with ACL 2020), is study of effect of context on Sarcasm detection in conversations of Social media. We present different techniques and models, mostly based on transformer for Sarcasm Detection with Context. We extended latest pre-trained transformers like BERT, RoBERTa, spanBERT on different task objectives like single sentence classification, sentence pair classification, etc. to understand role of conversation context for sarcasm detection on Twitter conversations and conversation threads from Reddit. We also present our own architecture consisting of LSTM and Transformers to achieve the objective.

1 Introduction

With advent of Internet and Social media platforms, it is important to know actual sentiments and beliefs of its users, and recognizing Sarcasm is very important for this. We can't always decide if a sentence is sarcastic or not without knowing its context. For example, consider below two sentences S1 and S2.

> S1: "What you love on weekends?"

> S2: "I love going to the doctor."

Just by looking at the 'S2' sentence we can tag the sentence 'S2' as *not sarcastic*", but imagine this sentence as a reply to the sentence 'S1' , now we would like to tag the sentence 'S2' as *"sarcastic"*. Hence it is necessary to know the context of a sentence to know sarcasm.

We were provided with conversation threads from two of popular social media, Reddit and Twitter. For this objective We used different pre-trained language model and famous transformer architecture like BERT (Devlin et al., 2019), RoBERTa (Liu et al., 2019) and spanBERT (Joshi et al., 2020). We

also propose our own architecture made of Transformers (Vaswani et al., 2017) and LSTM (Hochreiter and Schmidhuber, 1997).

2 Datasets

Two types of Datasets were used, corpus from Twitter conversations and conversation threads from Reddit.

Twitter Corpus Ghosh et al. (2018) introduced a self label twitter conversations corpus. The sarcastic tweets were collected by relying upon hashtags, like sarcasm, sarcastic, etc., that users assign to their sarcastic tweets. For non-sarcastic they adopted a methodology, according to which Nonsarcastic tweet doesn't contain sarcasm hashtag instead they were having sentiments hashtag like happy, positive, sad, etc.

Reddit Corpus Khodak et al. (2018) collected 1.5 million sarcastic statement and many of nonsarcastic statement from Reddit. They self annotated all of these Reddit corpus manually.

For both datasets, the training and testing data was provided in json format where each utterance contains the following fields: 1) "label" : SARCASM or NOT_SARCASM. For test data, label was not provided. 2) "response" : the sarcastic response, whether a sarcastic Tweet or a Reddit post. 3) "context" : the conversation context of the "response". 4) "id" : unique id to identify and label each data point in test dataset.

Twitter data set is of 5,000 English Tweets balanced between the "SARCASM" and "NOT_SARCASM" classes and Reddit dataset is of 4,400 Reddit posts balanced between the "SARCASM" and "NOT_SARCASM" classes.

3 Pre-Process

We used different text pre-processing technique to remove noise from text provided to us. We removed unwanted punctuation, multiple spaces, URL tags, etc. We changed different abbreviations to their

88

Proceedings of the Second Workshop on Figurative Language Processing, pages 88–92
July 9, 2020. ©2020 Association for Computational Linguistics
https://doi.org/10.18653/v1/P17

proper format, for example: "I'm" was changed to "I am", "idk" to "I don't know", etc.

4 Experiments

We experimented with different transformers and pretrained models like BERT , RoBERTa, spanBERT and our own architecture built over these Transformers.

For both datasets, each training and testing utterance contains two major fields: "response" (i.e, the sarcastic response, whether a sarcastic Tweet or a Reddit post), "context" (i.e., the conversation context of the "response"). The "context" is an ordered list of dialogue, i.e., if the "context" contains three elements, "c1", "c2", "c3", in that order, then "c2" is a reply to "c1" and "c3" is a reply to "c2". Further, if the sarcastic "response" is "r", then "r" is a reply to "c3". For instance, for the following example, "label": "SARCASM", "response": "Did Kelly just call someone else messy? Baaaahaaahahahaha", "context": ["X is looking a First Lady should", "didn't think it was tailored enough it looked messy"]. The response tweet, "Did Kelly..." is a reply to its immediate context "didn't think it was tailored..." which is a reply to "X is looking...".

For each utterance in datasets, We defined 'response' as response_string and concatenation of all the 'context' in reverse order as context_string.

response_string = "response"

context_string = "c3" + "c2" + "c1"

We approached this classification task in two ways, first as Single sentence classification task and second as Sentence pair classification tasks. We also experimented single sentence classification only with response_string. Throughout the experiment we used 'transformers' library by Hugging Face (Wolf et al., 2019) for experimenting with BERT and RoBERTa models and for spanBERT we used their official released code, and incorporated new methods to suit our task.

4.1 Single sentence Classification Task

As name indicates, to obtain a single sentence for classification, we concatenated response_string and context_string.

Figure 1 represents general architecture of models used in subsection 4.1.1, 4.1.2 and 4.1.3, for single sentence classification where:

- Input : response_string + context_string

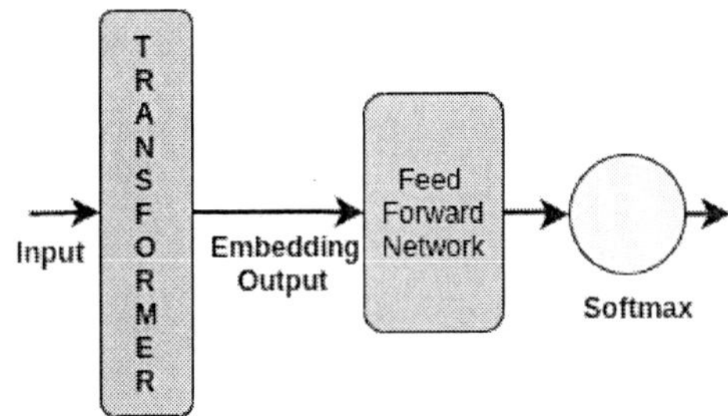

Figure 1: Transformer model for single sentence classification

- Transformer: layer could be any of the model from BERT, RoBERTa or spanBERT as transformer.

- Embedding output: is representation of "[CLS]" token by transformer, used for classification task.

- Feed Forward Network : has multiple dense and dropout layer.

- Softmax: classifier for binary classification.

4.1.1 BERT

Devlin et al. (2019) introduced Bidirectional Encoder Representations from Transformers(BERT). BERT's key technical innovation is applying bidirectional training of Transformers to language modeling. BERT is pre-trained on two objectives, Masked language modeling (MLM) and next sentence prediction (NSP).

We used 'bert-base-uncased' and 'bert-large-uncased' pretrained model in transformer layer. 'bert-base-uncased' has 12-layers, 768-hidden state size, 12-attention heads and 110M parameters, with each hidden state of (max_seq_len, 768) size and embedding output of 768 length. 'bert-large-uncased' has 24-layers, 1024-hidden state size, 16-attention heads and 340M parameters. it has each hidden state of (max_seq_len, 1024) size and embedding output of 1024 length. 'bert-large-uncased' gave better results than 'bert-base-uncased' on both datasets.

4.1.2 SpanBERT

Joshi et al. (2020) introduced pretraining method to represent and predict span instead of words. This approach is different from BERT based pretraining methods in two ways:

1. Masking contiguous random spans instead of masking random tokens.

2. Span Boundary Objective: Predicting entire content of masked span with help of hidden states of boundary token of masked span.

We used 'spanbert-base-cased' and 'spanbert-large-cased' pretrained model as transformer layer. 'spanbert-base-cased' has 12-layers, 768-hidden state size, 12-attention heads and 110M parameters, with each hidden state of (max_seq_len, 768) size and embedding output of 768 length. 'spanbert-large-cased' has 24-layers, 1024-hidden state size, 16-attention heads and 340M parameters. It has each hidden state of (max_seq_len, 1024) size and embedding output of 1024 length. 'spanbert-large-cased' gave better results than 'spanbert-base-cased', 'bert-base-uncased' and 'bert-large-uncased' respectively on both datasets .

4.1.3 RoBERTa

Liu et al. (2019) presented a replication study of BERT pre-training, related to impact of key hyper-parameter and size of training data on which it was pre-trained, and found BERT as significantly untrained.

We tried only roberta large models, which has 24-layers, 1024-hidden state size, 24-attention heads and 355M parameters. it has each hidden state of (max_seq_len, 1024) size and embedding output of 1024 length. 'roberta-large' gave better results than all previous models.

4.1.4 LSTM over Transformer

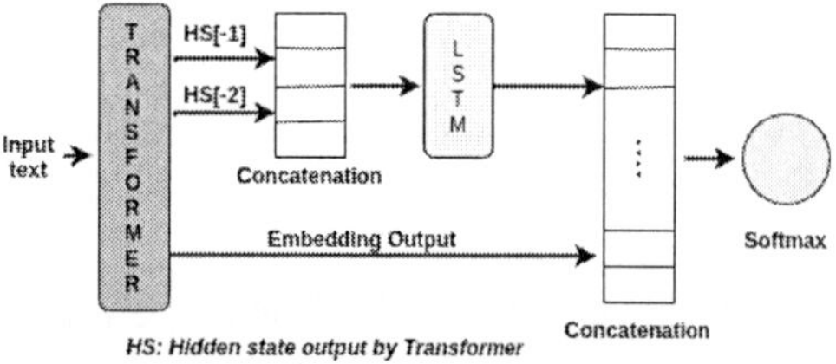

Figure 2: Architecture of model 4.1.4

To improvise, We modified previously used model architecture. Figure 2 represents architecture of our successful improvised model, where:

- HS[-1], HS[-2]: represent last hidden state and second last hidden state output by transformer respectively.

- Concatenation: layer concatenate two or more tensors along suitable axis.

- LSTM: Hochreiter and Schmidhuber (1997)

In this model, last two hidden states are concatenated and passed through LSTM to get more contextual representation of text. Later output of LSTM and embedding output of transformer is concatenated and fed through feed forward Neural network for classification.

We tried 'bert-large-uncased' and 'Roberta large' as transformer layer in this architecture. 'Roberta large' gave best f1-score among all. This model also gave best result on classification using only 'response_string' as input on both datsets.

4.2 Sentence pair Classification task

In this Sentence Pair classification task, we give a pair of text as input for binary classification. We present following two models:

4.2.1 Siamese Transformer

Our architecture was inspired from two things, first is intuition that it may be a case that only 'response' is Sarcastic but not concatenation of 'response' and 'context', and second, Siamese network (Mueller and Thyagarajan, 2016).

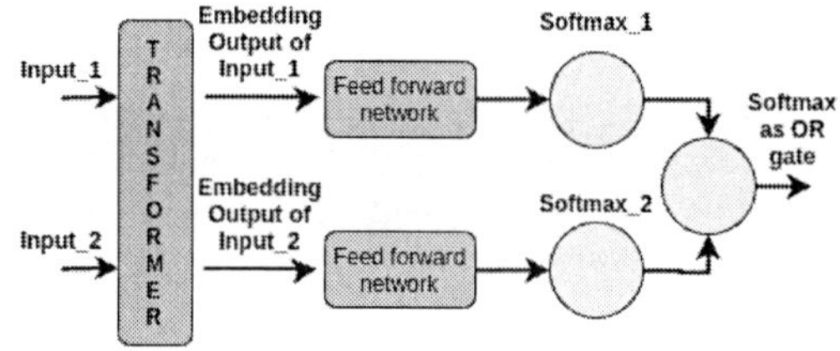

Figure 3: Architecture of Proposed Siamese Transformer

Figure 3 represents our Siamese Transformer, where: 'input_1' is response_string, 'input_2' is response_string + context_string, 'Softmax' is last softmax layer intuitively work as 'OR' logical gate.

We expected improvement in result over previous models, but it didn't happen. This also establishes that context is necessary for Sarcasm Detection.

4.2.2 Dual Transformer

Length of context_string is larger than response_string so it might be that their combined contextual representation is dominated by 'context_string'. To overcome this, we pass them through different transformers to get their individual representation of equal size. These representation are then concatenated and passed through Bi-LSTM to get contextual representation of the

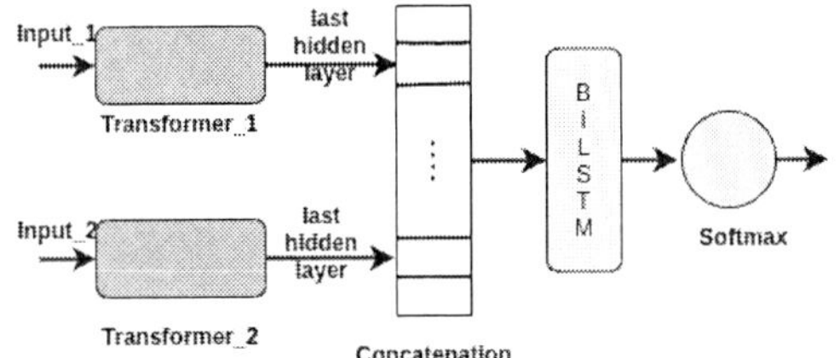

Figure 4: Architecture of Dual Transformer model

combination. Figure 4 represents our architecture of Dual transformer, where: 'input_1' is response_string, 'input_2' is context_string, 'BiLSTM' is bidirectional LSTM (Schuster and Paliwal, 1997)

Last hidden state output of both transformers are concatenated and passed over Bi-LSTM to get a better contextual, output of which is passed through a classification layer. This model didn't give better results as expected. We guessed lack of training data as one of the possible reason.

5   Results

Model	P	R	f1
response only$_{SS}$	68.7	71.8	67.50
bert-base$_{SS}$	74.7	74.8	74.62
bert-large$_{SS}$	75.1	75.1	75.03
roberta-large$_{SS}$	76.1	76.1	76.05
spanbert-base$_{SS}$	74.9	75.2	74.89
spanbert-large$_{SS}$	75.7	75.9	75.68
bert-large$_{LoT}$	76.5	76.7	76.44
roberta-large$_{LoT}$	77.3	77.4	**77.22**
roberta-large$_{ST}$	75.5	75.5	75.49
roberta-large$_{DT}$	75.9	76.2	75.88

Table 1: Result on Twitter

Model	P	R	f1
response only$_{SS}$	64.2	64.7	63.83
bert-base$_{SS}$	66.5	66.6	66.47
bert-large$_{SS}$	67.3	67.3	67.27
roberta-large$_{SS}$	67.5	67.5	67.49
spanbert-base$_{SS}$	66.9	67.3	66.75
spanbert-large$_{SS}$	67.4	67.4	67.36
bert-large$_{LoT}$	68.1	68.1	68.0
roberta-large$_{LoT}$	69.3	69.9	**69.11**
roberta-large$_{ST}$	67.9	68.1	67.86
roberta-large$_{DT}$	68.1	68.1	68.1

Table 2: Result on Reddit

Table 1 and Table 2 depict results of all models and tasks on Twitter and Reddit datasets respectively. In both table 'SS' denotes single sentence classification task, 'LoT' denotes LSTM over Transformer(4.1.4), 'DT' denotes Dual Transformer(4.2.2) and 'ST' denotes Siamese Transformer (4.2.1).

Using only 'response_string' (i.e without using context) we got best f1-score of 67.50 and 63.2 on Twitter and Reddit datsets respectively. Using response as well as context, LSTM over Transformer model (sub-section 4.1.4) with 'robert-large' as transformer layer performed best. We tried different maximum sequence legth, 126 on Twitter conversation and 80 on Reddit Conversation text gave the best results. We didn't benchmark our results with Ghosh et al. (2018), Zhang et al. (2016), etc. related works, becuase those models were trained on different datasets. To do a fair comparison, we would have to re-train those models on our dataset, but due to computational constraints we were unable to do this.

6   Related Work

Most of the existing works are on detecting sarcasm without considering context. Joshi et al. (2016) , Zhang et al. (2016) , Ghosh et al. (2018) have considered context and utterances separately for sarcasm detection and showed how context is helpful in sarcasm detection.

7   Conclusion

To conclude, we showed effective method for sarcasm detection and how much context is necessary for it. We didn't use any dataset (reddit and twitter) specific pre-processing or hyperparameter tuning in order to evaluate effectiveness of models across various types of data. In future, we would like to experiment with supplementing external data or merging different types of data on this task.

References

Jacob Devlin, Ming-Wei Chang, Kenton Lee, and Kristina Toutanova. 2019. BERT: Pre-training of deep bidirectional transformers for language understanding. In *Proceedings of the 2019 Conference of the North American Chapter of the Association for Computational Linguistics: Human Language Technologies, Volume 1 (Long and Short Papers)*, pages 4171–4186, Minneapolis, Minnesota. Association for Computational Linguistics.

Debanjan Ghosh, Alexander R. Fabbri, and Smaranda Muresan. 2018. Sarcasm analysis using conversation context. *Computational Linguistics*, 44(4):755–792.

Sepp Hochreiter and Jürgen Schmidhuber. 1997. Long short-term memory. *Neural Computation*, 9(8):1735–1780.

Aditya Joshi, Vaibhav Tripathi, Pushpak Bhattacharyya, and Mark J. Carman. 2016. Harnessing sequence labeling for sarcasm detection in dialogue from TV series 'Friends'. In *Proceedings of The 20th SIGNLL Conference on Computational Natural Language Learning*, pages 146–155, Berlin, Germany. Association for Computational Linguistics.

Mandar Joshi, Danqi Chen, Yinhan Liu, Daniel S. Weld, Luke Zettlemoyer, and Omer Levy. 2020. Spanbert: Improving pre-training by representing and predicting spans. *Transactions of the Association for Computational Linguistics*, 8:64–77.

Mikhail Khodak, Nikunj Saunshi, and Kiran Vodrahalli. 2018. A large self-annotated corpus for sarcasm. In *Proceedings of the Eleventh International Conference on Language Resources and Evaluation (LREC-2018)*, Miyazaki, Japan. European Languages Resources Association (ELRA).

Yinhan Liu, Myle Ott, Naman Goyal, Jingfei Du, Mandar Joshi, Danqi Chen, Omer Levy, Mike Lewis, Luke Zettlemoyer, and Veselin Stoyanov. 2019. Roberta: A robustly optimized BERT pretraining approach. *CoRR*, abs/1907.11692.

Jonas Mueller and Aditya Thyagarajan. 2016. Siamese recurrent architectures for learning sentence similarity. In *thirtieth AAAI conference on artificial intelligence*.

Mike Schuster and Kuldip K Paliwal. 1997. Bidirectional recurrent neural networks. *IEEE transactions on Signal Processing*, 45(11):2673–2681.

Ashish Vaswani, Noam Shazeer, Niki Parmar, Jakob Uszkoreit, Llion Jones, Aidan N Gomez, Ł ukasz Kaiser, and Illia Polosukhin. 2017. Attention is all you need. In I. Guyon, U. V. Luxburg, S. Bengio, H. Wallach, R. Fergus, S. Vishwanathan, and R. Garnett, editors, *Advances in Neural Information Processing Systems 30*, pages 5998–6008. Curran Associates, Inc.

Thomas Wolf, Lysandre Debut, Victor Sanh, Julien Chaumond, Clement Delangue, Anthony Moi, Pierric Cistac, Tim Rault, R'emi Louf, Morgan Funtowicz, and Jamie Brew. 2019. Huggingface's transformers: State-of-the-art natural language processing. *ArXiv*, abs/1910.03771.

Meishan Zhang, Yue Zhang, and Guohong Fu. 2016. Tweet sarcasm detection using deep neural network. In *Proceedings of COLING 2016, the 26th International Conference on Computational Linguistics: Technical Papers*, pages 2449–2460, Osaka, Japan. The COLING 2016 Organizing Committee.

A Novel Hierarchical BERT Architecture for Sarcasm Detection

Himani Srivastava
TCS Research
New Delhi
India
srivastava.himani
@tcs.com

Vaibhav Varshney
TCS Research
New Delhi
India
varshney.v
@tcs.com

Surabhi Kumari
TCS Research
New Delhi
India
surabhi.kumari6
@tcs.com

Saurabh Srivastava
TCS Research
New Delhi
India
sriv.saurabh
@tcs.com

Abstract

Online discussion platforms are often flooded with opinions from users across the world on a variety of topics. Many such posts, comments, or utterances are often sarcastic in nature, i.e., the actual intent is hidden in the sentence and is different from its literal meaning, making the detection of such utterances challenging without additional context. In this paper, we propose a novel deep learning-based approach to detect whether an utterance is sarcastic or non-sarcastic by utilizing the given contexts in a hierarchical manner. We have used datasets from two online discussion platform - Twitter and Reddit[1] for our experiments. Experimental and error analysis shows that the hierarchical models can make full use of history to obtain a better representation of contexts and thus, in turn, can outperform their sequential counterparts.

1 Introduction

In the current scenario, social media serves as the biggest platform for people to express their opinion and share information. Many organizations use this data to understand the choices of people and amend their policies accordingly. On these platforms, people often express their opinion sarcastically which is inherently difficult even for humans to analyze. For example *"It is a wonderful feeling to carry an expensive phone with short battery life."* is a sarcastic sentence that complains about the battery life of the phone but with the positive set of words like "wonderful". Therefore it is essential to identify sarcastic responses to comprehend the users' demands and complaints.

However, detecting sarcasm from a text is a difficult task as such sentences have positive surface sentiment but negative implied sentiment. For example, in the sentence *"Yeah Right! I bought that nice expensive phone for this only!"*, the phrase "nice expensive" may imply positive sentiment from the user, but, the phrase "Yeah Right!" may render the whole sentence as a negative statement given enough background or context.

Sarcasm detection is not an independent area of study and is closely related to sentiment analysis. In order to detect sarcasm, many works like, (Veale and Hao, 2010), (Maynard and Greenwood, 2014) have proposed the use of hand-crafted features to identify a sarcastic response.

However, with the advent of Deep Learning, it became possible to automatically learn and extract these features, thereby reducing both time and effort. Many of these approaches have also been applied in complex NLP problems, for example, (Kim, 2014) proposed a Convolution Neural Network (CNN) to extract n-gram features automatically from the text. (Nowak et al., 2017) and (Cho et al., 2014) showed the efficacy of Recurrent Neural Networks (RNNs) like LSTMs (Hochreiter and Schmidhuber, 1997) and GRUs (Cho et al., 2014) in handling the long term dependencies. Attention mechanisms (Bahdanau et al., 2014) have further improved the performance of complex NLP tasks like machine translation and reading comprehension by attending or focusing on the important words/ phrases from the inputs before making a decision. Recently, transformers (Vaswani et al., 2017) have outperformed many traditional and recent approaches in NLP by allowing one to learn from the huge amount of data.

In this paper, we present a Hierarchical BERT (Devlin et al., 2018) based model for sarcasm detection for a given response and its context. Our model, first, extracts the local features from the words in a sentence, and then uses a Convolution module to summarize all the sentences in a context.

---

[1] Both the dataset are provided by the organizers of Shared Task of Sarcasm Detection in FigLang-2020

Proceedings of the Second Workshop on Figurative Language Processing, pages 93–97
July 9, 2020. ©2020 Association for Computational Linguistics
https://doi.org/10.18653/v1/P17

The summarized context is then passed through a recurrent layer to extract the temporal features from the input. These temporal features are then convoluted with the input response to detect whether the response is sarcastic or not.

2   Related Work

The task of sarcasm detection can be formulated as a binary classification task i.e. given a sentence, the task is to predict whether it is sarcastic or not. Another area of study involves labeling utterances in a dialogue as sarcastic or non-sarcastic using sequence labeling. These approaches usually fall into three different categories namely, Rule-based, Statistical, and deep learning-based.

Rule Based Approaches In (Veale and Hao, 2010), (Maynard and Greenwood, 2014), (Bharti et al., 2015) and (Riloff et al., 2013) authors proposed the use of hand-crafted features and rule-based approaches to perform classification. In order to learn a decision boundary, one has to model all the hand-crafted features beforehand, which is a big disadvantage with such approaches.

Statistical Approaches In statistical approaches, features like bag-of-words, pattern-based, user mentions, emoticons, N-grams have been proposed in (Tsur et al., 2010), (González-Ibáñez et al., 2011), (Liebrecht et al., 2013), (Reyes et al., 2013). (Barbieri et al., 2014) included several sets of features such as minimum/ maximum/ average number of synset and synonyms, minimum/ maximum gap of the intensity of adverb and adjectives in the target text to build first automated system targeted for detecting irony [2] in Italian Tweets.

Deep Learning-based Approaches The above mentioned approaches suffer from generalization since it is hard to manually extract and define all the rules and features to detect sarcasm, whereas, deep learning approaches can generalize well by automatically learning from data. (Joshi et al., 2016) used similarity between word embeddings of utterances for sarcasm detection. (Amir et al., 2016) applied convolution operation on user embedding and the utterance embedding for sarcasm detection. User embedding allowed them to learn user-specific context. and auxiliary features [3] to train the convNet. (Cai et al., 2019) used a multi-modal fusion model to detect sarcasm in a tweet that may contain an image or video along with the text. In (Potamias et al., 2019), authors proposed use of transformer for detecting sarcastic text.

3   Dataset

For Sarcasm Detection, we have used 2 datasets namely: (1) Twitter Dataset and (2) Reddit Dataset provided for the FIG-LANG shared task[4]. Both the datasets have a 'Context' provided in the form of a conversation between the users, and the final 'Response' that has to be classified as Sarcastic or Non Sarcastic response, using context. The Twitter and Reddit dataset contains 5000 and 4400 train instances respectively and 1800 test instances each. The train set was further divided into an 80:20 ratio in a stratified fashion to obtain our final dev (evaluation) and train sets.

4   Approach

In our proposed approach, we hypothesize that the context must have a significant role in deciding the sarcastic orientation of the response. Hence, in order to capture the temporal features from the context, we processed the contexts in a hierarchical manner. In this section, we describe all the components of our proposed architecture.

Sentence Encoding Layer: To obtain the initial representation of the input, we used 2 separate encoder layers for the context and its response. The utterances in a context are passed through the first BERT layer to extract sentence level features of a context. For instance, if our context contains 'm' different utterances then, the output of this layer would be $s_{con} \in R^{(m,d_{sen},d_{bert})}$ where, d_{sen} is the maximum sentence length and d_{bert} is the length of word vector obtained from BERT. In our experiments, we have used *all the context* provided in the input to obtain initial context representation.

Similarly, the second BERT layer is used to encode the response in a fixed length vector $s_{res} \in R^{d_{sen},d_{bert}}$. This representation is further passed through a BiLSTM layer to capture the semantic relationship between the words of a response. The final response output is denoted by $o_{res} \in R^{d_{sen},d_{lstm}}$ where, d_{lstm} is the number of BiLSTM units.

Context Summarization Layer: The size of initial context vector s_{con} after the sentence en-

---

[2]Sarcasm is a form of irony.

[3]In this paper 5 auxiliary features are taken which are: count of (!, ?, ., capital letters, "or") in a tweet

[4]The shared task on sarcasm detection conducted at the ACL 2020 workshop on Figurative Language Processing.

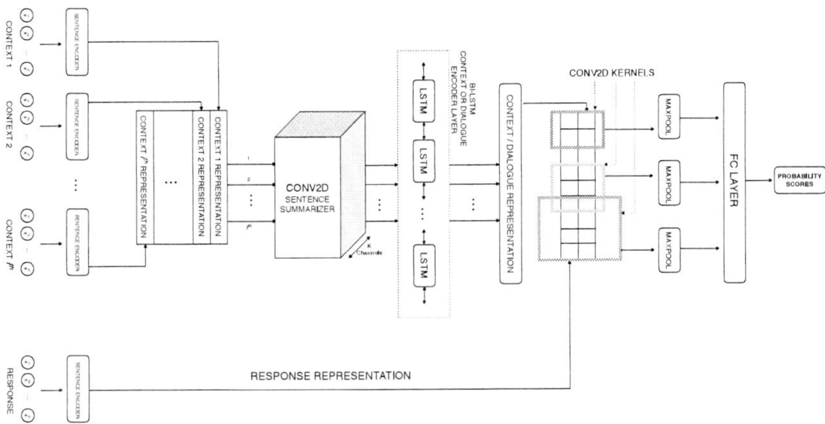

Figure 1: Proposed Architecture

coder layer becomes too large to process. For instance, if d_{bert} is 768, d_{sen} is 100 and m is 10 then our initial representation will be of size $10 \times 100 \times 768$. Thus, in order to obtain a summarized context, we projected the utterances to a lower dimension space using a convolution operation. To achieve this, we passed all the utterances through a 2D convolution layer with kernel size of (k_{row}, k_{col}) and a stride of 1. We obtain d_{sum} such feature maps to output our summary, $sum_{con} \in R^{(m-k_{row}, d_{sen}-k_{col}, d_{sum})}$.

Context Encoder Layer: Since the utterances are sequential in nature, i.e., one utterance is uttered in response to the previous one, it is essential to capture the contextual information between the utterances to obtain a better context representation. We have used BiLSTMs to output a sequence of hidden state vectors $[\mathbf{h^1}, \mathbf{h^2}, ..., \mathbf{h^M}]$ corresponding to each of the M input vectors, where M is $m - k_{row}$. The vector h^M can be seen as a short summary for whole the context just like a short summary of a paragraph or a book. The final output of this layer is $\mathbf{o_{con}} \in R^{(M, d_{lstm})}$

CNN Layer: In (Kim, 2014) author proposed a hybrid multi-channel CNN to capture the N-grams features in a text by varying the kernel size. As our final output $\mathbf{o}$, we again used a 2D convolution layer to extract relations between response $\mathbf{o_{res}}$ and context $\mathbf{o_{con}}$. To obtain different N-grams features as mentioned in (Kim, 2014), we used different shared matrices of sizes (2, 2), (2, 3), and (2, 5). Finally, we applied a Max-pool layer to extract the most relevant features from each of these N-gram features. Our final architecture is described in Figure 1.

Fully Connected Layer: The relevant N-grams from the last layer are then passed through a fully connected layer to obtain a score S, which is then passed through a sigmoid layer to compute the probability scores.

5 Experiments and Results

For our experiments, we compare proposed approach with two baselines defined next:

Baseline 1: Hierarchical Attention Network Proposed in (Yang et al., 2016), the authors applied attention mechanism to classify large documents. We used this model to visualize the attention given to a particular context and words in response while making a decision.

Baseline 2: Memory Networks This experiment is done based on the implementation of (Sukhbaatar et al., 2015). The intuition was to use (context, response) as a (key, value) pair, and given this information we predicted whether our value is sarcastic or not. Results have been shown in the table 1.

Experimental Settings All the parameters in our architecture were tuned on val set. We have used small version of BERT with $d_{bert} = 768$, the number of Bi-LSTMs, d_{lstm} were varied between the range 200, 300. Throughout our experiments on test and val sets, we found that the optimum value for (k_{row}, k_{col}) were (2,2) and were kept same throughout all other experiments. The maximum sentence length, d_{sen} was fixed to 100 and the dropout values were adjusted as described in (Srivastava et al., 2014). We used cross-entropy as the loss function and Adam as optimizer (with default values) for all the models. The F1 scores were used as an evaluation metric for validation set.

All these parameters were tuned on val F1 scores to determine the final optimal values.

6   Results and Analysis

We have reported the results of all the experiments table 1. As shown in table, our architecture outperformed all the other strong baselines in both the datasets. To further analyse the strengths of our network we further performed some experiments by visualizing the attention weights given to contexts and words in response.

As evidenced from Figure 2, we can see that the model correctly predicts the inputs in row 1 and 4. In row 1, the maximum attention is given to Utterance 2, while in the response, a strong negative phrase like "biggest bullies" were given maximum attention to classify the response as sarcastic. Also, we can see that the irrelevant words like "@USER" were given the least attention (shades of green determine the positive while, the shades of red determine the negative attention weights). Similarly in row 4, we can see that the context and response are consists of positive sentiment words and emoticons which helped the model to classify the input as non-sarcastic.

In row 2 and 3 there are examples of incorrect classification made by our model. Upon analysis, we found that the response contains the positive words used in negative sentiment thereby confusing the model. Similarly in row 3, the response contains the negative words/ phrases like "stop obsessing", "rude" but has positive sentiment. Such examples where, there is a very fine distinction between the sarcastic and non-sarcastic responses are likely to confuse our model.

We hypothesised that the false-positive produced by our models must be are of "boundary cases" which our model is not able to handle. To corroborate this fact, we plotted the embedding produced by our model before sigmoid layer using t-SNE (van der Maaten and Hinton, 2008). In Figure 3, green and blue points denotes correct non-sarcastic and sarcastic samples respectively while orange and red points denote the incorrect classifications. We can see that most of the miss-classifications form a cluster and can be seen as boundary examples. Also, to explain the difference between the val and test results we plotted the test samples on top of these points (denoted by cross markers). We can see in Figure 3, that the test samples fall on these boundary cases which might be the reason

for such discrepancy.

Dataset		HAN	KG-Mem	Our Approach
Twitter	train	0.76	0.79	**0.87**
	dev	0.74	0.79	**0.84**
	test	0.68	0.70	**0.74**
Reddit	train	0.69	0.69	**0.77**
	dev	0.67	0.68	**0.76**
	test	0.60	0.605	**0.639**

Table 1: Comparison with baselines

Figure 2: Error Analysis

7   Conclusion and Future work

In this paper, we proposed a novel Hierarchical BERT based neural network architecture to handle context and response. From analysis and results, we supported the facts that the hierarchical model can effectively model the context and can produce a better representation of input before making a decision.

Applying BERT on large documents and in hierarchical setting is still an open problem and we would like to explore this aspect in depth in our future works. Further, we would like to obtain a better representation of context by compressing the BERT representation of context in a much more efficient way (the context summarization layer).

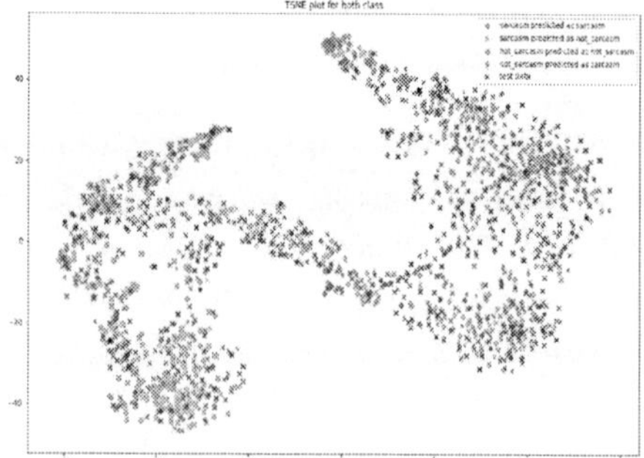

Figure 3: t-SNE plot for val and test data

References

Silvio Amir, Byron Wallace, Hao Lyu, Paula Carvalho, and Mário Silva. 2016. Modelling context with user embeddings for sarcasm detection in social media. pages 167–177.

Dzmitry Bahdanau, Kyunghyun Cho, and Y. Bengio. 2014. Neural machine translation by jointly learning to align and translate. *ArXiv*, 1409.

Francesco Barbieri, Francesco Ronzano, and Horacio Saggion. 2014. Italian irony detection in twitter: a first approach.

S. K. Bharti, K. S. Babu, and S. K. Jena. 2015. Parsing-based sarcasm sentiment recognition in twitter data. In *2015 IEEE/ACM International Conference on Advances in Social Networks Analysis and Mining (ASONAM)*, pages 1373–1380.

Yitao Cai, Huiyu Cai, and Xiaojun Wan. 2019. Multi-modal sarcasm detection in twitter with hierarchical fusion model. pages 2506–2515.

Kyunghyun Cho, Bart van Merrienboer, Çaglar Gülçehre, Fethi Bougares, Holger Schwenk, and Yoshua Bengio. 2014. Learning phrase representations using RNN encoder-decoder for statistical machine translation. *CoRR*, abs/1406.1078.

Jacob Devlin, Ming-Wei Chang, Kenton Lee, and Kristina Toutanova. 2018. BERT: pre-training of deep bidirectional transformers for language understanding. *CoRR*, abs/1810.04805.

Roberto González-Ibáñez, Smaranda Muresan, and Nina Wacholder. 2011. Identifying sarcasm in twitter: A closer look. In *Proceedings of the 49th Annual Meeting of the Association for Computational Linguistics: Human Language Technologies*, pages 581–586, Portland, Oregon, USA. Association for Computational Linguistics.

Sepp Hochreiter and Jürgen Schmidhuber. 1997. Long short-term memory. *Neural computation*, 9:1735–80.

Aditya Joshi, Kevin Patel, Vaibhav Tripathi, Pushpak Bhattacharyya, and Mark Carman. 2016. Are word embedding-based features useful for sarcasm detection?

Yoon Kim. 2014. Convolutional neural networks for sentence classification. In *Proceedings of the 2014 Conference on Empirical Methods in Natural Language Processing (EMNLP)*, pages 1746–1751, Doha, Qatar. Association for Computational Linguistics.

Christine Liebrecht, Florian Kunneman, and Antal van den Bosch. 2013. The perfect solution for detecting sarcasm in tweets #not. In *Proceedings of the 4th Workshop on Computational Approaches to Subjectivity, Sentiment and Social Media Analysis*, pages 29–37, Atlanta, Georgia. Association for Computational Linguistics.

Laurens van der Maaten and Geoffrey Hinton. 2008. Visualizing data using t-SNE. *Journal of Machine Learning Research*, 9:2579–2605.

Diana Maynard and Mark Greenwood. 2014. Who cares about sarcastic tweets? investigating the impact of sarcasm on sentiment analysis. In *Proceedings of the Ninth International Conference on Language Resources and Evaluation (LREC'14)*, pages 4238–4243, Reykjavik, Iceland. European Language Resources Association (ELRA).

Jakub Nowak, Ahmet Taspinar, and Rafal Scherer. 2017. Lstm recurrent neural networks for short text and sentiment classification. pages 553–562.

Rolandos Potamias, Georgios Siolas, and Andreas Stafylopatis. 2019. A transformer-based approach to irony and sarcasm detection.

Antonio Reyes, Paolo Rosso, and Tony Veale. 2013. A multidimensional approach for detecting irony in twitter. *Language Resources and Evaluation*, 47.

Ellen Riloff, A. Qadir, P. Surve, L. Silva, N. Gilbert, and R. Huang. 2013. Sarcasm as contrast between a positive sentiment and negative situation. *Proceedings of EMNLP*, pages 704–714.

Nitish Srivastava, Geoffrey Hinton, Alex Krizhevsky, Ilya Sutskever, and Ruslan Salakhutdinov. 2014. Dropout: A simple way to prevent neural networks from overfitting. *Journal of Machine Learning Research*, 15(56):1929–1958.

Sainbayar Sukhbaatar, Jason Weston, Rob Fergus, et al. 2015. End-to-end memory networks. In *Advances in neural information processing systems*, pages 2440–2448.

Oren Tsur, Dmitry Davidov, and Ari Rappoport. 2010. Icwsm - a great catchy name: Semi-supervised recognition of sarcastic sentences in online product reviews.

Ashish Vaswani, Noam Shazeer, Niki Parmar, Jakob Uszkoreit, Llion Jones, Aidan N. Gomez, Lukasz Kaiser, and Illia Polosukhin. 2017. Attention is all you need.

Tony Veale and Yanfen Hao. 2010. Detecting ironic intent in creative comparisons. pages 765–770.

Zichao Yang, Diyi Yang, Chris Dyer, Xiaodong He, Alex Smola, and Eduard Hovy. 2016. Hierarchical attention networks for document classification. In *Proceedings of the 2016 conference of the North American chapter of the association for computational linguistics: human language technologies*, pages 1480–1489.

Detecting Sarcasm in Conversation Context Using Transformer-Based Models

Adithya Avvaru[1,2], **Sanath Vobilisetty**[2] and **Radhika Mamidi**[1]
[1] International Institute of Information Technology, Hyderabad, India
[2]Teradata India Pvt. Ltd, India
[1]`adithya.avvaru@students.iiit.ac.in` [1]`radhika.mamidi@iiit.ac.in`
[2]`sanath.vobilisetty@teradata.com`

Abstract

Sarcasm detection, regarded as one of the sub-problems of sentiment analysis, is a very typical task because the introduction of sarcastic words can flip the sentiment of the sentence itself. To date, many research works revolve around detecting sarcasm in one single sentence and there is very limited research to detect sarcasm resulting from multiple sentences. Current models used Long Short Term Memory (Hochreiter and Schmidhuber, 1997) (LSTM) variants with or without attention to detect sarcasm in conversations. We showed that the models using state-of-the-art Bidirectional Encoder Representations from Transformers (Devlin et al., 2018) (BERT), to capture syntactic and semantic information across conversation sentences, performed better than the current models. Based on the data analysis, we estimated that the number of sentences in the conversation that can contribute to the sarcasm and the results agrees to this estimation. We also perform a comparative study of our different versions of BERT-based model with other variants of LSTM model and XLNet (Yang et al., 2019) (both using the estimated number of conversation sentences) and find out that BERT-based models outperformed them.

1 Introduction

For many NLP researchers from both academia and industry, sarcasm detection has been one of the most focused areas of research among many research problems like code-mixed sentiment analysis (Lal et al., 2019), detection of offensive or hate speeches (Liu et al., 2019), question-answering(Soares and Parreiras, 2018), etc. One of the main reasons why sarcasm finds a significant portion of research work is because of its nature that the addition of a sarcastic clause or a word can alter the sentiment of the sentence.

Sarcasm is used to criticize people, to provide political or apolitical views, to make fun of ideas, etc., and the most common form of sarcasm usage is through text. Some major sources of the sarcastic text are social media platforms like Twitter, Instagram, Facebook, Quora, WhatsApp etc. Out of these, Twitter forms the major source of sarcastic content drawing attention from researchers across the globe (Bamman and Smith, 2015; Rajadesingan et al., 2015; Davidov et al., 2010).

Due to its inherent nature of flipping the context of the sentence, sarcasm in a sentence is difficult to detect even for humans (Chaudhari and Chandankhede, 2017). Here, the context is considered only in one sentence. How do we deal with situations where the sarcastic sentence depends on a conversation context and the context spans over multiple sentences preceding the response sarcastic sentence? Addressing this problem may help in identifying the root cause of sarcasm in a larger context, which is even tougher because conversation sentences differ in number, some conversation sentences themselves may be sarcastic and response text may depend on more than one conversation sentences. This is the research problem that we are trying to address and are largely successful in building better models which outperformed the baseline F-measures of 0.6 for Reddit and 0.67 for Twitter datasets (Ghosh et al., 2018). We have achieved F-measures of 0.752 for Twitter and 0.621 for Reddit datasets.

2 Related work

Sarcasm is a form of figurative language where the meaning of a sentence does not hold and the interpretation is quite contrary. A quick survey about sarcasm detection and some of the earlier approaches is compiled by Joshi et al. (2017). The problem of sarcasm detection is targeted in

Proceedings of the Second Workshop on Figurative Language Processing, pages 98–103
July 9, 2020. ©2020 Association for Computational Linguistics
https://doi.org/10.18653/v1/P17

Field	Field Description
label	SARCASM or NOT_SARCASM
response	Tweet or a Reddit post
context	Ordered list of dialogue

Table 1: Fields used in the training data

different ways by the research community. Sarcasm detection is not wholly a linguistic problem but extra-lingual features like author and audience information, communication environment etc., also play a significant role in sarcasm identification (Bamman and Smith, 2015). Davoodi and Kosseim (2017) used semi-supervised approaches to detect sarcasm. Another approach is automatic learning and exploiting word embeddings to recognize sarcasm (Amir et al., 2016). Emojis also have a significant impact on the sarcastic nature of the text, which might help in detecting sarcasm better (Felbo et al., 2017). Other approaches to detect sarcasm include Bi-Directional Gated Recurrent Neural Network (Bi-Directional GRNU) (Zhang et al., 2016). Sarcasm detection in speech is also gaining importance (Castro et al., 2019).

Some of the earlier works involving conversation contexts in detecting sarcasm are trying to model conversation contexts and understand what part of conversation sentence was involved in triggering sarcasm (Ghosh et al., 2017, 2018) and identify the specific sentence that is sarcastic given a sarcastic post that contains multiple sentences (Ghosh et al., 2018). Humans could infer sarcasm better with conversation context which emphasises the importance of conversation context (Wallace et al., 2014).

The structure of the paper is as follows. In Section 3, we describe the dataset (fields provided in the train and the test data and an example data along with its explanation). Section 4 describes the feature extraction where the emphasis is on data preprocessing and the procedure to select conversation sentences. Section 5 describes the systems used in training the data whereas section 6 discusses the comparative results of various models. Section 7 presents concluding remarks and future direction of research.

3   Dataset Description

The data[1] we used for model building is taken from sarcasm detection shared task of the Second Workshop on Figurative Language Processing (FigLang2020). There are two types of data provided by the organizers: 1. Twitter dataset and 2. Reddit dataset. Training data contains the fields - "label", "response" and "context" and are described as shown in the Table 1.

If the "context" contains three elements, "c1", "c2", "c3", in that order, then "c2" is a reply to "c1" and "c3" is a reply to "c2". Further, if the sarcastic "response" is "r", then "r" is a reply to "c3". Consider the example provided by the organizers:

label: *"SARCASM"*
response: *"Did Kelly just call someone else messy? Baaaahaaahahahaha"*
context: [*"X is looking a First Lady should . #classact*, *"didn't think it was tailored enough it looked messy"*]

This example can be understood as *"Did Kelly..."* is a reply to its immediate context *"didn't think it was tailored..."* which is a reply to *"X is looking..."*. and the label of the response is *"SARCASM"*.

Testing data contains the fields - "id", "response" and "context" and are described as shown in the Table 2.

The data of both Twitter tweets and Reddit posts were organized into train and test sets. The number of samples in each of these datasets is shown in Table 3. It is clear from the table that the data is balanced with the same number of sarcastic and non-sarcastic samples (Abercrombie and Hovy, 2016).

Field	Field Description
id	Identification for each test sample
response	Tweet or a Reddit post
context	Ordered list of dialogue

Table 2: Fields used in the testing data

Datasets	Label	No. of Samples	
		Train	Test
Twitter	S	2500	1800
	NS	2500	
Reddit	S	2200	1800
	NS	2200	

Table 3: Dataset Composition Description
∗ *S : SARCASM, NS : NON_SARCASM*

[1] https://competitions.codalab.org/competitions/22247

4 Feature Extraction

4.1 Data Pre-processing and Cleaning

The corpus data contains consecutive occurrences of periods (.), multiple spaces between words, more or consecutive punctuation marks like exclamation (!), etc. Since the data is collected from Twitter handles and Reddit posts, the data also contain hashtags and emoticons, which are some of the properties of the text extracted from social media. Hence, there is a great need to clean the data before any further processing and we followed multiple steps, for cleaning the data, as described below:

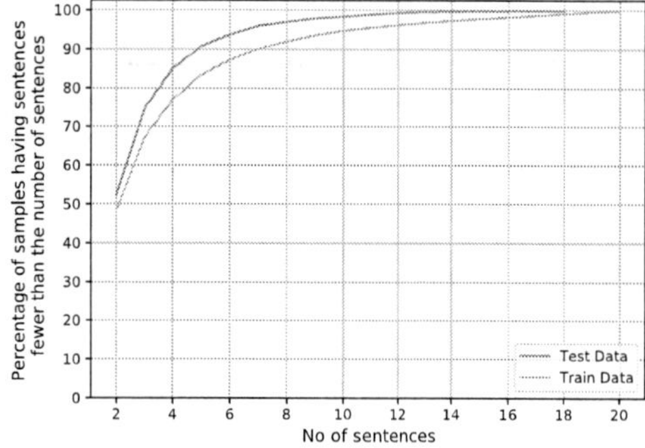

Figure 1: **Analysis of Twitter data:** Number of sentences Vs Percentage of samples

1. Replacing consecutive instances of punctuation marks with only one instance of it.

2. Demojizing the sentences that contain emoticons i.e., replacing emoticons with their corresponding texts. For example, 😛 is replaced with *:stuck_out_tongue:*.

3. There are two ways of handling hashtags - one, remove the hashtag and two, extract the hashtag content. We took the second approach as we believe certain hashtags contain meaningful text. For example, consider the text *Made $174 this month, I'm gonna buy a yacht! #poor*. There are two parts to this sentence - *Made $174 this month*, which doesn't have any sentiment but it is understood that the money he got is less and the second one, *I'm gonna buy a yacht!*, which is a positive statement that he can buy something very costly. The addition of hashtag *#poor* flipped the first statement to negative sentiment. Ignoring *#poor* will lose the sarcastic impact on the sentence.

No of sentences in a conversation	Training	Testing
5 or less	83%	90%
7 or less	90%	96%
10 or less	95%	98%

Table 4: Twitter Data - Percentage of samples having certain number of sentences in a conversation

No of sentences in a conversation	Training	Testing
5 or less	99.4%	70%
7 or less	99.9%	93.8%
10 or less	100%	99%

Table 5: Reddit Data - Percentage of samples having certain number of sentences in a conversation

4. Some punctuation marks like exclamation (!) have special significance in English text and are generally used to express emotions such as sudden surprises, praises, excitement or even pain. So, we decided to not remove punctuation marks.

5. We have identified contracted and combined words (for example, *we've, won't've*, etc,.) and replaced them with their corresponding English equivalents (in this case, *we have, will not have*, etc,.).

4.2 Selection of Conversation Sentences

Twitter Dataset: Since the number of conversation sentences range from two to twenty, it is important to understand how many sentences can contribute to the sarcastic behavior.

A quick analysis of Twitter data is provided by the Figure 1 and the Table 4. The behavior of training and testing data follows similar trend as observed from the Figure 1. We selected the last 7 conversation sentences out of all conversation sentences per Twitter tweet based on the following analysis:

- If we have chosen to select 10 sentences or more, then around 50 percent of samples which have 2 context sentences should be padded with zeros after tokenization. If we have chosen to select 2 sentences, then we will end up losing more context information. There is this trade-off while selecting conversation sentences.

- It is unlikely that the response text depends on the farther context sentences. So, the response text largely depends on context sentences that are closest to the response text.

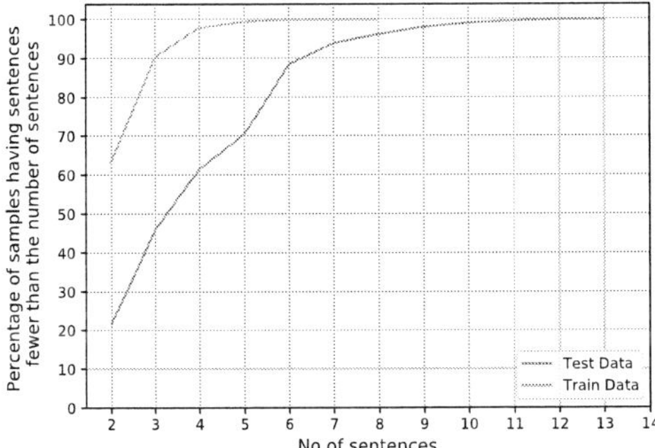

Figure 2: **Analysis of Reddit data:** Number of sentences Vs Percentage of samples

Reddit Dataset: Here, the dataset composition is different compared to that of Twitter Dataset. The number of conversation sentences ranges from two to eight in train data with 99 percent of samples having five or fewer sentences but the number of conversation sentences in test data ranges from two to thirteen with only 70 percent of samples having five or fewer sentences. Figure 2 and the Table 5 depict this behaviour of Reddit data.

4.3 Training text finalization

As discussed in Section 4.2, we considered the last 7 cleaned sentences from the conversation sentences. The response text is a direct result of the conversation sentences. Hence, we concatenate all the selected conversation sentences together and with the cleaned response text. This final text is fed to the model for training.

5 System description

There are several NLP models at our disposal to work with, some are pre-trained while others need to be trained from scratch. We have done experiments with LSTM, BiLSTM, Stacked LSTM and CNN-LSTM (Convolution Neural Network + LSTM) models which can be trained to capture sequence information. To avoid over-fitting, we have introduced dropout layers and taken early stopping measures while training. We split the training data into train data (to train the model) and validation data (10 percent of actual training data to validate the model and employ early stopping). We also

have worked with pre-trained Transformer based BERT (bert-base-uncased) model and XLNet. The following steps are used to fine-tune the pre-trained BERT model:

1. Tokenize the text (BERT requires the text to be in a predefined format with separators and class labels)

2. Create attention masks

3. Fine-tune the pre-trained BERT model so that the model parameters will conform to the input training data

In our model, training stops when F1-score on validation data goes below the earlier epoch's F1-score and the prediction is done on the earlier model for which validation F1-score is highest. Similar steps are performed to fine-tune XLNet model.

6 Results

The LSTM model variants - LSTM, BiLSTM, Stacked-LSTM and Conv-LSTM models are applied to Twitter dataset and the F1-scores on test data are 0.67, 0.66, 0.66 and 0.67 respectively. The F1-scores of variants of BERT models considering different lengths of conversation sentences and XLNet are depicted in Table 6.

	Twitter	**Reddit**
BERT-3	0.710	0.603
BERT-5	0.745	**0.621**
BERT-7	**0.752**	_*
BERT-all	0.724	0.592
XLNet	0.684	0.541

Table 6: Comparison of results for various models for Twitter and Reddit datasets
∗ indicates that the BERT-7 model is not trained as the number of samples in BERT-all model is just one sample more than that in BERT-7 model.

We experimented by considering the last 3, 5 and 8 sentences for Reddit dataset and found that model that used 5 sentences outperformed the other two, probably because the model which used 3 sentences captured the context well while training but failed to apply it as the range of sentences' length in the test set is large compared to the train set. Similarly model with 8 samples had a lot of padded zeros as 99 percent of samples have five or fewer sentences which resulted in poor performance. The results of the experiments on Reddit dataset are depicted in Table 6. Since LSTM variants did not perform well compared to BERT-based models, we focused more on data preparation part of our research work for Reddit dataset.

It can be inferred from the results table that our hypothesis of taking seven latest sentences, for Twitter dataset, falls in-line with the results.

7   Conclusion

Sarcasm detection in conversational context is an important research area which infuses more enthusiasm and encourages the researchers across the globe. We build models that outperformed the baseline results. Though the results in the Shared Task leaderboard shows that the top model achieved F-measure of 0.93 for the Twitter dataset and 0.83 for the Reddit dataset, there is a lot to work on the problem and find ways to improve the performance with a larger dataset. Use of a larger dataset might help in adding more context and help in improving accuracy. Currently, the models that are built are not generalised across datasets. Further research can focus on building a generalized model for multiple datasets.

References

Gavin Abercrombie and Dirk Hovy. 2016. Putting Sarcasm Detection into Context: The Effects of Class Imbalance and Manual Labelling on Supervised Machine Classification of Twitter Conversations. In *Proceedings of the ACL 2016 Student Research Workshop*, pages 107–113.

Silvio Amir, Byron C. Wallace, Hao Lyu, Paula Carvalho, and Mário J. Silva. 2016. Modelling context with user embeddings for sarcasm detection in social media. In *Proceedings of The 20th SIGNLL Conference on Computational Natural Language Learning*, pages 167–177, Berlin, Germany. Association for Computational Linguistics.

David Bamman and Noah A Smith. 2015. Contextualized Sarcasm Detection on Twitter. In *Ninth International AAAI Conference on Web and Social Media*.

Santiago Castro, Devamanyu Hazarika, Verónica Pérez-Rosas, Roger Zimmermann, Rada Mihalcea, and Soujanya Poria. 2019. Towards Multimodal Sarcasm Detection (An _Obviously_ Perfect Paper). *arXiv preprint arXiv:1906.01815*.

P. Chaudhari and C. Chandankhede. 2017. Literature survey of sarcasm detection. In *2017 International Conference on Wireless Communications, Signal Processing and Networking (WiSPNET)*, pages 2041–2046.

Dmitry Davidov, Oren Tsur, and Ari Rappoport. 2010. Semi-Supervised Recognition of Sarcastic Sentences in Twitter and Amazon. In *Proceedings of the fourteenth conference on computational natural language learning*, pages 107–116. Association for Computational Linguistics.

Elnaz Davoodi and Leila Kosseim. 2017. Automatic identification of AltLexes using monolingual parallel corpora. In *Proceedings of the International Conference Recent Advances in Natural Language Processing, RANLP 2017*, pages 195–200, Varna, Bulgaria. INCOMA Ltd.

Jacob Devlin, Ming-Wei Chang, Kenton Lee, and Kristina Toutanova. 2018. BERT: Pre-training of Deep Bidirectional Transformers for Language Understanding. *arXiv preprint arXiv:1810.04805*.

Bjarke Felbo, Alan Mislove, Anders Søgaard, Iyad Rahwan, and Sune Lehmann. 2017. Using millions of emoji occurrences to learn any-domain representations for detecting sentiment, emotion and sarcasm. *arXiv preprint arXiv:1708.00524*.

Debanjan Ghosh, Alexander R Fabbri, and Smaranda Muresan. 2018. Sarcasm analysis using conversation context. *Computational Linguistics*, 44(4):755–792.

Debanjan Ghosh, Alexander Richard Fabbri, and Smaranda Muresan. 2017. The Role of Conversation Context for Sarcasm Detection in Online Interactions. *arXiv preprint arXiv:1707.06226*.

Sepp Hochreiter and Jürgen Schmidhuber. 1997. Long Short-Term Memory. *Neural computation*, 9(8):1735–1780.

Aditya Joshi, Pushpak Bhattacharyya, and Mark J Carman. 2017. Automatic Sarcasm Detection: A Survey. *ACM Computing Surveys (CSUR)*, 50(5):1–22.

Yash Kumar Lal, Vaibhav Kumar, Mrinal Dhar, Manish Shrivastava, and Philipp Koehn. 2019. De-mixing sentiment from code-mixed text. In *Proceedings of the 57th Annual Meeting of the Association for Computational Linguistics: Student Research Workshop*, pages 371–377, Florence, Italy. Association for Computational Linguistics.

Ping Liu, Wen Li, and Liang Zou. 2019. NULI at SemEval-2019 task 6: Transfer learning for offensive language detection using bidirectional transformers. In *Proceedings of the 13th International Workshop on Semantic Evaluation*, pages 87–91, Minneapolis, Minnesota, USA. Association for Computational Linguistics.

Ashwin Rajadesingan, Reza Zafarani, and Huan Liu. 2015. Sarcasm Detection on Twitter: A Behavioral Modeling Approach. In *Proceedings of the eighth ACM international conference on web search and data mining*, pages 97–106.

Marco Antonio Calijorne Soares and Fernando Silva Parreiras. 2018. A literature review on question answering techniques, paradigms and systems. *Journal of King Saud University-Computer and Information Sciences.*

Byron C Wallace, Laura Kertz, Eugene Charniak, et al. 2014. Humans require context to infer ironic intent (so computers probably do, too). In *Proceedings of the 52nd Annual Meeting of the Association for Computational Linguistics (Volume 2: Short Papers)*, pages 512–516.

Zhilin Yang, Zihang Dai, Yiming Yang, Jaime Carbonell, Russ R Salakhutdinov, and Quoc V Le. 2019. XLNet: Generalized Autoregressive Pretraining for Language Understanding. In *Advances in neural information processing systems*, pages 5754–5764.

Meishan Zhang, Yue Zhang, and Guohong Fu. 2016. Tweet sarcasm detection using deep neural network. In *Proceedings of COLING 2016, the 26th International Conference on Computational Linguistics: Technical Papers*, pages 2449–2460, Osaka, Japan. The COLING 2016 Organizing Committee.

Using Conceptual Norms for Metaphor Detection

Mingyu Wan[1,3]*, Kathleen Ahrens[2], Emmanuele Chersoni[3]
Menghan Jiang[3], Qi Su[1], Rong Xiang[4], Chu-Ren Huang[3]

[1]School of Foreign Languages, Peking University
[2]Dept. of English, The Hong Kong Polytechnic University
[3]Dept. of Chinese and Bilingual Studies, The Hong Kong Polytechnic University
[4]Dept. of Computing, The Hong Kong Polytechnic University
{*wanmy*, *sukia*}*@pku.edu.cn*, {*emmanuelechersoni, xiangrong0302*}*@gmail.com*
{*kathleen.ahrens, menghanengl.jiang, churen.huang*}*@polyu.edu.hk*

Abstract

This paper reports a linguistically-enriched method of detecting token-level metaphors for the second shared task on Metaphor Detection. We participate in all four phases of competition with both datasets, i.e. Verbs and All-POS on the VUA and the TOFEL datasets. We use the modality exclusivity and embodiment norms for constructing a conceptual representation of the nodes and the context. Our system obtains an F-score of 0.652 for the VUA Verbs track, which is 5% higher than the strong baselines. The experimental results across models and datasets indicate the salient contribution of using modality exclusivity and modality shift information for predicting metaphoricity.

1 Introduction

Metaphors are one kind of figurative language that use conceptual mapping to represent one thing (target domain) as another (source domain). As proposed by Lakoff and Johnson (1980) in Conceptual Metaphor Theory (CMT), metaphor is not only a property of the language but also a cognitive mechanism that describes our conceptual system. Thus metaphors are devices that transfer the property of one domain to another unrelated or different domain, as in 'sweet voice' (use taste to describe sound).

Metaphors are prevalent in daily life and play a significant role for people to interpret/understand complex concepts. On the other hand, as a popular linguistic device, metaphors encode versatile ontological information, which usually involve e.g. domain transfer (Ahrens et al., 2003; Ahrens, 2010; Ahrens and Jiang, 2020), sentiment reverse (Steen et al., 2010) or modality shift (Winter, 2019) etc. Therefore, detecting the metaphors in texts is essential for capturing the authentic meaning of the texts, which can benefit many natural language

processing applications, such as machine translation, dialogue systems and sentiment analysis (Tsvetkov et al., 2014). In this shared task, we aim to detect token-level metaphors from plain texts by focusing on content words (Verbs, Nouns, Adjectives and Adverbs) of two corpora: VUA[1] and TOFEL[2]. To better understand the intrinsic properties of metaphors and to provide an in-depth analysis to this phenomenon, we propose a linguistically-enriched model to deal with this task with the use of modality exclusivity and embodiment norms (see details in Section 3).

2 Related Work

Many approaches have been proposed for automatic detection of metaphors, using features of lexical information (Klebanov et al., 2014; Wilks et al., 2013), semantic classes (Klebanov et al., 2016), concreteness (Klebanov et al., 2015), word associations (Xiao et al., 2016), constructions and frames (Hong, 2016) and systems such as traditional machine learning classifiers (Rai et al., 2016), deep neural networks (Do Dinh and Gurevych, 2016) and sequential models (Bizzoni and Ghanimifard, 2018).

Despite many advances in the above work, metaphor detection remains a challenging task. The semantic and ontological differences between metaphorical and non-metaphorical expressions are often subtle and their perception may vary from person to person. To tackle such problems, researchers resort to specific domain knowledge (Tsvetkov et al., 2014); lexicons (Mohler et al., 2013; Dodge et al., 2015); supervised methods (Klebanov et al., 2014, 2015, 2016) or using attention-based deep learning models to capture latent patterns (Igam-

---

[1]`http://www.vismet.org/metcor/documentation/home.html`
[2]`https://catalog.ldc.upenn.edu/LDC2014T06`

Proceedings of the Second Workshop on Figurative Language Processing, pages 104–109
July 9, 2020. ©2020 Association for Computational Linguistics
https://doi.org/10.18653/v1/P17

berdiev and Shin, 2018). These methods show different strengths on detecting metaphors, yet each has its respective disadvantages, such as having generalization problems or lack association of their results with the intrinsic properties of metaphors. In addition, the reported performances of metaphor detection so far (around 0.6 F1 in the last shared task) (Leong et al., 2018) are still not promising. This calls for further endeavours in all aspects.

In this work, we adopt supervised machine learning algorithms based on four categories of features, which include linguistic norms, ngram-word, -lemma and -pos collocations, word embeddings and cosine similarity between the target nodes and its neighboring words, as well as the strong baselines provided by the organizer of the shared task (Leong et al., 2018; Klebanov et al., 2014, 2015, 2016). Moreover, we use several statistical models and ensemble learning strategies during training and testing so as to test the cross-model consistency of the improvement using the various features. The methods are described in detail in the following sections.

3   Feature Sets

This work uses four categories of features (16 subsets in all) to represent the nodes and contextual information at hierarchical levels, which include the lexical and syntactic-to-semantic information, sensory modality scales, embodiment ratings (of verbs only), as well as word vectors of the nodes and cosine similarity of node-neighbor pairs, as detailed below.

- **Linguistic Norms:** Two linguistic norms are used to construct four linguistically-enriched feature sets in the jsonlines format: [3]

    - **ME** (modality exclusivity): 42 dimension of target nodes representation, containing the mapped sensorimotor values in the modality norms;

    - **DM** (dominant modality): 1×5 dimension of node-neighbor pairs (five lexical neighboring words) information, representing the dominant modality of the target nodes and the surrounding lexical words;

    - **EB** (embodiment): 2 dimension of nodes representation, including embodiment rating and standard deviation;

    - **EB-diff** (embodiment differences): 2×5 dimension of node-neighbor pairs (five lexical neighboring words) information.

The ME and DM feature sets are constructed by using the Lancaster Sensorimotor norms collected by Lynott et al. (2019). The data include measures of sensorimotor strength (0-5 scale indicating different degrees of sense modalities/action effectors) for 39,707 English words across six perceptual modalities: touch, hearing, smell, taste, vision and interception, and five action effectors: mouth/throat, hand/arm, foot/leg, head (excluding mouth/throat), torso.[4] As sensorimotor information plays a fundamental role in cognition, these norms provide a valuable knowledge representation to the conceptual categories of the target and neighboring words which serve as salient features for inferring metaphors.

The EB and EB-diff feature sets are constructed by using the embodiment norms for 687 English verbs which is collected by Sidhu et al. (2014). Research examining semantic richness effects has shown that multiple dimensions of meaning are activated in the process of word recognition (Yap et al., 2011). This data applies the semantic richness approach (Sidhu et al., 2014, 2016) to verb stimuli in order to investigate how verb meanings are represented. The relative embodiment ratings (1-7 scale indicating different degrees of bodily involvement) revealed that bodily experience was judged to be more important to the meanings of some verbs (e.g., dance, breathe) than to others (e.g., evaporate, expect), suggesting that relative embodiment is an important aspect of verb meaning, which can be a useful indicator of meaning mismatch of the figurative usage of verbs.

- **Collocations:** Three sets of collocational features are constructed to represent the lexical, syntactic, grammatical information of the nodes and their neighbors: **Trigram**, **FL** (Fivegram Lemma), **FPOS** (Fivegram POS tags). The two corpora are

---

105

lemmatized using the nltk WordNetLemmatizer[5] and POS tagged using the nltk averaged_perceptron_tagger[6] before constructing such features.

- **Word Embeddings:** For comparisons, we utilise distributional vector representation of word meaning to the nodes based on the distributional hypothesis (Firth, 1957; Lenci, 2018). Two pre-trained Word2Vec models (**GoogleNews.300d** and **Internal-W2V.300d** (pre-trained using the VUA and TOFEL corpora)) and the GloVe vectors are used. GoogleNews[7] in this work is pre-trained using the continuous bag-of-words architecture for computing vector representations of words (Church, 2017). GloVe[8] is an unsupervised learning algorithm for obtaining vector representations for words. We use the 300d vectors pre-trained on Wikipedia 2014+Gigaword 5 (Pennington et al., 2014).

- **Cosine Similarity:** We also investigate the cosine similarity (CS) measures for computing word sense distances between the nodes and their neighboring lexical words, based on the hypothesis that words of distant meaning are more likely to be metaphors. Three different sets of CS features are constructed in this work by using the above three different word embedding models: **CS-Google**, **CS-GloVe**, **CS-Internal**.

These features constitute a rather comprehensive representation of the mismatch of the nodes and their neighbors in terms of senses, domains, modalities, agentivity and concreteness etc, which are highly indicative of metaphorical uses and are hence hypothesized as more distinctive features than the strong baselines in Leong et al. (2018).

In addition, we replicate the three strong baselines provided by the organizer for comparison purposes:

- **B1**: lemmatized unigrams (UL)

- **B2**: lemmatized unigrams, generalized WordNet semantic classes, and difference in concreteness ratings between verbs/adjectives and nouns (UL + WordNet + CCDB)

- **B3**: baseline 2 and unigrams, pos tag, topic, concreteness ratings between nodes and up and down words respectively (UL + WordNet + CCDB + U + P + T + CUp + CDown)

4 Classifiers and Experimental Setup

Three traditional classifiers are used for predicting the metaphoricity of the tokens, including Logistic Regression, Linear SVC and a Random Forest Classifier. The Machine Learning experiments are run through utilities in the SciKit-Learn Laboratory (SKLL) (Pedregosa et al., 2011). [9]

For parameter tuning, we use grid search to find optimal parameters for the learners. Finally, we set up the following optimized parameters for the three classifiers:

- Logistic Regression (LR): *'class_weight':'balanced', 'max_iter':5000, 'tol':1*

- Linear SVC (LSVC): *'class_weight':'balanced', 'max_iter':50000, 'C':10*

- Random Forest Classifier (RFC): *'min_samples_split':8, 'max_features':'log2', 'oob_score':'True', 'random_state':10, 'class_weight':'balanced'*

5 Results and Discussions

5.1 Evaluation Results

In order to evaluate the discriminativeness of the various features for metaphor detection and their fitness to the three classifiers, we focus on the VUA Verbs phase and randomly select a development set (4380 tokens) from the training set in proportion to the Train/Test ratio. Experiments are run using the three classifiers and the setup in Section 4.

The evaluation results on the individual features in terms of F1-score are summarized in Table 1 below:

In Table 1, the top five features with the LR classifier are highlighted in bold. Results show that the best individual feature is ME, followed by

---

[5] https://www.nltk.org/_modules/nltk/stem/wordnet.html

[6] https://www.kaggle.com/nltkdata/averaged-perceptron-tagger

[7] https://github.com/mmihaltz/word2vec-GoogleNews-vectors

[8] https://nlp.stanford.edu/projects/glove/

[9] https://skll.readthedocs.io/en/latest/index.html

Individual	Features	LR	LSVC	RFC
Baseline	B1^{T2}	**.632**	.621	.618
Linguistic	ME^{T1}	**.637**	.636	.632
	DM	.616	.620	.623
	EB	.547	.548	.544
	EB-diff	.322	.321	.302
Collocation	Trigram^{T4}	**.626**	.625	.612
	FL^{T5}	**.624**	.623	.621
	FPOS	.378	.369	.335
Word2Vec	GoogleNews	.605	.607	.603
	GloVe^{T3}	**.630**	.627	.633
	Internal	.569	.555	.568
CS	GoogleNews	.448	.451	.445
	GloVe	.403	.404	.410
	Internal	.436	.421	.402

Table 1: Evaluation Results on Individual Features. T1-5 are the top five features in terms of F1 score.

B1, W2V.GloVe, Trigram and FL. For the conceptual representations, modality exclusivity features demonstrate outstanding performance, while the embodiment features perform quite poorly. This is due to the data sparseness of the embodiment feature representations. As the data in the embodiment norms only contains 687 English verbs, it cannot cover most of the words in the two corpora of the shared task, which causes many empty values in the feature matrix, resulting in a poor performance in the task. Despite of this, it still helps the overall performance, if concatenated with other features, as to be shown in the later section.

The performances of the three classifiers are quite close for all features, with LR performing slightly better. To test the combined power of these features for metaphor detection, we also conduct evaluation on fused features, as shown in Table 2 below:

Fused Features	LR	LSVC	RFC
B2	.641	.636	.635
B3	.631	.630	.628
Top3	.653	.649	.650
Top4	.668	.666	.659
Top5	.669	.665	.668
Linguistic+B2	.655	.654	.652
Collocation+B2	.659	.658	.655
Word2Vec+B2	.637	.636	.637
CS+B2	.639	.637	.636
Selected	.672	.670	.671

Table 2: Evaluation Results on Fused Features

Results in Table 2 show that B2 is a stronger baseline than B3, so we use B2 as the comparison basis. Among the four categories of features, the linguistic and collocational features in combination with B2 achieve the greatest improvement

by around 1.5% F1-score. The top three to five features also improve the performance by 1-2% F1-score. However, the word embeddings and cosine similarity features show no improvement over baseline 2. Finally, we selected 12 features (excluding the W2V features) using the automatic feature selection algorithm and have achieved the best results for evaluation (.672 F1 for LR).

5.2 Results on Test Sets

We use the best feature sets and classifier (LR) in the above evaluation for the final submission. The released results of our system on the test sets of the four phases in terms of F1-score are summarized in Table 3 below:

Phase/Method	B2	Top5	L+B2	Selected
VUA-Verbs	.600	.645	.642	**.652**
VUA-AllPOS	.589	.597	.591	**.603**
TOFEL-Verbs	.555	.588	.581	**.596**
TOFEL-AllPOS	.543	.550	.552	**.560**

Table 3: Released Final Results of Our System

In Table 3, 'L+B2' stands for 'Linguistic feature fused with baseline 2' and the best results are highlighted in bold. In addition to the best methods, we also submit the Top5 features and the 'L+B2' features which all show consistent improvement (1-5% F1) over baseline 2. The evaluation results prove the effectiveness of using the linguistic features, especially the Modality Exclusivity representations for metaphor detection.

5.3 Comparison to other Works

To demonstrate the effectiveness of our method, this section presents the comparisons of our system to some highly related works that participated in the same shared task (2018) of the VUA corpus. All the results are publicly available, as reported in Leong et al. (2018). We compare our results on the VUA-Verbs and VUA-AllPOS phases to the top three teams (T1-3), the baseline2 (B2) and the only team using linguistic features (Ling) in 2018. The detailed results are displayed in Table 4 below:

Obviously, our method obtains very promising results: it beats the Top 2 team for the Verbs phase and is close to Top3 for the AllPOS phase; moreover, our results are significantly superior to both the baseline and another linguistically-based approach. This suggests the effectiveness of using conceptual features for metaphor detection, echoing the hypothesis that metaphor is a concept mismatch between the source and target domains.

Phase	Method	F1
VUA-Verbs-T1	w2v+CNN+Bi-LSTM	.672
VUA-Verbs-us	**linguistic+LR**	**.652**
VUA-Verbs-T2	w2v+LSTM RNN	.642
VUA-Verbs-T3	dictionary-based+LSTM	.619
VUA-Verbs-B2	UL+WordNet+CCDB+LR	.600
VUA-Verbs-Ling	linguistic+CRF	.246
VUA-AllPOS-T1	w2v+CNN+Bi-LSTM	.651
VUA-AllPOS-T2	w2v+Bi-LSTM+linguistic	.635
VUA-AllPOS-T3	w2v+LSTM RNN	.617
VUA-AllPOS-us	**linguistic+LR**	**.603**
VUA-AllPOS-B2	UL+WordNet+CCDB+LR	.589
VUA-AllPOS-Ling	linguistic+CRF	.138

Table 4: Comparison of Results of Our System to Works in the last Shared Task

6 Conclusion

We presented a linguistically enhanced method for word-level metaphor detection using conceptual features of modality and embodiment based on traditional classifiers. As suggested by the results, the modality exclusivity and embodiment norms provide conceptual and bodily information for representing the nodes and the context, which help improve the performance of metaphor detection over the three strong baselines to a great extent. It is noteworthy that our system did not employ any deep learning architectures, showing advantages of simplicity and model efficiency, yet it outperforms many sophisticated neural networks. In the future work, we will use the current feature sets in combination with state-of-the-art deep learning models to further examine the effectiveness of this method for metaphor detection.

Acknowledgments

This work is partially supported by the GRF grant (PolyU 156086/18H) and the Post-doctoral project (no. 4-ZZKE) at the Hong Kong Polytechnic University.

References

Kathleen Ahrens. 2010. Mapping principles for conceptual metaphors. *Researching and applying metaphor in the real world*, 26:185.

Kathleen Ahrens, Siaw Fong Chung, and Chu-Ren Huang. 2003. Conceptual metaphors: Ontology-based representation and corpora driven mapping principles. In *Proceedings of the ACL 2003 workshop on Lexicon and figurative language-Volume 14*, pages 36–42. Association for Computational Linguistics.

Kathleen Ahrens and Menghan Jiang. 2020. Source domain verification using corpus-based tools. *Metaphor and Symbol*, 35(1):43–55.

Yuri Bizzoni and Mehdi Ghanimifard. 2018. Bigrams and bilstms two neural networks for sequential metaphor detection. In *Proceedings of the Workshop on Figurative Language Processing*, pages 91–101.

Kenneth Ward Church. 2017. Word2vec. *Natural Language Engineering*, 23(1):155–162.

Erik-Lân Do Dinh and Iryna Gurevych. 2016. Token-level metaphor detection using neural networks. In *Proceedings of the Fourth Workshop on Metaphor in NLP*, pages 28–33.

Ellen K Dodge, Jisup Hong, and Elise Stickles. 2015. Metanet: Deep semantic automatic metaphor analysis. In *Proceedings of the Third Workshop on Metaphor in NLP*, pages 40–49.

Raymond Firth. 1957. 2. a note on descent groups in polynesia. *Man*, 57:4–8.

Jisup Hong. 2016. Automatic metaphor detection using constructions and frames. *Constructions and frames*, 8(2):295–322.

Timour Igamberdiev and Hyopil Shin. 2018. Metaphor identification with paragraph and word vectorization: An attention-based neural approach. In *Proceedings of the 32nd Pacific Asia Conference on Language, Information and Computation*.

Beata Beigman Klebanov, Ben Leong, Michael Heilman, and Michael Flor. 2014. Different texts, same metaphors: Unigrams and beyond. In *Proceedings of the Second Workshop on Metaphor in NLP*, pages 11–17.

Beata Beigman Klebanov, Chee Wee Leong, and Michael Flor. 2015. Supervised word-level metaphor detection: Experiments with concreteness and reweighting of examples. In *Proceedings of the Third Workshop on Metaphor in NLP*, pages 11–20.

Beata Beigman Klebanov, Chee Wee Leong, E Dario Gutierrez, Ekaterina Shutova, and Michael Flor. 2016. Semantic classifications for detection of verb metaphors. In *Proceedings of the 54th Annual Meeting of the Association for Computational Linguistics (Volume 2: Short Papers)*, pages 101–106.

George Lakoff and Mark Johnson. 1980. Metaphors we live by. *Chicago, IL: University of Chicago*.

Alessandro Lenci. 2018. Distributional models of word meaning. *Annual review of Linguistics*, 4:151–171.

Chee Wee Leong, Beata Beigman Klebanov, and Ekaterina Shutova. 2018. A report on the 2018 vua metaphor detection shared task. In *Proceedings of the Workshop on Figurative Language Processing*, pages 56–66.

Dermot Lynott, Louise Connell, Marc Brysbaert, James Brand, and James Carney. 2019. The lancaster sensorimotor norms: multidimensional measures of perceptual and action strength for 40,000 english words. *Behavior Research Methods*, pages 1–21.

Michael Mohler, David Bracewell, Marc Tomlinson, and David Hinote. 2013. Semantic signatures for example-based linguistic metaphor detection. In *Proceedings of the First Workshop on Metaphor in NLP*, pages 27–35.

Fabian Pedregosa, Gaël Varoquaux, Alexandre Gramfort, Vincent Michel, Bertrand Thirion, Olivier Grisel, Mathieu Blondel, Peter Prettenhofer, Ron Weiss, Vincent Dubourg, et al. 2011. Scikit-learn: Machine learning in python. *the Journal of machine Learning research*, 12:2825–2830.

Jeffrey Pennington, Richard Socher, and Christopher D Manning. 2014. Glove: Global vectors for word representation. In *Proceedings of the 2014 conference on empirical methods in natural language processing (EMNLP)*, pages 1532–1543.

Sunny Rai, Shampa Chakraverty, and Devendra K Tayal. 2016. Supervised metaphor detection using conditional random fields. In *Proceedings of the Fourth Workshop on Metaphor in NLP*, pages 18–27.

David M Sidhu, Alison Heard, and Penny M Pexman. 2016. Is more always better for verbs? semantic richness effects and verb meaning. *Frontiers in psychology*, 7:798.

David M Sidhu, Rachel Kwan, Penny M Pexman, and Paul D Siakaluk. 2014. Effects of relative embodiment in lexical and semantic processing of verbs. *Acta psychologica*, 149:32–39.

Gerard J Steen, Aletta G Dorst, J Berenike Herrmann, Anna A Kaal, and Tina Krennmayr. 2010. Metaphor in usage. *Cognitive Linguistics*, 21(4):765–796.

Yulia Tsvetkov, Leonid Boytsov, Anatole Gershman, Eric Nyberg, and Chris Dyer. 2014. Metaphor detection with cross-lingual model transfer. In *Proceedings of the 52nd Annual Meeting of the Association for Computational Linguistics (Volume 1: Long Papers)*, pages 248–258.

Yorick Wilks, Adam Dalton, James Allen, and Lucian Galescu. 2013. Automatic metaphor detection using large-scale lexical resources and conventional metaphor extraction. In *Proceedings of the First Workshop on Metaphor in NLP*, pages 36–44.

Bodo Winter. 2019. Synaesthetic metaphors are neither synaesthetic nor metaphorical. *Perception metaphors*, pages 105–126.

Ping Xiao, Khalid Alnajjar, Mark Granroth-Wilding, Kat Agres, and Hannu Toivonen. 2016. Meta4meaning: Automatic metaphor interpretation using corpus-derived word associations. In *Proceedings of the 7th International Conference on Computational Creativity (ICCC)*. Paris, France.

Melvin J Yap, Sarah E Tan, Penny M Pexman, and Ian S Hargreaves. 2011. Is more always better? effects of semantic richness on lexical decision, speeded pronunciation, and semantic classification. *Psychonomic Bulletin & Review*, 18(4):742–750.

ALBERT-BiLSTM for Sequential Metaphor Detection

Shuqun Li, Jingjie Zeng, Jinhui Zhang, Tao Peng, Liang Yang and Hongfei Lin
Information Retrieval Laboratory of Dalian University of Technology,
Department of Computer Science, Dalian University of Technology
`{1397023717,jjwind,wszjh,1316785071}@mail.dlut.edu.cn`
`{liang,hflin}@dlut.edu.cn`

Abstract

In our daily life, metaphor is a common way of expression. To understand the meaning of a metaphor, we should recognize the metaphor words which play important roles. In the metaphor detection task, we design a sequence labeling model based on ALBERT-LSTM-softmax. By applying this model, we carry out a lot of experiments and compare the experimental results with different processing methods, such as with different input sentences and tokens, or the methods with CRF and softmax. Then, some tricks are adopted to improve the experimental results. Finally, our model achieves a 0.707 F1-score for the all POS subtask and a 0.728 F1-score for the verb subtask on the TOEFL dataset.

1 Introduction

As a common rhetorical device, we often use metaphors to express our feelings and ideas vividly and concisely in our daily life. Detecting metaphors in texts is of great significance for analyzing the meaning and polarity of sentences. It can also be used to generate sentences that are more suitable for human expression, and promote the development of chat robots, machine translation and other fields.

Metaphor detection generally recognizes metaphorical words or phrases from the metaphorical sentence, such as "she is a woman with a stone heart", in which "stone" is a metaphorical word modified "heart". However, the task of metaphor detection is very challenging. Firstly, metaphor detection is a sequence labeling task, and every word in a sentence needs to be classified. Secondly, the boundaries between metaphors and non metaphors are sometimes vague. Moreover, due to the different identities of authors, some metaphorical words involve knowledge in specific fields and are difficult to recognize

directly (Tsvetkov et al., 2014). The traditional lexicon based method cannot cover all possible words occurred in metaphors. It is difficult to recognize metaphors when certain words are out-of-vocabulary. Although the traditional machine learning method needs to extract features manually (Heintz et al., 2013), its performance is still insufficient.While with the further development of language model, different kinds of end-to-end pre-trained models almost dominate the field of natural language processing, and also improve the prediction accuracy of various tasks to a higher level. Hence, in this paper we use pre-trained models to deal with metaphor detection task.

The purpose of this metaphorical shared task is to identify the whole words and verbs in given sentences. In this paper, we design an ALBERT-BiLSTM structure to recognize metaphorical words in TOEFL dataset. Firstly, we conduct an experimental comparison on the form of input sentence, and then select the form of inputting the single sentence directly. Secondly, we compare the application of BERT on this sequence labeling problem, and extract the input form of the first part after the BPE word segmentation of BERT. Finally, the effect of conditional random field (CRF) and softmax with class weights in the output layer is compared and the result shows that softmax with class weights is better. At the same time, we also adopt some tricks in the training process, including semantic merge and loss with class weight. The final result in the test set achieves a 0.707 F1-score for the all POS subtask, and a 0.728 F1-score for the verb subtask on TOEFL dataset.

2 Related works

At present, researchers in the field of natural language processing have made a lot of effort in metaphor detection task. Shutova et al. (2016)

110

Proceedings of the Second Workshop on Figurative Language Processing, pages 110–115
July 9, 2020. ©2020 Association for Computational Linguistics
https://doi.org/10.18653/v1/P17

used unsupervised learning to detect metaphors, and applied the syntactically perceived distribution word vectors. Gong et al. (2017) used metaphorical language detection as a method to explore the composition of word vectors, and calculated cosine distance to distinguish metaphor from non-metaphor: words that are out of context in sentences may be metaphorical. Gao et al. (2018) proposed a model to connect the expression of Glove and Elmo for solving the sequence labeling task, which is also transferred to the following metaphor task. Gutiérrez et al. (2016) used the flexibility of word vectors to study metaphor and its possibility of modeling in semantic space. Mao et al. (2019) designed an end-to-end model based on Glove and Elmo, which could identify metaphors conveniently.

For metaphor often contains emotions, some researchers tended to carry on emotion analysis on metaphors. Veale (2012) constructed an lexicon based model for analyzing emotions of metaphors. Kozareva (2013) proposed a new method, which integrated the trigger factors of cognition, emotion and perception.

Verb metaphor recognition is also an important subtask of metaphor recognition. Jia and Yu (2008) used conditional random fields(CRF) model and maximum entropy(ME) model to recognize verb metaphor, and they pointed out that there were no mature syntactic and semantic tools for metaphor analysis in Chinese. Beigman Klebanov et al. (2016) studied the effectiveness of semantic generalization and classification in capturing the rules of verb behavior, and tried to analyze their metaphors from the orthographic words unigrams.

These studies also provided some guidance to our work. For example, the word vector concatenation in LSTM is similar to RNN_HG (Mao et al., 2019).

3 Task definition

The dataset of this metaphorical shared task includes two kinds: VUA (Steen, 2010) and TOEFL (Klebanov et al., 2018). This paper mainly conducts experiments on TOEFL data. TOEFL dataset contains 180 articles written by non-native English speakers in the TOEFL test, and 60 articles in the test set. Each article is divided into several parts by sentence. At the same time, the corresponding examination questions of each article are provided, and there are 8 kinds of questions. The details of the dataset are as follows in table 1.

We make statistics on the sentence length distribution in the data set, and the following is shown by the box chart.

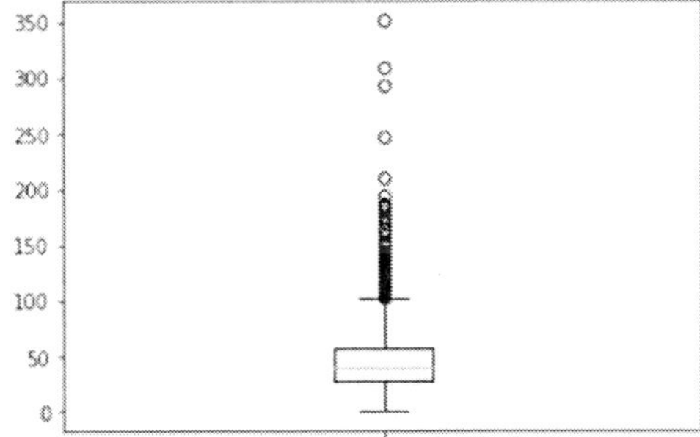

Figure 1: Sentence length distribution of train set.

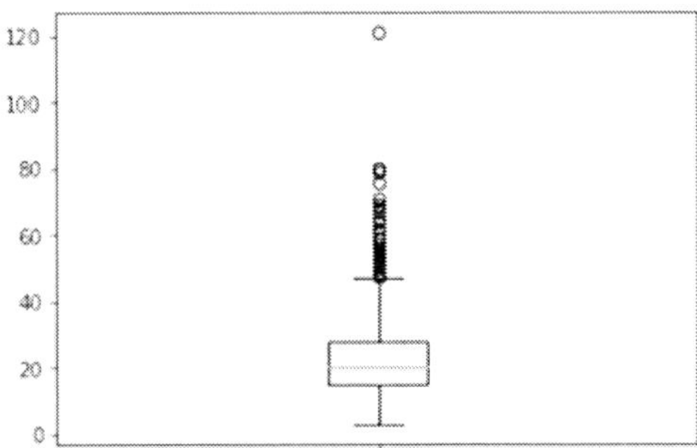

Figure 2: Sentence length distribution of test set.

It can be seen that the sentence length of training set is longer than that of test set, but most of them are distributed between 0 and 100, no more than 350 tokens. It is suitable for BERT model, because the maximum sentence length that BERT can support is 512.

This shared task subtask is divided into all POS recognition and verb recognition. It also provides some tokens' ID in sentences of the test set, and finally submits the recognition result corresponding to token ID. Final ranking and results are reported by Leong et al. (2020).

4 Method

In this section, we aim to introduce the method conducted on TOEFL dataset in this shared task. We use 'BERT+BiLSTM+softmax' as the baseline model, in which BERT (Devlin et al., 2019) is a pretrained language model proposed by Google in 2018, and BiLSTM is a bidirectional Recurrent Neural Network. The details of our method are described below.

	Number of articles	Total number of sentences	Average sentence length	Proportion of positive samples
Train	180	2741	45.5	0.03356
Test	60	968	22.9	/

Table 1: The details of the data set.

4.1 Data processing

Our data preprocessing method mainly includes two parts: data alignment and data augmentation. In data alignment part, we associate each word with its label in the sentence to transform the task into a sequential labeling task. In data augmentation part, we introduce context information and topic information of the sentences to expand the training data. There are three forms of our processed data: (1) single sentence; (2) the form of "sentence pair": considering that some metaphors are related to the context, we process the sentence into "sentence pair" form; (3) the form of "sentence-prompt pair": similar to form (2), we convert sentences into sentence pair, but we use prompt information instead of context information.The specific form is shown in table 2.

Format	Input	Label
single sentence	B	L
sentence pair	$A+B$	L
sentence-prompt pair	$B+P$	L

Table 2: Three different data input format. B is a sentence to be recognized and L is the label of B; A is the previous sentence of B in the text; P is the prompt of the text to which the sentence B belongs given in the TOEFL dataset.

The reason for this is that we believe the prompt information of the sentence will influence the prediction results of the model. In order to find the best form of data, we train the baseline model on three forms of data respectively. The results is shown in table 3.

Format	F1
single sentence	**0.687**
sentence pair	0.673
sentence-prompt pair	0.665

Table 3: Three different data input format preprocessing methods with baseline model.

The results show that the data format (1) performs best. After observing the dataset, we believe that the poor performance of data format (2) is due to the fact that the metaphor contained in the second sentence is not closely related to the first sentence. Additional input leads to the increased difficulty in model training. And the reason for the poor performance of data format (3) is that the sentence is less related to the given prompt. In conclusion, metaphors are more related to the local information in the sentence, and we use data format (1) as the input of our method.

In addition, we find that some sentences in TOEFL data are mainly written by people from non-native English speaking countries, and there are many spelling errors. So we try to use the SpellChecker package of Python to correct the spelling of words, the F1-score of the whole tokens in cross-validation before and after correction are 0.687 and 0.681 respectively. We initially thought word correction may be a useful method. However, the results show that the corrected data is not as good as expected, so we skip this step.

4.2 Our Model

The target of this evaluation is to identify metaphorical words in sentences, and we regard this task as a sequence labeling task. Our model consists of three layers: the pre-trained model layer, the contextual layer and the classification layer.

In pre-trained model layer, we use BERT for sequence labeling task. We find that the word segmentation algorithm BPE will divide the input words into smaller semantic units, i.e. subword, which leads to that the length of output sequence is greater than the length of input. To keep the length of the input and output in the same way, we propose three model input structures: (1) only the first subword of word is taken as input; (2) the input is unchanged, and only the first embedding of each word in output is taken as the representation of the current word; (3) the input is unchanged, and the embeddings of a word in output are merged into one embedding by convolutional neural networks which is taken as the representation of the current word. The results are as shown in table 4.

The results show that the structure (1) performances best, so we use only the first subword as the input of each word. We think the reason for the poor performance of structures (2) and (3) is

Input	F1
First segmentation	**0.687**
First vector	0.674
Aggregate vector	0.681

Table 4: The result of the three different word vector representation methods, where we use softmax as the classification layer.

Concatenation Format	F1
300-d	**0.709**
0-d	0.696
Linear mapping	0.695

Table 5: The result of the three different concatenation method. 300-d means concatenating LSTM output and the first 300 dimensions of ALBERT output as linear layer input; 0-d means taking only LSTM output as linear layer input; Linear mapping means mapping AL-BERT output through a linear layer to 300 dimensions and concatenating it with LSTM output as linear layer input.

that the provided TOEFL dataset is small and easy to be affected by input noise. The first subword is often the main part of a word, which can better express the semantic of the word compared to the rest subwords. Non-first subwords preserved by structure (2) and structure (3) will increase the input length of BERT, which brings noise while training, and makes it more difficult to learn from a small dataset.

In contextual layer, we use BiLSTM to get the context representation of the word based on the output embedding of BERT. In classification layer, we compare the performance of CRF and softmax. The cross-validation F1-score of the whole tokens are 0.671 for CRF and 0.687 for softmax. The results show that the softmax is better than the CRF model. We believe the reason is that there is no hard relation between the metaphor words and other words, so the constraint of CRF does not work well.

Finally, we adopt ALBERT+BiLSTM+softmax as our model. As a new pre-trained model released by Google, the performance of ALBERT-xxLarge-v1(ALBERT for short) (Lan et al., 2019) on natural language understanding task is better than BERT. Since the output dimension of ALBERT model is as high as 4096 dimensions, we just concatenate the first 300 dimension output embedding of ALBERT with the output embedding of BiLSTM. Then let the merged representation go through a full connection layer to get the probability distribution. Finally, the probability distribution is classified in the softmax layer. The reason for concatenating two parts of embedding is that we hope our model can predict by combining the context meaning and the word meaning. Table 5 shows that the concatenation method used performs better.

4.3 Tricks

In this subsections, we will introduce some useful tricks used in this evaluation.

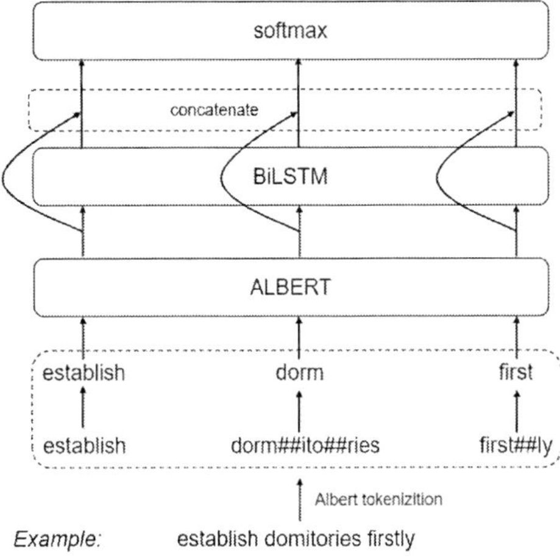

Figure 3: The architecture of our method.

4.3.1 Semantic merge

ALBERT has 12 layers in total. It is generally believed that each layer of language model learns different features of the text, so we make two attempts on the representation vectors for different layers: (1) we concatenate the average output of the last four layers as the final output; (2) we weighted sum the output of all 12 layers as the final output. The final online results show that method (1) is better. We believe that this is because the lower level of the language model is more inclined to learn the syntactic features of the text, while the higher level is more inclined to learn the semantic features of the text (Jawahar et al., 2019). The task of metaphor recognition is more challenging for the proposed model to understand the semantics. The addition of lower level feature representation will introduce noise information instead.

4.3.2   Loss with class weight

Due to the small proportion of metaphorical words in sentences, we consider to increase the loss value of positive metaphorical samples to balance the number difference between positive and negative samples. We try the weight value of positive sample loss between 0.8 and 4, based on the results we find that when weight value of positive samples is 2, we can get the best result.

The specific hyper-parameters of the model are as follows: ALBERT's learning rate is 1e-5, and weight decay is 0.01; BiLSTM has one layer, and the learning rate is 2e-3, hidden units are 256, dropout rate is 0.5; the optimizer is Adam, batch size is 2, early stopping is used. The loss weights corresponding to the positive and negative classes are set to 2 and 1 respectively. The results of our final model on the test sets are as shown in table 6:

	ALLPOS	VERB
TOEFL	0.707	0.728
VUA	0.712	0.755

Table 6: The F1-score of final model on TOEFL and VUA test sets.

Table 6 shows that our model performs well on the TOEFL dataset, and we also tests the results of the model on the VUA dataset. The results show that the proposed model in this paper can achieve good results on both datasets.

5   Conclusion

In this paper, we propose a method with AL-BERT+BiLSTM+softmax to identify metaphor words in the sentence. We extract text features through ALBERT's learning ability, and use BiL-STM to get contextual representation, then get the final prediction results with softmax layers. We also try several data preprocessing methods and utilize three tricks to improve the performance of our proposed model. Besides, we analyze and explain the results of each method according to the characteristics of the metaphor detection task. The experimental results show the effectiveness of our method.

References

Beata Beigman Klebanov, Chee Wee Leong, E. Dario Gutierrez, Ekaterina Shutova, and Michael Flor. 2016. Semantic classifications for detection of verb metaphors. In *Proceedings of the 54th Annual Meeting of the Association for Computational Linguistics (Volume 2: Short Papers)*, pages 101–106, Berlin, Germany. Association for Computational Linguistics.

Jacob Devlin, Ming-Wei Chang, Kenton Lee, and Kristina Toutanova. 2019. BERT: Pre-training of deep bidirectional transformers for language understanding. In *Proceedings of the 2019 Conference of the North American Chapter of the Association for Computational Linguistics: Human Language Technologies, Volume 1 (Long and Short Papers)*, pages 4171–4186, Minneapolis, Minnesota. Association for Computational Linguistics.

Ge Gao, Eunsol Choi, Yejin Choi, and Luke Zettlemoyer. 2018. Neural metaphor detection in context. In *Proceedings of the 2018 Conference on Empirical Methods in Natural Language Processing*, pages 607–613, Brussels, Belgium. Association for Computational Linguistics.

Hongyu Gong, Suma Bhat, and Pramod Viswanath. 2017. Geometry of compositionality. In *Proceedings of the Thirty-First AAAI Conference on Artificial Intelligence, February 4-9, 2017, San Francisco, California, USA*, pages 3202–3208. AAAI Press.

E.Dario Gutiérrez, Ekaterina Shutova, Tyler Marghetis, and Benjamin Bergen. 2016. Literal and metaphorical senses in compositional distributional semantic models. In *Proceedings of the 54th Annual Meeting of the Association for Computational Linguistics (Volume 1: Long Papers)*, pages 183–193, Berlin, Germany. Association for Computational Linguistics.

Ilana Heintz, Ryan Gabbard, Mahesh P. Srivastava, Dave Barner, Donald Black, Majorie Friedman, and Ralph M. Weischedel. 2013. Automatic extraction of linguistic metaphors with lda topic modeling.

Ganesh Jawahar, Benoît Sagot, and Djamé Seddah. 2019. What does BERT learn about the structure of language? In *Proceedings of the 57th Conference of the Association for Computational Linguistics, ACL 2019, Florence, Italy, July 28- August 2, 2019, Volume 1: Long Papers*, pages 3651–3657. Association for Computational Linguistics.

Yuxiang Jia and Shiwen Yu. 2008. Unsupervised Chinese verb metaphor recognition based on selectional preferences. In *Proceedings of the 22nd Pacific Asia Conference on Language, Information and Computation*, pages 207–214, The University of the Philippines Visayas Cebu College, Cebu City, Philippines. De La Salle University, Manila, Philippines.

Beata Beigman Klebanov, Chee Wee Leong, and Michael Flor. 2018. A corpus of non-native written english annotated for metaphor. In *Proceedings of the 2018 Conference of the North American Chapter of the Association for Computational Linguistics: Human Language Technologies, NAACL-IILT, New*

Orleans, Louisiana, USA, June 1-6, 2018, Volume 2 (Short Papers), pages 86–91. Association for Computational Linguistics.

Zornitsa Kozareva. 2013. Multilingual affect polarity and valence prediction in metaphor-rich texts. In *Proceedings of the 51st Annual Meeting of the Association for Computational Linguistics (Volume 1: Long Papers)*, pages 682–691, Sofia, Bulgaria. Association for Computational Linguistics.

Zhenzhong Lan, Mingda Chen, Sebastian Goodman, Kevin Gimpel, Piyush Sharma, and Radu Soricut. 2019. Albert: A lite bert for self-supervised learning of language representations.

Chee Wee Leong, Beata Beigman Klebanov, Chris Hamill, Egon Stemle, Rutuja Ubale, and Xianyang Chen. 2020. A report on the 2020 vua and toefl metaphor detection shared task. In *Proceedings of the Second Workshop on Figurative Language Processing*, Seattle, WA.

Rui Mao, Chenghua Lin, and Frank Guerin. 2019. End-to-end sequential metaphor identification inspired by linguistic theories. In *Proceedings of the 57th Annual Meeting of the Association for Computational Linguistics*, pages 3888–3898, Florence, Italy. Association for Computational Linguistics.

Ekaterina Shutova, Douwe Kiela, and Jean Maillard. 2016. Black holes and white rabbits: Metaphor identification with visual features. In *Proceedings of the 2016 Conference of the North American Chapter of the Association for Computational Linguistics: Human Language Technologies*, pages 160–170, San Diego, California. Association for Computational Linguistics.

Gerard J. Steen. 2010. A method for linguistic metaphor identification: From mip to mipvu.

Yulia Tsvetkov, Leonid Boytsov, Anatole Gershman, Eric Nyberg, and Chris Dyer. 2014. Metaphor detection with cross-lingual model transfer. In *Proceedings of the 52nd Annual Meeting of the Association for Computational Linguistics, ACL 2014, June 22-27, 2014, Baltimore, MD, USA, Volume 1: Long Papers*, pages 248–258. The Association for Computer Linguistics.

Tony Veale. 2012. A context-sensitive, multi-faceted model of lexico-conceptual affect. In *Proceedings of the 50th Annual Meeting of the Association for Computational Linguistics (Volume 2: Short Papers)*, pages 75–79, Jeju Island, Korea. Association for Computational Linguistics.

Character aware models with similarity learning for metaphor detection

Tarun Kumar
Department of CSIS
Birla Institute of Technology
and Science, Pilani, India
f2016005@pilani.bits-pilani.ac.in

Yashvardhan Sharma
Department of CSIS
Birla Institute of Technology
and Science, Pilani, India
yash@pilani.bits-pilani.ac.in

Abstract

Recent work on automatic sequential metaphor detection has involved recurrent neural networks initialized with different pre-trained word embeddings and which are sometimes combined with hand engineered features. To capture lexical and orthographic information automatically, in this paper we propose to add character based word representation. Also, to contrast the difference between literal and contextual meaning, we utilize a similarity network. We explore these components via two different architectures - a BiLSTM model and a Transformer Encoder model similar to BERT to perform metaphor identification. We participate in the Second Shared Task on Metaphor Detection on both the VUA and TOFEL datasets with the above models. The experimental results demonstrate the effectiveness of our method as it outperforms all the systems which participated in the previous shared task.

1 Introduction

Metaphors are an inherent component of natural language and enrich our day-to-day communication both in verbal and written forms. A metaphoric expression involves the use of one domain or concept to explain or represent another concept (Lakoff and Johnson, 1980). Detecting metaphors is a crucial step in interpreting semantic information and thus building better representations for natural language understanding (Shutova and Teufel, 2010). This is beneficial for applications which require to infer the literal/metaphorical usage of words such as information extraction, conversational systems and sentiment analysis (Tsvetkov et al., 2014).

The detection of metaphorical usage is not a trivial task. For example, in phrases such as *breaking the habit* and *absorption of knowledge*, the words *breaking* and *absorption* are used metaphorically to mean to destroy/end and understand/learn respectively. In the phrase, *All the world's a stage,*

the *world* (abstract) has been portrayed in a more concrete (*stage*) sense. Thus, computational approaches to metaphor identification need to exploit world knowledge, context and domain understanding (Tsvetkov et al., 2014).

A number of approaches to metaphor detection have been proposed in the last decade. Many of them use explicit hand-engineered lexical and syntactic information (Hovy et al., 2013; Klebanov et al., 2016), higher level features such as concreteness scores (Turney et al., 2011; Köper and Schulte im Walde, 2017) and WordNet supersenses (Tsvetkov et al., 2014). The more recent methods have modeled metaphor detection as a sequence labeling task, and hence have used BiLSTM (Graves and Schmidhuber, 2005) in different ways (Wu et al., 2018; Gao et al., 2018; Mao et al., 2019; Bizzoni and Ghanimifard, 2018).

In this paper, we use concatenation of GloVe (Pennington et al., 2014) and ELMo (Peters et al., 2018) vectors augmented with character level features using CNN and highway network (Kim et al., 2016; Srivastava et al., 2015). Such a method of combining pre-trained embeddings with character level representations has been previously used in several sequence tagging tasks - part-of-speech (POS) tagging (Ma and Hovy, 2016) and named entity recognition (NER) (Chiu and Nichols, 2016), question answering (Seo et al., 2016) and multi-task learning (Sanh et al., 2019). This inspires us to explore similar setting for metaphor identification as well.

We propose two models for metaphor detection[1] with the input prepared as above - a vanilla BiLSTM model and a vanilla Transformer Encoder (Vaswani et al., 2017) model similar to BERT (Devlin et al., 2019) (but without pre-training). To contrast the difference between a word's literal and contextual representation (Mao et al., 2019) con-

---

[1]Our code is available at: https://github.com/
Kumar-Tarun/metaphor-detection

Proceedings of the Second Workshop on Figurative Language Processing, pages 116–125
July 9, 2020. ©2020 Association for Computational Linguistics
https://doi.org/10.18653/v1/P17

catenated the two before feeding into the softmax classifier. Instead, we extend the idea of cosine similarity between two words in a phrase of signifying metaphoricity (Shutova et al., 2016; Rei et al., 2017) to similarity between the literal and contextual representations of a word and then feed this result into the classifier.

Finally, we participate in The Second Shared Task on Metaphor Detection[2] on both the VU Amsterdam Metaphor Corpus (VUA) (Steen et al., 2010) and TOEFL, a subset of ETS Corpus of Non-Native Written English (Beigman Klebanov et al., 2018) datasets with the above models and a vanilla combination of them. The combination of the models outperforms the winner (Wu et al., 2018) of the previous shared task (Leong et al., 2018).

2 Related Work

Previous metaphor detection frameworks include supervised machine learning approaches utilizing explicit hand-engineered features, approaches based on unsupervised learning and representation learning, and deep learning models to detect metaphors in an end-to-end manner. (Köper and Schulte im Walde, 2017) determine the difference of concreteness scores between the target word and its context and use this to predict the metaphoricity of verbs in the VUA dataset. (Tsvetkov et al., 2014) combine vector space representations with features such as abstractness and imageability and Word-Net Supersenses to model the metaphor detection problem in two syntactic constructions - subject-verb-object (SVO) and adjective-noun (AN). Evaluating their approach on the TroFi dataset (Birke and Sarkar, 2006), they achieve competitive accuracy. (Hovy et al., 2013) explore differences in compositional behaviour of a word's literal and metaphorical use in certain syntactic settings. Using lexical, WordNet supersense features and PoS tags of sentence tree, they train an SVM using tree-kernel. (Klebanov et al., 2016) use semantic classes of verbs such as orthographic unigram, lemma unigram, distributional clusters etc. to identify metaphors in the VUA dataset.

Some of the methods for metaphor detection utilize unsupervised learning. (Mao et al., 2018) train word embeddings on wikipedia dump and use WordNet compute a best-fit word corresponding to a target word in a sentence. The cosine similarity

between these two words indicates the metaphoricity of the target word. (Shutova et al., 2016) compute word embeddings and phrase embeddings on wikipedia dump. They extract visual features from CNNs using images from Google Images. Next, multimodal fusion strategies are explored to determine metaphoricity.

Recently, approaches based on deep learning have been proposed. The first in this line is Supervised Similarity network by (Rei et al., 2017). They capture metaphoric composition by modeling the interaction between source and target domain by a gating function and then using a cosine similarity network to compute metaphoricity. They evaluate their method on adjective-noun, verb-subject and verb-direct object constructions on the MOH (Mohammad et al., 2016) and TSV (Tsvetkov et al., 2014) datasets.

More recently, the problem has been modeled as a sequence labeling task, in which at each timestep the word is predicted as literal or metaphoric. (Wu et al., 2018) used word2vec (Mikolov et al., 2013), PoS tags and word clusters as input features to a CNN and BiLSTM network. They compared inference using softmax and CRF layers, and found softmax to work better. (Bizzoni and Ghanimifard, 2018) propose two models - a BiLSTM with dense layers before and after it and a recursive model for bigram phrase composition using fully-connected neural network. They also added concreteness scores to boost performance. (Gao et al., 2018) fed GloVe and ELMo embeddings into a vanilla BiLSTM followed by softmax. (Mao et al., 2019) proposed models based on MIP (Group, 2007) and SVP (Wilks, 1975, 1978) linguistic theories and achieved competitive performance on VUA, MOH and TroFi datasets.

3 Methodology

In this paper we propose two architectures for metaphor detection based on sequence labeling paradigm - a BiLSTM model and a Transformer Encoder model. Both the models are initialized with rich word representations. First, we describe the word representations, then, the similarity network, and subsequently the models (Figure 1).

3.1 Word Representations

The first step in building word representations is the concatenation of GloVe (Pennington et al., 2014) and ELMo (Peters et al., 2018) embeddings. The

[2] https://competitions.codalab.org/competitions/22188

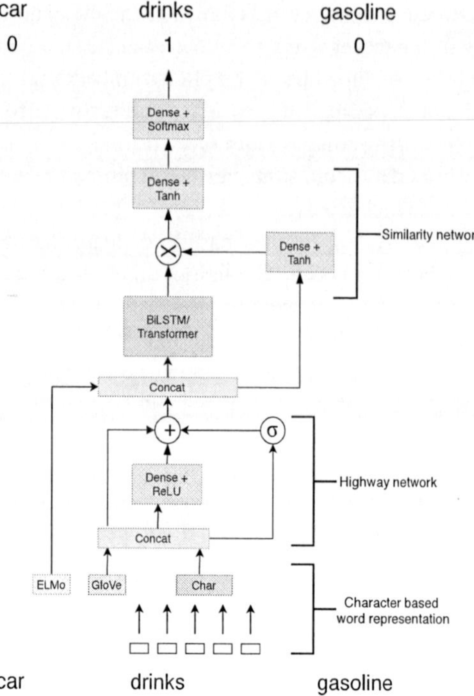

Figure 1: Proposed model which includes character embeddings and similarity network

combination of these two have shown good performance across an array of NLP tasks (Peters et al., 2018). While these two representations are based on corpus statistics and bidirectional language models respectively and serve as a good starting point as shown by (Gao et al., 2018) and (Mao et al., 2019), however to learn explicit lexical, syntactic and orthographic information (so as to be more suited for metaphor tasks) we augment these word representations with character level embeddings. We follow (Kim et al., 2016) to compute character-level representations by a 1D CNN (see Figure 2) followed by a highway network (Srivastava et al., 2015).

Let word at position t be made up of characters $[c_1, \ldots, c_l]$, where each $c_i \in R^d$, l is the length of word and d is dimensionality[3] of character embeddings. Let $C^t \in \mathbb{R}^{d \times l}$ denote the character-level embedding matrix of word t. This matrix is convolved with filter $H \in \mathbb{R}^{d \times w}$ of width w, followed by a non-linearity.

$$f^t = \tanh(C^t * H + b), f^t \in \mathbb{R}^{l-w+1} \quad (1)$$

Next, we apply max-pooling over the length of f

---

[3]d is chosen less than the $|C|$, the size of vocabulary of characters

to get a output for one filter.

$$y^t = \max_{1 \le j \le l-w+1} \{f_j^t\} \quad (2)$$

Now, we take multiple filters of different widths and concatenate the output of each to get a vector representation of word t. Let h be the number of filters and $y_1, \ldots, y_h$ be the outputs, then $c_t = [y_1^t, \ldots, y_h^t]$. We concatenate GloVe embedding (g_t) with c_t and run it through a single layer highway network (Srivastava et al., 2015).

$$a_t = [g_t; c_t] \quad (3)$$
$$t = \sigma(W_T a_t + b_T) \quad (4)$$
$$z_t = t \odot g(W_H a_t + b_H) + (1 - t) \odot a_t \quad (5)$$

z_t and a_t have same dimensionality by construction, W_H and W_T are square matrices, g is ReLU activation. t is called as transform gate and $(1 - t)$ as the carry gate. The role of highway network is to select the dimensions which are to be modified and which are to be passed directly to output. Thus, we allow the network to adjust the contribution of GloVe and character-based embeddings for better learning (thus an adjustment between semantic and lexical information). We also concatenated GloVe, ELMo and character embeddings and passed through highway layer, but the former approach performed better with lesser parameters. Our input representation is $[z_t; e_t]$ (where e_t is ELMo vector) which is fed to BiLSTM/Transformer.

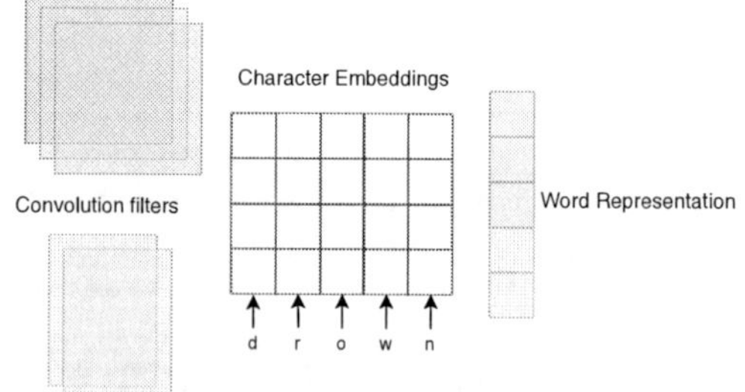

Figure 2: CNN for extracting character-level representations

3.2 BiLSTM model

We use a single-layer BiLSTM model (Graves and Schmidhuber, 2005) to produce hidden states h_t for each position t. These hidden states represent our contextual meaning, the meaning which we will contrast with the input literal meaning. Using hidden states as a candidate for contextual meaning has been done previously (Gao et al., 2018; Mao et al., 2019; Wu et al., 2018). A simple approach would be to pass h_t directly to softmax layer for predictions. But we condition our predictions both on h_t and input representation as shown in next sub-section.

3.3 Similarity Network

(Rei et al., 2017) use a weighted cosine similarity network to determine similarity between two word vectors in a phrase (Shutova et al., 2016). We extend this idea further to calculation of similarity between literal and contextual representations. To perform this computation, we first project the input embeddings to the size of hidden dimension of BiLSTM.

$$x_t = [z_t; e_t] \tag{6}$$

$$\tilde{x}_t = \tanh(W_z x_t) \tag{7}$$

This step serves two purposes - first reduces the size to enable calculation, second performs vector space mapping. Since input embeddings are in a different semantic vector space (due to the pre-trained vectors), we allow the network to learn a mapping to the more metaphor specific vector space. Next, we element-wise multiply $\tilde{x}_t$ with h_t.

$$m_t = \tilde{x}_t \odot h_t \tag{8}$$

m_t is input to a dense layer as follows,

$$u_t = \tanh(W_u m_t) \tag{9}$$

If u_t has length 1, W_u has all weights equal to 1 and linear activation is used instead of $\tanh$, then the above two steps mimic the cosine similarity function. But, to provide better generalization, $|u_t| > 1$ and $\tanh$ is used to allow the model to learn custom features for metaphor detection (Rei et al., 2017). u_t is fed to softmax classifier to make predictions.

$$p(\hat{y}_t | u_t) = \sigma(W_y u_t + b) \tag{10}$$

σ is the softmax function, W_y and b are trainable weights and bias respectively.

3.4 Transformer model

The advent of Transformer (Vaswani et al., 2017) and further general language models such as BERT (Devlin et al., 2019), GPT-2 (Radford et al., 2019) have shown excellent performance across multiple

Dataset	Train			Test	
	#T	#S	%M	#T	#S
VUA All-POS	72,611	12,122	15%	22,196	4,080
VUA Verb	17,240	12,122	28%	5,873	4,080
TOEFL All-POS	26,737	2741	7%	9,017	968
TOEFL Verb	7,016	2741	14%	2,301	968

Table 1: Dataset Statistics. #T denotes the number of tokens which are annotated. #S denotes the number of sentences. %M denotes the token-level metaphoricity percentage.

NLP, NLU and NLG tasks. Inspired by this, we explore a vanilla transformer model in this paper which consists of only the encoder stack and is not pre-trained on any corpus.

The input to the transformer model is the same as the BiLSTM model. To contrast the literal meaning with the contextual meaning, we employ equations 6,7,8,9,10 except that h_t would denote the output of the transformer at position t. (Mao et al., 2019) also explored transformers in their experiments, but they only computed word representations from a pre-trained BERT large model and fed it to BiLSTM, they did not train a transformer model from scratch. Since transformers do not track positional information, positional encodings are added for this purpose, but in our case adding such encoding did not improve performance. Furthermore, our transformer model is composed of only a single transformer block (that is depth=1) with a single head. Such a simple model is able to reach good score on the metaphor detection task.

4 Experiment

4.1 Dataset

We evaluate our models on two metaphor datasets on both ALL-POS and VERB track in the Second Shared Task on Metaphor Detection. Table 1 shows the dataset statistics.

First is the VU Amsterdam Metaphor Corpus (VUA) (Steen et al., 2010) widely studied dataset for metaphor detection. All the words in this dataset are labeled as either metaphoric or literal according to MIPVU (Steen et al., 2010; Group, 2007) protocol. This dataset was also used in the 2018 Shared Task on Metaphor Detection (Leong et al., 2018).

Second is the TOEFL corpus, a subset of ETS Corpus of Non-Native Written English

(Beigman Klebanov et al., 2018). This dataset contains the essays written by takers of the TOEFL test having either medium or high English proficiency. The words in this dataset are annotated for argumentation-relevant metaphors. The essays are in response to prompts, for which test-takers were required to argue for or against and in such process the metaphors used to support one's argument were annotated. So, the protocol used (Beigman Klebanov and Flor, 2013) is different from MIPVU.

4.2 Baselines

The first four baselines are evaluated on the VUA test set and the last two on the TOEFL test set. **CNN-BiLSTM** (Wu et al., 2018): This model is the winner of the previous shared task (Leong et al., 2018). They proposed an ensemble of CNN-BiLSTM network with input features as word2vec, PoS tags and word2vec clusters.
BiLSTM (Gao et al., 2018) : This model is a simple BiLSTM with inputs as concatenation of GloVe and ELMo embeddings.
BiLSTM-MCHA (Mao et al., 2019) : This model employs BiLSTM followed by a multi-head contextual attention which is inspired by SPV protocol of metaphor identification. They also use GloVe and ELMo as input features.
BiLSTM-Concat (Bizzoni and Ghanimifard, 2018) : This model achieved the second position in the previous shared task. They combined a BiLSTM (preceded and followed by dense layers) and a model based on recursive composition of word embedding. Concreteness scores were added to boost performance.
CE-BiLSTM : We add a variant of our proposed model without the Transformer model and the similarity network. All other components are kept same. CE denotes character embeddings.
Feature-based (Beigman Klebanov et al., 2018) : They use several hand-crafted features and train a logistic regression classifier to predict metaphoricity. This is the only known work on TOEFL dataset to the best of our knowledge.

We note that BiLSTM and BiLSTM-MHCA models above have different experimental settings than ours. They trained and tested their models on different amount of data when compared to the shared task. For a fair comparison, we evaluate (train and test) our method in the same data setting (Table 3).

4.3 Setup

The 300d pre-trained GloVe embeddings are used along with 1024d pre-trained ELMo embeddings. The dimension of character-level embeddings is set to 50. The filters used in CharCNN are $[(1, 25), (2, 50), (3, 75), (4, 100)]$, where first element of each tuple denotes the width of filter and second element denotes the number of filters used. Inspired by the effectiveness of PoS tags (Wu et al., 2018; Beigman Klebanov et al., 2014) in metaphor detection, we concatenate 30 dimensional PoS embeddings. We found 30d embeddings to work better than one-hot encodings. These embeddings are learned during model training. The uni-directional hidden state size of BiLSTM is set to 300. We apply Dropout (Srivastava et al., 2014) on input to BiLSTM and to the output of BiLSTM. The dimension of u_t, the output size of similarity network is set to 50.

The hidden state size of Transformer is set to 300 as well. We use a single head and single layer architecture. We also tried multiple heads (8, 16), but the performance dropped a little. The attention due to padded tokens is masked out in the attention matrix during forward pass. The feed-forward network which is applied after the self-attention layer consists of two linear transformations with ReLU activation in between (Vaswani et al., 2017). First transformation projects 300d to 1200d and second transformation projects 1200d back to 300d. Dropout is applied both before and after the feed-forward network. It can be seen that this transformer model is simplified in terms of number of parameters when compared to BERT (Devlin et al., 2019). Our focus here is on the power of transformer architecture rather than on transformer based huge language models.

We also explore the combination of both the models. Specifically, BiLSTM and Transformer model are combined at the pre-activation stage, that is, the logits of both networks are averaged and then input to the softmax layer for predictions. Both the models are trained in parallel, with their own losses, whereas the F1-score is calculated from the combined prediction.

The objective function used is weighted cross-entropy loss as used in (Mao et al., 2019; Wu et al., 2018).

$$L = -\sum_{n=1}^{M} w_{y_n} y_n \log(\hat{y_n}) \qquad (11)$$

Model	VUA ALL POS			VUA VERB		
	P	R	F1	P	R	F1
CNN-BiLSTM	60.8	70.0	65.1	60.0	76.3	67.1
BiLSTM-Concat	59.5	68.0	63.5	-	-	-
CE-BiLSTM-Transformer	60.6	73.9	66.6	62.7	82.2	71.2
CE-BiLSTM-Transformer (Ensemble)	63.0	71.6	**67.0**	66.7	77.5	**71.7**

Table 2: Comparison of our method against the baseline systems on the VUA test set.

Model	VUA ALL POS			VUA VERB		
	P	R	F1	P	R	F1
BiLSTM	71.6	73.6	72.6	68.2	71.3	69.7
BiLSTM-MHCA	73.0	75.7	74.3	66.3	75.2	70.5
CE-BiLSTM-Transformer	71.3	78.5	74.7	66.1	76.2	70.8
CE-BiLSTM-Transformer (Ensemble)	75.9	74.1	**75.0**	68.0	75.1	**71.4**

Table 3: Comparison of our method against the baseline systems on the VUA test set with different experimental setting.

Model	TOEFL ALL POS			TOEFL VERB		
	P	R	F1	P	R	F1
Feature-based	49.0	58.0	53.0	50.0	64.0	56.0
CE-BiLSTM	62.7	60.8	61.8	70.0	60.5	64.9
CE-BiLSTM-Transformer	62.3	61.7	**62.0**	66.9	63.8	**65.3**

Table 4: Comparison of our method against the baseline systems on the TOEFL test set.

where y_n is the gold label, $\hat{y}_n$ is the predicted score and w_{y_n} is set to 1 if y_n is literal and 2 otherwise. We use Adam optimizer (Kingma and Ba, 2014) and early stopping on the basis of validation F-score. Batch-size is set to 4.

TOEFL dataset contains essays annotated for metaphor and metadata mapping essays to the respective prompts and English proficiency of test-takers. We extract all sentences from all the essays and prepare our dataset considering one sentence as one example (batch-size x means x such examples). In this paper, we do not exploit the metadata of TOEFL corpus.

For both VUA and TOEFL datasets, we have a pre-specified train and test partition, so for hyper-parameter tuning we split the train set into train and validation in the ratio of 10:1 randomly. Since the models predict labels for all the words in a sequence, we train a single model and use it for evaluating both ALL-POS and Verb tracks. We report F-score on test set for metaphor class on both datasets and tasks. Section 6 presents an ablation study and explores the performance of different components.

5 Results

We first compare our method against the baseline systems which have the same experimental setting as ours on the VUA test set - CNN-BiLSTM and BiLSTM-Concat. Table 2 reports the results. As shown, our proposed model (comprising of both BiLSTM and Transformer) outperforms the other methods on both the tracks. Specifically, we achieve F-score of 66.6 on VUA All POS and 71.2 for VUA Verb set. Furthermore, we employ ensembling to boost our performance. This strategy mainly improves precision (60.6 to 63.0 for All POS, 62.7 to 66.7 for Verb). For ensembling we run the model 7 times which involves different dropout probabilities, changing the ratio of metaphoric to literal loss weights, increasing/decreasing number of epochs. Thus, we do not modify the number of parameters in any run. At the end, we take a majority vote to produce final predictions. Our best F-score on All POS track is 67.0 and Verb track is 71.7. We observe higher F-scores on Verb track than on All POS track, this might be due to fact that a higher percentage of verbs are annotated as being metaphoric, hence more training data.

We now compare our method with the other two baselines on a common experimental setting. We tune our hyperparameters in this setting due to difference in training and validation data. Specifically, since training set is of smaller size, we increase Dropout probabilities, and the dimension of PoS embedding is reduced from 30 to 10. As shown in Table 3, the single best model achieves a higher F-score than the baselines and the ensemble (with similar setting as above) improves the performance

Model	VUA Validation		
	P	R	F1
Vanilla BiLSTM	61.7	82.6	70.6
Vanilla Transformer	63.6	75.6	69.1
Vanilla BiLSTM + Transformer	67.1	77.7	72.0

Table 5: Performance of vanilla models on VUA validation set.

Model	VUA Validation		
	P	R	F1
CE + BiLSTM	65.7	78.8	71.6
CE + Transformer	67.3	74.7	70.8
CE + BiLSTM + Transformer	71.3	74.2	72.7

Table 6: Addition of Character embeddings to models.

a little more scoring 75.0 on All POS and 71.4 on Verb tracks.

Lastly, we explore the performance of our method on the TOEFL test set (Table 4). We added an extra baseline which does not include the Transformer model and the similarity network. Also, the CE-BiLSTM-Transformer model here does not include the similarity network. The reason for this is because it degraded performance. The similarity network contrasts the literal meaning with the contextual meaning of the target word which is in line with MIP (Steen et al., 2010) protocol. Since, TOEFL corpus is annotated for argument-specific metaphors and not MIP, we hypothesize that this might be the reason for lower performance. However, VUA is annotated according to MIP, thus similarity component improves performance here, as we show in the ablation section.

Table 4 shows that both our baseline (CE-BiLSTM) and baseline + Transformer improve upon the Feature-based model by 8.8 and 9.0 points respectively on All POS track and 8.9 and 9.3 points respectively on Verb track. Similar to VUA, here also Verbs score higher than All POS because of more training instances for verbs.

The scores on TOEFL dataset are lower than the VUA dataset. This is due to the lesser number of training instances in TOEFL dataset. Also, while we have higher recall on VUA, on TOEFL we have higher precision.

6 Ablation Study

This section considers the performance of different components of our method in isolation and combination on the VUA validation set unless otherwise specified. The reason for choosing validation set is because we were not able to evaluate some settings

on the test set due to limited time and number of submissions. Wherever we have test set results we report those as well.

Impact of Character Embeddings We first note the performances of vanilla BiLSTM and vanilla Transformer models and a simple combination of them in Table 5. Note that vanilla implementation still includes GloVe and ELMo vectors. We see that BiLSTM performs better than Transformer model and that a combination of them seems to complement each other.

Now, we see the impact of adding character-level embeddings on both the models. As Table 6 shows, addition of character embeddings improves both the networks. Particularly, Transformer benefits more from this addition as F1-score increases from 69.1 to 70.8. On the test set, our vanilla combination scores 65.2 whereas the combination of models with character embeddings scores 66.1. This helps in asserting the usefulness of character-based features in learning pro-metaphor features. (Beigman Klebanov et al., 2016) demonstrate the utility of unigram lemmas and orthographic features in metaphor detection. Our character embeddings computed from CNN combines features at different n-grams of a word and thus helps to learn lexical and orthographic information automatically which aids in improving performance.

We suspect that employing the baseline unigram features (Beigman Klebanov et al., 2014) provided by the organizers instead of learned character-embeddings may be seen as a way to achieve the same goal. But our method is more robust in the sense that, we allow for learning of different n-gram features of a word (including unigram itself). Particularly, our method is helpful in cases where the target word has incorrect spelling, because we learn representations instead of using fixed pre-computed features.

Impact of Similarity Network Table 7 depicts the performance after the addition of similarity network. As the similarity network is guided by the MIP protocol, it indeed boosts results for the VUA dataset. We observe that in this case too Transformer benefits more by the inclusion and the benefit (1.9 points) is even more than by adding character embeddings (1.7 points). However, for both the components increments in BiLSTM performance are equal. Also, the combination of both models with similarity network outperforms the combination with character embeddings although

Model	VUA Validation		
	P	R	F1
SN + BiLSTM	66.1	78.1	71.6
SN + Transformer	70.2	74.0	72.0
SN + BiLSTM + Transformer	68.7	77.8	73.0

Table 7: Addition of Similarity network to models. (SN is the Similarity network)

Model	VUA Validation		
	P	R	F1
CE + SN + BiLSTM	66.7	79.3	72.4
CE + SN + Transformer	67.7	77.8	72.4
CE + SN + BiLSTM + Transformer	68.5	79.1	73.4

Table 8: Addition of both SN and CE to the models.

by a small margin. The above reasoning indicates towards similarity network as being an important component for detection of MIP guided labeling of metaphors.

Table 8 reports the numbers when both character embeddings and similarity network are added to the base models. The results improve from either of the additions which indicate that they complement each other. Our best model so far contains both the base models and the components. This model on the VUA test set, scores 66.5 and the model in the last row of Table 6 scores 66.1.

In all the cases examined till now, Transformer based models have higher precision than the BiLSTM based models, and in 3 out of 4 cases of (Vanilla, CE, SN, CE + SN), the combination has as even better precision than either of the individual models. In terms of F-score, BiLSTM based models score higher than Transformer based ones in 2 cases (Vanilla and CE), equal in CE + SN and lower in SN.

Impact of PoS tags Incorporation of PoS tags proves to be beneficial. It improves the F-score of the last model in Table 8 from 73.4 to 73.5. On the test set, it improves the F-score from 66.5 to 66.6 which is in line with (Hovy et al., 2013; Wu et al., 2018).

7 Conclusion

We proposed two metaphor detection models, a BiLSTM model based on prior work and a Transformer model based on their success in NLP tasks. We augment these models with two components - Character Embeddings and Similarity network to learn lexical features and contrast literal and contextual meanings respectively. Our experimental results demonstrate the effectiveness of our method as we achieve superior performance than all the previous methods on VUA corpus and TOEFL corpus. Through an ablation study we examine the contribution of different parts of our framework in the task of metaphor detection.

In our future work we would explore metaphor detection in a multi-task setting with semantically similar tasks such as Word Sense Disambiguation and Co-reference Resolution. These auxiliary tasks may help to better understand the contextual meaning and reach of a word. For TOEFL dataset, future avenues would include strategies to exploit the metadata, and similarity measures more suitable for argumentation-relevant metaphors.

References

Beata Beigman Klebanov and Michael Flor. 2013. Argumentation-relevant metaphors in test-taker essays. In *Proceedings of the First Workshop on Metaphor in NLP*, pages 11–20, Atlanta, Georgia. Association for Computational Linguistics.

Beata Beigman Klebanov, Ben Leong, Michael Heilman, and Michael Flor. 2014. Different texts, same metaphors: Unigrams and beyond. In *Proceedings of the Second Workshop on Metaphor in NLP*, pages 11–17, Baltimore, MD. Association for Computational Linguistics.

Beata Beigman Klebanov, Chee Wee Leong, E. Dario Gutierrez, Ekaterina Shutova, and Michael Flor. 2016. Semantic classifications for detection of verb metaphors. In *Proceedings of the 54th Annual Meeting of the Association for Computational Linguistics (Volume 2: Short Papers)*, pages 101–106, Berlin, Germany. Association for Computational Linguistics.

Beata Beigman Klebanov, Chee Wee (Ben) Leong, and Michael Flor. 2018. A corpus of non-native written English annotated for metaphor. In *Proceedings of the 2018 Conference of the North American Chapter of the Association for Computational Linguistics: Human Language Technologies, Volume 2 (Short Papers)*, pages 86–91, New Orleans, Louisiana. Association for Computational Linguistics.

Julia Birke and Anoop Sarkar. 2006. A clustering approach for nearly unsupervised recognition of non-literal language. In *11th Conference of the European Chapter of the Association for Computational Linguistics*, Trento, Italy. Association for Computational Linguistics.

Yuri Bizzoni and Mehdi Ghanimifard. 2018. Bigrams and BiLSTMs two neural networks for sequential metaphor detection. In *Proceedings of the Workshop on Figurative Language Processing*, pages 91–101,

New Orleans, Louisiana. Association for Computational Linguistics.

Jason P.C. Chiu and Eric Nichols. 2016. Named entity recognition with bidirectional LSTM-CNNs. *Transactions of the Association for Computational Linguistics*, 4:357–370.

Jacob Devlin, Ming-Wei Chang, Kenton Lee, and Kristina Toutanova. 2019. BERT: Pre-training of deep bidirectional transformers for language understanding. In *Proceedings of the 2019 Conference of the North American Chapter of the Association for Computational Linguistics: Human Language Technologies, Volume 1 (Long and Short Papers)*, pages 4171–4186, Minneapolis, Minnesota. Association for Computational Linguistics.

Ge Gao, Eunsol Choi, Yejin Choi, and Luke Zettlemoyer. 2018. Neural metaphor detection in context. In *Proceedings of the 2018 Conference on Empirical Methods in Natural Language Processing*, pages 607–613, Brussels, Belgium. Association for Computational Linguistics.

Alex Graves and Jürgen Schmidhuber. 2005. Framewise phoneme classification with bidirectional lstm and other neural network architectures. *Neural networks*, 18(5-6):602–610.

Pragglejaz Group. 2007. Mip: A method for identifying metaphorically used words in discourse. *Metaphor and Symbol*, 22(1):1–39.

Dirk Hovy, Shashank Srivastava, Sujay Kumar Jauhar, Mrinmaya Sachan, Kartik Goyal, Huying Li, Whitney Sanders, and Eduard Hovy. 2013. Identifying metaphorical word use with tree kernels. In *Proceedings of the First Workshop on Metaphor in NLP*, pages 52–57.

Yoon Kim, Yacine Jernite, David Sontag, and Alexander M Rush. 2016. Character-aware neural language models. In *Thirtieth AAAI Conference on Artificial Intelligence*.

Diederik P Kingma and Jimmy Ba. 2014. Adam: A method for stochastic optimization. *arXiv preprint arXiv:1412.6980*.

Beata Beigman Klebanov, Chee Wee Leong, E Dario Gutierrez, Ekaterina Shutova, and Michael Flor. 2016. Semantic classifications for detection of verb metaphors. In *Proceedings of the 54th Annual Meeting of the Association for Computational Linguistics (Volume 2: Short Papers)*, pages 101–106.

Maximilian Köper and Sabine Schulte im Walde. 2017. Improving verb metaphor detection by propagating abstractness to words, phrases and individual senses. In *Proceedings of the 1st Workshop on Sense, Concept and Entity Representations and their Applications*, pages 24–30, Valencia, Spain. Association for Computational Linguistics.

George Lakoff and Mark Johnson. 1980. Metaphors we live by. *Chicago, IL: University of Chicago*.

Chee Wee (Ben) Leong, Beata Beigman Klebanov, and Ekaterina Shutova. 2018. A report on the 2018 VUA metaphor detection shared task. In *Proceedings of the Workshop on Figurative Language Processing*, pages 56–66, New Orleans, Louisiana. Association for Computational Linguistics.

Xuezhe Ma and Eduard Hovy. 2016. End-to-end sequence labeling via bi-directional LSTM-CNNs-CRF. In *Proceedings of the 54th Annual Meeting of the Association for Computational Linguistics (Volume 1: Long Papers)*, pages 1064–1074, Berlin, Germany. Association for Computational Linguistics.

Rui Mao, Chenghua Lin, and Frank Guerin. 2018. Word embedding and WordNet based metaphor identification and interpretation. In *Proceedings of the 56th Annual Meeting of the Association for Computational Linguistics (Volume 1: Long Papers)*, pages 1222–1231, Melbourne, Australia. Association for Computational Linguistics.

Rui Mao, Chenghua Lin, and Frank Guerin. 2019. End-to-end sequential metaphor identification inspired by linguistic theories. In *Proceedings of the 57th Annual Meeting of the Association for Computational Linguistics*, pages 3888–3898, Florence, Italy. Association for Computational Linguistics.

Tomas Mikolov, Ilya Sutskever, Kai Chen, Greg S Corrado, and Jeff Dean. 2013. Distributed representations of words and phrases and their compositionality. In *Advances in neural information processing systems*, pages 3111–3119.

Saif Mohammad, Ekaterina Shutova, and Peter Turney. 2016. Metaphor as a medium for emotion: An empirical study. In *Proceedings of the Fifth Joint Conference on Lexical and Computational Semantics*, pages 23–33.

Jeffrey Pennington, Richard Socher, and Christopher Manning. 2014. Glove: Global vectors for word representation. In *Proceedings of the 2014 Conference on Empirical Methods in Natural Language Processing (EMNLP)*, pages 1532–1543, Doha, Qatar. Association for Computational Linguistics.

Matthew Peters, Mark Neumann, Mohit Iyyer, Matt Gardner, Christopher Clark, Kenton Lee, and Luke Zettlemoyer. 2018. Deep contextualized word representations. In *Proceedings of the 2018 Conference of the North American Chapter of the Association for Computational Linguistics: Human Language Technologies, Volume 1 (Long Papers)*, pages 2227–2237, New Orleans, Louisiana. Association for Computational Linguistics.

Alec Radford, Jeffrey Wu, Rewon Child, David Luan, Dario Amodei, and Ilya Sutskever. 2019. Language models are unsupervised multitask learners. *OpenAI Blog*, 1(8):9.

Marek Rei, Luana Bulat, Douwe Kiela, and Ekaterina Shutova. 2017. Grasping the finer point: A supervised similarity network for metaphor detection. In *Proceedings of the 2017 Conference on Empirical Methods in Natural Language Processing*, pages 1537–1546, Copenhagen, Denmark. Association for Computational Linguistics.

Victor Sanh, Thomas Wolf, and Sebastian Ruder. 2019. A hierarchical multi-task approach for learning embeddings from semantic tasks. In *Proceedings of the AAAI Conference on Artificial Intelligence*, volume 33, pages 6949–6956.

Minjoon Seo, Aniruddha Kembhavi, Ali Farhadi, and Hannaneh Hajishirzi. 2016. Bidirectional attention flow for machine comprehension. *arXiv preprint arXiv:1611.01603*.

Ekaterina Shutova, Douwe Kiela, and Jean Maillard. 2016. Black holes and white rabbits: Metaphor identification with visual features. In *Proceedings of the 2016 Conference of the North American Chapter of the Association for Computational Linguistics: Human Language Technologies*, pages 160–170, San Diego, California. Association for Computational Linguistics.

Ekaterina Shutova and Simone Teufel. 2010. Metaphor corpus annotated for source-target domain mappings. In *LREC*, volume 2. Citeseer.

Nitish Srivastava, Geoffrey Hinton, Alex Krizhevsky, Ilya Sutskever, and Ruslan Salakhutdinov. 2014. Dropout: a simple way to prevent neural networks from overfitting. *The journal of machine learning research*, 15(1):1929–1958.

Rupesh K Srivastava, Klaus Greff, and Jürgen Schmidhuber. 2015. Training very deep networks. In *Advances in neural information processing systems*, pages 2377–2385.

Gerard Steen, Aletta Dorst, J Berenike Herrmann, Anna Kaal, Tina Krennmayr, and Trijntje Pasma. 2010. *A method for linguistic metaphor identification: From MIP to MIPVU*, volume 14. John Benjamins Publishing.

Yulia Tsvetkov, Leonid Boytsov, Anatole Gershman, Eric Nyberg, and Chris Dyer. 2014. Metaphor detection with cross-lingual model transfer. In *Proceedings of the 52nd Annual Meeting of the Association for Computational Linguistics (Volume 1: Long Papers)*, pages 248–258, Baltimore, Maryland. Association for Computational Linguistics.

Peter Turney, Yair Neuman, Dan Assaf, and Yohai Cohen. 2011. Literal and metaphorical sense identification through concrete and abstract context. In *Proceedings of the 2011 Conference on Empirical Methods in Natural Language Processing*, pages 680–690, Edinburgh, Scotland, UK. Association for Computational Linguistics.

Ashish Vaswani, Noam Shazeer, Niki Parmar, Jakob Uszkoreit, Llion Jones, Aidan N Gomez, Łukasz Kaiser, and Illia Polosukhin. 2017. Attention is all you need. In *Advances in neural information processing systems*, pages 5998–6008.

Yorick Wilks. 1975. A preferential, pattern-seeking, semantics for natural language inference. *Artificial intelligence*, 6(1):53–74.

Yorick Wilks. 1978. Making preferences more active. *Artificial intelligence*, 11(3):197–223.

Chuhan Wu, Fangzhao Wu, Yubo Chen, Sixing Wu, Zhigang Yuan, and Yongfeng Huang. 2018. Neural metaphor detecting with CNN-LSTM model. In *Proceedings of the Workshop on Figurative Language Processing*, pages 110–114, New Orleans, Louisiana. Association for Computational Linguistics.

Yuri Bizzoni
Saarland University
`yuri.bizzoni@uni-saarland.de`

Simon Dobnik
University of Gothenburg
`simon.dobnik@gu.se`

Abstract

This work explores the differences and similarities between neural image classifiers' mis-categorisations and visually grounded metaphors - that we could conceive as intentional mis-categorisations. We discuss the possibility of using automatic image classifiers to approximate human metaphoric behaviours, and the limitations of such frame. We report two pilot experiments to study grounded metaphoricity. In the first we represent metaphors as a form of visual mis-categorisation. In the second we model metaphors as a more flexible, compositional operation in a continuous visual space generated from automatic classification systems.

1 Introduction

Visually grounded metaphors are metaphors that function on the visual similarity between two objects. Humans use visually grounded metaphors to describe scenes or objects in a vivid way: we could call a large person an elephant, describe somebody's blue eyes as a clear summer sky; and so forth. The basic idea is that using a metaphoric element to "overlay" on the described object creates, in the imagination of the reader or listener of the metaphor, a stronger and effective mind picture. At the same time, the mechanisms and workings underlying metaphors remain unclear. Grounded metaphors are among several categories of metaphors that work on the interplay of all five senses plus the abstract dimension of language. Some of these metaphors and similes are harder to model: the precise reason why a *cold voice* creates the idea of a specific tone and sound of voice, or why some other synesthetic expressions like *a blue music* work in the human brain is difficult to define. Visually grounded metaphors, unlike metaphors that draw from several senses, could be easier to model: and we could try to study them

by applying the visual models used for image captioning in NLP. The central question of this paper is whether, and to to what degree human visual metaphors can be reproduced using image features trained in the image captioning scenario. This pilot study defines some possible lines of exploration through two small scale experiments that lead to further research in this area of connecting language and vision and modelling of metaphorical language. More data and analyses will be necessary to further deepen the topic.

2 State of the Art

A large bibliography has discussed the relation between language and perception and the way linguistic meaning is expressed linguistically and non-linguistically. This is done by grounding word meaning in visual perception (Siskind, 2001) and testing the compositionality of visually-enriched language representations (Gorniak and Roy, 2004), and more recently even using sensory-motor robotics to model lexico-grammatical patterns (Zhong et al., 2019), often for the construction of multimodal or dialogue agents (Roy, 2005; Roy and Reiter, 2005), under the general assumption that many aspects of language cannot be captured without extra-linguistic information (Barsalou, 2008). Despite this and the existence of consolidated linguistic work about the mechanisms of the underlying metaphor processing (Lakoff and Johnson, 2008), the research on the topic of metaphor and grounded language models is quite scarce and has focused on the use of visual features to identify metaphors (Shutova et al., 2016). The common practice in the domain is currently to attempt metaphor identification and modelling through linguistic data only (Zhang and Barnden, 2013; Do Dinh and Gurevych, 2016; Bizzoni and Lappin, 2018) Neurolinguistic studies such as De-

Proceedings of the Second Workshop on Figurative Language Processing, pages 126–135
July 9, 2020. ©2020 Association for Computational Linguistics
https://doi.org/10.18653/v1/P17

sai et al. (2013) show that the literal properties of terms are still activated if those terms are used metaphorically, confirming the idea that metaphors create a compositional feature transfer between source and target: for example, senso-motory verbs used in metaphorical ways still activate their "normal" senso-motory paths in the brain, a behaviour that distinguishes metaphors from idioms (Lai and Curran, 2013; Kemmerer, 2015). Other studies, such as Zanolie et al. (2012), show that some abstract concept, like *power*, seem linked, in the brain, to a spatial feature, like the vertical up-down dimension, which would, according to the study, account for the spatial metaphors of power that tend to visualise hierarchy on a vertical axis. In short, several studies in neurolinguistics support the idea that many metaphors do indeed rely on sensory knowledge (Lacey et al., 2012). Reproducing these mechanisms in computational models is the main idea behind our project. The goal of our study is to examine to what degree these observations are reflected in the performance of image classification deep neural models trained on images. The way image classification models both represent and categorise pictures can help us understand better to what extent grounded compositional metaphors are actually grounded (Section 4) and compositional (Section 6).

3   Models

For our study we use pre-trained visual object classification models available in Keras (Chollet et al., 2015). The two main models used in this work are ResNet50 (He et al., 2016) and VGG16 (Simonyan and Zisserman, 2014). For comparison we also use VGG19 (Simonyan and Zisserman, 2014) and InceptionResNetV2 (Szegedy et al., 2016). In the versions we use for this study, the networks were pre-trained on 1,000 object categories from ImageNet. Unlike the systems used for articulated image description, these models generate single token captions. (Deng et al., 2009). All models operate through in three steps: (i) the model takes an image as input; (ii) using the pre-trained weights the model transforms the image into a vector that represents its main features; (iii) the model's final layer operates a prediction or classification over such a vector. Since the categories are limited (here to 1,000) and the models imperfect, mis-categorisations occur.

4   Mis-categorisations

A classifier presented with an image will output a list of possible captions or descriptions, with confidence scores that indicate the similarity between the output category and the image. For example, if presented with a picture of a bird, ResNet50 will output the following probabilities:

1. brambling 0.473
2. house-finch 0.155
3. water ouzel 0.090
4. junco 0.005
5. robin 0.053

If presented with an airliner, the model will output captions like *airliner* (0.93), *warplane* (0.03), *airship* (0.001). If we use a good object classifier on a clear instance of an object that is well presented in its training data, the result is a high-probability prediction of the object category, followed by low-probability categories that share a decreasing number of features with the target object in the image. For example, if presented with a picture of an Indian elephant, ResNet50 outputs the following probabilities over categories:

1. Indian elephant 0.95
2. tusker 0.03
3. African elephant 0.01
4. triceratops 2.1814798e-05
5. water buffalo 1.0476451e-05
6. warthog 6.76768e-06
7. hippopotamus 6.4546807e-06
8. ice bear 3.6104445e-06

The gap in probabilities between the first and the second prediction is large, and the probabilities after the 4th item are insignificant. It is possible to notice how in all cases the model's predictions are based on the main features of the elephant's shape: the output's classes share some visual similarities with the Indian elephant, in a decreasing order of overlap. The model predicts, in order, the Indian elephants; other kinds of elephants; and other animals that in ResNet50's ontology share important properties with the Indian elephant. The reader can observe that the suggested alternative species have common characteristics of being massive four-legged animals and in many cases displaying prominent tusks. We can compare the network's behaviour with the strategies a human would adopt in the attempt to describe a specific animal to someone who has never seen it before: looking for other animals sharing some similarities with it. This mechanism becomes even more evident if we present the network with a category that was absent from its training data, or that was too rare in the training to allow the model to generalise on its features. Let's take for example Figure 1, an image of a fire on a dark background.

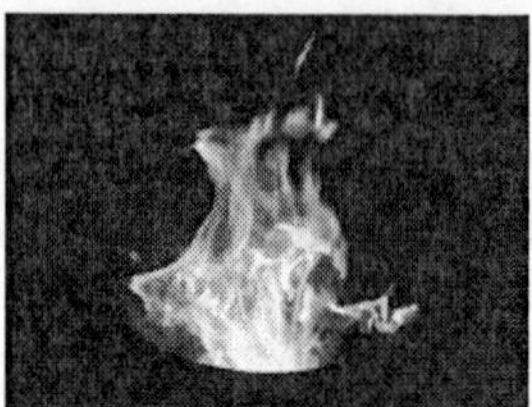

Figure 1: Fire!

The Keras' pre-trained model of ResNet50 lacks the category "fire" in its training dataset, and if presented with this picture, the model returns the following list of probabilities over categories: *stove* (0.85), *fire screen* (0.14), *dutch oven* (0.002).

The network identifies categories of objects in which fire is a likely component. Being unable to figure out the object's category with confidence, the model returns captions drawn from categories of objects that share some properties with the presented image. The picture's background and style play important roles as well. For example, ResNet50 categorises the leftmost image in Figure 2, a drawing representing a dragon, as *comic book* (0.28) or *laptop* (0.08), and the rightmost image Figure 2, a statue of dragon, as *pedestal* (0.61), *fountain* (0.38) or *palace* (0.0005). In both cases the classifier focuses on the "style" of the object - a drawing in the first case, a statue in the second case - to attempt a low-probability classification.

Figure 2: Two dragons

Mis-categorisations can happen if the object appears in a new or unusual way that confuses the network. For example, ResNet50 has various *bridge* categories in its ontology such as *steel arch bridge*,

but it tends to classify pictures of small bridges mirrored in the water as *viaduct* or *lakeside*, being confused by the elements present in the image. Similarly, it labels an aerial picture of a large modern bridge crossing the sea as *bannister* (0.44) or *dam* (0.03). As in the previous cases, the model looks for objects that pertain to the same field or conceptual area of the difficult image: to categorise bridges the models look for dams, viaducts and so on. In the same way, if presented with a picture of a church, the model suggests *church* (0.93), *bell cote* (0.02), *monastery* (0.02), and it tries to describe the Burj Khalifa as a *mosque* (0.13), a *palace* (0.08), a *bell cote* (0.07) or an *airship* (0.06). The last association is of particular interest for our study, since the model moves out of the conceptual domain of the picture to look for similarities in different areas. But what happens if the model is presented with an image belonging to a conceptual domain completely unknown? For example, "our" ResNet50 lacks in its pre-trained categories every thing pertaining to the sky: clouds, planets and stars are absent from its ontology. If presented with a classical image of Saturn, the model predicts *candle* (0.81). We suspect that the reason of this unexpected elaboration lies in the colour of Saturn's atmosphere, that is similar, in some pictures, to a candle's wax colour.

Figure 3: A guy.

In other situations, the network focuses on background elements that it recognises. For example, this model is also not trained on people: it cannot label a person as *person*. If presented with the image of a person in a bathtub, the suggested captions are *bathtub* (0.08), *bath towel* (0.07), *tub* (0.06). For similar reasons, and showing some politically incorrect bias, the model labels the person in Figure 3 as *prison* (0.05), *jean* (0.02) and *barrow* (0.06). In a picture representing a breaking storm over the sea, ResNet50 - not "knowing" what a storm is - pics the peripheral elements: *breakwater* and *pier*. The abundant literature on object classification has duly noted these systematic mistakes (Wang et al., 2009; Xu et al., 2015).

This behaviour also applies to different models. Many of VGG16's predictions in front of unknown or puzzling objects mirror those of ResNet50: *dam* (0.22) for the modern bridge picture, *pedestal* (0.55) for the dragon in Figure 2, *viaduct* (0.24) after *triumphal arch* (0.33) for the bridge mirrored in the water. For known objects, VGG16's second and third best guesses align with the ones produced by ResNet50: for example, the *church* prediction for the church is followed by *monastery* (0.02) and *bell cote* (0.02). In the case of the Burj Khalifa, the first prediction remains *mosque* (0.33), but VGG16 seems quicker to move out of the "buildings domain" to seek objects having the Burj's shape: *obelisk* (0.10), *missile* (0.09) and *projectile* (0.05). This possible predilection of VGG16 for shapes of elements, colour or "style" appears in other examples: Saturn is a *spotlight* (0.08) and a *ping pong ball* (0.07) rather than a *candle* (0.03), and the leftmost dragon in Figure 2 is labelled as *jersey* (0.68). Many of these mis-classifications are similar, in principle, to the operations underlying visually rooted metaphors. These metaphors give the listener or reader a clearer mind picture of a given element or scene through the parallel with something having similar visual properties, but pertaining to a different domain. To stick with the models' mistakes, it wouldn't be hard to imagine someone describing the Burj Khalifa as a "missile pointing to the sky" or the gigantic "obelisk of Dubai". Others of our models' mistakes, though, sound less natural to our sensibility: for example, describing Saturn as a candle in the sky or a ping pong ball in the sky is a less effective metaphor. ResNet50 captions an image of the setting Sun as a *ping pong ball* (0.58) and a *spotlight* (0.05) and only with lower confidence predicts similes used by humans to describe the sun in similar scenes, such as *orange* (0.017) and *balloon* (0.014). To give the reader a first hand idea of the descriptive qualities of these mis-categorisations, we present in Figure 4 a series of pictures with the first 5 categories assigned by the VGG16 model. Table 1 provides a small comparison of the mis-categorisations by VGG16 and ResNet50 on the same pictures.

The main intuition of this study is that some of these mis-categorisations seem to make a metaphoric sense for a human reader. For example, ResNet50 classifies a picture of lightnings as *spider web*. Although this may seem like an unexpected comparison, there are several pictures of lightnings on the Internet that are described by human annotators as *spider web lightning* due to their thread-like and branching shape. On the other hand, if a model labels the picture of a man sitting by a fire as a *volcano*, the metaphoric power of the classification becomes doubtful (although not necessarily absent).

To explore the parallels and differences between human visually rooted metaphors and visual models' mis-categorisations, we collected through manual online search a dataset of 100 pictures that human users had described with a metaphor or simile as shown in Figure 5. We exclusively selected metaphors that had *only* their target in the 1,000 ImageNet categories present in our models' ontology: for example, images of lightning (source, absent from the ontology) described as spider webs (target, present in the ontology), or fireworks (source, absent from the ontology) described as sea urchins (target, present in the ontology). With such a dataset it is possible to see, to a limited extent, whether the mis-categorisations performed by the models confronted with unforeseen elements go in the direction of the metaphors and similes humans conceive to provide a vivid description of an object.

If a human captioner described the image of a *sponge* (absent from the models' ontology) as a *harp* (present in the models' ontology), and our models categorise the same image as a *harp*, there is an overlap between the two frames. If, as in this case, our models categorise the same image as something else, e.g. a *barn spider*, there is a difference between the two frames. Table 2 shows the performance of four pre-trained models on metaphorical mis-categorisation. If we consider the first retrieved category for each picture, most models achieve an F-score between 0.23 and 0.26, with the exception of InceptionResNet that achieves an F-score of 0.0. If we relax the boundaries and take into consideration the first 5 results for each picture, most models' performance ranges between 0.3 and 0.4, and if we include the first 20 results they reach F-scores higher than 0.5. Considering the complexity of the task, we see F-scores of 0.3 and higher for the first 5 answers as an interesting result. At the same time, it is clear that this experimental frame remains limited: we were only able to use specific kinds of metaphors to work on the models' restricted ontology, and the metaphors had to be of

(a) Bubble, Alp, fireboat, mountain tent, fountain.

(b) Golf ball, gong, tick, chambered nautilus, spotlight.

(c) Matchstick, hook, spotlight, safety pin, flatworm.

(d) Comic book, jigsaw puzzle, book jacket, theater curtain, shower curtain.

(e) Shower curtain, pajama, ballpoint, maraca, rubber eraser.

(f) Volcano, fountain, seashore, space shuttle, lakeside.

Figure 4: The first 5 output categories of VGG16 for various pictures. Most of these pictures represent objects the network was not trained on. The reader can notice that some of the mis-classifications could work as metaphoric descriptions (as in b or f) more than others (as in a or e).

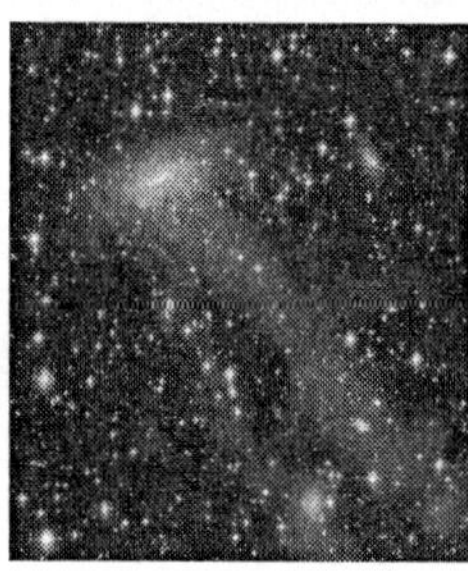

Figure 5: Two elements from our dataset. A galaxy described in the human-generated caption as a jellyfish, and a building described (and commonly known) as a cucumber/gherkin.

the single-word-to-single-word kind: the compositionality and flexibility present in many visually rooted metaphors, such as "the lawn is a *green* carpet" or "the snowflakes were *falling* dancers", are out of the scope of this kind of test. In the rest of the paper, we explore a different frame that allows more flexibility in the study of visually grounded metaphors.

5 Visual Spaces

The category of *cigarette* is absent from the ontology of the models we use in this study. If presented with a cigarette, most models see a *ruler* or a *band aid*. The classification step happens in the last layer of the networks: before that final layer, each model transforms its input picture in a 1x224x244x3 tensor that encodes the relevant visual features of the picture as a 4-dimensional set of weights. From such tensor the model draws a 1x1000 vector that represents the probability of such tensor to fall in each one of the 1000 categories.

This characteristic, shared by most neural classifiers, opens the possibility of exploring visually rooted metaphors as operations in a continuum, by using the final tensor extracted by each picture as a vector in a multi-dimensional space. Returning to the cigarette example, our VGG16 model cannot recognise any of the objects or symbols present in Figure 6.

The last picture confuses our model which mis-categories it in a different way than the previous two images: the model fails to pick the similarities evident to a human eye. But if we flatten the pre-categorisation final tensors created by the model to represent these three images and compute their cosine similarity, we might be able to overcome the rigidity of the classification step. Here are the results of such trial: the cosine similarity between the cigarette (a) and the danger sign (b) is 0.5, as the two pictures are different. But the similarity between (b) and the cigarettes are dangerous sign (c) is 0.68, while the similarity between (a) and (c) is as high as 0.83. In other words, the visual similarity that the multi-class classification frame kept latent clearly emerges.

Object	VGG16	ResNet50
Burj Khalifa	Mosque, obelisk, missile	Mosque, palace, bell cote
Mountain	Alp, valley, mountain tent	Alp, valley, mountain tent
Galaxy	Jellyfish, fountain, window screen	Volcano, ski mask, jellyfish
Mushrooms	Water tower, lampshade, table lamp	Mushroom, hen of the woods, fountain
Blanket clouds	Seashore, fountain, sandbar	Wing, seashore, sandbar
Sun(drawing)	Ping pong ball, envelope, maraca	Wall clock, analog clock, web site
Ballerinas	Spiny lobster, hoopskirt, fountain	Fountain, king crab, pole
Belt	Buckle, muzzle, hair slide	Buckle, muzzle, hair slide
Cloud looking like a bird	Geyser, lakeside, valley	Valley, lakeside, worm fence

Table 1: Comparing mis-categorisations between VGG16 and ResNet50. The first column names the object presented in the picture, the remaining two columns present the first 3 captions offered by the two models.

(a) ruler, band aid   (b) hatchet, electric guitar   (c) reel, croquet ball

Figure 6: Three pictures representing elements absent from our VGG16 ontology. The last picture shares obvious similarities with the first two images, but VGG16 classifies each picture in a completely different way.

Model	Top 1	Top 5	Top 20
VGG16	0.25	0.39	**0.57**
VGG19	0.23	0.33	0.54
InceptionResNet	0.00	0.01	0.05
ResNet50	**0.26**	0.39	0.53

Table 2: F1 scores for human-like metaphorical classification of 4 models considering the first 1, 5 and 20 results of each.

To strengthen this frame, we create visual vectors that represent several images of the same concept in order to create "conceptual" clusters or, in other words, new "classes" for our experiment without the need of a full new training set. For example, if we sum the flattened output tensors for two danger signs we obtain a new vector that "represents" both danger signs' relevant features. This approach seems to return better results. If we compute the cosine similarity between three different danger signs' tensors, we obtain an average similarity of 0.64. But if we sum two danger signs' tensors and compute the cosine similarity of the resulting tensor with the left-out picture's tensor, the average similarity rises to 0.73. In other words, by summing two danger signs' tensors we created a visually meaningful centroid in the feature space that represents better than any single image the essential appearance of a generic *danger sign*. It is possible to imagine that adding more pictures would make a more consistent representation. However, the most interesting aspect of this approach for our study is the possibility of obtaining a reasonable effect without the need of collecting large datasets or training the model from scratch. The same effect happens with the cigarette pictures: if the cosine similarity between two simple pictures of cigarettes as in Figure 6(a) is 0.95, the cosine similarity of a single cigarette vector with the summed vector of two other images of cigarettes rises to 0.99. Now we can compute the similarity between cigarettes, danger signs and cigarettes are dangerous disclaimers

(a) Sky

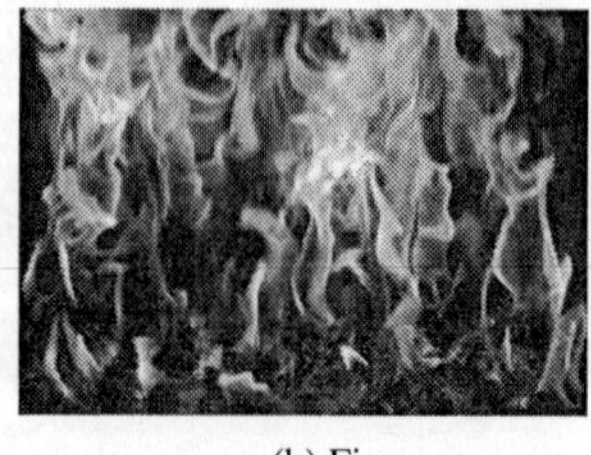

(b) Fire

(c) Sunset

Figure 7: Samples from the three compound visual vectors we create to serve as source, target and modifier of the metaphor *Sunset* is *Sky* on *Fire*.

of the kind presented in Figure 6 as a cosine similarity between vectors. Through this simple operation the similarity between the danger signs' vector and the disclaimers' vector rises up to 0.81, and the similarity between the cigarettes' vector and the disclaimers' vector rises to 0.87. If we sum the cigarettes' vector and the danger signs' vector and compare the result with the anti-smoke disclaimers' vector, the cosine similarity goes to 0.92. This high similarity does not seem to be the effect of noise: the similarity of the anti-smoke disclaimers' vector and a vector of an unrelated picture, such as an image of a firework, is -0.8.The essential visual similarities that make the symbolic disclaimer in Figure 6(c) understandable for humans are retrievable from the visual feature space. To prove the concept, we computed the cosine similarity between the danger signs' vector and the individual vectors of all the pictures present in the dataset described in this study. Despite more than 100 confounders, the three pictures of danger signs came with the highest ranking, followed by the two anti-smoke disclaimers. We then repeated the operation with the (danger+cigarette) vector, that retrieved all the cigarettes as most similar pictures. This leads to our final investigation.

6 Adding Fire to the Sky: Compositionality in Visually Grounded Metaphors

A visually grounded metaphor sometimes used to describe an impressive sunset is *the sky is on fire*. This is a simple and effective grounded metaphor: the reader or listener "adds" the colours and intensity of fire to the sky in order to imagine a vivid sunset. If this metaphor is indeed rooted in visual data and visual data only, this is the operation we should be able to perform in the visual space to "create" a sunset vector. Through online manual

search we collected 8 pictures of sunsets described as *Sky on fire* by their captioners. The individual vectors of some of these pictures already present the similarities necessary for the metaphoric shift: out of 8 pictures described as *Sky on fire* 2 retrieved as most similar picture in our dataset a picture of a fire with an average cosine similarity of 0.6, and another 4 had pictures of fire among the first ten most similar elements, with an average cosine similarity of 0.5.

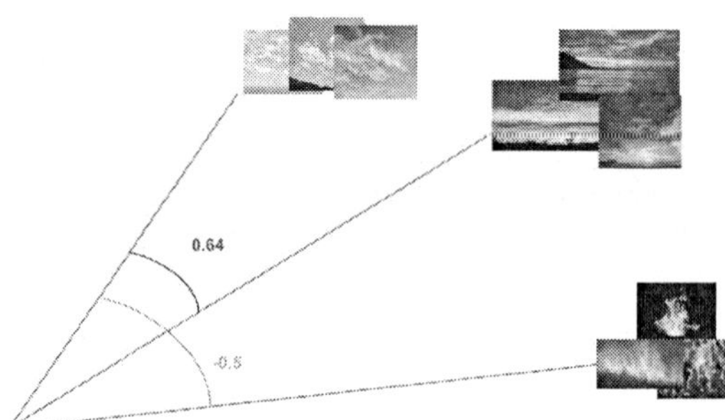

Figure 8: A schematic visualisation of the cosine similarities between the *sky*, the *fire* and the *sky on fire* vectors. The *sky* vector is relatively similar to the *sky on fire* vector and further away from the *fire* vector.

But is it possible to reproduce the compositionality of this metaphor in the visual space? To answer this question, we created a *sky* vector out of 10 pictures of (mainly blue) skies such as the one in Figure 7(a). The average cosine similarity of these pictures is around 0 (the lowest possible cosine similarity is -1). This relatively low similarity between sky pictures is probably due to the lack of stable and recognisable shapes in the "concept of sky": most of our sky pictures featured a of varying hue background sometimes with some clouds, and the clouds' shapes varied constantly. We then created a *fire* vector out of 13 pictures of fire such as the one in Figure 7(b) with average cosine similarity

132

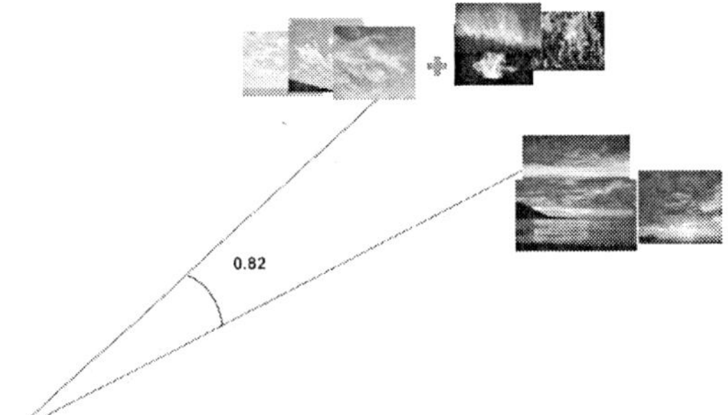

Figure 9: A visually grounded metaphor in the visual space. If we sum the *sky* vector with the *fire* vector, we create a "metaphoric" new vector which is closer to the *sky on fire* vector than the simple *sky* vector was: adding fire to the sky seems an effective way to recreate a sunset.

Metaphor	Sim ST	Sim (S+M)T
Sunset is sky on fire	0.64	0.82
Blonde hair are river of gold	0.01	0.1
Snow is white carpet	0.82	0.90
Lawn is green carpet	-0.3	0.4
Hair are white waterfall	-0.5	0.62

Table 3: Compositional metaphors: the similarity between two visual vectors representing the (S)ource and the (T)arget of a metaphor increases if a modifier's vector is added to the source - (S+M)T. For example, the cosine similarity of the *blonde hair* vector and *river* in the second row is 0.01. If we sum *river* with a vector representing its modifier *golden* (which is a vector created out of several pictures of gold and golden elements) the similarity goes up to 0.1.

of 0.6. Finally, we created a *sunset* vector out of 7 pictures of sunsets captioned by humans as *sky on fire*, as the one in Figure 7(c). The average cosine similarity between the pictures of this group is 0.74. As represented in Figure 8, the cosine similarity between the *sky* vector and the *fire* vector is low: -0.5. The objects, sky and fire, have little in common in terms of visual features. The cosine similarity between the *sky* and *sky on fire* vectors that represent the same object under different conditions is higher: 0.64. If we sum the vectors of *sky* and *fire*, we create a *sky-fire* vector as shown in Figure 9. The cosine similarity of this new vector with the *sky on fire* vector rises to 0.82. In other words, adding the metaphoric *fire* to the literal *sky* made the sky vector closer to the sunset vector. The compositional *sky on fire* metaphor seems to work in our visual space (see Figure 9 for a visualisation). Although this is a particularly clear case of visual compositionality, metaphoric compositionality of this kind seems to be present also in other examples. In Table 3 we give an overview of some of the metaphors we tried. We tried to select on metaphors that could be strongly visual, and that would not rely on excessively complex shapes or hues.

Collecting pictures that represent such metaphors from online data is a difficult task. The metaphors have to be compositional, visually grounded and included in captions. We thus collected a tiny dataset of 22 such metaphors (some of which we include in Table 3) with an average of 5 images associated with each element: source, target and modifier. To make negative examples

we created a "balancing" list of 22 false metaphors by randomly shuffling targets and modifiers. To keep the experiment clear in its scope, we tried to avoid for this negative counterpart borderline compositions that could work as unusual but still valid or evocative metaphors, since that would create a fascinating but hard to define grey area. For each of these metaphors, we operated the following steps:

1. We measured the cosine similarity of the source and target visual vectors: for example, the similarity of the Sky vector with the Sunset vector.

2. We either summed or multiplied the modifier's vector to the source's vector; for example, we added the Fire vector to the Sky vector.

3. We measured the cosine similarity of the new "modified source" vector with the target vector: the similarity of Sky+Fire with Sunset.

Every time the modifier increases the similarity between a true metaphor's source and target, we count it as a true positive. Every time the same happens for a false metaphor, we count it as a false positive . We show the performance of the InceptionResNet and ResNet50 models on this dataset in Table 4.[1] We find that most real metaphors improve through the addition of the modifier's vector, while most

---

[1] The other two models returned very similar results and therefore we do not discuss them specifically.

false metaphors do not, achieving the best F-score of 0.68 using ResNet50.

For both classifiers, the majority of the real metaphors improved (in terms of source-target cosine similarity) if we added the modifier with the source: in other words, in over 60 per cent of the cases we reproduced the mere visual compositionality of these metaphors. At the same time, the majority of the false metaphors got worse (in terms of souce-target cosine similarity) if we added the modifier to the source, confirming that the effect is linked to the visual compositionality of such expressions.

Multiply	**Precision**	**Recall**	**F1**
InceptionResNet	0.55	0.68	0.61
ResNet50	0.63	0.31	0.42
Sum	**Precision**	**Recall**	**F1**
InceptionResNet	0.60	0.64	0.62
ResNet50	0.64	0.73	**0.68**

Table 4: Precision, Recall and F1 for two models' metaphorical compositionality. The F-score measures to what extent the modifier improves the similarity between source and target in real metaphors (precision), but not in false metaphors (recall). We test the composition of visual vectors using multiplication (top) or sum (bottom).

7   Conclusions and Future Works

We conceived this study as an exploration of visually grounded metaphors in two experiments and two tiny datasets. In the first experiment we focus on categorisation: two image captioning models classified pictures of previously unseen elements and compared them with human-generated metaphors for the same pictures, returning a low overlap between human generated metaphors and models' mis-classifications. It is important to keep in mind that metaphors are flexible and diverse, and some of the mis-classifications of the models might be valid metaphors for humans - they were just absent from the specific dataset we collected. In this respect, an overlap of 30% between human metaphors and the first 5 captions produced by the models is encouraging. In a number of cases, the mis-classifications of the models do not seem to align with anything similar to a human-like metaphor, especially if variables like background or peripheral elements come into play. This doesn't mean that the so-called visually rooted metaphors

are not visually rooted: but they might rely on either more complex similarity that were not captured by our models, or on a composition of visual and extra-visual world knowledge. In the second experiment we focus on unsupervised composition using a multi-dimensional visual feature space that offers a flexible representation for our domain. Using an unsupervised approach we cannot produce a comparison against a labelled dataset as in the classification experiment. However, we do show that the apparent visual compositionality in several metaphors can be predicted in the visual feature space. In most cases adding the metaphoric modifier to the metaphor's source made the source and the target closer than they were before. This shift indicates that the metaphors are grounded in the visual features that are encoded by image classification models. The visual elements present in those metaphors are working in the visual space and account for the effectiveness and flexibility of the metaphoric expressions.

There are several ways to continue from this study. First of all, our datasets are very small. Collecting larger corpora of visually grounded metaphors and relative pictures would be necessary to expand our study. This would also imply finding more systematic ways of selecting both the metaphors and their pictures, since for these studies we used our sole sensibility to select and collect the examples. It would also be interesting to add more complex cases, especially when operating on the continuum visual space, and to compare the compositional efficiency of different metaphors. While such selection and collection steps are challenging due to the complex nature of the problem we study, the ever-growing wealth of annotated pictures makes us optimist about its feasability. An open question remains to what degree different metaphors are grounded visually and to what degree they can be predicted from the language models. It would also be interesting to check which visual clues are most useful to the classifiers when they reproduce human metaphorical combinations. Finally, even if no human ever produced a specific metaphor, this doesn't mean that such metaphor is bad: it would be interesting in the future to measure the level of human appreciation of visually grounded metaphors generated through image captioning. These will be the foci of our future work.

References

Lawrence W Barsalou. 2008. Grounded cognition. *Annu. Rev. Psychol.*, 59:617–645.

Yuri Bizzoni and Shalom Lappin. 2018. Predicting human metaphor paraphrase judgments with deep neural networks. In *Proceedings of the Workshop on Figurative Language Processing*, pages 45–55.

François Chollet et al. 2015. Keras.

Jia Deng, Wei Dong, Richard Socher, Li-Jia Li, Kai Li, and Li Fei-Fei. 2009. Imagenet: A large-scale hierarchical image database. In *Computer Vision and Pattern Recognition, 2009. CVPR 2009. IEEE Conference on*, pages 248–255. Ieee.

Rutvik H Desai, Lisa L Conant, Jeffrey R Binder, Haeil Park, and Mark S Seidenberg. 2013. A piece of the action: modulation of sensory-motor regions by action idioms and metaphors. *NeuroImage*, 83:862–869.

Erik-Lân Do Dinh and Iryna Gurevych. 2016. Token-level metaphor detection using neural networks. In *Proceedings of the Fourth Workshop on Metaphor in NLP*, pages 28–33.

Peter Gorniak and Deb Roy. 2004. Grounded semantic composition for visual scenes. *Journal of Artificial Intelligence Research*, 21:429–470.

Kaiming He, Xiangyu Zhang, Shaoqing Ren, and Jian Sun. 2016. Deep residual learning for image recognition. In *Proceedings of the IEEE conference on computer vision and pattern recognition*, pages 770–778.

David Kemmerer. 2015. Are the motor features of verb meanings represented in the precentral motor cortices? yes, but within the context of a flexible, multilevel architecture for conceptual knowledge. *Psychonomic Bulletin & Review*, 22(4):1068–1075.

Simon Lacey, Randall Stilla, and Krish Sathian. 2012. Metaphorically feeling: comprehending textural metaphors activates somatosensory cortex. *Brain and language*, 120(3):416–421.

Vicky Tzuyin Lai and Tim Curran. 2013. Erp evidence for conceptual mappings and comparison processes during the comprehension of conventional and novel metaphors. *Brain and Language*, 127(3):484–496.

George Lakoff and Mark Johnson. 2008. *Metaphors we live by*. University of Chicago press.

Deb Roy. 2005. Grounding words in perception and action: computational insights. *Trends in cognitive sciences*, 9(8):389–396.

Deb Roy and Ehud Reiter. 2005. Connecting language to the world. *Artificial Intelligence*, 167(1-2):1–12.

Ekaterina Shutova, Douwe Kiela, and Jean Maillard. 2016. Black holes and white rabbits: Metaphor identification with visual features. In *Proceedings of the 2016 Conference of the North American Chapter of the Association for Computational Linguistics: Human Language Technologies*, pages 160–170.

Karen Simonyan and Andrew Zisserman. 2014. Very deep convolutional networks for large-scale image recognition. *arXiv preprint arXiv:1409.1556*.

Jeffrey Mark Siskind. 2001. Grounding the lexical semantics of verbs in visual perception using force dynamics and event logic. *Journal of artificial intelligence research*, 15:31–90.

Christian Szegedy, Sergey Ioffe, and Vincent Vanhoucke. 2016. Inception-v4, inception-resnet and the impact of residual connections on learning. *CoRR*, abs/1602.07261.

Josiah Wang, Katja Markert, and Mark Everingham. 2009. Learning models for object recognition from natural language descriptions.

Kelvin Xu, Jimmy Ba, Ryan Kiros, Kyunghyun Cho, Aaron Courville, Ruslan Salakhudinov, Rich Zemel, and Yoshua Bengio. 2015. Show, attend and tell: Neural image caption generation with visual attention. In *International conference on machine learning*, pages 2048–2057.

Kiki Zanolie, Saskia van Dantzig, Inge Boot, Jasper Wijnen, Thomas W Schubert, Steffen R Giessner, and Diane Pecher. 2012. Mighty metaphors: Behavioral and erp evidence that power shifts attention on a vertical dimension. *Brain and cognition*, 78(1):50–58.

Li Zhang and John Barnden. 2013. Towards a semantic-based approach for affect and metaphor detection. *International Journal of Distance Education Technologies (IJDET)*, 11(2):48–65.

Junpei Zhong, Martin Peniak, Jun Tani, Tetsuya Ogata, and Angelo Cangelosi. 2019. Sensorimotor input as a language generalisation tool: A neurorobotics model for generation and generalisation of noun-verb combinations with sensorimotor inputs. *Autonomous Robots*, 43(5):1271–1290.

Recognizing Euphemisms and Dysphemisms Using Sentiment Analysis

Christian Felt and Ellen Riloff
School of Computing
University of Utah
christianfelt@comcast.net, riloff@cs.utah.edu

Abstract

This paper presents the first research aimed at recognizing euphemistic and dysphemistic phrases with natural language processing. Euphemisms soften references to topics that are sensitive, disagreeable, or taboo. Conversely, dysphemisms refer to sensitive topics in a harsh or rude way. For example, *"passed away"* and *"departed"* are euphemisms for death, while *"croaked"* and *"six feet under"* are dysphemisms for death. Our work explores the use of sentiment analysis to recognize euphemistic and dysphemistic language. First, we identify near-synonym phrases for three topics (FIRING, LYING, and STEALING) using a bootstrapping algorithm for semantic lexicon induction. Next, we classify phrases as euphemistic, dysphemistic, or neutral using lexical sentiment cues and contextual sentiment analysis. We introduce a new gold standard data set and present our experimental results for this task.

1 Introduction

Euphemisms are expressions used to soften references to topics that are sensitive, disagreeable, or taboo with respect to societal norms. Whether as a lubricant for polite discourse, a means to hide disagreeable truths, or a repository for cultural anxieties, veiled by idioms so familiar we no longer think about what they literally mean, euphemisms are an essential part of human linguistic competence. Conversely, **dysphemisms** make references more harsh or rude, often using language that is direct or blunt, less formal or polite, and sometimes offensive. For example, *"passed away"* and *"departed"* are common euphemisms for death, while *"croaked"* and *"six feet under"* are dysphemisms for death. Table 1 shows examples of euphemisms and dysphemisms across a variety of topics.

Following terminology from linguistics (e.g., (Allan, 2009; Rababah, 2014)), we use the term **x-phemism** to refer to the general phenomenon of euphemisms and dysphemisms. Recognizing x-phemisms could be valuable for many NLP tasks. Euphemisms are related to politeness, which plays a role in applications involving dialogue and social interactions (e.g., (Danescu-Niculescu-Mizil et al., 2013)). Dysphemisms can include pejorative and offensive language, which relates to cyberbullying (Xu et al., 2012; Van Hee et al., 2015), hate speech (Magu and Luo, 2014), and abusive language (Park et al., 2018; Wiegand et al., 2018). Recognizing euphemisms and dysphemisms for controversial topics could be valuable for stance detection and argumentation in political discourse or debates (Somasundaran and Wiebe, 2010; Walker et al., 2012; Habernal and Gurevych, 2015). In medicine, researchers found that medical professionals use x-phemisms when talking to patients about serious conditions, and have emphasized the importance of preserving x-phemisms across translations when treating non-English speakers (Rababah, 2014).

An area of NLP that relates to x-phemisms is sentiment analysis, although the relationship is complex. A key feature of x-phemisms is that their directionality (euphemism vs. dysphemism) is relative to an underlying topic, which itself often has affective polarity. X-phemisms are usually associated with negative topics that are culturally disagreeable or have a negative connotation, such as death, intoxication, prostitution, old age, mental illness, and defecation. However x-phemisms also occur with topics that are sensitive but not inherently negative, such as pregnancy (e.g., *"in a family way"* is a euphemism, while *"knocked up"* is a dysphemism). In general, dysphemistic language increases the degree of sensitivity, intensifying negative polarity or shifting polarity from neutral to negative. Conversely, euphemistic language generally decreases sensitivity. But euphemisms for inherently negative topics may still have negative polarity (e.g.,

136

Proceedings of the Second Workshop on Figurative Language Processing, pages 136–145
July 9, 2020. ©2020 Association for Computational Linguistics
https://doi.org/10.18653/v1/P17

Topic	Euphemisms	Dysphemisms
DEATH	passed away, eternal rest, put to sleep	croaked, six feet under, bit the dust
INTOXICATION	tipsy, inebriated, under the influence	hammered, plastered, sloshed, wasted
LYING	falsehood, misrepresent facts, untruth	bullshit, rubbish, whopper, quackery
PROSTITUTE	lady of the night, working girl, sex worker	whore, tart, harlot, floozy
DEFECATION	bowel movement, number two, pass stool	take a dump, crap, drop a load
VOMITING	be sick, regurgitate, heave	blow chunks, puke, upchuck

Table 1: Examples of Euphemisms and Dysphemisms

vomiting is unpleasant no matter how gently it is referred to).

This paper presents the first effort to identify euphemistic and dysphemistic language in text. Since affective polarity clearly plays a role in this phenomenon, our research explores whether sentiment analysis can be useful for recognizing x-phemisms. We deconstructed the problem into two subtasks. First, we identify phrases that refer to three sensitive topics: LYING, STEALING, and FIRING (job termination). We use a weakly supervised algorithm for semantic lexicon induction (Thelen and Riloff, 2002) to semi-automatically generate lists of *near-synonym phrases* for each topic. Second, we investigate two methods to classify phrases as *euphemistic*, *dysphemistic*, or *neutral*[1]. (1) We use dictionary-based methods to explore the value of several types of information found in sentiment lexicons: affective polarity, connotation, intensity, arousal, and dominance. (2) We use contextual sentiment analysis to classify x-phemism phrases. We collect sentence contexts around instances of each candidate phrase in a large corpus, and assign each phrase to an x-phemism category based on the polarity of its contexts. Finally, we introduce a gold standard data set of human x-phemism judgments and evaluate our models for this task. We hope that this new data set will encourage more work on x-phemisms. Our experiments show that sentiment connotation and affective polarity can be useful for identifying euphemistic and dysphemistic phrases, although this problem remains challenging.

2   Related Work

Euphemisms and dysphemisms have been studied in linguistics and related disciplines (e.g., (Allan and Burridge, 1991; Pfaff et al., 1997; Rawson, 2003; Allan, 2009; Rababah, 2014)), but they have received little attention in the NLP community.

Magu and Luo (2014) recognized code words in "euphemistic hate speech" by measuring cosine distance between word embeddings. But their code words conceal references to hate speech rather than soften them (e.g., the code word *"skypes"* covertly referred to Jews), which is different from the traditional definition of euphemisms that is addressed in our work.

The NLP community has explored several linguistic phenomena related to x-phemisms, such as metaphor (e.g., (Shutova, 2010; Wallington et al., 2011; Shutova et al., 2010; Kesarwani et al., 2017)), politeness (e.g., (Danescu-Niculescu-Mizil et al., 2013; Aubakirova and Bansal, 2016)), and formality (e.g., (Pavlick and Tetreault, 2016)). Pfaff et al. (1997) found that people comprehend metaphorical euphemisms or dysphemisms more quickly when they share the same underlying conceptual metaphor. For example, people are likely to use the euphemism *"parted ways"* to describe ending a relationship in the context of the conceptual metaphor A RELATIONSHIP IS A JOURNEY, but more likely to use the euphemism *"cut their losses"* in the context of the metaphor A RELATIONSHIP IS AN INVESTMENT.

Our research focuses on the relationship between x-phemisms and sentiment analysis. We take advantage of several existing sentiment resources, including the NRC EmoLex, VAD, and Affective Intensity Lexicons (Mohammad and Turney, 2013; Mohammad, 2018a,b) and Connotation WordNet (Feng et al., 2013; Kang et al., 2014). We also re-implemented the NRC-Canada sentiment classifier (Mohammad et al., 2013) to use in our work.

Allan (2009) examined the connotation of color terms according to how often they appear in dysphemistic, euphemistic, or neutral contexts. For instance, *"blue"* is often used as a euphemism for *"sad"*, while *"yellow"* can be dysphemistically used to mean *"cowardly"*. Our paper takes the reverse approach, recognizing x-phemisms by means of

---

[1] Direct ("straight-talking") references to a topic are called *orthophemisms*, but for simplicity we refer to them as neutral.

connotation.

Rababah (2014) studied how medical professionals use x-phemisms when talking to patients and found that serious conditions tend to inspire more euphemism. Rababah argued that translating x-phemisms appropriately is important when providing medical care to non-English speakers. It follows that it is important for machine translation systems to preserve euphemistic language across translations in medical applications. More generally, machine translation systems should be concerned not only with preserving the intended semantics but also preserving the intended discourse pragmatics, which includes translating euphemisms into euphemisms and translating dysphemisms into dysphemisms. When a speaker chooses to use a euphemistic or dysphemistic expression, that choice usually reflects a viewpoint or bias that is a significant property of the discourse. Consequently, it is important for NLP systems to recognize x-phemisms and their polarity, both for applications where views and biases are central (e.g., medicine, argumentation and debate, or stance detection in political discourse) and for comprehensive natural language understanding in general.

3 Overview of Technical Approach

X-phemisms are so pervasive in language that euphemism dictionaries have been published containing manually compiled lists (Bertram, 1998; Holder, 2002; Rawson, 2003). However these dictionaries are far from complete because new x-phemisms are constantly entering language, both for long-standing sensitive topics and new ones. For example, every generation of youth invents new ways of referring to defecation, and political trends can trigger heightened sensitivity to controversial topics (e.g., *"enhanced interrogation"* is a recently introduced euphemism for torture). Euphemistic terms can even become offensive with time and replaced by new euphemisms, a phenomenon known as "the euphemism treadmill." For instance, the phrase *"mentally retarded"* began its life as a euphemism. Now, even *"special needs"* is sometimes viewed as offensive. The goal of our research is to develop methods to automatically curate lists of euphemistic and dysphemistic phrases for a topic from a text corpus, which would enable emerging x-phemisms to be continually discovered.

We tackled this problem by decomposing the task into two steps: (1) identifying near-synonym phrases for a topic, and (2) classifying each phrase as *euphemistic*, *dysphemistic*, or *neutral*. For the first step, we considered using existing thesauri (e.g., WordNet, Roget's thesaurus, Wiktionary, etc.) but their synonym lists were relatively small.[2] Roget's thesaurus was among the best resources, but included only a few dozen entries for most topics. Furthermore, x-phemisms can stretch meaning to soften or harden a sensitive subject, so we wanted to include *near-synonyms* that have a similar (but not identical) meaning. For example, *laid off*, *resigned*, and *downsized* are not strictly synonymous with FIRING, but broadly construed they all refer to job termination.

Ultimately, we decided to use the Basilisk bootstrapping algorithm for weakly supervised semantic lexicon induction (Thelen and Riloff, 2002). Basilisk begins with a small set of seed terms for a desired category and iteratively learns more terms that consistently occur in the same contexts as the seeds. While there are other methods for near-synonym generation (e.g., (Gupta et al., 2015)), we chose Basilisk because it can learn phrases corresponding to syntactic constituents (e.g., NPs and VPs) and can use lexico-syntactic contextual patterns. For the bootstrapping process, we used the English Gigaword corpus because it contains a large and diverse collection of news articles. We focused on three sensitive topics that are common in news and rich in x-phemisms: LYING, STEALING, and FIRING (job termination).

4 Generating Near-Synonym Phrases with Semantic Lexicon Induction

The Basilisk algorithm learns new phrases for a category using a small list of "seed" terms and a text corpus. In an iterative bootstrapping framework, Basilisk extracts contextual patterns surrounding the seed terms, identifies new phrases that *consistently* occur in the same contexts as the seeds, adds the learned phrases to the seed list, and restarts the process. Our categories of interest (LYING, STEALING, FIRING) are actions, so we wanted to learn verb phrases as well as noun phrases (e.g., event nominals). Consequently, we provided Basilisk with two seed lists for each topic, one list of verb phrases (VPs) and one list of noun phrases

---

[2]We considered using the Paraphrase Database (PPDB) (Ganitkevitch et al., 2013) as well, but many of its paraphrases are syntactic variations (e.g., active vs. passive) which are not useful for our purpose, and many entries are noisy as they were automatically generated.

FIRE		LIE		STEAL	
NPs	**VPs**	**NPs**	**VPs**	**NPs**	**VPs**
dismissal	dismiss	exaggeration	deceive	larceny	defraud
downsizing	fire	fabrication	distort	misappropriation	embezzle
firing	force resignation	falsehood	exaggerate	pickpocketing	extort
forced retirement	furlough	fib	fabricate	pilfering	loot
layoff	lay off	lie	falsify	purloining	mug
redundancy	leave company	mendacity	lie	robbery	pilfer
reorganization	oust	misrepresentation	misinform	shoplifting	plunder
sacking	resign	misstatement	mislead	stealing	rob
suspension	sack	prevarication	misrepresent	theft	steal
termination	step down	untruth	misstate	theiving	swindle

Table 2: Seed Phrases per Topic

(NPs). To collect seed terms, we identified common phrases for each topic that had high frequency in the Gigaword corpus. The seed lists are shown in Table 2. We included both active and passive voice verb phrase forms for the verbs shown in Table 2, except we excluded *resign* in passive voice because *"was resigned to"* is a common expression with a different meaning.

Most previous applications of Basilisk have used lexico-syntactic patterns to represent the contexts around seed terms (e.g., (Riloff et al., 2003; Qadir and Riloff, 2012)). For example, a pattern may indicate that a phrase occurs as the syntactic subject or direct object of a specific verb. So we used the dependency relations produced by the SpaCy parser (https://spacy.io/)[3] for contextual patterns. For generality, we used word lemmas both for the learned phrases and the patterns.

4.1 Representing Contextual Patterns and Verb Phrases

We defined a contextual pattern as a dependency relation linked to/from a seed term, coupled with the head of the governing/dependent phrase. For example, consider the sentence *"The lie spread quickly"*. The contextual pattern for the noun *"lie"* would be ←**NSUBJ(spread)**, indicating that the NP with head *"lie"* occurred as the syntactic subject of a governing VP with head *"spread"*. We treated *"have"*, *"do"*, and *"be"* as special cases because of their generality and paired them with the head of their complement (subject, direct object, predicate nominal, or predicate adjective). For example, given the sentence *"The lie was horrific"*, the contextual pattern for *"lie"* would be ←**NSUBJ(be_horrific)**.

We also created compound relations for syntactic constructions that rely on pairs of constituents to be

meaningful. For example, a preposition alone is not very informative, so we pair each preposition with the head of its object (e.g., *"in_jail"*). Specifically, we pair the dependency relation "prep" with its "pobj," "agent" with its "pobj", and "dative" with the "dobj" of its governing verb. We also create compound dependencies for "pcomp," and "advcl" relations and resolve the relative pronoun with its subject for "relcl" relations.

Basilisk has not previously been used to learn multi-word verb phrases, so we needed to define a VP representation. We represented each VP using the following syntax: VP([voice]<verb>)MOD(<modifier>)DOBJ(<noun>). The VP() identifies the head verb and voice (Active or Passive), and MOD() contains the first of any adverbs or particles included in the verb phrase. DOBJ() contains the head noun of a VP's direct object, if present. As we did with the contextual patterns, we treat *"have"*, *"do"*, and *"be,"* as special cases and join the verb with its complement. As an example, the verb phrase *"is clearly distorting"* would be represented as **"VP([active]be_distort)MOD(clearly)"**.

We observed that many of the most useful contextual patterns for identifying near-synonyms captured conjunction dependency relations. For example, the contextual pattern ←**CONJ(distortion)** occured with 6 seed terms (*exaggeration, fabrication, falsehood, lie, misrepresentation,* and *untruth*), as well as several other near-synonyms such as *disinformation, inaccuracy, crap,* and *dishonesty*. Near-synonyms also frequently appeared in conjoined verb phrases, such as *"misstate and inflate"* or *"misstate and embellish"*. As an example of a different type of dependency relation that proved to be useful, the compound pattern →**AgentPhrase(by_looter)** occurred with several near-synonym VPs for STEAL, such as *seize, ran-*

---

[3]We used all relations except "punct" and "det".

sack and *clean out*.

4.2 Near-Synonym Generation Results

We had no idea how many near-synonyms we could expect to find for each topic, so we configured Basilisk to learn 1,000 phrases[4] to err on the side of overgeneration. Basilisk learns in a fully automated process, but the resulting lists are not perfect so must be manually filtered to ensure a high-quality lexicon. The filtering process took us approximately 1.5 hours to review each list.[5] Most of the correct entries were among the first 400 terms generated by Basilisk.

Topic	FIRE	LIE	STEAL
# Phrases	142	177	146

Table 3: Near-Synonym Phrases per Topic

Table 3 shows the total number of near-synonyms acquired for each topic, after conflating active and passive voice variants, typos, and including the seed terms. These numbers show that the semantic lexicon induction algorithm enabled us to quickly produce many more near-synonym phrases per topic than we had found in the synonym lists of thesauri. Some of the discovered terms were quite interesting, such as *"infojunk"* and *"puffery"* for LIE, and sometimes unfamiliar to us but relevant, such as *"malversation"* and *"dacoity"* for STEAL.

5 Gold X-Phemism Data Set

To create a high-quality gold data set for x-phemism classification, we asked three people (not the authors) to label the near-synonym phrases for each topic on a scale from 1 to 5, where 1 is most dysphemistic, 3 is neutral, and 5 is most euphemistic. For each phrase, we computed the average score across the three annotators and assigned each phrase to a "gold" x-phemism category: phrases with score < 2.5 were labeled *dysphemistic*, phrases with score > 3.5 were labeled *euphemistic*, and the rest were labeled *neutral*.

To assess inter-annotator agreement, we assigned each annotator's score to one of the three x-phemism categories using the same ranges as above, and measured the category agreement for

each pair of annotators using Cohen's kappa (κ). For LYING, the pairwise κ scores were $\{.64, .69, .77\}$ with average $\kappa = .70$. For FIRE, the κ scores were $\{.66, .68, .80\}$ with average $\kappa = .71$. For STEAL, the κ scores were $\{.66, .77, .79\}$ with average $\kappa = .74$. Since the mean κ scores were $\geq .70$ for all three topics, we concluded that the agreement was reasonably good.

Table 4 shows examples of near-synonym phrases[6] with their gold scores and category labels. For example, *crap* and *infojunk* were among the most dysphemistic phrases for LIE, while *invent* and *embellish* were among the most euphemistic phrases for LIE. Table 5 shows the distribution of labels in the gold data set.

FIRE	LIE	STEAL	GOLD	
ax	crap	gut	1.00	D
flush out	infojunk	snatching	1.33	D
oust	fool	thuggery	1.66	D
expel	fakery	mug	2.00	D
disbar	deceive	burgle	2.33	D
severance	falsehood	rob	2.66	N
fire	lie	steal	3.00	N
dismiss	mistruth	despoliation	3.33	N
decommission	fabrication	malversation	3.66	E
downsize	misinform	overcharge	4.00	E
leave company	exaggerate	confiscate	4.33	E
furlough	invent	legerdemain	4.66	E
retire	embellish	–	5.00	E

Table 4: Examples of Gold Data Scores and Labels (D = dysphemistic, N = neutral, E = euphemistic)

	FIRE	LIE	STEAL
Euphemism	.30	.42	.24
Neutral	.29	.30	.35
Dysphemism	.41	.28	.41

Table 5: Class Distributions in Gold Data

6 X-phemism Classification with Sentiment Lexicons

Euphemisms and dysphemisms capture softer and harsher references to sensitive topics, so one could argue that this phenomenon falls within the realm of sentiment analysis. But x-phemisms are a distinctly different phenomenon. It may be tempting to equate euphemisms with positive sentiment and dysphemisms with negative sentiment, but x-phemisms refer to sensitive topics that typically

---

[4]Basilisk ran for 200 iterations learning 5 words per cycle.

[5]One of the authors did this filtering. Our goal was merely to obtain a list of near-synonyms to use for x-phemism classification, and not to evaluate the near-synonym generation per se since that is not the main contribution of our work.

[6]We display the phrases here as n-grams for readability, but they are actually represented syntactically. For example, *"leave company"* is represented as an active voice VP with head *"leave"* linked to a direct object with head *"company"*.

have strong affective polarity (usually negative). For example, vomiting is never a pleasant topic, no matter how it is referred to. Consequently, most euphemisms for vomiting still have negative polarity (e.g., *"be sick"* or *"lose your lunch"*). However some euphemisms can have neutral polarity, such as scientific or formal terms (e.g., *"regurgitation"*), and occasionally a euphemism will evoke positive polarity for a negative topic through metaphor (e.g., *"pushing up daisies"* for death). In this section, we investigate whether sentiment information can be beneficial for recognizing euphemisms and dysphemisms and establish baseline results for this task. We explore five properties associated with sentiment: affective polarity, connotation, intensity, arousal, and dominance.

As our first baseline, we assess the effectiveness of using positive/negative affective polarity (valence) information to label x-phemism phrases using two sentiment lexicons: the NRC EmoLex and VAD Lexicons (Mohammad and Turney, 2013; Mohammad, 2018a). For the specific emotions, we considered *anger*, *disgust*, *fear*, *sadness*, and *surprise* to be negative, and *anticipation*, *joy*, and *trust* to be positive. Another sentiment property related to x-phemisms is connotation. Euphemisms often include terms with positive connotation to soften a reference, and dysphemisms may include terms with negative connotation to make a reference more harsh. But importantly, connotation and x-phemisms are not the same phenomenon. For one, many terms with a strong connotation are not x-phemisms. Also, as with polarity, euphemisms can retain a negative connotation because the underlying topic has negative polarity. But since connotation and x-phemisms are related, we investigate whether connotation polarities from ConnotationWN (Feng et al., 2013; Kang et al., 2014) can be valuable for labeling x-phemisms.

We also explored the effectiveness of using affective intensity, arousal, and dominance information from the NRC Affective Intensity and VAD Lexicons (Mohammad, 2018b,a) for recognizing euphemistic and dysphemistic phrases. Dysphemisms are often harsh and can be downright rude, so we hypothesized that terms with high arousal may be dysphemistic. Conversely, euphemisms use softer and gentler language, so they may be associated with low arousal. Dominant terms correspond to power and control, so it would be logical to expect that high dominance may be associated with

euphemisms and low dominance may be associated with dysphemisms (e.g., *"frail"* and *"weak"*) (Mohammad, 2018a).

For intensity, we used the NRC Affective Intensity Lexicon (Mohammad, 2018b), which associates words with specific emotions. We mapped the intensity scores so that high intensity values for negative emotions ranged from [0-0.5] (representing dysphemistic to neutral) and high intensity values for positive emotions ranged from [0.5-1] (representing neutral to euphemistic).

The sentiment resources provide scores between 0 and 1. For polarities and connotation, 0 represents the strongest negative score and 1 represents the strongest positive score. For arousal, and dominance, the range is low (0) to high (1). We expect high arousal to be associated with dysphemism, so to be consistent with the other properties we reverse its range and replace each score S with 1-S. We score multi-word phrases by taking the average score of their words. Once a phrase receives a score S, we map S to one of the three x-phemism categories as follows: $S \leq 0.25 \Rightarrow dysphemism$, $0.25 < S < 0.75 \Rightarrow neutral$, and $S \geq .75 \Rightarrow euphemism$. We chose these ranges to conservatively divide the space into quadrants, so that scores in the lowest quadrant represent dysphemism, scores in the highest quadrant represent euphemism, and scores in the middle are considered neutral.

6.1 Lexicon Results

Table 6 shows the results for the sentiment lexicon experiments. We report F-scores for the euphemism (**Euph**), neutral (**Neu**), and dysphemism (**Dysph**) categories as well as a macro-average F-score (**Avg**). The best-performing lexicon across all three topics was ConnotationWN (ConnoWN).

We also experimented with combining multiple dictionaries to see if they were complementary. For these experiments, each dictionary labeled a phrase as euphemistic, dysphemistic, or neutral (as described earlier) or none (i.e., no label if the word was not present in the lexicon). The most frequent label was then assigned to the phrase, except that 'none' labels were ignored. ConnotationWN's label was used to break ties. We evaluated all pairs of lexicons and the best pair turned out to be ConnotationWN plus Valence, which we refer to as BestPair in Table 6. We also tried using all of the dictionaries, shown as AllDicts in Table 6. Combining dictionaries did improve performance, with

BestPair performing best for FIRE and STEAL, and AllDicts performing best for LIE.

Overall, connotation and valence (affective polarity) were the most useful sentiment properties for recognizing x-phemisms. But, thus far we have considered only the words in a phrase. In the next section, we explore an approach that exploits the sentence contexts around the phrases.

FIRE	Euph	Neu	Dysph	Avg
EmoLex	.00	.00	.28	.09
Dominance	.00	**.40**	.07	.15
Intensity	.05	.29	.18	.17
Arousal	.05	.35	.15	.18
Valence	.05	.26	.25	.19
ConnoWN	.28	**.40**	**.50**	.39
AllDicts	.39	.30	.48	.39
BestPair	**.40**	.33	.47	**.40**
LIE	Euph	Neu	Dysph	Avg
EmoLex	.11	.04	.37	.17
Intensity	.03	.38	.15	.19
Dominance	.09	**.42**	.15	.22
Arousal	.03	**.42**	.25	.23
Valence	.12	.31	.37	.26
ConnoWN	.31	.32	.38	.34
BestPair	**.33**	.33	.38	.35
AllDicts	.32	.40	**.43**	**.39**
STEAL	Euph	Neu	Dysph	Avg
EmoLex	.20	.00	.21	.13
Intensity	.00	.19	.18	.13
Arousal	.00	.30	.21	.17
Valence	.20	.20	.23	.21
Dominance	.21	**.39**	.07	.22
ConnoWN	.20	.21	**.43**	.28
AllDicts	.28	.31	.41	.33
BestPair	**.40**	.33	.41	**.38**

Table 6: Results for Sentiment Lexicons (F-scores)

7 X-phemism Classification with Contextual Sentiment Analysis

We hypothesized that the contexts around euphemisms and dysphemisms would be different in terms of sentiment. People often use euphemisms when they want to be comforting, supportive, or put a positive spin on a subject. In obituaries, for example, euphemisms for death are often accompanied by references to peace, heaven, flowers, and courage. In contrast, grisly murder mystery novels often use dysphemisms, speaking about death using harsh or graphic language. X-phemisms are also prevalent in political discourse. People frequently use euphemisms to argue for the merits of a particular subject (e.g., *"enhanced interrogation"* is a euphemism invoked to justify the use of TORTURE). Conversely, people use dysphemisms when arguing against something (e.g., *"baby killing"* to refer to ABORTION).

To investigate this hypothesis, we developed models to classify a phrase with respect to x-phemism categories using sentiment analysis of its sentence contexts. We use the Gigaword corpus and experiment with both sentiment lexicons and a sentiment classifier to evaluate sentence polarity.

However polysemy and metaphor pose a major challenge: many phrases have multiple meanings. To address this problem, we create a subcorpus for each topic by extracting Gigaword articles that contain a seed term for that topic (see Table 2). The seed terms can also be ambiguous, but we expect that the resulting subcorpus will have a higher density of articles about the intended topic than the Gigaword corpus as a whole. Given a candidate x-phemism phrase for a topic, we then extract sentences containing that phrase from the topic's subcorpus. Our expectation is that most documents that contain <u>both</u> the x-phemism phrase <u>and</u> a seed term for the topic will be relevant to the topic.

Once we have a set of sentence contexts for an x-phemism phrase, our first contextual model uses sentiment lexicons to determine each sentence's polarity. For each topic, we use the best-performing lexicons reported in Section 6.1 (i.e., BestPair for FIRE and STEAL, and AllDicts for LIE). First, each word found in the lexicons is labeled positive for scores > 0.5 or negative for scores < 0.5.[7] We then assign a polarity to each sentence based on majority vote among its labeled words. Sentences with an equal number of positive and negative words, or no labeled words, are ignored.

X-phemisms are relative to a topic that itself often has strong affective polarity, so given a phrase P, our goal is to determine whether P's contexts are positive or negative *relative to the topic*. To assess this, we generate a polarity distribution across *all* sentences in the topic's subcorpus. We will refer to all sentences in the subcorpus for topic T as Sents(T) and the sentences in the subcorpus that mention phrase P as Sents(T, P). We define POS(S) as the percent of sentences S labeled positive, and

---

[7] If a word occurred in multiple lexicons, ConnotationWN was given precedence.

NEG(S) as the percent of sentences S labeled negative, and classify each phrase P as follows:

If POS(Sents(T, P)) > POS(Sents(T)) + γ
Then label P as *euphemistic*

If NEG(Sents(T, P)) > NEG(Sents(T)) + γ
Then label P as *dysphemistic*

Else label P as *neutral*

We set $\gamma = 0.10$ for our experiments.[8] Intuitively, the γ parameter dictates that a phrase is labeled as euphemistic (or dysphemistic) only if its sentence contexts have a positive (or negative) percentage at least 10% higher than the sentence contexts for the topic as a whole.

Our second contextual model uses a sentiment classifier instead of lexicons to assign polarity to each sentence. We used a reimplementation of the NRC-Canada sentiment classifier (Mohammad et al., 2013), which performed well in the SemEval 2013 Task 2. Given a sentence, the classifier returns probabilities that the sentence is positive, negative, or neutral. We label each sentence with the polarity that has the highest probability.

Since the classifier provides labels for all three polarities (whereas we only got positive and negative polarities from the lexicons), we use a slightly different procedure to label a phrase. First, we compute the percent of subcorpus sentences containing phrase P that are assigned each polarity (POS, NEG, NEU), and compute the percent of <u>all</u> subcorpus sentences assigned each polarity. Then we compute the difference for each polarity. For example, $\Delta(POS) = $ POS(Sents(T, P))-POS(Sents(T)). This represents the difference between the percent of Positive sentences containing P and the percent of Positive sentences in the subcorpus as a whole. Finally, we label phrase P based on the polarity that had the largest difference: POS $\Rightarrow$ *euphemistic*, NEG $\Rightarrow$ *dysphemistic*, NEU $\Rightarrow$ *neutral*.

7.1 Contextual Sentiment Results

Table 7 shows F-score results for the contextual models on our gold data. We evaluated three contextual models that use different mechanisms to label the affective polarity of a sentence: ContextNRC uses the NRC sentiment classifier, ContextAllDicts uses the AllDicts lexicon method, and ContextBestPair uses the BestPair lexicon method. For the sake of comparison, we also re-display the

<hr>

	Euph	Neu	Dysph	Avg
FIRE				
BestDictModel	.40	**.33**	**.47**	**.40**
ContextNRC	.28	.18	.37	.28
ContextAllDict	**.52**	.19	.18	.30
ContextBestPair	.31	.26	.45	.34
LIE				
BestDictModel	.32	.40	.43	.39
ContextBestPair	.42	.41	.35	.39
ContextNRC	.56	.19	**.46**	.40
ContextAllDicts	**.67**	**.42**	.31	**.47**
STEAL				
BestDictModel	.40	**.33**	.41	.38
ContextNRC	.24	.25	**.52**	.34
ContextBestPair	.42	.24	.47	.38
ContextAllDicts	**.61**	.29	.40	**.43**

Table 7: Results for Contextual Analysis (F-scores)

results for the best lexicon model (*BestDictModel*) presented in Section 6.1 for each topic.

For LIE and STEAL, the best contextual model outperformed the best lexicon method, improving the F-score from .39 $\rightarrow$ .47 for LIE and from .38 $\rightarrow$ .43 for STEAL. For FIRE, the contextual models showed lower performance. We observed that phrases for the FIRE topic exhibited more lexical ambiguity than the other topics, so the subcorpus extracted for FIRE was more noisy than for the other topics. This likely contributed to the inferior performance of the contextual models on this topic.

Table 8 shows the recall (R) and precision (P) breakdown for the best performing model for each topic. Euphemisms had the best recall and precision for LIE and STEAL, but lower recall for FIRE. Precision was lowest for the neutral category overall, indicating that too many euphemistic and dysphemistic phrases are being labeled as neutral.

	Euph		Neu		Dysph	
	R	P	R	P	R	P
FIRE	.31	.58	.47	.25	.44	.51
LIE	.64	.69	.52	.35	.24	.46
STEAL	.68	.56	.32	.26	.33	.50

Table 8: Recall and Precision of Best Models

Our observation is that the models perform best on strongly euphemistic or dysphemistic phrases, and they have the most trouble categorizing metaphorical expressions, such as *"ax"* for FIRE. It makes sense that the lexicon-based models would have difficulty with these cases, but we had hoped that the contextual models would fare better. We suspect that polysemy is especially problematic for metaphorical phrases, resulting in a subcorpus for the topic that contains many irrelevant contexts. Incorporating understanding of metaphor seems to be an important direction for future research.

8 Conclusions

This paper presented the first effort to recognize euphemisms and dysphemisms using natural language processing. Our research examined the relationship between x-phemisms and sentiment analysis, exploring whether information about affective polarity, connotation, arousal, intensity, and dominance could be beneficial for this task. We used semantic lexicon induction to generate near-synonyms for three topics, and developed lexicon-based and context-based sentiment analysis methods to classify phrases as *euphemistic, dysphemistic*, or *neutral*. We found that affective polarity and connotation information were useful for this task, and that identifying sentiment in sentence contexts around a phrase was generally more effective than labeling the phrases themselves. Promising avenues for future work include incorporating methods for recognizing politeness, formality, and metaphor. Euphemisms and dysphemisms are an exceedingly rich linguistic phenomenon, and we hope that our research will encourage more work on this interesting yet challenging problem.

Acknowledgments

We gratefully thank Shelley Felt, Shauna Felt, and Claire Moore for their help annotating the gold data for this research.

References

Keith Allan. 2009. The connotations of English colour terms: Colour-based X-phemisms. *Journal of Pragmatics*, 41.

Keith Allan and Kate Burridge. 1991. *Euphemism and Dysphemism: Language Used as Shield and Weapon*. Oxford University Press, New York.

Malika Aubakirova and Mohit Bansal. 2016. Interpreting neural networks to improve politeness comprehension. In *Proceedings of the 2016 Conference on Empirical Methods in Natural Language Processing*.

Anne Bertram. 1998. *NTC's Dictionary of Euphemisms*. NTC, Chicago.

Cristian Danescu-Niculescu-Mizil, Moritz Sudhof, Dan Jurafsky, Jure Leskovec, and Christopher Potts. 2013. A computational approach to politeness with application to social factors. In *Proceedings of the 51st Annual Meeting of the Association for Computational Linguistics, ACL 2013*.

Song Feng, Jun Seok Kang, Polina Kuznetsova, and Yejin Choi. 2013. Connotation Lexicon: A Dash of Sentiment Beneath the Surface Meaning. In *Proceedings of the 51st Annual Meeting of the Association for Computational Linguistics (ACL-2013)*.

Juri Ganitkevitch, , Benjamin Van Durme, and Chris Callison-burch. 2013. PPDB: The Paraphrase Database. In *Proceedings of the 2013 North American Chapter of the Association for Computational Linguistics: Human Language Technologies*.

D. Gupta, J. Carbonell, A. Gershman, S. Klein, and D. Miller. 2015. Unsupervised phrasal near-synonym generation from text corpora. In *Proceedings of the 29th AAAI Conference on Artificial Intelligence (AAAI 2015)*.

Ivan Habernal and Iryna Gurevych. 2015. Exploiting debate portals for semi-supervised argumentation mining in user-generated web discourse. In *Proceedings of the 2015 Conference on Empirical Methods in Natural Language Processing*.

R. W. Holder. 2002. *How Not To Say What You Mean: A Dictionary of Euphemisms*. Oxford University Press, Oxford.

Jun Seok Kang, Song Feng, Leman Akoglu, and Yejin Choi. 2014. ConnotationWordNet: Learning connotation over the word+sense network. In *Proceedings of the 52nd Annual Meeting of the Association for Computational Linguistics*.

Vaibhav Kesarwani, Diana Inkpen, Stan Szpakowicz, and Chris Tanasescu (Margento). 2017. Metaphor detection in a poetry corpus. In *Proceedings of the Joint SIGHUM Workshop on Computational Linguistics for Cultural Heritage, Social Sciences, Humanities and Literature*.

Rijul Magu and Jiebo Luo. 2014. Determining Code Words in Euphemistic Hate Speech Using Word Embedding Networks. In *Proceedings of the Second Workshop on Abusive Language Online (ALW2)*.

Saif M. Mohammad. 2018a. Obtaining reliable human ratings of valence, arousal, and dominance for 20,000 english words. In *Proceedings of The Annual Conference of the Association for Computational Linguistics (ACL)*, Melbourne, Australia.

Saif M. Mohammad. 2018b. Word affect intensities. In *Proceedings of the 11th Edition of the Language Resources and Evaluation Conference (LREC-2018)*, Miyazaki, Japan.

Saif M Mohammad, Svetlana Kiritchenko, and Xiaodan Zhu. 2013. NRC-Canada: Building the state-of-the-art in sentiment analysis of tweets. In *Proceedings of the Second Joint Conference on Lexical and Computational Semantics*.

Saif M. Mohammad and Peter D. Turney. 2013. Crowd-sourcing a word-emotion association lexicon. *Computational Intelligence*, 29(3):436–465.

Ji Ho Park, Jamin Shin, and Pascale Fung. 2018. Reducing gender bias in abusive language detection. In *Proceedings of the 2018 Conference on Empirical Methods in Natural Language Processing*.

Ellie Pavlick and Joel Tetreault. 2016. An empirical analysis of formality in online communication. *Transactions of the Association for Computational Linguistics*, 4:61–74.

Kerry L. Pfaff, Raymond W. Gibbs Jr., and Michael D. Johnson. 1997. Metaphor in using and understanding euphemism and dysphemism. *Applied Psycholinguistics*, 18.

A. Qadir and E. Riloff. 2012. Ensemble-based semantic lexicon induction for semantic tagging. In *Proceedings of the First Joint Conference on Lexical and Computational Semantics (*SEM 2012)*.

Hussein Abdo Rababah. 2014. The Translatability and Use of X-Phemism Expressions (X-Phemization): Euphemisms, Dysphemisms and Orthophemisms in the Medical Discourse. *Studies in Literature and Language*, 9.

Hugh Rawson. 2003. *Rawson's Dictionary of Euphemisms and Other Doubletalk*. Castle, Chicago, IL.

E. Riloff, J. Wiebe, and T. Wilson. 2003. Learning Subjective Nouns using Extraction Pattern Bootstrapping. In *Proceedings of the Seventh Conference on Natural Language Learning (CoNLL-2003)*, pages 25–32.

Ekaterina Shutova. 2010. Automatic metaphor interpretation as a paraphrasing task. In *Proceedings of the 2010 Annual Conference of the North American Chapter of the Association for Computational Linguistics*.

Ekaterina Shutova, Lin Sun, and Anna Korhonen. 2010. Metaphor identification using verb and noun clustering. In *Proceedings of the 23rd International Conference on Computational Linguistics*.

S. Somasundaran and J. Wiebe. 2010. Recognizing stances in ideological on-line debates. In *Proceedings of the NAACL HLT 2010 Workshop on Computational Approaches to Analysis and Generation of Emotion in Text*.

M. Thelen and E. Riloff. 2002. A Bootstrapping Method for Learning Semantic Lexicons Using Extraction Pa ttern Contexts. In *Proceedings of the 2002 Conference on Empirical Methods in Natural Language Processing*, pages 214–221.

Cynthia Van Hee, Els Lefever, Ben Verhoeven, Julie Mennes, Bart Desmet, Guy De Pauw, Walter Daelemans, and Veronique Hoste. 2015. Detection and fine-grained classification of cyberbullying events. In *Proceedings of the International Conference Recent Advances in Natural Language Processing*.

M. Walker, P. Anand, R. Abbott, and R. Grant. 2012. Stance classification using dialogic properties of persuasion. In *Proceedings of the 2012 Conference of the North American Chapter of the Association for Computational Linguistics: Human Language Technologies*.

Alan Wallington, Rodrigo Agerri, John Barnden, Mark Lee, and Tim Rumbell. 2011. Affect transfer by metaphor for an intelligent conversational agent. In *Affective Computing and Sentiment Analysis*, pages 53–66. Springer.

Michael Wiegand, Josef Ruppenhoffer, Anna Schmidt, and Clayton Greenberg. 2018. Inducing a lexicon of abusive words - a feature-based approach. In *NAACL-HLT 2018*.

Jun-Ming Xu, Kwang-Sung Jun, Xiaojin Zhu, and Amy Bellmore. 2012. Learning from bullying traces in social media. In *Proceedings of the 2012 Conference of the North American Chapter of the Association for Computational Linguistics*.

IlliniMet: Illinois System for Metaphor Detection with Contextual and Linguistic Information

Hongyu Gong   Kshitij Gupta   Akriti Jain   Suma Bhat
University of Illinois at Urbana-Champaign, IL, USA
{hgong6,kg9,akritij,spbhat2}@illinois.edu

Abstract

Metaphors are rhetorical use of words based on the conceptual mapping as opposed to their literal use. Metaphor detection, an important task in language understanding, aims to identify metaphors in word level from given sentences. We present IlliniMet, a system to automatically detect metaphorical words. Our model combines the strengths of the contextualized representation by the widely used RoBERTa model and the rich linguistic information from external resources such as WordNet. The proposed approach is shown to outperform strong baselines on a benchmark dataset. Our best model achieves F1 scores of 73.0% on VUA ALLPOS, 77.1% on VUA VERB, 70.3% on TOEFL ALLPOS and 71.9% on TOEFL VERB.

1 Introduction

Metaphors are a form of figurative language used to make an implicit or implied comparison between two things that are unrelated (Ortony and Andrew, 1993). They are widely used in natural language, conveying rich semantic information which deviates from their literal meaning. For instance, in the sentence "Tom has always been an early bird waking up at 5:30 a.m.", the phrase "early bird" does not mean a real animal but refers to someone doing something early.

The ubiquity and subtlety of metaphors present challenges to language understanding in natural language processing. Detecting metaphors is the first step towards metaphor understanding, which helps to uncover the meaning more accurately. Metaphor detection has been used in a variety of downstream applications such as sentiment classification (Rentoumi et al., 2012) and machine translation (Koglin et al., 2015).

Some existing approaches to metaphor detection rely on linguistic features such as lexicon based

metaphor constructions, lexical abstractness and word categories in WordNet (Dodge et al., 2015; Klebanov et al., 2016). Most of these approaches either do not consider the contextual information or only focus on limited contexts. Others use unigram based features regardless of their contexts (Köper and im Walde, 2017), and still others identify metaphors in the limited context of subject-verb-object triples (Bulat et al., 2017). We note that the contextual information is crucial for metaphor detection. As shown in Table 1, the word "fix" can be used both metaphorically and literally depending on its context.

Table 1: Metaphorical and Literal Usage of Word "Fix"

Metaphor: I think that we need to begin from facts and **fix** important data.
Literal: They couldn't **fix** my old computer, and I had to buy a new one.

Recent studies incorporating contextual information into metaphor detection include unsupervised approaches (Gong et al., 2017) and supervised models (Wu et al., 2018; Stowe et al., 2019). Neural networks such as Long Short Term Memory (LSTM) have achieved state-of-the-art performance in metaphor detection due to their ability to encode contextual information (Gao et al., 2018).

Recently proposed contextualized representation models that have been widely used include Embeddings from Language Models (ELMo) (Peters et al., 2018), Representations from Transformer (BERT) (Devlin et al., 2019) and Robustly Optimized BERT Pretraining Approach (RoBERTa) (Liu et al., 2019). Their use has shown dramatic improvements in the performance of several NLP tasks. These models are pretrained on large text corpora to encode rich contextualized knowledge into the semantic representation of words with deep network structures.

146

Proceedings of the Second Workshop on Figurative Language Processing, pages 146–153
July 9, 2020. ©2020 Association for Computational Linguistics
https://doi.org/10.18653/v1/P17

In this paper, we build our metaphor detection model upon RoBERTa to leverage its strength in capturing contextual information. In addition, we enhance the power of contextualized representation by using linguistic features. Using external resources our model integrates features such as word concreteness, which serves to complement the contextual knowledge in RoBERTa embeddings and aid the task of metaphor detection. This model was our contribution to the Second Shared Task on Metaphor Detection (Leong et al., 2020). Our best model achieves F1 scores of 73.0% and 77.1% on all words and verbs alone respectively for metaphors in the VUA dataset. Our model performance is 70.3% and 71.9% on all words and only verbs respectively in the TOEFL dataset. We make our implementation available for a wider exploration[1].

2   Related Work

Metaphor Detection. Metaphor detection has recently attracted a lot of research interest in the area of natural language processing. The metaphor detection task can be broadly classified into two categories. The first involves predicting whether a given word or phrase is a metaphor (Gong et al., 2017). The second category can be formulated as a sequential labeling task of predicting the metaphorical or literal usage of every word in a sentence (Leong et al., 2018). Our current study falls into the second category.

Feature-based approaches.   Many recent works have explored the use of various linguistic features for automatic metaphor detection. These features include word abstractness (Köper and im Walde, 2017), WordNet features, hypernyms and synonyms (Mao et al., 2018), syntactic dependencies and semantic patterns (Hovy et al., 2013), word imageability (Strzalkowski et al., 2013) as well as word embeddings (Köper and im Walde, 2017).

Neural network models. Deep learning models are becoming very popular in various downstream applications of natural language processing owing to the ability to train models in an end-to-end manner without explicit feature engineering. Approaches built upon neural networks have shown great successes in metaphor detection task as well. Different structures of neural networks have been extensively studied to better encode semantic knowledge by capturing metaphorical patterns (Leong et al., 2018).

Sequential models such as Recurrent Neural Networks (RNN) demonstrate strong performance in metaphor detection (Bizzoni and Ghanimifard, 2018). An LSTM is applied to identifying metaphors together with a Convolutional Neural Network (CNN) (Wu et al., 2018). The model utilizes pretrained word2vec word embeddings. Another approach built on sequential models is a Bidirectional LSTM model augmented with pretrained contextualized embeddings (Gao et al., 2018).

A recent work draws inspiration from linguistic theories, and proposes RNN_HG and RNN_MHCA, which are variants of RNN models (Mao et al., 2019). Assuming that pretrained GloVe embeddings carry literal meaning, the model RNN_HG detects metaphors by comparing GloVe embeddings with the contextualized word representations learned by the RNN. The other variant, RNN_MHCA, integrates the multi-head attention mechanism in model hidden states, and enriches word representations with information from broader contexts.

Contextualized representation model.   The linguistic theory of Selectional Preference Violation (SPV) states that a metaphorical phrase or word is semantically different from its context (Wilks, 1975, 1978). This suggests the importance of contextual information for metaphor detection. A few pretrained contextualized representation models have been recently proposed and shown to achieve better performance than commonly used sequential models in a variety of language understanding tasks. A few models that encode contextual knowledge include ELMo (Peters et al., 2018), BERT (Devlin et al., 2019) and RoBERTa (Liu et al., 2019). The advantages of these models are that they are trained on a large amount of text to encode rich semantic and contextual information into the representations giving them greater representation power than the models which are only trained on small task-specific datasets. In this work, we build our system upon RoBERTa to take advantage of its contextual representation for metaphor detection.

3   Metaphor Detection

In this section, we will introduce our model design, training and prediction for metaphor detection.

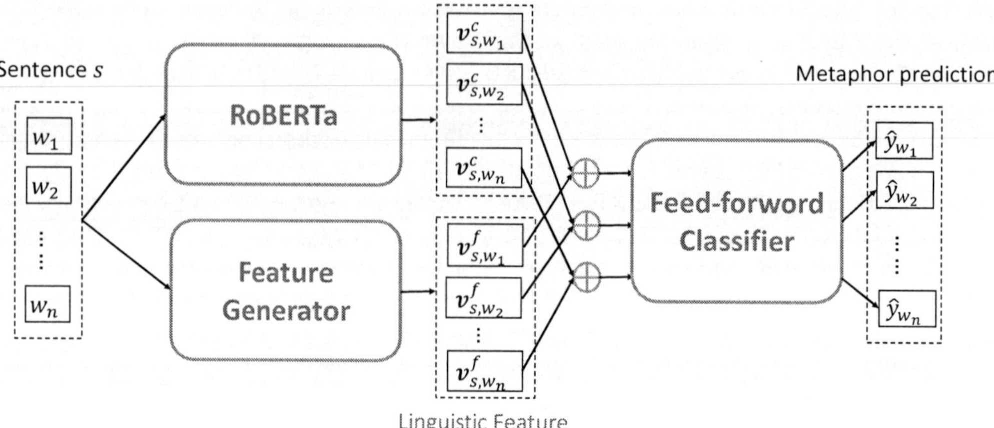

Figure 1: Model structure of IlliniMet system for metaphor detection. Its RoBERTa module learns contextualized representations, and the feature generator generates linguistic features for words. The outputs of RoBERTa and feature generator are combined as the word representations, which are sent to feed-forward classifier for metaphor classification.

3.1 Model

We cast the problem of metaphor detection as a sequence labeling task, where each word in the input sentence is classified as either metaphor or non-metaphor. As shown in Fig. 1, the framework of our IlliniMet model consists of three modules: RoBERTa, a feature generator and a feed-forward classifier. We will discuss each module in detail in the following parts.

RoBERTa. The meaning of words can vary subtly from one context to another, and RoBERTa generates contextualized word representations to capture the context-sensitive semantics of words (Liu et al., 2019). The use of word representations from RoBERTa has resulted in state-of-the-art performance in a variety of language understanding tasks. Given a sentence s consisting of n words $\{w_1, \ldots, w_n\}$, RoBERTa model generates their contextualized representations $\{\mathbf{v}^c_{s,w_1}, \ldots, \mathbf{v}^c_{s,w_n}\}$.

Linguistic features. The second module in our model is a feature generator. Previous works on metaphor detection have shown that linguistic features are useful for detecting metaphors. The features considered in our work are:

- Part-of-speech (POS) feature. We use the part-of-speech tags of the input words as the POS feature (Klebanov et al., 2014). Instead of using a one-hot vector as the POS feature, we create an embedding lookup table for POS tags, where each POS tag is mapped to a vec-

tor. All POS vectors are randomly initialized and are tuned during model training. We can obtain the representation of a given tag from the table during model training and prediction.

- Topic feature. The topic feature (Klebanov et al., 2014) is a distribution of a word over 100 topics extracted using Latent Dirichlet Allocation (LDA) (Blei et al., 2003).

- Word concreteness. Word concreteness is obtained from the database of (Brysbaert et al., 2014). Following (Klebanov et al., 2015), we binned words' concreteness rating ranging from 1 to 5 with upward and downward thresholds respectively. A word would be assigned to a bin with the upward threshold a if its concreteness is at least a. Similarly, it is assigned to a bin with the downward threshold b if its concreteness is at most b. Each word is represented with a binary vector indicating the bins in which its rating falls.

- WordNet feature. WordNet, a commonly used linguistic resource, provides the semantic classes of words such as verbs of communication and consumption. We use binary vectors corresponding to these classes as the WordNet feature for words (Klebanov et al., 2016).

- VerbNet feature. The VerbNet database classifies verbs based on their syntactic and seman-

148

tic patterns such as their frames, predicates, thematic roles and thematic role fillers. We again use binary feature vectors to represent the classes of verbs as in (Klebanov et al., 2016).

- Corpus-based feature. Verbs are clustered into 150 semantic clusters, and are assigned with corresponding one-hot vectors as the corpus-based features (Klebanov et al., 2016).

We note that some words may not have certain features; for instance, nouns do not have VerbNet features. We assign feature vectors of all zeros to those words without corresponding features.

The Feed-forward classifier. Lastly we have a feed-forward network based classifier as the inference module. The model derives word representations from the concatenation of contextualized representations and linguistic features. The concatenated representations are fed to the classifier and used to predict word labels (either metaphor or non-metaphor). We use a one-layer fully-connected feed-forward neural network for classification. For word w denote its RoBERTa embedding by $\mathbf{v}_{s,w}^c$ in sentence s and linguistic feature $\mathbf{v}_{s,w}^f$. The inference module predicts $\hat{\mathbf{y}}_w$, the probability over the two classes (both metaphor and non-metaphor).

$$\hat{\mathbf{y}}_w = \mathrm{softmax}(\mathbf{W}(\mathbf{v}_{s,w}^c \oplus \mathbf{v}_{s,w}^f) + \mathbf{b}), \quad (1)$$

where $\hat{\mathbf{y}}_w$ is a two-dimensional vector, and $\oplus$ is the concatenation operator. The weight matrix $\mathbf{W}$ and the bias vector $\mathbf{b}$ are both trainable model parameters.

As will be described in Section 4, the datasets we have are imbalanced with many more non-metaphorical words than metaphorical ones. Therefore, we used a weighted cross-entropy loss, and assign less weight to the more frequent label. We denote y_w as the true label of word w, and $\hat{y}_w$ as its predicted probability. Given a set of training sentences S, the training loss L is formulated as follows:

$$L = -\sum_{s \in S} \sum_{w \in s} \alpha_{y_w} \log \hat{y}_w, \quad (2)$$

where α_{y_w} is the weight coefficient of label y_w, and it is the total number of labels divided by the count of the label α_{y_w}.

3.2 Training and Prediction

Training. We divided the training data into train and dev sets with a split ratio of $4:1$, and trained the model to minimize the loss. The model which achieved the best F1 score on the dev set was used for testing. We used the pretrained RoBERTa model with 24 hidden layers in our system. Other model parameters were randomly initialized.

The system was trained end-to-end, and all model parameters including RoBERTa's parameters were tuned during model training. We set the dropout probability as 0.1, and the training epochs as 4 for all datasets. The learning rate was set as $2e-5$. We availed the warmup schedule by linearly increasing the learning rate from 0 to $2e-5$ within the first training epoch. The warmup schedule is a useful technique for tuning a pretrained model, while prevents the large deviation of the model from its pretrained parameters when it is tuned on a new dataset (Devlin et al., 2019).

Prediction. We use an ensemble method for the model prediction. Three models were trained independently with different train/dev splits, and we collect their predictions on the test data. Ensemble methods have been proposed to reduce the variance in predictions made by machine learning and deep learning models (Dietterich, 2000). In our experiments, we decide the word label by the majority vote of the predictions from these three models.

4 Experiment

We empirically evaluate our model for metaphor detection in this section. Precision, Recall and F1 score are the evaluation metrics used in our experiments. We report metaphor detection results on words of any POS tags as well as verbs alone in the test set provided by the shared task [2].

Dataset. Two datasets were used for the evaluation of metaphor detection – the VU Amsterdam Metaphor Corpus (VUA) (Steen, 2010) and the TOEFL dataset (Klebanov et al., 2018). The sentences in these two datasets were manually annotated for the task of metaphor detection at the word level.

The VUA dataset was collected from the BNC in four genres including news, academic, fiction and conversation. It provides $12,122$ sentences for training, and $4,080$ sentences for testing. Around

---

[2]https://competitions.codalab.org/
competitions/22188

Table 2: The Test Performance of Different Models on Metaphor Detection

Dataset	VUA						TOEFL					
Type	ALLPOS			VERB			ALLPOS			VERB		
Metric	P	R	F1	P	R	F1	P	R	F1	P	R	F1
RoBERTa w. feature (ensemble)	74.6	71.5	73.0	76.7	77.2	77.0	72.6	67.5	70.0	73.1	70.7	**71.9**
RoBERTa w. feature (single)	75.0	69.8	72.3	76.5	75.5	76.0	74.2	63.8	68.6	72.0	69.4	70.7
RoBERTa (ensemble)	74.4	70.3	72.3	76.1	78.1	**77.1**	70.9	69.7	**70.3**	70.8	72.7	71.8
RoBERTa (single)	75.6	68.6	72.0	77.4	75.2	76.3	70.6	67.5	69.0	68.2	70.4	69.3
CNN-LSTM	60.8	70.0	65.1	60.0	76.3	67.2	-	-	-	-	-	-
ELMo-LSTM	71.6	73.6	72.6	68.2	71.3	69.7	-	-	-	-	-	-
RNN_HG	71.8	76.3	**74.0**	69.3	72.3	70.8	-	-	-	-	-	-

11% of VUA tokens are metaphors in the training data.

The TOEFL dataset consists of essays written by non-native speakers of English. It contains 180 train essays with $2,741$ sentences and 60 test essays with 968 sentences. In the training partition, 7% of TOEFL tokens are metaphors.

Models. We report and compare the performance of the variants of our model. The methods we discuss in this work include:

1. RoBERTa w. feature (ensemble): our full model with both RoBERTa embeddings and linguistic features. The ensemble method is used to make predictions based on the votes of three separately trained models.

2. RoBERTa w. feature (single): a single full model trained to classify metaphors.

3. RoBERTa (ensemble): the model built on only RoBERTa and the classification layer without using linguistic features. Again, an ensemble method is applied to model predictions.

4. RoBERTa (single): the model has only RoBERTa and the classifier. A single model is trained to make predictions on test data.

Baselines. We also include three strong baselines for an empirical comparison in the task of metaphor detection.

- CNN-LSTM (Wu et al., 2018). This baseline combines CNN and LSTM layers to learn contextualized word embedding, and also includes additional features such as POS and word clusters. It has achieved the best performance on the VUA dataset in the 2018 VUA Metaphor Detection Shared Task (Leong et al., 2018).

- ELMo-LSTM (Gao et al., 2018). Built upon LSTM, this baseline makes use of pretrained contextualized embeddings from ELMo model (Peters et al., 2018).

- RNN_HG (Mao et al., 2019). This is the most recent model on metaphor detection reporting the state-of-the-art results on VUA dataset. It includes a bidirectional LSTM and makes use of GloVe and ELMo embeddings.

Results. Table 2 reports the results of our model variants as well as those of the three baselines discussed above. All variants of our model achieve better performance than the baselines, CNN-LSTM and ELMo-LSTM on both VUA ALLPOS and VUA VERB. The ensemble model of *RoBERTa with feature* falls behind the baseline RNN_HG by 1% in F1 score on VUA ALLPOS, while outperforming it by a large margin of 6.2%.

Ablation analysis. Ablation analysis was performed to compare the performance of our model variants. We can evaluate the effect of linguistic features by comparing our model with and without external features. When the ensemble method is used, the incorporation of external features does not influence the detection of metaphor verbs performance too much on both VUA and TOEFL data. When it comes to metaphor detection of all words, external features improve the F1 score by 0.7%

on VUA data, but degrades the performance on TOEFL data by 0.3%.

The gain in VUA ALLPOS is brought by the linguistic information of external features, which is not captured by the contextualized embeddings. The performance drop in TOEFL ALLPOS might have resulted from a larger search space of model parameters when the external features were added. Considering that the training data of TOEFL is much smaller in size compared tto that of VUA, the TOEFL model is likely to result in sub-optimal parameters after training when more parameters are introduced to the classification layer by the linguistic features.

We also evaluated the effectiveness of the ensemble method by comparing its performance with the performance of the single model. The ensemble model outperforms the single model regardless of whether external features were used. With external features, the ensemble model achieves gains of 0.7% and 1.4% in VUA and TOEFL dataset respectively when evaluated on all words.

Other model designs. We have only reported our best-performing models until now. In order to provide some empirical insights for those interested, we also discuss some designs which we had tried even though those did not yield performance gains. Besides RoBERTa embedding and linguistic features, we tried other features to expand the word representation. Borrowing ideas from (Devlin et al., 2018), we included the concatenation and the average of hidden state vectors of RoBERTa's last four layers. Another idea, which was inspired from (Mao et al., 2019), was to include the context-independent embedding from the bottom layer of RoBERTa. The intuition was that the model could identify metaphors more easily by comparing words' context-independent and context-sensitive embeddings.

Besides expanding word representation, we also experimented with different classification modules. We increased the layers of the feed-forward network, and also tried different activation functions in the feed-forward layer. We did not observe significant performance gains with these modifications to word representations and the inference module.

5 Discussion

In this section, we perform an analysis to explore the strengths and weaknesses of our model. Since we did not have ground truth labels for the test

instances, we divided the training data into train, dev and test sets with a ratio of $4 : 1 : 1$ for the purpose of error analysis. We trained and tuned our best performing model on the resulting train and dev sets respectively, and evaluated it on the test set.

Model performance on different POS tags. We evaluate the model performance on words of different part-of-speech tags. On the VUA dataset, determiners ("DT"), prepositions and conjunctions ("IN") had the highest F1 scores, while adjectives ("JJ") and plural nouns ("NNS") got the lowest F1 scores among all words. On the TOEFL dataset, the best-performing words were adjectives ("JJ") and verbs ("VB"). Words ranking at the bottom were prepositions and conjunctions ("IN") and nouns ("NN").

The nouns on both datasets received low F1 scores. One explanation is that nouns have a large vocabulary and often have multiple senses. As will be discussed in the error analysis below, the model may not make correct predictions if a noun and its different senses are not included in the training data. Interestingly, prepositions and conjunctions in the VUA dataset got good F1 scores while those in the TOEFL dataset got low scores. Since TOEFL data was collected from written texts of non-native English learners, we conjecture that there is more variety in the usage of prepositions in TOEFL dataset. The corresponding noise may have made it harder for the model to generalize from the training set to the test set.

Error analysis. We look through the examples where our model made wrong predictions, and summarize the patterns of these error examples below.

- Words that are unseen in the training set. Some metaphorical words in the test set do not occur in the training set. Examples are "whip-aerials", "puritans", "half-imagined" and "pandora box". Our model incorrectly classifies these words as non-metaphorical.

- Words that have senses unseen in the training set. We note that some words occur in both training and test sets, but they are used with different senses. For example, the word "wounded" is only used metaphorically in the training set. Our model incorrectly predicts its literal usage as metaphorical usage in the test data.

- Words whose test labels have inter-annotator

disagreement. Words "pack" and "bags" are labeled as metaphorical in the sentence " his job was to convince amaldi to pack his bags because there was a ship waiting at naples to take him to the united states". However, we think these words carry their literal senses in the given context.

- Inaccurate interpretation of contexts. In the long sentence "the 63-year-old head of pembridge investments , through which the bid is being mounted says ...", word "says" with the subject "the head" is not a metaphor. Our model may not capture its subject correctly given the long-distance dependency, which results in a false positive prediction.

6 Conclusion

In this paper, we introduced the IlliniMet system for the task of word-level metaphor detection. Our model leveraged contextual and linguistic information by combining contextualized representation and external linguistic features. We adopted an ensemble approach to reduce the variance of predictions and improve the model performance. The empirical results showed the effectiveness of our model. We also performed an error analysis to gain insights into the model behavior.

Acknowledgments

This work is supported by IBM-ILLINOIS Center for Cognitive Computing Systems Research (C3SR) - a research collaboration as part of the IBM AI Horizons Network. We would like to thank the anonymous reviewers for their constructive comments and suggestions.

References

Yuri Bizzoni and Mehdi Ghanimifard. 2018. Bigrams and bilstms two neural networks for sequential metaphor detection. In *Proceedings of the Workshop on Figurative Language Processing*, pages 91–101.

David M Blei, Andrew Y Ng, and Michael I Jordan. 2003. Latent dirichlet allocation. *Journal of machine Learning research*, 3(Jan):993–1022.

Marc Brysbaert, Amy Beth Warriner, and Victor Kuperman. 2014. Concreteness ratings for 40 thousand generally known english word lemmas. *Behavior research methods*, 46(3):904–911.

Luana Bulat, Stephen Clark, and Ekaterina Shutova. 2017. Modelling metaphor with attribute-based semantics. In *Proceedings of the 15th Conference of the European Chapter of the Association for Computational Linguistics: Volume 2, Short Papers*, pages 523–528.

Jacob Devlin, Ming-Wei Chang, Kenton Lee, and Kristina Toutanova. 2018. Bert: Pre-training of deep bidirectional transformers for language understanding. *arXiv preprint arXiv:1810.04805*.

Jacob Devlin, Ming-Wei Chang, Kenton Lee, and Kristina Toutanova. 2019. Bert: Pre-training of deep bidirectional transformers for language understanding. In *Proceedings of the 2019 Conference of the North American Chapter of the Association for Computational Linguistics: Human Language Technologies, Volume 1 (Long and Short Papers)*, pages 4171–4186.

Thomas G Dietterich. 2000. Ensemble methods in machine learning. In *International workshop on multiple classifier systems*, pages 1–15. Springer.

Ellen K Dodge, Jisup Hong, and Elise Stickles. 2015. Metanet: Deep semantic automatic metaphor analysis. In *Proceedings of the Third Workshop on Metaphor in NLP*, pages 40–49.

Ge Gao, Eunsol Choi, Yejin Choi, and Luke Zettlemoyer. 2018. Neural metaphor detection in context. In *Conference on Empirical Methods in Natural Language Processing*.

Hongyu Gong, Suma Bhat, and Pramod Viswanath. 2017. Geometry of compositionality. In *Thirty-First AAAI Conference on Artificial Intelligence*.

Dirk Hovy, Shashank Srivastava, Sujay Kumar Jauhar, Mrinmaya Sachan, Kartik Goyal, Huying Li, Whitney Sanders, and Eduard Hovy. 2013. Identifying metaphorical word use with tree kernels. In *Proceedings of the First Workshop on Metaphor in NLP*, pages 52–57.

Beata Beigman Klebanov, Ben Leong, Michael Heilman, and Michael Flor. 2014. Different texts, same metaphors: Unigrams and beyond. In *Proceedings of the Second Workshop on Metaphor in NLP*, pages 11–17.

Beata Beigman Klebanov, Chee Wee Leong, and Michael Flor. 2015. Supervised word-level metaphor detection: Experiments with concreteness and reweighting of examples. In *Proceedings of the Third Workshop on Metaphor in NLP*, pages 11–20.

Beata Beigman Klebanov, Chee Wee Leong, and Michael Flor. 2018. A corpus of non-native written english annotated for metaphor. In *Proceedings of the 2018 Conference of the North American Chapter of the Association for Computational Linguistics: Human Language Technologies, Volume 2 (Short Papers)*, pages 86–91.

Beata Beigman Klebanov, Chee Wee Leong, E Dario Gutierrez, Ekaterina Shutova, and Michael Flor. 2016. Semantic classifications for detection of verb metaphors. In *Proceedings of the 54th Annual Meeting of the Association for Computational Linguistics (Volume 2: Short Papers)*, pages 101–106.

Arlene Koglin et al. 2015. An empirical investigation of cognitive effort required to post-edit machine translated metaphors compared to the translation of metaphors. *Translation & Interpreting, The*, 7(1):126.

Maximilian Köper and Sabine Schulte im Walde. 2017. Improving verb metaphor detection by propagating abstractness to words, phrases and individual senses. In *Proceedings of the 1st Workshop on Sense, Concept and Entity Representations and their Applications*, pages 24–30.

Chee Wee Leong, Beata Beigman Klebanov, Chris Hamill, Egon Stemle, Rutuja Ubale, and Xianyang Chen. 2020. A report on the 2020 vua and toefl metaphor detection shared task. In *Proceedings of the Second Workshop on Figurative Language Processing*, Seattle, WA.

Chee Wee Leong, Beata Beigman Klebanov, and Ekaterina Shutova. 2018. A report on the 2018 vua metaphor detection shared task. In *Proceedings of the Workshop on Figurative Language Processing*, pages 56–66.

Yinhan Liu, Myle Ott, Naman Goyal, Jingfei Du, Mandar Joshi, Danqi Chen, Omer Levy, Mike Lewis, Luke Zettlemoyer, and Veselin Stoyanov. 2019. Roberta: A robustly optimized bert pretraining approach. *arXiv preprint arXiv:1907.11692*.

Rui Mao, Chenghua Lin, and Frank Guerin. 2018. Word embedding and wordnet based metaphor identification and interpretation. In *Proceedings of the 56th Annual Meeting of the Association for Computational Linguistics (Volume 1: Long Papers)*, pages 1222–1231.

Rui Mao, Chenghua Lin, and Frank Guerin. 2019. End-to-end sequential metaphor identification inspired by linguistic theories. In *Proceedings of the 57th Annual Meeting of the Association for Computational Linguistics*, pages 3888–3898.

Andrew Ortony and Ortony Andrew. 1993. *Metaphor and thought*. Cambridge University Press.

Matthew E Peters, Mark Neumann, Mohit Iyyer, Matt Gardner, Christopher Clark, Kenton Lee, and Luke Zettlemoyer. 2018. Deep contextualized word representations. In *Proceedings of NAACL-HLT*, pages 2227–2237.

Vassiliki Rentoumi, George A Vouros, Vangelis Karkaletsis, and Amalia Moser. 2012. Investigating metaphorical language in sentiment analysis: A sense-to-sentiment perspective. *ACM Transactions on Speech and Language Processing (TSLP)*, 9(3):1–31.

Gerard Steen. 2010. *A method for linguistic metaphor identification: From MIP to MIPVU*, volume 14. John Benjamins Publishing.

Kevin Stowe, Sarah Moeller, Laura Michaelis, and Martha Palmer. 2019. Linguistic analysis improves neural metaphor detection. In *Proceedings of the 23rd Conference on Computational Natural Language Learning (CoNLL)*, pages 362–371.

Tomek Strzalkowski, George Aaron Broadwell, Sarah Taylor, Laurie Feldman, Samira Shaikh, Ting Liu, Boris Yamrom, Kit Cho, Umit Boz, Ignacio Cases, et al. 2013. Robust extraction of metaphor from novel data. In *Proceedings of the First Workshop on Metaphor in NLP*, pages 67–76.

Yorick Wilks. 1975. A preferential, pattern-seeking, semantics for natural language inference. *Artificial intelligence*, 6(1):53–74.

Yorick Wilks. 1978. Making preferences more active. *Artificial intelligence*, 11(3):197–223.

Chuhan Wu, Fangzhao Wu, Yubo Chen, Sixing Wu, Zhigang Yuan, and Yongfeng Huang. 2018. Neural metaphor detecting with cnn-lstm model. In *Proceedings of the Workshop on Figurative Language Processing*, pages 110–114.

Adaptation of Word-Level Benchmark Datasets for Relation-Level Metaphor Identification

Omnia Zayed, John P. McCrae, Paul Buitelaar
Insight SFI Research Centre for Data Analytics
Data Science Institute
National University of Ireland Galway
IDA Business Park, Lower Dangan, Galway, Ireland
`{omnia.zayed, john.mccrae, paul.buitelaar}@insight-centre.org`

Abstract

Metaphor processing and understanding has attracted the attention of many researchers recently with an increasing number of computational approaches. A common factor among these approaches is utilising existing benchmark datasets for evaluation and comparisons. The availability, quality and size of the annotated data are among the main difficulties facing the growing research area of metaphor processing. The majority of current approaches pertaining to metaphor processing concentrate on word-level processing due to data availability. On the other hand, approaches that process metaphors on the relation-level ignore the context where the metaphoric expression. This is due to the nature and format of the available data. Word-level annotation is poorly grounded theoretically and is harder to use in downstream tasks such as metaphor interpretation. The conversion from word-level to relation-level annotation is non-trivial. In this work, we attempt to fill this research gap by adapting three benchmark datasets, namely the VU Amsterdam metaphor corpus, the TroFi dataset and the TSV dataset, to suit relation-level metaphor identification. We publish the adapted datasets to facilitate future research in relation-level metaphor processing.

1 Introduction

Metaphor is a ubiquitous figurative device that represents the interaction between cognition and language (Cameron and Low, 1999). A metaphor contains an implied analogy where a concept (represented by a word sense) is borrowed to represent another concept by exploiting common or single properties of both concepts. Generally, a metaphor has two main components, the tenor and the vehicle; the relation between them is called the ground. The tenor represents the topic of the metaphor while the vehicle is the term used metaphorically and the ground gives the metaphor its meaning (End, 1986). Perceiving these components is essential to fully comprehend the metaphor. In this work, we adopt the conceptual metaphor theory (CMT) by Lakoff and Johnson (1980) to view metaphor where there is an underlying mapping between a source domain (the vehicle) and a target domain (the tenor). For example, a concept such as *"fragile object"* (source domain/vehicle) can be borrowed to express another such as *"emotions"* (target domain/tenor). This conceptual metaphor *"Emotions are Fragile Objects"* can be expressed in our everyday language in terms of linguistic metaphors such as *"shattered my emotions"*, *"break his soul"*, *"crushed her happiness"*, *"fragile emotions"* and *"brittle feelings"*.

Due to their nebulous nature, metaphors are quite challenging to comprehend and process by humans, let alone computational models. This intrigued many researchers to develop various automatic techniques to process metaphor in text. Metaphor processing has many potential applications, either as part of natural language processing (NLP) tasks such as machine translation (Koglin and Cunha, 2019), text simplification (Wolska and Clausen, 2017; Clausen and Nastase, 2019) and sentiment analysis (Rentoumi et al., 2012) or in more general discourse analysis use cases such as in analysing political discourse (Charteris-Black, 2011), financial reporting (Ho and Cheng, 2016) and health communication (Semino et al., 2018).

The computational processing of metaphors can be divided into two tasks, namely metaphor identification and its interpretation. While the former is concerned with recognising the metaphoric word or expression in a given sentence, the latter focuses on discerning the meaning of the metaphor. Metaphor identification is studied more extensively than metaphor interpretation, in part due to the availability of datasets. Identifying metaphors in

Proceedings of the Second Workshop on Figurative Language Processing, pages 154–164
July 9, 2020. ©2020 Association for Computational Linguistics
https://doi.org/10.18653/v1/P17

text can be done on either the sentence, grammatical relation or word levels. Sentence-level approaches classify the whole sentence that contains the metaphoric word/expression without explicit annotation of the source and target domain words. Relation-level metaphor identification focuses on certain grammatical relations by looking at pairs of words where both the source and target domain words are classified as a metaphoric expression. It is also referred to as phrase-level metaphor identification due to the way a sentence is divided into sub-phrases with various syntactic structures (we use these two terms indistinguishably in the context of this paper). The most commonly studied grammatical relations are verb-noun and adjective-noun relations where the metaphoricity of the verb or the adjective (source domain/vehicle) is discerned given its association with the noun (target domain/tenor). Finally, word-level metaphor identification approaches treat the task as either sequence labelling or single-word classification. In both methods, only the source domain words (vehicle) are labelled either as metaphoric or literal given the context. Many approaches are designed to identify metaphors of different syntactic types on the word-level but the most frequently studied ones are verbs.

In this paper, we are interested in relation-level metaphor identification focusing on the data availability for this level of processing. The next section explains, in detail, the difference between word-level and relation-level metaphor analysis highlighting the research gap that we aim to tackle.

2 Word-Level vs. Relation-Level Metaphor Analysis

Although the main focus of both the relation-level and word-level metaphor identification is discerning the metaphoricity of the vehicle (source domain words), relation-level approaches attend to the tenor (target domain words) associated with the vehicle under study during processing the metaphor which, in turn, gives the model a narrower focus in a way that mimics human comprehension of metaphors. Thus, processing metaphors on the word-level could be seen as a more general approach where the tenor of the metaphor is not explicitly highlighted as well as the relation between the source and the target domains. On the other hand, relation-level metaphor identification explicitly analyses the tenor and the relation between

the source and the target domains. Figure 1 illustrates the difference between the levels of metaphor identification.

Stowe and Palmer (2018) highlighted the importance of integrating syntax and semantics to process metaphors in text. Through a corpus-based analysis focusing on verb metaphors, the authors showed that the type of syntactic construction (dependency/grammar relation) a verb occurs in influences its metaphoricity.

Relation-level metaphor processing requires an extra step to identify the grammatical relations (i.e. dependencies) that highlight both the tenor and the vehicle. Thus, it might be seen that processing metaphors on the word-level is more straight forward and raises the question: why do we need relation-level metaphor identification? Relation-level metaphor identification can be used to support metaphor interpretation and cross-domain mappings. Metaphor interpretation focuses on explaining or inferring the meaning of a given metaphorical expression. As explained earlier, the tenor (target domain words) is the topic of the metaphor that gives the metaphor its meaning. Therefore, relation-level identification is an important initial step that facilitates inferring the meaning of a given expression. Cross-domain mappings focuses on identifying the relation between the source and target domain concepts in a way that mimics the human formulation of metaphors. This mapping is produced by studying a set of multiple metaphorical expressions that describe one concept in terms of another. Hence, identifying metaphors on the relation-level is employed to support such mappings in order to create knowledge-bases of metaphoric language.

The levels of processing metaphors should be taken into consideration when designing and developing a computational model to identify metaphors and hence choosing the annotated dataset accordingly for evaluation and comparison. Shutova (2015), Parde and Nielsen (2018) and Zayed et al. (2019) provided extensive details about existing datasets for metaphor identification in English text. The authors highlighted the level of annotation for each dataset among other properties. The widely used benchmark datasets are TroFi (Birke and Sarkar, 2006), VU Amsterdam metaphor corpus (VUAMC) (Steen et al., 2010) and MOH (Mohammad et al., 2016) for word-level metaphor identification, whereas TSV (Tsvetkov et al., 2014), the adaptation of MOH by Shutova et al. (2016), and

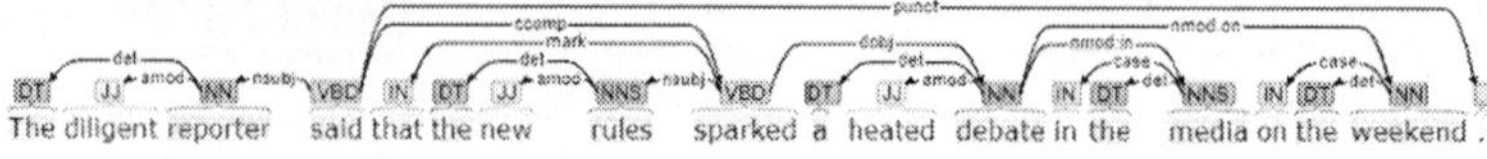

grammar relation	expression	
amod	**diligent** reporter	0
nsubj	reporter **said**	0
nsubj	rules **sparked**	1
amod	**heated** debate	1
dobj	**sparked** debate	1
case	**in** media	1
case	**on** weekend	1

Figure 1: An illustration of the difference between word-level and relation-level metaphor identification. Stanford CoreNLP is used to generate the dependencies.

Zayed's Tweets (Zayed et al., 2019) datasets are utilised for relation-level metaphor identification.

Approaches addressing the task on the word-level are not fairly comparable to relation-level approaches since each task deals with metaphor identification differently. Therefore, given the distinction of the tasks definition, the tradition of previous work in this area is to compare the word-level metaphor identification approaches against each other on either the TroFi, VUAMC or MOH datasets. On the other hand, relation-level approaches are compared against each other on either the TSV, Shutova's adaptation of MOH or Zayed's Tweets datasets. Although, the VUAMC is the most well-known and widely used corpus for metaphor identification, it is not possible to apply it to relation-level metaphor identification without further annotation effort. This is also the case for the TroFi dataset which is one of the earliest balanced datasets annotated to identify metaphoric verbs on the word-level. On the other hand, the TSV dataset is the only available annotated dataset for relation-level metaphor identification that addresses adjective-noun grammatical relations. However, the main issue with this dataset is the absence of full sentences in the training set leaving a relatively small test set that has full sentences which limits its usage for state-of-the-art approaches that rely on using the full context.

One limitation of word-level annotation is the implicit level of analysis discussed earlier. Direct mapping from word-level to relation-level annotation is not straight forward and requires extra annotation effort. Consider the following examples that contain verb metaphors:

(1) The speech stirred the emotions.

(2) "history will judge you at this moment."

(3) Citizens see hope in the new regulations.

Identifying metaphoric verbs on the word-level will result in recognising the verbs *"stirred"*, *"judge"* and *"see"* as metaphoric in examples (1), (2) and (3), respectively. In example (1), both the subject and the object are responsible for the metaphoricity of the verb; while in example (2), the subject gave the verb its metaphoricity and in example (3) the object did. This is done implicitly in word-level annotation/identification. On the other hand, if we consider relation-level processing, the tenor associated with the verb has to be explicitly highlighted. Thus, annotating the above examples on the relation-level focusing on verb-direct object relations (i.e. dobj) will result in identifying the expressions *"stirred the emotions"* and *"see hope"* as metaphoric in examples (1) and (3), respectively and ignoring example (2) since *"history will judge"* is a subject-verb (i.e. *nsubj*) relation. Therefore, adapting existing datasets annotated on the word-level is required to arrive at explicit analysis of the tenor and the relation between the source and the target domains.

In this work, we take a step towards filling this research gap by introducing an adapted version of benchmark datasets to better suit relation-level (phrase-level) metaphor identification. We adapt the VUAMC and the TroFi dataset to identify verb-noun metaphoric expressions. Moreover, we extend the relation-level metaphor identification TSV dataset by providing context for the adjective-noun relations in its training set. We publish the adapted version of the datasets according to the licensing type of each of them to facilitate research on metaphor processing.

3   Related Work

This work is inspired by Tsvetkov et al. (2014) and Shutova et al. (2016) who attempted to adapt existing word-level metaphor identification datasets to suit their relation-level (phrase-level) identification approaches. Shutova et al. (2010) was the first to create an annotated dataset for relation-level metaphor identification. The Robust Accurate Statistical Parsing (RASP) parser (Briscoe et al., 2006) was utilised to extract verb-subject and verb-direct object grammar relations from the British National Corpus (BNC) (Burnard, 2007). The dataset comprises around 62 verb-noun pairs of metaphoric expressions, where the verb is used metaphorically given the complement noun (tenor).

The TroFi dataset, which was designed to classify particular literal and metaphoric verbs on the word-level, was adapted by Tsvetkov et al. (2014) in order to extract metaphoric expressions on the relation-level. The authors parsed the original dataset using the Turbo dependency parser (Martins et al., 2010) to extract subject-verb-object (SVO) grammar relations. The final dataset consists of 953 metaphorical and 656 literal instances. In the same work, Tsvetkov et al. also prepared a relation-level metaphor identification dataset, referred to as the TSV dataset, focusing on adjective-noun grammar relations. We will further describe this dataset in Section 4.

More recently, Shutova et al. (2016) adapted the benchmark MOH dataset, which was initially created to extract metaphoric verbs on the word-level, to suit relation-level metaphor identification of verb-noun relations. Verb-direct object and verbs-subject dependencies were extracted and filtered yielding a dataset of 647 verb–noun pairs, out of which 316 instances are metaphorical and 331 instances are literal.

To the best of our knowledge, there is no attempt to adapt the benchmark VU Amsterdam metaphor corpus, referred to as VUAMC, to suit relation-level metaphor identification. This has discouraged other researchers focusing on relation-level approaches to employ this dataset such as the work done by Rei et al. (2017), Bulat et al. (2017), Shutova et al. (2016) and Tsvetkov et al. (2014) who did not evaluate or compare their approaches using this dataset. In this paper, we introduce the first adapted version of the VUAMC. Furthermore, we adapt the TroFi and the TSV datasets to better suit relation-level metaphor processing.

4   Datasets

As mentioned in Section 2, the widely used benchmark datasets for word-level metaphor identification are TroFi, VUAMC and MOH datasets, while TSV, Shutova's adaptation of MOH and Zayed's Tweets datasets are commonly used for relation-level metaphor identification. Table 1, adapted from (Zayed et al., 2019), revisits the properties of each dataset . In this work, we focus on the word-level VUAMC, and the TroFi dataset in addition to the relation-level TSV dataset as the largest and extensively used datasets for metaphor identification. In this section, we discuss each dataset in detail.

The VU Amsterdam Metaphor Corpus (VUAMC)[1], introduced by Steen et al. (2010), has become one of the most well-known metaphor corpus existing nowadays. It is the largest corpus annotated for metaphors and has been used extensively to train, evaluate and compare models that identify metaphors on the word-level. The corpus consists of 117 randomly selected texts from the BNC Baby version which comprises various text genres, namely academic, conversation, fiction and news. The corpus is annotated for metaphors on the word-level, regardless of the word's syntactic type, through a collaborative annotation scheme. The employed annotation scheme is referred to as the metaphor identification procedure (MIPVU) by

---

[1] Also referred to, in literature, as the VUA dataset or the VUA metaphor corpus.

Level of analysis	Dataset	Syntactic structure	Text type	Size	% Metaphors
word-level	TroFi Example Base (Birke and Sarkar, 2006)	verb	50 selected verbs (News)	3,727 sentences	57.5%
	VUAMC (Steen et al., 2010)	all POS	known-corpus (The BNC)	~16,000 sentences (~200,000 words)	12.5%
	MOH (Mohammad et al., 2016)	verb	selected examples (WordNet)	1,639 sentences	25%
relation-level (phrase-level)	TSV (Tsvetkov et al., 2014)	adjective–noun	selected examples (Web)	~2,000 adj-noun pairs	50%
	adaptation of MOH (Shutova et al., 2016)	verb-direct object; subject-verb	selected examples (WordNet)	647 sentences	48.8%
	Zayed's Tweets (Zayed et al., 2019)	verb-direct object	Tweets (general and political topics)	~2,500 tweets	54.8%

Table 1: Statistics of the widely used benchmark datasets for linguistic metaphor identification.

which a strong inter-annotator agreement of 0.84 is obtained, in terms of Fleiss' kappa (Fleiss, 1971), among four annotators. The dataset is published in an XML format; Figure 2 shows an example of the corpus where the metaphoric words are tagged as *function="mrw"*.

```
<w lemma="such" type="DT0">Such </w>
<w lemma="language" type="NN1">language </w>
<w lemma="focus" type="VVD-VVN">
  <seg function="mrw" subtype="PP" type="met"
  vici:morph="n">focused</seg>
</w>
<w lemma="attention" type="NN1">attention </w>
<w lemma="on" type="PRP">
  <seg function="mrw" type="met" vici:morph="n">on</seg>
</w>
<w lemma="the" type="AT0">the </w>
<w lemma="individual" type="NN2">individuals </w>
<w lemma="or" type="CJC">or </w>
<w lemma="group" type="NN2">groups </w>
<w lemma="who" type="PNQ">who </w>
<w lemma="be" type="VBD">were </w>
<c type="PUQ">,</c>
<w lemma="break" type="VVG">
  <seg function="mrw" type="met" vici:morph="n">breaking
  </seg></w>
<w lemma="the" type="AT0">the </w>
<w lemma="law" type="NN1">law</w>
```

Figure 2: An example form the VU Amsterdam metaphor corpus (VUAMC) showing the data annotation format and the metaphoric words labelled with the metaphor-related word tag *(function="mrw")*.

The NAACL 2018 Metaphor Shared Task (Leong et al., 2018) employed the VUAMC in order to develop, train and test systems to identify metaphors on the word-level. The shared task consisted of two tracks, which are 1) *All Part-Of-Speech (POS)* to identify nouns, verbs, adverbs and adjectives that are labelled as metaphorical; 2) *Verbs* track which is concerned only with identifying metaphorical verbs. All forms of the verbs: *"be, do,* and *have"* are excluded for both tracks. The corpus is then divided into training and test sets according to the focus of each track. A script is provided to parse the original

VUAMC.xml file[2] which contains the corpus, since the corpus is not directly downloadable due to licensing restrictions. In this paper, we utilise the dataset from the *Verbs* track from this shared task. Table 2 shows the statistics of the dataset as highlighted in (Leong et al., 2018).

Data	Training			Test		
	#texts	#tokens	%M	#texts	#tokens	%M
Academic	12	4,903	31 %	4	1,259	51%
Conversation	18	4,181	15%	6	2,001	15%
Fiction	11	4,647	25%	3	1,385	20%
News	49	3,509	42 %	14	1,228	46%

Table 2: Statistics of the training and test data in the "Verbs" track in the NAACL metaphor shared task. %M is the percentage of metaphors.

The main limitation of the VUAMC, and any dataset that stems from it, is that it only suits the identification of metaphors on the word-level. Thus, it is not possible to apply the VUAMC in its current state to relation-level metaphor identification and there are no larger dataset designated to support relation-level metaphor identification since the size of Shutova's adaptation of MOH and Zayed's Tweets datasets is relatively small for training state-of-the-art neural models.

The TroFi Dataset is one of the earliest metaphor identification datasets introduced by Birke and Sarkar (2006, 2007). The dataset focuses on the metaphoric usage of 50 selected verbs and comprises 3,727 English sentences extracted from the 1987-1989 Wall Street Journal (WSJ) corpus. The metaphoricity of the selected verbs on the word-level is identified by manual annotation. The inter-annotator agreement was calculated on a random sample of 200 annotated

---

[2]The VUAMC was available online at: `http://ota. ahds.ac.uk/headers/2541.xml` but the website was unresponsive at the time of this publication.

sentences scoring 0.77 in terms of Cohen's kappa (Cohen, 1960) among two annotators. The dataset had been used to evaluate the performance of many word-level metaphor identification systems. In order to use this dataset for relation-level metaphor identification of verb-noun relations, further annotation is required to highlight the complementing noun (tenor) of each metaphoric verb (vehicle).

The TSV Dataset (Tsvetkov et al., 2014) was created to support relation-level metaphor identification approaches that focus on adjective-noun grammatical relations. The dataset comprises ∼2,000 adjective-noun pairs which were selected manually from collections of metaphors on the Web. It is divided into 1,768 pairs as a train set and 200 pairs as a test set. As mentioned earlier, only the test set contains the full sentences which was obtained from the English Ten-Ten Web corpus (Jakubíček et al., 2013) by utilising SketchEngine[3] (Kilgarriff et al., 2014). The annotation scheme depended on the intuition of the human annotators to define the metaphoric expressions. An inter-annotator agreement of 0.76, in terms of Fleiss' kappa, was obtained among five annotators on the test set. The main limitation of this dataset is the absence of the full sentences in the training set which forces the models employing it to either ignore the context that surrounds the adjective-noun pairs or to use the small test set in a cross-validation experimental setting which makes the model prone to overfitting.

5 Dataset Adaptation Methodology

In this section, we discuss the methodology of adapting the VUAMC, TroFi and TSV datasets to better suit relation-level (phrase-level) metaphor processing.

5.1 VUAMC and TroFi dataset Adaptation

As discussed earlier, relation-level metaphor identification focuses on a specific grammatical relation that represents the source and target domains of the metaphor. The datasets that are initially annotated for word-level processing have the source domain words (vehicle) labelled as a metaphor regardless of its tenor since it is word-by-word classification. Therefore, in order to adapt them to suit relation-level processing, the associated target domain words (tenor) need to be identified.

Our approach towards adapting the datasets annotated on the word-level is as follows:

1. select the benchmark dataset which is originally annotated on the word-level;

2. extract particular grammatical relations focusing on the vehicle as the head of the relation (e.g. the verb in a *dobj* or adjective in *amod* relation);

3. retrieve the gold labels from the original dataset based on the metaphoricity of the vehicle;

4. verify the correctness of the retrieved relations and the assigned gold label.

In this work, we employ the Stanford dependency parser (Chen and Manning, 2014) to identify grammar relations. The recurrent neural network (RNN) parser, pre-trained on the WSJ corpus, is used from within the Stanford CoreNLP toolkit (Manning et al., 2014).

For the VUAMC adaptation, as discussed in Section 4, we utilise the training and test splits provided by the NAACL metaphor shared task in the *Verbs* track. We focus on this track since we are interested in verb-noun relations. The verbs dataset consists of 17,240 annotated verbs in the training set and 5,874 annotated verbs in the test set. First, we retrieved the original sentences of these verbs from the VUAMC since the shared task released their *ids* and the corresponding gold labels. This yielded around 10,570 sentences in both sets. Then, we parsed these sentences using the Stanford parser and extracted the verb-direct object (i.e. *dobj*) relations, discarding the instances with pronominal or clausal objects[4]. The extracted relations are then filtered to exclude parsing-related errors. Manual inspection is done to ensure that, in a given *dobj* relation, the verb is metaphoric due to the associated object (more details will be given in Section 6). The final adapted dataset comprises 4,420 sentences in the training set and 1,398 in the test set.

For the TroFi dataset adaptation, we utilise the 3,737 manually annotated English sentences from Birke and Sarkar (2006)[5]. Each sentence contains either literal or metaphorical use for one of 50 English verbs. These sentences were parsed to extract dependency information. Then, we filtered

---

[4]This is done automatically using regular expressions to select the grammatical relations with certain POS tags.

[5]http://natlang.cs.sfu.ca/software/trofi.html

the extracted relations to only select the *dobj* relations that include verbs from the 50 verbs list and to eliminate mis-parsing cases. This resulted in a dataset of 1,535 sentences.

Table 4 shows the statistics of the adapted VUAMC and TroFi dataset after applying the quality assessment in Section 6. Examples of the annotated sentences from the adapted VUAMC and TroFi dataset are listed in Table 5 as they appear in the adapted relation-level version.

5.2 TSV Dataset Adaptation

Our main goal when adapting the TSV relation-level dataset is to provide a context for the balanced training set of 1,768 metaphoric and non-metaphoric adjective-noun pairs. Table 3 gives examples for the adjective-noun expressions appearing in the original TSV training set[6]. This will allow the computational models to benefit from the contextual knowledge that surrounds the expression. The method used to achieve this goal is to query the Twitter Search API[7] using the adjective-noun pairs and retrieve tweets as the context around these expressions. Among the main motivations behind selecting the user-generated text (tweets) to expand this dataset are: 1) to encourage and facilitate the study of metaphors in social media contexts; 2) the availability of Twitter data as well as the ease of use of the Twitter API.

Metaphor	Non-metaphor
blind faith	blind patient
deep sorrow	deep cut
empty life	empty house
fishy offer	frozen food
heated criticism	heated oven
raw idea	raw vegetables
shallow character	shallow water
warm smile	warm day

Table 3: Examples of the annotated adjective-noun expressions in the TSV training dataset.

For each expression in the training set, a tweet is retrieved given that its length is more than 10 words and it does not contain more than four hashtags or mentions to ensure that the retrieved context has enough information. Then, the tweets are preprocessed to remove URLs and duplicate tweets. This yielded an adapted training set of 1,764 tweets that

[6]https://github.com/ytsvetko/metaphor
[7]https://developer.twitter.com/en/docs/api-reference-index

contains metaphoric and non-metaphoric expressions of adjective-noun relations. The next step is to ensure the quality of the retrieved content in terms of keeping the metaphoricity of the original expression. This is done manually as will be discussed in the next section. Table 4 provides the statistics of the adapted TSV training dataset after expanding it with full sentences (tweets). Examples of the annotated tweets from the adapted TSV training dataset are given in Table 5.

6 Quality Assessment and Enhancement

In order to assess the quality of the adapted datasets, we suggested a preliminary quality assessment scheme and tested it through an initial experiment on a randomly sampled subset from each dataset. We then employed this scheme to ensure the quality of the whole datasets.

6.1 Initial Quality Assessment Experiment

In this pilot experiment, we randomly sampled 100 sentences from each dataset. We then asked two native English speakers with background in (computational) linguistics to manually identify the quality of the retrieved sample. Since the datasets were previously annotated, our main concerns for evaluation are as follows:

For each instance in the VUAMC and the TroFi dataset:

1. to check that the *dobj* dependency is syntactically valid;

2. to ensure that the verb is metaphoric due to the associated object;

3. check if the expression is really a metaphor.

For each instance in the TSV dataset:

1. to ensure that the tweet is in understandable English;

2. to check that the *amod* dependency is syntactically valid;

3. to ensure that the provided context (scrapped tweets) preserves the metaphoricity of the expression.

For the VUAMC, the annotators agreed that in 81.1% of the metaphoric cases, the the metaphoricity of the verb is due to the complement direct-object. However, the annotators raised some issues regarding the original annotation of the VUAMC using the MIPVU procedure. Their main concerns

	VUAMC* (NAACL metaphor shared task data)		TroFi Dataset	TSV Dataset
	training set	test set		training set
targeted grammar relation	verb-direct object		verb-direct object	adjective-noun
# sentences	4,420	1,398	1,535	1,764
# metaphoric instances	1,675	586	908	881
# non-metaphoric instances	2,745	812	627	883
% metaphors	37.96%	41.92%	59.15%	49.94%

Table 4: Statistics of the adapted VUAMC, TroFi and TSV benchmark datasets. *The training and test sets from the "Verbs" track in the NAACL metaphor shared task.

	ID	Text	Expression	Label
VUAMC	fpb-..._1150_5	I want you to break the news gently to Gran.	break the news	1
	crs-..._35_12	The Community Health Team had major responsibility for assessing children and recommending provision.	recommending provision	0
TroFi	wsj13:9766_16	And even when that loophole was closed, in 1980, the Japanese decided to absorb the tariff rather than boost prices.	absorb the tariff	1
	wsj67:11208_14	Because they 're so accurate, cruise missiles can use conventional bombs to destroy targets that only a few years ago required nuclear warheads.	destroy targets	0
TSV (Training)	1248238...	@sacrebleu141 @FasslerCynthia But it's exactly what the left wants. Trains the people into blind obedience	blind obedience	1
	1248271...	Still have nightmares about waiting tables many years later. Hands down the hardest, most stressful job I've ever had.	stressful job	0

Table 5: Examples from the adapted VUAMC, TroFi and TSV benchmark datasets showing the targeted expression and the provided label (1:metaphor; 0:non-metaphor).

were: 1) the quality of the original annotation which is done on the word-level without explicitly highlighting the tenor or the ground of the metaphor; 2) the consistency of the annotations across the corpus which relied on the annotators' intuition of the basic meaning of the given word and the definition of metaphor. This informal discussion with our expert annotators confirmed our initial concerns that the VUAMC is not really sufficient for metaphor processing in its current state.

The annotators highlighted that the TSV and TroFi datasets have more reliable annotations that align well with the linguistic definition of metaphor than the VUAMC. We attribute that to the following reasons: 1) the TSV dataset was originally annotated on the relation-level with explicit labelling of the tenor; 2) the TroFi dataset comprises carefully selected examples of metaphoric and literal usages for 50 particular verbs. For the TroFi dataset, the annotators agreed that the all the verbs in the random set were used metaphorically due to the associated direct-object without raising any concerns regarding the original annotation of the dataset.

The manual inspection of the random subset of the TSV dataset revealed that, surprisingly, the provided context for the adjective-noun expressions

preserved the meaning and the metaphoric sense of all the queried expressions. We suspected that some ambiguous cases might led to ambiguous contexts. For example, the expression *"filthy man"*, which is marked as a metaphor in the dataset, could be used literally to describe the hygienic state of a person; however, the retrieved tweet preserved the metaphoric sense of this expression that describes the morality of a person. This might be due to the following reasons: 1) the conventionality and frequency of adjective-noun metaphoric expressions; 2) the nature of the user-generated (conversational) text of the tweets allows the usage of figurative and metaphoric expressions more frequently than their literal counterparts; 3) the nature of the expressions in the TSV dataset itself in terms of abstractness and concreteness. Further corpus studies are required to investigate this finding.

6.2 Data Filtering and Quality Enhancement

Based on the conclusions of the initial quality assessment, an expert annotator[8] is asked to review the three adapted datasets for quality enhancement following the same scheme. Table 6 includes de-

---

[8]by "expert" we mean having a computational linguistic background and extensive experience in metaphor processing.

tailed statistics of this quality assessment.

To enhance the **TSV** dataset and ensure its quality, if any of the aforementioned problems is detected the annotator provided another tweet by manually searching Twitter. This is done in a similar way to that adopted by Tsvetkov et al. (2014) while preparing the TSV test set. The annotator noticed that sometimes the tweets contain code-mixed text in English and other language written in Latin letters. These instances are replaced by understandable ones. For the **TroFi** dataset and the **VUAMC**, the annotator corrected the detected parsing errors if possible otherwise the erroneous instances are discarded. Moreover, if the expression is metaphoric due to the associated subject (not the direct object), the expression is corrected and labelled as having an *nsubj* dependency. These expressions are not excluded from the data. Finally, when the annotator disagrees about the metaphoricity of a given instance, it has to be checked first in the original VUAMC dataset and if no annotation error is detected then the instance is flagged to have an annotation disagreement with what the annotator believed to be a metaphor. Aligning with the other two annotators of the pilot experiment, quality and consistency issues are raised about the VUAMC annotation. For example, the verb *"commit"* is labelled five times as a metaphor with the nouns *"acts, bag, government,* and *offence(s)"* and three times as literal with the nouns *"rape,* and *offence(s)"* in very similar contexts. As shown in Table 6, the annotator flagged around 5% of the data for annotation doubt or inconsistency. The majority of the inconsistent annotations revolves around the verbs *"receive, form, create, use, make, recognise, feel, enjoy,* and *reduce"*.

7   Conclusion and Future Work

In this paper, we took a step towards filling the gap of the availability of large benchmark datasets for relation-level metaphor processing in English text by utilising existing word-level datasets. We employed a semi-automatic approach to adapt the VUAMC to better suit identifying metaphors on the relation-level without the need for extensive manual annotation. We also adapted the TroFi dataset, one of the earliest word-level datasets for metaphor identification of verbs, to support verb-noun metaphor identification. Furthermore, we extended the TSV dataset which was originally annotated on the relation-level focusing on

Dataset		Total % accepted by annotator
TSV	the Tweet is in understandable English?	70%
	the relation is syntactically valid?	82.75%
	did the context (tweet) kept the metaphoric sense of the expression?	99.36%
TroFi	the relation is syntactically valid?	98.52%
	the verb is metaphoric or literal due to the associated object?	100%
VUAMC	the relation is syntactically valid?	98.42%
	the verb is metaphoric or literal due to the associated object?	98.5%
	annotation disagreement or inconsistency	5.45%

Table 6: Statistics of the quality assessment of the three adapted datasets showing the total percentage of instances accepted by the annotator.

adjective-noun relations by assigning context to its expressions from Twitter. This will encourage research in this area to work towards understanding metaphors in social media. As a result of this work, we publish an adapted version of these benchmark datasets which will facilitate research on relation-level metaphor identification focusing on verb-direct object and adjective-noun relations.

This paper also provides an extensive review of the different levels of metaphor processing and the importance of relation-level metaphor identification. We question the reliability of word-level metaphor processing and annotation in general highlighting the reasons behind that. We provided a brief data analysis in this regard that we are planing to extend as a continuation of this work.

In future work, we will expand the adapted VUAMC to include verb-subject (i.e. *nsubj*) and adjective-noun (i.e. *amod*) relations. Moreover, we plan to consolidate these adapted datasets in one repository categorised by data source and text genre. We also plan to invest extra annotation effort to ensure the consistency of the annotated instances across the different datasets using weakly supervised approaches.

Acknowledgments

This work was supported by Science Foundation Ireland under grant number SFI/12/RC/2289_2 (Insight).

References

Julia Birke and Anoop Sarkar. 2006. A clustering approach for nearly unsupervised recognition of nonliteral language. In *In Proceedings of the 11th Conference of the European Chapter of the Association for Computational Linguistics*, EACL '06, pages 329–336, Trento, Italy.

Julia Birke and Anoop Sarkar. 2007. Active learning for the identification of nonliteral language. In *Proceedings of the Workshop on Computational Approaches to Figurative Language*, pages 21–28, Rochester, NY, USA.

Ted Briscoe, John Carroll, and Rebecca Watson. 2006. The second release of the RASP system. In *Proceedings of the Joint Conference of the International Committee on Computational Linguistics and the Association for Computational Linguistics*, COLING-ACL '06, pages 77–80, Sydney, Australia.

Luana Bulat, Stephen Clark, and Ekaterina Shutova. 2017. Modelling metaphor with attribute-based semantics. In *Proceedings of the 15th Conference of the European Chapter of the Association for Computational Linguistics*, EACL '17, pages 523–528, Valencia, Spain.

Lou Burnard. 2007. Reference guide for the British National Corpus (XML edition).

Lynne Cameron and Graham Low. 1999. *Researching and Applying Metaphor*. Cambridge Applied Linguistics. Cambridge University Press, Cambridge, UK.

Jonathan Charteris-Black. 2011. Metaphor in Political Discourse. In *Politicians and Rhetoric: The Persuasive Power of Metaphor*, pages 28–51. Palgrave Macmillan UK, London.

Danqi Chen and Christopher Manning. 2014. A fast and accurate dependency parser using neural networks. In *Proceedings of the 2014 Conference on Empirical Methods in Natural Language Processing*, EMNLP '14, pages 740–750, Doha, Qatar.

Yulia Clausen and Vivi Nastase. 2019. Metaphors in text simplification: To change or not to change, that is the question. In *Proceedings of the Fourteenth Workshop on Innovative Use of NLP for Building Educational Applications*, pages 423–434, Florence, Italy.

Jacob Cohen. 1960. A Coefficient of Agreement for Nominal Scales. *Educational and Psychological Measurement*, 20(1):37–46.

Laurel J End. 1986. Grounds for metaphor comprehension. *Knowledge and language*, pages 327–345.

Joseph L. Fleiss. 1971. Measuring nominal scale agreement among many raters. *Psychological Bulletin*, 76(5):378–382.

Janet Ho and Winnie Cheng. 2016. Metaphors in financial analysis reports: How are emotions expressed? *English for Specific Purposes*, 43:37 – 48.

Miloš Jakubíček, Adam Kilgarriff, Vojtěch Kovář, Pavel Rychlý, and Vít Suchomel. 2013. The TenTen corpus family. In *Proceedings of the 7th International Corpus Linguistics Conference*, CL '13, pages 125–127, Lancaster, UK.

Adam Kilgarriff, Vít Baisa, Jan Bušta, Miloš Jakubíček, Vojtěch Kovář, Jan Michelfeit, Pavel Rychlý, and Vít Suchomel. 2014. The Sketch Engine: ten years on. *Lexicography*, pages 7–36.

Arlene Koglin and Rossana Cunha. 2019. Investigating the post-editing effort associated with machine-translated metaphors: a process-driven analysis. *The Journal of Specialised Translation*, 31(01):38–59.

George Lakoff and Mark Johnson. 1980. *Metaphors we live by*. University of Chicago Press, Chicago, USA.

Chee Wee (Ben) Leong, Beata Beigman Klebanov, and Ekaterina Shutova. 2018. A report on the 2018 VUA metaphor detection shared task. In *Proceedings of the Workshop on Figurative Language Processing*, pages 56–66, New Orleans, LA, USA.

Christopher D. Manning, Mihai Surdeanu, John Bauer, Jenny Finkel, Steven J. Bethard, and David McClosky. 2014. The Stanford CoreNLP natural language processing toolkit. In *Proceedings of 52nd Annual Meeting of the Association for Computational Linguistics: System Demonstrations*, ACL '14, pages 55–60, Baltimore, MD, USA.

André Martins, Noah Smith, Eric Xing, Pedro Aguiar, and Mário Figueiredo. 2010. Turbo parsers: Dependency parsing by approximate variational inference. In *Proceedings of the 2010 Conference on Empirical Methods in Natural Language Processing*, EMNLP '10, pages 34–44, Cambridge, MA, USA.

Saif M. Mohammad, Ekaterina Shutova, and Peter D. Turney. 2016. Metaphor as a medium for emotion: An empirical study. In *Proceedings of the 5th Joint Conference on Lexical and Computational Semantics*, *Sem '16, pages 23–33, Berlin, Germany.

Natalie Parde and Rodney Nielsen. 2018. A corpus of metaphor novelty scores for syntactically-related word pairs. In *Proceedings of the 11th International Conference on Language Resources and Evaluation*, LREC '18, pages 1535–1540, Miyazaki, Japan.

Marek Rei, Luana Bulat, Douwe Kiela, and Ekaterina Shutova. 2017. Grasping the finer point: A supervised similarity network for metaphor detection. In *Proceedings of the 2017 Conference on Empirical Methods in Natural Language Processing*, EMNLP '17, pages 1537–1546, Copenhagen, Denmark.

Vassiliki Rentoumi, George A. Vouros, Vangelis Karkaletsis, and Amalia Moser. 2012. Investigating metaphorical language in sentiment analysis: A sense-to-sentiment perspective. *ACM Transactions on Speech and Language Processing*, 9(3):1–31.

Elena Semino, Zsofia Demjen, Andrew Hardie, Sheila Alison Payne, and Paul Edward Rayson. 2018. *Metaphor, Cancer and the End of Life: A Corpusbased Study*. Routledge, London, UK.

Ekaterina Shutova. 2015. Design and evaluation of metaphor processing systems. *Computational Linguistics*, 41(4):579–623.

Ekaterina Shutova, Douwe Kiela, and Jean Maillard. 2016. Black holes and white rabbits: Metaphor identification with visual features. In *Proceedings of the 2016 Annual Conference of the North American Chapter of the Association for Computational Linguistics: Human Language Technologies*, NAACL-HLT '16, pages 160–170, San Diego, CA, USA.

Ekaterina Shutova, Lin Sun, and Anna Korhonen. 2010. Metaphor identification using verb and noun clustering. In *Proceedings of the 23rd International Conference on Computational Linguistics*, COLING '10, pages 1002–1010, Beijing, China.

Gerard J. Steen, Aletta G. Dorst, J. Berenike Herrmann, Anna Kaal, Tina Krennmayr, and Trijntje Pasma. 2010. *A Method for Linguistic Metaphor Identification: From MIP to MIPVU*. Converging evidence in language and communication research. John Benjamins Publishing Company.

Kevin Stowe and Martha Palmer. 2018. Leveraging syntactic constructions for metaphor identification. In *Proceedings of the Workshop on Figurative Language Processing*, pages 17–26, New Orleans, LA, USA.

Yulia Tsvetkov, Leonid Boytsov, Anatole Gershman, Eric Nyberg, and Chris Dyer. 2014. Metaphor detection with cross-lingual model transfer. In *Proceedings of the 52nd Annual Meeting of the Association for Computational Linguistics*, ACL '14, pages 248–258, Baltimore, MD, USA.

Magdalena Wolska and Yulia Clausen. 2017. Simplifying metaphorical language for young readers: A corpus study on news text. In *Proceedings of the 12th Workshop on Innovative Use of NLP for Building Educational Applications*, pages 313–318, Copenhagen, Denmark. Association for Computational Linguistics.

Omnia Zayed, John Philip McCrae, and Paul Buitelaar. 2019. Crowd-sourcing a high-quality dataset for metaphor identification in tweets. In *Proceedings of the 2nd Conference on Language, Data and Knowledge*, LDK '19, Leipzig, Germany.

Generating Ethnographic Models from Communities' Online Data

Tomek Strzalkowski[1], Anna Newheiser[2], Nathan Kemper[2], Ning Sa[2], Bharvee Acharya[2]
and Gregorios Katsios[1]
[1]Rensselaer Polytechnic Institute, Troy, NY, USA
[2]University at Albany, SUNY, Albany, NY, USA
{tomek, katsig}@rpi.edu, {anewheiser, nkemper, nsa, bacharya}@albany.edu

Abstract

In this paper, we describe computational ethnography studies to demonstrate how machine learning techniques can be utilized to exploit bias resident in language data produced by communities with online presence. Specifically, we leverage the use of figurative language (i.e., the choice of metaphors) in online text (e.g., news media, blogs) produced by distinct communities to obtain models of community worldviews that can be shown to be distinctly biased and thus different from other communities' models. We automatically construct metaphor-based community models for two distinct scenarios: debates on gun rights and marriage equality. We then conduct a series of experiments to validate the hypothesis that the metaphors found in each community's online language convey the bias in the community's worldview.

1 Introduction

Recent advances in machine learning, particularly deep learning, have led to successful exploitation of vast amounts of human-generated internet data and have produced remarkably accurate computational models of complex semantic and social phenomena in language, speech, vision, and other media, thus bringing us closer to the practical reality of artificial intelligence. These models are often considered objective and universal because the volume of data on which they are based is so vast that it is believed to be free of sampling limitations plaguing earlier research. And yet, the models that can be derived are only as good as the data from which they are built; the data, however vast, may still be biased. For one, people who post on the internet are not necessarily representative of the general population. Furthermore, society is composed of various communities and groups whose opinions and worldviews differ dramatically on a range of important issues. When data are oversampled from some sources over others (which can easily happen due to different rates of production), the resulting model is bound to be biased accordingly. This bias can lead to unwanted consequences, for example in government planning or resource allocation.

The flip side of the data bias, however, is that each community produces a unique information footprint that may be used to understand how its members perceive the world. The objective of our project is to investigate whether online information generated by various communities can serve as raw data for developing reliable and accurate ethnographic models of these communities, thus augmenting costly and limited-scale field studies. Clearly, the methods of computational ethnography will be different from its traditional counterpart and will rely extensively on substantial volumes of largely un-directed data, from which the critical information (e.g., relationships, opinions, conceptualizations) can be learned. One rich source of data is language, which serves as a communication vehicle, but also, as it evolves, encodes social, cultural, and often physical experiences of its user communities. These experiences are often vividly captured in the use of figurative language constructs, such as metaphors, that directly link abstract notions to collective physical experiences (Lakoff & Johnson, 1980; Thibodeau & Boroditsky, 2011). This observation has been confirmed in earlier work that constructed metaphor repositories across language and cultural dimensions (Western/American, Latin American/Mexican, Eastern European/Russian, Middle Eastern/Persian) related to such notions as government, economic inequality, and democracy (e.g., Shutova, 2010; Strzalkowski et al., 2013;

165

Proceedings of the Second Workshop on Figurative Language Processing, pages 165–175
July 9, 2020. ©2020 Association for Computational Linguistics
https://doi.org/10.18653/v1/P17

Wilks et al., 2013; Mohan et al., 2013). Furthermore, within each linguistic-cultural society, various communities project their views on weighty social issues onto metaphorical language (Charteris-Black, 2002).

The objectives of the current Computational Ethnography (COMETH) project are thus twofold: (1) confirm experimentally that computational models of figurative language use capture communities' uniquely biased worldviews; and (2) demonstrate experimentally that such models, when used generatively, can mimic communities' reactions to novel information. Accordingly, the COMETH project developed an automated system that (a) rapidly ingests quantities of unstructured language data produced by communities of interest; and (b) uses natural language processing and machine learning techniques to construct ethnographic models for these communities. In this paper, we report preliminary results from applying this approach to two distinct scenarios: debates on gun rights and marriage equality.

2 Initial Case Study and Approach

Our initial approach was to develop and evaluate ethnographic models of two U.S. communities: (1) a community whose members prefer individual oversight of guns and prioritize gun rights, which we refer to as INDO; and (2) another community whose members prefer government oversight of guns and prioritize gun control, which we refer to as GOVTO. Our research demonstrates that these two communities' cultural models differ fundamentally from one another in their representation and valuation of concepts related to the gun debate. These concepts include broad notions such as gun rights and gun control, as well as narrower issues such as the Second Amendment, school shootings, and assault weapons. Each community is defined by the set of valuations they assign to these concepts. In order to extract these valuations, we identify culturally biased correlations, expressed in the use of metaphorical language, between key gun-related concepts and more basic, concrete, and imageable source domains, such as war, barrier, disease, animals, natural force, water, and foodstuffs. Additionally, we capture the prevalent sentiment that members of each community apply when referring to these concepts, in both literal and metaphorical contexts. We leverage language data available through public online sources produced by the target communities. These sources include mainstream media as well as public community blogs, newsletters, and websites. Data are collected and processed automatically using simple internet crawlers and natural language processing software capable of analyzing sentences for grammatical components, sentiment, and presence of metaphors. The processed data are then deposited in searchable structured repositories that are unique to each community. We estimate that the amount of data required to support both confirmatory and exploratory studies is approximately 5 million words per community. In the initial feasibility demonstration stage of this project, we collected 6 million words for both the INDO and GOVTO community.

In the remainder of this section, we provide detailed descriptions of data collection and processing procedures, as well as the repository construction process. These steps prepare us for the experiments described in Sections 5 and 6.

2.1 Data Harvesting and Processing

Our first objective was to identify the metaphors that are used to characterize the gun rights debate in the U.S. The topics of guns, gun rights, and gun control are well represented in U.S. media and finding related metaphors is not difficult. We use the automated system developed during the IARPA Metaphor Program (Strzalkowski et al., 2013) in order to extract examples of metaphors across a variety of information outlets.

For extracted metaphors to be useful for model development purposes, they must be assigned to a particular community or protagonist, in this case INDO or GOVTO, the two sides of the gun debate. To do so, we identified appropriate media outlets that cater to the INDO and GOVTO communities, as follows:

1. *Identification of spokespersons and spokesperson sites representing each community.* This step typically requires input from a cultural/political expert; however, it may be approximated using distance calculation based on metaphor distribution. For the gun debate scenario, we leveraged known correlations of opinions with the liberal-conservative political spectrum.

2. *Array sites along an opinion spectrum.* In most cases, there will be a spectrum of opinions within each community. We were initially particularly interested in the most orthodox

and extreme positions, because these provide the strongest contrast with other communities. This step is also assisted by input from cultural experts; however, it may be approximated by the Topical Positioning method (Lin et al., 2013) that tracks sentiment polarity in addition to metaphor choice. We leveraged Pew Research Center (2014, 2015, 2017) studies for establishing ground truth for both scenarios.

3. *Start collection of data from extreme positions.* This helps to establish a reasonably balanced collection of evidence from each community that can be used for confirmatory studies. Prior research (e.g., Shaikh et al., 2015) shows that the overall output of generally comparable communities may be quite unbalanced, depending on political context and related factors (Taylor et al., 2014).

4. *Data collection from sites of a more general nature.* These sites will be general news and opinion sites that may be considered relatively "opinion balanced" or "objective". These data provide a cultural backdrop against which the selected communities may be compared. In the current project, we collected such data as part of the exploratory marriage equality scenario.

This data collection and segmentation method is founded on the fact that language (including metaphors) is used as a group marker or a signal of group membership (Lakoff, 2001). Observation suggests that subgroups taking an extreme position define important markers for the more general group. Those in the middle of an opinion spectrum may employ language that reflects some of the extreme positions, some of the middling positions, and possibly some of the opposite positions – reflecting not only their middle-of-the-road approach to the issue, but also their willingness to identify with a range of views.

The positions of various participants in the U.S. gun debate range on a scale from radically in favor of government oversight of gun ownership, through a more moderate position in favor of this oversight, to a moderate position against such oversight, ending in a radical position against government oversight. In the U.S., this range corresponds roughly to a spectrum of U.S. political thought, arrayed typically on a scale from the radical left through the center to the radical right.

2.2 Identifying Metaphorical Targets

The process of identifying key concepts relevant to the case scenario has been fully automated. It proceeds in the following three steps:

1. *Locate frequently occurring topics in text.* The initial candidates are noun phrases, proper names (of locations, organizations, positions, events, and other phenomena, but less so of specific individuals). These are augmented with co-referential lexical items: pronouns, variants, and synonyms. The process of selection is quite robust but requires some rudimentary processing capability in the target language: part-of-speech tagging, basic anaphor resolution, and a lexicon/thesaurus.

2. *Down-select frequent topics to a set of 20-30 concepts.* The two key criteria are length and polarization. Topic length is measured by the number of references to the topic (either direct or indirect) that form "chains" across the "utterances" that are part of the scenario-related debate. Topic polarization is measured by the proportion of polarized references to the topic, either positive or negative. For example, the terms *gun rights* and *gun safety* are both frequently used and polarized in the gun debate.

3. *Select metaphorical targets.* Although all topics selected in Step 2 are important to the scenario, only some of them are likely to be targets of metaphors. We determine this simply by probing metaphor extraction for each of the selected topics and then eliminating these that do not bring back a sufficient number of metaphors or where the metaphor-to-literal ratio is too low. For example, "gun" is mostly used literally and is a poor metaphorical target. We used a 2% cut-off threshold for productive targets (a typical metaphor to literal ratio is 8-10%).

2.3 Data Collection Procedure

The data collection procedure consists of several steps as explained below. All steps are automated.

1. *Selection of target terms.* Target terms denote the key concepts of interest that the analyst wishes to investigate. For the gun debate, target concepts include *gun control*, *gun rights*, and *Second Amendment*, among others. This initial set of seed target terms need not be more than a few terms (e.g., less than 10).

2. *Search.* Selected data source websites were visited using an automated script. For sites that supported a search function, queries were posted directly to it. All text files matching any of the search terms were downloaded.

3. *Data cleaning.* All downloaded material was automatically segmented into passages so that at most five consecutive sentences were extracted: the sentence containing at least one search term, and up to two sentences on either side (before and after). Each full document yields one or more such passages, some of which may be overlapping.

4. *Data pre-processing.* All extracted passages were automatically pre-processed by a tokenizer that removes spurious characters and non-textual content and properly separates words.

5. *Target term set expansion.* Extracted passages were analyzed for presence of other terms besides the seed targets. All bigrams including only content words (not prepositions, determiners, etc.) were extracted and normalized for lexical variations. The most frequent bigrams were selected as additional target terms. This expansion was applied only once.

2.4 Scenarios Investigated

We investigated two distinct scenarios during the course of this project. The initial scenario involved two distinct views of gun rights versus gun control in the U.S. and developing ethnographic models of the communities representing these views. This initial scenario was partly based on the preliminary work conducted in the IARPA Metaphor program. The second scenario developed models for communities within the U.S. that hold different views on the topic of marriage equality, including same-sex marriage. Unlike the gun rights scenario that is essentially binary, the marriage equality topic produced multiple views, thus making the modeling task significantly harder. Nonetheless, we demonstrated that our approach can successfully support derivation of multi-faceted models. We summarize the first scenario only briefly; see Shaikh et al., 2015 for a complete description. The second scenario is described in more detail.

Gun Rights Scenario. Within the U.S., a public debate is ongoing concerning the Constitutionally and socially appropriate management of gun ownership, between those favoring Federal Government oversight (GOVTO) and those favoring individual oversight (INDO). At their extremes, the two sides are far apart. They view the issue in different conceptual terms, the GOVTO side relying heavily on DISEASE related metaphors and the INDO side relying on WAR related metaphors. These views appear reasonably constant over the years, even as the volume of output from each side changes.

Marriage Equality Scenario. Similar to gun rights versus gun control, people also disagree about the issue of marriage equality (i.e., same-sex marriage or gay marriage). Clashes in opinion on this topic became apparent during Obergefell v. Hodges (2015), the landmark case in which the U.S. Supreme Court ruled in favor of recognizing same-sex marriage. The lead-up to and aftermath of this case rippled through the media, with people voicing various stances on the issue. We identified seven basic stances one might take on the concept of marriage equality.

The first stance, labeled *expansion*, holds that we must nationally and internationally continue to expand rights for the LGBT community in regard to marriage, adoption, etc. The second stance, labeled *maintenance*, focuses on preserving the hard-won rights of gay couples and protecting them from infringement. The third stance, labeled *celebration*, is oriented toward commemorating the history of activism and legal battles that led to the Supreme Court decision legalizing same-sex marriage in the U.S. These three stances can be grouped together in the more general category of the *progressive community*, or those who believe that the institution of marriage should be open to all, regardless of sexual orientation or gender identity.

The fourth stance, labeled *reconciliation*, holds that traditional institutions such as the church should begin adapting to the changing moral and legal landscape surrounding marriage and family. The fifth stance, labeled *navigation*, is oriented toward working within changing laws surrounding marriage and family without compromising one's own values. These two stances can be grouped into the more general category of the *moderate community*, or those who default to legal precedent and consensus.

The sixth stance, labeled *incorrect interpretation*, holds that any extension of the institutions of marriage and family beyond heterosexual couples is an incorrect interpretation of the concept of marriage. Finally, the seventh stance, labeled *infringement,* focuses on preventing emerging legal definitions of marriage and family from infringing on personal and religious liberties. These last two stances can be grouped into the more general category of the *traditional community*, or those who believe that marriage and family should be reserved for heterosexual couples and that it is not the place of the government to define these terms.

2.5 Data Sources

For the gun debate case scenario, we identified 62 internet sources that include both extreme and moderate positions on both sides of the issue. These sources included both mainstream news reporting (e.g., New York Times, The New Yorker, Fox News) as well as blogs and websites of relevant organizations (e.g., nra.com). In selecting data sources for the gun debate scenario, we relied on the fact that in the U.S. these issues align quite closely with the political spectrum. We could thus utilize publications such as Pew Research Center reports to identify initial media on the political left and right. Our final collection consisted of 33,000 documents from which 55,000 passages were extracted, for a of approx. 6.1 million words.

Data collection for the marriage equality scenario involved 75 online sources that yielded nearly 1 million text passages. After removing duplicates and ill-formed content, we obtained 620,000 passages (each containing up to 5 sentences) with the cumulative content of approx. 30 million words. As with the gun debate scenario, we deployed search terms that represent the most frequently used concepts in the domain. The larger size of the marriage equality dataset reflects its greater complexity of stances.

3 Metaphor Extraction Approach

We distinguish two levels of metaphor identification: (1) text (or linguistic) metaphors that consist of a metaphorical target, typically an abstract concept, and a relation adopted from a concrete source domain; and (2) conceptual metaphors that generalize across multiple occurrences of text metaphors involving the same target. While text metaphors have the semantic form of *shared-property (Target, Source)*, the conceptual metaphor usually conveys a more definite mapping *Target=Source* or *Target ∈ Source*. For example, the textual metaphor "erosion of gun rights" alludes a shared property between gun rights and a geological landmark, thus invoking "Gun Rights is a Geological Landmark" conceptual metaphor. We note that conceptual metaphors are often implied rather than directly stated. Accordingly, the metaphor extraction process follows these two steps: we extract text metaphors first and then fuse them into conceptual ones. For ethnographic modeling purposes we use conceptual metaphors espoused in the language generated by a particular group of people.

We have developed a data-driven computational approach to extracting text metaphors that combines topical structure and imageability analysis in order to locate the candidate metaphorical expressions within text (Strzalkowski et al., 2013). To analyze topical structure, we identify nouns and verbs in a text passage and link their repeated occurrences, including co-references, synonyms, and hyponyms, and combine them into topic chains. Content words (e.g., verbs, nouns, adjectives) found outside these topical chains are candidate source relations if they also carry high imageability scores. Imageability ratings of most lexical items are looked up in an expanded MRC psycholinguistic database, which were built for several languages (Liu et al., 2014). The candidate relations are then used to compute and rank possible source domains in an emerging conceptual metaphor. Full details of the metaphor extraction process can be found in the cited papers.

Our approach to metaphor extraction is contrasted with more traditional computational approaches based on selectional restriction violations (Wilks, 1975; Fass, 1991; Martin, 1994; Carbonell, 1980; Feldman & Narayan, 2004; Shutova & Teufel, 2010; inter alia, also Shutova, 2010 for an overview) which do not scale well due to their heavy reliance on domain knowledge. More recent variants of this general approach (e.g., Rosen, 2018) utilize more robust deep learning methods but their utility remains limited to only some forms of text metaphors.

4 Metaphor-based Ethnographic Models

In this section, we outline the ethnographic models derived for each of the two scenarios. We provide only top-level characterization of each domain in terms of selection and distribution of metaphors that define each community's viewpoint: two communities for the gun debate scenario and three communities for the marriage equality scenario.

4.1 Characterization of the INDO and GOVTO Metaphor Repositories

We applied the metaphor extraction system (Broadwell et al., 2013) to the 2018 GOVTO and INDO datasets. All passages were processed by the software to determine whether a target term was used metaphorically or literally. In both cases, the semantic relation involving the target term was identified so that sentiment toward the target could be computed. For metaphorical cases, the relations were further classified into one of several dozen metaphorical source domains (see Table 1), such as War, Disease, or Barrier. The processed passages form the metaphor repository database, from which community models are derived.

SOURCE DOMAIN	DEFINITION	ANCHOR TERMS
BARRIER	anything blocking someone from going somewhere or from doing something	barrier, obstacle, wall, obstruction
WATER	the part of the earth's surface covered with water (such as a river or lake or ocean)	watercourse, ocean, lake, river, pond, sea
DISEASE	a disordered or incorrectly functioning organ, part, structure, or system of the body	illness, sickness, ailment, disease, cancer
MAZE	a confusing network of intercommunicating paths or passages; labyrinth.	labyrinth, web, tangle, snarl, warren, maze
MEDICINE	any substance or substances used in treating disease or illness; medicament; remedy	medication, drug, remedy, medicine
FORCEFUL EXTRACT	to get, pull, or draw out, usually with special effort, skill, or force	pull, draw, extract, force out
WAR	a conflict carried on by force of arms, as between nations or between parties within a nation; warfare	warfare, combat, hostilities, war, battle, conflict

Table 1. *A subset of metaphorical source domains used in this study*

We also analyzed the distribution of metaphors with respect to the source domains. A source domain is a concrete semantic class to which the target is likened. The assignment of a metaphor to a source domain is determined by metaphorical relations that are applied to the target in a particular instance. For example, in "the plague of gun

violence" the metaphorical relation is "plague," which is a sub-concept of DISEASE (e.g., in Wordnet; Miller, 1995). Therefore, this metaphor is classified as DISEASE metaphor – that is, "gun violence" is likened to disease.

Table 1 shows a partial list of source domains we used, along with definitions and anchor terms that are representative members of each domain. The complete list of 67 source domains was compiled by the IARPA Metaphor Program.

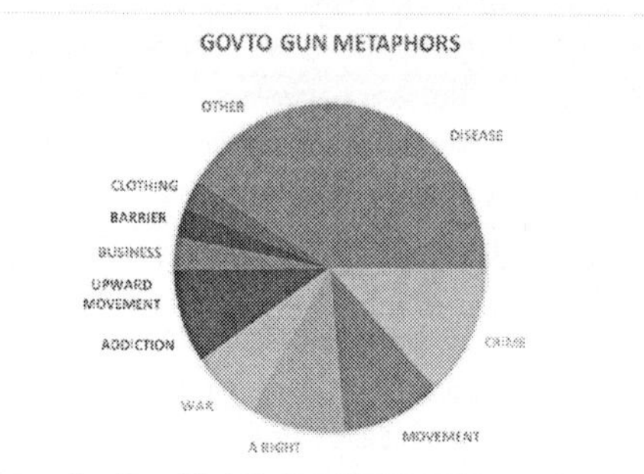

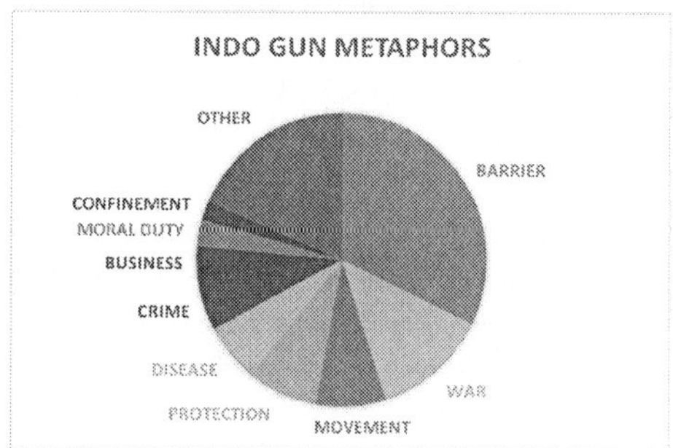

Figure 1: *Metaphor source domains for the gun debate scenario: DISEASE and CRIME dominate the GOVTO community, whereas BARRIER and WAR are most common within the INDO community.*

In Figure 1, we present the top choices of source domains for metaphors associated with the target concepts, including *gun control, gun rights*, and *gun violence*. We note that *DISEASE and CRIME* dominate on the GOVTO side, while *BARRIER and WAR* explain nearly half of INDO metaphors. This analysis illustrates one type of strong bias that is found in the data and confirms some earlier findings (Shaikh et al., 2015) over new data.

4.2 Characterization of Metaphors in the Marriage Equality Domain

We applied our metaphor extraction system to the marriage equality data, initially concentrating on the three major stances noted above (i.e., the progressive, moderate, and traditional communities). We used the same list of source domains as with the gun debate scenario. Overall, we extracted 8305 metaphors including targets such as *marriage equality, same-sex marriage,* and *gay rights*. As expected, the selection of source domains was different than in the gun debate scenario, but again it showed marked contrast across the stances. Moreover, unlike in the gun debate scenario, we did not have an *a priori* classification of media sources as representing a particular stance. Instead, the set of all metaphors was split 3-ways using K-means clustering applied on the metaphor distribution statistics, taking into account the metaphor target, the metaphoric relation, the target role in the relation, and the source domain. Figure 2 shows near-perfect 3-way separation between sources representing progressive, moderate, and traditional views on marriage equality. A further attempt to separate the finer-grained seven stances described above was somewhat less successful, producing an Adjusted Rand Index (ARI) score of only 0.27, partly due to soft boundaries between some of the stances and insufficient data.

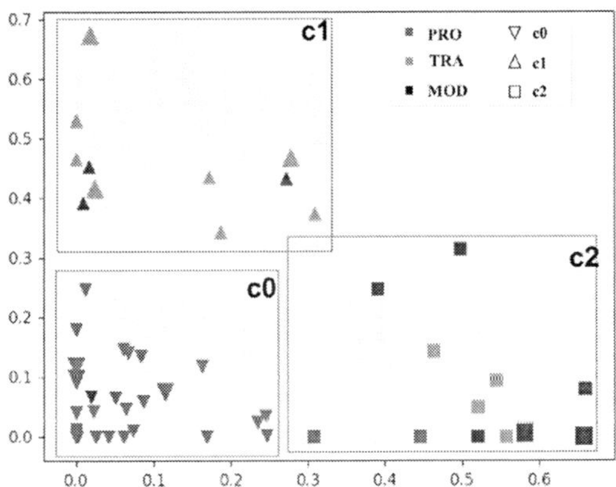

Figure 2. *Automatically derived clusters of information sources based on metaphor distribution show a good split between progressive (c0), traditional (c1), and moderate sources (c2), with ARI of 0.69.*

We note that alternative approaches to obtaining automatic separation of stances based on topic and sentiment distribution did not come close to the result seen in Figure 2. A doc2vec based method (Le & Mikolov, 2014) only achieved an ARI score of 0.17 on the 3-way split; an LDA-based approach (Blei et al, 2003) did only slightly better at 0.37.

Figures 3 to 5 show the metaphor distribution across the three main stances in the marriage equality domain. The first analysis (Figure 3, Table 2) shows metaphor distribution in language collected from progressive sources. The dominating metaphor is Forceful Extraction, which

involves relations such as "ban" and "prohibit." Other common metaphors, along with their frequent relations, are shown in Table 2.

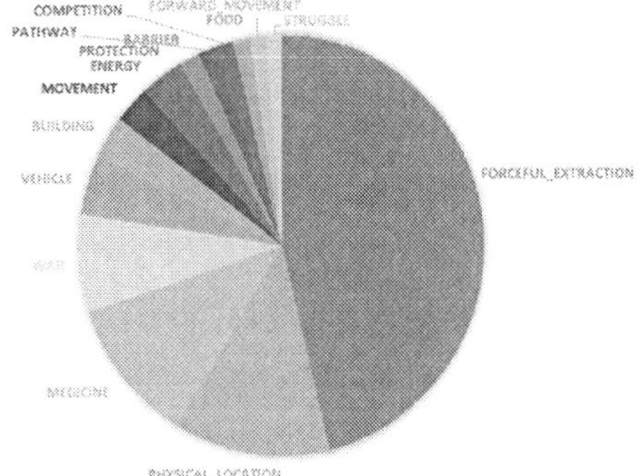

Figure 3. *Distribution of marriage equality metaphors in the progressive stance sources*

Marriage Equality is...	Sample Metaphorical Relations
forceful extraction (38.4%)	ban, prohibit
physical location (10.3%)	disagree, divide, poll, reiterate, strike, subject
medicine (9.3%)	legalize, ban, approve
war (6.2%)	battle, fight, defend, victory
vehicle (3.9%)	overturn, drive, ban
building (2.7%)	enter, condemn, preside, celebrate, way for
movement (3.4%)	embrace, move, movement, proceed

Table 2. *Selected metaphoric relations for the most frequent source domains in the progressive stance.*

Figure 4 and Table 3 show the analysis of the moderate stance. The most frequent metaphor, representing about 23% of all collected examples, is Physical Location. This is followed by Medicine, which explains another 14% of the examples. This community had a relatively low output volume, producing a mere 5% of metaphors in our data set, with another 20% attributed to "neutral" sources.

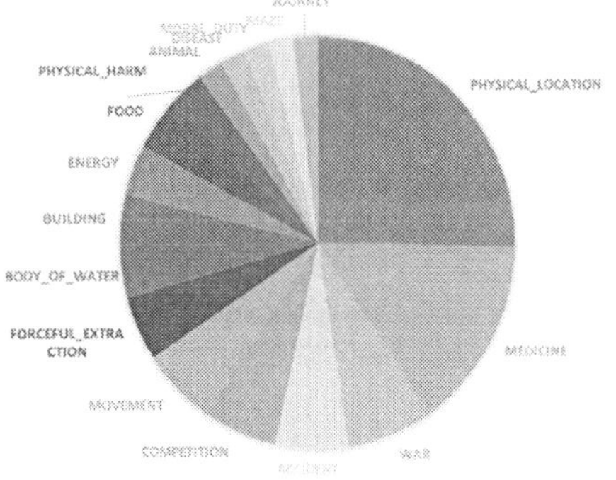

Figure 4. *Distribution of marriage equality metaphors in the moderate stance sources.*

MARRIAGE EQUALITY IS...	SAMPLE METAPHORICAL RELATIONS
physical location (22.7%)	argument, recognition
medicine (13.6%)	legalize, treat
war (6.4%)	undermine, authorize
accident (5.5%)	rule
competition (5.5%)	promote
movement (5.5%)	embrace, perform
forceful extraction (4.6%)	ban
body of water (3.6%)	spawn, surround
building (3.6%)	enter

Table 3. *Selected metaphoric relations for the most frequent source domains in the moderate stance.*

Figure 5 and Table 4 show the analysis of the traditional stance on marriage equality. Here the dominating metaphor is Medicine (20%). When coupled with a related and quite frequent metaphor of Addiction (5%), these two together form a hybrid "bad medicine" metaphor. Other frequent metaphors (Physical Location and Forceful Extraction) are also quite visible, which can be explained partly by the mixed content of the traditional stance cluster as well as frequent critical references to the progressive sources. At this time, we lack reliable means, beyond distribution frequency, of separating expressions that characterize one's own stance as compared to other people's stances. We note that sources representing traditional views account for only about 10% of extracted metaphors.

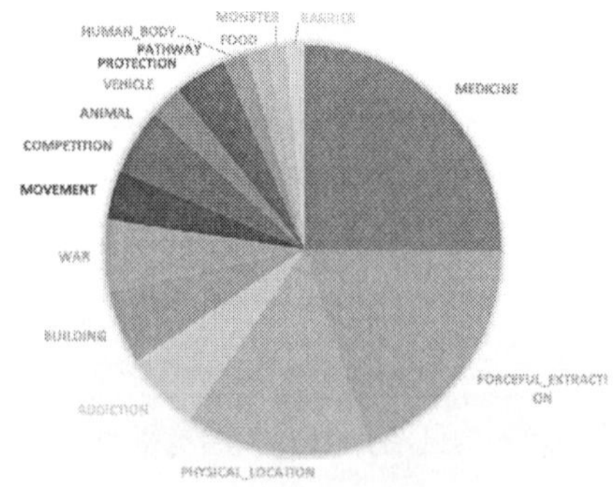

Figure 5. *Distribution of marriage equality metaphors in the traditional stance sources.*

MARRIAGE EQUALITY IS...	SAMPLE METAPHORICAL RELATIONS
medicine (20.2%)	legalize
forceful extraction (15.8%)	ban, prohibit, force
physical location (12%)	disagree, subject, argue
addiction (5%)	legalization
building (4.7%)	enter, way for, preside
war (4.5%)	fight, battle, defend, undermine
movement (3.1%)	perform, embrace

Table 4. *Selected metaphoric relations for the most frequent source domains in the traditional stance.*

5 Confirmatory Studies on the Gun Debate

We conducted a study to experimentally confirm the bias in community data in relation to the gun debate scenario. A subset of passages containing metaphors was selected from both the INDO and GOVTO communities' metaphor repository and were displayed to human participants, whose task was to categorize each passage as advocating for either individual or government oversight of guns. The objective of this study was to confirm that the bias was captured in the metaphors used by each community and that this bias can be detected by human raters. We thus predicted that participants would be able to categorize the passages as representing the intended community viewpoints at rates above chance. This result would confirm that our metaphor repositories accurately reflect the language use of the two communities relevant to this target scenario (i.e., INDO and GOVTO).

A sample of 338 respondents completed the study via Amazon Mechanical Turk. Raters viewed 20 passages from INDO sources and 20 passages from GOVTO sources. Overall accuracy scores were calculated by dividing the total number of correct categorizations by the total number of passages (i.e., 40). As predicted, participants categorized passages with above-chance accuracy (mean accuracy=66%, SD=14%), $t(337)$=21.94, $p<.001$, d=1.19. INDO and GOVTO categorization accuracy scores were calculated by dividing the number of correct categorizations for each passage type by 20. Participants categorized passages from GOVTO sources (mean accuracy=70%, SD=15%) more accurately than passages from INDO sources (mean accuracy=63%, SD=16%), $t(337)$=7.62, $p<.001$, d_z=0.41. Thus, human raters were able to determine whether passages came from INDO or GOVTO media sources at reliably greater-than-chance (above 50% accuracy) rates.

We replicated this study with another sample of 906 participants who rated 40 randomly selected (vs. researcher-selected, as in the previous study) passages from the same metaphor repositories on a continuous scale (0=*definitely in favor of government oversight* to 100=*definitely in favor of individual oversight*). As predicted, participants rated INDO passages as being reliably more in favor of individual oversight than the scale midpoint (M=56.48, SD=11.26), $t(905)$=17.47, p<.001, d=0.58. Participants also rated GOVTO passages as being reliably more in favor of government oversight than the scale midpoint (M=38.31, SD=12.71), $t(905)$=-27.62, p<.001, d=0.92. These results again suggest that participants were able to detect the bias present in the passages and rated them accordingly.

6   Confirmatory Study on the Marriage Equality Debate

We conducted a study to confirm the bias in community data in relation to the marriage equality scenario. Following the same procedure as in the first study, 285 participants categorized a total of 45 passages automatically selected from progressive, moderate, and traditional sources as representing a progressive, moderate, or traditional stance on marriage. As predicted, participants categorized passages with above chance accuracy, with 33% accuracy representing chance (mean accuracy=38%, SD=8%), $t(284)$=11.49, p<.001, d=0.68. Moreover, participants categorized passages from moderate sources (M=41%, SD=16%) more accurately than passages from progressive sources (mean accuracy=36%, SD=18%), $t(568)$=-3.70, $p_{bonferroni}$<.001, d_z=-0.20. Accuracy scores for passages from traditional sources (mean accuracy=38%, SD=15%) did not differ from any other accuracy score. Thus, human raters were able to determine whether passages regarding marriage equality originated from progressive, moderate, or traditional media sources at reliably greater-than-chance rates.

7   Conclusion

In this paper, we presented results from a project in which we built ethnographic models of communities based on the choice of metaphors in online language use. We investigated two distinct scenarios, a binary gun rights vs. gun control debate and a non-binary marriage equality debate. We demonstrated in both cases that metaphor choice provides strong clues to a community's identity and bias, and that automatically derived models can adequately delineate target communities. Future work will focus on improving the accuracy of metaphor classification and exploiting other forms of figurative language that capture deeply held collective meanings and stances.

This research explored a new avenue of computational ethnography, conducted entirely online. The long-standing benchmark is traditional field ethnography that involves typically small-scale field work, which takes months or years to complete. Such studies, while producing "thick" models, are not always feasible, especially in the areas of conflict or disturbance nor when a rapid response is required. Furthermore, field ethnography by its nature is heavily reliant on regional, local language speaking subject matter experts who may be hard to find due to lack of expertise or risks involved.

Current approaches to online ethnography include application of traditional methods of observation of online behavior aimed at modeling online communities, as opposed to the real-world communities (e.g., Miller & Salter, 2000; Safar & Mahdi, 2012). Efforts aimed at deriving offline models from online data are either small-scale (Martey et al., 2011) or limited to superficial analysis of social media (e.g., sentiment extraction) that cannot easily separate transient views from entrenched opinions (e.g., Turney & Littman, 2003). These approaches produce low-quality results also due to over-sensitivity to data noise and are thus unreliable. We believe that our research shows the value of advanced sociolinguistic analysis and natural language processing in studying the online human terrain.

Acknowledgments

This work was supported by the Defense Advanced Research Projects Agency (DARPA) under Contract No. HR0011-18-9-0016. All statements of fact, opinion or conclusions contained herein are those of the authors and should not be construed as representing the official views or policies of USN, DARPA, or the U.S. Government.

References

Blei, David M., Andrew Y. Ng, and Michael I. Jordan (2003) Latent dirichlet allocation. Journal of machine Learning research. (vol. 3, pp 993-1022).

Broadwell, George Aaron; Umit Boz, Ignacio Cases, Tomek Strzalkowski, Laurie Feldman, Sarah Taylor, Samira Shaikh, Ting Liu, Kit Cho (2013) Using Imageability and Topic Chaining to Locate Metaphors in Linguistic Corpora. SBP-2013 Conference, Washington, DC.

Carbonell, Jaime (1980) Metaphor: a key to extensible semantic analysis. *Proceedings of the 18th Annual Meeting on Association for Computational Linguistics.*

Charteris-Black, Jonathan (2002) Second language figurative proficiency: A comparative study of Malay and English. Appl Linguistics, 23(1):104–33.

Fass, Dan (1991) met*: A Method for Discriminating Metonymy and Metaphor by Computer. *Computational Linguistics, Vol 17:49-90*

Feldman, J. and S. Narayanan (2004) Embodied meaning in a neural theory of language. *Brain and Language*, 89(2):385–392.

Lakoff, George and Johnson, Mark (1980) *Metaphors We Live By*. University of Chicago Press.

Lakoff, George (2001) *Moral politics: what conservatives know that liberals don't*. University of Chicago Press, Chicago, Illinois.

Le, Quoc and Mikolov, Tomas (2014) Distributed representations of sentences and documents. In Proceedings of the 31st International Conference on Machine Learning, ICML'14.

Lin, Ching-Sheng; Samira Shaikh, Jennifer Stromer-Galley, Jennifer Crowley, Tomek Strzalkowski, Veena Ravishankar (2013) Topical Positioning: A New Method for Predicting Opinion Changes in Conversation. Proceedings of the Language Analysis in Social Media workshop, NAACL 2013 Conference, Atlanta, GA.

Liu, Ting; Kit Cho, George Aaron Broadwell, Samira Shaikh, Tomek Strzalkowski, John Lien, Sarah Taylor, Laurie Feldman, Boris Yamrom, Nick Webb, Umit Boz and Ignacio Cases (2014). Automatic Expansion of the MRC Psycholinguistic Database Imageability Ratings. LREC Conference, Reykjavik.

Martey, Rosa Mikeal, Jennifer Stromer-Galley, Mia Consalvo, Kelly Reene, Tomek Strzalkowski, Michelle Weihmann-Purcell, Kevin Shiflett, Jingsi Wu, Jaime Banks, Sharon Small and Michael Ferguson. (2011) "Gamer culture versus the culture of the game: An Analysis of Player Behavior and Gamer Identity in Second Life," in Proceedings of the 12th annual conference of the Association of Internet Researchers (AoIR), Seattle.

Miller, G. A. (1995). WordNet: A Lexical database for English. Comm. of the ACM, 38(11): 39-41.

Miller, D., and Slater, D. (2000) The Internet: An Ethnographic Approach, Oxford; New York: Berg.

Mohler, Michael; David Bracewell, David Hinote, and Marc Tomlinson (2013) Semantic signatures for example-based linguistic metaphor detection. In *Proceedings of the First Workshop on Metaphor in NLP, (NAACL)*, pages 46–54.

Pew Research Center (2013) A survey of LGBT Americans: Attitudes, experiences and values in changing times. Retrieved from https://www.pewsocialtrends.org/2013/06/13/a-survey-oflgbt-americans/

Pew Research Center (2014) Political polarization and media habits: From Fox News to Facebook, how liberals and conservatives keep up with politics. Retrieved from http://www.journalism.org/2014/10/21/political-polarization-media-habits/58

Pew Research Center (2017) America's complex relationship with guns: An in-depth look at the attitudes and experiences of U.S. adults. Retrieved fromhttp://www.pewsocialtrends.org/2017/06/22/a mericas-complex-relationship-with-guns/

Rosen, Zachary (2018) Computationally Constructed Concepts: A Machine Learning Approach to Metaphor Interpretation Using Usage-Based Construction Grammatical Cues. Proceedings of the ACL Workshop on Figurative Language Processing, New Orleans, Louisiana.

Safar, M., & Mahdi, K. (2012) Social Networking and Community Behavior Modeling: Qualitative and Quantitative Measures, (pp. 1-400). Hershey, PA: IGI Global. doi:10.4018/978-1-61350-444-4

Shaikh, Samira; Tomek Strzalkowski, Ting Liu, George Aaron Broadwell, Boris Yamrom, Sarah Taylor, Laurie Feldman, Kit Cho, Umit Boz, Ignacio Cases, Yuliya Peshkova and Ching-Sheng Lin (2014) A Multi-Cultural Repository of Automatically Discovered Linguistic and Conceptual Metaphors. LREC Conf., Reykjavik.

Shaikh, Samira; Tomek Strzalkowski, Sarah Taylor, Ting Liu, John Lien, George Aaron Broadwell, Laurie Feldman, Boris Yamrom, Kit Cho and Yuliya Peshkova (2015). Understanding Cultural Conflicts using Metaphors and Sociolinguistic Measures of Influence. Proc. of 3rd workshop on Metaphor in NLP, NAACL-2015, Boulder, CO.

Shutova, Ekaterina (2010) Models of metaphor in nlp. *Proc. of 48th Meeting of the Assoc. for Computational Linguistics*, pages 688–697.

Shutova, E. and S. Teufel (2010) Metaphor corpus annotated for source - target domain mappings. *In Proceedings of LREC 2010, Malta*

Strzalkowski, Tomek; George Aaron Broadwell, Sarah Taylor, Laurie Feldman, Boris Yamrom, Samira Shaikh, Ting Liu, Kit Cho, Umit Boz, Ignacio Cases and Kyle Elliott. (2013) Robust Extraction of Metaphors from Novel Data. Proceedings of NAACL Workshop on Metaphors in NLP. Atlanta, GA.

Strzalkowski, Tomek; George Aaron Broadwell, Sarah Taylor, Laurie Feldman, Boris Yamrom, Samira Shaikh, Ting Liu, Kit Cho, Umit Boz, Ignacio Cases and Kyle Elliott (2014) Computing Affect in Metaphors. Proceedings of the 2nd workshop on Metaphor in NLP, ACL-2014 Conference, Baltimore, MD.

Taylor, Sarah; Laurie Beth Feldman, Kit Cho, Samira Shaikh, Ignacio Cases,Yuliya Peshkova, George Aaron Broadwell Ting Liu, Umit Boz, Kyle Elliott. Boris Yamrom, and Tomek Strzalkowski (2014) Extracting Understanding from automated metaphor identification: Contrasting Concepts of Poverty across Cultures and Languages. AHFE Conference, Cracow, Poland.

Thibodeau, Paul, H. and Lera Boroditsky (2011) Metaphors We Think With: The Role of Metaphor in Reasoning. PLoS ONE 6(2): e16782.

Turney, P. D., & Littman, M. L. (2003) "Measuring Praise and Criticism," ACM Trans. Inf. Syst., 21(4), 315–346.

Wilks, Yorick (1975) Preference semantics. *Formal Semantics of Natural Language*, E. L. Keenan, Ed. Cambridge University Press, Cambridge, U.K., 329--348.

Wilks, Yorick; Lucian Galescu, James Allen, Adam Dalton (2013) Automatic Metaphor Detection using Large-Scale Lexical Resources and Conventional Metaphor Extraction. In the *Proceedings of the First Workshop on Metaphor in NLP, (NAACL)*. Atlanta.

Oxymorons: a preliminary corpus investigation

Marta La Pietra
University of Bologna Alumna
marta.lapietra93@gmail.com

Francesca Masini
University of Bologna
francesca.masini@unibo.it

Abstract

This paper contains a preliminary corpus study of oxymorons, a figure of speech so far under-investigated in NLP-oriented research. The study resulted in a list of 376 oxymorons, identified by extracting a set of antonymous pairs (under various configurations) from corpora of written Italian and by manually checking the results. A complementary method is also envisaged for discovering contextual oxymorons, which are highly relevant for the detection of humor, irony and sarcasm.

1 Why oxymorons?

The growing body of research on figurative language in NLP has recently witnessed an expansion from more traditional domains (like idioms, metaphors, metonymy) to other ubiquitous phenomena such as irony, puns and sarcasm. However, other – supposedly more marginal – figures of speech have received less attention so far. The oxymoron is a case in point.

The oxymoron, which has been studied mainly in rhetoric and literature, is "[a] figure of speech in which a pair of opposed or markedly contradictory terms are placed in conjunction for emphasis", although its meaning has expanded to comprise more generally "a contradiction in terms" (definitions from OED: www.oed.com). Typical examples of oxymorons would be *deafening silence*, *sweet sorrow* or *awfully good*.

The oxymoron is obviously closely intertwined with the semantic relation of antonymy: it is often the union of antonymous items that creates the oxymoron's paradoxical effect, thus generating a new meaning, which often heavily depends on context. As Gibbs & Kearney (1994: 86) observe, "[u]nderstanding oxymora requires that people access relevant world knowledge to constrain their creative interpretations of seemingly contradictory concepts".

In this paper, we set out a preliminary investigation of oxymorons based on naturally occurring data from Italian, with a view to contributing to the NLP-oriented research on figurative language by supplying an initial list of oxymorons and oxymoronic structures that can be used for further analyses and for evaluation tasks. The questions that drove our investigation are: What kind of oxymorons do we find in common language? What syntactic constructions are involved in their creation? And above all, how can we detect them in corpora?

In Section 2 we describe the methodology we used to detect oxymorons in corpora of contemporary written Italian. Although our study is based on Italian, the procedure we followed can easily be extended to other languages. In Section 3 we illustrate the main results of our analysis. The full list of oxymorons detected is available in the Appendix. Section 4 outlines another promising complementary methodology to be pursued in future research. Finally, Section 5 discusses possible further developments, with special attention to the challenges oxymorons pose for automatic identification and extraction.

2 Methodology

The procedure we devised to track down oxymorons in corpora of written Italian stems from the observation that these constructions are closely connected with antonymous pairs, which have been the subject of several studies based on their co-occurrence in texts (cf. e.g. Charles & Miller 1989; Justeson & Katz 1991; Lobanova 2012; Kostić 2017).

Proceedings of the Second Workshop on Figurative Language Processing, pages 176–185
July 9, 2020. ©2020 Association for Computational Linguistics
https://doi.org/10.18653/v1/P17

Our starting point was Jones' (2002) analysis of English antonyms, which makes use of a list of canonical antonymous pairs to be searched in a corpus of texts from *The Independent* (approx. 280M words). We therefore translated Jones' antonymous pairs into Italian and made a selection out of this set, driven mainly by the exclusion of predicative (e.g. *confirm* ~ *deny*) and adverbial (e.g. *badly* ~ *well*) couples.

This resulted in a list of 17 noun ~ noun antonymous pairs, displayed in Table 1.

Italian antonymous pairs	English translation
amore ~ odio	love ~ hate
attività ~ passività	activity ~ passivity
caldo ~ freddo	hot ~ cold
coraggio ~ paura	bravery ~ fear
distanza ~ vicinanza	distance ~ proximity
dolcezza ~ amarezza	sweetness ~ bitterness
felicità ~ infelicità	happiness ~ unhappiness
giustizia ~ ingiustizia	justice ~ injustice
guerra ~ pace	war ~ peace
leggerezza ~ pesantezza	lightness ~ heaviness
lentezza ~ velocità	slowness ~ speed
luce ~ buio	light ~ dark
realtà ~ irrealtà	reality ~ unreality
ricchezza ~ povertà	wealth ~ poverty
silenzio ~ rumore	silence ~ noise
vita ~ morte	life ~ death
vuoto ~ pieno	emptiness ~ fullness

Table 1: Starting list of Italian antonymous pairs.

Then we designed an inventory of potential oxymorons. All the constructed couples were searched, as lemmas, in two large corpora of contemporary written Italian: Italian Web 2016 (itTenTen16, through the SketchEngine platform: https://www.sketchengine.eu/) and CORIS (2017 version; Rossini Favretti et al. 2002; http://corpora.ficlit.unibo.it/coris _eng.html). The results were manually checked.

The above-mentioned inventory of potential oxymorons was built in the following way.

First, we matched each noun of each pair (e.g. *odio* 'hate') with its antonym (*amore* 'love') in either adjectival (*amoroso / amorevole* 'loving') or verbal (*amare* 'to love') form. With this first round of extractions, we obtained combinations such as *odio amoroso* (lit. hate lovely) and *amorevole odio* (lit. lovely hate) 'loving hate', as well as *l'amore odia* 'love hates', although sequences containing verbs were quite uncommon. However, the search for lemma verbs retrieved also a number of participial forms used as adjectives (as in *amore*

odiato 'hated love', where *odiato* is the past participle of *odiare* 'to hate').

Second, we added contrastive adjective ~ adverb pairs connected to the nouns in Table 1 (e.g. *felicità* 'happiness' > *felice* 'happy' > *felicemente* 'happily' + *infelicità* > *infelice* 'unhappy', gaining *felicemente infelice* 'happily unhappy').

In addition, to enrich data retrieval, we selected lexemes semantically related to the members of the antonymous pairs in Table 1 (synonyms, hyponyms, etc.) from the *Grande Dizionario Analogico della Lingua Italiana* (Simone 2010). This step was inspired by Shen's (1987: 109) definition of indirect oxymoron, i.e. an oxymoron where "one of [the] two terms is not the direct antonym of the other, but rather the hyponym of its antonym" (like *whistling silence*, where *whistling* is a type of *noise*). Related lexemes were also searched in the two above-mentioned corpora. For the sake of exemplification, we illustrate some of these paradigmatic expansions for the following three antonymous pairs, for which we retrieved a considerable amount of data:

- *caldo ~ freddo* (hot ~ cold) → *afa* 'stuffiness', *calura* 'heat', *fuoco* 'fire', *fiamma* 'flame' ~ *gelo* 'frost', *ghiaccio* 'ice', *grandine* 'hail', *neve* 'snow', *pioggia* 'rain';

- *felicità ~ infelicità* (happiness ~ unhappiness) → *allegria* 'glee', *contentezza* 'cheer', *gaiezza* 'gaiety', *gioia* 'joy' ~ *afflizione* 'distress', *depressione* 'depression', *disperazione* 'despair', *dolore* 'pain', *sconforto* 'discouragement', *scontento* 'discontentment', *tristezza* 'sadness';

- *silenzio ~ rumore* (silence ~ noise) → [*silenzio* only] ~ *boato* 'rumble', *fracasso* 'racket', *fragore* 'clamour', *grido* 'shout', *ululato* 'howling', *urlo* 'scream'.

The final phase of the analysis implied the interrogation of the Sketch Engine Word Sketch tool, which describes the collocational behavior of words by showing the lexemes that most typically co-occur with them, within specific syntagmatic contexts, by using statistical association measures. In this case, we searched for all nouns participating in the antonymous pairs in Table 1 and we manually revised all top results provided the Word Sketch function (thus focusing on the most statistically significant combinations). Beside oxymorons that we had already retrieved with the previous procedure (e.g. the very frequent *silenzio assordante* 'deafening silence'), this method allowed us to identify new configurations, for instance sentential patterns where the two opposite nouns are linked by the copula *è* 'is' (e.g. *la luce è tenebra* 'light is darkness') or prepositional phrases where the two opposite nouns are linked by a preposition (e.g. *il fragore del silenzio* 'the racket of silence').

3 Results

The multiple-step procedure described in Section 2 resulted in a final list of 376 oxymorons, the first of its kind in Italian, to the best of our knowledge. The full dataset (***Italian oxymorons 1.0***) is provided in the Appendix and released as an Excel file through the University of Bologna Institutional Research Repository (AMSActa):

`http://amsacta.unibo.it/id/eprint/6388`

Around 20% of the oxymorons were found in both corpora, whereas the vast majority (almost 80%) was retrieved in itTenTen16, which is much larger than CORIS (4.9 billion vs. 150 million words).

3.1 Syntactic structure

We classified the 376 oxymorons according to their syntactic structure. A quantitative summary is given in Table 2, which reports, for each of the 9 structures we could identify, the number of oxymorons with that structure and the number of antonymous pairs that generate oxymorons with that structure.

Syntactic structure	N. of oxymorons	N. of antonymous pairs
N A	140	17
A N	112	17
S	52	11
Adv A	50	16
N Prep N	14	7
A A	3	1
V V	2	1
V A	2	1
V Prep N	1	1
Total	**376**	**17**

Table 2: Syntactic structures of oxymorons in our dataset.

As expected, the vast majority of the oxymorons in our dataset belongs to noun-adjective combinations, in both orders: [N A] (e.g. *silenzio urlante* 'screaming silence', *attività passive* 'passive activities') and [A N] (e.g. *raggiante oscurità* 'glowing darkness', *disperata felicità* 'desperate happiness'). These are the only two structures that host oxymorons generated from all the 17 antonymous pairs in Table 1. In our data, [A N] sequences are quite numerous despite the fact that noun-adjective is the unmarked, neutral order in Italian. This may be linked to the fact that the prenominal position for Italian adjectives is generally associated with affect and emphasis (Ramaglia 2010), values that are highly compatible with the oxymoron as a rhetorical device. Several examples in these two classes display participial forms used in adjectival function, e.g. *fiamma bagnata* 'wet flame' ([N Prt]) or *infuocato gelo* 'inflamed frost' ([Prt N]). We found mostly past participles (see the aforementioned examples), but also a few present participles (e.g. *prossimità distanziante* 'distancing proximity').

The third most frequent structure in terms of number of oxymorons is Sentence (S). The examples belonging to this class emerged especially (though not entirely) through the exploration of the Word Sketch function (cf. Section 2). The antonymous nouns in our pairs were found both in copular sentences (e.g. *l'amore è odio* 'love is hate', *il silenzio è rumore* 'the silence is noise') and in subject-verb sentences (e.g. *il silenzio grida* 'the silence screams', *il buio illumina* 'the dark illuminates (something)'). Some sentence-level oxymorons are borderline cases, since they could be argued to qualify as paradoxes rather than oxymorons (e.g. *il buio è luce* 'the dark is the light'). We decided to keep them, since the divide between oxymorons and paradoxes is not so clear(-cut): as Flayih (2009) claims, the "oxymoron is sometimes taken as 'condensed paradox' and paradox as 'expanded oxymoron'".

We also retrieved a considerable number of adverbial oxymorons of the [Adv A] type (e.g. *allegramente depresso* 'cheerfully depressed', *luminosamente oscuro* 'brightly dark') – which is relevant also in terms of the number of antonymous pairs it represents (16 out of 17, cf. Table 2) – and some [N Prep N] oxymoronic expressions, such as *la tenebra della luce* 'darkness of the light'. As for the latter category, all examples contain the preposition *di* 'of', except for *il silenzio nel rumore* 'the silence into the noise', which contains *in* 'in'.

Finally, we found other less common structures, such as [A A] (e.g. *fredda calda* 'cold hot'), [V V] (where the second verb is a gerund, e.g. *gridare tacendo* 'to shout being silent'), [V A] (e.g. *urlare muto* 'to scream (staying) mute'), and [V Prep N] (e.g. *urlare in silenzio* 'to scream in silence').

3.2 Antonymous pairs

As for the antonymous pairs taken into consideration (Table 1), we observe a rather unequal distribution in our data in terms of their ability to create oxymorons. Some pairs – such as *caldo* ~ *freddo* (hot ~ cold), *silenzio* ~ *rumore* (silence ~ noise) or *felicità* ~ *infelicità* (happiness ~ unhappiness) – generate a high number of oxymoronic constructions, whereas others are definitely less exploited, like *coraggio* ~ *paura* (bravery ~ fear), *guerra* ~ *pace* (war ~ peace) or *leggerezza* ~ *pesantezza* (lightness ~ heaviness). Overall, the pairs with the higher number of oxymorons are also those displaying a wider array of syntactic structures (Table 2), but the differences are not so great. All the pairs are represented by at least 3 structures (out of 9 possibilities).

The complete quantitative picture is given in Table 3, where antonymous pairs are reported in English translation (like in the Appendix) for convenience.

Antonymous pair	N. of oxymorons	N. of syntactic structures
hot-cold	87	5
silence-noise	85	8
happiness-unhappiness	50	4
light-dark	30	5
distance-proximity	19	4
love-hate	18	5
life-death	13	4
reality-unreality	11	5
wealth-poverty	10	5
sweetness-bitterness	10	3
slowness-speed	9	3
bravery-fear	8	4
activity-passivity	7	3
justice-injustice	6	4
war-peace	5	4
emptiness-fullness	5	3
lightness-heaviness	3	3
Total	**376**	**9**

Table 3: Number of oxymorons and syntactic structures per each antonymous pair.

At first glance there does not seem to be a strong and clear driving principle behind the unequal distribution of the pairs in terms of semantics. For instance, we find abstract concepts (e.g. happiness ~ unhappiness, justice ~ injustice) or sensorial concepts (e.g. hot ~ cold, lightness ~ heaviness) at various points of the list in Table 3. However, a more fine-grained semantic analysis and a larger dataset would be necessary to draw more solid conclusions.

Of course, the higher number of semantically related lexemes investigated for some pairs plays a clear role (cf. Section 2). Also the entrenchment of some notorious cases might be relevant. Take for instance *silenzio assordante* 'deafening silence', which occurs 2564 times in the itTenTen16 corpus (plus 1517 times in the reverse adjective-noun order: *assordante silenzio*). The high token frequency of this specific oxymoron may favor the creation of new oxymorons in the very same conceptual domain (silence ~ noise).

3.3 Morphosyntactic variability

Although the morphosyntactic variation of oxymorons is not the focus of the present study, we can preliminary observe that, according to the data we collected so far, oxymorons are rather flexible structures. In other words, contrary to many multiword expressions (cf., among many others, Sag et al. 2002), oxymorons seem to show a low degree of fixedness.

Many combinations of a noun and an adjective are attested in both orders, although with different frequency (remember that noun-adjective is more neutral than adjective-noun): see the couple *silenzio assordante* vs. *assordante silenzio* mentioned at the end of Section 3.2, or *tenebra luminosa* (9 tokens in itTenTen16) vs. *luminosa tenebra* (4 tokens in itTenTen16) 'bright shadow'.

In [N Prep N] oxymorons, the second (non-head) noun may occur in both singular and plural (contrary to Italian multiword expressions belonging to the same pattern, where the non-head noun is morphologically fixed, cf. Masini 2009), although the singular form is generally preferred, e.g.: *suono del silenzio* 'sound of the silence' (380 tokens in itTenTen16) vs. *suono dei silenzi* 'sound of the silences' (7 tokens in itTenTen16).

As for sentential oxymorons, we often found different configurations for the same pair of items; for instance, *silenzio* 'silence' and *rumore* 'noise' are found as: *il silenzio è un rumore (che…)*

'silence is a noise (that…)', *il silenzio è rumore* 'silence is noise', *il silenzio è il rumore (di…)* 'silence is the noise (of…)' (all these variants are reported as a single entry – *il silenzio è rumore* 'silence is noise' – in the Appendix).

4 A complementary method

Another complementary technique to harvest oxymorons from corpora is, quite trivially, to search the word *ossimoro* 'oxymoron'. We noticed that, when they come across or use (what they believe to be) an oxymoron, speakers tend to comment on it metalinguistically, as in: *una guerra santa (grandissimo ossimoro)* 'a holy war (huge oxymoron)' (from CORIS). This behavior allows to detect oxymorons which would probably be missed otherwise.

To test this method we searched the string [.*ossimor.*] in CORIS (retrieving 223 hits). Upon preliminary manual checking, we found a number of valid oxymorons. A few were already included in our list, like *tenebra luminosissima* 'very bright shadow' (cf. *tenebra luminosa* 'bright shadow' in the Appendix). Another few were examples, related to one of the antonymous pairs we considered (cf. Table 1), which were not retrieved by our method, like *boato di silenzio* 'roar of silence' (belonging to the *silenzio ~ rumore* 'silence ~ noise' pair).

Most cases, however, were completely new oxymorons. Some could have been ideally identified with our method based on antonymous pairs (e.g. *normalmente eccezionali* 'normally exceptional', *piangendo rido* 'I laugh crying', *caoticamente ordinate* 'chaotically tidy'), but many others turned out to be hardly foreseeable and heavily dependent on context and on the speaker's beliefs and communicative intentions. Take for instance: *A Cala del Faro, villaggio superchic di Porto Cervo, l'ultimo business è un ossimoro applicato al calcio: il ritiro mondano* 'In Cala del Faro, a superchic village at Porto Cervo, the last business is an oxymoron applied to football: the social training camp', where the writer emphasizes the contradiction in hosting a *ritiro* 'training camp' (lit. retirement) in such a voguish and social place like Porto Cervo. Or: *vi attendono minacciosi decine di ristoranti tibetani, praticamente un ossimoro* […] *non essendo propriamente gli altopiani tibetani un paradiso dell'enogastronomia* '[there] tens of threatening Tibetan restaurants are waiting for you, basically an oxymoron […] since Tibetan uplands are not exactly the paradise of food and wine', where the writer's bad opinion about Tibetan food and wine is ironically expressed.

Therefore, this method might be especially promising for identifying creative, highly contextual oxymorons. In this respect, social media platforms are definitely one of the sources to be used for this kind of research, which we leave for future studies.

5 Future challenges

This short paper illustrates the results of an investigation aimed at tracking down oxymoronic constructions in corpora of written Italian. Far from being exhaustive, this is just a preliminary attempt, resulting in an initial list of 376 oxymorons that needs to be enriched.

On the one hand, this enrichment may be pursued by adding more antonymous pairs under the current approach, which however heavily relies on manual work at various stages and would benefit from a higher degree of automation.

On the other hand, different methods should be devised and tested for the (we suspect) wide set of oxymorons that cannot be traced back to antonymous pairs. For instance, some oxymorons actually contain synonymous or even identical elements, within specific structures, such as *suoni senza suono* 'sounds without sound' (retrieved from itTenTen16). More interestingly, as Gibbs (1993: 269) observes, "oxymora are frequently found in everyday speech, many of them barely noticed as such, for example, 'intense apathy,' 'internal exile,' 'man child,' 'loyal opposition,' 'plastic glasses,' 'guest host,' and so on. The ubiquity of these figures suggests some underlying ability to conceive of ideas, objects, and events in oxymoronic terms." But – we add – it also suggests that the detection of these tropes is yet another challenge for automatic extraction, especially considering that some are heavily contextual.

Moreover, many oxymorons are "jocular", as Horn (2018) observes, mentioning cases such as *military intelligence, congressional ethics, airplane food* and *open secrets*. Given this, a deeper investigation of oxymorons looks even more desirable. Beside advancing our knowledge of figurative language in general, it would have clear benefits for other mainstream challenges in NLP, like the detection of humor, irony and sarcasm.

References

Walter Charles and George Miller. 1989. Contexts of antonymous adjectives. *Applied Psycholinguistics*, 10(3):357-375.

Reja'a M. Flayih. 2009. A linguistic study of oxymoron. *Journal of Kerbala University*, 7(3):30-40.

Raymond W. Gibbs, Jr. 1993. Process and products in making sense of tropes. In *Metaphor and Thought (2nd ed.)*, Andrew Ortony (ed.). Cambridge: Cambridge University Press, pages 252-276.

Raymond W. Gibbs, Jr. and Lydia R. Kearney. 1994. When parting is such sweet sorrow: The comprehension and appreciation of oxymora. *Journal of Psycholinguistic Research*, 23(1):75-89.

Laurence R. Horn. 2018. Contradiction. In *The Stanford Encyclopedia of Philosophy* (Winter 2018 Edition), Edward N. Zalta (ed.).

Steven Jones. 2002. *Antonymy: A Corpus-based Perspective*. London and New York: Routledge.

John S. Justeson and Slava M. Katz. 1991. Co-occurrences of antonymous adjectives and their contexts. *Computational Linguistics*, 17(1):1-19.

Nataša Kostić. 2017. Adjectival antonyms in discourse: A corpus study of scalar and complementary antonyms. *Folia Linguistica*, 51(3):587-610.

Anna Lobanova. 2012. *The Anatomy of Antonymy: A Corpus-driven Approach*. Groningen University PhD dissertation.

Francesca Masini. 2009. Phrasal lexemes, compounds and phrases: A constructionist perspective. *Word Structure*, 2(2):254-271.

Lynne M. Murphy. 2006. Antonyms as lexical constructions: Or, why paradigmatic construction is not an oxymoron. *Constructions*, SV1-8/2006.

Francesca Ramaglia. 2010. Aggettivi. In *Enciclopedia dell'Italiano*. Treccani.

Rema Rossini Favretti, Fabio Tamburini and Cristiana De Santis. 2002. CORIS/CODIS: A corpus of written Italian based on a defined and a dynamic model. In *A Rainbow of Corpora: Corpus Linguistics and the Languages of the World*, Andrew Wilson, P. Rayson and A. M. McEnery (eds.). Munich: Lincom-Europa, pages 27-38.

Ivan A. Sag, Timothy Baldwin, Francis Bond, Ann Copestake and Dan Flickinger .2002. Multiword expressions: A pain in the neck for NLP. In *Computational linguistics and intelligent text processing: Third International Conference: CICLing-2002* (LNCS 2276), Alexander Gelbukh (ed.). Berlin/Heidelberg: Springer, pages 1-15.

Yeshayahu Shen. 1987. On the structure and understanding of poetic oxymoron. *Poetics Today*, 8(1):105-122.

Raffaele Simone (ed.). 2010. *Grande Dizionario Analogico della Lingua Italiana (CD-ROM)*. Torino: UTET.

A Appendix: *Italian oxymorons 1.0*

This Appendix contains the lemmatized version of the 376 oxymorons we retrieved, ordered by "Antonymous pair" (the pairs appear in their English translation). As for sentential oxymorons displaying variants (cf. Section 3.3), we chose to report a single version as representative of all variants, for the sake of simplicity.

Italian oxymoron	English translation	Structure	Antonymous pair	Corpus
attiva passività	active passivity	A N	activity-passivity	itTenTen16
attivamente passivo	actively passive	Adv A	activity-passivity	itTenTen16
attività inattiva	inactive activity	N A	activity-passivity	itTenTen16
attività passiva	passive activity	N A	activity-passivity	CORIS + itTenTen16
passiva attività	passive activity	A N	activity-passivity	itTenTen16
passivamente attivo	passively active	Adv A	activity-passivity	itTenTen16
passività attiva	active passivity	N A	activity-passivity	CORIS + itTenTen16
coraggiosa paura	brave fear	A N	bravery-fear	itTenTen16
coraggiosamente pauroso	bravely scared	Adv A	bravery-fear	itTenTen16
coraggiosamente vigliacco	bravely coward	Adv A	bravery-fear	itTenTen16
coraggiosamente vile	bravely cowardly	Adv A	bravery-fear	itTenTen16
il coraggio della paura	the bravery of fear	N Prep N	bravery-fear	itTenTen16
paura impavida	fearless fear	N A	bravery-fear	CORIS
pauroso coraggio	fearful bravery	A N	bravery-fear	CORIS
vile coraggio	cowardly bravery	A N	bravery-fear	itTenTen16
distante prossimità	far proximity	A N	distance-proximity	itTenTen16
distante vicinanza	far closeness	A N	distance-proximity	itTenTen16
distanza vicina	near distance	N A	distance-proximity	itTenTen16
la distanza avvicina	distance brings (sth) closer	S	distance-proximity	itTenTen16
la lontananza avvicina	distance brings (sth) closer	S	distance-proximity	itTenTen16
la vicinanza allontana	proximity pulls (sth) away	S	distance-proximity	itTenTen16
lontana vicinanza	distant proximity	A N	distance-proximity	itTenTen16
lontanamente vicino	remotely close	Adv A	distance-proximity	itTenTen16
lontananza vicina	near distance	N A	distance-proximity	itTenTen16
prossimità distante	far proximity	N A	distance-proximity	itTenTen16
prossimità distanziante	distancing proximity	N A	distance-proximity	itTenTen16
prossimità lontana	far proximity	N A	distance-proximity	itTenTen16
prossimità remota	distant proximity	N A	distance-proximity	itTenTen16
remota prossimità	distant proximity	A N	distance-proximity	itTenTen16

Italian	English	POS	Category	Source
vicina distanza	near distance	A N	distance-proximity	CORIS + itTenTen16
vicina lontananza	near distance	A N	distance-proximity	itTenTen16
vicinanza distante	far proximity	N A	distance-proximity	itTenTen16
vicinanza lontana	distant proximity	N A	distance-proximity	itTenTen16
vicinanza remota	remote proximity	N A	distance-proximity	CORIS
il vuoto riempie	the void fills (sth) up	S	emptiness-fullness	CORIS + itTenTen16
pienamente svuotato	fully emptied	Adv A	emptiness-fullness	itTenTen16
pieno vuoto	full void	A N	emptiness-fullness	itTenTen16
vuoto colmo	full void	N A	emptiness-fullness	itTenTen16
vuoto pieno	full void	N A	emptiness-fullness	CORIS + itTenTen16
addolorata contentezza	sorrowful gladness	A N	happiness-unhappiness	itTenTen16
allegra depressione	merry depression	A N	happiness-unhappiness	itTenTen16
allegra disperazione	merry despair	A N	happiness-unhappiness	itTenTen16
allegra infelicità	merry unhappiness	A N	happiness-unhappiness	itTenTen16
allegra tristezza	merry sadness	A N	happiness-unhappiness	itTenTen16
allegramente depresso	cheerfully depressed	Adv A	happiness-unhappiness	itTenTen16
allegramente disperato	cheerfully desperate	Adv A	happiness-unhappiness	itTenTen16
allegramente triste	cheerfully sad	Adv A	happiness-unhappiness	itTenTen16
allegria disperata	desperate glee	N A	happiness-unhappiness	CORIS + itTenTen16
allegria scontenta	displeased glee	N A	happiness-unhappiness	itTenTen16
allegria triste	sad glee	N A	happiness-unhappiness	itTenTen16
cupa felicità	gloomy happiness	A N	happiness-unhappiness	CORIS + itTenTen16
disperata allegria	desperate glee	A N	happiness-unhappiness	CORIS + itTenTen16
disperata felicità	desperate happiness	A N	happiness-unhappiness	itTenTen16
disperata gioia	desperate joy	A N	happiness-unhappiness	itTenTen16
disperatamente allegro	desperately merry	Adv A	happiness-unhappiness	itTenTen16
disperatamente contento	desperately glad	Adv A	happiness-unhappiness	itTenTen16
disperatamente felice	desperately happy	Adv A	happiness-unhappiness	CORIS + itTenTen16
disperatamente gioioso	desperately joyful	Adv A	happiness-unhappiness	itTenTen16
disperazione allegra	merry despair	N A	happiness-unhappiness	itTenTen16
dolore gioioso	joyful pain	N A	happiness-unhappiness	itTenTen16
felice disperazione	happy despair	A N	happiness-unhappiness	itTenTen16
felice infelicità	happy unhappiness	A N	happiness-unhappiness	itTenTen16
felice tristezza	happy sadness	A N	happiness-unhappiness	itTenTen16
felicemente infelice	happily unhappy	Adv A	happiness-unhappiness	itTenTen16
felicemente triste	happily sad	Adv A	happiness-unhappiness	itTenTen16
felicità disperata	desperate happiness	N A	happiness-unhappiness	itTenTen16
felicità triste	sad happiness	N A	happiness-unhappiness	itTenTen16
gaia disperazione	cheerful despair	A N	happiness-unhappiness	itTenTen16
gaia tristezza	cheerful sadness	A N	happiness-unhappiness	itTenTen16
gaiamente infelice	gaily unhappy	Adv A	happiness-unhappiness	itTenTen16
gioia cupa	gloomy joy	N A	happiness-unhappiness	CORIS + itTenTen16
gioia disperata	desperate joy	N A	happiness-unhappiness	CORIS + itTenTen16
gioia sconsolata	sorrowful joy	N A	happiness-unhappiness	itTenTen16
gioia triste	sad joy	N A	happiness-unhappiness	CORIS + itTenTen16
gioiosa disperazione	joyful despair	A N	happiness-unhappiness	itTenTen16
gioiosa tristezza	joyful sadness	A N	happiness-unhappiness	itTenTen16
gioiosamente disperato	joyously desperate	Adv A	happiness-unhappiness	itTenTen16
infelice felicità	unhappy happiness	A N	happiness-unhappiness	CORIS + itTenTen16
l'allegria (lo) fa triste	cheerfulness makes (sb) sad	S	happiness-unhappiness	itTenTen16
la gioia è dolore	joy is pain	S	happiness-unhappiness	itTenTen16
la tristezza (lo) fa allegro	sadness makes (sb) merry	S	happiness-unhappiness	itTenTen16
sconsolata allegria	sorrowful cheerfulness	A N	happiness-unhappiness	itTenTen16
triste allegria	sad cheerfulness	A N	happiness-unhappiness	itTenTen16
triste contentezza	sad gladness	A N	happiness-unhappiness	itTenTen16
triste felicità	sad happiness	A N	happiness-unhappiness	itTenTen16
triste gaiezza	sad gaiety	A N	happiness-unhappiness	itTenTen16
triste gioia	sad joy	A N	happiness-unhappiness	itTenTen16
tristezza allegra	merry sadness	N A	happiness-unhappiness	itTenTen16
tristezza felice	happy sadness	N A	happiness-unhappiness	CORIS + itTenTen16
acqua ignea	igneous water	N A	hot-cold	itTenTen16
acquoso fuoco	watery fire	A N	hot-cold	itTenTen16
ardente ghiaccio	burning ice	A N	hot-cold	itTenTen16
ardente pioggia	blazing rain	A N	hot-cold	itTenTen16
calda freddezza	warm coldness	A N	hot-cold	itTenTen16
calda fresca	hot cold	A A	hot-cold	itTenTen16
calda neve	hot snow	A N	hot-cold	itTenTen16
caldo freddo	hot cold	A N	hot-cold	CORIS + itTenTen16
caldo fresco	cool hot	N A	hot-cold	itTenTen16
caldo gelido	gelid hot	N A	hot-cold	itTenTen16
caldo gelo	hot frost	A N	hot-cold	itTenTen16
caldo ghiaccio	hot ice	A N	hot-cold	itTenTen16
calore freddo	cold warmth	N A	hot-cold	CORIS + itTenTen16
calore gelido	icy warmth	N A	hot-cold	itTenTen16
calore ghiacciato	frozen warmth	N A	hot-cold	itTenTen16
calorosamente freddo	warmly cold	Adv A	hot-cold	itTenTen16
cocente freddo	searing cold	A N	hot-cold	itTenTen16
fiamma bagnata	wet flame	N A	hot-cold	itTenTen16
fiamma congelata	frozen flame	N A	hot-cold	itTenTen16
fiamma fredda	cold flame	N A	hot-cold	CORIS + itTenTen16
fiamma fresca	cool flame	N A	hot-cold	CORIS + itTenTen16
fiamma gelida	freezing flame	N A	hot-cold	itTenTen16
fiamma glaciale	glacial flame	N A	hot-cold	itTenTen16
fredda calda	cold hot	A A	hot-cold	itTenTen16
fredda fiamma	cold flame	A N	hot-cold	CORIS + itTenTen16
freddezza calda	warm coldness	N A	hot-cold	itTenTen16
freddo bollente	scalding cold	N A	hot-cold	itTenTen16
freddo calore	cold warmth	A N	hot-cold	itTenTen16
freddo caloroso	warm cold	N A	hot-cold	itTenTen16
freddo fuoco	cold fire	A N	hot-cold	CORIS + itTenTen16
freddo incandescente	searing cold	N A	hot-cold	itTenTen16
freddo torrido	scorching cold	N A	hot-cold	itTenTen16
fresca calura	cool heat	A N	hot-cold	itTenTen16
fresca fiamma	cool flame	A N	hot-cold	itTenTen16

Expression	Gloss	POS	Category	Corpus
fresco caldo	cool hot	A N	hot-cold	itTenTen16
fresco calore	cool warmth	A N	hot-cold	itTenTen16
fresco fuoco	cool fire	A N	hot-cold	itTenTen16
fuoco acquoso	watery fire	N A	hot-cold	CORIS + itTenTen16
fuoco algido	cold fire	N A	hot-cold	CORIS + itTenTen16
fuoco congelato	frozen fire	N A	hot-cold	itTenTen16
fuoco freddo	cold fire	N A	hot-cold	CORIS + itTenTen16
fuoco fresco	cool fire	N A	hot-cold	itTenTen16
fuoco gelato	frozen fire	N A	hot-cold	itTenTen16
fuoco gelido	icy fire	N A	hot-cold	CORIS + itTenTen16
fuoco ghiacciato	icy fire	N A	hot-cold	itTenTen16
gelida fiamma	freezing flame	A N	hot-cold	itTenTen16
gelido caldo	gelid hot	A A	hot-cold	itTenTen16
gelido calore	icy warmth	A N	hot-cold	itTenTen16
gelido fuoco	icy fire	A N	hot-cold	CORIS + itTenTen16
gelo ardente	burning frost	N A	hot-cold	itTenTen16
gelo bruciante	burning frost	N A	hot-cold	itTenTen16
ghiaccio acceso	burning ice	N A	hot-cold	itTenTen16
ghiaccio ardente	burning ice	N A	hot-cold	itTenTen16
ghiaccio bollente	steaming ice	N A	hot-cold	CORIS + itTenTen16
ghiaccio caldo	hot ice	N A	hot-cold	CORIS + itTenTen16
ghiaccio cocente	searing ice	N A	hot-cold	itTenTen16
ghiaccio fiammeggiante	flaming ice	N A	hot-cold	itTenTen16
ghiaccio incandescente	incandescent ice	N A	hot-cold	itTenTen16
ghiaccio infuocato	inflamed ice	N A	hot-cold	itTenTen16
ghiaccio rovente	scorching ice	N A	hot-cold	itTenTen16
glaciale calore	glacial warmth	A N	hot-cold	itTenTen16
glaciale fiamma	glacial flame	A N	hot-cold	itTenTen16
grandine incandescente	incandescent hail	N A	hot-cold	itTenTen16
grandine rovente	scorching hail	N A	hot-cold	itTenTen16
il fuoco bagna	fire wets (sth)	S	hot-cold	CORIS + itTenTen16
il fuoco raffredda	fire chills (sth)	S	hot-cold	itTenTen16
il gelo infiamma	frost sets fire	S	hot-cold	itTenTen16
il ghiaccio brucia	ice burns	S	hot-cold	itTenTen16
infuocato gelo	inflamed frost	A N	hot-cold	itTenTen16
infuocato ghiaccio	inflamed ice	A N	hot-cold	itTenTen16
la fiamma bagna	flame wets	S	hot-cold	itTenTen16
la fiamma gela	flame freezes	S	hot-cold	itTenTen16
la neve brucia	the snow burns	S	hot-cold	itTenTen16
la pioggia infiamma	the rain sets fire	S	hot-cold	itTenTen16
neve ardente	burning snow	N A	hot-cold	CORIS + itTenTen16
neve bollente	steaming snow	N A	hot-cold	itTenTen16
neve calda	hot snow	N A	hot-cold	itTenTen16
neve incandescente	incandescent snow	N A	hot-cold	itTenTen16
neve infuocata	inflamed snow	N A	hot-cold	itTenTen16
pioggia ardente	blazing rain	N A	hot-cold	itTenTen16
pioggia bollente	steaming rain	N A	hot-cold	itTenTen16
pioggia bruciante	burning rain	N A	hot-cold	itTenTen16
pioggia incandescente	incandescent rain	N A	hot-cold	itTenTen16
pioggia infiammata	burning rain	N A	hot-cold	itTenTen16
pioggia infuocata	inflamed rain	N A	hot-cold	CORIS + itTenTen16
pioggia rovente	scorching rain	N A	hot-cold	itTenTen16
rovente ghiaccio	scorching ice	A N	hot-cold	itTenTen16
giusta ingiustizia	just injustice	A N	justice-injustice	itTenTen16
giustamente ingiusto	justly unjust	Adv A	justice-injustice	itTenTen16
giustizia ingiusta	unjust justice	N A	justice-injustice	CORIS + itTenTen16
ingiusta giustizia	unjust justice	A N	justice-injustice	CORIS + itTenTen16
ingiustizia giusta	just unjustice	N A	justice-injustice	itTenTen16
l'ingiustizia della giustizia	the injustice of justice	N Prep N	justice-injustice	itTenTen16
la morte è vita	death is life	S	life-death	itTenTen16
la morte vive	death lives	S	life-death	itTenTen16
la vita è morte	life is death	S	life-death	itTenTen16
mortalmente vivo	mortally alive	Adv A	life-death	itTenTen16
morte vitale	vital death	N A	life-death	itTenTen16
morte viva	living death	N A	life-death	CORIS + itTenTen16
morte vivente	living death	N A	life-death	CORIS + itTenTen16
morto vivente	living dead	N A	life-death	CORIS + itTenTen16
morto vivo	living dead	N A	life-death	CORIS + itTenTen16
vita morta	dead life	N A	life-death	itTenTen16
vitale morte	vital death	A N	life-death	itTenTen16
viva morte	living death	A N	life-death	CORIS + itTenTen16
vivente morte	living death	A N	life-death	itTenTen16
buia luce	dark light	A N	light-dark	CORIS + itTenTen16
buio chiarore	dark gleam	A N	light-dark	itTenTen16
buio lucente	shining dark	N A	light-dark	itTenTen16
buio luminoso	bright dark	N A	light-dark	CORIS + itTenTen16
chiaramente (o)scuro	brightly dark	Adv A	light-dark	itTenTen16
chiaramente buio	clearly dark	Adv A	light-dark	itTenTen16
chiarore scuro	dark gleam	N A	light-dark	itTenTen16
il buio è luce	dark is light	S	light-dark	itTenTen16
il buio illumina	the dark illuminates (sth)	S	light-dark	itTenTen16
l'oscurità della luce	the darkness of the light	N Prep N	light-dark	itTenTen16
l'oscurità illumina	darkness illuminates (sth)	S	light-dark	itTenTen16
la luce è ombra	light is shadow	S	light-dark	itTenTen16
la luce è tenebra	light is darkness	S	light-dark	itTenTen16
la luce oscura	light darkens (sth)	S	light-dark	itTenTen16
la tenebra della luce	darkness of the light	N Prep N	light-dark	itTenTen16
la tenebra è luce	darkness is light	S	light-dark	itTenTen16
luce (o)scura	obscure light	N A	light-dark	CORIS + itTenTen16
luce buia	dark light	N A	light-dark	CORIS + itTenTen16
luce oscurante	darkening light	N A	light-dark	itTenTen16
luce tenebrosa	gloomy light	N A	light-dark	itTenTen16
luminosa oscurità	bright darkness	A N	light-dark	itTenTen16
luminosa tenebra	bright shadow	A N	light-dark	itTenTen16
luminosamente oscuro	brightly dark	Adv A	light-dark	itTenTen16
oscuramente chiaro	darkly clear	Adv A	light-dark	itTenTen16
oscuramente luminoso	darkly bright	Adv A	light-dark	itTenTen16
oscurità lucente	glossy darkness	N A	light-dark	itTenTen16
oscurità luminosa	bright darkness	N A	light-dark	itTenTen16
raggiante oscurità	glowing darkness	A N	light-dark	itTenTen16

Italian	English	Type	Category	Source
tenebra lucente	glossy shadow	N A	light-dark	itTenTen16
tenebra luminosa	bright shadow	N A	light-dark	CORIS + itTenTen16
leggerezza pesante	heavy lightness	N A	lightness-heaviness	CORIS + itTenTen16
leggermente pesante	lightly heavy	Adv A	lightness-heaviness	CORIS + itTenTen16
pesante leggerezza	heavy lightness	A N	lightness-heaviness	CORIS + itTenTen16
amore odiato	hated love	N A	love-hate	itTenTen16
amore odioso	hateful love	N A	love-hate	itTenTen16
amorevole odio	loving hate	A N	love-hate	itTenTen16
amorevolmente odioso	lovely hateful	Adv A	love-hate	itTenTen16
detestabile amore	awful love	A N	love-hate	CORIS
l'amore detesta	love despises	S	love-hate	itTenTen16
l'amore è odio	love is hate	S	love-hate	itTenTen16
l'amore odia	love hates	S	love-hate	itTenTen16
l'odio dell'amore	the hatred of love	N Prep N	love-hate	itTenTen16
l'odio è amore	hate is love	S	love-hate	itTenTen16
odiato amore	hated love	A N	love-hate	itTenTen16
odio amar(ti/lo)	I hate to love you/it	S	love-hate	itTenTen16
odio amorevole	loving hate	N A	love-hate	itTenTen16
odio amoroso	loving love	N A	love-hate	CORIS + itTenTen16
odiosamente amabile	hatefully lovely	Adv A	love-hate	itTenTen16
odioso amore	hateful love	A N	love-hate	itTenTen16
ti amo, odio mio	I love you, my hate	S	love-hate	itTenTen16
ti odio, amore mio	I hate you, my love	S	love-hate	itTenTen16
irreale realtà	unreal reality	A N	reality-unreality	CORIS + itTenTen16
irrealmente reale	unreally real	Adv A	reality-unreality	itTenTen16
irrealtà reale	real unreality	N A	reality-unreality	itTenTen16
la finzione è realtà	pretence is reality	S	reality-unreality	itTenTen16
la irrealtà della realtà	the unreality of reality	N Prep N	reality-unreality	itTenTen16
la realtà è finzione	reality is pretence	S	reality-unreality	itTenTen16
la realtà è illusione	reality is an illusion	S	reality-unreality	itTenTen16
la realtà è sogno	reality is a dream	S	reality-unreality	itTenTen16
reale irrealtà	real unreality	A N	reality-unreality	itTenTen16
realmente irreale	really unreal	Adv A	reality-unreality	itTenTen16
realtà irreale	unreal reality	N A	reality-unreality	CORIS + itTenTen16
assordante silenzio	deafening silence	A N	silence-noise	CORIS + itTenTen16
bisbigliante silenzio	whispering silence	A N	silence-noise	itTenTen16
boato muto	mute thunder	N A	silence-noise	itTenTen16
eloquente silenzio	eloquent silence	A N	silence-noise	CORIS + itTenTen16
eloquentemente muto	eloquently mute	Adv A	silence-noise	itTenTen16
eloquentemente silenzioso	eloquently quiet	Adv A	silence-noise	CORIS + itTenTen16
fragore muto	mute racket	N A	silence-noise	itTenTen16
fragore silenzioso	hushed racket	N A	silence-noise	itTenTen16
fragorosamente silente	loudly silent	Adv A	silence-noise	itTenTen16
fragorosamente silenzioso	loudly quiet	Adv A	silence-noise	CORIS + itTenTen16
fragoroso silenzio	loud silence	A N	silence-noise	CORIS + itTenTen16
gridare silenzi	to shout silences	S	silence-noise	itTenTen16
gridare tacendo	to shout being silent	V V	silence-noise	itTenTen16
grido muto	mute shout	N A	silence-noise	CORIS + itTenTen16
grido silente	silent shout	N A	silence-noise	itTenTen16
grido silenzioso	quiet shout	N A	silence-noise	CORIS + itTenTen16
grido taciuto	silenced shout	N A	silence-noise	itTenTen16
il fragore del silenzio	the racket of silence	N Prep N	silence-noise	itTenTen16
il grido del silenzio	the shout of silence	N Prep N	silence-noise	itTenTen16
il rumore del silenzio	the noise of silence	N Prep N	silence-noise	itTenTen16
il silenzio del rumore	the silence of noise	N Prep N	silence-noise	itTenTen16
il silenzio è rumore	silence is noise	S	silence-noise	itTenTen16
il silenzio è un grido	silence is a cry	S	silence-noise	itTenTen16
il silenzio è un urlo	silence is a shout	S	silence-noise	itTenTen16
il silenzio è una voce	silence is a voice	S	silence-noise	itTenTen16
il silenzio grida	silence screams	S	silence-noise	CORIS + itTenTen16
il silenzio mormora	silence whispers	S	silence-noise	itTenTen16
il silenzio nel rumore	the silence into the noise	N Prep N	silence-noise	itTenTen16
il silenzio parla	silence speaks	S	silence-noise	itTenTen16
il silenzio rimbomba	silence roars	S	silence-noise	itTenTen16
il silenzio risuona	silence resounds	S	silence-noise	itTenTen16
il silenzio urla	silence cries	S	silence-noise	itTenTen16
il suono del silenzio	the sound of silence	N Prep N	silence-noise	itTenTen16
l'urlo di/del silenzio	the scream of silence	N Prep N	silence-noise	itTenTen16
mormorante silenzio	murmuring silence	A N	silence-noise	itTenTen16
mutamente eloquente	dumbly eloquent	Adv A	silence-noise	itTenTen16
muto fragore	mute racket	A N	silence-noise	itTenTen16
muto grido	mute shout	A N	silence-noise	CORIS + itTenTen16
muto suono	mute sound	A N	silence-noise	CORIS + itTenTen16
muto ululato	mute howling	A N	silence-noise	itTenTen16
muto urlo	mute cry	A N	silence-noise	itTenTen16
rumore muto	mute noise	N A	silence-noise	CORIS + itTenTen16
rumore silenzioso	quiet noise	N A	silence-noise	itTenTen16
rumore taciuto	silenced noise	N A	silence-noise	itTenTen16
rumorosamente silenzioso	noisily quiet	Adv A	silence-noise	itTenTen16
rumorosamente zitto	noisily mute	Adv A	silence-noise	itTenTen16
rumoroso silenzio	loud silence	A N	silence-noise	CORIS + itTenTen16
silenzio assordante	deafening silence	N A	silence-noise	CORIS + itTenTen16
silenzio bisbigliante	whispering silence	N A	silence-noise	itTenTen16
silenzio eloquente	eloquent silence	N A	silence-noise	CORIS + itTenTen16
silenzio fragoroso	loud silence	N A	silence-noise	CORIS + itTenTen16
silenzio gridato	shouted silence	N A	silence-noise	itTenTen16
silenzio mormorato	murmured silence	N A	silence-noise	itTenTen16
silenzio parlato	spoken silence	N A	silence-noise	itTenTen16
silenzio rumoroso	noisy silence	N A	silence-noise	itTenTen16
silenzio sonoro	resounding silence	N A	silence-noise	itTenTen16
silenzio urlante	screaming silence	N A	silence-noise	itTenTen16
silenzio urlato	screamed silence	N A	silence-noise	CORIS + itTenTen16
silenziosamente assordante	quietly deafening	Adv A	silence-noise	itTenTen16
silenziosamente eloquente	quietly eloquent	Adv A	silence-noise	itTenTen16
silenziosamente rumoroso	quietly noisy	Adv A	silence-noise	itTenTen16

silenzioso fracasso	silent racket	A N	silence-noise	itTenTen16
silenzioso fragore	silent racket	A N	silence-noise	itTenTen16
silenzioso grido	silent shout	A N	silence-noise	CORIS + itTenTen16
silenzioso rumore	silent noise	A N	silence-noise	itTenTen16
silenzioso suono	silent sound	A N	silence-noise	itTenTen16
silenzioso urlo	silent scream	A N	silence-noise	itTenTen16
suono muto	mute sound	N A	silence-noise	itTenTen16
suono silenzioso	silent sound	N A	silence-noise	itTenTen16
suono tacito	tacit sound	N A	silence-noise	itTenTen16
sussurro muto	mute whisper	N A	silence-noise	itTenTen16
tacitamente eloquente	tacitly eloquent	Adv A	silence-noise	itTenTen16
tacito grido	tacit shout	A N	silence-noise	itTenTen16
tacito suono	tacit sound	A N	silence-noise	itTenTen16
taciuto urlo	tacit scream	A N	silence-noise	itTenTen16
urlante silenzio	screaming silence	A N	silence-noise	itTenTen16
urlare (stando) muto	to scream (staying) mute	V A	silence-noise	itTenTen16
urlare (stando) silenzioso	to scream (staying) quiet	V A	silence-noise	itTenTen16
urlare in silenzio	to scream in silence	V Prep N	silence-noise	itTenTen16
urlare tacendo	to scream being silent	V V	silence-noise	itTenTen16
urlato silenzio	screamed silence	A N	silence-noise	itTenTen16
urlo muto	mute scream	N A	silence-noise	CORIS + itTenTen16
urlo silente	silent scream	N A	silence-noise	itTenTen16
urlo silenzioso	quiet scream	N A	silence-noise	CORIS + itTenTen16
voce muta	mute voice	N A	silence-noise	itTenTen16
calma veloce	quick calm	N A	slowness-speed	itTenTen16
lenta celerità	slow speed	A N	slowness-speed	itTenTen16
lenta rapidità	slow rush	A N	slowness-speed	itTenTen16
lentamente veloce	slowly fast	Adv A	slowness-speed	itTenTen16
lentezza rapida	fast slowness	N A	slowness-speed	CORIS
rapida lentezza	speedy slowness	A N	slowness-speed	itTenTen16
veloce calma	quick calm	A N	slowness-speed	itTenTen16
veloce lentezza	fast slowness	A N	slowness-speed	itTenTen16
velocemente lento	quickly slow	Adv A	slowness-speed	itTenTen16
acre dolcezza	acrid sweetness	A N	sweetness-bitterness	itTenTen16
amara dolcezza	bitter sweetness	A N	sweetness-bitterness	CORIS + itTenTen16
amaramente dolce	bitterly sweet	Adv A	sweetness-bitterness	itTenTen16
aspra dolcezza	sour sweetness	A N	sweetness-bitterness	itTenTen16
dolce amarezza	sweet bitterness	A N	sweetness-bitterness	CORIS + itTenTen16
dolcemente acido	sweetly acid	Adv A	sweetness-bitterness	itTenTen16
dolcemente amaro	sweetly bitter	Adv A	sweetness-bitterness	itTenTen16
dolcemente aspro	sweetly sour	Adv A	sweetness-bitterness	itTenTen16
dolcezza amara	bitter sweetness	N A	sweetness-bitterness	CORIS + itTenTen16
dolcezza aspra	sour sweetness	N A	sweetness-bitterness	itTenTen16
guerra pacifica	peaceful war	N A	war-peace	CORIS + itTenTen16
inoffensiva guerra	harmless war	A N	war-peace	itTenTen16
la guerra è pace	war is peace	S	war-peace	itTenTen16
la pace è guerra	peace is war	S	war-peace	itTenTen16
pacifica guerra	peaceful war	A N	war-peace	itTenTen16

la povertà arricchisce	poverty enriches	S	wealth-poverty	itTenTen16
la povertà è ricchezza	poverty is wealth	S	wealth-poverty	itTenTen16
la ricchezza della povertà	the wealth of poverty	N Prep N	wealth-poverty	itTenTen16
la ricchezza impoverisce	wealth impoverishes	S	wealth-poverty	itTenTen16
povera ricchezza	poor wealth	A N	wealth-poverty	CORIS + itTenTen16
poveramente ricco	poorly rich	Adv A	wealth-poverty	itTenTen16
povertà ricca	rich poverty	N A	wealth-poverty	itTenTen16
ricca povertà	rich poverty	A N	wealth-poverty	itTenTen16
riccamente povero	richly poor	Adv A	wealth-poverty	itTenTen16
ricchezza povera	poor wealth	N A	wealth-poverty	itTenTen16

Can Humor Prediction Datasets be used for Humor Generation?
Humorous Headline Generation via Style Transfer

Orion Weller
Brigham Young University
orionw@byu.edu

Nancy Fulda
Brigham Young University
nfulda@byu.edu

Kevin Seppi
Brigham Young University
kseppi@byu.edu

Abstract

Understanding and identifying humor has been increasingly popular, as seen by the number of datasets created to study humor. However, one area of humor research, humor generation, has remained a difficult task, with machine generated jokes failing to match human-created humor. As many humor prediction datasets claim to aid in generative tasks, we examine whether these claims are true. We focus our experiments on the most popular dataset, included in the 2020 SemEval's Task 7, and teach our model to take normal text and "translate" it into humorous text. We evaluate our model compared to humorous human generated headlines, finding that our model is preferred equally in A/B testing with the human edited versions, a strong success for humor generation, and is preferred over an intelligent random baseline 72% of the time. We also show that our model is assumed to be human written comparable with that of the human edited headlines and is significantly better than random, indicating that this dataset does indeed provide potential for future humor generation systems.

1 Introduction

Understanding and identifying humor has long been a goal for natural language understanding systems (Taylor and Mazlack, 2004; Hempelmann, 2008; Purandare and Litman, 2006; Mihalcea and Strapparava, 2005), with many attempts seeking to identify whether a sentence is a joke. These systems have seen impressive gains in recent years (Yang et al., 2015; Chen and Soo, 2018), with systems achieving scores in the mid 90's. As such, other areas of humor research have grown in popularity, including distinguishing between jokes (Weller and Seppi, 2019) and generating humorous text (He et al., 2019; Luo et al., 2019).

This rise in popularity has even translated to a SemEval task of predicting the level of humor in text (Hossain et al., 2019). In their work, as well as others (Mihalcea and Strapparava, 2005; Weller and Seppi, 2019) that seek to understand various aspects of humor, the authors note that their work may be influential in helping create systems that can automatically generate humor. To the best of our knowledge, however, no work has attempted to explore whether these humor prediction datasets encode information that can be used by a generative system. Instead current systems rely on retrieve-and-edit models (He et al., 2019) or models based on word senses (Luo et al., 2019).

The recent works of Hossain et al. (2019, 2020b) have created pairs of minimal changes that turn a regular news sentence into a humorous news sentence, by only changing one phrase. Because of its popularity and impact, as well as the clear insight that can be gained from minimal pair datasets (Kaushik et al., 2019; Gardner et al., 2020), we choose to examine the former as an initial exploration of what can be done. Our contributions include:

- Proposing the first model for humor style transfer, building a transformer model that "translates" from regular to humorous English[1]

- Examining whether the format of popular humor prediction datasets can be used to successfully generate humorous text. We explore this through a crowdsourced human evaluation, showing that our system performs equally to human edits (a difficult challenge for abstractive generative humor systems) as well as showing that our model provides more than random effects

---

[1] We publicly release our code and models at https://github.com/orionw/humorTranslate

Proceedings of the Second Workshop on Figurative Language Processing, pages 186–191
July 9, 2020. ©2020 Association for Computational Linguistics
https://doi.org/10.18653/v1/P17

Original Headline	Humorous Edit
Meet the wealthy **donors** pouring millions into the 2018 elections	Meet the wealthy **sadists** pouring millions into the 2018 elections
Trump has the upper hand in North Korea **talks**	Trump has the upper hand in North Korea **handshakes**
Manhattan DA reportedly dropped felony fraud case against Trump's kids after donation from Trump's **lawyer**	Manhattan DA reportedly dropped felony fraud case against Trump's kids after donation from Trump's **doppleganger**

Table 1: Example instances of the Humicroedit dataset, containing the original headline and a humorous edited version. Edited phrase is in bold. Note that the edited headlines are designed to be humorous in light of the original.

2 Related Work

Many humor datasets have been created in order to explore humor in different circumstances. These datasets include diverse domains such as puns (Yang et al., 2015), TV shows (Purandare and Litman, 2006), Ted Talks (Chen and Soo, 2018), and online forums (Weller and Seppi, 2019, 2020). Humor prediction has even been included in this year's SemEval Task 7 (Hossain et al., 2020a) with humorous data created by online crowdsourcers who modified news headlines. Concurrent to our work, Hossain et al. (2020b) generate additional crowd-sourced data through interactive online games.

In the humor generation area, previous approaches have relied strongly on templated approaches for specific types of puns or jokes (Ritchie, 2005; Binsted et al., 1997; Binsted, 1996), such as "I like my coffee like I like my [insert phrase here]." Others have used templates based on word similarity or uncommonness to generate humorous samples (Petrović and Matthews, 2013; Valitutti et al., 2016). Recent work has started to break off from the template trend, creating abstractive models such as an RNN that creates puns (Yu et al., 2018), a retrieve-and-edit model that adds surprise to create jokes (He et al., 2019), and a Pun GAN with a word-sense disambiguater as a discriminator (Luo et al., 2019). However, none of these models employ a humorous corpus to generate their jokes, leading to the question: are they useful for models attempting to generate humor?

Our work also utilizes methods from stylized text generation (Fu et al., 2018), where work has shown success with parallel data (Zhang et al., 2018; Dai et al., 2019) as well as dealing with the lack of such data (Prabhumoye et al., 2018; Shen et al., 2017). These methods, recently employing transformer models proposed by Vaswani et al. (2017), have also been applied to formality of language (Etinger

and Black, 2019) and sarcasm (Mishra et al., 2019). However, to the best of our knowledge we are the first to use style transfer for humor generation.

3 Experimental Setup

Dataset. In order to explore the utility of recently published humor corpora, we use the Humicroedit dataset created by Hossain et al. and used in the 2020 SemEval Task 7, containing more than 15,000 humorous headlines. These headlines were generated by taking a dataset of normal headlines and asking crowdsourced workers to make humorous edits. They specifically limited the workers to a single edit, where an edit was defined as the insertion of a single-word noun or verb to replace an existing entity or single-word noun or verb. Although our system will not enforce such strict edits, we use this data as a training set because of its popularity and its parallel corpus of minimal edits.

This dataset further assumes that the reader is aware of the original headline (from already popular news, for example), so that the additional word play in the edits will be humorous in light of the original headlines and topic (example instances are shown in Table 1). We note that the original Humicroedit dataset contains humor ratings for each crowdsourced edited headline: however, due to the scarcity of training data we include all headlines regardless of the humor level rating, as each edited headline was a human generated attempt at humor. In order to provide a fair training/test split, we remove all instances from the dataset which contain the same original headline, in order to prevent data leakage. We then divide the data into an 80/20 train test split, with 9000 and 2300 instances.

Model[2]. We build our model similarly to the trans-

---

[2]We do not report results from pre-trained models (i.e. BERT (Devlin et al., 2018), GPT-2 (Radford et al., 2019)) as we want to explore the effects of the HumicroEdit dataset apart from the effects of pre-training.

Original	President Trumps Golden Age of Trolling
Edited	President Trumps **Infinite** of Trolling
Random	President **Big Spenders Accentuation** Age of Trolling
Translated	President Trumps Golden Age of **Sassy** Trolling
Original	How CBS News reported the last national military parade in 1991
Edited	How CBS News reported the last national military **buffet** in 1991
Random	How **Ides Hemophiliac** reported the last national military parade in 1991
Translated	How CBS News **choreographed** the last national military parade in 1991
Original	Trump lawyers scramble to prepare for new stage of Russia probe
Edited	Trump lawyers scramble to prepare for new stage of **dog** probe
Random	Trump lawyers scramble to prepare for new **bailey** of Russia probe
Translated	Trump lawyers scramble to prepare for new **eggs** of Russia probe

Table 2: Example instances of all three systems: the human edited headlines, random edits, and our translated edits. Edited replacements of the original headline are in bold.

A/B Test	Ours	Other
Translated vs Edited	24	26
Translated vs Random	36*	14

Table 3: Results from A/B testing. * indicates statistical significance from a one sample test of proportions

former initially described in Vaswani et al. (2017), using an encoder-decoder architecture with eight attention heads and two layers in both encoder and decoder. We trained on the training set for 200 epochs and manually inspected checkpoint samples from the training data along the way. We chose the best performing model from the checkpoints to generate the samples for our evaluation.

Baseline. To show the effectiveness of our model on the data, we use a baseline that would generate similar surprisal effects in headline edits. We recognize the capacity of the human mind to make connections when there are none, thus, we want a baseline that randomly replaces words in a sentence and relies on that connective ability. However, a purely random model would be too naive, creating headlines that are ungrammatical and unintelligible. Thus, we create an intelligent random model that probabilistically replaces specific parts of speech with other words in that same part of speech, capitalizing the replacement phrase if the original was capitalized. We randomly replace nouns, noun-phrases, verbs, and adjectives, in order to replicate human edits in the original dataset.

4 Experiments

We use the test set described in Section 3, consisting of over 2k instances. In order to show a comprehensive view of our model, we compare the human and random edits with our translated samples. For convenience in writing, we term these models *edited*, *random*, and *translated*. We label the original non-humorous headlines, *original*. Example instances of each humor system are displayed in Table 2. We attempt to provide instances showing both positive and negative aspects of the human edited and random models. Samples examining limitations of our translation model are shown in Table 4.

We perform three experiments: a rating task, and two A/B tests between our model and the other systems. For each experiment we randomly sample 50 instances from the test set and employ users from Amazon's Mechanical Turk for feedback. We randomize the order of appearance for each trial of the A/B tests, so that order preference is controlled. We present the instances to the user and ask them "Which one of the following changes to this headline is more humorous," giving them the original headline for comparison. We limit each respondent to 5 annotations in order to avoid annotator burnout. The rating tasks are given by displaying an instance to the user and asking them to rate the headline on a 1-5 scale for fluency of language and level of humor. We then ask the user whether or not they think the headline is human generated. Our final score for both A/B tests and rating tasks consist of the average (or mode) of three annotators.

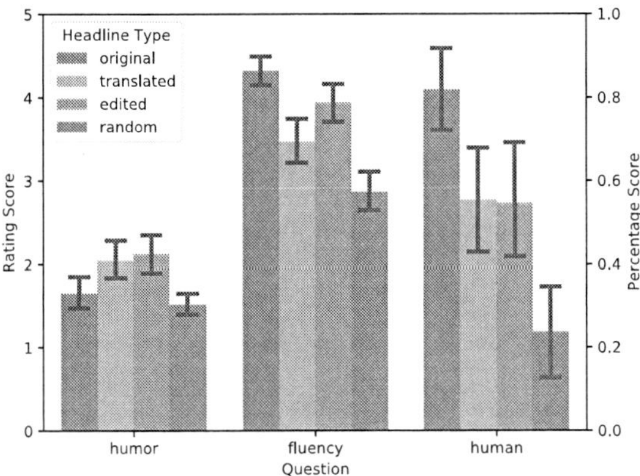

Figure 1: Results from human evaluation of headline humor, fluency, and proportion of whether or not they think it is human generated. Results are gathered from Mechanical Turk. Error bars indicate two standard errors from the mean.

5   Results

We see the results of the experiments in Table 3 and Figure 1. On the A/B tests, the human edited version of the original headline was preferred to the translated version 26 to 24 times, or 52% of the time. However, our system was preferred to the intelligent random baseline 36 times to 14, or 72% of the time. To determine significance, we conduct one-sample hypothesis tests ($\alpha = 0.05$), finding that our model is statistically significant compared to the random model, but not statistically different than the human edited version. Although this may not seem like a positive result at first glance, matching human performance on humor tasks is difficult to accomplish.

When we examine each headline in isolation, we find that the unedited human headlines are ranked significantly higher than all three systems in sentence fluency and proportion of users that thought the headline was human generated. This is to be expected, as humor does not always follow standard grammar rules. In the humor category, we see that the original headline ranked below the human edited and translated versions, also as expected. The random model performed significantly below all others in almost every task, indicating that the human edited and translated headlines contained elements that were more than random associations. We further see that the translated system performed statistically similar to the human edited version on all questions.

Example 1:	Repeats
Original:	Couple who rented condo to Pruitt pays fine to D.C.
Edit:	Couple who wore wizard to Pruitt pays to D.C. D.C. D.C.
Example 2:	Not Humorous
Original:	China says to ban some petroleum exports to North Korea
Edit:	China says to ban some 2005 to North Korea
Example 3:	No Change
Original:	California to sue Trump administration for repeal of fracking rules
Edit:	California to sue Trump administration for repeal of fracking rules

Table 4: Examples of poor performing samples from the humor translation model

We see instances in Table 4 where the translation system failed to generate a humorous edit. We observed the following categories of failure in the model: failure to change the sentence, repeated words, and non-humorous edits. From a manual inspection of a random sample of 100 instances, these errors occurred less than 5% of the time.

We see that despite the above mentioned limitations, our humor translation model matches the performance of human generated edits. As humor is a a linguistic phenomenon that depends upon the human receiving it to appreciate the humor, it is difficult to generate humor that is better than human generated content. However, our results indicate that the HumicroEdit dataset of pairs combined with our translation model is able to provide creative ways of reformulating headlines. As this work is exploratory and non-exhaustive, this gives a positive signal that the communities' efforts in humor collection have strong potential for further advances in humor generation.

6   Conclusion

In this work, we explored whether humor prediction data, such as the HumicroEdit dataset from SemEval Task 7, could be used to generate humor, examining whether this humor provides more than random surprisal effects. We use these human edited headlines as training for a machine translation system that automatically "translates" normal headlines into humor. We then build a intelligent random system as a baseline, showing that our generative headlines are significantly better than random effects, illustrating that our results are due to more than spurious correlations. We further find that our system's humorous headlines are preferred equally with those of the human generated edits, with equal proportions of crowdsourcers thinking these headlines are human generated and humorous. As this initial positive result shows that a humor prediction dataset can be used successfully for generating humor, we hope that future generative systems for humor will consider utilizing and improving from such resources.

References

Kim Binsted. 1996. Machine humour: An implemented model of puns.

Kim Binsted, Helen Pain, and Graeme D Ritchie. 1997. Children's evaluation of computer-generated punning riddles. *Pragmatics & Cognition*, 5(2):305–354.

Peng-Yu Chen and Von-Wun Soo. 2018. Humor recognition using deep learning. *Proceedings of the 2018 Conference of the North American Chapter of the Association for Computational Linguistics: Human Language Technologies, Volume 2 (Short Papers)*.

Ning Dai, Jianze Liang, Xipeng Qiu, and Xuanjing Huang. 2019. Style transformer: Unpaired text style transfer without disentangled latent representation. *arXiv preprint arXiv:1905.05621*.

Jacob Devlin, Ming-Wei Chang, Kenton Lee, and Kristina Toutanova. 2018. BERT: Pre-training of Deep Bidirectional Transformers for Language Understanding. *North American Chapter of the Association for Computational Linguistics*.

Isak Czeresnia Etinger and Alan W Black. 2019. Formality style transfer for noisy, user-generated conversations: Extracting labeled, parallel data from unlabeled corpora. In *Proceedings of the 5th Workshop on Noisy User-generated Text (W-NUT 2019)*, pages 11–16.

Zhenxin Fu, Xiaoye Tan, Nanyun Peng, Dongyan Zhao, and Rui Yan. 2018. Style transfer in text: Exploration and evaluation. In *Thirty-Second AAAI Conference on Artificial Intelligence*.

Matt Gardner, Yoav Artzi, Victoria Basmova, Jonathan Berant, Ben Bogin, Sihao Chen, Pradeep Dasigi, Dheeru Dua, Yanai Elazar, Ananth Gottumukkala, Nitish Gupta, Hanna Hajishirzi, Gabriel Ilharco, Daniel Khashabi, Kevin Lin, Jiangming Liu, Nelson F. Liu, Phoebe Mulcaire, Qiang Ning, Sameer Singh, Noah A. Smith, Sanjay Subramanian, Reut Tsarfaty, Eric Wallace, Ally Quan Zhang, and Ben Zhou. 2020. Evaluating nlp models via contrast sets. *ArXiv*, abs/2004.02709.

He He, Nanyun Peng, and Percy Liang. 2019. Pun generation with surprise. In *North American Association for Computational Linguistics (NAACL)*.

Christian F Hempelmann. 2008. Computational humor: Beyond the pun? *The Primer of Humor Research. Humor Research*, 8:333–360.

Nabil Hossain, John Krumm, and Michael Gamon. 2019. " president vows to cut¡ taxes¿ hair": Dataset and analysis of creative text editing for humorous headlines. *arXiv preprint arXiv:1906.00274*.

Nabil Hossain, John Krumm, Michael Gamon, and Henry Kautz. 2020a. Semeval-2020 Task 7: Assessing humor in edited news headlines. In *Proceedings of International Workshop on Semantic Evaluation (SemEval-2020)*, Barcelona, Spain.

Nabil Hossain, John Krumm, Tanvir Sajed, and Henry Kautz. 2020b. Stimulating creativity with funlines: A case study of humor generation in headlines. *ArXiv*, abs/2002.02031.

Divyansh Kaushik, Eduard Hovy, and Zachary C Lipton. 2019. Learning the difference that makes a difference with counterfactually-augmented data. *arXiv preprint arXiv:1909.12434*.

Fuli Luo, Shunyao Li, Pengcheng Yang, Baobao Chang, Zhifang Sui, Xu Sun, et al. 2019. Pun-gan: Generative adversarial network for pun generation. *arXiv preprint arXiv:1910.10950*.

Rada Mihalcea and Carlo Strapparava. 2005. Making computers laugh: Investigations in automatic humor recognition. In *Proceedings of the Conference on Human Language Technology and Empirical Methods in Natural Language Processing*, HLT '05, pages 531–538, Stroudsburg, PA, USA. Association for Computational Linguistics.

Abhijit Mishra, Tarun Tater, and Karthik Sankaranarayanan. 2019. A modular architecture for unsupervised sarcasm generation. In *Proceedings of the 2019 Conference on Empirical Methods in Natural Language Processing and the 9th International Joint Conference on Natural Language Processing (EMNLP-IJCNLP)*, pages 6146–6155.

Saša Petrović and David Matthews. 2013. Unsupervised joke generation from big data. In *Proceedings of the 51st Annual Meeting of the Association for Computational Linguistics (Volume 2: Short Papers)*, pages 228–232.

Shrimai Prabhumoye, Yulia Tsvetkov, Ruslan Salakhutdinov, and Alan W Black. 2018. Style transfer through back-translation. *arXiv preprint arXiv:1804.09000*.

Amruta Purandare and Diane Litman. 2006. Humor: Prosody analysis and automatic recognition for f*r*i*e*n*d*s*. *Proceedings of the 2006 Conference on Empirical Methods in Natural Language Processing*, pages 208–215.

Alec Radford, Jeffrey Wu, Rewon Child, David Luan, Dario Amodei, and Ilya Sutskever. 2019. Language models are unsupervised multitask learners. *OpenAI Blog*, 1(8).

Graeme Ritchie. 2005. Computational mechanisms for pun generation. In *Proceedings of the Tenth European Workshop on Natural Language Generation (ENLG-05)*.

Tianxiao Shen, Tao Lei, Regina Barzilay, and Tommi Jaakkola. 2017. Style transfer from non-parallel text by cross-alignment. In *Advances in neural information processing systems*, pages 6830–6841.

Julia M. Taylor and Lawrence J. Mazlack. 2004. Computationally recognizing wordplay in jokes. *In Proceedings of CogSci 2004*.

Alessandro Valitutti, Antoine Doucet, Jukka M Toivanen, and Hannu Toivonen. 2016. Computational generation and dissection of lexical replacement humor. *Natural Language Engineering*, 22(5):727–749.

Ashish Vaswani, Noam Shazeer, Niki Parmar, Jakob Uszkoreit, Llion Jones, Aidan N Gomez, Łukasz Kaiser, and Illia Polosukhin. 2017. Attention is all you need. In *Advances in neural information processing systems*, pages 5998–6008.

Orion Weller and Kevin Seppi. 2019. Humor detection: A transformer gets the last laugh. In *Proceedings of the 2019 Conference on Empirical Methods in Natural Language Processing and the 9th International Joint Conference on Natural Language Processing (EMNLP-IJCNLP)*, pages 3612–3616.

Orion Weller and Kevin Seppi. 2020. The rjokes dataset: a large scale humor collection. In *Proceedings of The 12th Language Resources and Evaluation Conference*, pages 6136–6141, Marseille, France. European Language Resources Association.

Diyi Yang, Alon Lavie, Chris Dyer, and Eduard Hovy. 2015. Humor recognition and humor anchor extraction. *Proceedings of the 2015 Conference on Empirical Methods in Natural Language Processing*, pages 2367–2376.

Zhiwei Yu, Jiwei Tan, and Xiaojun Wan. 2018. A neural approach to pun generation. In *Proceedings of the 56th Annual Meeting of the Association for Computational Linguistics (Volume 1: Long Papers)*, pages 1650–1660.

Zhirui Zhang, Shuo Ren, Shujie Liu, Jianyong Wang, Peng Chen, Mu Li, Ming Zhou, and Enhong Chen. 2018. Style transfer as unsupervised machine translation. *arXiv preprint arXiv:1808.07894*.

Evaluating a Bi-LSTM Model for Metaphor Detection in TOEFL Essays

Kevin Kuo
Computer Science
University of Maryland
kvkkuo@gmail.com

Marine Carpuat
Computer Science & UMIACS
University of Maryland
marine@cs.umd.edu

Abstract

This paper describes systems submitted to the Metaphor Shared Task at the Second Workshop on Figurative Language Processing. In this submission, we replicate the evaluation of the Bi-LSTM model introduced by Gao et al. (2018) on the VUA corpus in a new setting: TOEFL essays written by non-native English speakers. Our results show that Bi-LSTM models outperform feature-rich linear models on this challenging task, which is consistent with prior findings on the VUA dataset. However, the Bi-LSTM models lag behind the best performing systems in the shared task.

1 Introduction

In today's globalized world, text in a given language is not always written by native speakers. It is therefore important to evaluate to what degree NLP models and tools developed and evaluated primarily on edited text written and aimed at native speakers port to non-native language. The Metaphor Detection Shared Task at the Second Workshop on Figurative Language Processing offers the opportunity to perform such an evaluation on a challenging genre: argumentative essays written by non-native speakers of English as part of the Test of English as a Foreign Language (TOEFL).

We participate in the TOEFL ALLPOS task, a sequence labeling task where each word in running task is labeled with one of two tags: metaphorical (M) or literal (L). While the best-performing system described in this paper was submitted to other sections of the shared task, we focus on reporting a wider range of results for the TOEFL ALLPOS task.

Context determines whether a word or phrase is being used in a metaphorical sense. Consider an example from the TOEFL dataset: "The world is a huge **stage** and nearly everybody is an **actor**." The words "stage" and "actor" are used metaphorically to analogize the world to a stage and individuals to actors on that stage. A literal usage of these two words would be "The **actor** walked across the **stage**.", because "actor" and "stage" both occur within the context of a theatrical performance, which also matches the context of the sentence.

Beigman Klebanov et al. (2018) establish baselines for metaphor detection on TOEFL essays using feature-rich logistic regression classifiers, and show that use of metaphors is a strong predictor of the quality of the essay. The same year, Gao et al. (2018) establish a new state-of-the-art with a simple Bi-LSTM model on the VUA dataset drawn from multiple genres in the British National Corpus (BNC). Their approach departed from prior models built on linguistically motivated features (Turney et al., 2011; Hovy et al., 2013; Tsvetkov et al., 2014), visual features (Shutova et al., 2016) or learning custom word embeddings (Stemle and Onysko, 2018; Mykowiecka et al., 2018), and showed that contextualized word representations from Bi-LSTM can be more effective.

In this work, we investigate whether Gao et al. (2018)'s findings can be replicated when detecting metaphors in TOEFL essays rather than the BNC. In addition, we attempt to answer the following question: do contextualized word representations from a Bi-LSTM model detect metaphorical word use more accurately than feature-rich linear models? On the one hand, Bi-LSTM sequence labelers have proven quite successful at learning task-specific representations for many NLP problems. On the other hand, text written by non-native speakers of varying proficiency might include more variability that harms the models ability to learn useful contextual representations.

Our results show that Bi-LSTMs with word embedding inputs outperform feature-rich linear classifiers as in prior work, but their performances lag behind that of the top performing submissions in the shared task.

Proceedings of the Second Workshop on Figurative Language Processing, pages 192–196
July 9, 2020. ©2020 Association for Computational Linguistics
https://doi.org/10.18653/v1/P17

	Train	Test
Sentences	2741	968
Labeled Tokens	26647	9014
Labeled Tokens (+)	1878	-
Labeled Types	5587	2746

Table 1: TOEFL ALLPOS statistics for the provided training data (train) and the blind evaluation set (test).

2 Task Overview

The goal of the task is to accurately predict whether words are used in a literal or metaphorical sense in a sequence labeling setting. As shown in Table 1, the literal tokens heavily outnumber the metaphorical ones. To account for this imbalance, submissions are evaluated using the F1 score for the positive class (metaphorical). In the table, a "token" refers to a labeled word in the data (not all words are assigned labels/features). We will refer the reader to the shared task description paper for a detailed description of the task.

In addition to metaphor annotations, the corpus comes with pre-extracted features from Klebanov et al. (2015), labeled as *Provided features* in Table 2. These features include unigrams, Stanford POS tags, binned mean concreteness values (Brysbaert et al., 2013), and Topic-Latent Dirichlet Allocation (Blei et al., 2003). Unlabeled tokens are assigned a literal classification and values of zero for all non-word embedding features.

3 System Configurations

3.1 Classifiers

We ran our internal experiments using a simple baseline and two classifier architectures. The implementation, written in Python, will be made publicly available on Github. [1]

Baseline As a baseline (**BL**), we predict the probability $p(w)$ of a word lemma w to be positive (metaphorical) as m_w/c_w, where m_w and c_w are the number of positive occurrences and total occurrences of w respectively in the training data. If $c_w = 0$ (the word was not encountered during training), we automatically assign a negative (literal) prediction.

Linear Classifiers We use a logistic regression (**LR**) classifier implemented using scikit-learn (Pedregosa et al., 2011) with default training settings

Feature	Dim.	Name
Word embeddings		
GE	1324	GloVe + ELMo vectors
Provided features		
UL	5027	Unigram lemma
P	17	Stanford POS
WN	15	WordNet verb senses
T	100	Topic-LDA
C	34	Concreteness bins
CD	66	Concreteness difference

Table 2: Features available for use.

(LBFGS solver with L2 penalization). We predict a binary classification for each token independently, ignoring other predictions and features in the sequence.

Bi-LSTM Following Gao et al. (2018), we use a Bidirectional LSTM as a sequence labeler, simply using a feed-forward neural network to make a binary prediction at each time step, using the contextualized representations learned by the Bi-LSTM as input. Predictions are made for each sentence in an essay, independently of the document context. Our experiments are based on the implementation by Gao et al., with modifications to the code in order to apply their model to the TOEFL data and to incorporate different combinations of features.

The LSTMs have a hidden size of 300 units for each direction. Concatenating the forward and backward representations yields a 600-dimensional output. We feed this output through a single-layer (2 units) feedforward neural network and apply a softmax function, which outputs a probability distribution for the two output classes. Dropout is applied to the LSTM input ($p = 0.5$) and from LSTM output to the linear layer ($p = 0.1$). The models are trained using the Adam algorithm, with learning rates of $\eta = 0.005$ and 0.001 for epochs $0 - 10$ and $11 - 20$, respectively.

3.2 Features

We experimented with different input features within each model architecture, which are summarized in Table 2.

We obtain word embedding features for each word type by concatenating GloVe (Pennington et al., 2014) and ELMo (Peters et al., 2018) word embeddings into a 1324-dimensional vector, shown as "GE" in Table 2.

All the other features were provided with the

[1] https://github.com/imkevinkuo/metaphor-toefl.

Model	Features Used	P	R	F1	Test F1
BL	-	64.3	52.6	57.7	54.5
LR	UL	55.2	51.9	53.3	52.4
	UL, P, WN, T, C, CD	58.4	54.1	55.7	50.5
	GE	58.7	63.0	60.5	-
	GE, UL	55.7	60.6	57.9	**56.5**
	GE, UL, WN, CD	61.0	61.7	60.7	-
LSTM	UL, P, WN, T, C, CD	50.6	30.5	38.0	-
	GE	69.3	65.0	66.8	58.2
	GE, UL	73.3	61.9	67.1	**60.9**
	GE, UL, WN, CD	73.8	60.4	66.3	-

Table 3: Summary of results based on 5-fold cross validation on the unmodified training set (P,R,F1) as well as evaluation on the blind test set on CodaLab (Test F1).

TOEFL ALLPOS dataset, which we will refer to as 'provided' features. With the exception of Topic-LDA (T), all of them are represented with one-hot encodings (UL, P) or a vector of binary values (WN, C, CD).

Various combinations of all these features were concatenated together to form the input data on which we trained and evaluated the classifiers described above.

3.3 Data Versions

Default Data   We first build classifiers on the data as processed by the organizers, with the provided tokenization and no additional processing.

Since the TOEFL essays are written by non-native English speakers, many sentences contain misspellings or grammatical errors, such as "The problems of the pollution is one of the most ones of this century." We experiment two strategies to address these sources of variability.

Spelling Correction   We created a cleaned version of the dataset using the Python *pyspellchecker* library, which finds a given word's minimum Levenshtein distance neighbor in the OpenSubtitles corpus. In total, we replaced 1536 (train) and 492 (test) misspelled tokens in the data.

Error Injection   Anastasopoulos et al. (2018) showed that adding synthetic grammatical errors to training data improves neural machine translation of non-native English to Spanish text. To investigate the effect of such methods on metaphor detection, we separately inject the following errors (if applicable) into three copies of each training sentence and append them to the training set:

- RT: Missing determiner (includes articles)

- PREP: Missing preposition

- NN: Flipped noun number

For simplicity, unlike Anastasopoulos et al. we did not randomly replace determiners or prepositions with another member of their confusion set. Instead, we simply removed the word from the sentence.

3.4 Evaluation Settings

When training the logistic regression and Bi-LSTM classifiers, we ran cross-validation ($k = 5$) and used early stopping to select a final test model based on validation loss. We then selected a probability threshold that maximized our F1 score on the validation data before finally making predictions on the test set.

For our baseline model, we used the same model selection technique without early stopping, as there is no 'training' iteration involved in the baseline.

4 Results

4.1 Impact of Classifier and Feature Choice

We first compare classifiers and features when training on the default data. Table 3 includes our internal results averaged across 5-fold cross-validation on the training set, and for a subset of the models, results on the blind evaluation test set taken from official leader board on CodaLab.

The baseline model performs well on both the testing and validation sets, which suggests that the identify of the word is a strong indicator of metaphorical use even before taking context into account, for the TOEFL data as for other genres. Surprisingly, the linear classifiers that did not use word embedding features did not improve over the baseline, despite the fact that they include the identity of the current lemma (UL). The only models that produced improvements over the baseline on average used GloVe and ELMo embeddings. Additionally, the effect of adding the provided features is inconsistent - in some cases, performance degrades, but in others, it improves.

The difference in F1 score between Bi-LSTM and LR models is primarily due to precision: The Bi-LSTM models that use word embeddings achieve higher precisions than the logistic regression models, while the differences in recall are small. This constrasts with the findings of Gao et al. (2018) on the VUA dataset, where the Bi-LSTM model primarily benefited recall over precision.

The best results overall are obtained with the Bi-LSTM models that use GloVe and ELMo input. Interestingly, adding unigram lemma features (UL) further improves precision and the expense of a small decrease in recall, and overall yields the best F1 both by cross-validation and on the official test set. As expected, Bi-LSTM performance degrades heavily when trained on only the dataset-provided features. Investigating better ways to incorporate these features would be a useful direction for future research. Finally, Table 5 shows our best model's performance, broken down by Penn Treebank POS tags: F1 scores are the highest for verbs and lowest for nouns, mostly due to worse recall for nouns than for verbs.

4.2 Impact of Addressing Spelling and Grammatical Errors

Spell-checking and error injection experiments have an inconsistent impact. As shown in 4, this additional data processing improves the F1 score of the Logistic Regression model most. For the Bi-LSTM, spell-checking the data yields a small F1 improvement when using cross-validation, and no significant difference on the official test set (60.9 vs. 61.0). Injecting artificial errors leads to a small F1 decrease with cross-validation and was therefore not tested on the official test set.

5 Official Submission

Our best submission on the leaderboard is a Bi-LSTM network trained on a spell-checked dataset embedded with GloVe, ELMo, and one-hot unigram lemma vectors. This model yields an F1 score of 0.610, which is slightly below the median score of 0.653.

Model	Data	P	R	F1	Test F1
BL	Base	64.3	52.6	57.7	**54.5**
	Spell	60.6	54.7	57.4	54.3
LR	Base	55.7	60.6	57.9	-
	Spell	60.5	62.4	**61.3**	-
	Errors	58.7	62.5	60.5	-
LSTM	Base	73.3	61.9	67.1	60.9
	Spell	70.5	65.5	67.9	**61.0**
	Errors	70.8	63.5	66.8	-

Table 4: Comparison of averaged 5-fold cross validation results (P,R,F1) on the original text (Base), spell checked data (Spell) and error injected data (Error), as well as evaluation on the blind test set on CodaLab (Test F1). non-BL models use the GE and UL features.

POS	#	% M	P	R	F1
NN	8498	4.8	75.8	54.7	63.5
NNS	4328	2.4	72.2	50.0	59.1
JJ	4024	8.6	83.0	63.8	72.1
VB	2715	16.2	77.8	78.8	78.3
RB	1998	3.2	86.7	68.4	76.5
VBP	1402	6.6	68.2	78.9	73.2
VBG	1188	11.5	73.9	70.8	72.3

Table 5: Evaluation of best Bi-LSTM model per POS tag via cross-validation. We show statistics (count, % metaphoric) for the training set. Only POS tags with more than 1000 occurrences are displayed.

6 Conclusion

In summary, our experiments replicate existing metaphor detection models in the new settings provided by the TOEFL ALLPOS task. Adding GloVe vectors and ELMo contextual embeddings helped push the performance of the logistic regression model over a simple frequency baseline. The use of a Bi-LSTM network in combination with GloVe, ELMo, and one-hot unigram lemma vectors yields the highest performance out of all the models tested. This confirms the benefits of contextual representations learned by the Bi-LSTM for metaphor detection highlighted by Gao et al. (2018) on the VUA dataset. However, the more challenging TOEFL ALLPOS data also shows the limitation of the Bi-LSTM model, which yields smaller improvements over the baseline than on VUA, and lags behind the best systems on the shared task leader board.

References

Antonios Anastasopoulos, Marika Lekakou, Josep Quer, Eleni Zimianiti, Justin DeBenedetto, and David Chiang. 2018. Part-of-speech tagging on an endangered language: a parallel Griko-Italian resource. In *Proceedings of the 27th International Conference on Computational Linguistics*, pages 2529–2539, Santa Fe, New Mexico, USA. Association for Computational Linguistics.

Beata Beigman Klebanov, Chee Wee (Ben) Leong, and Michael Flor. 2018. A corpus of non-native written English annotated for metaphor. In *Proceedings of the 2018 Conference of the North American Chapter of the Association for Computational Linguistics: Human Language Technologies, Volume 2 (Short Papers)*, pages 86–91, New Orleans, Louisiana. Association for Computational Linguistics.

David M. Blei, Andrew Y. Ng, and Michael I. Jordan. 2003. Latent dirichlet allocation. *J. Mach. Learn. Res.*, 3(null):993–1022.

Marc Brysbaert, Amy Beth Warriner, and Victor Kuperman. 2013. Concreteness ratings for 40 thousand generally known english word lemmas. *Behavior Research Methods*, 46(3):904—-911.

Ge Gao, Eunsol Choi, Yejin Choi, and Luke Zettlemoyer. 2018. Neural metaphor detection in context.

Dirk Hovy, Shashank Srivastava, Sujay Kumar Jauhar, Mrinmaya Sachan, Kartik Goyal, Huying Li, Whitney Sanders, and Eduard Hovy. 2013. Identifying metaphorical word use with tree kernels. In *Proceedings of the First Workshop on Metaphor in NLP*, pages 52–57, Atlanta, Georgia. Association for Computational Linguistics.

Beata Klebanov, Chee Wee Leong, and Michael Flor. 2015. Supervised word-level metaphor detection: Experiments with concreteness and reweighting of examples.

Agnieszka Mykowiecka, Aleksander Wawer, and Malgorzata Marciniak. 2018. Detecting figurative word occurrences using recurrent neural networks. In *Proceedings of the Workshop on Figurative Language Processing*, pages 124–127, New Orleans, Louisiana. Association for Computational Linguistics.

F. Pedregosa, G. Varoquaux, A. Gramfort, V. Michel, B. Thirion, O. Grisel, M. Blondel, P. Prettenhofer, R. Weiss, V. Dubourg, J. Vanderplas, A. Passos, D. Cournapeau, M. Brucher, M. Perrot, and E. Duchesnay. 2011. Scikit-learn: Machine learning in Python. *Journal of Machine Learning Research*, 12:2825–2830.

Jeffrey Pennington, Richard Socher, and Christopher Manning. 2014. Glove: Global vectors for word representation. In *Proceedings of the 2014 Conference on Empirical Methods in Natural Language Processing (EMNLP)*, pages 1532–1543, Doha, Qatar. Association for Computational Linguistics.

Matthew E Peters, Mark Neumann, Mohit Iyyer, Matt Gardner, Christopher Clark, Kenton Lee, and Luke Zettlemoyer. 2018. Deep contextualized word representations. *arXiv preprint arXiv:1802.05365*.

Ekaterina Shutova, Douwe Kiela, and Jean Maillard. 2016. Black holes and white rabbits: Metaphor identification with visual features. In *Proceedings of the 2016 Conference of the North American Chapter of the Association for Computational Linguistics: Human Language Technologies*, pages 160–170, San Diego, California. Association for Computational Linguistics.

Egon Stemle and Alexander Onysko. 2018. Using language learner data for metaphor detection. In *Proceedings of the Workshop on Figurative Language Processing*, pages 133–138, New Orleans, Louisiana. Association for Computational Linguistics.

Yulia Tsvetkov, Leonid Boytsov, Anatole Gershman, Eric Nyberg, and Chris Dyer. 2014. Metaphor detection with cross-lingual model transfer. In *Proceedings of the 52nd Annual Meeting of the Association for Computational Linguistics (Volume 1: Long Papers)*, pages 248–258, Baltimore, Maryland. Association for Computational Linguistics.

Peter Turney, Yair Neuman, Dan Assaf, and Yohai Cohen. 2011. Literal and metaphorical sense identification through concrete and abstract context. In *Proceedings of the 2011 Conference on Empirical Methods in Natural Language Processing*, pages 680–690, Edinburgh, Scotland, UK. Association for Computational Linguistics.

Neural Metaphor Detection with a Residual biLSTM-CRF Model

Andrés Torres Rivera, Antoni Oliver, Salvador Climent, Marta Coll-Florit
Universitat Oberta de Catalunya
{*atorresrive, aoliverg, scliment, mcollfl*}*@uoc.edu*

Abstract

In this paper we present a novel resource-inexpensive architecture for metaphor detection based on a residual bidirectional long short-term memory and conditional random fields. Current approaches on this task rely on deep neural networks to identify metaphorical words, using additional linguistic features or word embeddings. We evaluate our proposed approach using different model configurations that combine embeddings, part of speech tags, and semantically disambiguated synonym sets. This evaluation process was performed using the training and testing partitions of the VU Amsterdam Metaphor Corpus. We use this method of evaluation as reference to compare the results with other current neural approaches for this task that implement similar neural architectures and features, and that were evaluated using this corpus. Results show that our system achieves competitive results with a simpler architecture compared to previous approaches.

1 Introduction

This paper presents a new model for automatic metaphor detection which has participated at the FigLang 2020 metaphor detection shared task (Leong et al., 2020). Our approach, which is based on neural networks, has been developed in the framework of the research project MOMENT (Coll-Florit et al., 2018), a project devoted to the analysis of metaphors in mental health discourses.

As it is well known in Cognitive Linguistics, a conceptual metaphor (CM) is a cognitive process which allows to understand and communicate an abstract or diffuse concept in terms of a more concrete one (cf. e.g. Lakoff and Johnson (1980)). This process is expressed linguistically by using metaphorically used words (MUW).

The study of metaphor is a prolific area of research in Cognitive Linguistics, being the Metaphor Identification Procedure (MIP) (Pragglejaz Group, 2007) and its derivative MIPVU (Steen et al., 2019) the most standard methods for manual MUW detection. MIPVU is the method that was used to annotate the VU Amsterdam Metaphor Corpus (VUA corpus), used in FigLang 2020. Moreover, in the area of Corpus Linguistics, some methods have been developed for a richer annotation of metaphor in corpora (Ogarkova and Soriano Salinas, 2014; Shutova, 2017; Coll-Florit and Climent, 2019).

CM is pervasive in natural language text and therefore it is crucial in automatic text understanding (Shutova, 2010). For this reason automated metaphor processing has become an increasingly important concern in natural language processing, as shown by the holding of the Metaphor in NLP workshop series (at NAACL-HLT 2013, ACL 2014, NAACL-HLT 2015, NAACL-HLT 2016 and NAACL-HLT 2018) and a growing body of research — see Veale et al. (2016) and Shutova (2017) for quite recent reviews.

Automatic metaphor processing involves two main tasks: identifying MUW (metaphor detection or recognition) and attempting to provide a semantic interpretation for the utterance containing them (metaphor interpretation). This work deals with metaphor detection.

This problem has been mainly approached in the last decade by supervised and semi-supervised machine learning techniques but recently this paradigm has largely shifted to the use of deep learning algorithms, such as neural networks. Leong et al. (2018) report that all but one of participating teams on the 2018 VUA Metaphor Detection Shared Task used this kind of architectures. Our system follows this trend by trying to improve on previous neural network methods.

Below we describe the main related works (section 2). Next we present our methodology and

197

Proceedings of the Second Workshop on Figurative Language Processing, pages 197–203
July 9, 2020. ©2020 Association for Computational Linguistics
https://doi.org/10.18653/v1/P17

model (section 3), experiments (section 4) and results (Section 5). We finish with the discussion and our overall conclusions (sections 6 and 7).

2 Background

Research on metaphor recognition and interpretation is changing from the use of features (linguistic and concreteness features), classical methods (as generalization, classification and word associations) and the use of theoretical principles (construction grammar, frame semantics and conceptual metaphor theory) to neural networks and other deep learning techniques.

Concreteness features are used by Klebanov et al. (2015) along with re-weighting of the training examples to train a supervised machine learning system. The trained system is able to classify all content words of a text in two groups: metaphorical and non-metaphorical.

Klebanov et al. (2016) study the metaphoricity of verbs using semantic generalization and classification using word forms, lemmas and several other linguistic features. They demonstrated the effectiveness of the generalization from orthographic unigrams to lemmas and the combination of lemmas and semantic classes based on WordNet. They also used automatically generated clusters to combine with unigram lemmas getting a competitive performance.

The Meta4meaning (Xiao et al., 2016) metaphor interpretation method uses word associations extracted from a corpus to retrieve approximate properties of concepts and provide interpretations for nominal metaphors of the form $NOUN_1$ is [a] $NOUN_2$ (where $NOUN_1$ is the tenor and $NOUN_2$ the vehicle). Metaphor interpretation is obtained as a combination of the saliences of the properties to the tenor and the vehicle. Combinations can be aggregations (the product or sum of saliences), salience difference or a combination of the results of the two. As an output, Meta4meaning provides a list of interpretations with weights.

The automatic metaphor detection system MetaNet (Hong, 2016) has been designed applying theoretical principles from construction grammar, frame semantics, and conceptual metaphor theory. The system relies on a conceptual network of frames and metaphors.

Rosen (2018) developed an algorithm using deep learning techniques that uses a representation of metaphorical constructions in an argument-structure level. The algorithm allows for the identification of source-level mappings of metaphors. The author concludes that the use of deep learning algorithms with the addition of construction grammatical relations in the feature set improves the accuracy of the prediction of metaphorical source domains.

Wu et al. (2018) propose to use a Convolutional Neural Network - Long-Short Term Memory (CNN-LSTM) with a Conditional Random Field (CRF) or Softmax layer for metaphor detection in texts. They combine CNN and LSTM to capture both local and long-distance contextual information to represent the input sentences. Meanwhile, Mu et al. (2019) argue that using broader discourse features can have a substantial positive impact for the task of metaphorical identification. They obtain significant results using document embeddings methods to represent an utterance and its surrounding discourse. With this material a gradient boosting classifier is trained.

Other works for specific tasks within the scope of metaphor recognition, such as detecting the metaphoricity of adjective-noun (AN) pairs in English as isolated units, include the works by Turney et al. (2011), Gutierrez et al. (2016), Bizzoni et al. (2017), and Torres Rivera et al. (2020). The main goal of this task is to classify AN collocations using external and internal linguistic features, or techniques such as transfer learning along with word embeddings.

We propose a model that uses residual bidirectional long short-term memory (biLSTM) with a CRF, using ELMo embeddings along with additional linguistic features, such as part of speech tags (POS) and semantically disambiguated WordNet[1] synonym sets (synsets) (Fellbaum and Miller, 1998). Our model could be grouped in the same category as the aforementioned approaches: deep neural networks models for metaphor detection.

3 Model Description

Most of the approaches mentioned in section 2 used the VUA corpus (Steen et al., 2010) in order to carry out model training and testing. They divided the training and test sets according to the VUA Metaphor Detection Shared Task specifications. To train and test our model we used the VUA corpus partitions, using ELMo embeddings to represent words and lemmas, and POS and synsets as

---

[1]Freeling implements WordNet version 3.0.

additional linguistic features. ELMo (*Embeddings from Language Models*) embeddings (Peters et al., 2018) are derived from a bidirectional language model (biLM) and they are contextualized, deep and character based. ELMo embeddings have been successfully used in several NLP tasks.

To process the VUA corpus we used the Natural Language Toolkit (NLTK) (Loper and Bird, 2002) for Python, with this tool we performed tokenization, lemmatization, and POS tagging. Then we used Freeling (Padró and Stanilovsky, 2012) to obtain the respective synset of each token. Although NLTK provides a method for obtaining synsets – using POS tags or Lesk's Algorithm–, Freeling implements UKB (Agirre et al., 2014), a graph-based word sense disambiguation (WSD) algorithm that is used to obtain semantically disambiguated synsets. These features along the ELMo embeddings were used –in different configurations– as input for our model. We set a sequence padding value equal to 116, which is the maximum sentence length observed in the corpus. This process normalizes the input in order to train in batches, but might contribute to sparsity on training data.

We used one-hot encoded representation for POS, and computed local 100-dimension embeddings for synsets. In the case of POS, we have a small set of tags (43), and therefore resulting in a low dimensionality of the one-hot embeddings. For synsets, the computation of local embeddings provides the semantically disambiguated relations that exist between the units that compose the training data. These embeddings, in addition with their EMLo counterparts, shall provide enough contextual and semantic data to understand metaphorical instances of words.

The main architecture of our model (shown in Figure 1) is composed by a residual biLSTM (Kim et al., 2017; Tran et al., 2017) for sequence labeling. One of the particularities of this architecture lies in the implementation of an additive operation that takes the outputs from each biLSTM layer and combines them to calculate the residual connection between them, in order to obtain previously seen information from both instances.

After computing the residual connection from both biLSTM layers, our model includes a dropout layer, followed by a time distributed layer in which a dense activation with 2 hidden units to each timestep is applied. We used ReLU (Nair and Hinton, 2010) as activation function in combination

with a He-normal (He et al., 2015) kernel initialization function for the time distributed layer, which results in a zero-mean Gaussian distribution with a standard deviation equal to $\sqrt{\frac{2}{\hat{n}_l}}$. Finally, after the time distributed layer we used a conditional random field (CRF) implemented for sequence labeling (Lafferty et al., 2001).

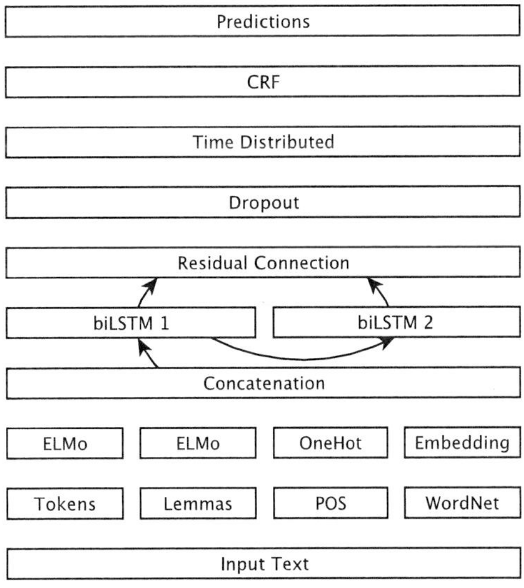

Figure 1: Summarized model diagram.

Given that the VUA corpus is composed by more negative –or literal– labels than positive –or metaphoric– labels, and that the sequence padding process added non-informative features to the input array, we opted to treat the training partition as an imbalanced dataset. We selected the Nadam optimizer (Dozat, 2016), which is based on Adam (Kingma and Ba, 2014) and tends to perform better with sparse data. This last optimization algorithm has two main components: a momentum and an adaptive learning rate component. Nadam modifies the momentum component of Adam using Nesterov's accelerated gradient (NAG). The Nadam update rule can be written as follows:

$$w_{t+1} = w_t - \frac{\alpha}{\sqrt{\hat{w}_t + \epsilon}} \left(\beta_1 \hat{m}_t + \frac{1 - \beta_1}{1 - \beta_1^t} \cdot \frac{\partial L}{\partial w_t} \right) \quad (1)$$

4   Experiments

To carry out the evaluation of our model we used the train and test splits provided in VUA shared task partitions (Shutova, 2017). In order to obtain a validation split we divided the training partition using the following percentages: 80% for training 20% for validation. With these partitions, we trained a total of 6 different model configurations: words and POS (W+POS); lemmas and POS (L+POS); words, POS and synsets (W+POS+SS); lemmas, POS and synsets (L+POS+SS); words, lemmas and POS (WL+POS); and words, lemmas, POS and synsets (WL+POS+SS).

In all cases we used the same training parameters, all model configurations were trained in batches for 5 epochs, using a learning rate = 0.0025. Then, the resulting models were evaluated –using the precision, recall and F_1 score metrics– on both the all POS metaphor detection task and the metaphoric verbs detection task.

5   Results

Regarding the all POS prediction task (Table 1) , the L+POS+SS model had the best performance with a 0.5729 in precision, 0.6027 in recall and an F_1 score equal to 0.5874. Overall, all configuration obtained a mean F_1 score of 0.58 being the WL+POS model the one with the lowest score (0.5615). Regarding the recall score, the highest observed value was obtained by the W+POS+SS model, with a recall equal to 0.6438.

Model	Precision	Recall	F_1
W+POS	0.5635	0.6098	0.5857
W+POS+SS	0.5313	**0.6438**	0.5822
L+POS	0.5685	0.5956	0.5817
L+POS+SS	**0.5729**	0.6027	**0.5874**
WL+POS	0.5064	0.6302	0.5615
WL+POS+SS	0.5601	0.6174	0.5873

Table 1: All POS task model comparison.

It could be said that a less diverse lexicon obtained by using lemmas instead of words to obtain embeddings, helped to improve the performance of the L+POS+SS model. Nevertheless, when comparing the W+POS and L+POS configuration, both obtained similar results, with less than 1% difference in performance between them. Meanwhile, when comparing the W+POS+SS and L+POS+SS models, it can be observed that both models obtained similar F_1 scores, but a variation of 4% between the precision and recall that favours precision in the L+POS+SS model, and recall in the W+POS+SS model.

In the case of the metaphoric verb labeling task (Table 2), the W+POS model obtained the best

scores in precision and F_1 score (0.6695 and 0.6543 accordingly), while the W+POS+SS model obtained the highest recall value (0.7032). Overall, the mean F_1 score of all configurations was equal to 0.6411, being the WL+POS the poorest performing configuration with a F_1 score of 0.6101. In a similar way to the all POS task, the W+POS+SS and L+POS+SS configurations obtained precision and recall scores with a difference of 6% in both metrics.

Unlike in the all POS task, combining features did not improve the performance of the models for verbs labeling. While using synsets to disambiguate the meaning of the different words or lemmas that were fed to the model, using ELMo embeddings and POS tags yielded better results in this task. One of the possible explanations for this behavior could be that verbs tend to be more polysemous than nouns and, therefore, obtain greater benefit from this feature. According to WordNet statistics[2], verbs have an average polisemy index of 2.17, while nouns have an average of 1.24.

Model	Precision	Recall	F_1
W+POS	**0.6695**	0.6397	**0.6543**
W+POS+SS	0.5933	**0.7032**	0.6436
L+POS	0.6398	0.6413	0.6405
L+POS+SS	0.6544	0.6474	0.6509
WL+POS	0.5576	0.6735	0.6101
WL+POS+SS	0.6201	0.6779	0.6477

Table 2: Verbs task model comparison.

It can be observed the all POS models set the W+POS architecture has a higher precision in comparison to the W+POS+SS configuration. This behaviour can also be observed in the Verbs task model set, where both configurations obtained the higher values for these metrics. On one hand, the W+POS classifier captures fewer instances of metaphoric words, but most of the metaphors it classifies are true positives whereas, on the other hand, the W+POS+SS is a greedier model that correctly classifies metaphors but its predictions tend to include instances of false negatives.

Such variation might be caused by the inclusion of synsets as training feature: when additional senses are linked to each training word, they provide a polysemous representation of words and cause an increase in semantic patterns for both

---

[2] https://wordnet.princeton.edu/ documentation/wnstats7wn

metaphoric and literal tokens. These semantically disambiguated patterns broaden the prediction scope of the model, as words with similar senses might occur in similar contexts. While the W+POS architecture correctly predicts metaphors to a certain degree, its scope is more precise but narrower than the W+POS+SS architecture in which words –particularly verbs– have a variety of senses that improve the recall metric at the expense of predicting literal tokens as metaphoric when compared to the W+POS model.

6 Discussion

Our proposed architecture has similarities to other current approaches such as Wu et al. (2018) who propose a LSTM with Softmax model, and Mu et al. (2019) who implement an XGBoost classifier using ELMo embeddings. In comparison to these approaches, our model shows an improvement in precision on the verb labeling task with a value equal to 0.6695, while Mu et al. (2019) reported a precision score of 0.600^3, and Mu et al. (2019) a precision equal to 0.589. Nevertheless Wu et al. (2018) reported the highest F_1 score (0.671), and Mu et al. (2019) the highest recall (0.771).

All POS task			
Model	**Precision**	**Recall**	**F_1**
Wu et al. (2018)	0.608	0.700	0.651
L+POS+SS	0.5729	0.6027	0.5874
Verbs task			
Wu et al. (2018)	0.600	0.763	**0.671**
Mu et al. (2019)	0.589	**0.771**	0.668
W+POS	**0.6695**	0.6397	0.6543

Table 3: Comparison with other current approaches.

Regarding the all POS labeling task, the model presented by Wu et al. (2018) performs better in all metrics, with a difference of 3% in precision, 10% in recall and 8% in F_1 score. It has to be noted that our model presents a simpler architecture (as shown in section 3). Wu et al. (2018) trained their model using 200 biLSTM hidden states and 100 CNN units for 15 epochs, and trained it 20 times using an ensemble method. On the other hand, the most simple W+POS architecture that we presented takes an average time of 5 minutes by epoch[4] to

train and validate, thus producing a less complex model that is faster and less expensive to train.

On both tasks the poorest performing configuration was WL+POS, combining these features improved recall but lowered both precision and F_1. Combining words and lemmas might create redundancy in certain features that is not possible to leverage using POS. On the other hand, while the dimensionality becomes higher than the previous configuration (1024 + 1024 + 43), once synsets are added in the WL+POS+SS architecture (and increasing the feature dimensionality by 100) the performance of the model improves on both precision and recall on the all POS task, and in all metrics on the verbs task.

One of the strategies that we implemented to leverage the imbalance of the training data was using a kernel initialization function. The He-normal function uses the size of the last layer in order to generate weights that have different ranges. In this case, the time distributed layer is activated using RELu, and takes the size of the dropout layer and then initializes it with a He-normal distribution.

7 Conclusions and further work

In this paper we have described the system we have presented at the FigLang 2020 metaphor detection shared task. Our approach is based on neural networks using a residual biLSTM with a CRF and using ELMo embeddings along with the inclusion of several combinations of words, lemmas and linguistic features as POS and WordNet synsets. The system achieves competitive results with a simpler architecture compared to systems found in the literature. Such systems implement similar elements such as the use of bidirectional LSTM, CRF and ELMo embeddings in different configurations, and with different combination of linguistic features.

As future work, we plan to further analyse which POS benefits most from the inclusion of synset information. Other aspect we want to explore is how to deal with imbalanced data, i.e. how we can leverage a dataset with only two classes (metaphoric/literal) where most of the samples are literal. Other interesting questions that deserve more research is the effects on optimal dimensionality of the addition of linguistic information. Other features that could be implemented are concreteness value of certain words, or as an strategy to balance classes according to the influence that this feature has on literal and metaphoric classes.

---

[3]Both authors reported metric results using three digits.

[4]The model was trained using a shared NVIDIA Tesla P100 GPU.

Other future lines of work might include the implementation of this type of model for the detection of metaphors and source domain identification in Spanish. Current developments on metaphor detection are being carried out mainly in English, while this is a great resource it could be interesting to create resources in other languages to broaden the scope of metaphor detection and interpretation. A possible pipeline could be configured with two separated model, one that performs the detection of metaphorical words, followed by another classifier that predicts the domain of those metaphors.

Acknowledgments

This research was conducted in the framework of "MOMENT: Metaphors of severe mental disorders. Discourse analysis of affected people and mental health professionals", a project funded by the Spanish National Research Agency (Agencia Estatal de Investigación, AEI) and the European Regional Development Fund (ERDF), within the Spanish Government's National Programme for Research Aimed at the Challenges of Society. Ref. FFI2017-86969-R (AEI/ERDF, EU).

References

Eneko Agirre, Oier López de Lacalle, and Aitor Soroa. 2014. Random walks for knowledge-based word sense disambiguation. *Computational Linguistics*, 40(1):57–84.

Yuri Bizzoni, Stergios Chatzikyriakidis, and Mehdi Ghanimifard. 2017. "Deep" Learning : Detecting Metaphoricity in Adjective-Noun Pairs. In *Proceedings of the Workshop on Stylistic Variation*, pages 43–52, Copenhagen, Denmark. Association for Computational Linguistics.

Marta Coll-Florit and Salvador Climent. 2019. A new methodology for conceptual metaphor detection and formulation in corpora. a case study on a mental health corpus. *SKY Journal of Linguistics*, 32:43–74.

Marta Coll-Florit, Salvador Climent, Martín Correa-Urquiza, Eulàlia Hernández, Antoni Oliver, and Asun Pié. 2018. MOMENT: Metáforas del trastorno mental grave. análisis del discurso de personas afectadas y profesionales de la salud mental [MOMENT: Metaphors of severe mental disorder. discourse analysis of affected people and mental health professionals]. *Procesamiento del Lenguaje Natural*, 61:139–142.

Timothy Dozat. 2016. Incorporating nesterov momentum into adam. In *Proceedings of the International Conference on Learning Representations (ICLR-2016) - Workshop Track*, San Juan (Puerto Rico).

C. Fellbaum and G.A. Miller. 1998. *WordNet: An Electronic Lexical Database*. Language, speech, and communication. MIT Press.

E.Dario Gutierrez, Ekaterina Shutova, Tyler Marghetis, and Benjamin Bergen. 2016. Literal and Metaphorical Senses in Compositional Distributional Semantic Models. In *Proceedings of the 54th Annual Meeting of the Association for Computational Linguistics (Volume 1: Long Papers)*, pages 183–193, Berlin, Germany. Association for Computational Linguistics.

Kaiming He, Xiangyu Zhang, Shaoqing Ren, and Jian Sun. 2015. Delving deep into rectifiers: Surpassing human-level performance on imagenet classification. *CoRR*, abs/1502.01852.

Jisup Hong. 2016. Automatic metaphor detection using constructions and frames. *Constructions and frames*, 8(2):295–322.

Jaeyoung Kim, Mostafa El-Khamy, and Jungwon Lee. 2017. Residual LSTM: design of a deep recurrent architecture for distant speech recognition. *CoRR*, abs/1701.03360.

Diederik P. Kingma and Jimmy Ba. 2014. Adam: A Method for Stochastic Optimization. *arXiv:1412.6980 [cs]*. ArXiv: 1412.6980.

Beata Beigman Klebanov, Chee Wee Leong, and Michael Flor. 2015. Supervised word-level metaphor detection: Experiments with concreteness and reweighting of examples. In *Proceedings of the Third Workshop on Metaphor in NLP*, pages 11–20.

Beata Beigman Klebanov, Chee Wee Leong, E Dario Gutierrez, Ekaterina Shutova, and Michael Flor. 2016. Semantic classifications for detection of verb metaphors. In *Proceedings of the 54th Annual Meeting of the Association for Computational Linguistics (Volume 2: Short Papers)*, pages 101–106.

John D. Lafferty, Andrew McCallum, and Fernando C. N. Pereira. 2001. Conditional random fields: Probabilistic models for segmenting and labeling sequence data. In *Proceedings of the Eighteenth International Conference on Machine Learning*, ICML '01, pages 282–289, San Francisco, CA, USA. Morgan Kaufmann Publishers Inc.

George Lakoff and Mark Johnson. 1980. *Metaphors we Live by*. University of Chicago Press, Chicago.

Chee Wee Leong, Beata Beigman Klebanov, Chris Hamill, Egon Stemle, Rutuja Ubale, and Xianyang Chen. 2020. A report on the 2020 vua and toefl metaphor detection shared task. In *Proceedings of the Second Workshop on Figurative Language Processing*, Seattle, WA.

Chee Wee (Ben) Leong, Beata Beigman Klebanov, and Ekaterina Shutova. 2018. A report on the 2018 VUA metaphor detection shared task. In *Proceedings of the Workshop on Figurative Language Processing*, pages 56–66, New Orleans, Louisiana. Association for Computational Linguistics.

Edward Loper and Steven Bird. 2002. Nltk: The natural language toolkit. In *Proceedings of the ACL-02 Workshop on Effective Tools and Methodologies for Teaching Natural Language Processing and Computational Linguistics*, pages 63–70.

Jesse Mu, Helen Yannakoudakis, and Ekaterina Shutova. 2019. Learning Outside the Box: Discourse-level Features Improve Metaphor Identification. *arXiv:1904.02246 [cs]*. ArXiv: 1904.02246.

Vinod Nair and Geoffrey E. Hinton. 2010. Rectified linear units improve restricted boltzmann machines. In *Proceedings of the 27th International Conference on International Conference on Machine Learning*, ICML'10, page 807–814, Madison, WI, USA. Omnipress.

Anna Ogarkova and Cristina Soriano Salinas. 2014. *Variation within universals: The 'metaphorical profile' approach to the study of ANGER concepts in English, Russian and Spanish*, Metaphor and Intercultural Communication. Bloomsbury, London. ID: unige:98101.

Lluís Padró and Evgeny Stanilovsky. 2012. Freeling 3.0: Towards wider multilinguality. In *Proceedings of the Language Resources and Evaluation Conference (LREC 2012)*, Istanbul, Turkey. ELRA.

Matthew Peters, Mark Neumann, Mohit Iyyer, Matt Gardner, Christopher Clark, Kenton Lee, and Luke Zettlemoyer. 2018. Deep contextualized word representations. In *Proceedings of the 2018 Conference of the North American Chapter of the Association for Computational Linguistics: Human Language Technologies, Volume 1 (Long Papers)*, pages 2227–2237, New Orleans, Louisiana. Association for Computational Linguistics.

Pragglejaz Group. 2007. MIP: A method for identifying metaphorically used words in discourse. *Metaphor and Symbol*, 22(1):1–39.

Zachary Rosen. 2018. Computationally Constructed Concepts: A Machine Learning Approach to Metaphor Interpretation Using Usage-Based Construction Grammatical Cues. In *Proceedings of the Workshop on Figurative Language Processing*, pages 102–109, New Orleans, Louisiana. Association for Computational Linguistics.

Ekaterina Shutova. 2010. Models of Metaphor in NLP. *Proceedings of the 48th Annual Meeting of the Association for Computational Linguistics*, pages 688–697.

Ekaterina Shutova. 2017. *Annotation of Linguistic and Conceptual Metaphor*, pages 1073–1100. Springer Netherlands, Dordrecht.

Gerard Steen, Lettie Dorst, J Berenike Herrmann, Anna Kaal, Tina Krennmayr, and Tryntje Pasma. 2019. *MIPVU: A manual for identifying metaphor-related words*, pages 24–40.

Gerard J. Steen, Aletta G. Dorst, J. Berenike Herrmann, Anna Kaal, Tina Krennmayr, and Trijntje Pasma. 2010. *A Method for Linguistic Metaphor Identification: From MIP to MIPVU*. John Benjamins.

Andrés Torres Rivera, Antoni Oliver, and Marta Coll-Florit. 2020. Metaphoricity detection in adjective-noun pairs. *Procesamiento del Lenguaje Natural*, 64:53–60.

Quan Tran, Andrew MacKinlay, and Antonio Jimeno-Yepes. 2017. Named entity recognition with stack residual LSTM and trainable bias decoding. *CoRR*, abs/1706.07598.

Peter Turney, Yair Neuman, Dan Assaf, and Yohai Cohen. 2011. Literal and Metaphorical Sense Identification through Concrete and Abstract Context. In *Proceedings of the 2011 Conference on Empirical Methods in Natural Language Processing*, pages 680–690, Edinburgh, Scotland, UK. Association for Computational Linguistics.

Tony Veale, Ekaterina Shutova, and Beata Beigman Klebanov. 2016. Metaphor: A Computational Perspective. *Synthesis Lectures on Human Language Technologies*, 9(1):1–160.

Chuhan Wu, Fangzhao Wu, Yubo Chen, Sixing Wu, Zhigang Yuan, and Yongfeng Huang. 2018. Neural Metaphor Detecting with CNN-LSTM Model. In *Proceedings of the Workshop on Figurative Language Processing*, pages 110–114, New Orleans, Louisiana. Association for Computational Linguistics.

Ping Xiao, Khalid Alnajjar, Mark Granroth-Wilding, Kat Agres, and Hannu Toivonen. 2016. Meta4meaning: Automatic metaphor interpretation using corpus-derived word associations. In *Proceedings of the 7th International Conference on Computational Creativity (ICCC). Paris, France*.

Augmenting Neural Metaphor Detection with Concreteness

Ghadi Alnafesah[1,2] and **Harish Tayyar Madabushi[1]** and **Mark Lee[1]**

[1] University of Birmingham, UK
(gxa713, H.TayyarMadabushi.1, m.g.lee)@bham.ac.uk

[2] Qassim University, KSA
gm.alnafesah@qu.edu.sa

Abstract

The idea that a shift in concreteness within a sentence indicates the presence of a metaphor has been around for a while. However, recent methods of detecting metaphor that have relied on deep neural models have ignored concreteness and related psycholinguistic information. We hypothesis that this information is not available to these models and that their addition will boost the performance of these models in detecting metaphor. We test this hypothesis on the Metaphor Detection Shared Task 2020 and find that the addition of concreteness information does in fact boost deep neural models. We also run tests on data from a previous shared task and show similar results.

1 Introduction

The automatic detection and processing of metaphor is an ongoing challenge for true deep semantic understanding of natural language text. Metaphors often convey unrelated concepts to their literal meaning and the meaning of metaphor involves more than just its words meaning, but it incorporates the whole context with a wider knowledge of their conceptual domain.

Traditional methods of metaphor detection that do not make use of neural networks have used concreteness scores to improve metaphor detection (Turney et al., 2011; Tsvetkov et al., 2013) . However, neural models that use distributional semantics (i.e. word embeddings: Mikolov et al. (2013)) have shown promising and often state-of-the-art results in a range of NLP tasks and have recently produced promising results in metaphor detection (Mao et al., 2018; Mishra et al., 2019; Rei et al., 2017). These models, however, focus on the textual information provided by the word embeddings and do not further explore the use and effect of combining other lexical information. This

paper reports the result of combining neural networks with a lexical resource for measuring concreteness for word-level metaphor detection.

Despite the success of deep neural models, we hypothesise that they do not have access to concreteness information with their structure. To test this, we explicitly add concreteness information to deep neural models and compare their performance with and without this information. Our experiments show that deep neural models, like more traditional models, do benefit from concreteness information.

2 Related Work

Early work, by Turney et al. (2011) on the use of concreteness to detect metaphor made use of the relatively small MRC psycholinguistic dataset (Coltheart, 1981) for concreteness scores. Their work uses a logistic regression model to detect the metaphoricity of adj-noun pairs in the TroFi dataset (Birke and Sarkar, 2006). Subsequently, Tsvetkov et al. (2013) made use of the same MRC dataset to detect subject-verb-obj metaphors from TroiFi dataset. They also train a supervised logistic regression classifier on English triples and test on a Russian dataset. Köper and Schulte im Walde (2017b) extend this work by using a significantly larger dataset (Brysbaert et al., 2014) of concreteness ratings and propagating the concreteness rating to phrases using word2vec (Mikolov et al., 2013). Their experiments use Leong et al. (2018)'s Logistic Regression classifier on VUAMC for verbs using ten-fold cross-validation process.

The context that a word occurs in plays an important role in metaphor detection (Klebanov et al., 2014). Words and phrases often convey very different meanings in different contexts. Consider the phrase *"cut down"* in the sentence *"She cut down his advances with her words."* In ab-

Proceedings of the Second Workshop on Figurative Language Processing, pages 204–210
July 9, 2020. ©2020 Association for Computational Linguistics
https://doi.org/10.18653/v1/P17

sence of the context, it is not clear that "*cut down*" is metaphorical. Many supervised learning approaches, including those described above, utilise bag of words methods, thus focusing on sets of features which do not capture context. Those that do consider context, do so only to a small extent, for example by focusing only on specific sentence constructs like *adj-noun* pairs (Bizzoni et al., 2017) or *subj-verb-obj* (Tsvetkov et al., 2013).

Given the importance of context and the power of neural models in capturing context, it was only natural to use deep neural models for metaphor detection. Gao et al. (2018) make use of deep neural networks to detect metaphor with significant success across multiple datasets including VUAMC. In particular they use Bidirectional Long Short Term Memory networks (Bi-LSTM) that capture relations in both directions for word-level metaphor classification with word-embeddings as input.

Other work on using concreteness and similar psycholinguistic features for metaphor detection include that by Bulat et al. (2017) who combined concreteness with property norms to formulate representations. Ljubešić et al. (2018) combine imageability scores with concreteness for cross-lingual metaphor detection and Dunn (2015) make use of abstractness.

This paper reports the result of applying concreteness score to individual words in the token-level metaphor classification for the Metaphor Detection Shared Task competition 2020. We build on Gao et al. (2018)'s sequence labelling network by adding concreteness scores to individual words.

The arrival of deep neural networks has meant that psycholinguistic features are no longer explicitly considered and, as mentioned in Section 1, we hypothesise that deep neural networks do not have access to this information. In this work, we show that this is the case and that access to this information improves the accuracy of deep neural networks by testing on multiple datasets.

3 Generalising Concreteness Scores

We used the resource created by Brysbaert et al. (2014) for concreteness scores. This is a list of about 40,000 English words rated for concreteness between 1 to 5 where 1 is most abstract and 5 is most concrete. As an illustration, "*wood*" has a rating of 4.85, "*counterargument*" a rating of 2.17 and "*conventionalism*" 1.18.

Before we can use concreteness scores for metaphor detection, we need a way of handling those words in our dataset that do not have corresponding concreteness scores in the concreteness lexical resource created by Brysbaert et al. (2014). The most obvious solution is to set the concreteness scores of these words to 0. However, the fact that a large number of words in our dataset do not have corresponding concreteness scores makes this impractical.

To get around this, we use the concreteness values available to train a Support Vector Machine. We use BERT (Devlin et al., 2018) embeddings as features to the SVM and the rounded up concreteness values as output classes. So as to use BERT embeddings as input to an SVM, we extract static, non-contextual BERT embeddings. We choose to use BERT, as opposed to static embedding like word2vec, due to BERT's unique tokenizer that allows for the generation of embeddings for all words in our dictionary. We use the following hyperparameters for the SVM: hidden layer sizes 100, activation identity, solver adam, alpha 0.0001, batch size auto, learning rate adaptive, learning rate init 0.001, powert 0.5, max iteration 200, shuffle True, random state None, tol 0.0001, verbose False, warm start False, momentum 0.9, nesterovs momentum True, early stopping False, validation fraction 0.1, beta1 0.9, beta2 0.999, epsilon 1e-08, and niter_no_change 10.

4 Neural Metaphor Detection with Concreteness

We use Gao et al. (2018)'s sequence labeling model as the baseline and modify it to include a concreteness rating as follows. For every input word x_i we modify w_i, the 300-D GloVe pretrained embedding for x_i, with the concreteness class assignment c_i of x_i. This results in a 301-D representation $[w_i : c_i]$ for each of the input words. These representations of words are fed to the sequence labeling model, which consists of a Bi-LSTM which generates a contextual representation of each word. These are then fed to feedforward neural networks which predict a label for each word. Figure 1 provides an illustration of the sequence labeling model, wherein the Bi-LSTM is represented by pink blocks and the blue blocks represent the feedforward neural networks.

We also test appending the probabilities of each of the four concreteness classes output by the

SVM. In this case the 300-D pre-trained representation w_i is concatenated with a vector p_i of length four, where each digit represents the probability of this word belonging to the output class 1, 2, 3 or 4 respectively. This results in a 304-D representation $[w_i : p_i]$ for each word. This method of using the probability distribution is unlike previous methods that have used a single concreteness score. We use the concreteness scorers generated by our SVM model even when a word and the corresponding concreteness score is included in the dataset provided (Brysbaert et al., 2014) and used as the training data for our SVM. We find that the addition of probabilities is far more effective than the addition of a single score possibly because this provides more of a signal for the model to pick up on (4 features not 1).

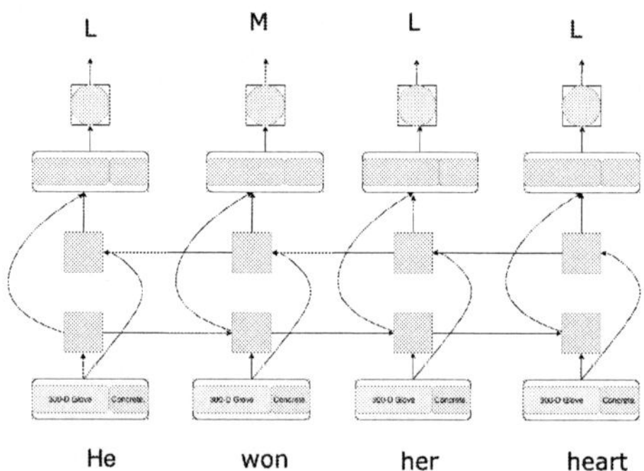

Figure 1: The sequence classification model architecture used in the experiment.

Importantly, if pre-trained embeddings (in our case GloVe) contained concreteness information, the explicit addition of this information by means of appending it to the embeddings should not improve the performance of a well trained Bi-LSTM model as such models are capable of extracting relevant information from their input. An improvement in performance with the addition of concreteness information would imply that such information is not contained in the pre-trained embeddings we use.

5   Results

The metaphor detection shared task allowed multiple submissions and we use this to evaluate different models, both with and without concreteness scores. We present this comparative analysis of our models first before describing our performance in Section 5.2. We also test our models on the previous shared and present these results in Section 5.3.

5.1   Comparitive Analysis

Table 1 summarises the results of our experiments on the VUA ALLPOS dataset. The results on the Shared Task data without concreteness rating is considered the baseline for measuring the model's performance. "Single Class Rating" refers to the model where a single number representing the class of the word was appended to the word's embedding, "Probability Rating" refers to the model where the probability for each class output by the SVM was was concatenated to the word embeddings.

Experiment	Precision	Recall	F1
Gao et al. (2018) with Shared Task Dataset	64.9%	48.9%	55.8%
Single class rating	60.3%	53.7%	56.8%
Probability rating	63.6%	52.9%	57.8%
Probability with rating 2 layers	65.5%	53.2%	58.7%
Probability rating with 3 layers	65.3%	54.8%	**59.6%**

Table 1: A comparison of models with and without concreteness.

Interestingly, the model that used the probabilities of each of the output classes performs the best. Further hyperparameter optimisation (by increasing the number of layers by one) increased F1 score to reach 59.6%. Modifying other hyperparameters did not improve performance. The values of the hyperparameters we use are: 10 epochs, hidden size of 300, batch size of 64, learning rate of 0.005, 1 hidden layer, and LSTM dropouts of 0.5 0 and .1 for input hidden and output layers respectively. So as to ensure that the addition of concreteness rankings is not simply introducing noise, we plot the loss for training and validation which is presented in Figure 2. A subjective analysis of these results is presented in Section 6.

5.2   Shared Task Results

We test our model on the VU Amsterdam Metaphoricial Corpus (VUAMC) by participating in the The Second Shared Task on Metaphor Detection for VUA AllPOS dataset. Our performance

206

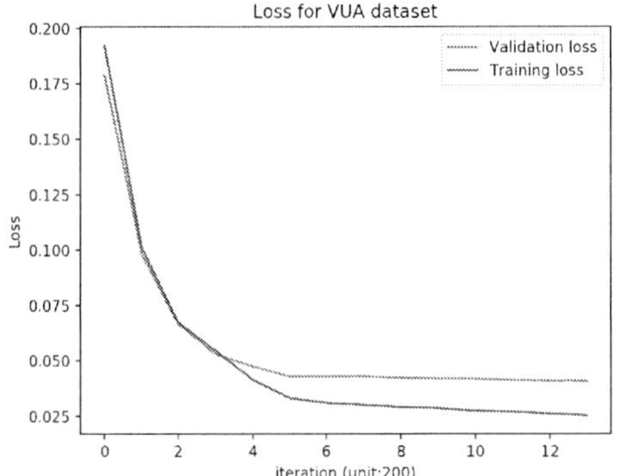

Figure 2: The training and validation loss for the sequence classification model.

on the task is show in Table 2

Rank	Team	F1
1	DeepMet	76.9%
2	xchenets	73.4%
3	meta-phor	73.0%
	...	
13	**UoB Team**	59.6%
14	eduardgzaharia	55.2%

Table 2: Our performance on the shared task.

The lackluster performance on the task can possibly be attributed to our use of static embeddings as opposed to the more powerful contextual pre-trained embeddings such as BERT. We intend to integrate concreteness into BERT models for metaphor detection in our future experiments (Section 7).

5.3 Further Experiments with Verbal Metaphor Detection

In addition to participating in the shared task we also experiment with the Gao et al. (2018)'s version of VUAMC dataset published by Leong et al. (2018) for 2018 Metaphor Shared Task. It should be noted that Gao et al. (2018) modify the task of metaphor detection to one of classification. While the shared task required the classification of metaphor at the word-level, Gao et al. (2018) provide a verb and a sentence containing that verb as input and required classifying that verb into either "Metaphor" or "Not Metaphor".

Once again, we use our reproduced results[1] of the target classification model by Gao et al.

---

[1]Gao et al. (2018) note that the model that they make available does not include the final hyperparameters used to generate their reported results.

(2018) as our baseline and augment it with concreteness scores as we did for this year's tasks. The classification model, like the sequence labeling model feeds word representations to a Bi-LSTM which generates a contextual representation of each word. Unlike in the sequence labeling model, the BiLSTM includes attention and these representations are concatenated and fed to a single feedforward neural network which predicts the label of the verb. Figure 3 provides an illustration of the classification model, wherein the Bi-LSTM is represented by pink blocks, the concatenated representation as the red square and the blue block represents the feedforward neural network. The coloured in circle represents the (highlighted) verb of interest in the sentence.

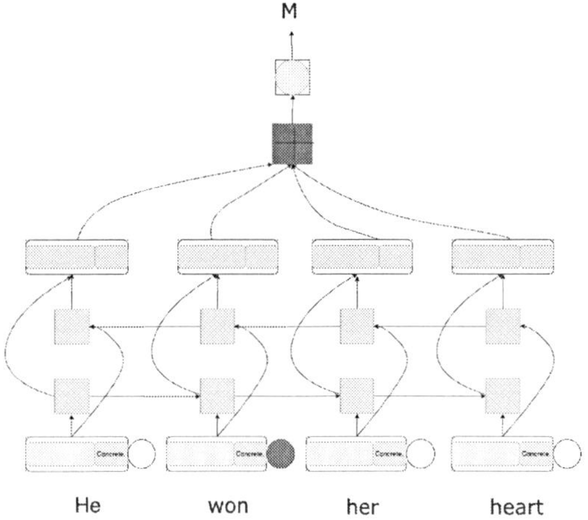

Figure 3: The classification model used for verb metaphor detection.

The values of the hyperparameters we use: 20 epochs, hidden size of 128, batch size of 16, learning rate of 0.01, hidden layers 1, and LSTM dropouts of 0.5 0.0 and 0.2 for input hidden and output layers respectively. The results of our experiments are presented in Table 3.

The classification model also has ELMo Peters et al. (2018) embeddings concatenated to the GloVe embeddings and concreteness score. The incorporation of ELMo embeddings ensures that we capture contextual information. The fact that the addition of concreteness to contextual embeddings shows improvement implies that contextual embeddings do not have access to concreteness information either.

Experiment	Precision	Recall	F1
Gao et al. (2018) classification *reproduced*	55.85%	49.80%	52.65%
Single class rating	57.93%	44.57%	50.38%
One-hot encoding	54.66%	52.18%	55.41%
Probability rating	52.02%	62.86%	56.92%
Probability rating + hyperparameter tuning	54.21%	62.46%	**58.04%**

Table 3: Summary of the experiments results on the classification task.

6 Analysis and Discussion

The training data from the VUAMC dataset has 181,501 tokens, 19,177 of which are labeled metaphor with 162,324 labeled literal. An exploration of the results shows that the most frequently occurring words in the dataset are prepositions. The word *of*, for example, occurs 4,638 but is labeled as a metaphor only 151 times. *With*, on the other hand, appears 995 times and is labelled as a metaphor 620 times and *up* is labelled 137 times as metaphor out of 335 occurrences. Table 5 shows a couple of most frequent words in the dataset along with the number of true positives and false negatives. It appears that prepositions appear so frequently that the distinction between their literal and metaphorical sense is hard to distinguish. For example, the model incorrectly classified the word *of* as literal in the the sentence "*Francesca Simon describes some of the pitfalls and how to avoid them.*"

In addition, prepositions also appear as part of phrases, such as in "*some of the*" making it harder still to classify them correctly. Often, the meaning of a phrasal verb differs significantly from that meaning of its parts. Additionally, concreteness of each of the individual parts is also different from that of the phrase. For example, in the sentence "*The use of role play, incorporating previously discussed difficulties (i.e. homework assignment session 4) in real or set up situations provide an opportunity for testing these skills.*", the overall meaning of the phrase *set up* is different from the meaning of *set* and *up*. Additionally, we were able to successfully classified *set* as a metaphor, but failed to classify *up* as a metaphor in this context.

The partial sentence "*real or set up situations*"

has the following information: The word *real*, a literal, has concreteness rating equals to 2 is correctly classified as literal. The word *or* is correctly labelled as literal has concreteness rating of 1. The word *set* is correctly classified as metaphor has concreteness rating of 3. Followed by the word *up* which is incorrectly labelled as literal has concreteness of 3. Lastly, the word *situations* is incorrectly classified as literal has concreteness rating of 2. The noticeable shift in concreteness from rating 1 to 3 for *or* and *set* could lead to successfully classifying set as a metaphor but failed to classify *up* as also a metaphor, although the two forms the meaning of the phrasal vary, because *up*'s rating is not very far from *set*'s rating. A similar error occurs when classifying the phrasal verb "*put up with*" in the sentence "*they also have to put up with the heaviest police presence .*"

Each word meaning by itself differs from the meaning of the whole phrase. *Put* means to place something physically, *up* means the position *up* and *with* mean accompanied by someone or something; however, these three together refer "*to accept an unpleasant situation, something or someone* (willingly or not)." As for their and their near context degrees of abstractness are as follows: The word *to* is correctly labelled as literal has rating equal to metaphor, *put* is correctly labelled as literal has rating 2 as its concreteness rating, followed by the word *up* that is correctly labelled as literal and has a rating of 3. Next is the word *with* that is incorrectly classified as literal has concreteness of 2 and lastly, the word *the* is correctly classified as literal has concreteness of 1. Since there is no drastic shift in concreteness or their senses, the model fails to spot the hits and labels them all as literal.

Of the 15,439 unique tokens in the dataset, 7527 tokens appear exactly once. For example, "*There were others , but Lucy never disclosed any of them to us*" the word *disclosed* is labelled as metaphor but incorrectly classified as literal. There are two interpretations for this sentence. The metaphorical sentence talks about uncovering "*people's identities*" Lucy knew when referencing *others* and *them*, or could literally talks about uncovering of "*secrets*" Lucy hides, which are referenced by *them* and *others*. As for the concreteness ratings for the sentence's words, the rating range between 1 and 2, other than *Lucy* that has rating of 4; therefore, we could say that the rating did not help to

The sentence	The label	The Predicted Label	Concrete-ness Rating
And they told it without onscreen questioning , though the programme is *skilfully* structured to give it a coherence it might have lacked .	0	0	1
The burn threads a wild and inhospitable crevice of the hills , where the wind blows cold and the sense of *isolation* grows with each lonely mile .	1	0	2
Although that is the position in law , the court emphasised that as a matter of sense a tenant should first complain to the landlord before *exercising* the right to prosecute .	1	1	2

Table 4: Sample of sentences that contain words used only once throughout the dataset, their label, predicted label and their concreteness rating.

Word	True Positive	False Negative	Count
of	3	148	4638
to	538	239	3731
in	1198	285	2811
with	510	110	995
go	24	40	258

Table 5: Sample of words with the highest word counts in the dataset, and their counts for how many times the model correctly classified them as metaphors or failed by classifying them as literal.

clarify the meaning. To better understand the intended meaning (literal or metaphorical), this ambiguous sentence needs more context. The same can be said about the word *corruption* in "*Bribery and corruption!*" This sentence word's concreteness ratings are (2, 1, and 2) respectively; thus, to correctly classify *corruption* as metaphor, more context is required. Table 4 show more sentences containing words that appeared only once along with their labels, predicted labels and concreteness classes.

7 Conclusion and Future Work

This paper reports the results of providing deep neural models with concreteness information by appending a measure of concreteness to word embedding for all content words. Our hypothesis is that explicitly adding a concreteness rating to the word representation will boost the neural network performance in detecting metaphors as neural models do not have access to this information. We tested two representations of concreteness, one as a scale and the other is class probabilities using the VUA ALLPOS data from the Second Metaphor Detection Shared Task 2020 and data from the First Metaphor Detection Shared Task

2018 and find that this information does boost performance in all cases.

We plan on testing the effectiveness of incorporating other psycholinguistic information, such as imageability, into deep neural models so as to establish their impact on metaphor detection. We also intend to incorporate these features into contextual pre-trained models, such as BERT (Devlin et al., 2018) as context is critical to identifying metaphor. In this current work, BERT pre-trained representations were used only in training an SVM and not in the Bi-LSTM that detects metaphor.

We also intend to use more complex models to expand concreteness, imageability and other such features to a larger vocabulary. These models will be designed to perform classification better and also capture context so as to better identify the concreteness of words in context. Finally, we intend to extend our work to include phrases a significant source of errors in this task.

References

Julia Birke and Anoop Sarkar. 2006. A clustering approach for nearly unsupervised recognition of non-literal language. In *11th Conference of the European Chapter of the Association for Computational Linguistics*.

Yuri Bizzoni, Stergios Chatzikyriakidis, and Mehdi Ghanimifard. 2017. "deep" learning: Detecting metaphoricity in adjective-noun pairs. In *Proceedings of the Workshop on Stylistic Variation*, pages 43–52.

Marc Brysbaert, Amy Beth Warriner, and Victor Kuperman. 2014. Concreteness ratings for 40 thousand generally known english word lemmas. *Behavior research methods*, 46(3):904–911.

Luana Bulat, Stephen Clark, and Ekaterina Shutova. 2017. Modelling metaphor with attribute-based semantics. *Proceedings of the 15th Conference of the*

European Chapter of the Association for Computational Linguistics.

Max Coltheart. 1981. The mrc psycholinguistic database. *The Quarterly Journal of Experimental Psychology Section A*, 33(4):497–505.

Jacob Devlin, Ming-Wei Chang, Kenton Lee, and Kristina Toutanova. 2018. Bert: Pre-training of deep bidirectional transformers for language understanding. *arXiv preprint arXiv:1810.04805.*

Jonathan Dunn. 2015. Modeling abstractness and metaphoricity. *Metaphor and Symbol*, 30(4):259–289.

Ge Gao, Eunsol Choi, Yejin Choi, and Luke Zettlemoyer. 2018. Neural metaphor detection in context. *arXiv preprint arXiv:1808.09653.*

Beata Beigman Klebanov, Ben Leong, Michael Heilman, and Michael Flor. 2014. Different texts, same metaphors: Unigrams and beyond. In *Proceedings of the Second Workshop on Metaphor in NLP*, pages 11–17.

Maximilian Köper and Sabine Schulte im Walde. 2017b. Improving verb metaphor detection by propagating abstractness to words, phrases and individual senses. In *Proceedings of the 1st Workshop on Sense, Concept and Entity Representations and their Applications*, pages 24–30, Valencia, Spain. Association for Computational Linguistics.

Chee Wee Leong, Beata Beigman Klebanov, and Ekaterina Shutova. 2018. A report on the 2018 vua metaphor detection shared task. In *Proceedings of the Workshop on Figurative Language Processing*, New Orleans, LA.

Nikola Ljubešić, Darja Fišer, and Anita Peti-Stantić. 2018. Predicting concreteness and imageability of words within and across languages via word embeddings. *arXiv preprint arXiv:1807.02903.*

Rui Mao, Chenghua Lin, and Frank Guerin. 2018. Word embedding and wordnet based metaphor identification and interpretation. In *Proceedings of the 56th Annual Meeting of the Association for Computational Linguistics*. Association for Computational Linguistics (ACL).

Tomas Mikolov, Kai Chen, Greg Corrado, and Jeffrey Dean. 2013. Efficient estimation of word representations in vector space. *arXiv preprint arXiv:1301.3781.*

Pushkar Mishra, Marco Del Tredici, Helen Yannakoudakis, and Ekaterina Shutova. 2019. Author profiling for hate speech detection. *arXiv preprint arXiv:1902.06734.*

Matthew E. Peters, Mark Neumann, Mohit Iyyer, Matt Gardner, Christopher Clark, Kenton Lee, and Luke Zettlemoyer. 2018. Deep contextualized word representations. In *Proc. of NAACL.*

Marek Rei, Luana Bulat, Douwe Kiela, and Ekaterina Shutova. 2017. Grasping the finer point: A supervised similarity network for metaphor detection. *arXiv preprint arXiv:1709.00575.*

Yulia Tsvetkov, Elena Mukomel, and Anatole Gershman. 2013. Cross-lingual metaphor detection using common semantic features. In *Proceedings of the First Workshop on Metaphor in NLP*, pages 45–51.

Peter D Turney, Yair Neuman, Dan Assaf, and Yohai Cohen. 2011. Literal and metaphorical sense identification through concrete and abstract context. In *Proceedings of the Conference on Empirical Methods in Natural Language Processing*, pages 680–690. Association for Computational Linguistics.

Supervised Disambiguation of German Verbal Idioms with a BiLSTM Architecture

Rafael Ehren[1], Timm Lichte[2], Laura Kallmeyer[1], Jakub Waszczuk[1]
[1]Heinrich Heine University, Düsseldorf, Germany
[2]University of Tübingen, Tübingen, Germany
{ehren|kallmeyer|waszczuk}@phil.hhu.de
timm.lichte@uni-tuebingen.de

Abstract

Supervised disambiguation of verbal idioms (VID) poses special demands on the quality and quantity of the annotated data used for learning and evaluation. In this paper, we present a new VID corpus for German and perform a series of VID disambiguation experiments on it. Our best classifier, based on a neural architecture, yields an error reduction across VIDs of 57% in terms of accuracy compared to a simple majority baseline.

1 Introduction

Figurative language is not just a momentary product of creativity and associative processes, but a vast number of metaphors, metonyms, etc. have become conventionalized and are part of every speaker's lexicon. Still, in most cases, they can simultaneously be understood in a non-figurative, literal way, however implausible this reading might be. Take, for example, the following sentence:

(1)   He is in the bathroom and talks to Huey on the big white telephone.

The verbal phrase *talk to Huey on the big white telephone* can be understood as a figurative euphemism for being physically sick. But it could also be taken literally to describe an act of remote communication with a person called Huey. Despite the ambiguity, a speaker of English will most probably choose the figurative reading in (1), also because of the presence of certain syntactic cues such as the adjective sequence *big white* or the use of *telephone* instead of, for example, *mobile*. Omitting such cues generally makes the reader more hesitant at selecting the figurative meaning. There is thus a strong connection of non-literal meaning and properties pertaining to the form of the expression, which is characterstic for what Baldwin and

Kim (2010) call an idiom. Since the figurative expression in (1) consists of a verb and its syntactic arguments, we will furthermore call it a Verbal Idiom (VID) adapting the terminology in Ramisch et al. (2018).

While it is safe to assume that the VID *talk to Huey on the big white telephone* almost never occurs with a literal reading, this does not hold for all idioms. The expression *break the ice* for example can easily convey both a literal (*The trawler broke the ice*) and a non-literal meaning (*The welcome speech broke the ice*) depending on the subject. Although recent work suggests that literal occurrences of VIDs generally are quite rare in comparison to the idiomatic ones (Savary et al., 2019), it remains a qualitatively major problem with the risk of serious errors due to wrong disambiguation.

However, tackling this problem with supervised learning poses special demands on the learning and test data in order to be successful. Most importantly, since the semantic and morphosyntactic properties of VID types (and idioms in general) are very diverse and idiosyncratic, the data must contain a sufficient number of tokens of both the literal and non-literal readings for each VID. In addition, each token should allow access to the context because the context can provide important hints as to the intended reading.

In this paper, we investigate the supervised disambiguation of potential occurrences of German VIDs. For training and evaluation, we have created COLF-VID (Corpus of Literal and Figurative Readings of Verbal Idioms), a German annotated corpus of literal and semantically idiomatic occurrences of 34 preselected VID types. Altogether, we have collected 6985 sentences with candidate occurrences that have been semantically annotated by three annotators with high inter-annotator agreement. The annotations overall show a relatively low idiomaticity rate of 77.55 %, while the idiomaticity

Proceedings of the Second Workshop on Figurative Language Processing, pages 211–220
July 9, 2020. ©2020 Association for Computational Linguistics
https://doi.org/10.18653/v1/P17

rates of the single VIDs vary greatly. The derived corpus is made available under the Creative Commons Attribution-ShareAlike 4.0 International license.[1] To the best of our knowledge, it represents the largest available collection of German VIDs annotated on token-level.

Furthermore, we report on disambiguation experiments using COLF-VID in order to establish a first baseline on this corpus. These experiments use a neural architecture with different pretrained word representations as inputs. Compared to a simple majority baseline, the best classifier yields an error reduction across VIDs of 57% in terms of accuracy.

2   Related Work

2.1   VID Resources

In this section, we discuss previous work on the creation of token-level corpora of VID types.

Cook et al. (2007) draw on syntactic properties of multiword expressions to perform token-level classification of certain VID types. To this end they created a dataset of 2984 instances drawn from the BNC (British National Corpus), covering 53 different verb-noun idiomatic combination (VNIC) types (Cook et al., 2008). The annotation tag set includes the labels LITERAL, IDIOMATIC and UNKNOWN which correspond to three of the four labels used for COLF-VID, albeit the conditions for the application of UNKNOWN where a bit different, since the annotators only had access to one sentence per instance. The overall reported unweighted Kappa score, calculated on the dev and test set, is 0.76. Split decisions were discussed among the two judges to receive a final annotation.

The VU Amsterdam Metaphor Corpus (Steen et al., 2010) is currently probably the largest manually annotated corpus of non-literal language and is freely available. It comprises roughly 200,000 English sentences from different genres and provides annotations basically for all non-functional words following a refined version of the Metaphor Identification Procedure (MIP) (Pragglejaz Group, 2007). Regarding only verbs, this yields an impressive overall number of 37962 tokens with 18.7% "metaphor-related" readings (Steen et al., 2010; Herrmann, 2013). Due to its general purpose and the lack of lexical filtering, however, this is hardly comparable with COLF-VID.

The IDIX (IDioms In Context) corpus created by Sporleder et al. (2010) can be seen as the English counterpart of COLF-VID. It is an add-on to the BNC XML Edition and contains 5836 annotated instances of 78 pre-selected VIDs mainly of the form V+NP and V+PP. As for our corpus, expressions were favoured that presumably had a high literality rate. The employed tag set was more or less identical with ours. Quite remarkably, and in stark contrast to COLF-VID and other comparable corpora, the literal occurrences in the IDIX corpus represent the majority class with 49.4% (vs. 45.4% instances being tagged as NON-LITERAL). They report a Kappa score of 0.87 which was evaluated using 1,136 instances that were annotated independently by two annotators.

Fritzinger et al. (2010) conduct a survey on a German dataset similar to ours. They extracted 9700 instances of 77 potentially idiomatic preposition-noun-verb triples from two different corpora. Two annotators independently classified the candidates according to whether they were used literally or idiomatically in a given context. The tag set also included an AMBIGUOUS label, but, as was the case with Cook et al. (2008), only single sentences were available as context to determine the correct reading. An agreement rate of 97.9% was computed on the basis of 6,690 instances. The biggest difference to our and other presented corpora is the very high idiomaticity rate of 96.12%. However, this dataset does not seem to be publicly available.

Horbach et al. (2016) are concerned with German infitive-verb compounds such as *sitzen lassen* ('let sit'⇒'leave someone'), i.e. verb groups with an idiomatic reading that consist of an inflected head verb and an infinitive modifier. In order to conduct experiments on automatic detection and disambigution of these kinds of VIDs they created a corpus of 6000 instances of 6 different infinitive-verb compounds which were annotated by two experts with the label set LITERAL, IDIOMATIC and ? (for undecidable). In contrast to Cook et al. (2008) and Fritzinger et al. (2010), a context of one sentence to the left and one sentence to the right of the candidate was taken into account. The annotation process proved to be especially challenging since some of the examined compounds had several literal and figurative meanings. Nevertheless, they achieved high agreement values of $(0.6 < \kappa < 0.8)$ or $(\kappa > 0.8)$ for most expressions with a mean idiomaticity rate of 65.5%.[2]

---

[2]Kappa scores and idiomaticity rates were reported independently for each expression.

2.2 VID Disambiguation

Even though literal occurrences of VIDs seem to be a rare phenomenon (Savary et al., 2019), it is still desirable to account for them, i.e. to disambiguate between idiomatic and literal reading. It may be a quantitatively minor problem, but qualitatively it continues to be a major challenge for NLP, for instance for machine translation systems.

VIDs exhibit a variety of properties exploitable for determining the correct reading of a candidate expression. On the morphosyntactic level a lot of VIDs are less flexible than their literal counterparts, e.g. the idiomatic *kick the bucket* is not readily passivizable. On the semantic level VIDs often disrupt the cohesion of a sentence, because of their non-compositionality, or they violate selectional preferences, for example in the sentence *The city shows its teeth*.

Examples for a morphosyntactic approach are the works of Cook et al. (2007) and Fazly et al. (2009). They show that it is possible to leverage automatically acquired knowledge about the syntactic behaviour of VNICs, i.e. their syntactic fixedness, to perform token-level disambiguation.

Katz and Giesbrecht (2006) draw on semantic properties by using dense word vectors to identify literal and idiomatic occurrences of the German VID *ins Wasser fallen* (idiomatically 'to be cancelled', literally 'to fall into the water'). They assumed that the contexts of the literal and idiomatic use of this expression differ which in turn is represented by their distributional vectors. Test instances are then compared to these vectors in order to classify them.

Li and Sporleder (2009) and Ehren (2017) both used cohesion-based graphs for the disambiguation task, the assumption being that semantically idiomatic expressions disrupt the cohesion of the context they appear in. The former used Normalized Google Distance, while the latter used the cosine between word embeddings to capture the semantic similarity of words. To classify the test instances in an unsupervised way, graphs were built based on the two mentioned metrics and if the mean value rose after the removal of the instance, it was classified as idiomatic.

Shutova et al. (2010) and Haagsma and Bjerva (2016) employ the knowledge that metaphors tend to violate selectional preferences to detect them in running text.

Building on these insights from previous work, in this paper, we will use a BiLSTM architecture based on different types of word embeddings that is intended to capture the semantic properties of the VID itself, together with the context and the morphosyntactic flexibility of the specific VID instance.

3 The Creation of the Corpus

3.1 The Data

As mentioned above, literal occurrences of VIDs usually seem to occur quite rarely. The German dataset of the PARSEME 1.1 corpus (Ramisch et al., 2018) consists of 8996 sentences with 1341 instances of VIDs. These 1341 instances have an idiomaticity rate of 98%, i.e. the whole dataset only includes a handful of literal occurrences. Training and evaluating a classifier with such an imbalance of classes would prove rather difficult. Thus, it is not feasible to gather a sufficient amount of data by selecting sentences at random – at least if human resources are limited – and it is not possible to build a huge dataset so that the natural occurrence rate will give us enough literal readings. In order to alleviate the data sparsity, we hand-picked a number of VID types with presumably high numbers of literal occurrences. Afterwards we extracted sentences (along with their contexts) from the German newspaper corpus TüPP-D/Z[3] that contained the lexical components of our VID types as lemmas. We then manually filtered out coincidental occurrences with an undesired coarse syntactic structure (Savary et al., 2019), leaving us with only valid candidates for our corpus. Table 1 shows the 34 different types. One thing that immediately stands out is the fact that most of the pre-chosen VID types (26 to be exact) consist of a prepositional phrase (PP) and a verb. The rest consists of verb-noun combinations with the noun in direct object position. Another salient property of this dataset is the high variance with respect to the number of candidates per type. For the VID *an Glanz verlieren* ('loose sheen'⇒'loose attractivity'), we only found 5 instances, while *auf dem Tisch liegen* ('lay on the table'⇒'be topic') is represented by 951 candidates.

3.2 The Annotation Labels

Besides the labels LITERAL, IDIOMATIC we also use the labels UNDECIDABLE and BOTH in cases

---

[3]http://hdl.handle.net/11858/
00-1778-0000-0007-5E99-D

VID type	Lit.	Idiom.	Und.	Both	I%
am Boden liegen	35	11	0	1	23.4
an Glanz verlieren	0	15	1	0	93.75
an Land ziehen	25	235	0	0	90.38
am Pranger stehen	0	5	0	0	100.0
den Atem anhalten	10	30	0	0	75.0
auf dem Abstellgleis stehen	15	11	0	0	42.31
auf den Arm nehmen	39	50	0	0	42.31
auf der Ersatzbank sitzen	16	5	0	0	23.81
auf der Straße stehen	93	156	1	0	62.4
auf der Strecke bleiben	4	616	1	0	99.19
auf dem Tisch liegen	262	678	10	1	71.29
auf den Zug aufspringen	5	121	0	0	96.03
eine Brücke bauen	109	238	1	0	68.39
die Fäden ziehen	9	164	0	0	94.8
im Blut haben	29	7	0	0	19.44
in den Keller gehen	34	91	0	0	72.8
in der Luft hängen	28	256	0	0	90.14
im Regen stehen	69	302	4	4	79.68
ins Rennen gehen	11	51	0	0	82.26
in eine Sackgasse geraten	2	99	0	0	98.02
im Schatten stehen	7	52	0	1	86.67
in Schieflage geraten	3	40	1	0	90.91
ins Wasser fallen	67	186	0	0	73.52
Luft holen	100	66	4	0	38.82
mit dem Feuer spielen	9	74	2	0	87.06
einen Nerv treffen	1	284	0	0	99.65
die Notbremse ziehen	51	275	0	0	84.36
eine Rechnung begleichen	89	162	0	0	64.54
von Bord gehen	45	48	0	0	51.61
vor der Tür stehen	189	409	1	1	68.17
ein Zelt aufschlagen	53	41	6	0	41.0
über Bord gehen	62	52	1	0	45.22
über Bord werfen	54	389	0	0	87.81
über die Bühne gehen	2	198	0	0	99.0
Total	1527	5417	33	8	77.55

Table 1: Statistics of COLF-VID

where an expression can be seen as LITERAL and
IDIOMATIC at the same time for different reasons.

As to UNDECIDABLE, the disambiguation of an
expressions is not possible due to the lack of context. For instance, this is notoriously difficult for
metonymic expressions whose literal meaning describes a bodily action that typically co-occurs with
the idiomatic meaning. An example of that is the
German expression *sich die Haare raufen* ('to scuf-
fle one's hair' ⇒ 'to be worried/upset'): A person
that is upset can often be seen scuffling their hair.[4]

By contrast, the label BOTH applies to cases
where the literal and idiomatic readings seem to be
both intended, as illustrated in (2):

(2) Wer möchte, könnte ihm den Kopf waschen,
     Who wants, could him the head wash,
     ihm mal auf den Zahn fühlen oder ihn gar
     him once on the tooth feel   or   him even
     auf den Arm nehmen [...].
     on the arm take   [...].

This sentence originates from an article depicting
proposals on how to proceed with the statue of
a certain historic personality and it contains the

VIDs *jmdm. den Kopf waschen* ('wash someone's
head' ⇒ 'scold someone'), *jmdm. auf den Zahn
fühlen* ('feel someone's tooth' ⇒ 'interrogate someone') and *jmdn. auf den Arm nehmen* ('take someone on your arm' ⇒ 'taunt someone'[5]). The author
of the sentence suggests to tear the statue down and
to perform the aforementioned actions in an effort
to demystify the person represented by the statue.
The wordplay used here relies on the fact that all
the VIDs relate to bodily actions and could be performed on a statue. Thus, both readings, literal and
idiomatic, are active at the same time.

3.3 The Annotation Guidelines

The annotation guidelines basically consisted of
definitions of the applicable labels, coupled with
examples. A condensed version of the definitions
is given below:

- **LITERAL**: In the context of this annotation
  task we equate literality with compositionality. We understand compositionality as the
  property that the semantics of an expression
  is determined by the most basic meanings of
  its components without any form of figuration
  involved.

- **IDIOMATIC**: According to Baldwin and Kim
  (2010)[6] there are different forms of idiomaticity: lexical, syntactic, semantic, pragmatic
  and statistical. In the context of this annotation task, "idiomatic" is used synonymously
  with "semantically idiomatic", i.e. the property of an expression that it is not possible to
  fully derive its meaning by only considering
  the semantics of its components. Thus we
  understand semantic idiomaticity as a lack of
  compositionality.

- **UNDECIDABLE**: This label is for cases in
  which it is not possible to decide whether the
  target expression is literal or idiomatic.

- **BOTH**: While the label UNDECIDABLE means
  that there is only one possible reading, but it's
  not feasible to decide which, the label BOTH
  denotes the phenomenon of the two readings
  being activated at the same time.

---

[4] *Pull out one's hair* would be the English equivalent, but
very seldomly, if not for huge emotional distress, people actually pull out their hair when upset.

[5] The literal meaning of *jmdn. auf den Arm nehmen* would
be 'pick someone up'. A translation to English that keeps
reference to a corresponding bodily action would be *to pull
someone's leg*.

[6] The annotators were required to read Baldwin and Kim
(2010) prior to the annotation.

The annotation task then consisted of applying one of the labels to each candidate.

4 Annotation Results

The annotation was performed by three trained linguists on the whole dataset. The annotation results are summarized in Table 1. Columns 2 to 5 contain the counts of the majority decisions for the different labels, while column 6 contains the idiomaticity rate of a VID type. Figure 1 shows an example for an instance of the VID type *die Notbremse ziehen* ('pull the emergency breaks' ⇒ 'quickly terminate a process')[7] in the column format of the corpus. The

```
# global.columns = ID FORM LEMMA
POS ANNO_1 ANNO_2 ANNO_3 MAJORITY_ANNO
# article_id = T890825.128
# text = Bundesbahn will die
Notbremse ziehen
# context_judgement_1 = 0
# context_judgement_2 = 0
1 Bundesbahn Bundesbahn NN * * * *
2 will wollen VMFIN * * * *
3 die die ART * * * *
4 Notbremse Notbremse NN 2 2 2 2
5 ziehen ziehen VVINF 2 2 2 2
```

Figure 1: A sample idiomatic instance in COLF-VID

last four columns contain the annotations: columns 5 to 7 are the annotations of the three different annotators, the last column contains the majority annotation. Since all the annotators agreed that the reading of this instance is idiomatic (2 stands for the tag IDIOMATIC), this is an example for a clear-cut decision. In the rare cases where there was a split decision and every annotator chose a different label, the label UNDECIDABLE was employed.

What immediately stands out is that the overall idiomaticity rate is not nearly as high as the 98% reported for the German PARSEME dataset mentioned in Section 3.1 It ranges from 19.44% (*im Blut haben* 'be in one's blood') to 99.65%[8] (*den Nerv treffen*) and is 77.55% in total. But one has to keep in mind that these two datasets are hardly comparable regarding their statistics, since COLF-VID was created with the intention to maximize the number of literal occurrences by only choosing VID types with a presumably high literality count. Even though there are some VID types with

an unexpectedly high idiomaticity rate (*auf der Strecke bleiben, in eine Sackgasse geraten* or *über die Bühne gehen* to name a few), the large majority of the chosen VID types is indeed represented with a relatively low idiomaticity rate.

Only 0.59 of the instances received the labels UNDECIDABLE or BOTH (see Figure 2), but this is hardly surprising. We nevertheless wanted to include these tags for the sake of completeness and linguistic interest.

For the three annotators we calculated the following Cohen's Kappa scores on the basis of the whole dataset:

- annotator 1 – annotator 2: 0.9
- annotator 2 – annotator 3: 0.8
- annotator 1 – annotator 3: 0.77

Thus, the agreement is high for all three annotators, which is expected given the nature of the task and the equally high agreement scores reported for comparable corpora (Cook et al. (2008), Sporleder et al. (2010), Fritzinger et al. (2010)).

Another feature of COLF-VID is the context judgement provided by two of the annotators. These judgements can be seen in Figure 1 in the last two lines (starting with a hash tag) before the beginning of the sentence. They indicate whether the annotators needed more than one sentence to determine the reading of an instance. The two zeros denote that this was not the case for this candidate expression ("1" would indicate the opposite). Even if the sentence is rather short with only five words, the fact that the pulling of an emergency break requires an animate agent if used literally was enough information for both annotators to make their decisions. The context judgement feature provides the possibility of excluding candidates where none of the annotators was able to determine the reading only from a single sentence. As a result, instances where one sentence is not sufficient to make an informed decision would be prevented from entering a given system (e.g. a classifier which aims to disambiguate the candidates).

5 VID Disambiguation Experiments

5.1 Setup

The Task The goal of the presented experiments is to train a classifier capable of distinguishing the different readings of a candidate expression. It is important to emphasize that this task is different

---

[7]Translation: "The federal railway wants to pull the emergency breaks". The combination of *federal railway* and *pull emergency breaks* is very frequent in COLF-VID for obvious reasons.

[8]*Am Pranger stehen* 'stand in the pillory' has an idiomaticity rate of 100%, but its 5 candidates might not be that representative.

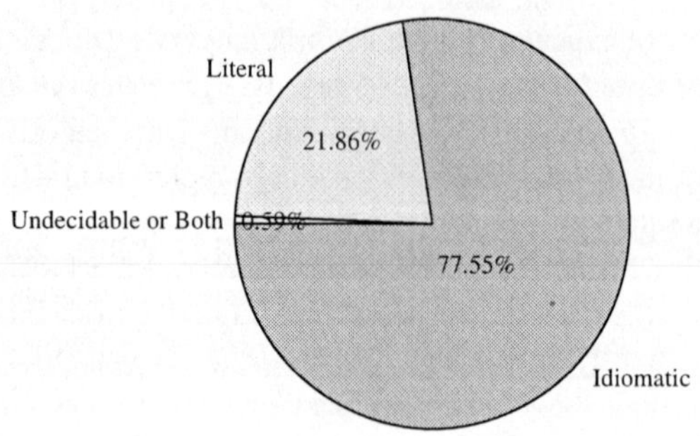

Figure 2: Distribution of annotation labels in COLF-VID

from *identification*, where all the VID occurrences are to be identified in a sentence, e.g. by applying a sequential model to label every token as a VID component or not. The reason for this is that COLF – for now – is a lexical sample corpus, which means it consists of a pre-selected set of target expressions annotated with respect to their contexts. In other words, the sentences could contain non-annotated instances of VID types that weren't part of the pre-selected set, which in turn could confuse the system during training and skew the evaluation results (we will further address this issue in section 6.)

Thus, we modeled the task assuming another process had pre-identified the candidate expressions, which is the usual approach when it comes to the disambiguation of VIDs (Constant et al., 2017). The classifier then only has to decide which label to apply given a certain instance and its context. This means that, although all components of a VID instance received a label during annotation[9] (cf. Figure 1), during classification we conflated all labels of a VID instance into one label for the whole expression. This is possible, since we did not allow for components of an instance to have different labels. For example, the verb cannot be literal while the noun is idiomatic.

Word Representations   During the experiments we employed word representations that were pretrained on other, considerably larger corpora with three different models: Word2vec (Skip-gram) (Mikolov et al., 2013), fastText (CBOW) (Bojanowski et al., 2016) and ELMo (Embeddings from Language Models) (Peters et al., 2018). We trained the Word2vec embeddings ourselves[10] on

a variant of the German web corpus DECOW16 (Schäfer and Bildhauer, 2012) which consists of 11 billion tokens and shuffled sentences. The resulting vectors have 100 dimensions. As for the other models we reverted to already existing resources. The fastText embeddings were trained on Common Crawl and Wikipedia with a dimensionality of 300[11]. The German ELMo model was trained on a special Wikipedia corpus that also included the comments besides the articles (May, 2019)[12]. The underlying bidirectional language model provided us with 3 different word representations of size 1024 for each input token. These were averaged to give us one embedding per token.

Architecture   There are different properties on the morphosyntactic and semantic level we can leverage during the disambiguation process. E.g. some VIDs do not possess the same lexical or morphological flexibility as their literal counterparts. The VID *kick the bucket*, for instance, does not allow for *bucket* to be replaced by a synonym like *pail* or for it to be in plural form, hence both would be strong indicators for literality. On the semantic level the surrounding context can of course give clues about the correct readings. An observation made during annotation was that, over and over again, the violation of selectional preferences gave a strong indication on how to annotate a candidate. For example in a sentence like *Berlin holds its breath*, *Berlin* is no animate subject which immediately gives away the non-literal nature of the sentence. This is why we settled for a classifier architecture that is best suited for taking the context into account. Figure 3 shows a graph of our architecture.

For an input sentence s of length n with words $w_1, ..., w_n$ we associate every word w_i with its corresponding pretrained word embedding which gives us our input sequence of vectors $x_{1:n}$:

$$x_i = e(w_i)$$

In the case we use Word2vec embeddings, a sequence $w_{1:n}$ consists of lemmas, while for fastText it consists of tokens, because the former model was trained on lemmas and the latter on n-grams.

After the embedding assignment the sequence $x_{1:n}$ is fed into a bidirectional recurrent neural net

---

[9]In order to allow for a different kind of task at a later point.

[10]We used the word2vec implementation of the python package gensim (Řehůřek and Sojka, 2010).

[11]https://fasttext.cc/docs/en/crawl-vectors.html

[12]https://github.com/t-systems-on-site-services-gmbh/german_elmo_model

$$(Score_{Literal}, Score_{Idiomatic}, Score_{Undecidable}, Score_{Both})$$

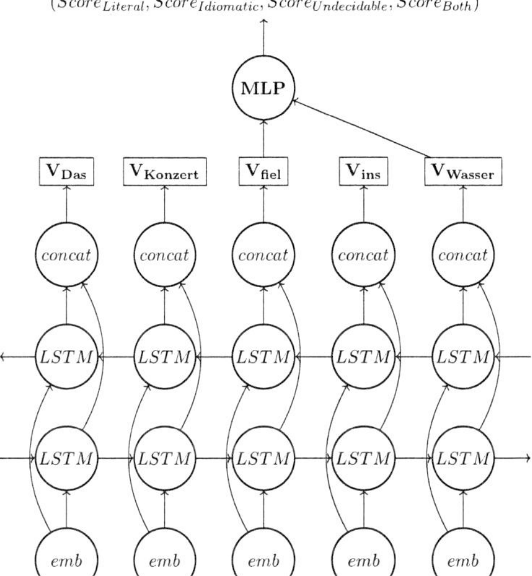

Figure 3: Architecture of the neural model

with LSTM (Hochreiter and Schmidhuber, 1997) units (BiLSTM) in order to receive contextualized representations v_i of each input element w_i:

$$v_i = LSTM_{\theta_F}(x_{1:n}, i) \circ LSTM_{\theta_B}(x_{1:n}, i)$$

The contextualized representation v_i is the concatenation (denoted by $\circ$) of the outputs computed by the forward ($LSTM_{\theta_F}$) and backward ($LSTM_{\theta_B}$) LSTM. Hence, v_i ideally contains information about all the preceding and succeeding items.

We then take two of those vectors, namely those for the verb and noun of the potential VID[13], concatenate them and feed the result into a multi-layer perceptron (MLP) to obtain the final scores:

$$SCORE(v_i \circ v_j) = MLP(v_i \circ v_j)$$

where v_i and v_j are the contextualized representations of the verb and the noun of the potential VID, respectively. We did not include prepositions into the input for the final scoring, because some expressions in COLF come without a lexicalized preposition (even though most do).

Till now, we only considered Word2vec and fastText embeddings as inputs. However, for ELMo things are a bit different on the input level. While Word2vec and fastText are functions that map each word to exactly one embedding, ELMo assigns different embeddings to the same word, depending on its context:

$$x_i = ELMo(w_{1:n}, i)$$

This means, we introduce context already at the very beginning, which we assume is a great advantage for the system, since the components of the candidates receive different vectors depending on their context. E.g. during the classification process with Word2vec or fastText embeddings, the word *ice* in the sentences *The weight of the ship broke the ice* and *With a joke he broke the ice* would receive the same vector, while ELMo should assign them different representations.

Training and Hyperparameters We split the COLF-VID dataset into train (70%), validation (15%) and test (15%) data. During the split we had to consider the high variance of the number of instances per VID type as to make sure that every split mirrors the distribution of types in the original data. E.g. *am Boden liegen* (48 instances) and *auf dem Tisch liegen* (951 instances) are represented with the same ratio in all three data sets.

The objective of the training was to minimize the cross entropy loss and for optimization we used the gradient descent variant Adam with a learning rate of 0.01. As for the labels we chose the majority annotation. We trained the models for 15 (Word2vec, fastText) respectively 18 (ELMo) epochs with a batch size of 30. The input size of our models was dependent on the dimensionality of the pretrained embeddings which had 100 (Word2vec), 300 (fastText) and 1024 (ELMo) dimensions. The forward and backward LSTMs were one-layered and the size of the hidden state was 100 for all three models, despite the considerable difference in input sizes which could have warranted testing larger hidden states for larger embeddings. But we refrained from doing so to keep the numbers of parameters in the MLP constant and thereby the model computationally less expensive. Hence, the MLP itself had an input size of 400 for all models, coupled with a hidden layer of size 100 and an output layer of size 4. The implementations of the three models are available on GitHub.[14]

5.2 Results

In this section we will present the results of our experiments on the disambiguation of German VIDs in context (see Table 2). We report precision, recall

---

[13]Remember, we assume for this task that another process already has identified the candidate expressions.

[14]https://github.com/rafehr/
colf-bilstm-classifier

Validation set:

Model	class idiomatic			class literal			weighted macro average			
	Pre	Rec	F1	Pre	Rec	F1	Pre	Rec	F1	Acc
Majority baseline	75.39	100.00	85.97	0	0	0	56.78	75.32	64.75	75.32
Word2vec+LSTM+MLP	90.60	90.25	90.42	70.47	72.76	71.60	85.30	85.59	85.44	85.59
fastText+LSTM+MLP	91.77	92.85	92.31	77.41	75.20	76.29	87.86	88.14	87.99	88.14
ELMo+LSTM+MLP	90.70	96.36	93.44	85.71	70.73	77.51	89.05	89.71	89.14	89.71

Test set:

Model	class idiomatic			class literal			weighted macro average			
	Pre	Rec	F1	Pre	Rec	F1	Pre	Rec	F1	Acc
Majority baseline	76.95	100.00	86.98	0	0	0	59.22	76.95	66.93	76.95
Word2vec+LSTM+MLP	90.40	87.38	88.86	61.05	69.66	65.07	83.17	82.76	82.88	82.76
fastText+LSTM+MLP	91.23	93.94	92.56	77.42	71.79	74.50	87.45	88.29	87.83	88.29
ELMo+LSTM+MLP	93.70	93.94	93.82	78.24	79.91	79.07	89.54	90.10	89.82	90.10

Table 2: Evaluation results

Test set:

VID	#	I%	ELMo+LSTM+MLP		
			Pre	Rec	F1
am Boden liegen	8	23.4	77.50	87.50	81.94
an Glanz verlieren	3	93.75	100.00	100.00	100.00
an Land ziehen	39	90.38	100.00	100.00	100.00
am Pranger stehen	1	100.0	100.00	100.00	100.00
den Atem anhalten	6	75.0	88.89	83.33	83.81
auf dem Abstellgleis stehen	4	42.31	56.25	75.00	64.29
auf den Arm nehmen	14	42.31	93.88	92.86	92.89
auf der Ersatzbank sitzen	4	23.81	50.00	50.00	50.00
auf der Straße stehen	38	62.4	87.30	86.84	87.00
auf der Strecke bleiben	94	99.19	97.88	98.94	98.41
auf dem Tisch liegen	143	71.29	89.13	90.21	89.44
auf den Zug aufspringen	19	96.03	100.00	94.74	97.30
eine Brücke bauen	53	68.39	92.45	92.45	92.45
die Fäden ziehen	26	94.8	90.86	88.46	89.49
im Blut haben	6	19.44	100.00	100.00	100.00
in den Keller gehen	19	72.8	95.18	94.74	94.68
in der Luft hängen	43	90.14	89.24	88.37	88.74
im Regen stehen	57	79.68	82.42	85.96	84.09
ins Rennen gehen	10	82.26	64.00	80.00	71.11
in eine Sackgasse geraten	16	98.02	100.00	100.00	100.00
im Schatten stehen	9	86.67	100.00	100.00	100.00
in Schieflage geraten	7	90.91	100.00	100.00	100.00
ins Wasser fallen	38	73.52	92.98	89.47	90.15
Luft holen	26	38.82	83.85	76.92	75.11
mit dem Feuer spielen	13	87.06	85.21	92.31	88.62
einen Nerv treffen	43	99.65	100.00	100.00	100.00
die Notbremse ziehen	49	84.36	92.09	89.80	90.51
eine Rechnung begleichen	38	64.54	78.95	78.95	78.95
von Bord gehen	14	51.61	82.86	71.43	70.24
vor der Tür stehen	90	68.17	83.20	82.22	82.54
ein Zelt aufschlagen	15	41.0	76.67	66.67	65.08
über Bord gehen	18	45.22	84.03	88.89	86.30
über Bord werfen	67	87.81	98.66	98.51	98.54
über die Bühne gehen	20	99.0	90.25	95.00	92.56

Table 3: Evaluation results (weighted macro) per VID on the test set.

and F1-score for the two classes with the most instances – IDIOMATIC and LITERAL – as well as the weighted macro-average for all classes combined. Since there was such a low number of instances with the labels UNDECIDABLE and BOTH for the system to train on (only 28 in the train set), it did not do well on those classes which it always misclassified. In order to account for this stark imbalance in classes, we settled for the weighted macro average instead of the normal macro average and did not include detailed (precision/recall/F1) scores for the two low-number classes.

Overall Results   As a baseline we chose a simple majority classifier which already represents a non-trivial hurdle, because of the high idiomaticity rate of COLF-VID. Still, with respect to the F1-score, our system clears it with all three different input types and shows some considerable improvements. Furthermore, as was our hypothesis, the fastText embeddings were an enhancement over Word2vec, which in turn were bested by ELMo. Table 2 shows the increased performance across both classes for the validation and the test set. The highest F1-score on the validation (89.14) and the test (89.82) set were achieved when using ELMo embeddings.

We suspect the superiority of fastText and ELMo over Word2vec lies in the fact that the two former models incorporate subword information. This should allow the classifier to detect morphosyntactic features that give clues on the correct reading of an expression, e.g. when it encounters a form of inflection unusual for a VID which tends to be morphosyntactically fixed. This is something our Word2vec model cannot accomplish, since it was trained on lemmas. Also, it would have been surprising if ELMo's ability to handle polysemy would not have been an advantage in a disambiguation task. This way context is already introduced at the input level.

One apparent weakness of our system is its weaker performance on the LITERAL class in comparison to the IDIOMATIC class – hardly a surprise when considering the unbalanced distribution of labels. Still, a maximum F1-score of 79.07 for LITERAL shows that our efforts to keep the idiomaticity rate of COLF-VID low bear some fruit.

VID-specific Evaluation   Table 3 shows a more fine-grained evaluation of the best performing system by listing the results per VID on the test set. The classifier achieves its best results (100.00 F1-score) for *an Glanz verlieren*, *an Land ziehen*, *am Pranger stehen*, *im Blut haben*, *in eine Sackgasse geraten*, *im Schatten stehen*, *in Schieflage geraten* and *einen Nerv treffen*. That was to be expected, since all these VIDs have a high rate of idiomatic or literal readings – a fact the classifier very likely learnt during training, thus assigning a higher probability to the majority label. Nonetheless, even for those VID types it does not seem to mindlessly apply one label all the time. E.g. for *an Land ziehen* and *im Blut haben*, it correctly classifies the relatively few instances of their respective minority class.

Still, arguably the most interesting VID types with respect to the disambiguation task are those with a (relatively speaking) more balanced distribution of classes, like *auf der Straße stehen*, *auf dem Tisch liegen*, *eine Brücke bauen*, *in den Keller gehen*, *im Regen stehen ins Wasser fallen*, *Luft holen*, *eine Rechnung begleichen*, *von Bord gehen*, *vor der Tür stehen*, *ein Zelt aufschlagen* or *über Bord gehen*, all of which have idiomaticity rates between 38.82% and 79.68%. For all but four of those expressions, the system achieves F1-scores between 82.54 and 94.45. For *ein Zelt aufschlagen* (65.08), *von Bord gehen* (70.24), *Luft holen* (75.11) and *eine Rechnung begleichen* (78.95), the F1-scores are below 80. It would be interesting to investigate whether the difference in performance for the various VID types correlates with the inter-annotator agreement (IAA). We leave this question to future work.

6   Conclusion/Future Work

In this paper we presented COLF-VID, a new corpus with annotated instances of German VIDs and their literal counterparts. Furthermore, we experimented with VID disambiguation on the new corpus and showed that significant improvements can be gained from applying a neural architecture in comparison with a simple majority baseline. The experiments additionally demonstrated the effects of the different word representations on the resulting performance.

For the future we plan on extending the annotation of COLF-VID with those VIDs that were not in the set of pre-chosen expressions and con-sequently were not annotated. This would allow to use the corpus as a basis for an identification task and not just disambiguation. Concerning the disambiguation task itself, a cornucopia of different approaches – be it supervised or unsupervised – can be imagined. We plan on conducting a survey of different approaches in an attempt to reveal which architectures, context sizes and features are best suited for the task. Last but not least, cross-linguistic experiments with comparable corpora (e.g. IDIX) could be interesting in order to explore language-specific properties of VIDs.

Acknowledgements

We would like to thank Julia Fischer and Kevin Pochwyt for their annotations. We also would like to thank the anonymous reviewers for their helpful reviews and suggestions. This work has been supported by the Deutsche Forschungsgemeinschaft (DFG) within the CRC 991 "The Structure of Representations in Language, Cognition, and Science".

References

Timothy Baldwin and Su Nam Kim. 2010. Multiword expressions. *Handbook of natural language processing*, 2:267–292.

Piotr Bojanowski, Edouard Grave, Armand Joulin, and Tomas Mikolov. 2016. Enriching word vectors with subword information. *arXiv preprint arXiv:1607.04606*.

Mathieu Constant, Gülşen Eryiğit, Johanna Monti, Lonneke van der Plas, Carlos Ramisch, Michael Rosner, and Amalia Todirascu. 2017. Survey: Multiword expression processing: A Survey. *Computational Linguistics*, 43(4):837–892.

Paul Cook, Afsaneh Fazly, and Suzanne Stevenson. 2007. Pulling their weight: Exploiting syntactic forms for the automatic identification of idiomatic expressions in context. In *Proceedings of the Workshop on A Broader Perspective on Multiword Expressions*, pages 41–48, Prague, Czech Republic. Association for Computational Linguistics.

Paul Cook, Afsaneh Fazly, and Suzanne Stevenson. 2008. The vnc-tokens dataset. In *Proceedings of the LREC Workshop Towards a Shared Task for Multiword Expressions (MWE 2008)*, pages 19–22.

Rafael Ehren. 2017. Literal or idiomatic? identifying the reading of single occurrences of German multiword expressions using word embeddings. In *Proceedings of the EACL Student Research Workshop*, pages 103–112, Valencia, Spain.

Afsaneh Fazly, Paul Cook, and Suzanne Stevenson. 2009. Unsupervised type and token identification of idiomatic expressions. *Computational Linguistics*, 35(1):61–103.

Fabienne Fritzinger, Marion Weller, and Ulrich Heid. 2010. A survey of idiomatic preposition-noun-verb triples on token level. In *Proceedings of the Seventh International Conference on Language Resources and Evaluation (LREC'10)*, pages 2908–2914, Valletta, Malta. European Language Resources Association (ELRA).

Hessel Haagsma and Johannes Bjerva. 2016. Detecting novel metaphor using selectional preference information. In *Proceedings of the Fourth Workshop on Metaphor in NLP*, pages 10–17.

Julia B. Herrmann. 2013. *Metaphor in academic discourse: Linguistic forms, conceptual structures, communicative functions and cognitive representations*. Phd thesis, Vrije Universiteit Amsterdam, Amsterdam.

Sepp Hochreiter and Jürgen Schmidhuber. 1997. Long short-term memory. *Neural computation*, 9(8):1735–1780.

Andrea Horbach, Andrea Hensler, Sabine Krome, Jakob Prange, Werner Scholze-Stubenrecht, Diana Steffen, Stefan Thater, Christian Wellner, and Manfred Pinkal. 2016. A corpus of literal and idiomatic uses of German infinitive-verb compounds. In *Proceedings of the Tenth International Conference on Language Resources and Evaluation (LREC'16)*, pages 836–841, Portorož, Slovenia. European Language Resources Association (ELRA).

Graham Katz and Eugenie Giesbrecht. 2006. Automatic identification of non-compositional multiword expressions using latent semantic analysis. In *Proceedings of the Workshop on Multiword Expressions: Identifying and Exploiting Underlying Properties*, pages 12–19, Sydney, Australia. ACL.

Linlin Li and Caroline Sporleder. 2009. A cohesion graph based approach for unsupervised recognition of literal and non-literal use of multiword expressions. In *Proceedings of the 2009 Workshop on Graph-based Methods for Natural Language Processing (TextGraphs-4)*, pages 75–83, Suntec, Singapore.

Philip May. 2019. German ELMo Model.

Tomas Mikolov, Ilya Sutskever, Kai Chen, Greg S Corrado, and Jeff Dean. 2013. Distributed representations of words and phrases and their compositionality. In *Advances in neural information processing systems*, pages 3111–3119.

Matthew Peters, Mark Neumann, Mohit Iyyer, Matt Gardner, Christopher Clark, Kenton Lee, and Luke Zettlemoyer. 2018. Deep contextualized word representations. In *Proceedings of the 2018 Conference of the North American Chapter of the Association for Computational Linguistics: Human Language Technologies, Volume 1 (Long Papers)*, pages 2227–2237, New Orleans, Louisiana. Association for Computational Linguistics.

Pragglejaz Group. 2007. MIP: A method for identifying metaphorically used words in discourse. *Metaphor and Symbol*, 22(1):1–39.

Carlos Ramisch, Silvio Ricardo Cordeiro, Agata Savary, Veronika Vincze, Behrang QasemiZadeh, Marie Candito, Verginica Barbu Mititelu, Voula Giouli, Ivelina Stoyanova, Nathan Schneider, and Timm Lichte. 2018. Edition 1.1 of the PARSEME shared task on automatic identification of Verbal Multiword Expressions. In *Proceedings of LAW-MWE-CxG 2018*, Santa Fe, USA.

Radim Řehůřek and Petr Sojka. 2010. Software Framework for Topic Modelling with Large Corpora. In *Proceedings of the LREC 2010 Workshop on New Challenges for NLP Frameworks*, pages 45–50, Valletta, Malta. ELRA. http://is.muni.cz/publication/884893/en.

Agata Savary, Silvio Ricardo Cordeiro, Timm Lichte, Carlos Ramisch, Uxoa Iñurrieta, and Voula Giouli. 2019. Literal occurrences of multiword expressions: Rare birds that cause a stir. *The Prague Bulletin of Mathematical Linguistics*, 112(1):5–54.

Roland Schäfer and Felix Bildhauer. 2012. Building large corpora from the web using a new efficient tool chain. In *Proceedings of the Eighth International Conference on Language Resources and Evaluation (LREC-2012)*, pages 486–493, Istanbul, Turkey. European Language Resources Association (ELRA). ACL Anthology Identifier: L12-1497.

Ekaterina Shutova, Lin Sun, and Anna Korhonen. 2010. Metaphor identification using verb and noun clustering. In *Proceedings of the 23rd International Conference on Computational Linguistics*, pages 1002–1010. Association for Computational Linguistics.

Caroline Sporleder, Linlin Li, Philip Gorinski, and Xaver Koch. 2010. Idioms in context: The IDIX corpus. In *Proceedings of the Seventh International Conference on Language Resources and Evaluation (LREC'10)*, Valletta, Malta. European Language Resources Association (ELRA).

Gerard J. Steen, Aletta G. Dorst, J. Berenike Herrmann, Anna Kaal, Tina Krennmayr, and Trijntje Pasma. 2010. *A Method for Linguistic Metaphor Identification*. Number 14 in Converging Evidence in Language and Communication Research. John Benjamins, Amsterdam, The Netherlands.

Metaphor Detection Using Context and Concreteness

Rowan Hall Maudslay[1]   **Tiago Pimentel**[1]   **Ryan Cotterell**[1,2]   **Simone Teufel**[1]

[1] Department of Computer Science and Technology, University of Cambridge
[2] Department of Computer Science, ETH Zürich

`{rh635,tp472,sht25}@cam.ac.uk` `ryan.cotterell@inf.ethz.ch`

Abstract

We report the results of our system on the Metaphor Detection Shared Task at the Second Workshop on Figurative Language Processing 2020. Our model is an ensemble, utilising contextualised and static distributional semantic representations, along with word-type concreteness ratings. Using these features, it predicts word metaphoricity with a deep multilayer perceptron. We are able to best the state-of-the-art from the 2018 Shared Task by an average of 8.0% F_1, and finish fourth in both subtasks in which we participate.

1 Introduction

Metaphor detection is the task of assigning a label to a word (or sometimes a sentence) in a piece of text, to indicate whether or not it is metaphorical. Some metaphors occur so frequently as to be considered word senses in their own right (so-called *conventional metaphors*), whilst others are creative, and involve the use of words in unexpected ways (*novel metaphors*). Sometimes whole phrases or even sentences can lend themselves to metaphorical or literal interpretations.[1] For these reasons and others, human annotators might disagree about what constitutes a metaphor—computational metaphor detection is no doubt a challenging problem.

In this work, we participate in the 2020 Metaphor Detection Shared Task (Leong et al., 2020). First, we offer a description of metaphoricity, framing it in terms of the concreteness of a word in different contexts. Concreteness of a word in context is not a quantity for which there exists large-scale annotated data. In lieu of this, we train a metaphor detection model using input features which we expect to

---

[1] Consider *drowning student*, which could refer to students submerged in water, or students struggling with coursework (Tsvetkov et al., 2014), or the more idiomatic phrase, *they stabbed him in the back*, which could be taken literally or (more likely) metaphorically, depending on its context.

		Max concreteness (any sense)	
		low	*high*
Concreteness (this sense)	*low*	"she *considered* the problem", "they *hated* the film"	"she *attacked* the problem" "he *showered* her with love"
	high		"she *attacked* the soldier", "he *showered* at 8am"

Figure 1: Examples of verbs with varying levels of concreteness—metaphors are in green

contain the information needed to derive this contextual concreteness. This model outperforms the highest performing system of the previous shared task (Leong et al., 2018), and finishes 4th in the two subtasks in which we participate.

2 Concreteness and Context

Metaphor is a device which allows one to project structure from a source domain to a target domain (Lakoff and Johnson, 1980). For instance, in the sentence "he *attacked* the government", *attacked* can be seen as a conventional metaphor, which applies structure from the source domain of war to the target domain of argument. Intuitively, it seems that the context in which a word appears tells us about the target domain, whilst the word itself (and some knowledge about how it is used non-metaphorically) tells us about the source. Several existing models have exploited this difference (e.g. Mao et al., 2019; Gao et al., 2018).

Usually, the target domain is something intangible, whilst the source domain relates more closely to our real-world experience. *Concreteness* refers to the extent to which a word denotes something that can be experienced by the senses, and is gener-

Proceedings of the Second Workshop on Figurative Language Processing, pages 221–226
July 9, 2020. ©2020 Association for Computational Linguistics
https://doi.org/10.18653/v1/P17

ally measured by asking annotators to rate words on a numeric scale (Paivio et al., 1968; Spreen and Schulz, 1966); abstractness is then the inverse of concreteness. Using concreteness ratings for metaphor identification is clearly well motivated, as evidenced by previous work (e.g. Tsvetkov et al., 2014, 2013; Beigman Klebanov et al., 2015).

For a word to be metaphorical in a particular context, then, it needs to have a concrete sense and an abstract sense, with the abstract sense activated in that context. The concrete sense would belong to the source domain, and the abstract sense to the target domain. For instance, the meaning of the word *attacked* in "she *attacked* the soldier" is concrete, but in "she *attacked* the problem" it is abstract—and thus that usage is metaphorical. Polysemy of the word is a necessary condition; the existence of an abstract sense is not enough, otherwise a monosemously abstract word such as *considered* in "he *considered* the problem" would be metaphorical.

Figure 1 shows examples of words with different maximum concreteness levels elicited by certain senses (columns) appearing in contexts which result in different values of concreteness for that particular sense (rows). The most concrete sense of a word is a lexical property, and thus context independent. The metaphors (green) are found in the top right quadrant—they have an abstract meaning in context, but a concrete sense exists (as evidenced by the examples in the bottom right quadrant). The bottom left quadrant is greyed out, since it is conceptually impossible for a word to exist there—the concreteness of one sense of a word cannot be greater than the concreteness of any of its senses.

3 Model Architecture

We now describe a model which uses semantic representations of a word in and out of context to predict metaphoricity. Ideally, we would only provide the model with a representation of the concreteness of a word in context (since we believe that would do most of the lifting), but to our knowledge, no large-scale annotated datasets exist for context-dependent concreteness. In most popular datasets of concreteness annotation (e.g. Coltheart, 1981; Brysbaert et al., 2014), concreteness is a property assigned to each word type—but we would need the concreteness of a word *instance*. In this respect, our work resembles the abstractness classifier in Turney et al. (2011)—although this work uses word senses

instead of instances as we do. Because contextualised concreteness data is unavailable, we instead choose features which, when given to a multi-layer perceptron (MLP), should provide enough information about a word for the MLP to be able to differentiate between each cell in Figure 1.

We first provide the model with contextualised word embeddings, which we expect will provide some information about the target domain of the metaphor. In the contextualised representations, we expect there to exist a space of concrete meanings and some space of abstract meanings—which would help the network differentiate between the top and bottom rows of Figure 1. Along with this, we provide static word embeddings, to provide information about the source domain. Since these static type-level embeddings will clearly contain information about both source and target, we compliment them with type-level concreteness ratings. Such ratings should reflect the concreteness of the most concrete sense of the word, thus allowing the network to differentiate between the left and right columns of Figure 1.

Figure 2 shows an overview of our architecture. In the following paragraphs, we detail each individual component of the model.

Contextual Word Embedding For contextualised embeddings, we fine-tune BERT (Devlin et al., 2019). BERT is a sentence encoder which utilises a transformer architecture (Vaswani et al., 2017), and is trained with two separate tasks—masked language modelling (a cloze task), and next-sentence prediction. The latent space (the final hidden state of the encoder) contains vector representations of each input token, which change in different contexts. Several pre-trained BERT models are available—we use BERT large.[2]

Concreteness Model We define a simple model which represents the concreteness of a word as a linear interpolation between two vectors, representing maximal concreteness and abstractness, $\mathbf{v}_{con}$ and $\mathbf{v}_{abs}$ respectively. For each word w we obtain a real number estimate of its concreteness, c, from Brysbaert et al. (2014), where $c = 5$ indicates maximum abstractness, and $c = 0$ indicates maximum

---

[2]BERT accepts WordPiece units (Wu et al., 2016) as tokens, rather than words. There is not a single accepted way of converting multiple WordPiece unit vector representations into a single word. Following Devlin et al. (2019), we simply use the first token of any word. This is clearly a naïve method of compositionality; improving this may strengthen our results.

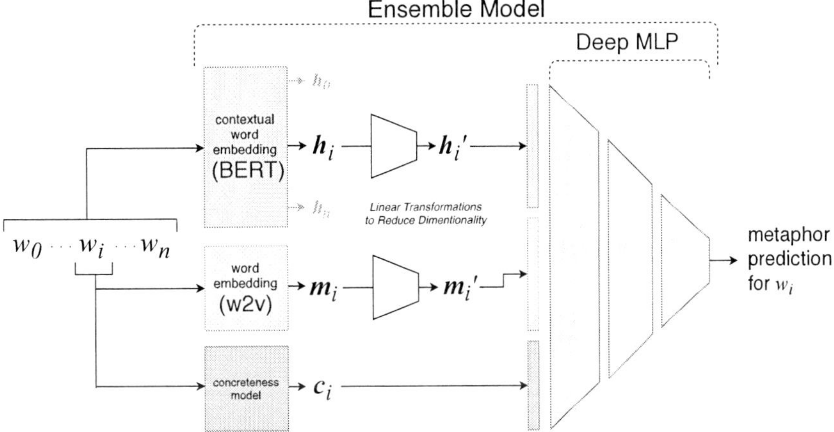

Figure 2: Architecture of our ensemble

concreteness. The output vector of the model is defined as

$$\mathbf{c} = \frac{c}{5} \cdot \mathbf{v}_{\mathrm{con}} + \frac{5-c}{5} \cdot \mathbf{v}_{\mathrm{abs}} \tag{1}$$

Out-of-vocabulary words have their own vector, $\mathbf{v}_{\mathrm{unk}}$. Each of $\mathbf{v}_{\mathrm{abs}}$, $\mathbf{v}_{\mathrm{con}}$, and $\mathbf{v}_{\mathrm{unk}}$ are randomly initialised and learned from data. The dimensionality of these vectors is a hyperparameter which is tuned—a higher dimensionalality will likely place more emphasis on this feature when it is fed into the MLP as part of the ensemble model.

Static Word Embedding We initialise a matrix of static 300-dimensional word embeddings from the *Word2Vec* Google News pretrained model (Mikolov et al., 2013), then fine tune it to the data. Out-of-vocabulary words are given their lemma's embedding, if present, otherwise they are initialised randomly.

Multi-Layer Perceptron We define a deep multi-layer percepton (MLP), which at each layer has four components: a linear transformation, layer normalisation, a ReLU activation function, and finally dropout (Srivastava et al., 2014). The structure is parameterised with three parameters—the input size k, number of layers n, and first hidden layer size h. The first linear layer of the network has an input of size k, and an output of size h. Each successive layer halves the size of the hidden state. After n layers, a final linear layer converts to a single output, which is then passed through a sigmoid to yield the prediction. Based on this design, we have the constraint that $2^n \leq h \leq k$, which imposes that (1) the first hidden layer is not larger than the input, and (2) the size of the hidden layer does not reach 1 before the final layer.

Ensemble Model Tying all of the aforementioned models together is an ensemble model. First, it passes each input sentence $w_0, \cdots, w_n$ through the contextual embedding component to yield the embeddings $\mathbf{h}_1, \cdots, \mathbf{h}_n$. To reduce their dimensionality, these are each passed through a simple linear transform, yielding $\mathbf{h}_1', \cdots, \mathbf{h}_n'$. Each word is then passed through the static embedding component, yielding embeddings $\mathbf{m}_1, \cdots, \mathbf{m}_n$, which are also projected down to $\mathbf{m}_1', \cdots, \mathbf{m}_n'$. Each word is also fed to the concreteness model, yielding concreteness vectors $\mathbf{c}_1, \cdots, \mathbf{c}_n$. For each word, the three representations ($\mathbf{h}_i'$, $\mathbf{m}_i'$, and $\mathbf{c}_i$) are concatenated, and passed into a deep multi-layer perceptron which makes the final metaphor prediction (per-word). This model is depicted in Figure 2. Crucially, though this model accepts sentences (needed to process the contextualised word representations), it makes predictions using the MLP on a per-word basis—but back-propagates through BERT for all annotated words in each sentence.

4 Experiments

Data We use the VUA corpus (Steen et al., 2010) which was made available for the shared task (Leong et al., 2020).[3] We train a model on all

---

[3] This corpus consists of four different genres from the British National Corpus: academic, news, conversation, and fiction. For the Shared Task, these were all merged, but clearly each categories' data will be of radically different forms. We expect our system to underperform on the transcriptions of conversations, since this will be very different from the data BERT was trained on.

Subset	Train	Dev	Total
By Tokens			
Verbs	15,323	1,917	17,240
All-POS	64,537	8,074	72,611
Everything	161,335	20,169	181,504
By Sentences			
Verbs	7,127	746	7,873
All-POS	9,809	1,085	10,894
Everything	10,738	1,371	12,109

Table 1: Number of tokens and sentences in the data

Parameter	Value
n-layers	4
Hidden size (h)	140
Size of c_i	50
Size of h'_i	150
Size of m'_i	200
Learning rate I	2×10^{-4}
Learning rate II	2×10^{-5}
Weight Decay	0.05
Dropout	0.4

Table 2: Hyperparameters of the final model

Ensemble Model			
CWE	*SWE*	*CM*	**F$_1$ Dev**
✓			0.574
✓		✓	0.586
✓	✓		0.636
✓	✓	✓	0.644

Table 3: Ablation study results

the available training data—not just those marked for the *verbs* or *all-pos* subtasks, because we found this improved performance. We split the data in an 8:1 ratio, ensuring that the split puts 1/9 of each subtask's data in the development set—details of the splits are shown in Table 1.

Training Details We train in batches of 32 sentences, and employ early stopping after 20 stable steps (based on F$_1$ on dev). As an optimizer, we use AdamW (Loshchilov and Hutter, 2017). We experimented with three fine-tuning options: (1) unfreezing the whole network and training it all at once, (2) freezing BERT and training until early stopping activates, then unfreezing BERT and training until early stopping again, and (3) freezing BERT and training until early stopping, then sequentially unfreezing and training a single layer of BERT at a time, and finally the whole model at once (inspired by Felbo et al., 2017). We used option (2) in the end, since it offered a large improvement over (1) when we used a lower learning rate for the second phase. We found that (3) offered no additional advantage. To find hyperparameters, we performed a random search over the parameter space; final hyperparameters are reported in Table 2.

Threshold Shifting The ratio of metaphors to non-metaphors in the entire VUA dataset was not the same as that of the verb and all-pos subsets used by the Shared Task. Having trained the model on all the data, we then adjust it to each different distribution. To do this, we find the threshold for the sigmoid output that maximises the F$_1$ score on each particular development set.[4]

Ablation Study To verify that each feature contributes useful information over just using a contextualised representation, we first conduct a simple ablation study, to see the performance impact of removing either the static word embeddings or concreteness ratings. We train four models (with the same hyperparameters as in Table 2), with different combinations of the concreteness model (CM) and static word embedding (SWE) model removed.[5] Table 3 shows the results on the development set. The contextualised word embeddings (CWE) on their own performs the worst. Adding the embeddings in particular really bolsters the performance (increasing it from 0.574 to 0.636 F$_1$). The type-level concreteness annotation also helps, but not quite as much. The combination of all three features achieves the highest F$_1$ score.

Shared Task Performance The Shared Task results are computed as the F$_1$ Score on held-out test data. Our results are presented in Table 4, alongside the results from the previous highest-performing system (Wu et al., 2018) from the 2018 Shared Task (Leong et al., 2018), and the highest-performing system on this shared task. Through the use of contextualised representations and concreteness rat-

---

[4]We also experimented with fine-tuning the network to each subset, but found this led to overfitting, and was detrimental to performance.

[5]For this experiment we use early stopping after 5 stable results (based on loss), BERT base rather than large, and did not fine-tune BERT.

	Subtask F_1	
Model	*Verbs*	*All-POS*
Us	0.755	0.718
2018 Winner	0.672	0.651
2020 Winner	0.804	0.769

Table 4: Shared Task results

ings, we are able to improve substantially over the best submission to the 2018 shared task (Wu et al., 2018) for metaphor detection on the VUA corpus (Steen et al., 2010), by 8.0% F_1. We trail the winner of the 2020 task by an average of 5.0% F_1.

5 Conclusion

We participated in the 2020 Metaphor Identification Shared Task (Leong et al., 2020). Our model was designed to try and exploit knowledge of lexical concreteness and contextual meaning to identify metaphors. Our results improved over the previous best performing system by an average of 8.0% F_1, but trailed behind the leader of the task by 5.0%.

In future work, we are keen to explore first training a model to identify concreteness in context, then fine-tuning this to metaphor identification, based on the reasoning presented in §2.

References

Beata Beigman Klebanov, Chee Wee Leong, and Michael Flor. 2015. Supervised word-level metaphor detection. Experiments with concreteness and reweighting of examples. In *Proceedings of the Third Workshop on Metaphor in NLP*, pages 11–20, Denver, Colorado. Association for Computational Linguistics.

Marc Brysbaert, Amy Beth Warriner, and Victor Kuperman. 2014. Concreteness ratings for 40 thousand generally known English word lemmas. *Behavior Research Methods*, 46(3):904–911.

Max Coltheart. 1981. The MRC psycholinguistic database. *The Quarterly Journal of Experimental Psychology Section A*, 33(4):497–505.

Jacob Devlin, Ming-Wei Chang, Kenton Lee, and Kristina Toutanova. 2019. BERT: Pre-training of deep bidirectional transformers for language understanding. In *Proceedings of the 2019 Conference of the North American Chapter of the Association for Computational Linguistics: Human Language Technologies, Volume 1 (Long and Short Papers)*, pages 4171–4186, Minneapolis, Minnesota. Association for Computational Linguistics.

Bjarke Felbo, Alan Mislove, Anders Søgaard, Iyad Rahwan, and Sune Lehmann. 2017. Using millions of emoji occurrences to learn any-domain representations for detecting sentiment, emotion and sarcasm. In *Proceedings of the 2017 Conference on Empirical Methods in Natural Language Processing*, pages 1615–1625, Copenhagen, Denmark. Association for Computational Linguistics.

Ge Gao, Eunsol Choi, Yejin Choi, and Luke Zettlemoyer. 2018. Neural metaphor detection in context. In *Proceedings of the 2018 Conference on Empirical Methods in Natural Language Processing*, pages 607–613, Brussels, Belgium. Association for Computational Linguistics.

George Lakoff and Mark Johnson. 1980. *Metaphors We Live By*. University of Chicago Press.

Chee Wee Leong, Beata Beigman Klebanov, Chris Hamill, Egon Stemle, Rutuja Ubale, and Xianyang Chen. 2020. A report on the 2020 vua and toefl metaphor detection shared task. In *Proceedings of the Second Workshop on Figurative Language Processing*, Seattle, WA.

Chee Wee (Ben) Leong, Beata Beigman Klebanov, and Ekaterina Shutova. 2018. A report on the 2018 VUA metaphor detection shared task. In *Proceedings of the Workshop on Figurative Language Processing*, pages 56–66, New Orleans, Louisiana. Association for Computational Linguistics.

Ilya Loshchilov and Frank Hutter. 2017. Decoupled weight decay regularization.

Rui Mao, Chenghua Lin, and Frank Guerin. 2019. End-to-end sequential metaphor identification inspired by linguistic theories. In *Proceedings of the 57th Annual Meeting of the Association for Computational Linguistics*, pages 3888–3898, Florence, Italy. Association for Computational Linguistics.

Tomas Mikolov, Kai Chen, Greg Corrado, and Jeffrey Dean. 2013. Efficient estimation of word representations in vector space.

Allan Paivio, John C Yuille, and Stephen A Madigan. 1968. Concreteness, imagery, and meaningfulness values for 925 nouns. *Journal of Experimental Psychology*, 76(1, Pt.2):1–25.

Otfried Spreen and Rudolph W. Schulz. 1966. Parameters of abstraction, meaningfulness, and pronunciability for 329 nouns. *Journal of Verbal Learning and Verbal Behavior*, 5(5):459–468.

Nitish Srivastava, Geoffrey Hinton, Alex Krizhevsky, Ilya Sutskever, and Ruslan Salakhutdinov. 2014. Dropout: A simple way to prevent neural networks from overfitting. *The Journal of Machine Learning Research*, 15(1):1929–1958.

Gerard J. Steen, Aletta G. Dorst, J Berenike Herrmann, Anna A. Kaal, and Tina Krennmayr. 2010. Metaphor in usage. *Cognitive Linguistics*, 21(4):765–796.

Yulia Tsvetkov, Leonid Boytsov, Anatole Gershman, Eric Nyberg, and Chris Dyer. 2014. Metaphor detection with cross-lingual model transfer. In *Proceedings of the 52nd Annual Meeting of the Association for Computational Linguistics (Volume 1: Long Papers)*, pages 248–258, Baltimore, Maryland. Association for Computational Linguistics.

Yulia Tsvetkov, Elena Mukomel, and Anatole Gershman. 2013. Cross-lingual metaphor detection using common semantic features. In *Proceedings of the First Workshop on Metaphor in NLP*, pages 45–51, Atlanta, Georgia. Association for Computational Linguistics.

Peter Turney, Yair Neuman, Dan Assaf, and Yohai Cohen. 2011. Literal and metaphorical sense identification through concrete and abstract context. In *Proceedings of the 2011 Conference on Empirical Methods in Natural Language Processing*, pages 680–690, Edinburgh, Scotland, UK. Association for Computational Linguistics.

Ashish Vaswani, Noam Shazeer, Niki Parmar, Jakob Uszkoreit, Llion Jones, Aidan N. Gomez, Łukasz Kaiser, and Illia Polosukhin. 2017. Attention is all you need. In I. Guyon, U. V. Luxburg, S. Bengio, H. Wallach, R. Fergus, S. Vishwanathan, and R. Garnett, editors, *Advances in Neural Information Processing Systems 30*, pages 5998–6008. Curran Associates, Inc.

Chuhan Wu, Fangzhao Wu, Yubo Chen, Sixing Wu, Zhigang Yuan, and Yongfeng Huang. 2018. Neural metaphor detecting with CNN-LSTM model. In *Proceedings of the Workshop on Figurative Language Processing*, pages 110–114, New Orleans, Louisiana. Association for Computational Linguistics.

Yonghui Wu, Mike Schuster, Zhifeng Chen, Quoc V. Le, Mohammad Norouzi, Wolfgang Macherey, Maxim Krikun, Yuan Cao, Qin Gao, Klaus Macherey, Jeff Klingner, Apurva Shah, Melvin Johnson, Xiaobing Liu, Łukasz Kaiser, Stephan Gouws, Yoshikiyo Kato, Taku Kudo, Hideto Kazawa, Keith Stevens, George Kurian, Nishant Patil, Wei Wang, Cliff Young, Jason Smith, Jason Riesa, Alex Rudnick, Oriol Vinyals, Greg Corrado, Macduff Hughes, and Jeffrey Dean. 2016. Google's neural machine translation system: Bridging the gap between human and machine translation.

Being neighbourly: Neural metaphor identification in discourse

Verna Dankers[1], Karan Malhotra[1], Gaurav Kudva[1],
Volodymyr Medentsiy[1], Ekaterina Shutova[2]
[1]University of Amsterdam, The Netherlands
[2]Institute for Logic, Language and Computation, University of Amsterdam, The Netherlands
`vernadankers@gmail.com`
`{karan.malhotra,gaurav.kudva,volodymyr.medentsiy}@student.uva.nl`
`e.shutova@uva.nl`

Abstract

Existing approaches to metaphor processing typically rely on local features, such as immediate lexico-syntactic contexts or information within a given sentence. However, a large body of corpus-linguistic research suggests that situational information and broader discourse properties influence metaphor production and comprehension. In this paper, we present the first neural metaphor processing architecture that models a broader discourse through the use of attention mechanisms. Our models advance the state of the art on the all POS track of the 2018 VU Amsterdam metaphor identification task. The inclusion of discourse-level information yields further significant improvements.

1 Introduction

Metaphor widely manifests itself in natural language. It is used to make an implicit comparison between two distinct domains that have certain common aspects (Lakoff and Johnson, 1980). For instance, in the sentence "The *price* of the commodity is *rising*", the target domain of quantity (*price*) can be understood through the source domain of directionality (*rising*).

The majority of computational approaches to metaphor focus on the task of its identification in text. Early approaches utilised hand-crafted features based on word classes (Beigman Klebanov et al., 2016), concreteness and imageability ratings (Turney et al., 2011; Broadwell et al., 2013) or selectional preferences (Wilks et al., 2013). Succeeding research has moved on to corpus-based techniques, such as the use of distributional and vector space models (Shutova, 2011; Gutierrez et al., 2016; Bulat et al., 2017), and more recently, deep learning methods (Rei et al., 2017). Current metaphor identification approaches cast the problem in the sequence labelling paradigm

and apply convolutional (Wu et al., 2018), recurrent (Gao et al., 2018; Mao et al., 2019; Dankers et al., 2019) and transformer-based neural models (Dankers et al., 2019).

However, these approaches model only local linguistic context, i.e. information about the sentence in which the metaphor resides. Yet, a large body of corpus-linguistic research suggests that metaphor production and comprehension is influenced by situational information and wider discourse properties (Musolff, 2000; Semino, 2008; Jang et al., 2015b). Previously presented computational models of metaphor incorporating discourse use hand-crafted features (Jang et al., 2015a) or neural sentence embeddings (Mu et al., 2019) within a simple classification paradigm. Since these methods employ shallow classification models, their task performance is subpar compared to deep neural architectures. Nonetheless, these studies established that discourse-level information is beneficial for metaphor detection.

Improving upon prior methods, we present a novel neural metaphor identification architecture that incorporates broader discourse. To model discourse, we investigate two types of attention mechanisms: a shallow general attention mechanism and a hierarchical one (Yang et al., 2016). The former builds a sentence representation by applying word-level attention. The latter combines attention at both word and sentence level. We apply our models to the 2018 VU Amsterdam (VUA) metaphor identification shared task (Leong et al., 2018), specifically to the all POS subtask. This task involves metaphor detection for all open-class words – i.e. verbs, adjectives, nouns and adverbs. Our results confirm that modelling discourse is beneficial for metaphor detection and our models improve upon the previous state-of-the-art task performance (Wu et al., 2018) by 5.2 and 6.4 F1-points, for our best-performing baseline and discourse models, respec-

227

Proceedings of the Second Workshop on Figurative Language Processing, pages 227–234
July 9, 2020. ©2020 Association for Computational Linguistics
https://doi.org/10.18653/v1/P17

tively. To the best of our knowledge, this is the first end-to-end neural approach investigating the effect of broader discourse on metaphor identification.

2 Related Work

2.1 Deep Learning for Metaphor Identification

The approach of Wu et al. (2018) obtained the highest performance in the 2018 VUA metaphor identification task. Their model combined a convolutional neural network and a bidirectional LSTM (Bi-LSTM), thus utilising local and long-range contextual information in the immediate sentence. F1-scores of 65.1% and 67.2% were obtained in the task's all POS and verbs-only subtasks, respectively. See Leong et al. (2018) for an overview of other systems submitted to the task.

Afterwards, Gao et al. (2018) proposed a sequence labelling model for metaphor identification that employed GloVe (Pennington et al., 2014) and ELMo (Peters et al., 2018) embeddings as input to a Bi-LSTM followed by a classification layer. The main difference compared to previously presented neural models was the inclusion of contextualised word embeddings, which significantly improved metaphor detection. Gao et al. (2018) reported results on the full sequence labelling task using the VUA metaphor corpus. However, their performance is not comparable to the all POS subtask of the 2018 shared task. The evaluation of Gao et al. (2018) included both closed- *and* open-class words and their models were trained on a different subset of the VUA metaphor corpus, causing incomparable main task performance measures.[1]

Mao et al. (2019) and Dankers et al. (2019) recently presented improved approaches to modelling metaphors by relying on (psycho)linguistically motivated theories of human metaphor processing. Mao et al. (2019) proposed two adaptations of the model of Gao et al. (2018): Firstly, concatenating the hidden states of the Bi-LSTM to a context representation capturing surrounding words within the current sentence, to model selectional preferences. Secondly, including word embeddings both at the input and classification layer, to explicitly model the discrepancy between a word's literal and its contextualised meaning. Dankers et al.

(2019) improved metaphor identification through joint learning with emotion prediction, motivated by the finding that metaphorical phrases tend to be more emotionally evocative than their literal counterparts. Joint learning was applied to the model of Gao et al. (2018) as well as to BERT (Devlin et al., 2019). The latter setup is the current state-of-the-art approach in metaphor identification. Mao et al. (2019) and Dankers et al. (2019) used the data subset and evaluation setup of Gao et al. (2018), which complicates direct performance comparisons to the 2018 shared task. We only compare to these studies in our performance breakdown per POS tag, for the four open-class POS categories.

2.2 Metaphor Identification and Discourse

The work of Jang et al. (2015a) was the first to investigate the effects of broader discourse in a computational model of metaphor. Their approach used hand-crafted features and coarse-grained lexical information extracted from a broader discourse such as topical information, lexical chains and unigram features. However, they did not directly model the effect of including neighbouring sentences in metaphor identification.

Mu et al. (2019) considered metaphor identification for the verbs-only subtask of the 2018 shared task. They obtained the broader context of verbs by embedding the surrounding paragraph with a range of methods: GloVe, ELMo, skip-thought (Kiros et al., 2015) and doc2vec (Le and Mikolov, 2014). The context embedding, along with the verb lemma and syntactic arguments, was used to train a gradient boosting decision tree classifier. The authors have shown that metaphor identification is positively influenced by including paragraph-level context. Their best-performing model achieved an F1-score of 66.8% falling just shy of the 2018 verbs-only subtask's highest performance of Wu et al. (2018).

3 Data

The task revolves around performing binary classification – identifying whether a word is metaphorical or literal – on the all POS subtask of the 2018 VUA metaphor identification shared task. This task uses a dataset consisting of 117 text excerpts from the British National Corpus (Clear, 1993), labelled in the VUA metaphor corpus (Steen et al., 2010). Each excerpt has been retrieved from one of the following four genres: academic, news, conver-

---

[1] Closed-class function words such as prepositions are considerably easier to classify than open-class words. The systems evaluated in the 2018 shared task setup essentially addressed a more challenging task, which would make a task performance comparison unfair.

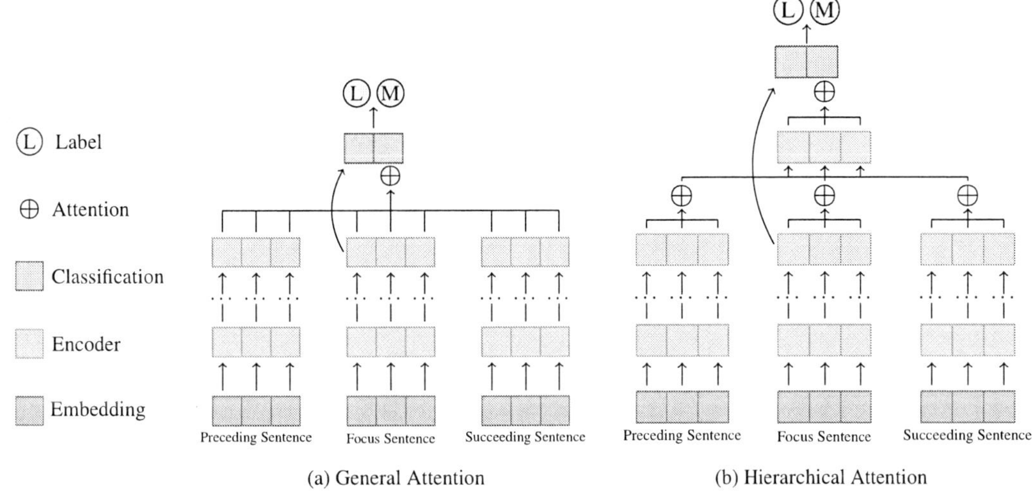

Figure 1: Visualisation of the sequence labelling architecture, for the two discourse computation mechanisms with context window size $k = 1$. To avoid visual clutter, only the classification of the first word in the focus sentence is shown.

sation, and fiction. Metaphorical expressions are annotated at word level. Following the shared task setup, we evaluate our models on open-class words only – i.e. verbs, adjectives, nouns and adverbs. The dataset contains 72,611 and 22,196 labelled words in the training and test set, respectively. 15% and 18% of these words are metaphorical for the two sets, respectively. We randomly sample 10% of the training data texts for validation purposes.

4 Methods

We construct a neural architecture that is optimised to predict binary metaphoricity at word level, by embedding the input words, applying encoder layers followed by a classification layer and softmax activation to yield per-word predictions. We present two variants of the model. The first method is *feature-based*, similar to the model of Gao et al. (2018). We embed input words through the concatenation of their non-contextualised (GloVe) and contextualised (ELMo) embeddings. The concatenation of GloVe and ELMo feeds into a one-layer Bi-LSTM encoder. During optimisation, we learn the parameters of the Bi-LSTM and classification layer.

As our second method, we use a *fine-tuning* architecture, similar to Dankers et al. (2019), in which the embeddings and recurrent encoder are replaced with the pretrained BERT$_{base}$ model (Devlin et al., 2019). BERT uses embeddings for subword units that are encoded with twelve transformer en-

coder layers. During optimisation we fine-tune BERT and learn the parameters of the classification layer. A word is considered metaphorical if any of its subword units is labelled as metaphorical. This choice is based on the assumption that it is more likely that a common prefix or suffix is not considered metaphorical while a word's main piece is than the other way around.

To include discourse information in both architectures, the output of the last encoder layer is concatenated to a discourse representation and fed to the classification layer, such that the classification layer contains dedicated parameters for both the discourse and (sub)word representations. We further detail the two mechanisms employed to compute the discourse representations below.

4.1 Modelling Discourse

Discourse Definition To represent discourse, we use a context window of size $2k + 1$ sentences. It comprises k preceding sentences, the immediate sentential context of the word to be classified (the *focus* sentence), and k succeeding sentences. However, based on the position of the focus sentence in the corresponding text, the number of preceding or succeeding sentences can be less than k. A value of 0 for k implies a context window containing the focus sentence only.

General Attention The first attention mechanism constructs a discourse representation by applying general attention to all tokens within the

Model	k	P	R	F1
Wu et al. (2018)	-	60.8	70.0	65.1
ELMo-LSTM				
- General Att.	0	66.3	64.8	65.5±.3
	1	66.3	66.6	66.4±.4
	2	66.8	67.8	**67.3±.2**
	3	66.6	67.3	66.9±.4
- Hierarchical Att.	1	67.5	65.5	66.5±.4
	2	67.6	66.1	66.8±.3
	3	68.1	66.1	67.1±.6
BERT				
- General Att.	0	73.5	67.4	70.3±.5
	1	72.6	69.8	71.1±.6
	2	73.7	68.9	71.1±.5
	3	72.8	70.0	71.3±.5
- Hierarchical Att.	1	73.1	69.1	71.0±.4
	2	73.5	69.6	**71.5±.5**
	3	73.8	68.9	71.3±.5

Table 1: Main task performance for the all POS 2018 VUA metaphor identification task. The highest performance per model type is shown in bold font.

Model	k	VB	ADJ	NN	ADV
Mu et al. (2019)[†]	-	66.8	-	-	-
Wu et al. (2018)	-	67.4	65.1	62.9	58.8
Gao et al. (2018)[†]	-	69.9	58.3	60.4	-
Mao et al. (2019)[†]	-	70.8	62.2	63.4	63.8
ELMo-LSTM					
- General Att.	0	69.7	62.0	62.5	57.3
	2	71.2	63.5	65.0	57.6
- Hierarchical Att.	3	71.5	63.2	64.2	57.1
BERT					
- General Att.	0	74.6	65.9	67.5	64.3
	3	75.6	66.4	68.9	64.0
- Hierarchical Att.	2	75.7	66.0	69.3	63.2

Table 2: Task performance (F1-score) breakdown per POS category, for the baseline systems and best-performing setup per model and attention module type. [†]Due to differences in the data subset used and evaluation setup these results are not directly comparable to ours.

context window. The encoder layers are applied to each of the sentences within the context window individually. The discourse representation is the weighted combination of the outputs, where the weights are computed by applying a linear layer followed by the softmax function. The architecture is shown in Figure 1a.

Hierarchical Attention Secondly, we replace the general attention with hierarchical attention inspired by the work of Yang et al. (2016) to combine word- and sentence-level attention. The former type provides fine-grained information needed for disambiguation and possibly co-reference resolution, whereas the latter is more suited to capture coarse-grained topical information. First, the individual sentences from the context window are encoded, and general attention is applied per sentence, yielding sentence representations. Second, the sentence representations are fed to a sentence-level encoder, and sentence-level attention is utilised to produce a discourse representation. For the recurrent architecture, the encoder is a Bi-LSTM, and for BERT, it is a transformer layer. The hierarchical attention module is visualised in Figure 1b.

5 Experiments and Results

5.1 Experimental Setup

The *feature-based* approach uses GloVe and ELMo embeddings of dimensionalities 300 and 1,024, respectively. The hidden state dimensionality of the Bi-LSTM is 128. Training lasts for 10 epochs, with a maximum learning rate of 0.005 and batches of size 64.

The *fine-tuning* method includes the BERT$_{base}$ model that has 12 pretrained transformer layers with a hidden dimensionality of 768. The BERT model is fine-tuned for 4 epochs with a batch size of 16, and a maximum learning rate of 5e−5.

Both model types are trained using the AdamW optimiser with a cosine-based learning rate scheduler and a warm-up period of 10%. Tokens with a POS tag other than the four open-class categories are included in the sentence, albeit that their metaphoricity is not considered during optimisation. We use the negative log-likelihood loss along with class weights to account for the class imbalance. The weights are annealed during training from 0.9 and 0.1 to 0.7 and 0.3 for the metaphorical and literal classes, respectively. We report the precision (P), recall (R), and F1-scores for the metaphor class achieved by each model averaged over ten randomly initialised runs.

5.2 Results

Table 1 presents our main task performance. We compare our models to the previous highest performing system designed by Wu et al. (2018). Our baseline systems using $k = 0$ only incorporate the sentential context of the focus sentence. The recurrent and BERT-based models with $k = 0$ already outperform the approach of Wu et al. (2018) by the margins of 0.4 and 5.2 F1-points, respectively.

The inclusion of discourse representations further improves the F1-scores over the baseline methods, for both model types and both attention modules. The performance differences are significant as per a t-test ($p < 5e{-}3$) for all experimental setups including wider discourse ($k > 0$). This finding is in accordance with the findings of Mu et al. (2019). Generally, the largest performance gain is achieved by increasing k from 0 to 1. This indicates that the immediate neighbouring sentences are the most informative. This claim is supported by Bizzoni and Ghanimifard (2018) who mention that the metaphors in the VUA metaphor corpus generally do not require long-distance information for their resolution. The top-performing model is the BERT setup with hierarchical attention and $k = 2$ that achieves a state-of-the-art F1-score of 71.5%. Overall, we observe that using the hierarchical attention module is more effective at increasing the precision, while the general attention module is more likely to improve the recall.

Table 2 displays more fine-grained F1-scores per POS category for the best-performing experimental setups per model type and attention module. We notice that the increase in performance is mainly achieved by increments in the F1-scores for verbs and nouns rather than adjectives and adverbs.

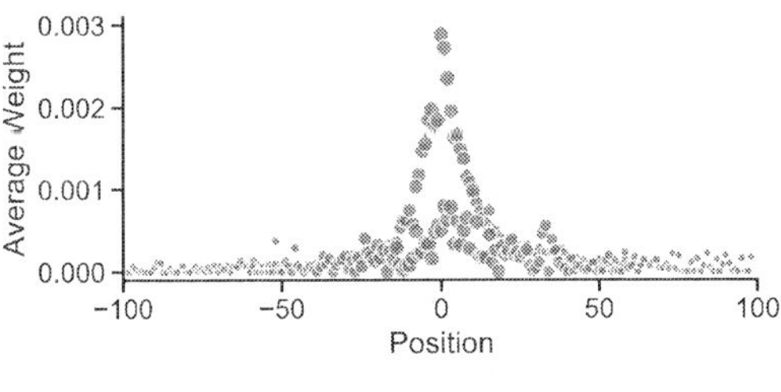

(a) ELMo-LSTM, general attention, $k = 1$

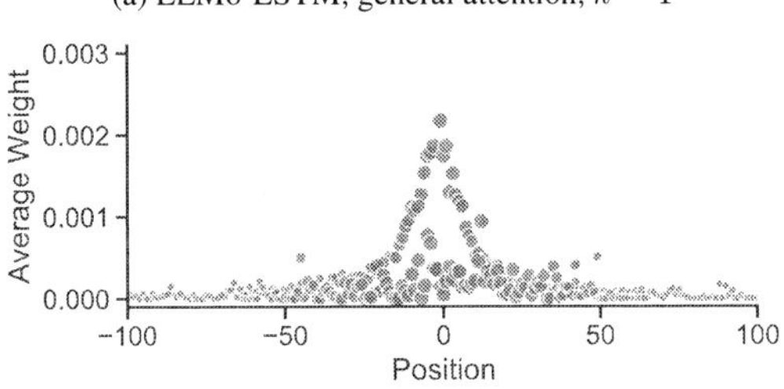

(b) BERT, general attention, $k = 1$

Figure 2: Distribution of the attention weight per token position, for (1) all test sentences and (2) the test sentences whose metaphoricity labels were corrected by including discourse information.

6 Analysis and Discussion

In order to investigate the types of information that discourse provides, we have conducted a qualitative analysis of the sentences where our discourse-aware models improved the labelling of a word over the discourse-agnostic baselines. We found that discourse helps primarily in two ways: (1) it provides information about the topic of the text, which is often needed for disambiguation, particularly for shorter sentences; and (2) it allows the models to implicitly perform co-reference resolution through the use of word-level attention.

We observe that while the attention distributions of the hierarchical mechanisms are rather diffused, the general attention mechanism uses very sparse weights. We hypothesise that the former type is more suited for modelling coarse-grained topical information. The latter is able to highlight specific words and phrases in neighbouring sentences that may be needed for disambiguation and co-reference resolution. The attention distributions displayed in Table 3 are exemplary of distributions in the hierarchical and general attention modules with regard to sparseness. This observation holds for both the recurrent and BERT-based models.

To further investigate the internal functioning of the attention modules and the influence of discourse, we use majority voting across the randomly initialised runs to obtain samples that are consistently improved by all discourse setups compared to the baseline per model type. For the recurrent models, this subset contains 109 samples: 53 metaphorical tokens and 56 literal ones. For BERT, these statistics are 57 and 19, respectively. To assert that within these subsets, the surrounding sentences affect the discourse representation, we visualise the average weight per word position, as measured from the middle of the focus sentence. Figure 2 demonstrates that for sentences in this subset, the distribution is more diffused compared to all test sentences. Thus, on average, the broader discourse has a more substantial effect on the model's classification for these samples. This finding supports the hypothesis that the numerical performance gain observed is caused by the inclusion of discourse representations.

The examples listed in Table 3 are drawn from the consistently improved subset for all recurrent discourse setups. Specifically, the annotations of the words *mincemeat*, *spread* and *hurry* were corrected. In the first example, the context contains

Hierarchical Attention		General Attention
Sentence	*Word*	
.297	I 've got_L some cooking_L apples_L out there Oh is n't he , I could hit_L him !	apples_L
.419	Why does n't he make_L make_L your own bloody_M mincemeat_L then !	bloody_M, mincemeat_L
.284	Yeah that 's cos_L I make_L the the pastry_L and you can	-
.276	As you always_L still_L continue_L to tell_L them yes_L you do .	-
.321	If I want_L it spread_M around .	spread_M, around
.403	That gives_M you your bit_M of character_M .	gives_M, bit_M, character_M
.344	The accelerator_L is the one on the right_L sir_L !	-
.268	He is an old_L gentleman_L , dear_L but er_L he is n't in a hurry_L what so ever_L .	hurry_L
.388	Look_L he 's slowing_L down there !	Look_L, slowing_L, down

Table 3: Visualisation of the attention distributions for three example sentences in which the underlined token was correctly labelled after including wider discourse information, for ELMo-LSTM with $k = 1$. The colour intensity represents the word-level attention weights. For hierarchical attention, the sentence weights (first column) influence the effect of the word-level weights (second column). Since the general attention distributions were rather sparse, we only include the key words (column three).

food references ("cooking apples" and "make the pastry") and hence provides the required topical information, emphasising that *mincemeat* is used in a text about cooking. If "making mincemeat of something" were used metaphorically, one would expect neighbouring sentences to discuss defeats, demolition or devastation. The second example illustrates a case where the wider context is needed for anaphora resolution: the meaning of *it* is unclear from the sentence itself, which hinders the metaphoricity resolution of *spread*. While the context does not specify the referent of *it*, it still incorporates clues through the phrases "continue to tell them" and "gives you character" that indicate something is not spread physically but socially. When looking into the even broader context (available to models with $k > 1$), *it* appears to be gossip about a wild night involving alcohol. This example indicates that the directly neighbouring sentences are not always sufficient for complete clarity – i.e. that increasing k beyond 1 can occasionally be helpful. In the final example, it becomes apparent from the metaphor's discourse context that "being in a hurry" in fact concerns the actual speed of the accelerator, as opposed to the metaphorical use of hurrying: the obstacle that keeps us all from living life fully.

The results in Table 2 show that the use of discourse information primarily improves performance for verbs and nouns, and less so for adjectives and adverbs. We hypothesise that much of this improvement is due to pronominal co-reference resolution, which is most critical for verbs and nouns. Pronouns replace nouns and noun phrases in sentences and are themselves in direct grammatical relations with the verbs (as their subject or object). A verb may be used metaphorically or literally, but without knowing the identity of its subject or object, its metaphoricity may be difficult to determine. For adverbs and adjectives that would not be the case, as they never modify a pronoun.

7 Conclusion

In this work, we presented deep neural architectures that make use of attention mechanisms to investigate the impact of discourse in the task of word-level metaphor detection. Our models establish new state-of-the-art results in the all POS track of the 2018 VUA metaphor identification shared task (Leong et al., 2018). Two attention mechanisms were experimented with for modelling discourse, a general and hierarchical one. Both modules yield significant performance increases, but our qualitative analysis indicates that they serve a different purpose.

Considering the high variety in the corpus's sentence lengths, future work could include defining the context window in terms of words instead of sentences and the merging of techniques to reap the benefits of both co-reference resolution and capturing topical information.

References

Beata Beigman Klebanov, Chee Wee Leong, E. Dario Gutierrez, Ekaterina Shutova, and Michael Flor. 2016. Semantic classifications for detection of verb metaphors. In *Proceedings of the 54th Annual Meeting of the Association for Computational Linguistics (ACL)*, volume 2, pages 101–106.

Yuri Bizzoni and Mehdi Ghanimifard. 2018. Bigrams and BiLSTMs two neural networks for sequential metaphor detection. In *Proceedings of NAACL-HLT 2018 Workshop on Figurative Language Processing*, pages 91–101.

George Aaron Broadwell, Umit Boz, Ignacio Cases, Tomek Strzalkowski, Laurie Feldman, Sarah Taylor, Samira Shaikh, Ting Liu, Kit Cho, and Nick Webb. 2013. Using imageability and topic chaining to locate metaphors in linguistic corpora. In *International Conference on Social Computing, Behavioral-Cultural Modeling, and Prediction*, pages 102–110. Springer.

Luana Bulat, Stephen Clark, and Ekaterina Shutova. 2017. Modelling metaphor with attribute-based semantics. In *Proceedings of the 15th Conference of the European Chapter of the Association for Computational Linguistics (EACL)*, volume 2, pages 523–528.

Jeremy H. Clear. 1993. The British National Corpus. In *The Digital Word: Text-Based Computing in the Humanities*, page 163–187. MIT Press, Cambridge, MA, USA.

Verna Dankers, Marek Rei, Martha Lewis, and Ekaterina Shutova. 2019. Modelling the interplay of metaphor and emotion through multitask learning. In *Proceedings of the 2019 Conference on Empirical Methods in Natural Language Processing and the 9th International Joint Conference on Natural Language Processing (EMNLP-IJCNLP)*, pages 2218–2229.

Jacob Devlin, Ming-Wei Chang, Kenton Lee, and Kristina Toutanova. 2019. Bert: Pre-training of deep bidirectional transformers for language understanding. In *Proceedings of the 2019 Conference of the North American Chapter of the Association for Computational Linguistics: Human Language Technologies (NAACL-HLT)*, volume 1, pages 4171–4186.

Ge Gao, Eunsol Choi, Yejin Choi, and Luke Zettlemoyer. 2018. Neural metaphor detection in context. In *Proceedings of the 2018 Conference on Empirical Methods in Natural Language Processing (EMNLP)*, pages 607–613.

E Dario Gutierrez, Ekaterina Shutova, Tyler Marghetis, and Benjamin Bergen. 2016. Literal and metaphorical senses in compositional distributional semantic models. In *Proceedings of the 54th Annual Meeting of the Association for Computational Linguistics (ACL)*, volume 1, pages 183–193.

Hyeju Jang, Seungwhan Moon, Yohan Jo, and Carolyn Rosé. 2015a. Metaphor detection in discourse. In *Proceedings of the 16th Annual Meeting of the Special Interest Group on Discourse and Dialogue*, pages 384–392.

Hyeju Jang, Miaomiao Wen, and Carolyn Rose. 2015b. Effects of situational factors on metaphor detection in an online discussion forum. In *Proceedings of the Third Workshop on Metaphor in NLP*, pages 1–10.

Ryan Kiros, Yukun Zhu, Ruslan Salakhutdinov, Richard S. Zemel, Antonio Torralba, Raquel Urtasun, and Sanja Fidler. 2015. Skip-thought vectors. In *Proceedings of the 28th International Conference on Neural Information Processing Systems (NeurIPS)*, volume 2, pages 3294–3302.

George Lakoff and Mark Johnson. 1980. *Metaphors we Live by*. University of Chicago Press, Chicago.

Quoc Le and Tomas Mikolov. 2014. Distributed representations of sentences and documents. In *Proceedings of the 31st International Conference on Machine Learning (ICML)*, pages 1188–1196.

Chee Wee (Ben) Leong, Beata Beigman Klebanov, and Ekaterina Shutova. 2018. A report on the 2018 VUA metaphor detection shared task. In *Proceedings of NAACL-HLT 2018 Workshop on Figurative Language Processing*, pages 56–66.

Rui Mao, Chenghua Lin, and Frank Guerin. 2019. End-to-end sequential metaphor identification inspired by linguistic theories. In *Proceedings of the 57th Annual Meeting of the Association for Computational Linguistics (ACL)*, pages 3888–3898.

Jesse Mu, Helen Yannakoudakis, and Ekaterina Shutova. 2019. Learning outside the box: Discourse-level features improve metaphor identification. In *Proceedings of the 2019 Conference of the North American Chapter of the Association for Computational Linguistics: Human Language Technologies (NAACL-HLT)*, volume 1, pages 596–601.

Andreas Musolff. 2000. *Mirror images of Europe: Metaphors in the public debate about Europe in Britain and Germany*. Iudicium, Muenchen.

Jeffrey Pennington, Richard Socher, and Christopher Manning. 2014. GloVe: Global vectors for word representation. In *Proceedings of the 2014 Conference on Empirical Methods in Natural Language Processing (EMNLP)*, pages 1532–1543. Association for Computational Linguistics.

Matthew Peters, Mark Neumann, Mohit Iyyer, Matt Gardner, Christopher Clark, Kenton Lee, and Luke Zettlemoyer. 2018. Deep contextualized word representations. In *Proceedings of the 2018 Conference of the North American Chapter of the Association for Computational Linguistics: Human Language Technologies (NAACL-HLT)*, volume 1, pages 2227–2237, New Orleans, Louisiana. Association for Computational Linguistics.

Marek Rei, Luana Bulat, Douwe Kiela, and Ekaterina Shutova. 2017. Grasping the finer point: A supervised similarity network for metaphor detection. In *Proceedings of the 2017 Conference on Empirical Methods in Natural Language Processing (EMNLP)*, pages 1537–1546.

Elena Semino. 2008. *Metaphor in Discourse.* Cambridge University Press, Cambridge.

Ekaterina Shutova. 2011. *Computational Approaches to Figurative Language.* Ph.D. thesis, University of Cambridge.

Gerard J Steen, Aletta G Dorst, J Berenike Herrmann, Anna Kaal, Tina Krennmayr, and Trijntje Pasma. 2010. *A Method for Linguistic Metaphor Identification: From MIP to MIPVU*, volume 14. John Benjamins Publishing.

Peter D Turney, Yair Neuman, Dan Assaf, and Yohai Cohen. 2011. Literal and metaphorical sense identification through concrete and abstract context. In *Proceedings of the Conference on Empirical Methods in Natural Language Processing*, pages 680–690. Association for Computational Linguistics.

Yorick Wilks, Adam Dalton, James Allen, and Lucian Galescu. 2013. Automatic metaphor detection using large-scale lexical resources and conventional metaphor extraction. In *Proceedings of the First Workshop on Metaphor in NLP*, pages 36–44.

Chuhan Wu, Fangzhao Wu, Yubo Chen, Sixing Wu, Zhigang Yuan, and Yongfeng Huang. 2018. Neural metaphor detecting with CNN-LSTM model. In *Proceedings of the Workshop on Figurative Language Processing*, pages 110–114, New Orleans, Louisiana. Association for Computational Linguistics.

Zichao Yang, Diyi Yang, Chris Dyer, Xiaodong He, Alex Smola, and Eduard Hovy. 2016. Hierarchical attention networks for document classification. In *Proceedings of the 2016 Conference of the North American Chapter of the Association for Computational Linguistics: Human Language Technologies*, pages 1480–1489, San Diego, California. Association for Computational Linguistics.

Go Figure! Multi-task transformer-based architecture for metaphor detection using idioms: ETS team in 2020 metaphor shared task

Xianyang Chen, Chee Wee (Ben) Leong, Michael Flor, and Beata Beigman Klebanov
Educational Testing Service
`xchen002,cleong,mflor,bbeigmanklebanov@ets.org`

Abstract

This paper describes the ETS entry to the 2020 Metaphor Detection shared task. Our contribution consists of a sequence of experiments using BERT, starting with a baseline, strengthening it by spell-correcting the TOEFL corpus, followed by a multi-task learning setting, where one of the tasks is the token-level metaphor classification as per the shared task, while the other is meant to provide additional training that we hypothesized to be relevant to the main task. In one case, out-of-domain data manually annotated for metaphor is used for the auxiliary task; in the other case, in-domain data automatically annotated for idioms is used for the auxiliary task. Both multi-task experiments yield promising results.

1 Introduction

We use metaphors in our everyday life as a means of relating our experiences to other subjects and contexts (Lakoff and Johnson, 2008); it is commonly used to help us understand the world in a structured way, and oftentimes in an unconscious manner while we speak and write. It sheds light on the unknown using the known, explains the complex using the simple, and helps us to emphasize the relevant aspects of meaning resulting in effective communication.

There is a large body of work in the literature that discusses how metaphor has been used in the context of political communication, marketing, mental health, teaching, assessment of English proficiency, among others (Beigman Klebanov et al., 2018; Gutierrez et al., 2017; Littlemore et al., 2013; Thibodeau and Boroditsky, 2011; Kaviani and Hamedi, 2011; Kathpalia and Carmel, 2011; Landau et al., 2009; Beigman Klebanov et al., 2008; Zaltman and Zaltman, 2008; Littlemore and Low, 2006; Cameron, 2003; Lakoff, 2010; Billow et al., 1997; Bosman, 1987); see chapter 7 in Veale et al. (2016) for a recent review.

In the NLP universe, there's been substantial recent interest in automated detection of metaphor (Dankers et al., 2019; Mikhalkova et al., 2019; Mao et al., 2019; Igamberdiev and Shin, 2018; Marhula et al., 2019; Markert, 2019; Saund et al., 2019).

This paper describes the ETS entry to the 2020 Metaphor Detection shared task held as a part of the 2nd Workshop on Processing Figurative Language, at ACL 2020[1]. The shared tasks consists of four tracks: all content parts of speech – nouns, verbs, adjectives, and adverbs (AllPOS) and a verbs-only track (Verbs) for two corpora – (a) a corpus of well-edited BNC articles from a variety of genres annotated using the MIP-VU protocol, and (b) a corpus of medium to high quality timed, non-native essays written for the Test of English as a Foreign Language annotated under a different protocol. We participated in all the four tracks.

Our contribution consists of a sequence of experiments using BERT, starting with a baseline, then strengthening it by spell-correcting the TOEFL corpus (section 4). We then devised a multi-task learning setting, where one of the tasks is the token level metaphor classification as per the shared task, while the other is meant to provide additional training that we hypothesized to be relevant to the main task (section 5).

The first multitask learning is the utilization out-of-domain data annotated for metaphor, albeit under a different annotation protocol, by using data from the other competition corpus. Thus, we use metaphor prediction on the VUA corpus as an auxiliary task for the main TOEFL task, and vice versa. We show that this setup resulted in an improved performance on the TOEFL test data but not on VUA data. A sanity-check experiment where the two training datasets were simply merged together yielded performance that was inferior to the baseline for all tracks (section 5.1).

---

[1] https://sites.google.com/view/figlang2020/home

Proceedings of the Second Workshop on Figurative Language Processing, pages 235–243
July 9, 2020. ©2020 Association for Computational Linguistics
https://doi.org/10.18653/v1/P17

The second auxiliary task is utilization of a large in-domain corpus that we automatically tagged for occurrence of a different type of figurative language phenomenon – idioms. We hypothesize that the affinity between the two ways of figuration might help the system become more sensitive to metaphor by learning to attend to idioms. Our results provide support to the hypothesis, as this setting yielded our best result on the VUA dataset (section 5.2). We provide a discussion of our findings in section 7.

2 Datasets

2.1 VUA corpus

We use the VU Amsterdam Metaphor Corpus (VUA) (Steen et al., 2010) as provided by the shared task organizers. The dataset consists of 117 fragments sampled across four genres from the British National Corpus: Academic, News, Conversation, and Fiction. Each genre is represented by approximately the same number of tokens, although the number of texts differs greatly, where the news archive has the largest number of texts. The data is annotated using the MIP-VU procedure with a strong inter-annotator reliability of $\kappa > 0.8$. It is based on the MIP procedure (Pragglejaz, 2007), extending it to handle metaphoricity through reference (such as marking *did* as a metaphor in *As the weather broke up, so did their friendship*) and allow for explicit coding of difficult cases where a group of annotators could not arrive at a consensus. Note that we only considered words marked as metaphors decided as such by the shared task organizers. The VUA dataset and annotations is the same as the one used in the first shared task on metaphor detection (Leong et al., 2018).

2.2 TOEFL corpus

This data labeled for metaphor was sampled from the publicly available ETS Corpus of Non-Native Written English[2] (Blanchard et al., 2013) and was first introduced by (Beigman Klebanov et al., 2018). The annotated data comprises essay responses to eight persuaisve/argumentative prompts, for three native languages of the writer (Japanese, Italian, Arabic), and for two proficiency levels – medium and high. The data was annotated using the protocol in Beigman Klebanov and Flor (2013), that emphasized argumentation-relevant

metaphors. Average inter-annotator agreement was $\kappa = 0.56 - 0.62$, for multiple passes of the annotation (see (Beigman Klebanov et al., 2018) for more details). For the experiments, we used the metaphor annotations marked as such by the organizers. We used 180 essays for training and 60 essays for testing, as provided by the shared task organizers. Tables 1 and 2 show some descriptive characteristics of the data: the number of texts, sentences, tokens, and class distribution information for Verbs and AllPOS tracks for the two corpora – VUA and TOEFL.

3 Baseline system

We build our baseline system based on BERT (Devlin et al., 2018). BERT (**B**idirectional **E**ncoder **R**epresentations from **T**ransformers) is a transformer (Vaswani et al., 2017) model that is pre-trained on a large quantity of texts, and obtained state-of-the-art performance on many NLP benchmarks (Wang et al., 2018; Zellers et al., 2018; Rajpurkar et al., 2016). Since its introduction, there have been many improvements over the original BERT model, such as RoBERTa (Liu et al., 2019), ERNIE (Sun et al., 2019), XLNet (Yang et al., 2019); we use the most basic model (**bert-base-uncased**).

We fine-tune the BERT model as a standard token classification task, that is, after obtaining the contextualized embeddings of a sentence, we apply a linear layer followed by softmax on each token to predict whether it is metaphorical or not. Fig 1 shows the architecture of the baseline model. We tune the hyperparameters based on cross-validation on training data. The fold partitions for the VUA corpus are the same as the ones used for experiments in Beigman Klebanov et al. (2016). For the TOEFL corpus, we obtained the folds information from the shared task organizers directly. We select batch size in $\{16, 32, 64\}$, number of training epochs in $\{2, 3, 4, 5\}$, and use a fixed learning rate of 3×10^{-5}. We also apply the learning rate scheduler known as *slanted triangular* (Howard and Ruder, 2018). Due to the imbalanced class distribution in our data (see Table 2), the positive class is up-weighted by a factor of 3. The same setting applies to experiments described in all the following sections.

---

[2]https://catalog.ldc.upenn.edu/LDC2014T06

Datasets	VUA		TOEFL	
	Train	Test	Train	Test
#texts	90	27	180	60
#sents	12,123	4,081	2,741	968

Table 1: Number of texts and sentences for both VUA and TOEFL datasets.

Datasets	VUA				TOEFL			
	Verbs		All POS		Verbs		All POS	
	Train	Test	Train	Test	Train	Test	Train	Test
#tokens	17,240	5,873	72,611	22,196	7,016	2,301	26,737	9,014
%M	29%	—	18%	—	13%	—	7%	—

Table 2: Number of tokens and percentage of metaphors breakdown for both VUA and TOEFL datasets, grouped by Verbs and AllPOS.

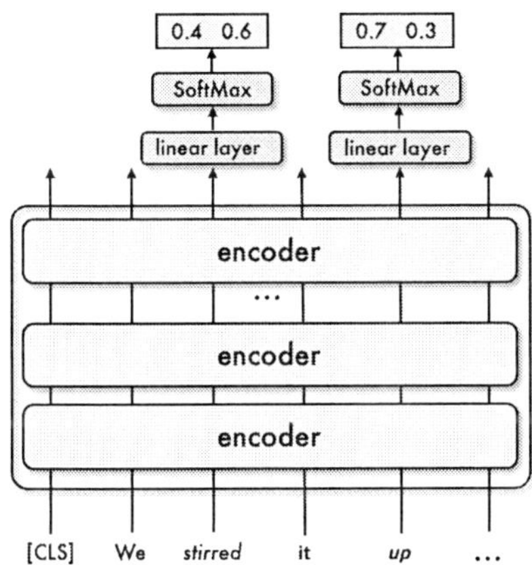

Figure 1: Baseline system architecture. The output is a pair of probabilities – the first for class 0 (non-metaphor) and the second for class 1 (metaphor).

4 Experiment 1: Spell correction system

Proper automatic detection of lexically-anchored phenomena in text often depends on availability of correct spelling in the text. The contribution of spelling correction to other tasks has been documented previously, especially for English texts produced by non-native learners of English (Rozovskaya and Roth, 2016; Granger and Wynne, 1999). Essays written by TOEFL test-takers are known to contain a considerable amount of spelling errors (Flor et al., 2015). To alleviate this, we used a state-of-the-art automatic spelling corrections system (Flor et al., 2019) to correct spelling in the TOEFL dataset. Specifically, for the training partition of the TOEFL dataset, the

system corrected 1553 errors in 180 essays, and 510 errors in 60 essays of the test partition.

5 Multi-task system

As we fine-tune BERT on relatively small datasets, we attempted to enrich the learning with partially relevant additional materials through a multi-task setting - adding auxiliary tasks and train the metaphor detection task with them. The auxiliary tasks are described in sections 5.1 and 5.2.

The model we use for multi-task learning is as follows: Instead of directly making predictions based on the output embeddings of BERT, the embeddings are first projected to a lower-dimensional representation by a linear layer; each task then has its own classifier on top of that linear layer. The architecture of the model is shown in Fig. 2.

During training, the data in batches of the metaphor task (our main task) and the auxiliary tasks are mixed and trained on in an interleaved manner; the specifics will be described for each of the auxiliary tasks separately. In order for the main task to dominate the learning, we also scale the gradient of the auxiliary tasks by a factor of 0.1. The hyperparameters are selected in the same way as described in section 3.

5.1 Experiment 2: Learning from out-of-domain data

Since both the VUA and the TOEFL corpora are annotated for metaphors, using one to help the other during learning could potentially provide additional relevant training data. However, since the data is from different types of texts and dif-

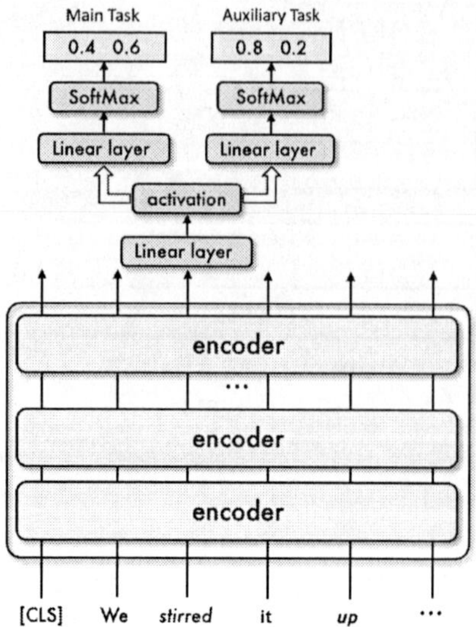

Figure 2: Multi-task system architecture. The output is a pair of probabilities – the first for class 0 (non-metaphor) and the second for class 1 (metaphor).

ferent genres (well-edited BNC text in academic, news, conversation and fiction genres vs relatively short English language learner essays), and since the guidelines under which the two datasets were annotated are different, it is possible that each corpus is only partially or indirectly relevant to the other. We experimented with both a straight-forward merging of the training sets of the two datasets (as a preview – this did not produce good results) and with a multi-task setting where the other corpus is used for the auxiliary task.

We use the same batch size and learning rate for the main task and the auxiliary task. The batches from the two tasks are interleaved uniformly; as there are roughly four times more sentences in the VUA corpus than in the TOEFL corpus, there are five batches of the VUA task following every batch of the TOEFL task. We do not sub-sample the VUA corpus or over-sample the TOEFL corpus.

5.2 Experiment 3: Learning from another type of figurative language

Differently from Experiment 2, where we utilized an out-of-domain dataset annotated for the same phenomenon (albeit under somewhat different annotation protocol), in Experiment 3 we are attempting to make use of a different but related phenomenon – a different type of figurative language, namely, idioms. The metaphorical underpinnings of many idiomatic expressions have been noted

in psycholinguistic literature (Gibbs and O'Brien, 1990; Nunberg et al., 1994; Glucksberg, 2001).

The main idea here is that one or more of the words participating in idiomatic expressions are often used metaphorically. Thus, in CUT-TING EDGE both the words are used metaphorically; in PAY *attention*, *false* STEP, *helping* HAND, GOLDEN *opportunity*, and *social* LADDER, the capitalized word is a metaphor while the other is not. There are also idioms where none of the words are used metaphorically such as *matter of fact*, *other than*, and *once in a while*. Still, it appears likely that the preponderance of metaphors within idiomatic expressions would be higher than in non-idiomatic language. It is also possible that learning to detect idioms – a different but related type of figurative language – could help with metaphor detection, as these might tend to be used in similar contexts. Experiment 3 is an attempt to explore these observations by setting idiom detection as an auxiliary task for the main metaphor detection task.

Although there exists considerable prior research on automatic detection of idioms (for a brief review see Flor and Beigman Klebanov (2018)), idiom detection systems are typically constrained to very small sets of idioms or to particular types of expressions (e.g. verb-noun constructions). We opted to use a system that marks candidate expressions but does not verify their idiomaticity in the given context. The advantage of this particular system is that it has very wide coverage. We assume that many of the idioms found in a particular corpus might be well-known idioms that are listed in various dictionaries. Our system (Flor and Beigman Klebanov, 2018) is equipped with a dictionary of about 5000 English idiomatic expressions (culled from Wiktionary), and performs a flexible search for idioms and their syntactic and lexical variants in running text. In fact, it performs a simultaneous flexible pattern matching. The idiom detection system looks only for expressions that have more than one word, and excludes common greeting phrases (e.g. 'have a nice day'), phrasal verbs and verb+preposition constructions (unless they are part of a larger idiom). The system marks expressions that potentially might be instances of idioms, but it does not perform idiom/non-idiom classification. For the present experiment we used this system with rather conservative settings that yielded precision of 0.571 in our previous evaluations on a subset of the TOEFL data; see the leftmost column in Figure 1-A in Flor and Beigman Klebanov (2018) for the details of the configuration. Based on the prior evaluation, for this system configuration, most of the errors were cases where the expression is identified correctly but it is used literally rather than idiomatically.

We ran the idiom-candidate marking system on TOEFL-11[3] essays and on the BNC corpus (excluding texts of the shared task). In total, the system detected 3,581 different idiom types in the BNC, with 179,967 instances of (candidate) idioms; in the TOEFL-11 data, we found 504 different idiom types, with 3,908 instances. There is somewhat more idiom usage per sentence in the BNC than in the TOEFL data: The system identified an idiom in 3% of all BNC sentences and in 2.2% for of TOEFL-11 sentences. Table 3 shows the 20 most frequently found (candidate, or unverified) idioms in the BNC and TOEFL data; the lists contain a mix of idioms that contain and do not contain metaphors.

The idiom detection auxiliary task is also formalized as a token classification task: Given a sentence, predict for each token whether it is part of an idiom. Given the size of the BNC corpus, we only sample a small subset of it for training: 10,000 sentences with idioms and 10,000 sentences without idioms. For the TOEFL-11 data, we keep all sentences with idioms and sample the same number (3,908) of sentences without idioms.

6 Results

Tables 4 and 5 show performance of the various systems on AllPOS and Verbs-only tasks, respectively, for both VUA and TOEFL data. Since it is clear that spelling correction is useful for improving performance on TOEFL data, we used the spell corrected version of the data for all the systems from experiments 2 and 3 on TOEFL data. Our best-performing systems reported here are also benchmarked against other participating systems in the shared task summary report (Leong et al., 2020). We obtained a ranking of 2nd and 4th in the VUA and TOEFL tasks, respectively.

Since VUA data contains well-edited BNC text, we did not run spelling correction on VUA data. For the Verbs tracks, we experimented with both (a) training on AllPOS data and evaluating on the

Verbs-only subset of the test data, and (b) training and testing on Verbs only subsets. Version (a) yielded better results, which are reported here.

7 Discussion

First, we observe that comparative results across the different systems are highly consistent for AllPOS and Verbs-only settings; we therefore focus on AllPOS in the discussion.

Combining the training data from TOEFL and VUA sets does not result in better performance on either test set (see D_{all} in Tables 4, 5). This could be due to both out-of-domain nature of the two corpora with respect to each other, to the difference in the guidelines under which the two corpora were annotated, and/or to the difference in the distribution of metaphors vs non-metaphors in the two corpora (see Table 2 for class distribution information).

However, when set up as a multi-task system with a shared representation, using data from VUA as part of the training process results in better performance on TOEFL test data, with a 2.6 points F1 score gain for AllPOS (0.666 vs 0.692 in Table 4). Thus, it appears that using the VUA data as part of the training process through the shared representation but without the TOEFL training process sustaining a loss for mis-classifying instances from VUA (as was the case when the training sets were merged), the system has apparently successfully acquired useful information that helped boost performance on TOEFL test data.

It is interesting to note that the multi-task version of the setting for using out-of-domain data did not result in improvements on VUA test data (F1 score of 0.717 vs 0.715). The drop in recall and increase in precision observed for the D_{mt} model on VUA data is consistent with the direction of the results where the two training datasets were simply merged into a bigger training dataset (D_{all}). It appears that under the guidelines in which TOEFL data was annotated where argumentation-relevant metaphors are detected intuitively, without recourse to a standard dictionary, the annotation outcomes are more conservative: Some instances that the system trained on VUA data considered metaphorical were not considered so in a system that was exposed to TOEFL data

---

[3] https://catalog.ldc.upenn.edu/LDC2014T06

BNC	TOEFL 11
find oneself	long time
other than	need-to-know
long time	pay attention
great deal	matter of fact
once again	other than
ups and downs	day-to-day
once more	find oneself
much less	long run
come through	stay at home
old woman	play games
bear in mind	great deal
cup of tea	jack of all trades
day-to-day	side effect
ask the question	much less
let alone	change one's mind
need-to-know	ask the question
common law	again and again
close one's eyes	well and good
blue-eyed	tell the truth
change one's mind	once again

Table 3: Top 20 most frequently observed (unverified) idioms in the BNC and TOEFL 11 corpora. Note: Hyphens are treated as between-word delimiters and are optionally matched. Thus, both "stay-at-home" and "day to day" will be matched, even though these are not the canonical forms of the idioms on the list.

All POS						
Sys-	VUA			TOEFL		
tem	P	R	F	P	R	F
BL	.721	.713	.718	.701	.563	.624
Sp	–	–	–	.656	.676	**.666**
D_{all}	.728	.676	.701	.576	.637	.605
D_{mt}	.741	.692	.715	.669	.717	**.692**
I_{mt}	.721	.749	**.734**	.718	.616	.663

Table 4: AllPOS performance. BL = baseline BERT system; Sp = baseline BERT system trained and tested on spell-corrected TOEFL data; D_{all} = baseline BERT system trained on combined TOEFL and VUA data; D_{mt} = a multi-task system using out-of-domain metaphor annotated data; I_{mt} = multi-task system using idiom detection as an auxiliary task.

Verbs						
Sys-	VUA			TOEFL		
tem	P	R	F	P	R	F
BL	.725	.790	.756	.624	.694	.657
Sp	–	–	–	.674	.694	**.684**
D_{all}	.747	.733	.740	.614	.664	.638
D_{mt}	.754	.772	.762	.747	.661	**.702**
I_{mt}	.732	.823	**.775**	.705	.631	.667

Table 5: Verbs performance. BL = baseline BERT system; Sp = baseline BERT system trained and tested on spell-corrected TOEFL data; D_{all} = baseline BERT system trained on combined TOEFL and VUA data; D_{mt} = a multi-task system using out-of-domain metaphor annotated data; I_{mt} = multi-task system using idiom detection as an auxiliary task.

during training. For example, the three underlined words in the following sentence were classified as metaphors by the version that was trained on VUA data only, but were classified as non-metaphors after augmentation with the TOEFL data: "A less direct measure which is applicable only to the most senior management is to observe the fall or rise of the share price when a particular executive leaves or joins a company." Of these, *senior* and *leaves* are metaphors according to VUA ground truth, while *observe* is not. Overall, the drop in recall was not sufficiently offset by the increase in precision (although there is a small improvement in F1 score for the Verbs only data – from 0.756 to 0.762, see Table 5). Still, our results suggest that if one is interested in a precision-focused system, using TOEFL data in a multi-task setting when training and testing on VUA could be beneficial, as D_{mt} achieved the best precision on the VUA dataset among all the compared systems.

We next turn to the experiments with an auxiliary idiom detection task. We observe that on VUA data this resulted in a 2-point increase in F1 score – with no penalty in precision, the system gained about 3.5 points in recall (0.713 vs 0.749 on AllPOS; 0.790 vs 0.823 on Verbs). This confirms the usefulness of attending to a related type of figurative language through an auxiliary task – even though the identification of idioms was done using an automated procedure and therefore is quite noisy.

To examine the impact of the idiom auxiliary task, we used one of the cross-validation folds as development set. Looking at instances tagged as non-metaphor by the baseline model and as metaphor by the current model, there are two observations. First, of the 236 VUA sentences with newly tagged metaphors, only 9 sentences contained an idiom, according to our idiom detection system. Thus, it does not appear to be the case that it is specifically metaphors within known idioms that the system has now learned to find; this is a tentative conclusion, however, as it is also possible that these sentences did contain idioms that were either not on the list of the 5,000 the system is searching for, or are on the list and are present in the text but are not detected by the system. Secondly, it appears that the system has learned some sentence-level characteristics of sentences that contain figurative language, in that quite often multiple words in the same sentence got tagged as metaphors: the 236 sentences contained 323 newly tagged metaphors. The most extreme case is that of 4 new words in the same sentence being tagged as metaphors (italicized): "This desire that can not find its *name* (though it would *dare speak*, if it could) is *pleasurable*."

Using idioms for an auxiliary task did not help with TOEFL data. We also tried using the BNC idiom data instead of the TOEFL 11 idiom data; this resulted in comparable performance, still without improvement over the spell-checked single-task version. Since results on VUA suggest that idioms could provide useful information for metaphor detection, we intend to further pursue this line of work by attending more closely to the different types of idiomatic expressions that might be more or less useful for metaphor detection, and by improving the idiom detection mechanism.

8 Conclusion

This paper describes the ETS entry to the 2020 Metaphor Detection shared task held as a part of the 2nd Workshop on Processing Figurative Language, at ACL 2020. We participated in all four tracks – Verbs and AllPOS for each of VUA and TOEFL datasets. Our contribution consists of a sequence of experiments using BERT, starting with a baseline, then strengthening it by spell-correcting the TOEFL corpus, followed by a multi-task learning setting, where one of the tasks is the token-level metaphor classification as per the shared task, while the other is meant to provide additional training that we hypothesized to be relevant to the main task.

The first multitask learning is the utilization of out-of-domain data annotated for metaphor, albeit under a different annotation protocol, by using data from the other competition corpus; this manipulation helped improve F1 scores for metaphor class on TOEFL test data, but not on VUA data. The second auxiliary task is utilization of a large in-domain corpus that we automatically tagged for occurrence of a different type of figurative language phenomenon – idioms. This manipulation resulted in an improved performance on VUA data, but not on TOEFL data. Given the promising results with idiom auxiliary task, we intend to continue work in this direction by improving automatic detection of idioms and by a finer-grained analysis of the contribution of various types of idioms to improve metaphor detection.

References

Beata Beigman Klebanov, Daniel Diermeier, and Eyal Beigman. 2008. Lexical cohesion analysis of political speech. *Political Analysis*, 16(4):447–463.

Beata Beigman Klebanov and Michael Flor. 2013. Argumentation-relevant metaphors in test-taker essays. In *Proceedings of the First Workshop on Metaphor in NLP*, pages 11–20.

Beata Beigman Klebanov, Chee Wee Leong, and Michael Flor. 2018. A corpus of non-native written English annotated for metaphor. In *Proceedings of the 2018 Conference of the North American Chapter of the Association for Computational Linguistics: Human Language Technologies, Volume 2 (Short Papers)*, pages 86–91, New Orleans, Louisiana. Association for Computational Linguistics.

Beata Beigman Klebanov, Chee Wee Leong, E Dario Gutierrez, Ekaterina Shutova, and Michael Flor. 2016. Semantic classifications for detection of verb metaphors. In *Proceedings of the 54th Annual Meeting of the Association for Computational Linguistics (Volume 2: Short Papers)*, volume 2, pages 101–106.

Richard M Billow, Jeffrey Rossman, Nona Lewis, Deberah Goldman, and Charles Raps. 1997. Observing expressive and deviant language in schizophrenia. *Metaphor and Symbol*, 12(3):205–216.

Daniel Blanchard, Joel Tetreault, Derrick Higgins, Aoife Cahill, and Martin Chodorow. 2013. Toefl11: A corpus of non-native english. *ETS Research Report Series*, 2013(2):i–15.

Jan Bosman. 1987. Persuasive effects of political metaphors. *Metaphor and Symbol*, 2(2):97–113.

Lynne Cameron. 2003. *Metaphor in educational discourse*. A&C Black.

Verna Dankers, Marek Rei, Martha Lewis, and Ekaterina Shutova. 2019. Modelling the interplay of metaphor and emotion through multitask learning. In *Proceedings of the 2019 Conference on Empirical Methods in Natural Language Processing and the 9th International Joint Conference on Natural Language Processing (EMNLP-IJCNLP)*, pages 2218–2229.

Jacob Devlin, Ming-Wei Chang, Kenton Lee, and Kristina Toutanova. 2018. Bert: Pre-training of deep bidirectional transformers for language understanding. *arXiv preprint arXiv:1810.04805*.

Michael Flor and Beata Beigman Klebanov. 2018. Catching idiomatic expressions in EFL essays. In *Proceedings of the Workshop on Figurative Language Processing*, pages 34–44, New Orleans, LA.

Michael Flor, Michael Fried, and Alla Rozovskaya. 2019. A benchmark corpus of English misspellings and a minimally-supervised model for spelling correction. In *Proceedings of the Fourteenth Workshop on Innovative Use of NLP for Building Educational Applications*, page 76–86, Florence, Italy.

Michael Flor, Yoko Futagi, Melissa Lopez, and Matthew Mulholland. 2015. Patterns of misspellings in L2 and L1 English: a view from the ETS spelling corpus. *Bergen Language and Linguistics Studies*, 6.

R. W. Gibbs and J. E. O'Brien. 1990. Idioms and mental imagery: The metaphorical motivation for idiomatic meaning. *Cognition*, 36:35–68.

Sam Glucksberg. 2001. *Understanding Figurative Language: from metaphors to idioms*. Oxford University Press, New York, NY.

Sylviane Granger and Martin Wynne. 1999. Optimising measures of lexical variation in EFL learner corpora. In *Corpora Galore*, pages 249–257, Amsterdam. Rodopi.

E Dario Gutierrez, Guillermo Cecchi, Cheryl Corcoran, and Philip Corlett. 2017. Using automated metaphor identification to aid in detection and prediction of first-episode schizophrenia. In *Proceedings of the 2017 Conference on Empirical Methods in Natural Language Processing*, pages 2923–2930.

Jeremy Howard and Sebastian Ruder. 2018. Universal language model fine-tuning for text classification. *arXiv preprint arXiv:1801.06146*.

Timour Igamberdiev and Hyopil Shin. 2018. Metaphor identification with paragraph and word vectorization: An attention-based neural approach. In *Proceedings of the 32nd Pacific Asia Conference on Language, Information and Computation*.

Sujata S Kathpalia and Heah Lee Hah Carmel. 2011. Metaphorical competence in ESL student writing. *RELC Journal*, 42(3):273–290.

Hossein Kaviani and Robabeh Hamedi. 2011. A quantitative/qualitative study on metaphors used by persian depressed patients. *Archives of Psychiatry and Psychotherapy*, 4(5-13):110.

George Lakoff. 2010. *Moral politics: How liberals and conservatives think*. University of Chicago Press.

George Lakoff and Mark Johnson. 2008. *Metaphors we live by*. University of Chicago press.

Mark J Landau, Daniel Sullivan, and Jeff Greenberg. 2009. Evidence that self-relevant motives and metaphoric framing interact to influence political and social attitudes. *Psychological Science*, 20(11):1421–1427.

Chee Wee Leong, Beata Beigman Klebanov, Chris Hamill, Egon Stemle, Rutuja Ubale, and Xianyang Chen. 2020. A report on the 2020 vua and toefl metaphor detection shared task. In *Proceedings of the Second Workshop on Figurative Language Processing*, Seattle, WA.

Chee Wee Leong, Beata Beigman Klebanov, and Ekaterina Shutova. 2018. A report on the 2018 vua metaphor detection shared task. In *Proceedings of the Workshop on Figurative Language Processing*, pages 56–66.

Jeannette Littlemore, Tina Krennmayr, James Turner, and Sarah Turner. 2013. An investigation into metaphor use at different levels of second language writing. *Applied linguistics*, 35(2):117–144.

Jeannette Littlemore and Graham Low. 2006. Metaphoric competence, second language learning, and communicative language ability. *Applied linguistics*, 27(2):268–294.

Yinhan Liu, Myle Ott, Naman Goyal, Jingfei Du, Mandar Joshi, Danqi Chen, Omer Levy, Mike Lewis, Luke Zettlemoyer, and Veselin Stoyanov. 2019. Roberta: A robustly optimized bert pretraining approach. *arXiv preprint arXiv:1907.11692*.

Rui Mao, Chenghua Lin, and Frank Guerin. 2019. End-to-end sequential metaphor identification inspired by linguistic theories. In *Proceedings of the 57th Annual Meeting of the Association for Computational Linguistics*, pages 3888–3898.

Joanna Marhula, Justyna Polak, Maria Janicka, and Aleksander Wawer. 2019. Recognizing metaphor: how do non-experts and machines deal with a metaphor identification task? In *BOOK OF ABSTRACTS*, page 70.

Katja Markert. 2019. Literature list ps/hs ss2019 figurative language resolution.

Elena Mikhalkova, Nadezhda Ganzherli, Vladislav Maraev, Anna Glazkova, and Dmitriy Grigoriev. 2019. A comparison of algorithms for detection of "figurativeness" in metaphor, irony and puns. In *International Conference on Analysis of Images, Social Networks and Texts*, pages 186–192. Springer.

Geoffrey Nunberg, Ivan A. Sag, and Thomas Wasow. 1994. Idioms. *Language*, 70(3):491–538.

Pragglejaz. 2007. MIP: A method for identifying metaphorically used words in discourse. *Metaphor and symbol*, 22(1):1–39.

Pranav Rajpurkar, Jian Zhang, Konstantin Lopyrev, and Percy Liang. 2016. Squad: 100,000+ questions for machine comprehension of text. *arXiv preprint arXiv:1606.05250*.

Alla Rozovskaya and Dan Roth. 2016. Grammatical error correction: Machine translation and classifiers. In *Proceedings of the 54th Annual Meeting of the Association for Computational Linguistics (Volume 1: Long Papers)*, pages 2205–2215, Berlin, Germany. Association for Computational Linguistics.

Carolyn Saund, Marion Roth, Mathieu Chollet, and Stacy Marsella. 2019. Multiple metaphors in metaphoric gesturing. In *2019 8th International Conference on Affective Computing and Intelligent Interaction (ACII)*, pages 524–530. IEEE.

Gerard J Steen, Aletta G Dorst, J Berenike Herrmann, Anna Kaal, Tina Krennmayr, and Trijntje Pasma. 2010. *A method for linguistic metaphor identification: From MIP to MIPVU*, volume 14. John Benjamins Publishing.

Yu Sun, Shuohuan Wang, Yukun Li, Shikun Feng, Xuyi Chen, Han Zhang, Xin Tian, Danxiang Zhu, Hao Tian, and Hua Wu. 2019. Ernie: Enhanced representation through knowledge integration. *arXiv preprint arXiv:1904.09223*.

Paul H Thibodeau and Lera Boroditsky. 2011. Metaphors we think with: The role of metaphor in reasoning. *PloS one*, 6(2):e16782.

Ashish Vaswani, Noam Shazeer, Niki Parmar, Jakob Uszkoreit, Llion Jones, Aidan N Gomez, Łukasz Kaiser, and Illia Polosukhin. 2017. Attention is all you need. In *Advances in neural information processing systems*, pages 5998–6008.

Tony Veale, Ekaterina Shutova, and Beata Beigman Klebanov. 2016. Metaphor: A computational perspective. *Synthesis Lectures on Human Language Technologies*, 9(1):1–160.

Alex Wang, Amanpreet Singh, Julian Michael, Felix Hill, Omer Levy, and Samuel R Bowman. 2018. Glue: A multi-task benchmark and analysis platform for natural language understanding. *arXiv preprint arXiv:1804.07461*.

Zhilin Yang, Zihang Dai, Yiming Yang, Jaime Carbonell, Russ R Salakhutdinov, and Quoc V Le. 2019. Xlnet: Generalized autoregressive pretraining for language understanding. In *Advances in neural information processing systems*, pages 5754–5764.

Gerald Zaltman and Lindsay H Zaltman. 2008. *Marketing metaphoria: What deep metaphors reveal about the minds of consumers*. Harvard Business Press.

Rowan Zellers, Yonatan Bisk, Roy Schwartz, and Yejin Choi. 2018. Swag: A large-scale adversarial dataset for grounded commonsense inference. *arXiv preprint arXiv:1808.05326*.

Metaphor Detection using Ensembles of Bidirectional Recurrent Neural Networks

Jennifer Brooks
The George Washington University
Washington, DC
jtbrooks@gwu.edu

Abdou Youssef
The George Washington University
Washington, DC
ayoussef@gwu.edu

Abstract

In this paper we present our results from the Second Shared Task on Metaphor Detection, hosted by the Second Workshop on Figurative Language Processing. We use an ensemble of RNN models with bidirectional LSTMs and bidirectional attention mechanisms. Some of the models were trained on all parts of speech. Each of the other models was trained on one of four categories for parts of speech: "nouns", "verbs", "adverbs/adjectives", or "other". The models were combined into voting pools and the voting pools were combined using the logical "OR" operator.

1 Introduction

Figurative language is common in everyday speech and generally easy for humans who are speaking the same language to interpret, yet machines have trouble with it, limiting our interaction with them. If a machine has trouble understanding our natural language, then it will have trouble interpreting our intentions and translating them correctly to another language or human. Therefore, the goal of our research is to improve metaphor detection to facilitate the interpretation and translation of natural language in discourse.

The Second Shared Task on Metaphor Detection used the Vrije University Amsterdam Metaphor Corpus (VUAMC) (Steen et al., 2010), which has been the most widely used database for training machines to detect metaphors. The metaphor labels in the VUAMC are per word and indicate whether the word is a metaphor related word (mrw) or not. An mrw may be an indirect, direct, or implicit metaphor. The VUAMC contains text from four sources: academic texts, newspapers, conversations, and fiction. Each word was labeled using the MIPVU procedure, with greater than 0.8 inter-annotator reliability (Steen et al., 2010). About 13% of the words in the VUAMC are labeled as metaphor related words.

The Second Shared Task on Metaphor Detection with the VUAMC demonstrated state of the art performance with the best performer achieving an F1 score of 0.769. On the same training and test sets, we were able to achieve an F1 score of 0.703, and when we randomly split the VUAMC data around sentences vs. fragments (which may contain more than one related sentence), we were able to achieve an F1 score of 0.730. Leong et al. (2020) provide a summary of the results from all participants in the shared task.

Listed below are our major findings and contributions:

- When forwarding information from a bidirectional LSTM to an attention layer, better performance can be obtained when each attention cell receives output from only one bidirectional LSTM cell (vs a fully connected architecture where the output of every bidirectional LSTM cell is forwarded to every attention cell). For reference, see the architectural differences between Figures 2 and 1.

- It is possible to get better performance from logically combining the outputs of an ensemble, compared with using only the usual ensemble approaches of combining models: boosting, bagging, or stacking.

- Splitting the training and data sets by randomly sampling sentences rather than fragments (or paragraphs), which contain more than one sentence, provides for better results.

- Concatenating ELMo (Peters et al., 2018) with GloVe (Pennington et al., 2014) word embeddings gives better results than using either one alone.

Proceedings of the Second Workshop on Figurative Language Processing, pages 244–249
July 9, 2020. ©2020 Association for Computational Linguistics
https://doi.org/10.18653/v1/P17

Next we present related work followed by a discussion of our approach. Then we present a summary of our results followed by conclusions. We conclude with a brief discussion about our future research plan.

2 Related Work

Dinh et al. (2016) showed that using only word embeddings to train a neural network to detect metaphor related words in the VUAMC resulted in performance that was comparable to the performance of approaches that incorporated additional features, such as parts-of-speech. Using only word embeddings they achieved 52.4% recall with 58.3% precision on the shared task data, covering all parts of speech, from the NAACL 2018 Workshop on Figurative Language Processing.

Wu et al. (2018) used a layered model with lemmatized-word embeddings. They layered a bidirectional LSTM (bi-LSTM) on top of a CNN. For the output layer, they experimented with Conditional Random Fields (CRF) vs. softmax. Their best performance was with softmax. They used 300d word2vec embeddings and the RMSProp optimizer. They also input one-hot vectors for parts-of-speech and one-hot vectors for cluster ids from clustering the word embeddings with k-means. They demonstrated the best performance on the VUAMC shared task, over all parts of speech, with 70% recall and 60.8% precision.

Bizzoni and Ghanimifard (2018) presented two alternative architectures, a bidirectional LSTM and a novel bigram model which is a sequence of fully connected neural networks (concatenation and ReLU for each network in the sequence). They experimented with different word embeddings (300d GloVe and word2vec) and the inclusion of concreteness scores. They used a maximum sentence length of 50 words. Sentences with more than 50 words were broken up into smaller chunks. Sentences with less than 50 words were padded. The best performance between the two models was with the bidirectional LSTM using the GloVe embeddings and concreteness scores, but an ensemble of the bidirectional LSTM and novel bigram model performed even better. Over all parts of speech on the VUAMC, they achieved 68% recall with 59.5% precision.

Stemle and Onysko (2018) also split sentences into segments depending on a maximum sequence length. Shorter sequences were padded. They used a layered model with input to a bidirectional LSTM which provided input to a fully connected output layer that was activated by the softmax function. The length of the output equaled the length of the input. The output predicted whether each word from the input layer was a metaphor related word or not. They used a categorical cross-entropy loss function to address the imbalance of non-metaphor related words to metaphor related words. They experimented with word embeddings from various models that were pre-trained on corpora that varied in their language proficiency levels. On the VAUMC shared task data sets for all parts of speech, they achieved 69.8% recall with 55.3% precision.

Leong et al. (2018) used logistic regression and random forest classifiers with lemmatized unigrams, generalized WordNet semantics, and difference in concreteness ratings between verbs/adjectives and nouns (Leong et al., 2018; Beigman Klebanov et al., 2016). During training, each class was weighted by the inverse of its frequency. For the optimization function, they used the f1-score. They achieved 69.6% recall with 51% precision on the VUAMC shared task data sets for all parts of speech.

Mykowiecka et al. (2018) trained an LSTM on 300d GloVe embeddings. They also experimented with using part-of-speech information and features from the General Inquirer, which worsened their results on the test data. Swarnkar and Singh (2018) presented an architecture that used a context encoder inspired by a bidirectional LSTM. The output of the encoder was fed to a feature selection module to select features for the token word. They showed that re-weighting examples and using parts of speech, WordNet, and concreteness ratings improved the performance of their model. Skurniak et al. (2018) presented a CRF sequence model that was trained using GloVe word embeddings and contextual information. Pramanick et al. (2018) used a hybrid model of bi-LSTM and CRF trained with word2vec embeddings for the token word and its lemma, 20d vectors representing the POS, and one-hot vectors for whether the lemma and the token were the same, and whether the lemma was present in the token.

Other researchers have made progress in metaphor detection at the word level, but the results were reported for data sets other than the VUAMC. Hovy et al. (2013) used SVMs with tree kernels on syntactic features and achieved an f1-score of 75%.

They built a corpus of 3872 labeled metaphors which they also released. Su et al. (2017) presented results from using the theory of meaning to identify metaphors in a subset of the BNC, which they labeled themselves. They achieved an f1-score of 87%. (The VUAMC is also a subset of the BNC.) Krishnakumaran and Zhu (2007) used WordNet bigram counts to identify metaphors in the Master Metaphor List created by (Lakoff, 1994). They reported 58% accuracy, 70% precision, and 61% recall.

3   Method

We designed and experimented with various RNN architectures using bidirectional LSTMs and attention mechanisms (Bahdanau et al., 2014; Zhou et al., 2016). The input was an 11-gram for each word in the training set (or test set during testing). Each word was represented by an 11-gram and appeared at the center of the 11-gram. Furthermore, each word in the 11-gram was represented by a 1,324 dimensional word embedding which was the result of concatenating a 1,024 dimensional ELMo (Peters et al., 2018) embedding with a 300 dimensional GloVe (Pennington et al., 2014) embedding, because preliminary testing revealed that ELMo concatenated with GloVe resulted in better performance than either one of them alone.

The 11-grams were from one sentence; i.e., they never extend across two sentences. Padding was used if the center word was not in the context of exactly 5 words to the left or right, so the first word in a sentence would always have 5 pads to its left and the last word in a sentence would always have 5 pads to its right. Five was chosen for the window size because it produced the best results in preliminary experiments.

The output was a two-dimensional vector representing the probabilities for the center word being a metaphor or not. Softmax was used to choose the highest probability.

Two architectures were used for our final results on the Shared Task. They are described below.

The first architecture is a many-to-one bidirectional LSTM with bidirectional attention (see Figure 1). In this architecture, the outputs of the forward and backward LSTM cells in the attention layer are concatenated only at the output for the center, target word, of the 11-gram. The expected output is a 1 or 0 for the center word in the 11-gram, depending on whether it is a metaphor related word

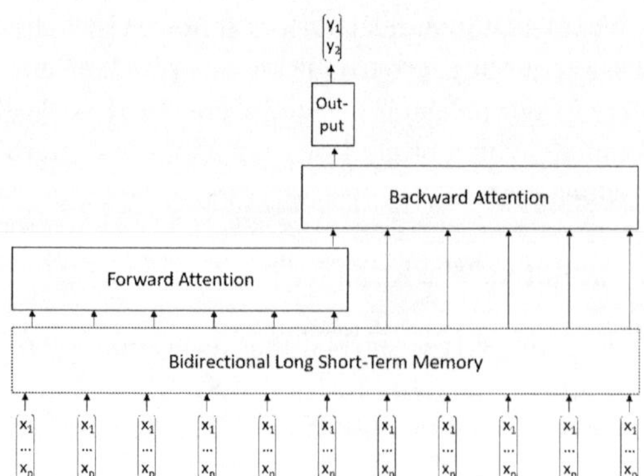

Figure 1: Many-to-One Bidirectional LSTM with Bidirectional Attention

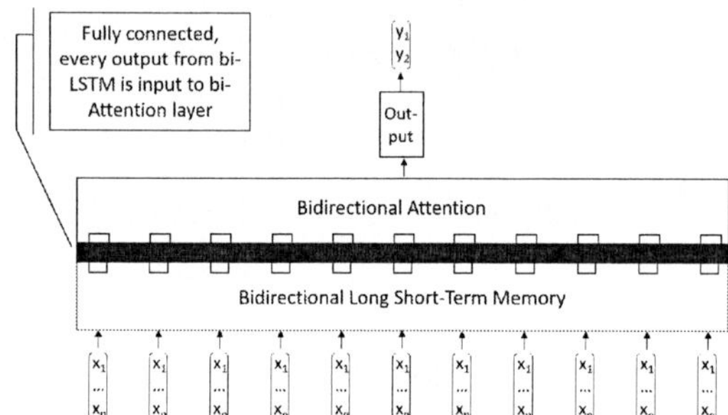

Figure 2: Many-to-One Fully-Connected Bidirectional LSTM with Bidirectional Attention

or not. Each attention cell receives output from only one bidirectional LSTM cell (vs. a fully connected architecture where the output of every bidirectional LSTM cell is forwarded to every attention cell). See the difference between Figures 2 and 1 for reference. The intuition behind the choice to forward only one cell's output per attention cell is that the attention cells are intended to process input in a sequential order (i.e., one word at a time). Providing each step with the entire matrix of weights for all words from the bidirectional LSTM seems to violate the design of the attention mechanisms. We tried both architectures and got better results with the architecture in which each attention cell receives output from only one bidirectional LSTM cell.

The second model is a many-to-many bidirectional LSTM with bidirectional attention (see Figure 3). The expected output is a 1 or 0 for each word in the 11-gram, depending on whether the word is a metaphor related word or not. However, in the trained model, only the output for the center word, w, is used to assign a prediction to w.

	Precision	Recall	F1
Many-to-Many	**0.683**	0.678	0.681
Many-to-One	0.655	**0.715**	0.684

Table 1: Performance from voting with many-to-many vs. many-to-one models

The key difference between this model and the first model is that the many-to-many model updates its weights based on the performance of the model on the target word's context words, in addition to the performance of the model on target word. The performance feedback includes whether or not the target word is in the context (within a window of 5 words on either side) of another metaphor related word. This is also why we must split across sentences and not allow a sentence from the training set to also appear in the test set. The many-to-many model was chosen because its performance complements the first model (i.e., the many-to-one bidirectional LSTM with bidirectional attention). Voting among trained instances of the many-to-many model gives better precision, while voting among trained instances of the many-to-one model gives better recall. Both have comparable F1 scores. Table 1 shows results from voting with five models of each architecture type. If at least two of the five models labeled the word as a metaphor related word, then it was scored as a metaphor related word.

Another important note about the many-to-many model is that the output of the backward attention layer starting at the last word in the 11-gram, w_{10}, is concatenated with the output of the forward attention layer for w_10; the output of the backward attention layer for w_9 is concatenated with the output of the forward attention layer for w_9; and so on until the output of the backward attention layer for w_0 is concatenated with the output of the forward attention layer for w_0.

We used a training batch size of 200. An Adam optimizer was used with a learning rate 0.006 and a decay rate of 0.001. The loss function was categorical cross entropy. A dropout rate of 0.2 was used for the bi-LSTM layer and a dropout of 0.1 was used for both the forward and backward attention. The hidden states for both the bi-LSTM and attention layers were vectors of length 128. The output layer of each model used the softmax activation function. Keras with a Tensorflow backend was used for the implementation.

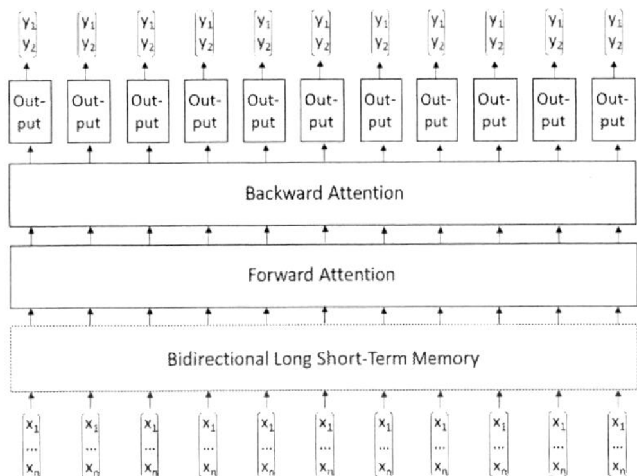

Figure 3: Many-to-Many Bidirectional LSTM with Bidirectional Attention

We trained and tested our models independently on two data splits. For the first split, 25% of the data samples (11-grams from the VUAMC) were randomly selected and held out for testing. Among the remaining 75%, one-third of the samples were randomly selected and preserved, along with all of the positive samples (labeled 1) in the remaining two-third. The rest of the training samples were discarded to achieve a more balanced training set. (However, testing was always performed on the entire test set.)

For the second split, we used the training and test sets from the Second Shared Task on Metaphor Detection. For the Shared Task, the training and test sets were sampled by fragments, in which a fragment (e.g., a paragraph) may contain more than one sentence. We initially used one-third of the training samples, the same way we did with the first split, but then we tried using the entire training set and passed class weights to the Adam optimizer to mitigate the imbalanced number of samples per class. The class weights were proportional to the percentage of samples in each class. We got better results using all of the samples in the training set. (We did not go back to the first split to train with all of the training samples and class weights, but we hypothesize that we'd get better results if we did.)

First, we trained and tested our model using 300 dimensional GloVe vectors (Pennington et al., 2014). Next, we tried 1024 dimensional ELMo vectors (Peters et al., 2018). Finally, we used 1324 dimensional vectors from combining GloVe with ELMo. In the last case, for each word, we simply concatenated the ELMo vector representation for that word with the GloVe vector representation for

247

	All POS	Verbs	Adv/Adj	Nouns	Other
Many-to-Many	0.681	0.726	0.643	0.665	0.647
Many-to-One	0.684	0.721	0.627	0.672	0.702
Ensemble	0.689	0.737	0.641	0.677	0.672

Table 2: F1 score per models and ensembles per part-of-speech category

that word, resulting in a vector of length 1324.

We trained each architecture independently multiple times on all parts of speech and then on each of four categories for parts of speech: "nouns", "verbs", "adverbs/adjectives", or "other". We used the NLTK toolkit (Bird et al., 2009) to derive the parts of speech.

4 Results

We achieved the best results with an ensemble of trained models. The ensemble consisted of five models per architecture trained on all parts of speech, and five models per architecture trained independently on each of four parts-of-speech categories: "nouns", "verbs", "adverbs/adjectives", or "other". The five models per architecture per part-of-speech category (including "all parts of speech") were assembled into a voting pool, so there were ten models total per category. Each set of ten models were combined into a voting pool and the voting pools were combined using the logical "OR" operator.

Table 2 shows the F1 score per part-of-speech category that resulted from voting on whether or not the target word was a metaphor related word (mrw). For the many-to-many and many-to-one models, if at least two of the five models per category labeled a word as an mrw, then it was scored as an mrw. The row for "Ensemble" shows the results from voting among the many-to-many and many-to-one models per category. The Ensemble row is meant to show the level of improvement that can be obtained by combining all ten models per category. An overall F1 score of 0.703, with 0.702 precision and 0.704 recall, was obtained by combining the "All POS" label with the appropriate part-of-speech category using the "OR" operator. For example, if the target word is a verb, then the verb was labeled as an mrw if the Ensemble for "All POS" labeled it as an mrw OR the Ensemble for "Verbs" labeled it as an mrw.

We also evaluated our many-to-one model with respect to the novelty scores provided by Dinh (Do Dinh et al., 2018) for the VUAMC. On novel metaphors (i.e. metaphors with a novelty score of at least 0.5 from (Do Dinh et al., 2018)) the many-to-one architecture found 52/77, or 67.5% in the shared task test set.

5 Conclusions and Next Steps

We have described two model architectures and an ensemble approach for metaphor detection. We have shown that splitting the training and data sets by randomly sampling sentences rather than fragments (or paragraphs), which may contain more than one sentence, may lead to better results. We believe this may be because there are patterns of language in the test fragments that were not seen in the training fragments. Allowing a model to train on some sentences from a fragment and then test on the other sentences in the same fragment may produce better results overall.

We shared that when forwarding information from a bidirectional LSTM to an attention layer, better performance can be obtained when each attention cell receives output from only one bidirectional LSTM cell.

Finally, we have revealed that it is possible to get better performance from logically combining the outputs of an ensemble.

In future work, we will continue improving metaphor detection with a focus on novel metaphors. According to Shutova et al. (2013), "Cameron (2003) conducted a corpus study of the use of metaphor in educational discourse for all parts of speech. She found that verbs account for around 50% of the data, the rest shared by nouns, adjectives, adverbs, copula constructions and multi-word metaphors." About 43% of metaphors in the VUAMC are verbs, while verbs are only 23% of all tokens in the VUAMC database. However, Do Dinh et al. (2018) found that only about 24% of the novel metaphors are verbs and 41% are nouns. The rest are adjectives and adverbs. (Other POS were not included.) Therefore, future work in detecting novel metaphors may place a heavier weight on nouns (vs. verbs as has been the case with conventional metaphors).

References

Dzmitry Bahdanau, Kyunghyun Cho, and Yoshua Bengio. 2014. Neural machine translation by jointly learning to align and translate. *CoRR*, abs/1409.0473.

Beata Beigman Klebanov, Chee Wee Leong, E Dario Gutierrez, Ekaterina Shutova, and Michael Flor. 2016. Semantic classifications for detection of verb metaphors. In *Proceedings of the 54th Annual Meeting of the Association for Computational Linguistics (Volume 2: Short Papers)*, pages 101–106.

Steven Bird, Edward Loper, and Ewan Klein. 2009), publisher = O'Reilly Media Inc. *Natural Language Processing with Python*.

Yuri Bizzoni and Mehdi Ghanimifard. 2018. Bigrams and bilstms: two neural networks for sequential metaphor detection. In *Proceedings of the Workshop on Figurative Language Processing*, pages 91–101.

Lynne Cameron. 2003. Metaphor in educational discourse.

do Dinh, Erik-Lân, and Iryna Gurevych. 2016. Token-level metaphor detection using neural networks. In *Proceedings of the Fourth Workshop on Metaphor in NLP*, pages 28–33.

Erik-Lân Do Dinh, Hannah Wieland, and Iryna Gurevych. 2018. Weeding out conventionalized metaphors: A corpus of novel metaphor annotations. In *Proceedings of the 2018 Conference on Empirical Methods in Natural Language Processing*, pages 1412–1424, Brussels, Belgium. Association for Computational Linguistics.

Dirk Hovy, Shashank Shrivastava, Sujay Kumar Jauhar, Mrinmaya Sachan, Kartik Goyal, Huying Li, Whitney Sanders, and Eduard Hovy. 2013. Identifying metaphorical word use with tree kernels. In *Proceedings of the First Workshop on Metaphor in NLP*, pages 52–57.

Saisuresh Krishnakumaran and Xiaojin Zhu. 2007. Hunting elusive metaphors using lexical resources. In *Proceedings of the Workshop on Computational approaches to Figurative Language*, pages 13–20. Association for Computational Linguistics.

George Lakoff. 1994. *Master metaphor list*. Berkeley, CA: University of California.

Chee Wee Leong, Beata Beigman Klebanov, and Ekaterina Shutova. 2018. A report on the 2018 vua metaphor detection shared task. In *Proceedings of the Workshop on Figurative Language Processing*, pages 56–66.

Chee Wee Leong, Beata Beigman Klebanov, Chris Hamill, Egon Stemle, Rutuja Ubale, and Xianyang Chen. 2020. A report on the 2020 vua and toefl metaphor detection shared task. In *Proceedings of the Second Workshop on Figurative Language Processing*, Seattle, WA.

Agnieszka Mykowiecka, Aleksander Wawer, and Malgorzata Marciniak. 2018. Detecting figurative word occurrences using word embeddings. In *Proceedings of the Workshop on Figurative Language Processing*, pages 124–127.

Jeffrey Pennington, Richard Socher, and Christopher D. Manning. 2014. Glove: Global vectors for word representation. In *Empirical Methods in Natural Language Processing (EMNLP)*, pages 1532–1543.

Matthew E. Peters, Mark Neumann, Mohit Iyyer, Matt Gardner, Christopher Clark, Kenton Lee, and Luke Zettlemoyer. 2018. Deep contextualized word representations. *CoRR*, abs/1802.05365.

Malay Pramanick, Ashim Gupta, and Pabitra Mitra. 2018. An lstm-crf based approach to token-level metaphor detection. In *Proceedings of the Workshop on Figurative Language Processing*, pages 67–75.

Ekaterina Shutova, Barry Devereux, and Anna Korhonen. 2013. Conceptual metaphor theory meets the data: A corpus-based human annotation study. *Language Resources and Evaluation*, 47.

Filip Skurniak, Maria Janicka, and Aleksander Wawer. 2018. Multi-module recurrent neural networks with transfer learning. a submission for the metaphor detection task. In *Proceedings of the Workshop on Figurative Language Processing*, pages 128–132.

Gerard J Steen, Aletta G Dorst, J Berenike Herrmann, Anna Kaal, Tina Krennmayr, and Trijntje Pasma. 2010. *A method for linguistic metaphor identification: From MIP to MIPVU*, volume 14. John Benjamins Publishing.

Egon Stemle and Alexander Onysko. 2018. Using language learner data for metaphor detection. In *Proceedings of the Workshop on Figurative Language Processing*, pages 133–138.

Chang Su, Shuman Huang, and Yijiang Chen. 2017. Automatic detection and interpretation of nominal metaphor based on the theory of meaning. *Neurocomputing*, 219:300–311.

Krishnkant Swarnkar and Anil Kumar Singh. 2018. Di-lstm contrast: a deep neural network for metaphor detection. In *Proceedings of the Workshop on Figurative Language Processing*, pages 115–120.

Chuhan Wu, Fangzhou Wu, Yubo Cen, Sixing Wu, Zhigang Yuan, and Yongfeng Huang. 2018. Neural metaphor detecting with cnn-lstm model. In *Proceedings of the Workshop on Figurative Language Processing*, pages 110–115.

Peng Zhou, Wei Shi, Jun Tian, Zhenyu Qi, Bingchen Li, Hongwei Hao, and Bo Xu. 2016. Attention-based bidirectional long short-term memory networks for relation classification. In *Proceedings of the 54th Annual Meeting of the Association for Computational Linguistics (Volume 2: Short Papers)*, pages 207–212.

Metaphor Detection Using Contextual Word Embeddings From Transformers

Jerry Liu, Nathan O'Hara, Alexander Rubin, Rachel Draelos, Cynthia Rudin
Department of Computer Science, Duke University
{jwl50, nmo4, acr43, rlb61}@duke.edu, cynthia@cs.duke.edu

Abstract

The detection of metaphors can provide valuable information about a given text and is crucial to sentiment analysis and machine translation. In this paper, we outline the techniques for word-level metaphor detection used in our submission to the Second Shared Task on Metaphor Detection. We propose using both BERT and XLNet language models to create contextualized embeddings and a bi-directional LSTM to identify whether a given word is a metaphor. Our best model achieved F1-scores of 68.0% on VUA AllPOS, 73.0% on VUA Verbs, 66.9% on TOEFL AllPOS, and 69.7% on TOEFL Verbs, placing 7th, 6th, 5th, and 5th respectively. In addition, we outline another potential approach with a KNN-LSTM ensemble model that we did not have enough time to implement given the deadline for the competition. We show that a KNN classifier provides a similar F1-score on a validation set as the LSTM and yields different information on metaphors.

1 Introduction

A metaphor is a form of figurative language that creates a link between two different concepts and conveys rich linguistic information (Lakofi and Johnson, 1980). The complex information that accompanies a metaphorical text is often overlooked in sentiment analysis, machine translation, and information extraction. Therefore, the detection of metaphors is an important task in order to achieve the full potential of many applications in natural language processing (Tsvetkov et al., 2014).

The differences between a metaphorical text and a non-metaphorical text can be subtle and require specific domain information. For instance, in the phrase

the trajectory of your legal career

the word *trajectory* is used metaphorically. To identify this metaphor, both the meaning of the word in the context of the sentence and its literal definition must be recognized and compared. In this case, the word *trajectory* is used to describe the path of a legal career in the sentence, whereas its basic definition involves the path of a projectile. As a result of the ambiguity present in determining the basic meaning of a word, as well as whether it deviates significantly from a contextual use, detecting metaphors at a word-level can be challenging even for humans. Additionally, the Metaphor Identification Procedure used to label the datasets (MIPVU) accounts for multiple kinds of metaphors (Steen et al., 2010). Capturing implicit, complex metaphors may require different information than capturing direct, simple metaphors.

This paper describes the techniques that we utilized in the Second Shared Task on Metaphor Detection. The competition provided two datasets: a subset of ETS Corpus of Non-Native Written English, which contains essays written by test-takers for the TOEFL test and was annotated for argumentation relevant metaphors, and the VU Amsterdam Metaphor Corpus (VUA) dataset, which consists of text fragments sampled across four genres from the British National Corpus (BNC) – Academic, News, Conversation, and Fiction. For each dataset, participants could compete in two tracks: identifying metaphors of all parts of speech (AllPOS) or verbs only (Verbs).

Our final submission uses pretrained BERT (Devlin et al., 2018) and XLNet (Yang et al., 2019) transformer models, part-of-speech (POS) labels, and a two-layer bi-directional long short-term memory (Bi-LSTM) neural network architecture. BERT and XLNet are used to generate contextualized word embeddings, which are then combined with POS tags and fed through the Bi-LSTM to predict metaphoricity for each word. By creating contex-

Proceedings of the Second Workshop on Figurative Language Processing, pages 250–255
July 9, 2020. ©2020 Association for Computational Linguistics
https://doi.org/10.18653/v1/P17

tualized word embeddings using transformers, we hoped to capture more long-range interdependencies between words than would be possible using methods such as word2vec, GloVe, or fastText. Indeed, our model achieved F1-scores of 68.0% on VUA AllPOS and 73.0% on VUA Verbs, improving upon results from the First Shared Task (Leong et al., 2018). On the TOEFL task, we achieved F1-scores of 66.9% on AllPOS, and 69.7% on Verbs. Our scores placed 7th, 6th, 5th, and 5th respectively in the Second Shared Task on Metaphor Detection (Leong et al., 2020).

2 Related Works

Historically, approaches to automatic metaphor detection have focused on hand-crafting a set of informative features for every word and applying a supervised machine learning algorithm to classify words as metaphorical or non-metaphorical. Previous works have explored features including POS tags, concreteness, imageability, semantic distributions, and semantic classes as characterized through SUMO ontology, WordNet, and VerbNet (Beigman Klebanov et al., 2014; Tsvetkov et al., 2014; Dunn, 2013; Mohler et al., 2013).

Deep learning methods have also been employed for automatic metaphor detection. In the First Shared Task on Metaphor Detection, the top three highest scoring teams all employed an LSTM model with word embeddings and additional features (Leong et al., 2018). Stemle and Onysko (2018) trained fastText word embeddings on various native and non-native English corpora, and passed the sequences of embeddings to an Bi-LSTM. The highest-performing model from Bizzoni and Ghanimifard (2018) employed a Bi-LSTM on GloVe embeddings and concreteness ratings for each word. Wu et al. (2018) appended POS and semantic class information to pretrained word2vec word embeddings, and utilized a CNN in addition to a Bi-LSTM in order to better capture local and global contextual information. In all these cases, the word embeddings used are context-independent: the same word appearing in two different sentences will nonetheless have the same embedding. Thus, these embeddings may not be able to fully capture information about multi-sense words (for example, the word *bank* in *river bank* and *bank robber*), which is crucial for properly identifying metaphors.

More recently, Mao et al. (2019) proposed two RNN models for word-level metaphor detection based on linguistic theories of metaphor identification. GloVe and ELMo embeddings are used as input features that capture literal meanings of words, which are compared with the hidden states of Bi-LSTMs that capture contextual meaning. We chose to explore transformer-based embeddings as an alternative way to capture contextual information.

Transformer-based models have shown state-of-the-art results on a wide variety of language tasks, including sentence classification, question answering, and named entity recognition. These models rely on self-attention mechanisms to capture global dependencies, and can be used to generate contextualized word embeddings. We chose to examine the models BERT, GPT2, and XLNet. These three models all achieve remarkable performances on various NLP tasks, but they capture long-distance relationships within the text in different ways. BERT is an autoencoder model, consisting of a stack of encoder layers, and is able to capture bi-directional context using masking during training (Devlin et al., 2018). GPT2 is an autoregressive model, consisting of a stack of decoder layers, and thus is only able to capture unidirectional context (Radford et al., 2018). XLNet is also autoregressive, but it captures bi-directional context by considering all permutations of the given words (Yang et al., 2019). Each of these models has its advantages and disadvantages that are worth exploring in the context of metaphor detection.

3 Methodology

Our method for metaphor detection begins with generating contextualized word embeddings for each word in a sentence using the hidden states of pretrained BERT and XLNet language models. Next, those embeddings are concatenated together, POS tags for each word are appended to the embeddings, and a Bi-LSTM reads the features as input and classifies each word in the sentence.

Word Embeddings Due to limited metaphor-annotated data, rather than training a transformer model on our downstream task, we instead opted to take a feature-based approach to generating contextualized word embeddings from pretrained transformer models. This idea was inspired by the approach to the token-level named entity recognition task described in Devlin et al. (2018), which used a number of strategies for combining hidden

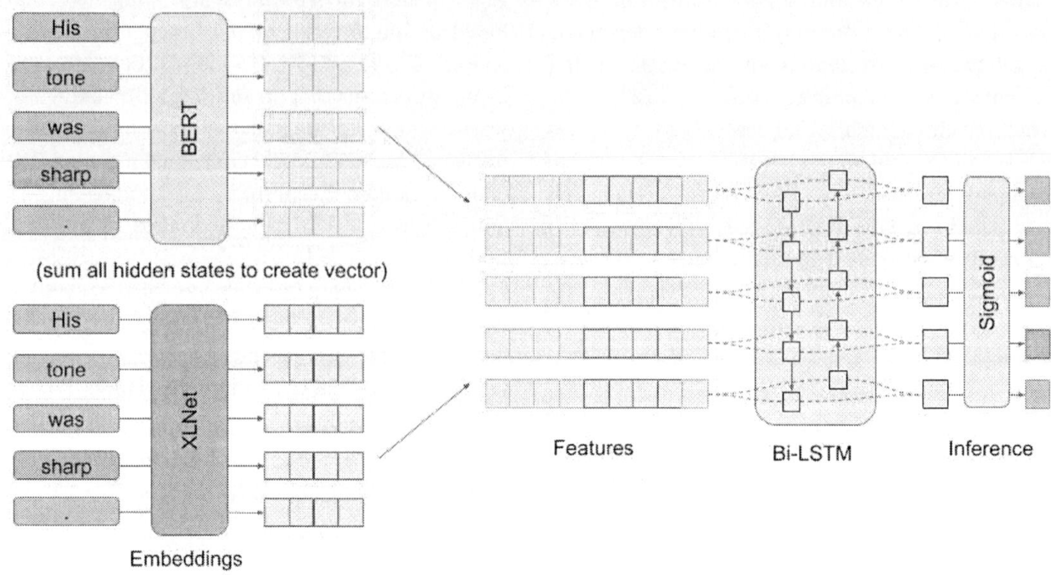

Figure 1: Our model architecture. Sentences are fed through pretrained BERT and XLNet models, concatenated along with POS tags, passed to a Bi-LSTM, and a sigmoid layer outputs probabilities.

state representations of words from a pretrained BERT model to generate contextualized word embeddings.

We installed the Python transformers library developed by huggingface (Wolf et al., 2019), which includes a PyTorch (Paszke et al., 2019) implementation of BERT and several pretrained BERT models. We opted to use the BERT base uncased model, which consists of 12-layers, 768-hidden, 12-heads, and 110M parameters. For each line in the VUA and TOEFL datasets, we use the BERT tokenizer included in the transformers package to pre-process the text, then generate hidden-state representations for each word by inputting each line into the pretrained BERT model. Each token is given a 12x768 hidden-state representation from BERT. We generate 768-dimension word embeddings by summing the values from each of the 12 hidden layers for each token. Words out-of-vocab for BERT are split into multiple tokens representing subwords. To generate embeddings for these words, embeddings are generated for each subword token, then averaged together.

Similarly, we installed the huggingface implementation of XLNet and used its pretrained XLNet base uncased model to generate embeddings for each word in the dataset using the same method as with BERT.

Once both embeddings are generated, we con-catenate the BERT and XLNet embeddings for each word to generate 1536-dimensional word embeddings. By combining word embeddings from multiple high-performing pretrained transformers, we are able to capture more contextual information for each word. Additionally, we supplement these word embeddings with the POS tag for each word as generated by the Stanford parser (Toutanova et al., 2003). POS tags were shown to improve metaphor detection in the 2018 Metaphor Detection Shared Task (Leong et al., 2018), and we find a small improvement by including them here.

Neural Network We pass the features from each sentence into a Bi-LSTM. The purpose of this network is to capture long-range relationships between words in the same sentence which may reveal the presence of metaphors. We use a dense layer with a sigmoid activation function to obtain the predicted probability of being a metaphor for each word in the sentence. During training, we employ a weighted binary cross entropy loss function to address the extreme class imbalance, since nonmetaphors occur significantly more frequently than metaphors. Hyperparameters were tuned via crossvalidation. For the testing phase, we use an ensemble strategy which was effective for Wu et al. (2018): we trained four copies of this Bi-LSTM with different initializations and averaged the predictions from each model.

Additionally, we noted that our model tended to assign similar probabilities to different instances of the same word in different contexts, and that a prediction significantly higher than the average prediction for that word was a good indicator of the presence of metaphor, even if the prediction fell lower than the ideal threshold. Thus, we used the following procedure for the testing phase: label the word as a metaphor if its predicted probability is higher than the threshold, or if its probability is three orders of magnitude higher than the median predicted probability for that word in the evaluation set. We found this to be a useful way of addressing the domain shift between the training and the test data. This concept is further explored in Section 4.1.

4 Experiments

Word Embeddings Devlin et al. (2018) suggest that for different token-level classification tasks, different methods for combining hidden states from BERT may prove effective in generating contextualized word embeddings. For our task, to determine the optimal embedding strategy, we evaluated four different methods of combining information from hidden states of the transformer models. To determine which performed best prior to training LSTM models, we tested each strategy using logistic regression on the word embeddings with an 80/20 training-test split. Results from logistic regression on BERT embeddings from the VUA AllPOS data are in Table 1. We note that the F1 scores using different methods of generating contextualized word embeddings differ substantially. We use the "sum-all-layers" method of generating word embeddings for our further experiments.

	VUA AllPOS			TOEFL AllPOS		
Method	P	R	F1	P	R	F1
Sum all layers	**0.672**	0.531	**0.593**	0.569	**0.596**	**0.582**
Concat. last 4 layers	0.614	**0.552**	0.581	**0.644**	0.473	0.546
Sum last 4 layers	0.623	0.534	0.575	0.594	0.550	0.571
Second to last layer	0.580	0.547	0.563	0.633	0.482	0.547
Last layer	0.628	0.493	0.553	0.542	0.551	0.546

Table 1: Logistic regression on various BERT word embeddings, VUA and TOEFL AllPOS.

Transformers Table 2 compares the performance of the Bi-LSTM using the embeddings from BERT, GPT2, and XLNet. Because the true test labels were not made available to us, here we report results on an 80/20 training-test split of the given training data. We make the following observations.

- The LSTM models perform far better than their logistic regression counterparts. Of the single embedding LSTM models, the BERT and XLNet embeddings have the best performances. Combining BERT and XLNet embeddings and using an ensemble strategy further improved our performance.

- In general, the AllPOS task is more challenging than the Verbs task. Different parts of speech are used metaphorically in different ways, and these multiple varieties of metaphor must all be captured by a single model in the AllPOS task. Correspondingly, all models perform worse on AllPOS than Verbs in both VUA and TOEFL datasets.

- Additionally, the models achieve a lower F1 score on the TOEFL dataset than the VUA in both AllPOS and Verbs track. We believe this is in part due to the smaller size of the TOEFL dataset, and in part because linguistic characteristics can differ substantially between native and non-native text. Since we used transformer models pretrained on a native corpus, the word embeddings were likely less informative for the TOEFL track.

- GPT2 and XLNet are both autoregressive language models, but GPT2+LSTM performs significantly worse than the other LSTM models. This result suggests that bi-directional relationships between words play a crucial role in metaphor detection. Because XLNet considers every possible permutation of the given words during training, the XLNet embeddings likely contain more bi-directional context than the GPT2 embeddings.

4.1 A Promising Future Approach: K-Nearest Neighbors

In our experiments, we noted that our LSTM models tended to output similar probabilities for different instances of the same word independent of context. For example, although 4 out of 14 of the occurrences of the word *capacity* in the validation set were metaphor-related, all of the LSTM predictions were less than 10^{-5}. This suggested that although word embeddings from transformer models

Model	VUA AllPOS			VUA Verbs			TOEFL AllPOS			TOEFL Verbs		
	P	R	F1	P	R	F1	P	R	F1	P	R	F1
Baseline*	0.608	0.700	0.651	0.600	0.763	0.672	N/A	N/A	N/A	N/A	N/A	N/A
BERT+LSTM	0.644	0.689	0.666	**0.662**	0.730	0.694	0.618	0.648	0.633	0.611	0.670	0.639
GPT2+LSTM	0.592	0.573	0.582	0.618	0.648	0.633	0.579	0.589	0.584	0.555	0.681	0.612
XLNet+LSTM	0.622	0.622	0.622	0.650	0.684	0.667	0.644	0.646	0.645	0.633	0.681	0.656
BERT+XLNet +LSTM	0.665	0.688	0.676	0.655	0.736	0.693	0.649	**0.664**	0.656	0.618	**0.724**	0.667
BERT+XLNet +LSTM (ensemble)	**0.675**	**0.710**	**0.692**	0.656	**0.768**	**0.708**	**0.686**	0.654	**0.669**	**0.722**	0.659	**0.689**

Table 2: Performance of LSTM models. The baseline is the highest achieved score from the First Shared Task on Metaphor Detection.

contain more contextual information than embeddings from word2vec or GloVe, the model could be improved by including even more contextual information. We explored the idea of ensembling an LSTM with a K-Nearest Neighbors (KNN) classification approach. We believe that the LSTM approach would give information as to which types of words tend to be metaphors in context, whereas the KNN approach would clue into whether a specific use of a specific word is more likely to be metaphorical. We were unable to fully implement such an ensemble model for the competition, but we detail some promising results below.

We trained a KNN-only model using our contextualized word embeddings. First, we lemmatized each word in the VUA and TOEFL datasets. For VUA, we classified each word based on a KNN classifier trained on all instances of the same lemmatized word in the training data. If no such lemmatized word existed in the training data, we classified that word using a prediction from an LSTM model, though that occurred in only 2% of cases. For TOEFL, we compared using training data from TOEFL combined with VUA due to the limited dataset. We achieved F1 scores of 0.642 and 0.608 on 80/20 training-test splits of VUA and TOEFL respectively, not much worse than our LSTM models.

There is reason to believe the LSTM and KNN approaches capture significantly different information on metaphors. On the VUA validation data, the LSTM method predicted 3751 metaphors and the KNN predicted 3190. However, only 2372 words were predicted as metaphors by the two models together. Since both models have similar F1 scores, this implies that a superior classifier can be constructed using information from both classifiers.

For our final submissions, we were able to adopt a simplified implementation of this approach, la-

beling an instance of a word as metaphorical if its LSTM prediction either was higher than a certain threshold, or higher by a significant amount than the median LSTM prediction of all instances of that word. This procedure improved our F1 scores by about 1% during the testing phase.

k	Precision	Recall	F1
1	0.665	0.599	0.630
2	**0.722**	0.514	0.600
3	0.676	**0.611**	**0.642**
4	0.703	0.538	0.610
5	0.679	0.604	0.639

Table 3: KNN using sum-all BERT word embeddings, VUA AllPOS

5 Conclusion

In this paper, we describe the best performing model that we submitted for the Second Shared Task on Metaphor Detection. We used BERT and XLNet language models to create contextualized embeddings, and fed these embeddings into a bidirectional LSTM with a sigmoid layer that used both local and global contextual information to output a probability. Our experimental results verify that contextualized embeddings outperform previous state-of-the-art word embeddings for metaphor detection. We also propose an ensemble model combining a bi-directional LSTM and a KNN, and show promising results that suggest the two models encode complementary information on metaphors.

Acknowledgments

The authors thank the organizers of the Second Shared Task on Metaphor Detection and the rest of the Duke Data Science Team. We also thank the anonymous reviewers for their insightful comments.

References

Beata Beigman Klebanov, Ben Leong, Michael Heilman, and Michael Flor. 2014. Different texts, same metaphors: Unigrams and beyond. In *Proceedings of the Second Workshop on Metaphor in NLP*, pages 11–17, Baltimore, MD. Association for Computational Linguistics.

Yuri Bizzoni and Mehdi Ghanimifard. 2018. Bigrams and BiLSTMs two neural networks for sequential metaphor detection. In *Proceedings of the Workshop on Figurative Language Processing*, pages 91–101, New Orleans, Louisiana. Association for Computational Linguistics.

Jacob Devlin, Ming-Wei Chang, Kenton Lee, and Kristina Toutanova. 2018. Bert: Pre-training of deep bidirectional transformers for language understanding. *arXiv*, arXiv:1810.04805.

Jonathan Dunn. 2013. What metaphor identification systems can tell us about metaphor-in-language. In *Proceedings of the First Workshop on Metaphor in NLP*, pages 1–10, Atlanta, Georgia. Association for Computational Linguistics.

George Lakofi and Mark Johnson. 1980. *Metaphors we live by*. University of Chicago Press, Chicago, IL.

Chee Wee Leong, Beata Beigman Klebanov, Chris Hamill, Egon Stemle, Rutuja Ubale, and Xianyang Chen. 2020. A report on the 2020 vua and toefl metaphor detection shared task. In *Proceedings of the Second Workshop on Figurative Language Processing*, Seattle, WA.

Chee Wee (Ben) Leong, Beata Beigman Klebanov, and Ekaterina Shutova. 2018. A report on the 2018 VUA metaphor detection shared task. In *Proceedings of the Workshop on Figurative Language Processing*, pages 56–66, New Orleans, Louisiana. Association for Computational Linguistics.

Rui Mao, Chenghua Lin, and Frank Guerin. 2019. End-to-end sequential metaphor identification inspired by linguistic theories. In *Proceedings of the 57th Annual Meeting of the Association for Computational Linguistics*, pages 3888–3898, Florence, Italy. Association for Computational Linguistics.

Michael Mohler, David Bracewell, Marc Tomlinson, and David Hinote. 2013. Semantic signatures for example-based linguistic metaphor detection. In *Proceedings of the First Workshop on Metaphor in NLP*, pages 27–35, Atlanta, Georgia. Association for Computational Linguistics.

Adam Paszke, Sam Gross, Francisco Massa, Adam Lerer, James Bradbury, Gregory Chanan, Trevor Killeen, Zeming Lin, Natalia Gimelshein, Luca Antiga, Alban Desmaison, Andreas Kopf, Edward Yang, Zachary DeVito, Martin Raison, Alykhan Tejani, Sasank Chilamkurthy, Benoit Steiner, Lu Fang, Junjie Bai, and Soumith Chintala. 2019. Pytorch: An imperative style, high-performance deep learning library. In *Advances in Neural Information Processing Systems 32*, pages 8024–8035. Curran Associates, Inc.

Alec Radford, Jeffrey Wu, Rewon Child, David Luan, Dario Amodei, and Ilya Sutskever. 2018. Language models are unsupervised multitask learners.

Gerard J. Steen, Aletta G. Dorst, J. Berenike Herrmann, Anna A. Kaal, Tina Krennmayr, and Trijntje Pasma. 2010. *A Method for Linguistic Metaphor Identification: From MIP to MIPVU*. John Benjamins Publishing.

Egon Stemle and Alexander Onysko. 2018. Using language learner data for metaphor detection. In *Proceedings of the Workshop on Figurative Language Processing*, pages 133–138, New Orleans, Louisiana. Association for Computational Linguistics.

Kristina Toutanova, Dan Klein, Christopher D. Manning, and Yoram Singer. 2003. Feature-rich part-of-speech tagging with a cyclic dependency network. In *Proceedings of the 2003 Human Language Technology Conference of the North American Chapter of the Association for Computational Linguistics*, pages 252–259.

Yulia Tsvetkov, Leonid Boytsov, Anatole Gershman, Eric Nyberg, and Chris Dyer. 2014. Metaphor detection with cross-lingual model transfer. In *Proceedings of the 52nd Annual Meeting of the Association for Computational Linguistics (Volume 1: Long Papers)*, pages 248–258, Baltimore, Maryland. Association for Computational Linguistics.

Thomas Wolf, Lysandre Debut, Victor Sanh, Julien Chaumond, Clement Delangue, Anthony Moi, Pierric Cistac, Tim Rault, R'emi Louf, Morgan Funtowicz, and Jamie Brew. 2019. Huggingface's transformers: State-of-the-art natural language processing. *arXiv*, arXiv:1910.03771.

Chuhan Wu, Fangzhao Wu, Yubo Chen, Sixing Wu, Zhigang Yuan, and Yongfeng Huang. 2018. Neural metaphor detecting with CNN-LSTM model. In *Proceedings of the Workshop on Figurative Language Processing*, pages 110–114, New Orleans, Louisiana. Association for Computational Linguistics.

Zhilin Yang, Zihang Dai, Yiming Yang, Jaime Carbonell, Ruslan Salakhutdinov, and Quoc V. Le. 2019. Xlnet: Generalized autoregressive pretraining for language understanding. *arXiv*, arXiv:1906.08237.

Testing the role of metadata in metaphor identification

Egon W. Stemle
Eurac Research / Bolzano-Bozen (IT)
Masaryk University / Brno (CZ)
egon.stemle@eurac.edu

Alexander Onysko
University of Klagenfurt / Klagenfurt (AT)
alexander.onysko@aau.at

Abstract

This paper describes the adaptation and application of a neural network system for the automatic detection of metaphors. The LSTM BiRNN system participated in the shared task of metaphor identification that was part of the Second Workshop of Figurative Language Processing (FigLang2020) held at the Annual Conference of the Association for Computational Linguistics (ACL2020). The particular focus of our approach is on the potential influence that the metadata given in the ETS Corpus of Non-Native Written English might have on the automatic detection of metaphors in this dataset. The article first discusses the annotated ETS learner data, highlighting some of its peculiarities and inherent biases of metaphor use. A series of evaluations follow in order to test whether specific metadata influence the system performance in the task of automatic metaphor identification. The system is available under the APLv2 open-source license.

1 Introduction

Research on metaphors, particularly in the framework of conceptual metaphor theory, continues to grow in all genres of language use and across diverse disciplines of linguistics (cf., among others, Littlemore, 2019; Gibbs Jr, 2017; Charteris-Black, 2016; Kövecses, 2020; Callies and Degani for recent and forthcoming overviews and extensions, and Veale et al., 2016 for a book-length discussion of computational linguistic perspectives). While the importance of metaphor in thought and everyday language use has long been acknowledged (Lakoff and Johnson, 1980), the practice of metaphor research still faces two methodological and analytical challenges: first of all, the identification of metaphors and, secondly, their actual description through source and target domains.

In computational linguistics, a great amount of recent work has been concerned with addressing the challenge of identifying metaphors in texts. This is evident in the series of four Workshops on Metaphor in NLP from 2013 to 2016 and in the two Workshops on Figurative Language Processing in 2018 (Beigman Klebanov et al., 2018b) and 2020 (Leong et al., 2020), each of which involved a shared task (ST) in automatic metaphor detection. Identification systems that achieved the best results in the first shared task relied on neural networks incorporating long-term short-term memory (LSTM) architectures (see Mu et al., 2019 for a discussion). Further advances in the field using deep learning approaches have been reported in Dankers et al. (2019), Gao et al. (2018), and Rei et al. (2017).

This paper extends a system proposed in Stemle and Onysko (2018), which combines word embeddings (WEs) of corpora like the BNC (British National Corpus Consortium, 2007) and the TOEFL11 language learner corpus (see Blanchard et al., 2013). With the modified system, we participated in *The Second Shared Task on Metaphor Detection*. The difference to the 2018 edition of the ST is a new set of data. As in the first task, one part of the dataset is based on the VU Amsterdam (VUA) Metaphor Corpus manually annotated according to the MIPVU procedure (Steen et al., 2010). Additionally, the second task includes a sample of 240 argumentative learner texts. These texts are taken from the ETS Corpus of Non-Native Written English (synonymous to the TOEFL11 corpus) and have been manually annotated (Beigman Klebanov et al., 2018a).

Since the learner essays are a very specific kind of data, the aim of this study is to build upon observations from Stemle and Onysko (2018), who found that a combination of word embeddings from the BNC and the TOEFL11 learner corpus yielded the best results of metaphor identification in a bi-

256

Proceedings of the Second Workshop on Figurative Language Processing, pages 256–263
July 9, 2020. ©2020 Association for Computational Linguistics
https://doi.org/10.18653/v1/P17

directional recursive neural network (BiRNN) with LSTM. These results triggered the hypothesis that learner language can lead to an information gain for neural network based metaphor identification. To explore this hypothesis further, the current study puts an explicit focus on the metadata provided for the ETS Corpus of Non-Native Written English and specifically tests the potential influence of proficiency ratings, essay prompt, and the first language (L1) of the author. In addition, we also test whether a combined training on the diverse datasets and the sequence of this training will have an impact on our system of neural network based metaphor identification.

To address these aims, our paper is structured as follows: Section 2 provides observations on the annotated learner corpus dataset. Section 3 describes the system of metaphor identification. This is followed in Section 4 by the results of the experiments, which are briefly discussed in light of the observations on the annotated learner corpus data.

2 Observations on the data

The VUA Metaphor Corpus and its application in the first shared task has been concisely described in Leong et al. (2018). The authors have reported the relatively high inter-annotator agreement ($\kappa > 0.8$), which is in part due to the MIPVU protocol (Steen et al., 2010) and the close training of annotators in the Amsterdam Metaphor Group. Interestingly, the results of the first task across all submitted systems showed a clear genre bias with academic texts consistently displaying the highest correct identification rates and conversation data (i.e. spoken texts) the lowest Leong et al. (2018, p.60). This might be related to the fact that academic discourse is more schematic and formulaic (e.g. in the use of sentential adverbials and verbal constructions) and might rely to a greater extent on recurrent metaphorical expressions than spoken conversations, which are less schematic and can thus display a higher degree of syntactic and lexical variation. In other words, similarities in the data between training and test sets might be higher in the academic than in the conversation genre, leading to different genre-specific training effects in neural networks.

Apart from the VUA metaphor corpus, the second shared task introduces a novel dataset culled from the ETS Corpus of Non-Native Written English. In their description, Beigman Klebanov et al.

(2018a) report an average inter-annotator agreement of $\kappa = 0.62$ on marking argumentation-relevant metaphors. Disagreement in the annotations was positively compensated in that all metaphor annotations were included even if only given by one of the two raters. While a focus on argumentation-relevant metaphors coheres with the genre of short argumentative learner essays written in response to one of eight prompts during TOEFL examinations in 2006-2007 (Blanchard et al., 2013), the scope of metaphor annotation is more restricted in the ETS sample than in the VUA corpus, which follows the more stringent MIPVU protocol. This explains to some extent why the overall amount of metaphor-related words in the training sets is considerably lower in the ETS sample (an average of 7% in All-POS and 14% among verbs; see Beigman Klebanov et al., 2018a, p.88) than in the VUA Metaphor Corpus (15% in All-POS and 28.3% among verbs; see Leong et al., 2018, p.58).

The relatively small size of the ETS sample inspired us to look into the structure of the data more closely to check whether any potential biases exist that might play a role for the automatic detection of metaphors. Beigman Klebanov et al. (2018a, p.89) report a significant positive correlation of the number of metaphors and the proficiency ratings of the texts as medium or high in the data. This relationship is confirmed by an independent samples t-test in the training partition of the data (180 texts). The group of highly proficient learners ($N = 95$) uses more metaphors ($M = 13.98, SD - 8.23$) compared to the group of medium proficient learners ($N = 85, M = 9.55, SD = 5.96$) at a significantly higher rate ($t = 4.07, p = 0.000071$). The L1 background of the learners (i.e. Arabic, Italian, Japanese) did not influence the mean number of metaphors in the texts as confirmed by a one-way ANOVA ($F = 1.619, p = 0.201$; L1 Arabic: $N = 63, M = 12.48, SD = 8.37$; L1 Italian: $N = 59, M = 12.71, SD = 7.79$; L1 Japanese: $N = 59, M = 10.44, SD = 6.38$).

Since the Corpus of Non-Native Written English consists of argumentative learner essays that were written in response to one of eight different prompts, another factor to consider in the annotated ETS sample is the role the prompt might have on metaphor use. Table 1 summarizes the descriptive statistics on the number of metaphors per prompt.

From left to right, the columns in Table 1 re-

Prompt	# words	# metaph. types	# metaph. tokens	Metaph. type/toks	% metaph. per words	mean # of metaph.
P1	8059	205	361	0.57	4.5	15.696
P2	7493	199	330	0.60	4.4	15.714
P3	7947	222	397	0.59	4.8	17.227
P4	8076	146	173	0.84	2.1	7.522
P5	8455	172	206	0.83	2.4	8.957
P6	8446	134	188	0.71	2.2	7.833
P7	7516	170	243	0.70	3.2	11.045
P8	7923	197	260	0.76	3.3	11.818

Table 1: Number of metaphors (types and tokens) per prompt in the annotated ETS training set.

port, per prompt, the total number of words, the number of metaphor types, the overall number of metaphor tokens (i.e. all words annotated for metaphor), the type token ratio of metaphors, the relative amount of metaphor tokens among all words, and the mean values of metaphors. The two rightmost columns illustrate an uneven occurrence of metaphors across the diverse prompts. Three groups emerge from the data according to their similarly high (or low) values: P1, P2, P3 as the highest scoring group, P4, P5, P6 as the lowest scoring group, and P7, P8 whose values are in-between the other two groups. A one-way ANOVA for independent samples ($F = 7.0919, p = .00001$) confirms a significant difference between the groups. T-tests comparing the minimal and maximal numerical distances between the high, the medium, and the low clusters show that the high cluster is significantly different from the low cluster (P1: $N = 23, M = 15.70, SD = 8.138$ compared to P5: $N = 23, M = 8.96, SD = 4.117$) at $t(44) = 3.54, p = .000948$. The differences between the low and the medium groups as well as the high and the medium group do not reach a significance threshold of $p < .01$.

When looking for an explanation of these biased metaphor occurrences, some interesting patterns emerge among the high frequency group (P1, P2, and P3). In all these instances, the prompts trigger certain metaphor-related words (MRW) that occur at a high rate. Table 2 provides an overview of the metaphorical expressions triggered by the prompts P1, P2, and P3. The 30 most frequent MRW were closely analyzed for each of the prompts.

In Table 2, MRW that cannot be related to the prompt are preceded by an asterisk. All the other terms are triggered by the prompts. For P1, the expression "broad knowledge" from the prompt that instantiates an objectification metaphor of knowledge (KNOWLEDGE IS AN OBJECT) is frequently reiterated in the test takers' essays and is by far the most frequent metaphorical expression among all annotated MRW in P1. The metaphorical uses of the lexeme *focus* as in "focus on a particular subject/field" is triggered by the prompt as a synonymous phrase for "…specialize in one specific subject". Similarly, the term *wide/-er* is used by some learners as a synonym of "broad knowledge". In P2, the metaphorical phrase "have time" is prevalent. It is thematically triggered by the phrase "enjoy life", which stimulates people to write about time as a (precious) possession that allows you to enjoy life. The metaphorical expression of "spending time" is evoked by the same conceptual metaphor. The LIFE IS A JOURNEY metaphor triggered by P2 is instantiated in the recurrent expression of stages in life. The mention of "time" in P3 evokes the same TIME IS A PRECIOUS POSSESSION conceptual metaphor as in P2. Again, the by far most recurrent MRW are the verbs *give, have,* and *spend* that objectify time in that metaphor. In addition, the use of the verb *support* as in "support communities" is directly related to the prompt ("…to helping their communities") as are the metaphorical collocations "free time" and "dedicate time".

In all the other prompts, trigger effects do not occur or are not as quantitatively relevant as in P1 to P3. P4, for example, does not show any spikes in metaphor frequencies with the most frequent MRW (*image*) merely occurring 5 times. The same is true in P5 with the terms *ruining, reach, comfortable,* and *advancement* being mentioned 4 times each as the most frequent MRW. A weak effect can be observed in P6 where the prompt "The best way to travel is in a group led by a tour guide" triggers the metaphorical collocation to "take a trip" that recurs 14 times across the learner texts. In P7 and P8, the most frequent MRW are not stimulated by the prompt, and there are similarly low token frequencies leading to a flat frequency distribution among the MRW. Incidentally, P8 ("Successful people try new things and take risks rather than only

P1: It is better to have broad knowledge of many academic subjects than to specialize in one specific subject.

P2: Young people enjoy life more than older people do.

P3: Young people nowadays do not give enough time to helping their communities.

metaphorical expression	# of occur.	metaphorical expression	# of occur.	metaphorical expression	# of occur.
P1		**P2**		**P3**	
"broad(er) knowledge"	60	have/-ing/has "have time"	55	give/-s/-ing/-en "give time", "give help"	29
focus/-ed "focus on a particular subject/field"	12	spend/-s/-ing "spend time/hours/years"	14	have/-ing/has "have time"	24
*give/-s/-ing	10	*face "face problems / change / responsibilities"	6	spend/-ing/-t "spend time"	16
wide/-er	9	*get	5	support/-s/-ing/-ed "support communities"	14
*lead/-s	7	stage "stage of life"	4	*strong/-er/-ly	14
*spend	6			free "free time"	9
				dedicate/-s "dedicate time"	9

Table 2: Most frequent metaphorical expressions in P1, P2, and P3.
(*) MRW does not occur verbatim in the prompt

doing what they already know how to do well") contains the metaphorical expression "take risks" that recurs in the learner essays 43 times. However, it has not been manually annotated as an MRW in the ETS Corpus.

If we take a look at how the MRW are distributed across the different parts of speech, it is interesting to note that verbs are by far more often marked as metaphors than nouns and adjectives/adverbs. Among the 30 most frequent MRW per prompt in the training set, 416 metaphorical verbs precede over 198 adjectives/adverbs and 141 nouns.

Finally, the learner data poses another peculiarity that is worth considering in the automatic metaphor identification. There is a total of 99 misspelled MRW across all prompts in the data (4.6% of all MRW) as in *messege, actractivity, strenght, knowled, isolte, dangerousness*, and *broadn* to randomly pick out a few. Finding a way to factor in the out-of-vocabulary words will increase the performance of automatic metaphor detection.

3 Design and implementation

Our approach extends the system from Stemle and Onysko (2018), which combines a small set of established machine learning (ML) methods and tools. In particular, the system uses fastText[1] word embeddings from different corpora in a bi-directional recursive neural network architecture with long-term short-term memory (LSTM BiRNN) and implements a flat sequence-to-sequence neural network with one hidden layer using TensorFlow+Keras (Abadi et al., 2015) in Python. With the goals we introduced in Section 1, it seemed sufficient to use a successful system from the last ST instead of improving the overall system by integrating the latest, highly successful[2] developments from the field of NLP (see, e.g., Wang

---

[1] https://fasttext.cc/

[2] The current development of increasing the complexity in neural network architectures by adding more processing layers in systems comes with the trade-off of loosing insights into the mechanisms of how the improvements are achieved. See also Mikolov (2020).

et al., 2020 for an overview).

In their experimental design Stemle and Onysko (2018) use word embeddings from corpora such as Wikipedia[3] and BNC[4] as well as from texts of language learners (TOEFL11). This is to follow the intuition that the use of metaphors can vary depending on the competence of the learners and that these differences can be helpful in training a metaphor detection system.

For the current ST, the system was slightly extended. We

- bumped the requirements of the used tools to current versions (in particular for Tensor-Flow+Keras, gensim[5], FastText, and scikit-learn[6]),

- adapted the system to the new format of the TOEFL data set,

- improved the use of sub-word information encoded in FastText word representations (we fixed a bug that prevented the system to use proper subword character n-gram representations in some cases), and

- added an option to integrate metadata into the input representations for the neural network.

For the last point, we adapted the way the input for the neural network is represented: The number of input layers corresponds to the number of features, i.e. for multiple features, e.g. multiple WE models or additional PoS tags, sequences are concatenated on the word level such that the number of features for an individual word grows. For the metadata, we added an input layer with the number of dimensions varying with the number of encoded metadata.

We maintain the implementation in a source code repository[7]. The system is available under the APLv2 open-source license.

4 Experiments

4.1 Combining VUA and TOEFL

In our first experiment, we tried to extend the training data and combine the two available datasets.

Given the discussion in Section 2, we expected confounding effects due to the fact that the manual classification of the All-POS- and Verb-metaphors are different in these two sets.

First, we shuffled both datasets individually and then combined them in three ways: A re-shuffled combination of the two sets and two combinations where we put one set at the beginning and the other one at the end. For the evaluation we emulated a 10-fold CV, with training on combinations of the original datasets and testing on a held out part of one of the datasets: We trained on one of our combined sets and tested on one of 10 parts of the uncombined dataset, which had been held out from the training, and repeated this for all 10 parts. As word embeddings, we used BNC and the complete TOEFL11 data.

Table 3 shows that, most notably, the highest recall is achieved on the Verbs task when using first the VUA data and subsequently the TOEFL data, and testing on the TOEFL data. We interpret that in a way that the learning of the VUA data is mostly 'forgotten' by the neural network, but its focus on Verb-metaphors leaves a strong initialization bias towards verbs.

Overall, the results of the various runs show that the much larger VUA data dominates the learnt properties of the model, and that the matching focus on Verb-metaphors in both datasets improves recall.

4.2 Metadata

In this experiment, we added available metadata as additional information to learn from. The difference is that compared to other information, such as POS tags, this metadata applies to whole sentences and the entire texts. Also, this experiment only addresses the TOEFL dataset.

The available metadata are the following:

- Prompt: The prompt that triggered the production of the respective sentence and text (P1-P8)

- Proficiency: The proficiency of the language learner who produced the text (medium or high)

- L1: The language learner's L1 (ARA, JPN, ITA)

- Text ID: The text's unique ID (which represents the individual language learner)

[3]https://fasttext.cc/docs/en/english-vectors.html
[4]https://embeddings.sketchengine.co.uk/static/index.html
[5]https://radimrehurek.com/gensim/
[6]https://scikit-learn.org/
[7]https://github.com/bot-zen/

Training		Test on VUA		Test on TOEFL	
		Verbs	All-POS	Verbs	All-POS
Shuffled	Pr	**0.58 (+/- 0.03)**	0.55 (+/- 0.04)	0.46 (+/- 0.09)	0.42 (+/- 0.04)
VUA + TOEFL	Re	0.65 (+/- 0.03)	0.64 (+/- 0.05)	0.69 (+/- 0.07)	0.67 (+/- 0.07)
	F1	**0.61 (+/- 0.02)**	0.59 (+/- 0.02)	0.54 (+/- 0.06)	0.52 (+/- 0.03)
Sequential	Pr	0.56 (+/- 0.05)	0.55 (+/- 0.06)	0.43 (+/- 0.06)	0.44 (+/- 0.04)
1:VUA 2:TOEFL	Re	0.67 (+/- 0.06)	0.64 (+/- 0.09)	**0.71 (+/- 0.07)**	0.68 (+/- 0.04)
	F1	0.60 (+/- 0.03)	0.58 (+/- 0.03)	0.53 (+/- 0.04)	0.53 (+/- 0.03)
Sequential	Pr	0.56 (+/- 0.04)	0.53 (+/- 0.06)	0.46 (+/- 0.06)	0.42 (+/- 0.05)
1:TOEFL 2:VUA	Re	0.68 (+/- 0.04)	0.67 (+/- 0.08)	0.69 (+/- 0.08)	0.70 (+/- 0.06)
	F1	0.61 (+/- 0.03)	0.59 (+/- 0.02)	0.55 (+/- 0.05)	0.52 (+/- 0.04)
Baseline:	Pr	0.55 (+/- 0.04)	0.55 (+/- 0.03)	0.57 (+/- 0.07)	0.53 (+/- 0.06)
VUA and TOEFL	Re	0.69 (+/- 0.04)	0.68 (+/- 0.04)	0.63 (+/- 0.08)	0.68 (+/- 0.06)
individually	F1	0.61 (+/- 0.01)	0.61 (+/- 0.01)	0.59 (+/- 0.03)	0.59 (+/- 0.03)

Table 3: 10-fold CV comparison of training on (un)shuffled VUA and TOEFL data for the Verbs and All-POS Tasks.

- Text length: The length (in tokens) of the complete text the respective sentence belongs to

Given the discussion in Section 2, we expected confounding effects for some of the metadata, and we hoped to improve the results when factoring in the metadata that showed significant effects on the number and use of metaphors.

As word embeddings, we used only the BNC. The input data was constructed for both tasks (All-POS and Verbs) by adding the metadata information for every single word in the input sequence. Testing was done by 10-fold cross-validation.

Table 4 shows that, most notably, the overall metadata does *not* improve the results in a systematic, meaningful way. Also, some metadata, like the *Text ID* even considerably degrades performance. Overall, there is no clear tendency towards metadata being more – if at all - helpful.

The complete held-out test set was not available at the time of writing, but we had evaluated some combinations of metadata during the shared task (via CodaLab) and found that the Verbs task - contrary to our 10-fold CV - gained slightly from the use of metadata. An evaluation on the complete test set would have been preferable. Additionally, representing the metadata at the level of the entire sequence instead of for each word individually could also noticeably influence the results.

		Verbs	All-POS
Baseline (no metadt.)	Pr	0.53 (+/- 0.04)	0.53 (+/- 0.04)
	Re	0.64 (+/- 0.07)	0.63 (+/- 0.05)
	F1	0.57 (+/- 0.02)	0.57 (+/- 0.03)
Prompt	Pr	0.50 (+/- 0.06)	0.51 (+/- 0.05)
	Re	0.66 (+/- 0.10)	0.64 (+/- 0.05)
	F1	0.56 (+/- 0.02)	0.56 (+/- 0.03)
Proficiency	Pr	0.51 (+/- 0.07)	0.51 (+/- 0.05)
	Re	0.68 (+/- 0.09)	0.65 (+/- 0.07)
	F1	0.57 (+/- 0.02)	0.57 (+/- 0.04)
L1	Pr	0.49 (+/- 0.05)	0.53 (+/- 0.06)
	Re	0.68 (+/- 0.08)	0.60 (+/- 0.06)
	F1	0.57 (+/- 0.02)	0.56 (+/- 0.03)
Prom.+ Prof. + L1	Pr	0.54 (+/- 0.07)	0.52 (+/- 0.06)
	Re	0.62 (+/- 0.07)	0.64 (+/- 0.05)
	F1	0.57 (+/- 0.03)	0.57 (+/- 0.03)
Text ID	Pr	0.42 (+/- 0.08)	0.48 (+/- 0.08)
	Re	0.72 (+/- 0.08)	0.60 (+/- 0.10)
	F1	0.52 (+/- 0.05)	0.52 (+/- 0.03)
Text length	Pr	0.50 (+/- 0.06)	0.53 (+/- 0.05)
	Re	0.66 (+/- 0.11)	0.62 (+/- 0.05)
	F1	0.56 (+/- 0.03)	0.57 (+/- 0.03)
All	Pr	0.45 (+/- 0.07)	0.44 (+/- 0.08)
	Re	0.68 (+/- 0.08)	0.64 (+/- 0.08)
	F1	0.54 (+/- 0.04)	0.51 (+/- 0.04)

Table 4: 10-fold CV comparison of training with different metadata on the TOEFL dataset.

5 Conclusion

This paper has focused on the structure of the learner data used in the Second Shared Task of Metaphor Identification. We aimed at exploring possible factors that influence this kind of data and tested whether these play a role for the automated identification using word embeddings in an established LSTM BiRNN system from the first ST in 2018. A descriptive investigation of the manually annotated sample of the ETS Corpus of Non-Native Written English (TOEFL11 corpus) shows that the factors of proficiency and especially the essay prompt exhibit significant correlations to the amount and type of metaphors found in the annotated training set. The data also show a numerical bias towards the annotation of verbs as metaphors compared to other content words.

A sequential training of the bidirectional neural network using both the VUA and the TOEFL partitions of the shared task points to the different structure of the datasets, in particular towards an emerging bias of overidentifying verbal metaphors in the neural network based classification. The hypothesized influence of the metadata in the TOEFL set, in particular the observed dependencies on proficiency and the essay prompt, was not confirmed by the results of the automated identification. While the factors of L1, proficiency, prompt and essay length did not influence the baseline results, the essay ID (i.e. the individual learner) reduced the performance of the system as did a combination of all metadata. For the future, more tests with different ways of modelling the metadata in the neural network architecture and on the test set of the task will provide further insights.

Acknowledgments

The computational results presented have been achieved in part using the Vienna Scientific Cluster (VSC).

References

Martín Abadi, Ashish Agarwal, Paul Barham, Eugene Brevdo, Zhifeng Chen, Craig Citro, Greg S. Corrado, Andy Davis, Jeffrey Dean, Matthieu Devin, Sanjay Ghemawat, Ian Goodfellow, Andrew Harp, Geoffrey Irving, Michael Isard, Yangqing Jia, Rafal Jozefowicz, Lukasz Kaiser, Manjunath Kudlur, Josh Levenberg, Dandelion Mané, Rajat Monga, Sherry Moore, Derek Murray, Chris Olah, Mike Schuster, Jonathon Shlens, Benoit Steiner, Ilya Sutskever, Kunal Talwar, Paul Tucker, Vincent Vanhoucke, Vijay Vasudevan, Fernanda Viégas, Oriol Vinyals, Pete Warden, Martin Wattenberg, Martin Wicke, Yuan Yu, and Xiaoqiang Zheng. 2015. TensorFlow: Large-scale machine learning on heterogeneous systems. Software available from tensorflow.org.

Beata Beigman Klebanov, Chee Wee (Ben) Leong, and Michael Flor. 2018a. A corpus of non-native written english annotated for metaphor. In *Proceedings of the 2018 Conference of the North American Chapter of the Association for Computational Linguistics: Human Language Technologies, Volume 2 (Short Papers)*, pages 86–91, New Orleans, Louisiana. Association for Computational Linguistics.

Beata Beigman Klebanov, Ekaterina Shutova, Patricia Lichtenstein, Smaranda Muresan, and Chee Wee. 2018b. *Proceedings of the Workshop on Figurative Language Processing*. Association for Computational Linguistics, New Orleans, Louisiana.

Daniel Blanchard, Joel Tetreault, Derrick Higgins, Aoife Cahill, and Martin Chodorow. 2013. TOEFL11: A corpus of non-native english. *ETS Research Report Series*, 2013(2):i–15.

British National Corpus Consortium. 2007. The British National Corpus, version 3 (BNC XML Edition).

Marcus Callies and Marta Degani, editors. *Metaphor in Language and Culture across World Englishes*. Bloomsbury, London. Forthcoming.

Jonathan Charteris-Black. 2016. *Fire Metaphors: Discourses of Awe and Authority*. Bloomsbury Academic.

Verna Dankers, Marek Rei, Martha Lewis, and Ekaterina Shutova. 2019. Modelling the interplay of metaphor and emotion through multitask learning. In *Proceedings of the 2019 Conference on Empirical Methods in Natural Language Processing and the 9th International Joint Conference on Natural Language Processing (EMNLP-IJCNLP)*, pages 2218–2229, Hong Kong, China. Association for Computational Linguistics.

Ge Gao, Eunsol Choi, Yejin Choi, and Luke Zettlemoyer. 2018. Neural metaphor detection in context. In *Proceedings of the 2018 Conference on Empirical Methods in Natural Language Processing*, pages 607–613, Brussels, Belgium. Association for Computational Linguistics.

Raymond W. Gibbs Jr. 2017. *Metaphor Wars: Conceptual Metaphors in Human Life*. Cambridge University Press, Cambridge.

Zoltán Kövecses. 2020. *Extended Conceptual Metaphor Theory*, first edition. Cambridge University Press.

George Lakoff and Mark Johnson. 1980. *Metaphors we Live by*. University of Chicago Press.

Chee Wee Leong, Beata Beigman Klebanov, Chris Hamill, Egon Stemle, Rutuja Ubale, and Xianyang Chen. 2020. A report on the 2020 VUA and TOEFL metaphor detection shared task. In *Proceedings of the Second Workshop on Figurative Language Processing*, Seattle, WA.

Chee Wee (Ben) Leong, Beata Beigman Klebanov, and Ekaterina Shutova. 2018. A report on the 2018 VUA metaphor detection shared task. In *Proceedings of the Workshop on Figurative Language Processing*, pages 56–66, New Orleans, Louisiana. Association for Computational Linguistics.

Jeannette Littlemore. 2019. *Metaphors in the Mind: Sources of Variation in Embodied Metaphor*, first edition. Cambridge University Press.

Tomáš Mikolov. 2020. Complexity and simplicity in machine learning. Keynote at the GeCKo symposium (Integrating Generic and Contextual Knowledge) 2020.

Jesse Mu, Helen Yannakoudakis, and Ekaterina Shutova. 2019. Learning outside the box: Discourse-level features improve metaphor identification. In *Proceedings of the 2019 Conference of the North American Chapter of the Association for Computational Linguistics: Human Language Technologies, Volume 1 (Long and Short Papers)*, pages 596–601, Minneapolis, Minnesota. Association for Computational Linguistics.

Marek Rei, Luana Bulat, Douwe Kiela, and Ekaterina Shutova. 2017. Grasping the finer point: A supervised similarity network for metaphor detection. In *Proceedings of the 2017 Conference on Empirical Methods in Natural Language Processing*, pages 1537–1546, Copenhagen, Denmark. Association for Computational Linguistics.

Gerard J. Steen, Aletta G. Dorst, J. Berenike Herrmann, Anna A. Kaal, Tina Krennmayr, and Trijntje Pasma. 2010. *A Method for Linguistic Metaphor Identification: From MIP to MIPVU*. John Benjamins.

Egon Stemle and Alexander Onysko. 2018. Using language learner data for metaphor detection. In *Proceedings of the Workshop on Figurative Language Processing*, pages 133–138, New Orleans, LA. Association for Computational Linguistics.

Tony Veale, Ekaterina Shutova, and Beata Beigman Klebanov. 2016. Metaphor: A computational perspective. *Synthesis Lectures on Human Language Technologies*, 9(1):1–160.

Yuxuan Wang, Yutai Hou, Wanxiang Che, and Ting Liu. 2020. From static to dynamic word representations: a survey. *International Journal of Machine Learning and Cybernetics*.

Sarcasm Detection Using an Ensemble Approach

Jens Lemmens and **Ben Burtenshaw** and **Ehsan Lotfi**
and **Ilia Markov** and **Walter Daelemans**
CLiPS, University of Antwerp
Lange Winkelstraat 40
2000, Antwerp (Belgium)
`firstname.lastname@uantwerpen.be`

Abstract

We present an ensemble approach for the detection of sarcasm in Reddit and Twitter responses in the context of The Second Workshop on Figurative Language Processing held in conjunction with ACL 2020[1]. The ensemble is trained on the predicted sarcasm probabilities of four component models and on additional features, such as the sentiment of the comment, its length, and source (Reddit or Twitter) in order to learn which of the component models is the most reliable for which input. The component models consist of an LSTM with hashtag and emoji representations; a CNN-LSTM with casing, stop word, punctuation, and sentiment representations; an MLP based on Infersent embeddings; and an SVM trained on stylometric and emotion-based features. All component models use the two conversational turns preceding the response as context, except for the SVM, which only uses features extracted from the response. The ensemble itself consists of an adaboost classifier with the decision tree algorithm as base estimator and yields F1-scores of 67% and 74% on the Reddit and Twitter test data, respectively.

1 Introduction

In this paper, an ensemble approach for the detection of sarcasm in social media data is described. The ensemble was designed in the context of The Second Workshop on Figurative Language Processing held in conjunction with ACL 2020[1]. It was the goal of the shared task to create a robust sarcasm detection model for tweets and Reddit comments and investigate the role of conversational context in automatic sarcasm detection models.

Detecting sarcasm can be a challenging task, not only for machines, but also for humans, because sarcasm is subjective and culturally dependent, and because an utterance on its own can be both sarcastic and non-sarcastic (Ghosh et al., 2018; Joshi

---

[1]https://sites.google.com/view/figlang2020/

et al., 2017). Context is therefore vital for a correct interpretation of a comment on social media (Wallace et al., 2014). For example, "Well done, guys!" generally has a positive meaning, whereas it is used sarcastically in the context of a social media post about the governments mismanagement. Therefore, conversational context is used in our approach described below to identify sarcasm.

2 Related research

In this section, recent advances and papers related to sarcasm detection are described. The first advance is related to automatic annotation methods where the annotators use computational methods to obtain the labels (Joshi et al., 2017), for instance by searching for "#sarcasm" in tweets (e.g. González-Ibáñez et al. (2011)). Automatic labelling is often preferred to manual labelling, because it is faster, cheaper, allows for the creation of larger data sets, and because the author of an utterance knows best whether it was meant sarcastically or not. Note that automatically annotated data can contain more false positives and/or false negatives than manually labeled data if the labeling method is not robust enough. An automatic method was used to label the data used in the present study and a more detailed description of that data can be found in Section 3.

A second advance in the field of sarcasm detection are pattern-based features (Joshi et al., 2017). This term refers to using linguistic patterns as features. For example, Riloff et al. (2013) use the pattern "presence of a positive verb and a negative situation" (e.g., "I love queueing for hours") as a feature. They hypothesized that this pattern is highly indicative of sarcasm. Their approach achieved an F1-score of 51%.

Similarly, Van Hee et al. (2018) hypothesized that sentiment incongruity within an utterance signifies sarcasm. They did not only consider explicit expressions of sentiment, but also attempted to deal with sentiment implicitly embedded in world

Proceedings of the Second Workshop on Figurative Language Processing, pages 264–269
July 9, 2020. ©2020 Association for Computational Linguistics
https://doi.org/10.18653/v1/P17

knowledge. To achieve this, the annotators gathered all real-world concepts that carried an implicit sentiment and labeled them with either a "positive" or "negative" sentiment label (e.g., "going to the dentist", which is usually associated with a negative sentiment). Three approaches were then proposed that implemented these implicit sentiment labels. None of these approaches, however, outperformed the baseline (70% F1-score). Thus, although sarcasm can be seen as an expression of sentiment, this study showed that successfully implementing sentiment in a classifier is not trivial.

A third advance in the sarcasm detection field is using context as feature (Joshi et al., 2017). Three types of context can be distinguished: author context, e.g., (Joshi et al., 2016), conversational context, e.g., (Wang et al., 2015), and topical context, e.g., (Wang et al., 2015). Author context refers to the name of the author of the comment. The intuition behind using this type of context is that one individual uses sarcasm more regularly than another individual and can therefore improve the performance of sarcasm detection models. Conversational context, on the other hand, refers to the conversational turns preceding (or following) the relevant utterance. As mentioned in the introduction, this type of context can clarify whether an utterance is sarcastic or not if that utterance can be perceived as both. Finally, topical context is used, because it is hypothesized that certain topics (e.g., religion or politics) trigger more sarcastic responses than other topics.

Further, previous research has shown that for statistical models, SVM performs best (Joshi et al., 2017, 2016; Riloff et al., 2013). Conversely, the most successful deep learning algorithms are long-short term memory (LSTM) networks and convolutional neural networks (CNN) (Ghosh and Veale, 2016; Amir et al., 2016).

More recently, Ghosh et al. (2018) presented an LSTM network with sentence-level attention heads that achieved the state-of-the-art performance: they reported F1-scores of 84% for sarcastic comments and 83% for non-sarcastic comments. The goal of their study was to investigate the role of conversational context in sarcasm detection and their experiments suggested that conversational context significantly improves the performance of their model.

Joshi et al. (2017) provide a survey of previous sarcasm detection studies and can be consulted for a more extensive overview of related research.

3 Data

The training data comprises 5,000 tweets and 4,400 Reddit comments, and was annotated automatically (Khodak et al., 2018; Ghosh et al., 2018). Each comment or "response" is accompanied by its context, i.e., an ordered list of all previous comments in the conversation, and a binary label indicating whether the response is sarcastic. Both the Twitter and Reddit data are balanced.

The test data contains 1,800 tweets and the same number of Reddit comments. Similar to the training data, the test responses are accompanied by their conversational context, and are balanced. In all instances, user mentions and URLs are replaced with placeholders: "@USER" and "<URL>", respectively. All data that was used in the present study was provided by the organizers of the workshop. However, the participating teams were allowed to collect extra data if desired.

4 Methodology

Four component models were used to construct the ensemble classifier. All of these models use conversational context as feature, with the exception of the SVM model described in Section 4.1.3, which focuses only on stylometric and emotion-based properties of the response. All other models use the two conversational turns preceding the response as context, since this was the minimum amount of context that was provided for each response.

4.1 Component models

4.1.1 LSTM

Preliminary studies showed that non-word features have a noticeable effect on sarcasm transparency. For example, hashtags and emojis were used as signifiers to modify the rest of a sentence. A bidirectional LSTM model was used to recognize these modifications in relation to the main embedded vocabulary and predict binary sarcasm (Zhou et al., 2016).

Context and response words were vectorized using pretrained GloVe embeddings (Pennington et al., 2014). Emojis were embedded using Emoji2Vec (Eisner et al., 2016). All words were then further embedded using an RNN model, trained on tweets from the Chirps corpus to predict hashtags (Shwartz et al., 2017); comparable to a sentence summarization task (Jing et al., 2003), which contributed to the Reddit task as well as Twitter, by using base text alone.

These 3 embedding layers were combined for the bidirectional LSTM to iterate over. To mitigate overfitting, dropout was applied two times and optimized: (i) to the embedding layers, and (ii) within the LSTM layers. Finally the concatenated output was passed to a sigmoid layer for prediction.

4.1.2 CNN-LSTM

This model uses word embeddings of the response and context pretrained with GloVe embeddings (Pennington et al., 2014)), and punctuation, casing, sentiment and stop word features. The punctuation features contain the absolute and relative numbers of exclamation marks, quotation marks, question marks, periods, hashtags, and at-symbols in the response. Conversely, the casing features comprise the absolute and relative numbers of uppercase, lowercase and other characters (e.g. digits) in the response. The sentiment features, obtained with NLTK's Vader sentiment analyzer (Bird et al., 2009), are represented by a negative, neutral, positive, and global sentiment score of both the response and its context. Finally, stop word features were obtained by constructing a count vectorizer with scikit-learn (Pedregosa et al., 2011) out of NLTK's English stop word list.

The response and context word embeddings were twice fed to a sequence of a convolutional layer with max pooling, and to a bidirectional LSTM layer. The other feature vectors were each passed to a dense layer. To avoid overfitting, dropout was applied and optimized after each embedding, convolutional, LSTM, and dense layer. Finally, the outputs of all of the above were concatenated and passed to a sigmoid layer for prediction.

4.1.3 SVM

In this approach, the response messages were represented through a combination of part-of-speech (POS) tags (obtained using the StanfordNLP library (Qi et al., 2018)), function words (i.e., words belonging to the closed syntactic classes[2]), and emotion-based features from the NRC emotion lexicon (Mohammad and Turney, 2013). From this representation, n-grams (with n from 1 to 3) were built. Character n-gram features (with n from 1 to 3) were added as a separate feature vector. This approach captures the stylometric and emotion characteristics of a textual content and is described in detail in (Markov et al., 2020).

---

[2] https://universaldependencies.org/u/pos/

The features were weighted using the term frequency (tf) weighting scheme and fed to liblinear SVM with optimized parameters (the optimal liblinear classifier parameters were selected: penalty parameter (C), loss function (loss), and tolerance for stopping criteria (tol) (based on grid search). The liblinear scikit-learn (Pedregosa et al., 2011) implementation of SVM was used.

4.1.4 MLP

This model consists of simple multi-layer perceptron (MLP) classifier based on sentence embeddings from the Infersent model developed by Facebook (Conneau et al., 2017). Infersent is trained on natural language inference data, which is a motivation to use this model in our ensemble approach, since it might spot the logical discrepancies that often play a role in creating and detecting sarcasm. Infersent works with GloVe or Fasttext word embeddings as input and gives a 4092-dimensional sentence embedding. For this task we concatenated the response and context embeddings (with GloVe) and fed the resulting 8184-dimensional vector to an MLP with Relu non-linearity and a sigmoid at the end for classification. This was attempted with different architectures among which a [8184-2048-128-16-2] composition showed the best results.

Before they were converted to embeddings, the responses and their context were preprocessed as follows: hashtags were added as descriptions at the end of the string and links were removed.

4.2 Ensemble

We used 10-fold cross-validation to train the component models. For each fold, the predicted validation labels were stored in a dataframe. This allowed us to collect predictions for all comments in the training data without the models being trained on the comments for which they predicted the label. These predictions were then used to train the ensemble model, which consisted of a decision tree classifier implemented as the base estimator in a scikit-learn adaboost classifier. In addition to the predicted labels, the character length of the response and context, their source (Twitter or Reddit) and NLTK's Vader sentiment scores for the response and its two preceding turns were used as features, so that the ensemble could learn which component model was the most reliable and for which input (e.g., long positive tweet as response and short negative tweet as context).

5 Results

In this section, the performance of the component models and of the ensemble model are described. The models were evaluated on the Reddit test set and Twitter test set separately, and F1-score was used as the official evaluation metric.

In Table 1, the 10-fold cross-validation precision, recall, and F1-score of the component models on the training data can be found. The ensemble itself yields precision, recall, and F1 scores of 77.2%, 76.9% and 76.9% under 10-fold cross-validation (Reddit and Twitter combined). Table 2 represents an overview of the scores obtained on the held-out evaluation set by the different component models and the ensemble architecture.

From these results, it can be concluded that the ensemble model has higher precision, recall, and F1-score than the models in isolation. This suggests that the ensemble does not simply predict the same label as the overall best performing component model, but learns which model performs best and when. What component model is globally the most robust, depends on the type of data (Reddit or Twitter) and on the setting (training or test data). Nevertheless, each component model contributes to the results and therefore seems to capture different sarcasm characteristics, as evidenced by the increase in performance when all the models are combined through the ensemble and by an ablation study we conducted: removing any of the component models results in a decrease in performance.

Further, the results show that both official test sets contain comments that are, on average, more challenging to classify than the training data, since the 10-fold cross-validation scores (Table 1) are substantially higher than the scores on the official test sets (Table 2). Moreover, it can be observed that all models achieve lower scores on Reddit comments than on Twitter comments. Since not only recall, but also precision are lower for all models, this does not only suggest that sarcasm is more challenging to detect, but that it is generally more difficult to distinguish between non-sarcastic and sarcastic utterances in Reddit comments. One plausible explanation for this imbalance is that tweets are limited in length, whereas Reddit comments are not. Therefore, the models may have more difficulties with interpreting the context in the longer Reddit comments, resulting in a lower performance. However, more research is needed to determine why Reddit comments are more challenging to clas-

	Reddit			Twitter		
Model	Pre	Rec	F1	Pre	Rec	F1
LSTM	64.3	64.0	63.8	75.6	75.2	75.2
CNN	62.1	62.0	62.0	76.1	75.9	75.9
SVM	64.2	64.2	64.2	74.5	74.4	74.4
MLP	65.1	65.3	65.1	74.1	74.9	73.9

Table 1: Precision (%), recall (%), and F1-score (%) of the component models on the training data under 10-fold cross-validation.

	Reddit			Twitter		
Model	Pre	Rec	F1	Pre	Rec	F1
LSTM	63.6	63.7	63.5	67.7	68.0	67.5
CNN	59.1	59.1	59.1	67.1	67.2	67.0
SVM	62.0	62.0	62.0	66.6	66.7	66.5
MLP	60.2	61.9	58.6	68.3	68.3	68.3
Ens.	**67.0**	**67.7**	**66.7**	**74.1**	**74.6**	**74.0**

Table 2: Precision (%), recall (%), and F1-score (%) of the models on the official evaluation data.

sify than tweets.

6 Conclusion

We described an ensemble approach for sarcasm detection in Reddit and Twitter comments. The model consists of an adaboost classifier with the decision tree algorithm as base estimator and learns the sarcasm probabilities predicted by four different component models: an LSTM model that uses word, emoji and hashtag representations; a model that uses CNNs and LSTM networks to learn word embeddings, and dense networks to learn punctuation, casing, sentiment and stop word features; an MLP based on Infersent embeddings; and an SVM approach that captures the stylometric and emotional characteristics of sarcastic content. All component models (except SVM) use conversational context to make predictions, namely the two turns preceding the response.

The sarcasm probabilities used to train the ensemble were obtained by training the component models using 10-fold cross-validation and saving the labels predicted for the validation set in each fold. In order to learn which model performs best and for what input, the ensemble also uses the lengths, the source and sentiment scores of the response and context as features.

The ensemble yields F1-scores of 67% and 74% on the Reddit and Twitter test data, respectively. The imbalance between the Reddit and Twitter scores is consistent in all component models, suggesting that the Reddit data is inherently more challenging to classify. However, more research on why this is the case is needed. Future work may also include experimenting with other component models to improve the overall performance of the ensemble.

Acknowledgments

This research received funding from the Flemish Government (AI Research Program).

References

Ilia Markov et al. 2020. Exploring stylometric and emotion-based features for multilingual cross-domain hate speech detection (in preparation).

Silvio Amir, Byron C. Wallace, Hao Lyu, and Paula Carvalho Mario J. Silva. 2016. Modelling context with user embeddings for sarcasm detection in social media. In *Proceedings of The 20th SIGNLL Conference on Computational Natural Language Learning*, pages 167–177, Berlin, Germany. Association for Computational Linguistics.

Steven Bird, Ewan Klein, and Edward Loper. 2009. *Natural Language Processing with Python*. O'Reilly Media Inc.

Alexis Conneau, Douwe Kiela, Holger Schwenk, Loïc Barrault, and Antoine Bordes. 2017. Supervised learning of universal sentence representations from natural language inference data. In *Proceedings of the 2017 Conference on Empirical Methods in Natural Language Processing*, pages 670–680, Copenhagen, Denmark. Association for Computational Linguistics.

Ben Eisner, Tim Rocktäschel, Isabelle Augenstein, Matko Bošnjak, and Sebastian Riedel. 2016. Emoji2vec: Learning emoji representations from their description. In *Proceedings of The Fourth International Workshop on Natural Language Processing for Social Media*, pages 48–54, Austin, Texas, USA. Association for Computational Linguistics.

Aniruddha Ghosh and Tony Veale. 2016. Fracking sarcasm using neural network. In *Proceedings of the 7th Workshop on Computational Approaches to Subjectivity, Sentiment and Social Media Analysis*, pages 161–169, San Diego, California. Association for Computational Linguistics.

Debanjan Ghosh, Alexander R. Fabbri, and Smaranda Muresan. 2018. Sarcasm analysis using conversation context. *Computational Linguistics*, 44(4):755–792.

Roberto González-Ibáñez, Smaranda Muresan, and Nina Wacholder. 2011. Identifying sarcasm in Twitter: A closer look. In *Proceedings of the 49th Annual Meeting of the Association for Computational Linguistics: Human Language Technologies*, pages 581–586, Portland, Oregon, USA. Association for Computational Linguistics.

Hongyan Jing, Daniel Lopresti, and Chilin Shih. 2003. Summarization of noisy documents: A pilot study. In *Proceedings of the HLT-NAACL 03 Text Summarization Workshop*, pages 25–32.

Aditya Joshi, Pushpak Bhattacharyya, Mark Carman, Jaya Saraswati, and Rajita Shukla. 2016. How do cultural differences impact the quality of sarcasm annotation?: A case study of Indian annotators and American text. In *Proceedings of the 10th SIGHUM Workshop on Language Technology for Cultural Heritage, Social Sciences, and Humanities (LaTeCH) 2016*, pages 95–99, Berlin, Germany. Association for Computational Linguistics.

Aditya Joshi, Pushpak Bhattacharyya, and Mark J. Carman. 2017. Automatic sarcasm detection: A survey. *ACM Computing Surveys*, 50(5):73.

Mikhail Khodak, Nikunj Saunshi, and Kiran Vodrahalli. 2018. A large self-annotated corpus for sarcasm. In *Proceedings of the Eleventh International Conference on Language Resources and Evaluation (LREC 2018)*, Miyazaki, Japan. European Language Resources Association (ELRA).

Saif Mohammad and Peter Turney. 2013. Crowdsourcing a word-emotion association lexicon. *Computational Intelligence*, 29:436–465.

Fabian Pedregosa, Gaël Varoquaux, Alexandre Gramfort, Vincent Michel, Bertrand Thirion, Olivier Grisel, Mathieu Blondel, Peter Prettenhofer, Ron Weiss, Vincent Dubourg, Jake Vanderplas, Alexandre Passos, David Cournapeau, Matthieu Brucher, Matthieu Perrot, and Édouard Duchesnay. 2011. Scikit-learn: Machine learning in Python. *Journal of Machine Learning Research*, 12(0):2825–2830.

Jeffrey Pennington, Richard Socher, and Christopher D. Manning. 2014. GloVe: Global vectors for word representations. In *Proceedings of the 2014 Conference on Empirical Methods in Natural Language Processing (EMNLP)*, pages 1532–1543, Doha, Qatar. Association for Computational Linguistics.

Peng Qi, Timothy Dozat, Yuhao Zhang, and Christopher Manning. 2018. Universal dependency parsing from scratch. In *Proceedings of the CoNLL 2018 Shared Task: Multilingual Parsing from Raw Text to Universal Dependencies*, pages 160–170, Brussels, Belgium. Association for Computational Linguistics.

Ellen Riloff, Ashequl Qadir, Prafulla Surve, Lalindra De Silva, Nathan Gilbert, and Ruihong Huang.

2013. Sarcasm as contrast between a positive sentiment and negative situation. In *Proceedings of the 2013 Conference on Empirical Methods in Natural Language Processing*, pages 704–714, Seattle, Washington, USA. Association for Computational Linguistics.

Vered Shwartz, Gabriel Stanovsky, and Ido Dagan. 2017. Acquiring predicate paraphrases from news tweets. In *Proceedings of the 6th Joint Conference on Lexical and Computational Semantics (*SEM 2017)*, pages 155–160, Vancouver, Canada. Association for Computational Linguistics.

Cynthia Van Hee, Els Lefever, and Véronique Hoste. 2018. We usually don't like going to the dentist: Using common sense to detect irony on Twitter. *Computational Linguistics*, 44(4):793–832.

Byron C. Wallace, Do Kook Choe, Laura Kertz, and Eugene Charniak. 2014. Humans require context to infer ironic intent (so computers probably do, too). In *Proceedings of the 52nd Annual Meeting of the Association for Computational Linguistics (Volume 2: Short Papers)*, pages 512–516, Baltimore, Maryland, USA. Association for Computational Linguistics.

Zelin Wang, Zhijian Wu, Ruimin Wang, and Yafeng Ren. 2015. Twitter sarcasm detection exploiting a context-based model. In *Proceedings, Part I, of the 16th International Conference on Web Information Systems Engineering — WISE 2015 - Volume 9418*, page 77–91, Berlin, Heidelberg. Springer-Verlag.

Peng Zhou, Zhenyu Qi, Suncong Zheng, Jiaming Xu, Hongyun Bao, and Bo Xu. 2016. Text classification improved by integrating bidirectional LSTM with two-dimensional max pooling. In *Proceedings of COLING 2016, the 26th International Conference on Computational Linguistics: Technical Papers*, pages 3485–3495, Osaka, Japan. The COLING 2016 Organizing Committee.

A Transformer Approach to Contextual Sarcasm Detection in Twitter

Hunter Gregory, Steven Li, Pouya Mohammadi, Natalie Tarn, Rachel Draelos, Cynthia Rudin
Department of Computer Science, Duke University
{hlg16, sl561, pm201, nt94, rlb61}@duke.edu, cynthia@cs.duke.edu

Abstract

Understanding tone in Twitter posts will be increasingly important as more and more communication moves online. One of the most difficult, yet important tones to detect is sarcasm. In the past, LSTM and transformer architecture models have been used to tackle this problem. We attempt to expand upon this research, implementing LSTM, GRU, and transformer models, and exploring new methods to classify sarcasm in Twitter posts. Among these, the most successful were transformer models, most notably BERT. While we attempted a few other models described in this paper, our most successful model was an ensemble of transformer models including BERT, RoBERTa, XLNet, RoBERTa-large, and ALBERT. This research was performed in conjunction with the sarcasm detection shared task section in the Second Workshop on Figurative Language Processing, co-located with ACL 2020.

1 Introduction

Sarcasm detection is an important step towards complete natural language comprehension since a sarcastic phrase typically expresses a sentiment contradictory to its literal meaning. Humans usually detect sarcasm with contextual clues, especially intonation, which is not available in text-based social media data.

One challenge of sarcasm is the frequent necessity of prior knowledge. Consider an example:

Context: driver tailgating a cyclist gets instant justice
Response: maybe he tried to save gas like you do when you tailgate a transport truck

As humans, we can discern this response is sarcastic since we know a large car behind a small bike would not improve aerodynamics and hence gas mileage. This is a Herculean inference for an algorithm. In other situations, sarcastic inference relies on knowledge about science, sports, politics, or movies.

A broader challenge in classifying sarcasm is that a model trained on one dataset does not necessarily generalize to another one.

Using a Twitter dataset from the Second Workshop on Figurative Language Preprocessing, we tackle this difficult challenge of sarcasm detection and its specific issues as discussed above.

2 Datasets

The workshop provided two balanced sarcasm datasets from both Twitter and Reddit with 5,000 and 4,400 observations respectively. The workshop collected and labeled the Twitter data using the hashtags #sarcastic and #sarcasm, and preprocessed the data by replacing URLs and user mentions with placeholders. The Reddit dataset is a subset of that from Khodak et al. (2017). Both datasets consist of a sarcasm label, response, and conversation context. Both the test datasets contained 1800 observations.

Unfortunately, there were notable limitations in the Twitter data. We removed 300 observations that were duplicates (further discussed in Preprocessing). Nuances in twitter data such as acronyms, hashtags, and emojis needed to be processed. Furthermore, the Twitter dataset had missing hashtags, affecting the meaning of the response. Some tweets also contained images in the response, but there were no images in the data. For example, one tweet contained "they gave me the most (#beautiful, removed in the dataset) eggs for breakfast" with an image of chickens, but without the image it would be hard to determine its label.

There was also a considerable domain shift between training and test data for the workshop. For all models, training and validation scores were significantly higher than test scores.

Proceedings of the Second Workshop on Figurative Language Processing, pages 270–275
July 9, 2020. ©2020 Association for Computational Linguistics
https://doi.org/10.18653/v1/P17

3 Related Works and How We Use Them

A wide variety of models have been created for sarcasm detection. Our baseline model stems from the work of Ghosh et al. (2018) about sarcasm analysis using conversation context. This model involves one LSTM reading the context and another reading the response. While Ghosh and Veale (2017) proposed a similar architecture based on bidirectional LSTMs to detect sarcasm in Twitter, we found that bidirectional LSTMs performed similarly to unidirectional LSTMs. We used two different word embedding architectures, one from a previous paper trained on a separate Twitter data set and one using CBOW with position-weights, with character n-grams of length 5, a window of size 5 and 10 negatives (Ghosh et al., 2018; Grave et al., 2018). Sentence embeddings were obtained from averaging the word embeddings. We experimented with both word-level and sentence-level attention models, but we found that attention-based models performed similarly to those without (Yang et al., 2016).

The GRU architecture seemed to be a promising alternative option to the LSTM. Exploring tasks on audio, handwriting, and musical classification, Greff et al. (2016) discovered that GRUs performed the same as LSTMs. Their finding across multiple domains suggested that GRUs would perform similarly to LSTMs in the Twitter domain. Given the small size of our dataset and the reduced parameter size and complexity in GRUs, we believed this architecture could generalize better than LSTMs.

We also experimented with transformer models, which have been very successful for other applications such as sentiment analysis, question answering, and recently even for sarcasm detection (Devlin et al., 2019; Peters et al., 2018; Kayalvizhi et al., 2019; Potamias et al., 2019). We experimented with using pre-trained representations from BERT as well as RoBERTa, obtained from a bidirectional approach of a masked language model and ELMo which uses a concatenation of representations obtained from a left-to-right and a right-to-left language model (Peters et al., 2018; Liu et al., 2019). We applied ensemble learning using various pretrained transformer models (BERT, RoBERTa, XLNet, RoBERTa-large, ALBERT with no fine-tuning on the transformer weights), where each model has a learned weighted sum for the hidden layers that is concatenated with hand-made features, that is then fed into a dense layer for classification similar to the work of Wang et al. (2015).

4 Methodology

4.1 Preprocessing

For the Twitter dataset, we had to perform preliminary preprocessing. In the data, we removed several exact duplicates of observations and several almost-exact duplicates, where the context or responses would only have minor differences in punctuation (e.g. including or excluding a period) or a few characters. Text in this dataset also had an issue where a space was always placed on both sides of an apostrophe (e.g. "ol' Pete isn't happy" would become "ol ' Pete isn ' t happy"). To fix this, we created a list of English contractions and slang terms paired with their expanded form (e.g. "ol'" with "old" and "isn't" with "is not") and then cleaned all the text using the list. We also removed all occurrences of "<URL>" and "@USER" in the text. Lastly, we expanded hashtags using the python package ekphrasis (Baziotis et al., 2017).

For both this cleaned Twitter data and the Reddit data, we proceeded with the following preprocessing and feature creation. We lower-cased text, removed punctuation (including hashtag symbols), and expanded contractions and slang terms using our list mentioned above. For additional features, We created most of the extra features that Ghosh et al. (2018) used when they were feasible (e.g. did not require paying for a dataset). These included binary features encoding whether any word in the response was entirely capitalized and whether the response contained quotation marks. We also created a ternary feature for whether zero, one, or multiple exclamation points were used in the response. Additionally, we developed features that were duplicated for both the context and response. These included a binary feature indicating if any word in the text had unnecessary repeating letters as well as a ternary feature for the sentiment of the context or response (positive, negative, or neutral) using TextBlob (Loria, 2018). In addition, we had a binary feature for whether a positive sentiment emoji was in the text, and similar features for negative and neutral sentiment emojis based on a table from Kralj Novak et al. (2015).

We also created a political feature after noticing that a large number of the sarcastic tweets were political in nature. More specifically, from a sample of 200 tweets that we took, we saw that 67.7% of the political tweets were sarcastic while 31.8% of the non-political tweets were sarcastic. We created this feature by conducting a boolean search on the

Word	Train set	Extra Set
joy	6.5%	76.9%
wonderful	6.7%	69.7%
voted	67.6%	6.0%
love	30.4%	72.7%

Table 1: Sarcasm frequencies in different corpora

response and context for key words and phrases that we deemed to be political. These included the names of famous politicians and words or phrases associated with relevant political issues such as "elections", "capitalists", "planned parenthood", or "sanctuary city". In order to reduce our false positive rate for political classification, we were careful to exclude words that are often political but could easily be used in a non-political context such as "president" (e.g. the president of a basketball team) or "immigrant" (e.g. a person referencing their life story).

After running an XGBoost model with sentence-level response embeddings and our features, all seemed to have relatively equal feature importances. Therefore, we proceeded with including all of the features above in our final models.

We also thought certain words or certain topics other than politics might be good predictors of sarcasm. We calculated the frequency of sarcasm for all k-grams and discovered certain words (unigrams) appeared almost strictly in sarcastic or non-sarcastic responses in the Twitter training data. As a sanity check, we calculated the same word frequencies for an extra Twitter dataset with over 65,000 responses gathered in the same way as the training set (Ptáček et al., 2014). Many comparisons between frequencies, some displayed in Table 1, proved that the patterns in the training set were not representative of Twitter posts as a whole.

We also found that the LDA topic models with the best coherence were not predictive of sarcasm. Predicting a tweet based on its top three topics with a SVM or Logistic Regression Classifier yielded 53% training accuracy. Such low accuracy scores suggested these features would not be likely to generalize. Thus, we did not use topic models or frequency-based features in our final models.

4.2 Final Models and Performance

For all of our models, we focused on classifying the Twitter dataset and left classifying the Reddit dataset to future works.

For our final baseline model, we used Twitter embeddings (Ghosh et al., 2018), and we em-

ployed a bidirectional LSTM with sentence-level embeddings for context and a bidirectional LSTM with word-level embeddings for response. These LSTMs outputted sequences, which were modified by the dimension-reducing attention scheme proposed by Yang et al. (2016). Finally, these outputs were concatenated with our extra features and passed into a dense layer. Switching to unidirectional LSTMs, changing the number of LSTM units, or adding an extra dense layer yielded no improvement. Despite our hopes, replacing LSTMs with GRUs also did not impact training/validation performance.

As our two datasets have different distributions, mainly due to differences in text structure, formatting, and content, training by combining the two datasets together reduced our testing performance on the Twitter data. This was due to some features that are characteristic of the Reddit data, but may not generalize to the Twitter data. In order to fully leverage both of the given datasets for predicting sarcasm on the Twitter datasets, we utilized a weighted binary cross entropy loss, where we weighed each batch of Reddit data less than our Twitter data. By doing so, the model picked up on more universal sarcasm characteristics inherent to both datasets, while still being tailored primarily to the Twitter dataset. While we only tested this for our LSTM based models, this approach could be generalized to our other models.

We also utilized pre-trained transformer models to create sentence-level embeddings for classification and word-level embeddings to feed into our LSTM model. For our testing, we chose to not fine-tune the weights of the transformer models themselves, however future works may consider doing so. Instead, we use a feature-based approach as suggested in Devlin et al. (2019), where we extract features from the hidden states of the pre-trained transformer model for prediction.

Two different approaches were used to incorporate context into the transformer inputs. The first approach was to concatenate the full context and response sentences into a single input. A potential downside to this method is that the concatenated sentences exceeded the transformer's sequence length limit for certain observations, and we were forced to remove words from the front of the context until the string was compatible with the transformer. The second approach was to feed the full context and responses into the transformer separately and concatenate the outputs. The second approach has the benefit of allowing for sentences that are longer than the transformer's sequence length limit, allowing for more context to be utilized. We also create a baseline model trained solely on the responses. From our validation results (Table 3), we decided to use the second approach for our final submissions.

We obtained token representations for each of the hidden states in the transformer model, which were then averaged across the whole sentence to obtain a sentence representation for each of the hidden states. To determine the best way to combine these hidden representations into a single sentence embedding, we experimented with using a weighted sum of all layers, a weighted average of the last four layers, using only the last layer, summing all of the layers, and concatenating the last four layers. We obtained the best validation results from using a weighted sum of all hidden states (Table 2), and used this for our final model. From here, we concatenated our additional features to this embedding and pass it through two dense layers for prediction.

For our final submission, we applied this method to five separate pretrained transformer models and ensembled their results, which boosted our F1-macro score by a significant margin on the test set (0.733 for a single model to 0.756). The models we chose to ensemble were BERT-base-uncased, RoBERTa-base, XLNet-base-cased, RoBERTa-large, and ALBERT-base-v2 from the Huggingface transformers library (Wolf et al., 2019).

We also developed an LSTM on a weighted sum of the BERT hidden layer outputs. This model was similar to the baseline LSTM. BERT outputs from context were passed into one bidirectional LSTM, and BERT outputs from response were passed into another; however, these LSTMs outputted final states instead of sequences. These results were concatenated with the extra features and passed into two dense layers. On the test set, this model had an approximate 2.2% increase in F1-macro score compared to the other LSTM baseline.

Additionally, we implemented an ensemble learning approach in the hopes of highlighting the strengths of the many models that we developed. We were hopeful after seeing the improvement from the multiple transformers model that this model could achieve similar success. The assumption was that if we allowed models that were extremely confident in certain observations or per-

| | RoBERTa | | | BERT | | |
Method	Precision	Recall	F1	Precision	Recall	F1
Weighted sum of last four hidden layers	0.770	0.769	0.768	0.782	**0.776**	0.776
Sum all layers	**0.786**	0.767	0.771	0.767	0.750	0.751
Last layer only	0.761	0.760	0.760	0.772	0.767	0.768
Concatenate last four layers	0.773	0.772	**0.773**	0.769	0.751	0.751
Weighted sum of all layers	0.764	**0.774**	**0.773**	**0.785**	**0.776**	**0.778**

Table 2: Macro-averaged validation scores using various methods of combining the hidden states. Best scores for each transformer are in bold

| | RoBERTa | | | BERT | | |
Method	Precision	Recall	F1	Precision	Recall	F1
Response only	0.757	0.754	0.755	0.752	0.754	0.752
Concatenated context and response	**0.791**	0.762	0.765	0.776	0.761	0.762
Separate context and response	0.764	**0.774**	**0.773**	**0.785**	**0.776**	**0.778**

Table 3: Macro-averaged validation scores for our transformer architecture with varying levels of contexts

formed best on observations with certain characteristics to classify on those observations while allowing other models to classify observations in which this was not the case. In order to implement this, we first trained and validated a multitude of models on only half of the training data given, returning classification probabilities on the other fifty percent of our training data and all of the test data. These models included the LSTM model and BERT model embeddings passed through an SVM, both discussed earlier, in addition to an LDA topic model, an XGBoost model, and a Gaussian Process Classifier, all of which seemed to perform decently on their own (besides LDA) and implement varying logic to the same classification problem. We chose a 50/50 split for our first training since we wanted to supply these initial models with enough training data to develop accurate classifications while leaving enough data for our ensemble classifier to train on. Once obtaining these outputs, we trained a Logistic Regression model on the prediction probabilities generated by the many models for the remaining 50 percent of the training set as well as the sarcasm features that we had developed. We chose Logistic Regression because it seemed to overfit less than polynomial kernel SVM or decision forest, and there has been research on the benefits of Logistic Regression on accuracy for ensemble learning (Wang et al., 2015). We then used this Logistic Regression to predict whether the test data was sarcastic or not. This model achieved a validation score of 0.779 and a test score of 0.686, indicating that the model did not generalize well. This ensemble model also worsened scores of our best models, which would achieve a higher F1-macro validation score when trained on the entirety of our training dataset. However, the best transformer models and RNN models would drop from a validation score of above 0.703 and 0.682 to 0.667 and 0.504 respectively, when trained on half of the data as done in the ensemble model. Therefore, we believe that the ensemble model would have achieved better scores if it were trained on a larger data set than the one we worked with. However, it appears that the weighted transformers model above performed best given our dataset.

As seen in Table 5, all our final models outperformed the LSTM with attention (our implementation of the baseline from Ghosh et al., 2018). Transformer representations seemed to capture the most relevant information for sarcasm detection, and having context tends to improve results.

5 Error Analysis

These results, however, are far below the F1-macro scores that were achieved in validation, which led us to believe that our training data may have come from a different distribution than our test data. In order to investigate this further, we calculated distributions of our features for both the train and test set. We found a few differences between the distributions indicating that there may be a covariate shift between the training and test sets. We provide a few results from this analysis in Table 4. Notably, we see that there was a difference of .0816 in the percentage of tweets that were political between the test set and the training set. We also see far less observations with quotes or fully capitalized words in the test set than the training set. While this may be due to a small dataset and a high variance in the distribution of tweets, it still provides us with enough information to believe that there is a covariate shift between the training and test sets.

As mentioned above, we also saw a large difference between our validation and test scores. For example, we achieved a validation F1-macro score of 0.767 for our LSTM model with attention. However, this model achieved an F1-macro score of 0.669 on the test set. Additionally, our ensemble model went from a validation F1-macro score of 0.779 to a test F1-Macro score of 0.686. In conjunction with the covariate shift, we believe that our training and test set come from different distributions which would greatly increase our error.

Features	Train	Test	Difference
Contains a Capitalized Word	0.034	0.002	-0.032
Contains a Quote	0.078	.056	-0.022
Positive Emoji in Context	0.192	0.223	0.031
Political	**0.397**	**0.315**	**-0.082**

Table 4: Feature Distribution in Train and Test Sets

Final Models	Precision	Recall	F1-macro
Transformer Ensemble	**0.758**	**0.767**	**0.756**
Solo RoBERTa Transformer	0.733	0.734	0.733
BERT embeddings + LSTM	0.695	0.704	0.692
Ensemble model	0.687	0.689	0.686
LSTM w/ attention	0.669	0.669	0.669

Table 5: Test Scores of Final Models

6 Discussion and Conclusions

This research can hopefully guide future work on the topic of detecting sarcasm in social media. On that note, we would like to provide a few suggestions that others may find helpful in tackling the problem and a few of the findings that resulted in the largest improvements for our results.

First, utilizing multiple transformers and weighting them by performance seems to perform far better than a single transformer approach. Presumably, this allows the model to contain the information provided in each of the embeddings as opposed to a single form of embeddings. Next, we believe that this task requires a large amount of training data. We believe the reason the transformers performed so well was that they were pre-trained on large datasets. The models that we trained from scratch did not have as much training data, and we believe that they would have performed better with more training data. We believe that the weighted binary cross-entropy loss function to incorporate both datasets is a potential approach to help with this, and a future step would be to incorporate this into our final transformer models. Additionally, as emojis are an incredibly prevalent form of communication on social media, as a future step, we would like to incorporate emojis into the embedding space of our models. Finally, sarcasm detection is a difficult task. Even for humans, it is difficult to determine whether individuals are being sarcastic online. There are many complex variables that are difficult to quantify when determining if a short post is sarcastic. Therefore, capturing this notion of sarcasm within a model is difficult as well. We hope our techniques may be improved and expanded upon to solve other challenging natural language tasks.

References

Christos Baziotis, Nikos Pelekis, and Christos Doulk-eridis. 2017. Datastories at semeval-2017 task 4: Deep LSTM with attention for message-level and topic-based sentiment analysis. In *Proceedings of the 11th International Workshop on Semantic Evaluation (SemEval-2017)*, pages 747–754, Vancouver, Canada. Association for Computational Linguistics.

Jacob Devlin, Ming-Wei Chang, Kenton Lee, and Kristina Toutanova. 2019. BERT: Pre-training of deep bidirectional transformers for language understanding. In *Proceedings of NAACL-HLT 2019*, pages 4171–4186.

Aniruddha Ghosh and Tony Veale. 2017. Magnets for sarcasm: Making sarcasm detection timely, contextual and very personal. In *Proceedings of the 2017 Conference on Empirical Methods in Natural Language Processing*, pages 482–491.

Debanjan Ghosh, Alexander R. Fabbri, and Smaranda Muresan. 2018. Sarcasm analysis using conversation context. *Computational Linguistics*, 44(4):755–792.

Edouard Grave, Piotr Bojanowski, Prakhar Gupta, Armand Joulin, and Tomas Mikolov. 2018. Learning word vectors for 157 languages. In *Proceedings of the International Conference on Language Resources and Evaluation (LREC 2018)*.

Klaus Greff, Rupesh K Srivastava, Jan Koutník, Bas R Steunebrink, and Jürgen Schmidhuber. 2016. LSTM: A search space odyssey. *IEEE transactions on neural networks and learning systems*, 28(10):2222–2232.

S. Kayalvizhi, D Thenmozhi, B Senthil Kumar, and Chandrabose Aravindan. 2019. SSN_NLP@IDAT-FIRE 2019: Irony detection in arabic tweets using deep learning and features-based approaches. In *FIRE*.

Mikhail Khodak, Nikunj Saunshi, and Kiran Vodrahalli. 2017. A large self-annotated corpus for sarcasm. *arXiv preprint arXiv:1704.05579*.

Petra Kralj Novak, Jasmina Smailović, Borut Sluban, and Igor Mozetič. 2015. Sentiment of emojis. *PLoS ONE*, 10(12):e0144296.

Yinhan Liu, Myle Ott, Naman Goyal, Jingfei Du, Mandar Joshi, Danqi Chen, Omer Levy, Mike Lewis, Luke Zettlemoyer, and Veselin Stoyanov. 2019. RoBERTa: A robustly optimized BERT pretraining approach. *arXiv preprint arXiv:1907.11692*.

Steven Loria. 2018. textblob documentation. *Release 0.15*, 2.

Matthew Peters, Mark Neumann, Mohit Iyyer, Matt Gardner, Christopher Clark, Kenton Lee, and Luke Zettlemoyer. 2018. Deep contextualized word representations. In *NAACL*.

Rolandos Alexandros Potamias, Georgios Siolas, and Andreas Georgios Stafylopatis. 2019. A transformer-based approach to irony and sarcasm detection.

Tomáš Ptáček, Ivan Habernal, and Jun Hong. 2014. Sarcasm detection on czech and english twitter. pages 213–223.

Hong Wang, Qingsong Xu, and Lifeng Zhou. 2015. Large unbalanced credit scoring using lasso-logistic regression ensemble. *PloS one*, 10(2).

Thomas Wolf, Lysandre Debut, Victor Sanh, Julien Chaumond, Clement Delangue, Anthony Moi, Pierric Cistac, Tim Rault, R'emi Louf, Morgan Funtowicz, and Jamie Brew. 2019. Huggingface's transformers: State-of-the-art natural language processing. *ArXiv*, abs/1910.03771.

Zichao Yang, Diyi Yang, Chris Dyer, Xiaodong He, Alex Smola, and Eduard Hovy. 2016. Hierarchical attention networks for document classification. In *Proceedings of the 2016 conference of the North American chapter of the association for computational linguistics: human language technologies*, pages 1480–1489.

Transformer-based Context-aware Sarcasm Detection in Conversation Threads from Social Media

Xiangjue Dong
Computer Science
Emory University
Altanta, GA, USA
xiangjue.dong@emory.edu

Changmao Li
Computer Science
Emory University
Altanta, GA, USA
changmao.li@emory.edu

Jinho D. Choi
Computer Science
Emory University
Altanta, GA, USA
jinho.choi@emory.edu

Abstract

We present a transformer-based sarcasm detection model that accounts for the context from the entire conversation thread for more robust predictions. Our model uses deep transformer layers to perform multi-head attentions among the target utterance and the relevant context in the thread. The context-aware models are evaluated on two datasets from social media, Twitter and Reddit, and show 3.1% and 7.0% improvements over their baselines. Our best models give the F1-scores of 79.0% and 75.0% for the Twitter and Reddit datasets respectively, becoming one of the highest performing systems among 36 participants in this shared task.

1 Introduction

Sarcasm is a form of figurative language that implies a negative sentiment while displaying a positive sentiment on the surface (Joshi et al., 2017). Because of its conflicting nature and subtlety in language, sarcasm detection has been considered one of the most challenging tasks in natural language processing. Furthermore, when sarcasm is used in social media platforms such as Twitter or Reddit to express users' nuanced intents, the language is often full of spelling errors, acronyms, slangs, emojis, and special characters, which adds another level of difficulty in this task.

Despite of its challenges, sarcasm detection has recently gained substantial attention because it can bring the last gist to deep contextual understanding for various applications such as author profiling, harassment detection, and irony detection (Van Hee et al., 2018). Many computational approaches have been proposed to detect sarcasm in conversations (Ghosh et al., 2015; Joshi et al., 2015, 2016). However, most of the previous studies use the utterances in isolation, which makes it hard even for human to detect sarcasm without the contexts. Thus, it's essential to interpret the target utterances along with

contextual information comprising textual features from the conversation thread, metadata about the conversation from external sources, or visual context (Bamman and Smith, 2015; Ghosh et al., 2017; Ghosh and Veale, 2017; Ghosh et al., 2018).

This paper presents a transformer-based sarcasm detection model that takes both the target utterance and its context and predicts if the target utterance involves sarcasm. Our model uses a transformer encoder to coherently generate the embedding representation for the target utterance and the context by performing multi-head attentions (Section 4). This approach is evaluated on two types of datasets collected from Twitter and Reddit (Section 3), and depicts significant improvement over the baseline using only the target utterance as input (Section 5). Our error analysis illustrates that the context-aware model can catch subtle nuance that cannot be captured by the target-oriented model (Section 6).

2 Related Work

Just as most other types of figurative languages are, sarcasm is not necessarily complicated to express but requires comprehensive understanding in context as well as commonsense knowledge rather than its literal sense (Van Hee et al., 2018). Various approaches have been presented for this task.

Most earlier works had taken the target utterance without context as input. Both explicit and implicit incongruity features were explored in these works (Joshi et al., 2015). To detect whether certain words in the target utterance involve sarcasm, several approaches based on distributional semantics were proposed (Ghosh et al., 2015). Additionally, word embedding-based features like distance-weighted similarities were also adapted to capture the subtle forms of context incongruity (Joshi et al., 2016). Nonetheless, it is difficult to detect sarcasm by considering only the target utterances in isolation.

276

Proceedings of the Second Workshop on Figurative Language Processing, pages 276–280
July 9, 2020. ©2020 Association for Computational Linguistics
https://doi.org/10.18653/v1/P17

Non-textual features such as the properties of the author, audience and environment were also taken into account (Bamman and Smith, 2015). Both the linguistic and context features were used to distinguish between information-seeking and rhetorical questions in forums and tweets (Oraby et al., 2017). Traditional machine learning methods such as Support Vector Machines were used to model sarcasm detection as a sequential classification task over the target utterance and its surrounding utterances (Wang et al., 2015). Recently, deep learning methods using LSTM were introduced, considering the prior turns (Ghosh et al., 2017) as well as the succeeding turns (Ghosh et al., 2018).

3   Data Description

Given a conversation thread, either from Twitter or Reddit, a target utterance is the turn to be predicted, whether or not it involves sarcasm, and the context is an ordered list of other utterances in the thread. Table 1 shows the examples of conversation threads where the target utterances involve sarcasm.[1]

	Utterance
C_1	This feels apt this morning but I don't feel fine ... <URL>
C_2	@USER it is what's going round in the heads of many I know ...
T	@USER @USER I remember a few months back we were saying the Americans shouldn't tell us how to vote on brexit

(a) Sarcasm example from Twitter.

	Utterance
C_1	Promotional images for some guy's Facebook page
C_2	I wouldn't let that robot near me
T	Sounds like you don't like science, you theist sheep

(b) Sarcasm example from Reddit.

Table 1: Examples of the conversation threads where the target utterances involve sarcasm. C_i: i'th utterance in the context, T: the target utterance.

The Twitter data is collected by using the hashtags #sarcasm and #sarcastic. The Reddit data is a subset of the Self-Annotated Reddit Corpus that consists of 1.3 million sarcastic and non-sarcastic posts (Khodak et al., 2017). Every target utterance is annotated with one of the two labels, SARCASM and NOT_SARCASM. Table 2 shows the statistics of the two datasets provided by this shared task.

---

^[1] Note that the target utterance can appear at any position of the context although its exact position is not provided in this year's shared task data.

Notice the huge variances in the utterance lengths for both the Twitter and the Reddit datasets. For the Reddit dataset, the average lengths of conversations as well as utterances are significantly larger in the test set than the training set that potentially makes the model development more challenging.

	NC	**AU**	**AT**
TRN	5,000	4.9 ($\pm$3.2)	140.4 ($\pm$112.8)
TST	1,800	4.2 ($\pm$1.9)	128.5 ($\pm$78.8)

(a) Twitter dataset statistics.

	NC	**AU**	**AT**
TRN	4,400	3.5 ($\pm$0.8)	45.8 ($\pm$17.3)
TST	1,800	5.3 ($\pm$2.0)	93.6 ($\pm$57.8)

(b) Reddit dataset statistics.

Table 2: Statistics of the two datasets provided by the shared task. TRN: training set, TST: test set, NC: # of conversations, AU: Avg # of utterances per conversation (including the target utterances) and its stdev, AT: Avg # of tokens per utterance and its stdev.

4   Approach

Two types of transformer-based sarcasm detection models are used for our experiments:

a) The target-oriented model takes only the target utterance as input (Section 4.1).

b) The context-aware model takes both the target utterance and the context utterances as input (Section 4.2).

These two models are coupled with the latest transformer encoders e.g., BERT (Devlin et al., 2019), RoBERTa (Liu et al., 2020), and ALBERT (Lan et al., 2019), and compared to evaluate how much impact the context makes to predict whether or not the target utterance involves sarcasm.

4.1   Target-oriented Model

Figure 1a shows the overview of the target-oriented model. Let $W = \{w_1, \ldots, w_n\}$ be the input target utterance, where w_i is the i'th token in W and n is the max-number of tokens in any target utterance. W is first prepended by the special token c representing the entire target utterance, which creates the input sequence $I^{to} = \{c\} \oplus W$. I^{to} is then fed into the transformer encoder, which generates the sequence of embeddings $\{e^c\} \oplus E^w$, where $E^w = \{e_1^w, \ldots, e_n^w\}$ is the embedding list for W and (e^c, e_i^w) are the embeddings of (c, w_i) respectively. Finally, e^c is fed into the linear decoder to generate the output vector o^{to} that makes the binary decision of whether or not W involves sarcasm.

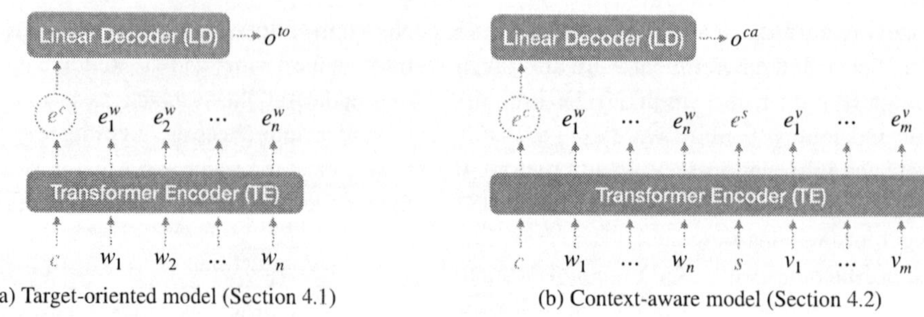

(a) Target-oriented model (Section 4.1)   (b) Context-aware model (Section 4.2)

Figure 1: The overview of our transformer-based target-oriented and context-aware models.

4.2 Context-aware Model

Figure 1b shows the overview of the context-aware model. Let L_i be the i'th utterance in the context. Then, $V = L_1 \oplus \cdots \oplus L_k = \{v_1, \ldots, v_m\}$ is the concatenated list of tokens in all context utterances, where k is the number of utterances in the context, v_1 is the first token in L_1 and v_m is the last token in L_k. The input sequence I^{to} from Section 4.1 is appended by the special token s representing the separator between the target utterance and the context, and also V, which creates the input sequence $I^{ca} = I^{to} \oplus \{s\} \oplus V$. Then, I^{ca} gets fed into the transformer encoder, which generates a sequence of embeddings $\{e^c\} \oplus E^w \oplus \{e^s\} \oplus E^v$, where $E^v = \{e_1^v, \ldots, e_m^v\}$ is the embedding list for V, and (e^s, e_i^v) are the embeddings of (s, v_i) respectively. Finally, e^c is fed into the linear decoder to generate the output vector o^{ca} that makes the same binary decision to detect sarcasm.

5 Experiments

5.1 Data Split

For all our experiments, a mixture of the Twitter and the Reddit datasets is used. The Twitter training set provided by the shared task consists of 5,000 tweets, where the labels are equally balanced between SARCASM and NOT_SARCASM (Table 2). We find, however, 4.82% of them are duplicates, which are removed before data splitting. As a result, 4,759 tweets are used for our experiments. Labels in the Reddit training set are also equally balanced and no duplicate is found in this dataset.

	Twitter		Reddit	
	TRN	DEV	TRN	DEV
SARCASM	2,020	239	1,973	227
NOT_SARCASM	2,263	237	1,987	213

Table 3: Statistics of the data split used for our experiments, where 10% of each dataset is randomly selected to create the development set.

5.2 Models

Three types of transformers are used for our experiments, that are BERT-Large (Devlin et al., 2019), RoBERTa-Large (Liu et al., 2020), and ALBERT-xxLarge (Lan et al., 2019), to compare the performance among the current state-of-the-art encoders. Every model is run three times and their average scores as well as standard deviations are reported. All models are trained on the combined Twitter + Reddit training set and evaluated on the combined development set (Table 3).

5.3 Experimental Setup

After an extensive hyper-parameter search, we set the learning rate to 3e-5, the number of epochs to 30, and use different seed values, 21, 42, 63, for the three runs. Additionally, based on the statistics of each dataset, we set the maximum sequence length to 128 for the target-oriented models while it is set to 256 for the context-aware models by considering the different lengths of the input sequences required by those approaches.

5.4 Results

The baseline scores are provided by the organizers, that are 60.0% for Reddit and 67.0% for Twitter using the single layer LSTM attention model (Ghosh et al., 2018). Table 4 shows the results achieved by our target-oriented (Section 4.1) and the context-aware (Section 4.2) models on the combined development set. The RoBERTa-Large model gives the highest F1-scores for both the target-oriented and context-aware models. The context-aware model using RoBERTa-Large show an improvement of 1.1% over its counterpart baseline so that this model is used for our final submission to the shared task. Note that it may be possible to achieve higher performance by fine-tuning hyperparameters for the Twitter and Reddit datasets separately, which we will explore in the future.

	P	R	F1
B-L	77.3 (±0.6)	79.9 (±0.8)	78.6 (±0.1)
R-L	73.4 (±0.6)	88.5 (±1.4)	**80.2** (±0.5)
A-XXL	76.1 (±1.4)	83.3 (±2.3)	79.5 (±0.2)

(a) Results from the target-oriented models (Section 4.1).

	P	R	F1
B-L	76.3 (±1.0)	82.7 (±1.6)	79.4 (±0.5)
R-L	77.3 (±3.8)	86.1 (±4.0)	**81.3** (±0.2)
A-XXL	76.5 (±3.3)	82.7 (±3.1)	79.4 (±2.2)

(b) Results from the context-aware models (Section 4.2).

Table 4: Results on the combined Twitter+Reddit development set. B-L: BERT-Large, R-L: RoBERTa-Large, A-XXL: ALBERT-xxLarge.

Table 5 shows the results by the RoBERTa-Large models on the test sets. The scores are retrieved by submitting the system outputs to the shared task's CodaLab page.[2] The context-aware models significantly outperform the target-oriented models on the test sets, showing improvements of 3.1% and 7.0% on the F1 scores for the Twitter and the Reddit datasets, respectively. The improvement on Reddit is particularly substantial due to the much greater lengths of the conversation threads and utterances in the test set compared to the ones in the training set (Table 2). As the final results, we achieve 79.0% and 75.0% for the Twitter and Reddit datasets respectively that mark the 2nd places for both datasets at the time of the submission.

	P	R	F1
Twitter	75.5 (±0.7)	76.4 (±0.6)	75.2 (±0.8)
Reddit	67.9 (±0.5)	69.2 (±0.7)	67.4 (±0.5)

(a) Results from the target-oriented RoBERTa-Large models.

	P	R	F1
Twitter	78.4 (±0.6)	78.9 (±0.3)	**78.3** (±0.7)
Reddit	74.5 (±0.6)	74.9 (±0.5)	**74.4** (±0.7)

(b) Results from the context-aware RoBERTa-Large models.

Table 5: Results on the test sets from CodaLab.

6   Analysis

For a better understanding in our final model, errors from the following three situations are analyzed (TO: target-oriented, CA: context-aware):

- TwCc: TO is wrong and CA is correct.

- TcCw: TO is correct and CA is wrong.

- TwCw: Both TO and CA are wrong.

[2] https://competitions.codalab.org/competitions/22247

Table 6 shows examples for every error situation. For TwCc, TO predicts it to be NOT_SARCASM. In this example, it is difficult to tell if the target utterance involves sarcasm without having the context. For TcCw, CA predicts it to be NOT_SARCASM. It appears that the target utterance is long enough to provide enough features for TO to make the correct prediction, whereas considering the extra context may increase noise for CA to make the incorrect decision. For TwCw, both TO and CA predict it to be NOT_SARCASM. This example seems to require deeper reasoning to make the correct prediction.

	Utterance
C_1	who has ever cared about y * utube r * wind .
C_2	@USER Back when YouTube was beginning it was a cool giveback to the community to do a super polished high production value video with YT talent . Not the same now . The better move for them would be to do like 5-6 of them in several categories to give that shine .
T	@USER @USER I look forward to the eventual annual Tubies Awards livestream .

(a) Example when TO is wrong and CA is correct.

	Utterance
C_1	I am asking the chairs of the House and Senate committees to investigate top secret intelligence shared with NBC prior to me seeing it.
C_2	@USER Good for you, sweetie! But using the legislative branch of the US Government to fix your media grudges seems a bit much.
T	@USER @USER @USER you look triggered after someone criticizes me, are conservatives skeptic of ppl in power?

(b) Example when TO is correct and CA is wrong.

	Utterance
C_1	If I could start my #Brand over, this is what I would emulate my #Site to look like .. And I might, once my anual contract with #WordPress is up . Even tho I don't think is very; I can't help but to find ... <URL> <URL>
C_2	@USER There is no design on it except for links ?
T	@USER It's the of what #Works in this current #Mindset of #MassConsumption; wannabe fast due to caused by, and being just another and. is the light, bringing color back to this sad world of and.

(c) Example when both TO and CA are wrong.

Table 6: Examples of the three error situations. C_i: i'th utterance in the context, T: the target utterance.

7   Conclusion

This paper explores the benefit of considering relevant contexts for the task of sarcasm detection. Three types of state-of-the-art transformer encoders are adapted to establish the strong baseline for the target-oriented models, which are compared to the context-aware models that show significant improvements for both Twitter and Reddit datasets and become one of the highest performing models in this shared task.

All our resources are publicly available at Emory NLP's open source repository: `https://github.com/emorynlp/figlang-shared-task-2020`

Acknowledgments

We gratefully acknowledge the support of the AWS Machine Learning Research Awards (MLRA). Any contents in this material are those of the authors and do not necessarily reflect the views of AWS.

References

David Bamman and Noah Smith. 2015. Contextualized Sarcasm Detection on Twitter. In *International AAAI Conference on Web and Social Media*, pages 574–577.

Jacob Devlin, Ming-Wei Chang, Kenton Lee, and Kristina Toutanova. 2019. BERT: Pre-training of Deep Bidirectional Transformers for Language Understanding. In *Proceedings of the Conference of the North American Chapter of the Association for Computational Linguistics: Human Language Technologies*, pages 4171–4186.

Aniruddha Ghosh and Tony Veale. 2017. Magnets for Sarcasm: Making Sarcasm Detection Timely, Contextual and Very Personal. In *Proceedings of the 2017 Conference on Empirical Methods in Natural Language Processing*, pages 482–491, Copenhagen, Denmark. Association for Computational Linguistics.

Debanjan Ghosh, Alexander Richard Fabbri, and Smaranda Muresan. 2017. The Role of Conversation Context for Sarcasm Detection in Online Interactions. *Proceedings of the 18th Annual SIGdial Meeting on Discourse and Dialogue*, pages 186–196.

Debanjan Ghosh, Alexander Richard Fabbri, and Smaranda Muresan. 2018. Sarcasm Analysis using Conversation Context. *Comput. Linguist.*, 44(4):755–792.

Debanjan Ghosh, Weiwei Guo, and Smaranda Muresan. 2015. Sarcastic or Not: Word Embeddings to Predict the Literal or Sarcastic Meaning of Words. In *Proceedings of the 2015 Conference on Empirical Methods in Natural Language Processing*, pages 1003–1012, Lisbon, Portugal. Association for Computational Linguistics.

Aditya Joshi, Pushpak Bhattacharyya, and Mark J. Carman. 2017. Automatic Sarcasm Detection: A Survey. *ACM Computing Surveys*, 50(5):1–22.

Aditya Joshi, Vinita Sharma, and Pushpak Bhattacharyya. 2015. Harnessing Context Incongruity for Sarcasm Detection. In *Proceedings of the 53rd Annual Meeting of the Association for Computational Linguistics and the 7th International Joint Conference on Natural Language Processing (Volume 2: Short Papers)*, pages 757–762, Beijing, China. Association for Computational Linguistics.

Aditya Joshi, Vaibhav Tripathi, Kevin Patel, Pushpak Bhattacharyya, and Mark Carman. 2016. Are Word Embedding-based Features Useful for Sarcasm Detection? In *Proceedings of the 2016 Conference on Empirical Methods in Natural Language Processing*, pages 1006–1011, Austin, Texas. Association for Computational Linguistics.

Mikhail Khodak, Nikunj Saunshi, and Kiran Vodrahalli. 2017. A Large Self-Annotated Corpus for Sarcasm. *Proceedings of the Eleventh International Conference on Language Resources and Evaluation (LREC 2018)*, abs/1704.05579.

Zhenzhong Lan, Mingda Chen, Sebastian Goodman, Kevin Gimpel, Piyush Sharma, and Radu Soricut. 2019. ALBERT: A Lite BERT for Self-supervised Learning of Language Representations. *arXiv*, 11942(1909).

Yinhan Liu, Myle Ott, Naman Goyal, Jingfei Du, Mandar Joshi, Danqi Chen, Omer Levy, Mike Lewis, Luke Zettlemoyer, and Veselin Stoyanov. 2020. RoBERTa: A Robustly Optimized BERT Pretraining Approach. In *Proceedings of the International Conference on Learning Representations*.

Shereen Oraby, Vrindavan Harrison, Amita Misra, Ellen Riloff, and Marilyn Walker. 2017. Are you serious?: Rhetorical Questions and Sarcasm in Social Media Dialog. In *Proceedings of the 18th Annual SIGdial Meeting on Discourse and Dialogue*, pages 310–319, Saarbrücken, Germany. Association for Computational Linguistics.

Cynthia Van Hee, Els Lefever, and Véronique Hoste. 2018. SemEval-2018 Task 3: Irony Detection in English Tweets. In *Proceedings of The 12th International Workshop on Semantic Evaluation*, pages 39–50, New Orleans, Louisiana. Association for Computational Linguistics.

Zelin Wang, Zhijian Wu, Ruimin Wang, and Yafeng Ren. 2015. Twitter Sarcasm Detection Exploiting a Context-Based Model. In *WISE*.

Author Index

Association for Computational Linguistics
209 N. Eighth Street
Stroudsburg, Pennsylvania 18360

ISBN 978-1-7138-1378-1